"Bound to be a best seller! First Edition. Awaiting critics review."

"Talented writer. Excellent reading. A remarkable debut!"

"Inspirational, motivating and encouraging."

"It's no exaggeration to say that Achille Paladini's autobiography could be one of the most entertaining ever written!"

"Enthralling and captivating."

"A remarkable story that is indeed Beyond the Bounds of Possibility!"

PERSEVERANCE

BEYOND THE BOUNDS OF POSSIBILITY

ACHILLE PALADINI

Palmetto Publishing Group
Charleston, SC

Perseverance
Copyright © 2019 by Achille Paladini

First Edition

Printed in the United States

ISBN-13: 978-1-64111-254-3
ISBN-10: 1-64111-254-9

PROLOGUE

My family has been urging me to write a book about my tumultuous existence and how I miraculously shadowed the life of my famous grandfather, Achille Paladini, who was prominently titled "The Fish King."

Achille was born in 1844 in Ancona Italy, a modest, colorful fishing seaport on the Adriatic Sea. In his early twenties, he came to the United States, arriving in San Francisco in 1865 aboard a sailing schooner by way of the Drake Passage, which was the preferred, shorter route by most ship captains, since there was open water for hundreds of miles, though it was often plagued by extremely rough conditions and harrowing high winds.

Achille was a short, stocky man, exhibiting a pronounced nose, and had an outgoing personality with the demeanor to succeed. His only possessions were an old wooden trunk containing just a change of clothes and a pair of boots. Intrigued with the affect that the California Gold Rush had on the prosperity of the city by the bay, he sought to somehow seek out a livelihood by capitalizing on the remnants of the gold dust that may have still been in the pockets of the wealthy miners taking up residency in the city. Now hungry and with no money, he thought of the fishing seaport where he was born and started fishing off a local dock for his dinner while pondering his uncertain future. Several passersby asked if they could buy his extra fish, and the idea was planted—and the rest is history. He eventually created the largest wholesale seafood distribution and processing company on the West Coast and became the second wealthiest Italian in all of California, second to none but A. P. Giannini, the founder of Bank of America. Achille and Amadeo eventually became the best of friends and had a Friday ritual of meeting at the Palace Hotel each week for lunch.

Immediately after the 1906 earthquake and fire that devastated the city, Giannini was arranging for loans to the dismayed local business and homeowners needing to rebuild from a small collapsible table on the corner of Montgomery and Clay Streets. It has been said that Achille advanced him money to help keep the bank's liquidity solvent due to the overwhelming demand from the property owners. I find it funny that I still need to swipe my card to show my ID at Bank of America. If only they knew what had transpired just over a century ago!

In 1908, both Paladini and Giannini coincidentally built their main offices less than half a block from one another; A. Paladini, Inc. at 542 Clay Street, and Giannini's Bank of Italy, later to become the Bank of America, on the corner of Clay and Montgomery streets. The bank's original location, though no longer in operation, is now a National Historic Site. As you once entered the structure, done in the architecture style known as Second Renaissance Revival, you felt as if you were experiencing the grandeur of an Italian villa, stepping onto white and black, grained marble floors with similarly colored marble walls and counters, while a crystal chandelier pretentiously hovered above; an era now gone.

The phrase "deep pockets" factually originated from when Achille had his pockets lengthened to carry an abundance of gold coins since his method of payment was in cash.

Achille also amassed a fortune in commercial real estate in San Francisco. The skyline of the city is now proudly dominated by the Transamerica Pyramid on Clay Street, one of his most renowned properties. It currently sits almost entirely upon the land of the once-main office of the wholesale fish distribution business, and now proudly reaches into the sky like a monument to its predecessor. The property was sold to Transamerica for its construction in 1968. Facetiously, we call it the "Paladini Tombstone."

He died in 1921. I was posthumously named after him fifteen years later. Was I somehow fatefully genetically engineered, predetermined to carry on his legacy after the unexpected collapse of his empire that lasted 109 years?

The thought is incomprehensible! Oddly enough, his revered old wooden trunk, pursued by all the family, was given to me, without my having asked for it, by his eldest daughter Henrietta just before her death. She told me, "Your grandfather sat on this trunk while putting on his boots every morning before going to work. You do the same, and it will bring you good luck!

How strange can it be that we have lived the past twenty-five years a mere half block from the Giannini estate, with it being the largest parcel, and ours the second largest within our immediate area on the peninsula in San Mateo bordering Hillsborough. Is it indeed fate or just coincidence? Or am I indeed *shadowing* my grandfather?

Regarding my decision to write a book: I tried to explain to my family that my mind had always been so preoccupied and filled with dreams that I'd never even *read* a book—how could I possibly write one?

I don't mean to use the word "I, I, I" at the start of each phrase, but how in the hell does one write a memoir without using "I"? And I must say—see, I just used it again—it sure makes one sound egotistical, narcissistic, and self-centered.

Furthermore, if I do finish writing this book, my preference would be that it be published after my death. But I know that won't happen, so I must use discretion. There are incidents that I am not proud of; above all, the fact that I hurt my wife so deeply during one self-absorbed phase, and I fear some of my revelations may open old wounds that will only cause hurt again. I am very fortunate that my wife had the tenacity and deeply embedded love to stay with me to this very day. I have always truly loved and adored her.

Since this book is factual, the incidents that occurred during that egregious, iniquitous phase, shamefully must be disclosed. I will do so, but again, with discretion.

I hope you find the following chapters intriguing and compelling, which reveal my life's venture that was compounded with so many challenges, setbacks, and heartbreak. There also may be an essential lesson or two for any entrepreneur aspiring to inaugurate a business, who possesses just the knowledge of their industry as their only asset. It just may be possible to nurture and develop that lonely asset into a successful business venture by reading the narrative exemplifying the inception of my business. If you behold tenacity, confidence, and optimism you should exploit your dream, which will inspire your rise to greatness! *There is nothing like a dream to create the future.*

My story starts with several joyous and humorous adventures during the innocence of my youth while growing up in the Marina District of San Francisco.

Later as a young adult, several stimulating and lascivious romantic encounters with tales of glitz and glamour while in Hollywood, dating models and starlets and living a fairy-tale, carefree life with illusions of grandeur; finally settling down and marrying a wonderful girl, the beautiful and talented stage, screen, and television actress, Joan Lora; then the *shocking* cataclysmic revelation in my mid-twenties that devastated my youthful illusions and led to confusion, hopelessness, dire despair, and struggle. This resulted in complete disillusionment and sincere concern over my impending future and the subsequent fortuity of my young family.

However, with merely a basic knowledge of the seafood industry, and the inherent blessing to behold the virtues of tenacity, fortitude, determination, and a bit of courage, I was driven to eventually accomplish the virtually impossible task of rebuilding the Paladini empire from *nothing*, with *nothing*. This resulted in unexpected, indisputable success and substantial wealth, having shadowed my grandfather. A legacy relived. Freud postulated that dreams are wishes.

Unfortunately, during one phase of this newfound success, narcissistic and sociopath-like tendencies, and ego mixed with my Italian-fueled level of testosterone, almost caused the collapse of my marriage, which led to alcoholism and despair. I was also concurrently repudiating the audacity of the West Coast Mafia's attempt to take over my dominance in the seafood industry while fiercely battling the Butchers Union that was pursuing to decimate my achievements with a long and costly tumultuous two-year strike, proclaiming unwarranted demands, causing upheaval and disruption of my entire operation that could have resulted in potential catastrophic economic turmoil.

My story contains factual experiences that most will conclude are fictional; however, everything stated in this book is true and unembellished.

Was it really my grandfather's old wooden trunk that held the secrets for success, if so, what powers could it conceivably covertly conceal that made me so driven to succeed?

Or, was it just my inherent *perseverance?*

INTRODUCTION
HOW IN THE HELL DID ALL THIS HAPPEN——AND SO QUICKLY?

It was about eight in the morning during the middle of the summer of 1980, and we had only been in the new plant six months.

I had to go upstairs to my office for some reason, and upon returning to go down to the sales office and face the hustle and bustle of the morning's activities, I hesitated on the landing at the top of the stairs, then stopped and looked out the window.

I was dumbfounded. I saw a sea of white Paladini trucks wherever I looked; in the parking area and out on the street, and as far as I could see to the corner. There were also several forty-foot tractor trailers from the production plant parked in front, proudly displaying the name like a billboard announcing its return to the industry.

Drivers were in line to gas up their trucks from the underground tank as others were backing into the loading docks and several more were leaving to make deliveries.

The scene I was viewing was one of an obviously very successful business that appeared to have been in business for decades, yet it had only been in operation for a little less than five years!

I sat on one of the chairs on the landing in the reception area that was close to the switchboard, and heard Doris answering call after call, saying, "Thank you for calling Paladini. May I help you?" Then saying, "Yes sir, but all lines into the sales office are busy. May I ask you to wait just a minute, please?" My God, it was as if we were the only seafood wholesaler in the Bay Area.

I remained there for several minutes, maybe ten or so, staring out the window, mesmerized by the chaotic activity taking place, when my secretary Beverly came up behind me and said, "Are you looking at what you created, boss?" I looked at her, bewildered, and asked, "How in the hell did all this happen—and so quickly?"

My mind started to wander, remembering just a few years ago, sitting all alone in that tiny old dingy plant with just a single-line black phone with *no* customers, *no* inventory, and *no* money; then thinking back even further at the intense struggle it had been getting to this point, and everything that had taken place, all the hurdles and all the disappointments. I never thought this could ever have been possible—my God!

I then thought back to my childhood days without a care or need in the world, not knowing what the future held for me, just a little kid with no vision of my fate, playing on the steps on Baker Street, believing in Superman.

CHAPTER 1
THE AGE OF INNOCENCE

It was just past two in the afternoon on a typical overcast day in San Francisco when I emerged into the world. Low-cast clouds clung to the majestic soaring towers of the Golden Gate Bridge while a mosaic of water-colored misty fog cloaked the bay below. It was Tuesday, June 8, 1936. The fog horns on the soon-to-be-completed bridge were triumphantly announcing its genesis as I took my first breath—a coincidentally fitting metaphor for the birth of a child innocently accepting its unknown forthcoming future.

This is pretty much the story of my life ever since I first said the word "mama."

It came to pass that I was a twin. My God! Two raucous, intolerable sons; however, I ousted the other guy early on, possibly saving my mother's sanity. That also gave me total reign of my soon-to-be imaginary kingdom.

Being a true Gemini, my personality has no middle. I'm either calm and passive or uncontrollably tempestuous. It's either black or white; there are no gray zones.

I was named Achille Paladini, innocuously after my legendary grandfather. Was this truly a harmless, innocent, unplanned thought process? Or was there a subliminal predetermined plan for me? Could it be possible that my future was predestined to eventually shadow his life? And yet, how can that be? Only God and fate could possibly know what was in store for this little guy with his soul still so pure and unblemished. If only we all knew what junctures the future held for us. Could we change it, should we want to? Where would this journey take me?

Regarding my name—or should I say, *names*—as if Achille weren't bad enough, when I was a baby my mom nicknamed me "Kiki." As a teenager, when asking a girl to dance, my name was

1

the last thing I wanted to discuss! The world was much smaller back then, with unusual names uncommon.

I grew up at 3159 Baker Street in the Marina District of San Francisco, an upscale section of the city in a large home just a block away from the Palace of Fine Arts.

We possibly had the only home in the city that stood alone with no other homes surrounding; quite unique in San Francisco. A triangular-shaped piece of property, it was encompassed by Baker and Francisco Streets and Richardson Boulevard. That came about when the Golden Gate Bridge was being constructed and the other surrounding homes were moved, allowing Richardson Boulevard to be a main entrance to the bridge, leaving us an island all to ourselves.

Well, I thought I was royalty living in that three-story grandeur of a home, and after all, every time I would go out with my mom and dad, people would say, "Oh, you're the famous Paladini fish people! I see your trucks all over!" At such a young age, I didn't know what that all meant, but it made me somewhat egotistical, thinking my family was well known and well off. To a degree we were, but—the "but" will come later.

I was totally spoiled as a youth. Just about everything I wanted, I got. I just asked my mom for it and it would magically appear. My room was made up every day by the maid, Gertie. My mother would ask each morning what I wanted for dinner that night, and she would cook it for me. After all, isn't that just the way it is for all kids? Well, my brother Walter and four sisters, Lorraine, Catherine, Tina, and Audrey didn't think so; they never got treated like that. They were all much older, and hey, what did I know? The next youngest, my sister Audrey, a cute, spunky brunette, was eight years older, and the others were as much as seventeen years older than me. I was always pampered by my four sisters. They loved to dress me up and put my long blond hair into curls. It's a wonder I didn't get confused what sex I was.

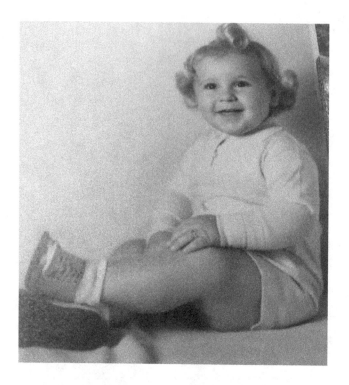

I got used to being surrounded by females and I liked it! *Even back then.*

In this cloistered life I was enjoying, I wasn't aware of the horrendous suffering other people were experiencing throughout the world at the time. There was no television, no CNN to blast us with the news of the world, only the radio and the daily Call Bulletin, which I of course never read, being so young. But I did overhear my parents talking about a war every night during dinner; they referred to it as a "world war." War? What was a war?

I was five and a half years old to the very date on December 8, 1941, when we went to war with Japan. I had some realization of the fright of war only because we lived just a block away from the Presideo. There were often unannounced air raid drills during the night, and all the lights had to be turned off. It was pitch black, and that was scary. I remember during one of the drills, my sister Kay, a vivacious blonde with a gregarious and amusing personality, looked so scared. I asked her, "What's the matter, sis?" And she said, "I'm just worried. We never know when it's for real, we could be bombed." I innocently said, "Don't worry, sis. Superman will save us!" However, this was a time of worry and hardship for all Americans. If only there really was a Superman.

How innocent, how pure, how trusting of the world one is at that young age, having no realization of the cruelty of mankind and the implausible suffering people have had to endure. Sadly, during that time while I was living in my blissful world, people were being bombed out of their homes in parts of Europe, and even worse, Jews, both parents and children, were being taken to concentration camps and separated, ultimately suffering excruciating pain and horrible death. Jews in Poland were living in sewers trying to escape capture from the Nazi Fascist rule. And there I was, living in the lap of luxury. I naturally didn't understand war or cruelty, or even death. Sensing turmoil in the world, I couldn't help to wonder why I was so privileged. It didn't seem or feel right.

Speaking of death, what was death? They say a child learns about death from losing a pet. I experienced that a few months later when our dog Corky, a little white Maltese poodle was run over by my brother while backing the car out of the garage. She was old and mostly blind, and partially deaf. Everyone was devastated, especially my dad. Corky was my dad's dog; they were inseparable.

I asked my mom where Corky went, and she said, "To heaven." "So, where's heaven, Mom?" I asked. "Up there," she said. "Up there where?" I replied.

Speaking of heaven, I was told a funny—or possibly better yet, *strange*—story from my humorous and entertaining, and sometimes "wacky" (said with love) sister Kay.

Our home on Baker Street was very large and could be rather spooky at times. After climbing well over twenty brick steps and reaching the front door on the second level, you would enter the foyer with the guest's coat room just ahead. Semi-circular steps leading to the third-floor bedrooms were just off to the right of the foyer, where a large antique grandfather clock imposingly stood at the bottom of the steps. To the left, you would take three steps down to enter the front room, as the smell of embers still burning in the fireplace at midnight invited you in to sit on one of the large cushy chairs and repose. To the right, was the formal dining room that held a huge crystal chandelier hanging over the dining table, which was always pre-set for ten, then a small cocktail room at the end. There was a long hallway parallel to the dining room, and at the end of the hallway you entered the kitchen. The door was always open, as it is in any Italian home.

Kay *claims* that one night after coming home from a date sometime after midnight, she entered the second-floor foyer, about to go upstairs to bed, when she saw the light on in the kitchen at the end of the hallway. As she entered the kitchen and walked to the far-left end to turn off the light at the switch near the ironing board compartment (that's where I used to ditch my vegetables I didn't eat as a kid), she noticed three men on the far right side dressed in old-fashioned black suits wearing dice box hats like they wore in the 1890s. She said one had a dirty-blond handlebar mustache with blue eyes. As she stopped in her tracks in horror and amazement, she said they turned toward her and gestured with their wine glasses up, like you would as if toasting someone! She said they were drinking red wine. Possibly Kay had also been drinking red wine—and too much! However, she swears that she saw it, and it truly happened.

Now frightened out of her wits, she ran upstairs to wake up mom and dad, screaming, "Dad, there are three men downstairs in the kitchen—and they're drinking your red wine!" Well, being awoken from a sound sleep, he told her to go to bed and that she was nuts! If you knew Kay, you may have a tendency to agree with him.

Kay insisted, so he reluctantly went downstairs, and of course, no one was there. However, the light was still on! Kay naturally said she had never turned it on. Okay, what was weird was that my dad said he had been noticing that someone had been drinking his red wine, and had been wondering who, since no one else in the family liked it. To make this even more intriguing, my mom said Kay's description of the man with the dirty-blond hair and blue eyes and handlebar mustache matched the description of her father!

I was basically raised as an only child, and yes, spoiled as I said previously—okay, really spoiled. I'm sure you already concluded that. However, I had been a mistake, and a big one! I would bring that up to my mom and she would say, "But I love you." And I would respond, "I know you do, Mom, but don't tell me that you had five children, were also raising Tommie, and were in your forties, and you said to Dad, 'Walter, let's have another child!'"

I had a wonderful relationship with my mother. Her name was Jennie. She was pure Italian, born in San Francisco; a brunette, not too tall, she possessed innocence and a heart of gold. She was a kind, caring, and loving mother, and a dear, sweet person. Telling her I loved her was easy. She was a down-to-earth mother and housewife, never having any responsibility regarding financial matters, or the need to.

My father, Walter, was rather short and stocky, and always a bit overweight for as long as I can remember. He had an extremely outgoing personality and was mostly jovial all the time. He was the big businessman that took care of all the expenses. My dad was like a God to me. I thought he was the only man on earth who may have referred to God as his associate.

We never did much of anything together as a father and son. No bike rides or throwing a football or fishing, stuff dads do with their son. Possibly that was due to his age. Consequently, I had to learn most everything by myself, be that right or wrong.

But still, life was good. The only not-so-nice experience that I can recall was, as a youth, attending Winfield Scott Grammar School in the first grade. We were sitting in class in desk-type chairs, and a girl with long dark hair was sitting directly in front of me. During class, I noticed that her little purse fell off the back of her chair, so I picked it up and put it back on the rear corner of her chair where it had fallen from, thinking I was being nice. She turned around and shouted, "What are you doing?!" I said, "Your purse fell, and I put it back for you." She then said, "Oh, you're Italian—and I don't trust you!"

When I got home, I asked my mom if we were bad people and explained what happened. She said, "You will learn that some people just don't like other people."

"Is that why we're at war?" I asked. I didn't understand.

Meanwhile, I had been going to catechism class, getting ready to receive my First Holy Communion at St. Vincent de Paul's Church. It was a two-week class, every other day after school, if I recall correctly. Upon completion and getting ready to receive my First Holy Communion on that Sunday, we all had to go to confession the Friday before. We were told to "keep our houses clean" to receive the lord. Meaning, don't sin; keep our souls pure and unblemished. You didn't want to receive the lord in your "house" (soul) if it was dirty.

Well, that Saturday, having nothing to do, I looked at a *National Geographic* magazine that I found on the table in the cocktail room. While casually browsing through the pages, I suddenly saw a picture of an African woman with her breasts exposed. Oh my gosh—breasts. I had never seen breasts! And there were more breasts on the ensuing pages. I looked at every one!

Then suddenly, I panicked. I'd sinned—my house was dirty! I was to receive the Lord the very next morning, and my house was dirty. Well, I didn't eat or sleep that night. I had been warned! What was I to do?

The next morning while I got dressed, the only thing I could think about was that I'd sinned, and was hours away from taking the Lord into my tarnished, dirty soul.

We were now sitting in the pews attending mass, and before I knew it, it was time to get up and get in line with the other kids to receive communion. I was sweating and seeing black spots. I was weak from hunger and fright.

It was now my turn to receive the Eucharist, the Lord. I opened my mouth and the priest placed the host on my tongue. The Lord was now entering my awful, dirty house. My heart started beating fast; I felt faint but had to make it back to the pew. I did . . . then promptly passed out.

My sister Kay, who had taken me to church—no, not my mom or dad—said she knew that it had to be me who fainted, since she noticed how nervous I'd been that morning!

I remember to this day, sitting outside the church on the fire escape in a cold sweat and getting fresh air to recover.

I don't know how I survived having the Lord in my dirty house, since I had sinned. He must be very forgiving. As he is.

CHAPTER 2
ADOLESCENCE

I was now about eight years old, still living the good life and getting even more egotistical by the day, thinking I was the son of this big shot. School wasn't really a priority, and no one told me otherwise or urged me to study . . . so I didn't. I thought I had it made.

Strangely, and for whatever reason, I started to stutter. There were times I had real difficulty talking, and sometimes it was really bad. My heart would beat fast and my chest would tighten when I wanted to say something. I just couldn't get the words out. I was often afraid to talk. I didn't understand this, or why it was happening.

At school I would keep my head down and hope that the teacher wouldn't call on me to speak. What a horrible feeling, living in fear that I would have to get up and talk in class.

I went to speech therapy and they taught me how to try to overcome this impediment by taking a deep breath and taking my time when speaking. That seemed to help, but not all the time. My stutter would appear when I *thought* about what I was going to say beforehand, but if I just blurted it out with no forethought, I was fine—how weird.

Though now seldom, it has plagued me all my life, and to this very day. Few, if anyone, has ever noticed it—I think. It happens mostly when I'm tired, or if something in my life isn't right, and/or something is bothering me. Mostly emotional. I don't understand that. However, I have learned how to cover it. If I feel tense, and can't get out what I wanted to say, I redirect to another subject, sometimes never saying what I intended. Frustrating!

I have often wondered if this stemmed from a subconscious, deeply rooted feeling of insecurity. But at such a young age, why? Especially since I thought I was already a big shot. Maybe deep down I knew I really wasn't?

Later during my teenage years, when calling a girl to ask her for a date, there were times I would call and couldn't get anything out—and had to hang up. Thank God they didn't have caller ID back then! It was frustrating, embarrassing, and humiliating.

Then later in my adult life, running my business, having sales and staff meetings with dozens of employees staring at me—their boss—or giving a speech, I always had the fear I would stutter. Jeez, I couldn't. I was supposed to be this big, powerful guy. Funny, when I got mad and swore, I would never stutter! However, I declared this was a small handicap compared to what so many other unfortunate people must endure.

Living close to the Palace of Fine Arts, my friends and I would often play ball on the lawn area. The main structures were closed off with a chain-link fence to keep people from entering because it was in very bad disrepair, and obviously dangerous. This was during the Second World War, remember, so there was no money or plans to improve the structure. However, being a kid, and as kids do, my friends and I decided to go exploring, and found an area in the fence we were able to stretch that allowed us passage into the large pavilion of the Palace of Fine Arts main buildings, ignoring the warning signs that read, "No Trespassing"—no *what*?

We found a door at the bottom of one of the large sixty-foot-tall pillars and played with the lock . . . okay, we broke it with a large rock! We now had access to get inside. We then looked at each other with bewildered expressions, now wondering if we should really proceed. Reluctantly, we bravely decided to go in; none of us would want to be declared a coward, though we were indeed all frightened. As we entered, it smelled foul; the aroma of pigeon poop was quite prominent, and it was dark. The only light coming in was from several cracks in the decaying structure. It was rather scary, especially with the cobwebs collecting on our faces as we walked. We had barely enough light to see our way and wondered what the soft squishy stuff was that we were stepping on. We also had no clue where we were going—or what we were doing.

Upon proceeding, we saw what looked like a makeshift, flimsy wooden stepladder going straight up, so naturally we undertook the task of seeing where it went. We climbed and climbed, and finally reached an area that had large beams stretching over what appeared to be the very top of the pavilion of the main structure. "Wow! Let's go," I said. Yes, I was the leader, of course. We started climbing up and up, then over on our knees on a beam, now discovering it was covered with several inches of the very pigeon poop we had smelled that had built up over the years. Actually, this was a place that only pigeons should have been, or any winged being that could take flight. While slowly edging over this narrow, two-foot-wide beam, we were very scared, because it would be one heck of a drop if we fell—and who in the hell would find us?

After some time, we finally reached the very top, the exact middle of the pavilion of the Palace of Fine Arts. It was circular and about six feet in diameter. Feeling like Christopher Columbus, I declared it "my clubhouse!"

So why was it just *my* clubhouse? Well, I was Christopher Columbus; the other guys were just my deck hands who I allowed to be members. Yes, just a kid's fantasy, and yes, maybe just a bit pompous! After proudly sitting there for about twenty minutes, I suddenly realized that we had to get back down, as it was getting close to dinner time. This was going to be scary, going down, especially with all the poop, but we slowly inched our way down safely as the occasional pigeon flew by and checked us out.

Well, as time went on, I brought comics books up there, potato chips, and cookies, and—oh, yes—finally a flash light. I was getting resourceful, and oh, sure, I allowed my friends free membership. I even invited a girl to come up to my clubhouse one day, even though it was an all-guys club. That was okay back then by the way! Of course, I was the only one allowed that privilege.

I recall one day sitting up there and silently thinking, *Wow, I have a clubhouse on the top of a palace and live on an island. How many kids can say that?*

One afternoon when we were going through that same door at the base of the pillar, we saw a man lying there. His skin was pale—no, white, very white! We said, "Hey, mister, you okay?" He didn't respond, and he didn't move. We suddenly realized he was dead!

We went flying out of there and shot out the opening of the chain-link fence and ran home and told my mom. She called the police to tell them that there could be a dead man at the base of one of the pillars. Well, that was a mistake, because when the policeman came to the house, he asked me if I'd seen the sign that read "No Trespassing. Well, this was my first visit to juvenile hall.

A strange and rather creepy occurrence happened that I would like to mention. Near the end of World War II, my brother Walter had not been heard from for several months, and we were all concerned, but knew he wasn't able to write, naturally due to the obvious circumstances. So, my four sisters pulled out the Ouija board, just playing around, yet hoping to get a prophetical obscure clue as to where he was. Two of my sisters sat across from one another, their hands on the planchette, and said, "Ouija, where is our brother Walter?" Then after a few moments, it very slowly and mysteriously started to move, going in a large circle, and then another even larger circle, as if it was thinking, searching. Then it slowed even further. It gradually went to the letter L, then slowly went to the letter U, then to the letter Z, then to O, then to N. Then it stopped. It had spelled out the word LUZON.

So now my sisters, curious, had to find out if there was indeed a place in the world called Luzon. Remember, this was back in early 1945, so there was no Google Earth. They then pulled out a map of the world, and after some time, discovered there was a place called Luzon in the Philippines, and as a matter of fact, it was the largest island.

Well, they found that amusing, as well as baffling, but also creepy, because they had never heard of the island before. Though the war was being fought in Luzon, the news was not as prevalent as it is today. The Battle of Luzon was fought January 9th through August 15th, 1945.

In the meantime, it came to pass that a week later we received a letter from my brother apologizing for not having written in such a long time, saying he wasn't allowed due to the ongoing war. He said he had been slightly injured by a falling palm tree, but was fine, and said it had happened while they were building an airstrip on the island of Luzon. This is, as a matter of fact, true!

My mom would occasionally have me go to the store on Chestnut Street a few blocks away. My friends would be over, so I would take them with me. On the way back after shopping, I would have my friends carry all the groceries. There were at least three guys following me in a march-like formation. I would sound off, "March, march, march," leading as they dutifully followed. I guess I unknowingly already thought I was a leader. One of my sisters, upon noticing this, called to my attention that it was inappropriate for me to have them carry everything for me, and to act as if I was superior. I really didn't realize I had done anything wrong. Wasn't that just the way it is? Often one does something inappropriate unaware or without realizing it, until someone calls attention to it.

During my primary days of development, I felt omnipotent—or at least I thought so. That premise was perceived to be true until inquiry and reality set in many years later.

Well, just about this time, my cousin was getting married and asked me to be in her wedding. She said I would be walking down the aisle with her youngest sister, who had just turned eight. A couple of weeks later she brought her over to the house so we could meet. Oh, jeez—she was sooooo cute! I was eight and a half years old. If you'll notice, I added that *half*, and was in love at first glance. This was it, I thought! I couldn't sleep, thinking about her.

Well, the wedding day eventually came. I was the ring bearer and she, the flower girl, and as I walked down the aisle, my heart fluttered like *we* were the ones getting married!

A few weeks passed, and I couldn't get her out of my mind; I had to see her again. The only means of transportation, of course, was my bike. I had gotten a new post-war model BA-107 Schwinn bicycle for Christmas—yes, I just asked, and I received. It was the new streamlined model with an embossed tank, an electric horn, a headlight, and a spring-fork shock absorber. It was two-tone, maroon with cream accents. It was hot! Well, hot or not, she lived in South San Francisco, at least fifteen miles away! It may not sound far, but there were no direct routes to take like nowadays. I had to travel entirely through the city. Keep in mind, I lived near the entrance to the Golden Gate Bridge in the Marina District, the opposite end of the city from South San Francisco. But I didn't care.

It was early in the morning during the summer when I was brainstorming as I laid in bed. I had an early breakfast and told my mom I was going out for a bike ride and wouldn't be back for lunch. She said, "Be back by five." "Okay, sure, Mom," I replied. I then set off peddling, peddling, no water, no snacks, no money. While venturing through the busy streets of San Francisco, dodging cars and occasionally forcing a pedestrian to flee the sidewalk, I was now getting tired—very tired and thirsty—but was amazed that I was figuring out how to get there. I remembered the route my dad had taken while going on Sunday rides down the Peninsula near where she lived. No GPS or Google maps back then, remember.

It was now approaching four o'clock in the afternoon, and I was finally just a few blocks from her house. Well, guess what, I got a flat tire! Now I was thinking, *how do I get home? I never thought it would take this long! My mom is going to be looking for me for dinner. Oh, jeez!*

I pushed my bike the next few blocks and arrived at my love's house. I rang the doorbell and it rang . . . and rang . . . and rang—yep, no one was home! No, I hadn't called to see if she was going to be home.

Sitting on her doorstep as five o'clock approached, I wondered what my mom was thinking, and even worse, how was I going to call her? How in the heck was I going to explain to her where I was? And how would I get back home?

A few minutes later, the girl's father drove up and promptly asked, "Kiki, what are you doing here?" Then, bewildered, he exclaimed, "And how did you get here?!" "On my bike," I answered. I then asked, "Is your daughter coming home soon?" I heard him chuckling as he talked to my mom, advising her of my day's adventure.

My brother then drove down and picked me up, along with my disabled bike. In the car he asked, "Did you at least call her before you left?" I looked at him with a smirk, and he knew.

So why did I bring this immature and silly adventure up? It's because I question my motivation for doing it. Was there inherent drive and *perseverance* prevalent within me at such a young age to strive for what I wanted, no matter the consequences? Or was I motivated on this crusade to the opposite ends of the earth while putting all obstacles aside, the beginning of my extreme attraction for the opposite sex?

Well, after that little fanciful excursion, my parents soon decided I should find an interest other than the allure of pubescent lassies, so they had me join the Boy Scouts of America for so-called character development. It sounded very militant and disciplinary. I wasn't too keen about the idea.

Well, it was somewhat fun at first, but I soon found I had to study to advance, and I hated studying. Mr. McGrevy, the scout leader, urged me—or should I be forthright and say that he constantly bugged me—to study to earn merit badges, and often spoke of the ultimate achievement of being an Eagle Scout. You know, I was never a goody-two-shoes, as the saying goes, so wasn't really into that. I ended up staying in it for over a year until I got thrown out.

There was a camp-out in Marin County one weekend and, being mischievous, I brought some sparklers to camp to play with at night. No, of course they weren't allowed. We were there to learn outdoor skills, and play was not on the agenda. Well, I played with them to show off and ended up catching the deck of the cabin on fire. Oh, heck, it was just a little fire. My parents were called to pick me up. Goodbye, Boy Scouts!

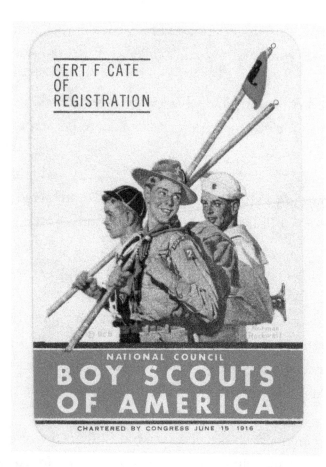

By the way, their motto is, "Be prepared." Well, just at the forefront of learning about sex, I took that to mean always carry condoms.

Then my parents had me take piano lessons. Jeez, I must have been a problem kid! Well, that also started out as fun, but soon became demanding, having to practice. I hate anything repetitious, or that has to do with studying, i.e., practicing. However, the piano lessons lasted for several years, and I ended up enjoying it. But don't ask me to even play Chopsticks now.

Well, during this time, I was in my last year at Winfield Scott, and one of my very studious friends, quite contrary to my make up, came running up to me. He said, "Kiki, they're having auditions for the San Francisco Opera Boy's Chorus on Friday in the gym. I'm so excited! Why don't you come?" I must have looked at him with I can only imagine what kind of look, thinking, *Oh, how terribly dull*, and said, "Uh, don't think so, but thanks."

So that Friday came, and I heard that a lady from the San Francisco Opera was in the gym doing the auditions. Well, my curiosity must have gotten the best of me, and I probably also wondered how my sedulous friend had done. So, to the gym, I went.

My gosh! There was a lineup of boys. I hadn't known this was such a big deal; who would have wanted to sing in a chorus, anyway? It was said they only needed two boys, and evidently all these guys must have been bad—really bad—because they weren't singing very long and were then asked to leave.

Well, the line for the auditions was now coming to an end, and I saw my friend over in a corner eyeing out what was going on. He then noticed me and came running over and said, "Hey, Kiki, they can't find the second boy. I'm the only one she chose so far. Come on over and try out. Her name is Miss Bacon!" I replied, "Wow! You made it. That's cool . . . I guess." He was now being insistent and wouldn't give up. I suppose misery likes company, as the saying goes, so I finally gave in. Now shaking, I walked up to this rather diminutive but stoic young lady and asked, "Are you still auditioning, Miss Bacon?"

Little did I know, I was standing there talking to an eventual icon with the San Francisco Opera Company, the now legendary Madi Bacon. Madi was in the process of forming the first year of the San Francisco Opera Boys Chorus.

She turned, looked down at me, and said, "Oh, yes, I am. Would you like to sing for me?" I wanted to say no, but for whatever reason said, "Sure." She then asked my name and I said Achille, figuring that might scare her away, but no luck. I forget what the song or the lines were that she asked me to sing. I never really sang. This wasn't something my family did, other than sing "Happy Birthday" at parties.

I nervously sang whatever she'd asked me to, whatever it was. However, it certainly wasn't "Happy Birthday"! Relieved it was now over and I could go outside and play baseball with my real guy friends, she stopped me, grabbed my arm, and said, "That was very good, Achille. By the way, is there another name they call you by?"

I said, "Yes, Miss Bacon. Kiki." She then said, "Well, Kiki, *you* are the second boy I have chosen. Congratulations!"

I guess I turned pale, because she then said, "Aren't you happy?" "Oh, oh, uh . . . yes, of course, Miss Bacon, thank you," I reluctantly replied.

Oh my God, what had I just done? Why had I let my four-eyed friend talk me into this? Then I wondered if my mom and dad would be happy or would think their son was a "cherry picker." Then thought, *Hey, maybe they won't sign the papers and I can get out of it.* Well, my mom and dad thought it was great . . . and I was committed.

Rehearsals started a month later, and the first opera was *La Boheme.* Well, after months of rehearsals and dress rehearsals, we were ready for the opening night.

For whatever reason, the night of the opening, Madi chose me to go on stage for the opening scene *alone*—that's right, all by myself. I guess it was a compliment.

She said, "Kiki, when the curtain rises, I will tell you when, and then run out to stage center and warm your hands on the bonfire"—simulated, of course. "Stay there, rubbing your hands over the fire, for about the count of thirty, then run back." She cautioned me to *not* look out at the crowd. "Do not look out at the audience," she said. "Yes, Miss Bacon," I replied, while standing there dressed as a young French peasant boy in tattered, baggy clothes with a dirty face.

The immense curtain then soon rose. The massive resounding forte of the entire San Francisco Opera Orchestra started to resonate, and the stage was now vibrating from the intense sound, with symbols crashing and drums thundering as the entire brass section announced my entrance. "Go," Miss Bacon said. So out I daringly ran onto this enormous stage. I'd seen it many times during rehearsals, but it hadn't looked that big. I thought, *Oh my God. Just concentrate and warm your hands. That's good. You're doing great. Now don't look out at the crowd, but I want to. No, don't. Actors don't look into the camera. You'll mess up.* These thoughts were rampaging through me as I stood there . . . and I guess by then, it had been too long! Just then, I heard Madi saying, "Kiki, come back! Come back!"

Okay, but just one look—so I did! I looked out and saw thousands upon thousands of people looking at me, just me! I guess I said, "Oh, shoot"—maybe even, "Oh, shit,"—because the entire audience started laughing!

When I got backstage, Madi asked, "Why did they laugh Kiki?" I nervously stammered, "I don't know… m-maybe t-they t-thought I w-was cute!"

We sang in many operas that year, including, *La Boheme*, *Boris Godunov*, and *Carmen*.

I must say, though I originally didn't want to be in the chorus, it was a wonderful experience. During rehearsals I met many famous people, such as Gaetano Merola, the actual founder of the San Francisco Opera Company, as well as Kurt Herbert Adler. Gaetano Merola and Kurt Herbert Adler were the company's first two general directors. I also met many famous opera singers, and have Merola's and Adler's autographs, along with many of the opera stars.

Funny, I remember sitting on Merola's lap one day during rehearsals with him saying to me, "My, my, you have a famous old San Francisco last name, Kiki." Little did I know at the time, who *he* was, or that *he* was the famous one! *So goes the innocence of a child.*

BOYS CHORUS OF SAN FRANCISCO OPERA COMPANY

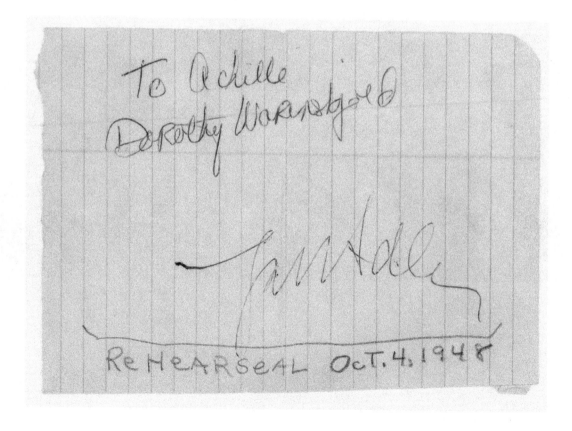

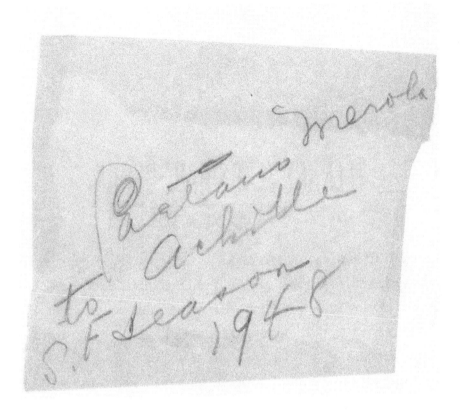

It came to pass that many current notable artists were once members of the famed San Francisco Opera Boy's Chorus, and in 1992, the chorus won a Grammy.

Flash forward many years—like sixty-five years—and I recently served as vice president of the board of directors and helped with fundraising for the yearly gala—once again, I was involved with many of the principal people of the San Francisco Opera Boys Chorus.

CHAPTER 3

TEENAGE YEARS HAVE BEGUN

When I was about fifteen, my dad took me to work one day during the summer. He was running the Oakland plant. I felt being with him all day could give us some time to really bond, something I had always wanted and craved. I was excited about that. I had never really seen a wholesale fish business in action, though heard him talking about it at the dinner table often. Upon arriving at the plant, I was surprised to see that he had a sea lion living in a stainless-steel tank, right there among all the commotion of the wholesale fish business. Can you imagine a sea lion swimming about in a seafood establishment? Was this paradise for him, or what, having to never hunt for fish again, but to only bark or roar, and he could have an hourly seafood meal of his choice! I heard his favorite meal was calamari. Calamari, or squid as it is more commonly known, is an inexpensive seafood. So, he was very frugal with his demands.

My dad was an animal lover, as our entire family is. It came to pass that he heard his drag boats talking to one another on the shortwave radio late one night, saying that a baby sea lion got caught in one of the drag nets and they were going to shoot it. My dad promptly got on the radio phone and explicitly said to leave it alone; to get it on board and bring it to the Oakland plant the next morning. He repeated, "Don't harm it!"

He immediately had a large stainless-steel tank built for it and called him "Oscar."

Every day during lunch my dad would put on a top hat—yes, an old-fashioned-style top hat like Lincoln wore. Though it symbolizes aristocracy, his intention was to be anything but fashionable; he was a real character. And he probably got it from the "GW" (Goodwill), as he called it, which was next door to the plant. He would take Oscar on a walk with him every day up to Broadway, the main street in Oakland. They would walk side by side . . . if that's what a sea lion does. My dad would then go into the Tele-News at the theater and watch the news for an hour, and Oscar would ceremoniously wait for him outside. I'm surprised he didn't buy a seat for him and bring him into the movie theater and eat popcorn together!

As Oscar matured, my dad would occasionally walk him down to the Oakland estuary several blocks from the plant and urge him to swim in the waters of the bay; it would hopefully allow him to find some fellow sea lions, and just maybe he would choose to swim away to be in his own natural environment. Knowing my dad, it would hurt to lose him, but I'm sure he didn't feel it was fair for Oscar to live out his life in a twenty-by-fifteen-foot tank. Oscar learned to love swimming in the estuary, and would often disappear for hours, but would always return to the exact place where my dad was attentively waiting for him, patiently smoking his cigarette and I'm sure occasionally dozing off while basking in the warm summer sun.

This routine repeated time and again; however, one day Oscar didn't return after the usual hour or so. My dad waited and waited for him, and several hours passed, now fearing Oscar had indeed caught up with other sea lions, or possibly a flirtatious sea lion lady, and was now gone. My dad returned to the plant with a sad heart and an ache in his gut; after all, they were buddies, and he probably loved the guy—if you can love a sea lion.

It was just a little before four in the afternoon, and time to close the plant, so my dad must have now sadly realized that his once-devoted friend was not coming back.

Just as he started walking to his car, he heard the sound of flippers flapping, flapping on the sidewalk, approaching him—yes, it was Oscar. He found his way back all the way from the estuary at least a half mile away. Can you imagine the site of a sea lion walking up Broadway Street in downtown Oakland—by itself?!

So, my dad had his beloved Oscar back. I'm sure if a sea lion could smile, Oscar was doing so at that moment. I know my dad was! They probably went back into the plant and enjoyed some calamari together. I have a picture of my dad and Oscar in the fish market together that I cherish. He and Oscar were written up in the *Oakland Tribune* many times.

On that first day of my adventure visiting the plant, my dad asked if I wanted to make a few bucks, so I said sure! He said the chef at a restaurant on Jack London Square needed a block of ice, and for me to take it to him, mentioning that it was about a half mile away. It just so happened that it was also a very hot day, close to ninety degrees. I then left on my first ever work assignment, taking this huge block of ice down to the restaurant on a hand truck. Well, after walking several blocks on the sidewalk, I noticed the ice was rapidly melting, so I frantically started to run, maneuvering around the countless tourists in Jack London Square, attempting to avoid hitting their heels with the clumsy, old, oversized wooden hand truck while leaving a trail of water behind me. By the time I got to the restaurant, the block of ice was now the size of a loaf of bread, a very small loaf of bread. The chef, who was this burly, tall, imposing, bearded man, fearlessly started to holler at me as I meekly cowered. He stated that he'd wanted a *whole* block of ice—not this puny, melting nothing—and promptly sent me back to fetch another. When I got back to the plant, my dad then also hollered at me, and asked what the hell had taken me so long to get there. The chef had obviously called him and was really pissed off!

He said for me to take another one down there, and this time to hurry up, for Christ sake! Jeez, I felt really lame. I didn't want to screw up on my first day on the job; I wanted my dad to be proud of me. So the second time I ran there as fast as I could, sounding out, *Beep, beep! Beep, beep!* as I ran past all the tourists, who were jumping off the sidewalk to get out of my way. Well, upon arriving the second time, the ice block was now just the size of a somewhat-larger loaf of bread than the first one had been. The chef now screamed at me again, saying, "What the hell is the matter with you kid?!" He then said he was going to call my dad—again!

Walking back, I felt deflated. I'd let my dad down on my first job assignment; I was a failure. When I got back to the plant, my T-shirt was soaking wet with perspiration, I was exhausted, thirsty, and downhearted. I then saw my dad standing outside . . . laughing—yes, laughing! He had a big belly, and I can still see it bellowing in and out! Okay, he got me. It had all been a setup! He'd had his fun.

Some of the things he did when I was a kid I remember to this day. On Sundays, my mom and dad would go for Sunday drives, and being only about twelve or so, I naturally had to tag along. I sat in the back seat of the Dodge coupe as my dad drove with Corky, his dog, on his shoulders. There were times he would drive slowly, gazing at things as his left arm hung out the window holding a half-smoked Camel cigarette. One day as he was doing his gazing at something, he got a ticket for going too slow. I remember that day so well, because later that same day, he got a ticket for going too fast! When the cop pulled him over, I asked him from the backseat, "Were you trying to average it out, Dad?" There was no response. On another one of those Sunday drives, he went through a stop sign. I remarked to him, "Dad, you just went through a stop sign!" He responded, "I'll stop twice tomorrow!" When the police officer approached the driver side window of the car, I asked my dad if he was going to tell that to the officer?

One day several months later, I had the realization that I never told my dad I loved him, and this bothered me; however, he never told me he loved me either. I decided it was important for me to tell him and set out to do it. He would go downstairs every night after dinner to his stamp room, turn on his overhead desk light, and fool around with his stamp collection. That was the perfect time for me to say it; we would be alone, and it should be easy.

Well, one night after dinner he went downstairs as usual, and I decided this was the night I was going say it once and for all. I waited awhile so he could get situated doing his thing with his stamp collection, then went downstairs and entered his stamp room. While hovering over his desk light, I nervously said, making small talk, "So how's the stamps doing, Dad?" While intensely looking through a magnifying glass, he said, "This one could be valuable. It's the Wright Brother's First Flight air mail stamp." (I still have that very stamp.) Then he said, "So what's up, kid?" This shocked me for a moment, but was the perfect introduction for me to say it . . . but I couldn't. It had nothing to do with stuttering; my heart started pounding and I ended up saying something stupid, like, "Oh, nuttin'. Just wanted to see what you were doin'."

I couldn't get those words out. Why, I'll never know. Maybe it was because back then, guys didn't tell other guys they loved each other, even if they were father and son. I attempted this at least a half dozen times, but never succeeded. So, it went unsaid, forever. I regret it to this day.

When I was about fourteen, I was losing interest in the homemade roller-skate wooden wagons we made, and the now-mundane riding of bicycles, so I transitioned into cars. Don't all guys around this age? I watched my dad and brother drive, so basically taught myself. Of course, I knew nothing about, or cared about, the traffic laws, however.

Even though we lived in this huge home, there was only room for one car in the garage since the home had been built in the 1920s, and cars weren't a big issue back then. My dad's car, an older, tan Dodge Coupe, was in a perfect position—straight in—for me and my buddies to push it out of the garage and start it in compression without making any noise. My dad would play cards several times a week in his card room adjacent to the garage, so he could hear the car starting if we started it with the ignition. I must add that my dad had an old cowbell on the garage door, so his paisanos could ring it to enter without going upstairs to the front-door entrance. Several of these paisanos were rather threatening-looking, such as "One-Eyed Ike"; then there was Nunzio, who allegedly packed a gun. They both had sizable seafood restaurants with retail stands on Fisherman's Wharf.

Well, on occasion when I felt gutsy, several of my friends would push the car out of the garage. It had a slight downward slope, so it would start in compression. I would leave the garage door open so we could coast back in without making a sound. This worked like a charm for several ventures, driving around the neighborhood and showing off for the girls, or just cruising on Chestnut or Lombard Streets, having a good time. I knew just the exact time we had to get the car back into the garage before the card game would break up, so my dad wouldn't get wise. No, of course I had no license or permit.

One night, my mom came downstairs for some reason and found the garage doors open, so she closed them, I guess thinking my brother had taken the car and forgotten to close them. My buddies and I knew it was now time to get back home and had no time to waste. Coming around

Richardson Avenue onto Francisco Street, I turned off the ignition as I always did and came around the corner just fast enough to go up the slight incline and into the garage, then silently turn off the ignition. As I approached the garage, still going relatively fast . . . I suddenly noticed the garage doors were shut! "Oh, shit!" I said—and slammed into them, with the goddamn cowbell clanging with all its might! I was now half in, half out of the garage with parts of the garage door surrounding the car, me stuck in the driver's seat. My friends flew out of the car like jackrabbits being chased by a fox, leaving me to be devoured alone!

I was dead meat. My dad came out saying—no, came out *yelling* at me— "I suspected you've been doing something like this!" And used profanities yet unheard of by me at such a young age. The garage door needed to be repaired, and there were now several permanent, good-sized dings in the car. I figured he couldn't take my license away; I didn't have one.

Many months later it was now time for my dad to get a new car, not due to that incident, however. For whatever reason, he liked Dodges. I hated them, especially because he always got the basic, stripped-down models.

One night at dinner he said he'd just ordered a new car, another Dodge, of course. "What model, Dad?" I asked. He said, "Oh, just a business Coupe." *Oh, damn,* I thought. *I'll be driving legally soon and want to look good for the girls. I don't want to be driving around in that drab, plain ole thing. Jeez,* I thought to myself, *why always a crummy business coupe?*

Well, it just so happened that he had brought home a brochure from the dealership of all the new models with the salesman's card stapled to it. I saw that there was a cool model called the Dodge Diplomat, a coupe that looked like a hard-top convertible, with lots of chrome, and the windows folded all the way down just like on a real convertible. *Wow, I'd look good in that!* I thought.

I don't know where in the hell I got the guts at such a young age, but the next day I called the salesman and told him that my dad was busy; he'd asked me to call to tell him that he'd changed his mind and wanted the Diplomat model instead. The salesman then said, "Oh, all right, well, let's see. Okay, we have one in stock. Is blue okay?" he asked me. I said, "Oh, I'm sure that will be just fine with him." After I hung up, I thought, *Jeez, what in the hell did I just do?!*

The next day, I anxiously yet very apprehensively waited until my dad came home. To my surprise, he indeed drove up in this really sharp-looking, light-blue hard-top convertible; and yes, with lots of cool, shiny chrome. Yea! *Yea,* baloney. What the hell would he say if the salesman told him I'd called?

When he walked in, I said meekly, "I thought you ordered a business coupe, Dad," and he replied, "Well, seems like they got the order mixed up and had this one ready for me, so I took it."

Oh my God! I couldn't believe what I'd just pulled off! Man, oh man, was I one happy guy. I was now all set for dating in a couple years when I got my license!

Did I really just pull that off? I later thought.

CHAPTER 4
FINALLY, A TEENAGER

I was now a teenager and attending Saint Ignatius High School. This was punishment—no girls! The teachers were all Jesuits and very strict, and I hated it.

I had to get out of there somehow. I thought maybe if I just didn't study or if I got into enough trouble, I would get thrown out, expelled. After all, I had always had a contention for defiance to guidance and discipline. Anyway, I didn't have to study and get good grades. For what? I had it made with my dad's business—*so I thought*.

I tried just about everything to get thrown out. Never studied, never did homework, fooled around in class, and got almost all Cs, a few Ds, and an occasional F—actually, several Fs . . . good! This was working great. I was eventually even successfully threatened with expulsion unless my grades improved drastically. This was a scholastic Jesuit school, serious stuff, a college preparatory linked to the University of San Francisco, so they didn't stand for any nonsense.

Well, one day they had a mandatory IQ test. I actually found it to be fun and didn't give it much thought. I didn't really know what it was, so I just rushed through it. A few days later, I was called into the principal's office. He was a tall, thin, dark-haired, rather good-looking man. I noticed he looked upset, but why? I wondered. I hadn't done anything wrong lately. He then said in that stern voice he used so often when I got in trouble, "Paladini, we're not going to tolerate your grades anymore. You have an IQ of 155. You're obviously no dummy! You're capable of straight As if you wanted to!" Heck, the only A I ever got on my report card was the first letter of my first name. I had no clue what that number meant anyway. So what did "IQ" stand for, anyway? I wondered. I thought possibly, "Interesting Quiz," or "Impressive Questions," or maybe even "I Quit!" Didn't really matter, because it got me into further trouble.

I then figured I would just have to get around that and get into more trouble to get tossed out. There was a very short Jesuit teacher named Father Rock; he was about five feet one or two. He taught religion; I hated religion. One day he was telling us about when Jesus calmed the stormy sea. He then went into a long dissertation about it, ending as Jesus said, "Peace! Be still!" Then the wind ceased and there was a dead calm.

I asked Father Rock, "How could that possibly happen? How could that be?" Well, he dismissed my question by answering, "Don't question the Bible or the word of God." I then said, "Baloney!" (Actually, I said "Bullshit!") He then screamed at me, "Go down the hall right now and see Father Leonard, the principal!" I then said, "Yes, Father Pebble!"

He turned pale and started to chase me. As I went out the classroom door, I held the door behind me as if it was locked; the door opened inward. He was tugging at it, tugging at it with all his might. I then let go and he fell backwards onto the floor as the entire class erupted into hysterical laughter! Okay, I'd gotten my first warning . . . this was working.

Then there was the time we were all having lunch out in the yard. I was eating a peach, a nice fat, soft, ripe peach. I had noticed that Father Spohn, a tall, robust man, was walking across the yard about fifty to sixty feet from me and was looking the other way. I said, "Watch this, guys," and I threw the peach at him. *Splat!* It hit him right on the side of his face. I never thought in a million years I would have or could have hit him. Oh boy, I was in big trouble now!

Well, the school was now on lock down that afternoon. It was soon announced over the loud speaker that all students had to stay until the boy who'd hit Father Spohn with the peach came forward. So, I bravely walked in and saw the principal, Father Leonard, and admitted to it. I told him, "I was aiming at a pigeon."

Still didn't get thrown out, damn it! Just another warning with lots of homework . . . that I didn't do.

I'll never forget the time when there was an old junk of a car parked up on the hill near the store where we bought our lunch. It had been there for weeks, and the guys would always egg me on saying, "Kiki, try it out!" Well, one day, showing off, I got behind the wheel of this old junk. The wheels were turned into the curb, as you must do in the city when parked on a hill, so I turned the wheels straight, making as if I was driving. It then started going down the hill rather fast, toward the school, then faster and faster. I tried the brakes. *Shit! No brakes! Oh, jeez, what do I do?!* There was a big intersection coming up at the end of the block. Well, the front entrance of

Saint Ignatius had a slight hill in front with a lawn. I thought maybe if I turned the car up onto the front lawn, it would slow down and stop—hopefully.

As I approached the front of the school, I turned the wheel to the right and drove up onto the lawn . . . however, it didn't slow down, at least not enough, and I slammed into the large plate-glass window of Father Leonard's office—yes, my now very familiar, good acquaintance, the principal! I can still see him spinning around in his swivel chair, looking at me through the gaping opening of the plate-glass window, now in a million pieces on his office floor, saying, "Paladini, you again!" That was a bad one, but it had been unplanned. Unintended! My dad was called, and I was in deep shit, but still didn't get expelled. *What the hell more must I do?!* I thought.

Yep, Saint Ignatius wasn't a good experience. There are many more tales about my adventures there, but I won't get into details. I was the court jester in high school, thinking I would someday be king. I only slowed down my antics somewhat when my father threatened me with the New Mexico Military Academy. He was casually reading a brochure from the academy at the dinner table a few nights later. That was not good.

CHAPTER 5
GETTING CLOSE TO ADULTHOOD

I'd just graduated somehow from Saint Ignatius High School. I think it was more than likely just because they were happy to get rid of me! Deep down, I really wanted to be a lawyer, but still knew I was going to work for my dad. I was slated to start the University of San Francisco's Law School at the end of the summer.

Just after graduating high school, I went down to Southern California; my dad had gone down a few months prior in an attempt to save the Los Angeles plant, as sales were declining. Hard to believe, I know. How could sales decline with the then-rapid influx of population into Southern California?

Arriving down south, I found that I loved the weather, never realizing the sky was blue, having come from the Marina District in San Francisco. The warm nights were amazing, and oh yes, the girls—the girls, my God, they were even more amazing, and all so gorgeous, prancing around in their skimpy little sun dresses. What a fun summer this was going to be.

I had just bought a 1950 Mercury convertible, quite suitable for Southern California, but that would not suffice. I wanted to date that summer while there, and needed something snazzier to drive around in. I had a government bond that had been given to me when I was a little boy, so with trading in the Mercury, I had just enough for the down payment on a brand new, white 1957 Thunderbird convertible—yah-hoo!

I now needed some money to date, and oh yes, to make the car payments, but luckily not for rent or food, because I was living with my mom and dad, who rented a home in Santa Monica near the Brentwood Farmers Market. I asked my dad if I could work for him for the summer—but just the summer—after all, I had to get back up north to start law school (though that was a futile pursuit, I thought).

I met several girls, mostly Jewish, and we got along great. One in particular, was adorable and seductive, only about five foot one, with short blonde hair and tiny, hard boobs; however, never being satisfied, I looked further. I then met the cute daughter of a salesman who worked for my dad, and she had magnificent breasts—oh my, did she! I'm sure she had other qualities, too. Now, mind you, I'm not totally into breasts. I'm really a leg man, and I'm not talking about fried chicken. Anyway, we dated for several weeks until she introduced me to her friend who would be in her senior class the next year at Van Nuys High in the Valley, the same school where Natalie Wood and Robert Redford were going to at the time. She was sixteen, and an absolutely gorgeous, voluptuous five-foot-seven knockout, with long blonde hair flowing over her shoulders. Yes, I had to stand up straight when meeting her. She had glaring, cobalt-blue eyes, with a magnificent, enticingly sexy figure, and looooong, provocative legs! Oh. My. God!

I remember that first date with her so well. I picked her up at her home in the Valley. She was wearing an alluring, black, skin-tight pantsuit, and looked so very seductive. We drove over Laurel Canyon and had dinner at the Seven Seas, a Tahitian-themed supper club on Hollywood Boulevard, almost directly across from the famed Grauman's Chinese Theater. Later, we went to a movie at the Egyptian Theater a few blocks away, then after the movie, drove back towards the Valley over Coldwater Canyon up to Mulholland Drive. There were still a few undeveloped cliff-side lots there at the time, which conveniently allowed there to be an alluring setting for a romantic interlude. Little did I know, my choice to respite that evening was directly next to Errol Flynn's famed playboy home. You can't say I don't have good taste.

I recall being with her that night up on Mulholland Drive in the T-Bird with the top down—not hers (at least not yet), the car's—on that crescent-moonlit night overlooking the brilliant, shimmering lights of the San Fernando Valley below. The warm breeze coming from the valley seemed to embrace us as I nervously sat there in anticipation of pulling her towards me. My heart was beating, beating ever-so-fast; I wanted to kiss her, kiss her so badly, but was frozen with fright. I wasn't that experienced with this stuff. But I had to—I had to. I said to myself, "Just get your guts up, and grab her shoulder and pull her over next to you, for Christ sake." So I did. And oh, she felt so good in my arms. I was immediately mesmerized looking into her beautiful blue eyes just inches away, her long blonde hair off to one side and her leg now crossed over onto mine. I was excited. I now found it easy to kiss her.

We kissed softly at first, then hard, and then ever-so-passionately, she kissed me back with equal desire. I now ran my lips down on her neck, hers on mine, and we were now locked in a vise-like embrace. Our electricity was on overload, my hands now attempting to move across her body, wanting to enjoy her silk-like skin. As I reached for her breast, I was soon halted, as if a circuit breaker had tripped. She whispered, "Slow down, honey."

I had never felt such excitement, such pleasure; our energy together was magic. My God, what was this? This incredible newfound joy. Does everyone feel like this at first? We almost lost the ability to control our senses, but eventually recovered and regained restraint of ourselves. The truth is, she flatly halted my attempts; after all, it was our first date.

I was immediately nuts about her and didn't want to see anyone else. Why would I? But how could this happen so suddenly? I just wanted to have fun, not get serious, and I was only in L.A. for the summer. But I couldn't get her out of my mind, and so looked forward to seeing her again as soon as I could. The following week while at work, and she at school, it was a struggle to get through the day, only looking forward to getting home to call her. I was infatuated with her; nothing else seemed important other than being with her.

Well, Saturday night finally came. It seemed like it had taken forever. I drove from Santa Monica, over winding Sepulveda Boulevard, and through the two-lane tunnel (no freeways back then), finally reaching her home a half hour later. Her folks weren't home, so we—correction, I—started getting affectionate. After messing up her hair and ruining her makeup, I was asked to please cool it!

She straightened up again, and we left for dinner in the T-Bird with the top down. As we drove out of her driveway she waved at a guy in front of his house, and said it was Audie Murphy, the highly decorated World War II Medal of Honor hero, now actor. He lived directly across the street from her. I was surprised to notice how short he was. "See, you don't have to be tall to be a super hero," I jokingly commented. She looked over at me, unimpressed.

We drove over Benedict Canyon to West Hollywood since there wasn't much exciting going on in the Valley in those days, then drove over Sunset Boulevard to the famed Chateau Marmont to get an appetizer before dinner. The hotel was an old Hollywood haunt and a perfect place for actors to remain anonymous while reviewing a script for an upcoming film. Coincidentally, Humphrey Bogart was sitting at the end of the bar alone that evening, pensively smoking a cigarette, possibly waiting for Lauren Bacall to arrive. Meanwhile, I guess it wasn't in the script for me to impress my girl that night, since we were both asked for our IDs, and we ended up drinking Pepsi. What the hell was I thinking to attempt that? Being a good sport, she laughed and said, "That was a good try, Kiki!" Well at least the shrimp appetizer was good.

Unfortunately, the appetizer and the two Pepsis cost almost as much as I had planned for the entire dinner later. No, of course I hadn't realized how expensive the place was. Yes, I should have. Thankfully, we hadn't gone out the night before because I would have ended up washing dishes to pay for it. Oh yeah, sure, I never washed a dish in my life. Well, that whole idea bombed—served me right!

As we were leaving, walking out through the lobby, she saw a girl she knew and stopped to talk to her. She was an adorable young brunette, about the same age as my date. She was sitting on one of the immense, overstuffed sofas with an older woman. My date referred to the girl as Natalie. I must admit, my adrenaline started to surge upon noticing her. She was so damn cute, not beautiful, but cute. I loved her dark chestnut-brown hair, that was rather short and combed off to one side. Her deep brown eyes penetrated my senses when I met her. *Whew.* My immediate thought was to get in on the conversation and try to get to know her better . . . you know, to ask her out later! Well, I quickly squashed that thought, thinking what the hell was the matter with me? My girl was beyond gorgeous. Damn it, why aren't I ever satisfied?

As we walked out, I asked my date who the girl was, and she said, "Oh, just a friend in my senior class with me at Van Nuys High, Natalie Zacharenko, and her mother, you know, the actress Natalie Wood." Oh, jeez! *That* Natalie! Now thinking, *Oh, sure, she'd go out with me, the son of a fishmonger. Hey, but my dad's the Fish King! Oh, whoopee! That would go far in Hollywood. That's not the kind of king it takes to date someone like her!*

Now I felt glum. The stinkin' fish business isn't very glamorous, is it? Hey, but Leslie Caron married George Hormel of the Hormel Ham Company. Ham's come from pigs, and what the hell smells more than pigs?

Put your pecker back in your pants, Kiki, and let it go. Enjoy the night, for Christ sake.

Shrugging it off and re-entering my fictive world again, we then got into the T-Bird and went to dinner at Hollywood's oldest restaurant, the Musso & Frank Grill, not too far away on Hollywood Boulevard. Well, not encouraging her to eat anything too elaborate, I luckily had just enough money to pay for dinner. I had to stiff the waiter on his tip a bit, though, and got the hell out of there before he picked up the check.

As we walked out of the restaurant, I was suddenly overwhelmed with the realization that I really was living a delusional and pretentious fantasy. The Hormel guy wouldn't have had to stiff the waiter. *I better sit back and rethink just who I am, who I really am. But hell, later, not tonight* . . . Immediately dismissing that thought, we walked a few blocks further south on Hollywood Boulevard to North Ivar to the Hollywood Knickerbocker Hotel. I just wanted to kiss her under the immense, fabled chandelier in the lobby where so many stars had done so. That was fun, and heck, it was free!

We then drove out on Sunset Boulevard to the Pacific Coast Highway to Malibu. It was a magnificent, warm Southern California night. We parked at the beach and watched the waves pounding the huge rocks lit by the fluorescent moon above. It was as if the intense sound of the crashing surf was orchestrating the ever-increasing excitement and eagerness that was building between us. We were both nervously yet anxiously anticipating the overwhelming desire to make love, to eagerly continue where we had left off. We kissed, but this time we kissed hard—really hard—our lips sealed, never parting. While now passionately kissing her lower neck and slowly moving toward her breasts, it was as if the magnitude of the crashing waves had intensified like symphonic drums, while trumpets heralded the anticipated moment. My hands now moved freely over her body, but this time without resistance, caressing her young, firm breasts, feeling her nipples so hard, then touching her inner thigh, then moving even further inward and upward. I was now thoroughly, lustfully aroused as she vigorously wrenched about with erotic, orgasmic cravings, wildly lurching back and forth; our body heat felt as if we were going to implode. Now totally out of my mind, I suddenly experienced the complete ecstasy of intense intercourse. We were enjoying erogenous and carnal pleasures never experienced before, then eventually, simultaneously climaxing with the explosive intensity resembling a nuclear fusion ignition unleashing its energy.

We had both just encountered our first sexual experience. I now realized I was desperately in love with her, and it wasn't because of the sex. Yes, we had bewitching desires of intimacy, but there was also karma and a real connection between us.

The feeling of loving and being loved in return by a girl was an exhilarating experience.

She was now clutched in my arms as we embraced, reflecting upon our newfound experience. My body was still upon hers as our breathing slowed and our hearts began beating at a somewhat-normal pace again. Our intense heat had fogged up the windows of the tiny car, giving the feeling we were all alone somewhere in a capsule. My legs were under the dashboard of the T-Bird, a very uncomfortable position due to the low seats and tight leg room, but I was still in a state of ecstasy and unaware of any discomfort. My head was still buried in her neck, my eyes closed while holding her. Then suddenly, there was a tap on the window. It was a cop saying, "Break it up, break it up!"

The cuff on the left leg of my pants was caught on the heater cable under the dashboard and I couldn't get it loose. The cop was now getting mad, hollering, "Break it up! Break it up, I said!" I tugged and tugged at it, finally ripping the entire left pant leg off from the crotch! Well, the mood then cooled drastically as I rolled down the window and meekly said, "Yes, officer."

Later, upon arriving at her home, I suggested I just drop her off at the front door, and said, "How would I explain to your dad my bringing you home with only one pant leg. Doubt he would believe a dog did it!" I, of course, tossed them out when I got home so my mom wouldn't see them.

Well, I was in love and in paradise driving around Tinseltown in the T-Bird with my beautiful girl, and I loved showing her off. There was a huge billboard with her on it on Olympic Boulevard for a cosmetic advertisement. I would pass by it every morning and blow her a kiss while driving to the seafood plant in east Los Angeles from Santa Monica. She had also just been selected to compete in the Miss California Beauty Contest.

Wow, how in the hell did I ever land such a fantastic girl? I wasn't very tall, about five feet nine—okay, five feet eight. Oh, jeez! Okay, okay five feet seven . . . *and a half.* I had a pronounced nose—masculine, as I like to call it—and had an uncertain future. But I concluded even a beautiful girl had to love someone.

Not to sound conceited or presumptuous, but there appears to be some kind of compelling magnetism between myself and women. I don't really know why; however, I won't question it.

As we dated, we hit all the hot spots in West Hollywood and Beverly Hills every weekend, only leaving when I was out of the little money I was making working for my dad part-time. I usually had just enough money to make it through Friday and Saturday night. On Sunday morning, I couldn't buy a cup of coffee.

I vividly remember one evening, after having dinner at the Arabian Nights Restaurant on Sunset Boulevard, as we were leaving, we came upon a fortune teller in the lobby. My girl said she wanted to have our fortunes told. She had her fortune told first. The tarot cards revealed several enlightening things about her future, mainly that she would do well modeling and would have, I forget now, how many kids, plus all the usual B.S. We scoffed and laughed at the results. I'm sure the lady wasn't impressed with our review of her findings.

Then it was my turn. After a few more B.S. things, she then surprisingly said, "Sir, someday you will have many trucks with your name on them, and they will be seen all over California." *Wow, this is weird,* I thought. *Why did she say "you," as in "my" trucks?* My dad's business already had a lot of trucks all over the state with the name on it. *Hey, it's all nonsense, anyway,* I concluded.

Well, I promptly dismissed her findings and thought she was a wacko. Aren't all fortune tellers?

Later that night we stopped in at a small intimate cafe on Hollywood Boulevard down the street from the Capital Records building, and Johnny Carson was there. Surprisingly, they knew each other. She had just made an appearance as a model on his show, unknown to me. Meeting him was nice.

We often frequented Ciro's and the Mocambo, and other nightclubs on the Sunset Strip staying out until early morning, many times until closing at 2 a.m., or until I was out of money.

I used to love going with her and her folks to the Alpine Village in downtown Los Angeles. It was an authentic German restaurant with a dance floor and a live polka band playing while you ate. I'd never done the polka before, but I was out there with her hopping around in circles and loved it! I can still vividly remember us being on the dance floor twirling around and around while the accordions resounded their happy, jumpy tunes, as her long blonde hair wildly flung in the air as we circled the dance floor. Those memories are embedded within me.

It was now the middle of summer and we had never been to Las Vegas, so I asked her if she wanted to go the next weekend, and she immediately said yes!

This would be fun, taking my girl to Vegas in the T-Bird. I couldn't wait to go. Friday soon came, and we took off on our three-hour journey to Vegas. The top was down, and we enjoyed the warmth of the desert sun upon us.

Arriving in Vegas we checked in at the Sands, the *in* place at the time. We then drove around and looked for shows and saw that Louie Prima and Keely Smith were appearing at the Desert Inn; we both loved their music.

We had dinner, then went to the Desert Inn. They were performing in the lounge. We got there early and had front-row seats. What a blast that was. We enjoyed their performance so much, we stayed for the second show starting at 11 p.m.

We ended up having a great weekend, and I was so in love with such a fun, exciting, and beautiful woman—well, not quite a woman just yet.

Life was good, and I didn't have a care in the world. I had my car and I had my gal—that's all I wanted—and that's all I needed.

Since we had such a great time in Vegas, I asked her if she would like to drive down to Mexico in two weeks for the weekend. Summer was ending, and I thought we should spend the last weekend together before school started for her again. University of San Francisco was still several weeks away before I had to get back up to San Francisco. However, thoughts of leaving her were gut wrenching.

Two weeks eventually came; it seemed like it took forever. We embarked on our journey down to Mexico, and I had no clue where I was going or how to get there, just knew to follow the water down and make sure it was always on the right. I also had no clue where we were going to stay. Crossing the border was a breeze, not like it is now; a driver's license was all you needed luckily, since I'd never even thought of the requirements. When you're young, those were frivolous non-essentials. Thinking of bringing a bathing suit and dark-tanning sun lotion was paramount.

As we crossed the border entering Tijuana, we were surprised to see the condition of the roads; they were just dirt, and the lack of signage of what was ahead was nonexistent, but I figured if I followed the main road, if you could call it that, and stay on the coast, we would eventually come to a beach resort—at least I had hoped.

Somehow, we ended up in an area where kids were happily playing alongside the dirt road in their bare feet with little or no clothing. It was warm so that wasn't odd, but what *was* odd, was that the people were living in little huts made of old sheet metal, Coca-Cola signs propped up forming the sides and a sort of roof. Was that the way they lived? What was even more amazing was that all the kids were so happy! I guess they didn't know any better and their needs were simple. So, who's to say what happiness really is? I felt guilty driving the T-Bird, so I stopped and gave several of the kids a buck each. That proved to be a mistake, because like seagulls when you throw bread, they swarmed around me. After all, it wasn't like I had a lot of bucks to hand out.

We then finally found the main road and down the coast we went. We drove about an hour and a half with the dirt and dust kicking up behind us. I had to keep moving since the top was down, because upon slowing or stopping, we would be covered with the Mexico landscape. As we came around a turn, and now getting concerned about a depleting gas tank, a beautiful resort came upon us. The entrance had a large stone archway above and the entry road was lined with tall palm trees, and a sign over the archway said, Al Rosarita. The Rosarita Beach Resort. Now I just hoped they had a room. Well luckily, they did, and with an ocean view. The resort was almost empty. We had our choice of just about any room we wanted. While checking in with the hombre at the front desk, I noticed him looking at me, then at her, then back at me again, and he said, "Tener un buen tiempo, mi amigo." Well, we intended to, let me tell you!

We then laid by the pool for the rest of the day with the blistering sun upon us, and not being asked for our ID's, we indulged sipping on vodka-laden tropical drinks, as I coyly but mischievously played with the strings holding up her tiny bikini top. Her curvaceous figure and provocative breasts were arousing and so tempting, it was difficult to leave her alone.

That evening we had dinner at the outdoor restaurant by the pool surrounded by tall palm trees while a gentle, warm sea breeze from the nearby Pacific comforted us as we were serenaded by a trio of Mariachi musicians all dressed in white. While waiting for dinner, we danced in a small cleared area, most likely designated for serving trays, but we declared it our dance floor. As I gently pulled her into my arms, the softness and the warmth of her breasts against my chest impassioned my desire for her. I recall saying out loud, "Oh my God." That primal attraction between a man and a woman was now overwhelming. My desire to make love to her was paralyzing. Upon concluding the three or four songs, the trio obviously expected a tip. I had already given several dollars to the kids on the road, so didn't have too many extra dollars, so I just thanked them. We never saw them again after that!

After dinner the sun was setting, so we went down to the beach and walked barefoot on the soft, white sand, as an occasional light breeze brushed against our backs, setting the mood for romance as the darkness of the night approached. She was wearing a brightly colored, above-the-knee, strapless sundress with no bra, and her firm young breasts were now teasingly exhibiting her protruding nipples. Just looking at her caused my testosterone to churn within me. I found a hidden spot behind a huge boulder and aggressively grabbed her and threw her to the ground, pouncing on her as if a starved wild cougar was attacking. The velvet-like sand was still warm, almost hot; possibly what we felt was our own heat emanating through our bodies as the yearning for each other had uncontrollably intensified. It felt as if the sand could turn into glass.

The waves were pounding against the nearby rocks with a thundering roar, concealing the sound of my heartbeat as it raged with excitement. I laid her onto her back and passionately but gently kissed her, then discreetly pulled down her sundress, exposing her breasts, then lightly brushed my lips over her nipples while tenderly caressing her bosom. As she lay beneath me, I could feel the sweat from between her breasts trickling off to the side and down the small of her back. I then ran my hand between her legs; she was now moist, so moist and so ready for me. I could feel her heart pounding in unison with mine; her body now pulsated with excitement and carnal desire. My lips were locked on her neck as she now thrusted her head back. Her face was flushed, her vagina aqueous with the fury of passion. She moaned softly at first, then began to groan. Loud, then louder, then she screamed, "Oh my God!" when I entered her.

We made love for hours. It wasn't until the waning gibbous moon cast its light upon us that we realized we could possibly be noticed by more than just the sand fleas that were now pestering us. We then went to the room and to bed, embracing our intimacy as we closed our eyes. I can still see the entrance to the resort, and so rememeber the amazing time we had together. I often wonder if it is still there.

Anxious to see each other, we dated several times a week. We had our favorite make-out place just off Ventura Boulevard in Encino on Louisa Street, but forget now just how we came upon it. We had to drive about a half mile up from Ventura Boulevard to get to "our spot." It was perfect since it was dark, so dark at night with the absence of street lights to glare upon us. I remember a huge tree in the center of the narrow road. It was a country setting; not many homes were built there yet and there would be no cops to knock on the window telling us to break it up—that is, if they could see through the fogged-up windows.

We later learned that we had been parking not thirty feet from the entrance to Clark Gable's estate. His home was written up in a magazine that we happened to read one day and noticed the gates were just a short distance from *our* spot. But to quote Rhette Butler (Clark Gable), as he said to Scarlett O'Hara (Vivian Leigh) in *Gone With the Wind*, "Frankly, my dear, I don't give a damn!"

The summer was now coming to an end. *What do I do with my plans to go to USF to attend law school?* I pondered. I thought maybe I could apply to a college down there but didn't think I had the grades for UCLA or the like. I only got into USF because Saint Ignatius was the college prep school for it. Somehow, I was accepted; maybe they felt there could be aspiration or potential, and even optimism, for me to transmute my ways, kind of like a metamorphosis? Oh, sure.

CHAPTER 6
LIFE GETS INTERESTING

As I mired in a quandary the next week, not knowing what to do with my future, I got a surprise phone call from my girl. She was crying, crying intensely, she was almost hysterical—then said her period was late, very late, and she was worried she was pregnant! *Oh, shit!* I was instantly frantic, and now ashamed. I felt so damn stupid for allowing my overly fueled Italian testosterone to have taken over my better judgment when deciding whether to take proper precautions and putting her in this position.

Another week had passed, and her senior year had now started, and still no period. My intentions for college were now not my immediate priority.

I remember being at home one evening during that worrisome time, with my nerves raw with fright, when a strange thing happened. I was still living in Santa Monica with my parents and sister Kay and her husband Jack, who was working for my dad at the time. My sister had given birth just a couple of months prior and that evening the baby was crying, crying, relentlessly crying. It was unnerving and was driving me crazy; it was like fingernails on a blackboard. I couldn't help it. I projected myself now possibly having a baby way before my time and I was scared out of my mind.

Something about the baby crying taunted me. I suddenly jumped up and stormed out of the house, screaming, screaming at the top of my lungs, "I can't take it! I can't take it anymore! I can't take the baby crying!"

My mom followed me as I was going out the front door, scolding me, saying, "Kiki, what's the matter with you? Someday you will have a baby of your own!"

Oh my God, that was all I needed to hear. I said under my breath, "Oh, Mom, if you only knew!"

After spending several sleepless nights, I decided to call my brother Walter in San Francisco. Being named after our dad, we called him "Brother." He was thirteen years older than me, and was a calm, soft-spoken, slim, good-looking, level-headed guy. He was married with four kids and his wife was expecting again.

I knew he would know what to do and would advise me properly. Should we get married now? Or just live together, then get married later? I certainly will have to get a full-time job, that was for sure, and forget about college. There went law school; there was no other option, as I saw it. Anyway, I was sure my older brother would advise me as to what direction to take.

I called him and said, "Brother, I need to talk to you about something really urgent. I can drive up on Saturday." He casually and unassumingly said, "Well, okay, if you must."

I was a mess that Saturday morning while driving up on Highway 101 alone. Thinking, thinking nonstop while on my arduous journey up north. I was really screwed up, especially since I'd just heard that my dad was considering selling the company's branch in LA. Then what the hell would I do? I had no real job skills; how in the hell could I support a wife and a child? What about a lot of things? My mind was reeling with anxiety and disparity of the unknown.

We had agreed to meet near our parent's home at a small pub on Lombard near Lyon street at one thirty that afternoon. Upon arriving, I immediately felt an uncomfortable coolness from him, sort of like, why was I bothering him? But I quickly brushed it off.

After I'd spilled my guts out for some time, telling him of my dilemma and occasionally getting choked up, I pleaded for his advice. He could obviously see that I was visibly shaken and desperate. Patiently waiting in anticipation for his advice, my wise older brother flippantly looked over at me and said, "What can I tell you, kid?"

I'll never forget those words: "What can I tell you, kid?"

I then immediately sank back in my seat while my stomach churned with gut wrenching spams. That's the advice my wise older brother had given me: "What can I tell you, kid?"

Jesus Christ. So I asked him again. "But really, Brother, what should I do? She's only seventeen, and an abortion is out of the question. I love her, and I would never just walk away, so what do you think? Please give me your thoughts." This time he very casually, but with an almost irritated, lackluster, unconcerned, disturbing expression on his face, looked over at me and just shrugged his shoulders.

He didn't say that he didn't know, didn't say "let me think about it"; that would have been acceptable, but he said nothing. It was as if he just didn't care; he didn't give a shit about the predicament I was in. It was like he almost enjoyed the dilemma I was in, and I was now taking up too much of his Saturday. That hurt.

I drove back down south that afternoon, forlorn and even more confused and scared than when I'd driven up. Keep in mind, there was no Highway 5 back then, just the old two-lane Highway 101, and you had to drive through dozens of small towns at a reduced speed, so the drive was at least seven hours between the far end of San Francisco to Santa Monica—plenty of time to ponder over my predicament.

I was now in a state of mind of senseless motor phenomena, such as one would expect when experiencing a catatonic trance, as I stared at the road ahead, wondering what I would soon be facing. I had to make a life-altering decision about what to do. You know what? I just did. We would just get married and I'd find a job, and just do what I had to do. That's what you do in life—do what you must do!

Arriving at her house rather late that same evening, she answered the door. Her folks were home. I whispered, "If it ends up that you're really pregnant, let's just get married and now!" She jumped into my arms with overwhelming love and complete trust, and we drove off to talk about it. We started planning about getting a small apartment and just how we were going to do this. I was working, sort of; we would make it, no matter what.

As we aimlessly drove around, we came upon a small, brown log-cabin-like chapel on Coldwater Canyon just before you get to Riverside Drive in Studio City. It is called the "Little Brown Church." We drove by it so many times on dates and often remarked on how cute it was. Many celebs got married there. I stopped in front of it, thinking I'd better find out the procedure of just how to get married. I ventured up to the office door of the tiny chapel and rang the bell. There was no answer. I repeatedly rang the bell. Still no answer. Of course not, it was Saturday night at ten o'clock. The chapel was closed. Hmm . . . and I thought God worked twenty-four-seven. We needed to know the process, so we could plan. We would just have to return.

We got back into the T-Bird and went back to her house and agreed that I would call them in the morning. Certainly, they would be open on Sunday morning, the day of worship.

Well, Sunday morning came, and I called and spoke to a very nice lady and asked about the procedure. She then calmly asked how old I was. "Well, uh, just turned nineteen," I said. Then she asked about the girl. "Uh . . . seventeen." Then she asked if we had gotten a marriage license yet. "Well, n-n-no . . . n-not yet," I stammered. Oh, shit! Of course! We needed a license!

Then she dropped a bomb and said that a girl under the age of eighteen needed her parents' signatures and a court order. *Okay, I'm dead.*

How in the hell were we going to tell her parents we wanted to get married? And not in a few years, but *now.* Better yet, *why?* She was also still in high school for several more months. Furthermore, I wouldn't survive her father's rage if he knew she was pregnant!

More sleepless nights. More anguish. More anxiety.

Well, a few more days had passed, and I concluded that I would just have to face up to it and tell her parents. However, she would most likely be a widow before she had a husband. So, I figured it was best to wait until we knew for sure that she was pregnant, at least a couple more weeks.

A few weeks more had now passed, and still no period. This was going to be a life-changing event, I concluded. I started to adjust to that fact and began feeling even closer to her. I suddenly felt a different kind of love for her, a deeply embedded love. *My God, she's carrying my baby.*

Well, the following week on Thursday morning while I was at work, she called about nine o'clock and excitedly said, "Kiki, Kiki, I just got my period!" *Oh, thank you God, thank you.* And thank goodness I hadn't talked to her folks yet. Whew!

Then suddenly a feeling of loss came over me; strange. I was now sort of depressed, which I thought was odd. Possibly I had adjusted to the idea of our marrying and having a child, and now . . . and now . . .

I then later wondered what had caused her period to be late. I have since learned that there could have been many reasons, but what did we know back then as teenagers?

We continued dating, but something was just slightly missing. Maybe it was the once deeply rooted love for the mother of my child that I had just experienced that was now gone. That reverence. Maybe, just maybe, we should have married anyway, soon after all of that, but of course, in the traditional way. We still deeply loved each other.

In retrospect, as far as the meeting with my brother and my brother's reaction, I feel he enjoyed seeing the torment and despair I was going through. I expected compassion and love and advice from my older brother and received cold dismissal.

Maybe it was true that he was jealous or envious of all the "stuff" I had gotten as a child that he hadn't, or possibly, he just didn't like me. *Envy begets hatred.*

But he was my brother. I wasn't aware of how much more I'd gotten than he and my sisters had. Heck, I was just a kid.

I was hurt, disappointed, and bewildered by his reaction. Maybe this is the reason for never having gotten close to another guy for most of my adult life. Since then, I didn't want or find the company of another guy to be comfortable, rewarding or sufficient. After all, my sisters idolized me, and I felt very comfortable with women.

This may have been the precursor of my hidden internal scarring and skepticism regarding guy friends, and for whatever reason, I never had a close male friend.

CHAPTER 7
GETTING CLOSE TO THE BIG TWENTY-ONE

Summer had now passed, and USF was down the drain, but that was okay, because I loved it in Southern California. I eventually did try to get into UCLA but of course didn't have the grades, as expected. Funny, when I went to the UCLA admissions office, there was a sign on the front door that read, No Admission! Uh, okay. Maybe that was a clue? Of course, it just meant "use the side entrance."

I now started wishing that my folks had instilled within me the need to study. I possibly would have listened and would have striven to do better at Saint Ignatius. I possibly could have gotten into a good college. Hell, maybe I would have even learned how to type, which would have sped up the writing of this book by several months!

I ended up at Santa Monica City College—SMCC, which stood for "Santa Monica Country Club," and a country club, it was. Brand new, just opened that fall. Serving hamburgers, fries, and milk shakes, with live music to dance to out on the patio of the restaurant at noon every day. An abundance of pretty girls was everywhere. Life was good again.

I majored in accounting and psychology, figuring that would be helpful when running my dad's business, since law school was now unrealistic. All my classes started in the early afternoon, allowing me to work in the morning until noon.

My dad made me foreman of production—yes, at nineteen. I didn't know what the hell I was doing but was the boss of twenty-four adult men overseeing the packing of the orders that were to be delivered that day. It was my responsibility to open the plant up at five o'clock every morning. Several times I would come straight from a date and drive to the plant at 1320 East Newton Street, far across the city in east LA.

It was in a terrible old industrial location, near Watts. Arriving just before 5 a.m., all alone was a bit unnerving, to say the least. I once found a dead man lying in front of the plant against the metal roll-up doors, a victim of a shooting in the less-than-respectable neighborhood back at that time.

One morning, I guess I'd either had too much to drink or had too much fun or both, and it was now a quarter to six in the morning and I was still deep in the San Fernando Valley with a forty-five-minute drive in front of me. I remember driving over Laurel Canyon, then down through east LA, hoping the men didn't think it was a holiday and had all gone home. What the hell would I do? My dad would kill me. This was before cell phones, so I couldn't call anyone to say I was on my way.

Arriving at six thirty, all the men were still standing out in front of the plant—thank God! I rushed in and rolled up my dress slacks, so the smock would cover them, since there was no time to change. My dad and Jack, my brother-in-law, who was the manager, arrived promptly at seven every morning. I had to get things in motion!

I said to the men, "Guys, we have a half hour to do what we normally do in two hours!" They were great; they immediately pulled out the fresh fish, shoveled the ice into bins to load the trucks, and set up the plant to start packing the orders. They hectically worked so I wouldn't get an ass-chewing, but we were still way behind, and my dad was due to arrive in a few minutes! I was frantic.

I told the guys to get several dozen of empty boxes and fill them with ice and put names of accounts on them—any account, it didn't matter—and close them up so my dad and Jack would see all the orders that we had already packed, and everything would look like normal for that time of day.

Well, they did, and just in time. It was like a movie set; nothing in them, just empty boxes.

My dad and Jack walked in. Jack went to his office as usual, and my dad looked around the production floor as he normally did each morning; however, sometimes he would inspect a few of the orders. I was trying to keep my composure. *Oh, please dear Lord, don't let him open any of the boxes!*

He looked around, and looked around, as my heart was pounding. Then he took the cigarette out of his mouth and slung it across the floor. He then went up to his office. Once he slung that cigarette, I knew I was okay; that was his daily ritual! *Whew.*

I bought the men their coffee and donuts that morning from the coffee truck. Anything they wanted was fine! Of course, I had to borrow the money from the company's cash box and pay it back on Friday, payday. Thankfully, my dad's bookkeeper liked me!

One Friday night after a casual date (with whom, I forget; she must have just been a "fill-in"), I was driving home and was hungry. It was about one in the morning, and I stopped at Stan's Drive-in on Melrose Avenue in Beverly Hills and ordered a burger, fries, and a shake.

I was sitting in the T-Bird, eating and listening to music, when I noticed a couple of guys that I went to SMCC with who were in the car beside mine. They said, "Hey, Kiki, bring your food over into our car with us."

So I did. We had been talking for a while, when suddenly, there was tapping on the front driver-side window. It was the Beverly Hills police. They then proceeded to tell the driver to get out of the car, and then ordered the other guy and me to get out, as well. *What the hell is this all about?* I thought. Then they looked in the trunk. I had no clue what was going on.

We all ended up in the patrol car and were taken to the Beverly Hills jail, where they took each of our finger prints and a picture holding a long number, then locked us up in separate cells.

I had no idea what the hell they'd done. I told the sergeant that I'd gotten into the car just a few minutes before the officers arrived, but he didn't want to talk about it until the next morning. *The next morning? Oh, great,* I thought. And my car was unlocked. Thankfully, it was Friday night and I didn't have to go to work, or heaven forbid, school, the next day.

I was allowed one phone call, so I called my father. It was now about three in the morning. He answered after many rings, and I told him I was in the Beverly Hills jail; could he do anything to get me out? He said—and I'll never forget it — "The way you got in, get out!" And promptly hung up. I shouted, "Dad! Dad!" But there was just a dial tone. What the heck had he meant by that? *The way you got in, get out.* I'd never get out the way I got in.

In the morning, they served me mush. Mush . . . ugh, I hated mush. I asked for some sugar and the officer on duty said, "Sugar? This isn't the Beverly Hilton, kid!"

It wasn't until three o'clock the next afternoon when I was released. It came to pass that my dad called the sergeant and told him to keep me there as long as possible. He evidently wanted to teach me a lesson. But about what? I hadn't done anything wrong, at least not that time.

All I can say is, okay. I was tossed in jail briefly, but at least it was the cleanest, nicest jail in the country.

But what's this no sugar thing?

CHAPTER 8
AT LAST, AN ADULT!

I had just turned twenty-one, and my cousin was getting married at the Olympic Golf and Country Club at Lakeside in San Francisco, so I took my beautiful blonde girlfriend with me for the weekend. Heck, I wanted to show her off!

We drove up the coast on Highway 101 in the T-Bird, with her long blonde hair flowing in the wind, listening to the latest hits on the radio and rocking back and forth in rhythm. We were having so much fun it seemed like it took no time at all to travel the roughly four hundred miles. This was going to be a fun weekend, and I looked forward to showing her my city.

My folks came up for the wedding, as well. We stayed at my parent's home in the marina; my mom insisted we have separate bedrooms, of course. That was okay. It was way down at the end of the hall from my mom and dad's room, so I could sneak into her room in the middle of the night—if I dared.

That Saturday morning, we drove around San Francisco and I showed her the Palace of Fine Arts, where I'd had my clubhouse, along with some of the more interesting sights of the city.

At four o'clock that afternoon, we attended the long boring church ceremony, and then immediately afterward, drove out to the swanky Olympic Country Club Lakeside for the reception.

There were at least a couple of hundred people in attendance, all dressed up in their most conservative best. Upon quick observation, they mostly looked as if they'd just come from a funeral, and were dispassionate about life, emitting a stoic, serious attitude.

In sharp contrast, my date wore a silk, form-fitting, spaghetti-strap dress, her blonde hair wrapped in a French twist. It was much more conservative for her than usual, however she still looked quite dramatic and breathtaking, and certainly stood out in this refined, cultured, sophisticated crowd. She looked very Hollywood—well, she was. I thought I was hot stuff, being there with her, and enjoyed showing her off. The guys were drooling—but she was mine!

We drank an abundance of champagne and ate the typical country-club-type canapes that were being passed around. Several made me gag, since I had no clue what I was eating.

We then danced, or at least tried to, since it was a string quartet playing music that sounded as if it was from the 1930s. But we were still having a grand time being immersed within each other.

I remember so vividly standing and talking with my date, when I noticed this stunning brunette across the room. I then suddenly caught her looking back at me. Was I flirting, of course! Was she? Hmm.

A few minutes later I heard a whistle—a loud whistle—the kind when you put your fingers in your mouth. It was my father! I looked over at him across the spacious hall and saw that he was motioning for me to come over. *Oh, my God! What the hell is he up to? This can't be good.* However, I noticed that same beautiful brunette was now standing beside him. *Uh oh!*

The two of us walked over and as I approached him, he screamed in a commanding voice, "I want you to meet a nice Italian girl!" "Jeez, Dad, don't say that in front of my girlfriend!" I whispered to him. I almost died; I was so embarrassed and shocked that my dad would say such a thing in front of her. Obviously perturbed, and most likely hurt, she excused herself and said she was going to the ladies room—to cry, I assume.

I then got myself together and caught my breath. I now looked over at this "nice Italian girl," and will never forget that moment. She was the most mesmerizing woman I'd ever seen. Yes, she appeared to be nice and Italian, but who in the hell cared. That wasn't a priority or a necessity.

She introduced herself as Joan. We spoke, but only briefly. She mentioned that she lived down south and had just come up for the wedding since she was friends with my cousin. As I was about to quickly ask for her phone number, she was suddenly called away. I then, presumably in a loud voice, must have said, "Damn it!" Well, her Aunt Josephine, who was quite tipsy by now, was standing nearby and must have overheard my exclamation of frustration. She then inquisitively, and with a little chuckle, asked me, "What did you want, Kiki? Her phone number?" She then seemed pleased and offered to give me her phone number and address. However, I only had the cocktail napkin that was under my drink to write on, which was now torn and soggy. I then borrowed a pen from a passing waitress and quickly scribbled it down on the ragged napkin as

I nervously rushed to write. My girlfriend would be back any moment, and she couldn't see me doing this. *Christ, I hope I got it right,* I thought! I never had time to look to see what the hell I'd written before putting it my pocket and concealing it. Then it dawned on me that I'd never gotten her last name—but there was no time to ask now.

I had to see her again, I had to, but also needed to get myself together—and quickly!

Just then, my girlfriend appeared and abruptly said, "Shall we dance, Kiki?" I then felt badly that I had wandering thoughts while being with her; I really loved her.

Well, I soon got my composure back, somewhat. However, the allure of that amazing brunette was still within my thoughts.

I can still see my dad gleaming with joy at what he'd done. He had just been very naughty and mischievous, and obviously enjoyed it. That moment was so bittersweet; sweet that I had met her, but bitter, not knowing if I would ever see her again.

I couldn't get that gorgeous, radiant girl out of my mind. She stood about five feet five, and had long dark-chestnut-brown hair with searing brown eyes. Her amazing figure and teasing smile could melt a bronze statue.

I had confusing feelings now. *Is it possible I could fall in love while being in love? But what the heck, maybe she already has a boyfriend, and why would I think she would be interested in me?*

Soon after returning down south, I had to call her, but where had I put that crumpled napkin? I hoped I still had it. I wouldn't have discarded it. I may have left it in my suit jacket, but what if my mom had sent it to the cleaners?!

I remembered the suit I'd worn that day and looked in the jacket pocket—and there it was! I tried to read what the hell I'd written, but it was all scrambled. Shoot! I'd had a lot of champagne that evening and was rushed and really nervous while writing it—damn it!

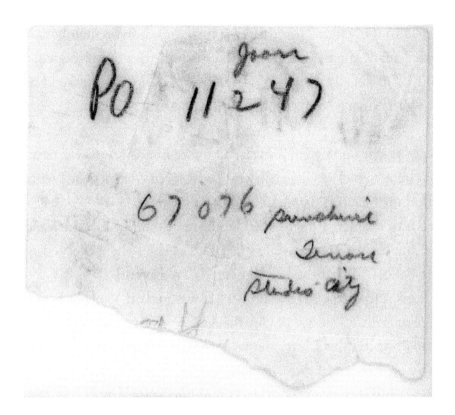

All I could read were the numbers one, one, two, four, seven—but what else? That couldn't be the phone number (phone numbers were much shorter back then). Something was missing, at least in part. Or was this her address? Nah, that was too long for an address. Then I thought, *You know, maybe she won't even remember me. But never assume!*

I started calling all the different prefix combinations I could come up with, but none were working. Damn it, I'll never see her again. I have to find her—somehow. I suddenly had a flashback to my bike-riding days, when I was eight and had ridden for hours to see my young love. At least I had a car now. *I'll find her. I must! Have perseverance...*

I recalled her having said something about the "sun." Was it that she lived on a street that started with "sun"? This was before MapQuest or Google Earth, might I add.

I started looking in the phone book. She'd said she lived in the Valley, the San Fernando Valley. What cities in the valley started with or had something in them with "sun"? I couldn't find any. Now I was feeling like the sleuth, Inspector Clouseau, unable to find a train on a track. What about street names? Yes, maybe street names. So, I looked at a map. I found a "Sunnyslope" in Sherman Oaks, and of course there was Sunset Boulevard, but it ran from Pacific Palisades to

Los Angeles; she lived in the Valley. Now thinking further, I didn't remember any street addresses up north having that many digits, but maybe down south they did—I hoped. Maybe it was her phone number and I'd just really screwed up badly. Not giving up, I looked further and found a "Sunrise Court" in Van Nuys, a "Sunswept Circle" in Beverly Hills, and a "Sunshine Terrace" in Studio City.

Well, I had my work cut out for me if I wanted to see her again. It was now a Saturday, and I had all day. I didn't have to pick up my girlfriend until seven o'clock that evening, so I set out on my adventure to find my beautiful brunette.

Starting from Santa Monica, I drove over Sepulveda Boulevard to the Valley. I drove to Van Nuys and checked out Sunrise Court, but still no "11247." I then checked out Sunnyslope in Sherman Oaks; no "11247." What the hell did "11247" represent?

Then I found Sunshine Terrace in Studio City. It was just off Ventura Boulevard up on a hill, a narrow, winding street. It was a hot day in the Valley, and now about two thirty in the afternoon. I had the top down on the T-Bird and was smoking a pipe and had a straw hat on. I don't know why. I didn't wear hats and I didn't smoke.

As I started up the hill, I noticed the address numbers started at 11200. My God, had I really figured it out? My heart started pounding and I was getting short of breath. But if this was her address, what would I do if she wasn't home? Or even worse, if she was with a date, or just didn't really want to see me and was just playing along with my dad that day.

Suddenly I got chicken. If I did indeed find her, what would the outcome be? I wondered. And what would I say? Maybe she wouldn't even remember me!

I now thought, *Just keep on driving to see if this is the right 11247. Don't even look over.*

I approached 11241, then 11243, then 11245. Oh my God, this was it: 11247 Sunshine Terrace! My heart raced. I then very slowly and inquisitively approached the home on the right side. Remember, the top was down, so I was very conspicuous and visible while staring over at the driveway.

An old lady was sweeping the front porch; she looked very Italian. Short and plump—no, not plump, *fat*—and you could see she was feisty! I slouched down in the driver seat as I drove by, hoping to just slowly mosey on by, but she noticed me and shouted in a heavy Italian accent, "Looking for-ah someone-ah?"

I hesitated, but then said, "Oh, hi there. By any chance does Joan live here?" She answered, "Who-ah you-ah?" I replied, "My name is Kiki." She said, "Who-ah?" This wasn't working, so I said, "Achille Paladini." She then put the broom aside and approached the car. That had worked: I was Italian! She said "Yes-ah, she-ah does-ah, but she's-ah at-ah Universal-ah Studio now." Oh my God, I'd *found* her!

So, if she's at Universal Studios, I wonder if she's an actress, I thought.

The Italian lady and I talked a bit. She was a sweet old lady, and her name was Ernestina. She said she was Joan's grandma. I asked for her phone number, and this time, I wrote it down correctly.

Consequently, I discovered that I had accidentally, during the moment of my rushed surge of enthusiasm at the Olympic Club, inverted her phone number with her address, and to make it worse, it was scribbled all over the paper and difficult to decipher.

I have to mention that I discovered just a few years ago that Joan actually saved that little piece of paper! I had no idea. I don't even know how she got it. I was very touched by that. My gosh, it had been almost sixty years.

I called the next day about noon. It was Sunday and she answered. With my heart pounding, I said, "Hi, Joan. This is Kiki. Remember me? I met you at—" She then interrupted me and said, "Yes, of course I remember you. What the hell took you so long to call?" I now sank back in the chair and with a deep sigh, replied, "Can I come over and say hi?" She said, "Sure. When?" "How about in an hour?" I said.

Arriving at her home in Studio City, and now hat-less and smoke-less,

I rang the bell and her grandma answered. It was a warm and pleasant welcome. Then Joan came into the room, and I got weak in the knees. *What do I say to her now that I'm actually here? And don't stutter, for Christ's sake!*

Making conversation was easy; she was so outgoing and animated. We talked about the coincidence of her knowing my cousin up north, and that her aunt lived in San Francisco. It was mostly nervous small talk, at least on my part. I then, without hesitation, courageously got up the guts and asked her out for that upcoming Saturday night. To my surprise, she immediately said yes.

As I drove away, my stomach was churning with anxiety. Then it churned with a gut-wrenching ache when I realized I was now in a pickle. What would I tell my girlfriend I was doing that Saturday night? We always went out on Friday and Saturday nights. I would have to lie to her. That wasn't nice. That wasn't fair. That wasn't—oh, hell! I had to see this girl.

Then I thought, *Thankfully Joan didn't ask me if I was dating someone, or worse, if I had a girlfriend. How would I have answered that? With another lie? You know, I didn't ask her either. I would rather not know, anyway.* Maybe that's the way she felt, too.

That Friday night my girl and I went out as usual and ended up at the Mocambo on the Sunset Strip in West Hollywood. It was a Latin-American-themed nightclub. Along the walls were glass cages with live colorful exotic birds such as parrots, macaws and cockatoos. They had a live band that made the club one of the town's most popular dance till dawn spots. Ella Fitzgerald was currently appearing there.

We got there in plenty of time for the dinner show, and purposely sat in a corner so we could be promiscuous and hopefully unseen. The "Mocambo Misfits" were playing dance music as we arrived. We then ordered our drinks and danced before dinner. For dinner, we both always started out with a jumbo prawn cocktail—had to support my dad. She ordered the Lobster Thermidor Prince De Monaco, and I, their Broiled Half Spring Chicken Macombo. For dessert, Crepes Suzette.

As we ate our crepes, Ella sang songs in her deep-throated voice that put us in a steamy mood. Unfortunately, still too young to drink alcoholic beverages, we had to be satisfied with sodas and the like, but our fury for passion was easily ignited, and by now, we didn't notice anyone else in the club. After all, she was singing "Do I Love You?" as if it were just for the two of us. We were getting pretty handsy, and I was all over my girl, as she was with me. I recall, as Ella started singing "Too Darn Hot," my girl disappeared under the small round table. I thought she had dropped her purse, that is, until . . .

At that very moment, the waiter came by and asked, "Another soft drink for you and the young lady, sir?" I meekly answered, "Uh, not now, but I'll ask the lady when she returns." He decorously replied, "When she returns, sir? Oh yes, whatever you say, sir."

No, no, nothing like that. Shame on you! What are you thinking? She really had just dropped her purse!

We soon ended up at the Sands Motel, just blocks away on Sunset. The time it took to check in was agony, as the overweight, bespectacled, balding nerd at the check-in desk insisted on the color, make, and license plate number of my car. I wanted to scream at him and say, "Who in the eff remembers the goddamn license plate number of their car, you damn peon?" So now I had to go outside and write it down, wasting time, and I didn't want her to cool off! He was most likely jealous of my obvious intentions and his inability to ever experience such pleasure, especially with such a magnificent young girl.

We finally got into the room, and I immediately approached her from behind and unzipped her strapless, bra-less dress while kissing the back of her neck. As it dropped to the floor, I spun her around and kissed her and pulled her towards me as her firm breasts with protruding hard nipples pressed against my chest. With her black lace panties now off, her long legs in black nylons and garter belt framed her sumptuous mound of Venus, causing me uncontrollable aspirations for wild, salacious sex. I then threw her onto the bed and we instantly indulged like we never had before. It seemed like the craving couldn't be satisfied, only wanting more of her, and she of me. I had her down on her back, her long blonde hair was now flung off the end of the bed as I lasciviously made love to her, time and time again. Her head repeatedly lunged back and forth as her nails ripped into the skin on my back as she screamed "Fuck me, fuck me!" Her vagina rocked me from side to side in an erogenous, rocking motion, allowing me to discover her like never before. We kissed with such passion and loved from within.

The night was one never to be forgotten. I then drove her home over Coldwater Canyon sometime just before sunrise.

Now the following paragraph is going to sound sociopathic, narcissistic, crude, or whatever description you would like to place upon me, but recall that I hadn't yet dated this nice Italian girl, so calm down and don't be so hard on me.

Reeling with excitement that I was taking this incredibly stunning brunette out the next night, I had to make up something as to why my girl and I couldn't go out that night. I think I told her there was a family function going on that Saturday night. I didn't enjoy lying to the girl I was still in love with, but what other option was there?

Yes, we had just made love for most of the night, and now I was looking forward to being with another girl.

It was now Saturday morning, and I was recovering from the night before. I was hungover and exhausted from all the extracurricular activity but was anxiously anticipating seeing this amazing brunette later that evening. Well, stupidly and without forethought, I had used up most of the money I'd made that week the night before with the clubbing, a fancy dinner, and a motel room. Normally if we went out on the town one night, the next night would just be casual, and we would do something like go to the drive-in movie—so I'd really messed up!

I'm going to be on a wing and a prayer tonight with money.

Well, Saturday night soon came, and I was to pick up Joan at her house at seven. Upon arriving, I talked with her Grandma Ernestina while Joan got ready. Ernestina was a kick. She told me she loved the horse races, and had just returned from Hollywood Park, and that she had lost again . . . as usual. Joan was dressed rather conservatively, but looked amazingly beautiful, and so classy.

I didn't really have a specific plan for the evening. I wanted to see what she enjoyed doing. We drove over towards Hollywood on Coldwater Canyon (by the way, I'd just driven on that same road in the opposite direction less that twelve hours ago with my girlfriend) and we ended up at the bar of the Hollywood Roosevelt Hotel—an "in" place for Hollywood starlets and actors. Susan Hayward was sitting at the end of the bar in a full-length mink coat, looking beautiful and alluring. Sure, I was dressed well, and was driving a new Thunderbird Convertible, playing the big shot, but only had about thirty bucks on me. It was sufficient back then for a drink and a casual dinner, a very casual dinner. It was going to be tight.

Sitting at the bar, the bartender approached and asked what we wanted. Joan said, "Do you know how to make a pousse-café?" *Okay, a pousse-café. Don't look ignorant, Kiki. Act like you know what it is. Be worldly.* Well, I had no clue what the hell it was! I casually said, "Oh, I'll have an Amer Picon on the rocks."

We talked, and really got along great. I was having a wonderful time with her. She told me that she was indeed an actress, and that her stage name was "Joan Lora." I told her that she looked a lot like Pier Angeli, only prettier, and she replied that several casting agents had mentioned that. She said she'd just completed filming several television series and had recently had a part in *Around the World in Eighty Days*. I asked what other films she'd appeared in, but she was modest, and hesitant to boast, and just said, "Oh, quite a few." I didn't push her. She briefly mentioned that she was currently doing a live theater play at the Santa Monica Playhouse off Wilshire and Fourth, but didn't elaborate or invite me. Hmm.

The drinks were now empty, and knowing I had to conserve what little money I had, I asked for the bill to get the hell out of there. I knew I could be in for a shock with the bill when the bartender very cautiously started pouring different liquors over a spoon, making for seven individually colored layers—her pousse-café. Well, I almost fell over when I saw the bill! The pousse-café was thirteen dollars; mine was three dollars. With a couple of bucks for a tip, it came to eighteen dollars. *Oh, Christ*, I thought. *hat the hell are we going to do for the rest of the evening with twelve dollars? Certainly, no expensive dinner, I hope. Uh . . .* I thought for a moment. *Look at what she just ordered for a drink. What could dinner be like?* What was she going to think of me if I admitted I didn't have much money left? No credit cards back then. *I didn't plan on a thirteen-dollar pousse—whatever the hell you call it. That will teach me to play the big shot, and even more so, having two girls at the same time!*

I hesitantly asked where she would like to go for dinner, and she thankfully said she wasn't hungry, and for us to just take a drive out to Malibu. Immediately relieved that I'd been pardoned from embarrassment, my mind quickly shifted. *Hmm . . . Malibu. To make out, maybe*, I thought. *Nah, she's a nice girl, remember? And this is only our first date. Hey, but maybe—settle down, Kiki. No maybes. Behave.*

We drove over Sunset Boulevard, winding down to the Pacific Coast Highway, then drove up to Zuma Beach, and turned around and ended up at the Holiday Lodge in Malibu, a beach-front restaurant and bar, perilously cresting on a cliff, another "in" spot with the Hollywood crowd. Walking down the steps, we bumped into Leslie Caron. Having a flashback, I thought to myself, *Hey, she's the dancer and actress who just married the guy that sells stinky pigs. Well, I sell stinky fish, and I'm out with an actress, too, so there!* Joan was also a dancer, and they had just been on a set together; I think she said it was *Gigi*. They chatted for a few minutes before we went into the bar. However, this Mr. Big Shot now only had twelve bucks left to his name. I hoped I could pull this off!

Well, I did. We had only one drink each, the normal type, thankfully, and still had a couple of bucks left. I hoped she didn't want to go someplace later, like Hamburger Hamlet, for a late-night bite, I now worried. I was hungry and could have sure gone for one.

Leaving the beach-front property, she said, "Let's take a walk on the beach." "Great idea," I said. We walked along the white sandy beach, now holding hands. This was good.

We sat down on the soft sand and talked for a while. I then put my arms around her, and this was even better! Then after some time, I boldly leaned over and kissed her. It was short, but we really connected—and she kissed me back! When I tried to proceed further, she pulled away and exclaimed, "Behave yourself! I'm a good girl. Remember what your father said." Trying to reason, I said, "But it was only a kiss." She responded, "Yeah, then what?" She wasn't going to be easy!

So changing the mood, we then played, running up to the waves and back, seeing who could get the closest and not get wet. Well, on one of my showing-off attempts, I got drenched from the waist down!

Now with my trousers totally soaked, how was I going to drive home? Joan then said, "So, take your pants off."

It came to pass that she was just being nice and thinking of me trying to drive and not ruin the leather seats on the T-Bird. So, I threw them into the trunk and we proceeded to drive back to the Valley. Yes, of course I had shorts on.

It started to drizzle slightly on the way home, and she asked me to pull up the soft convertible top on the T-Bird. Well, I didn't have one. I only had one top for it—the hard top—and that was at home in my garage. I hadn't had the money when I'd bought the car for the option of buying a soft top, as well. Not to divulge that little fact, I said I didn't think I would need one in Southern California. She didn't respond.

There we were, driving back to the Valley over Malibu Canyon Road. It was at least an hour-and-a-half drive, with no top on the car and no pants on. The seats were now very damp, as we both were, so I guess my pants being wet wouldn't have really mattered. The thought then occurred to me, how would this look if I was stopped by the California Highway Patrol with no pants on? Thankfully, she was a good sport about it, laughing most of the way, and didn't complain about her hair that was now drenched. I wasn't so sure I was making a very good first impression on her at this point.

She asked me about the T-Bird, and what other cars I'd owned, and of course I fibbed a little bit. She then told me that she had dated James Dean when he'd been filming *Rebel Without a*

Cause, and he'd taken her out in his Porsche 356 Speedster (not the Porsche RS 550 race car he was killed in), and he'd driven through Griffith Park so fast that he'd scared the heck out of her. They had met on the set, and become good friends, and she said he often came to her house and loved her homemade pizza. "So, I guess my little T-Bird is no big deal then, huh?" I said. She promptly and rather intimidatingly replied, "No!"

Then I went silent. My head started to wander, thinking, thinking. *So, she'd dated James Dean, and was friends with all the young up-and-coming actors from the film. She had a great career going, and yet she was out with me tonight.* That left me with an odd feeling.

Deep down, I wasn't very proud of myself as an individual. I had nothing to be proud of. My life at the time was just a facade, an illusion, everything in front and nothing in back, just like a movie set. I had nothing to back up my lifestyle as I was portraying it, not even a career objective like she had, other than working for my dad's company. *Why don't I make a life for myself instead of taking the easy way out? She's out on her own, making a career for herself. But do what? Be a lawyer? I'd have to go back up north.*

Suddenly, all these thoughts were rushing through my head. *Why am I trying to impress? I have been acting so impetuous, without thinking. Maybe I'm doing the wrong thing, giving the girls the impression I'm from money. Why am I doing that? Maybe because I have no self-assurance that they would go out with me, just for me. But I have money. Hmm . . . let's see. Yeah, I have six bucks left! Ha, and here I am, out with this amazing classy young woman tonight. I wonder what she thinks of me? I have to snap out of this!*

Joan was now looking over at me with a bewildered look. Just then, she said, "What are you thinking so intensely about?" So, I fibbed and said, "I was just thinking how much fun it has been to be with you tonight." She didn't buy it. This gal was in my head. She already knew me.

I immediately went back to making small talk while driving over Malibu Canyon, and eventually reached Sunshine Terrace at the bottom of the hill intersecting Ventura Boulevard. She said, "Let me go in first. I better make sure my grandma is asleep. Not sure how she would perceive you walking in with no pants on!" Joan's folks were in Capri, the Isle of Capri, on vacation visiting her father's family.

Now coming back to the car, she said, "The coast is clear. Here's my father's robe. I'll put your pants in the dryer." We sat there for about a half hour or so talking while my pants were drying, and I tried to kiss her again. Hey, I didn't have much on. Again, I was promptly put in my place. When I was leaving, I gave her a soft, meaningful kiss, and it went on for a bit longer, a lot longer than the first one, but I was not brave enough to venture any further.

I didn't feel that the first date was a very compelling start for me, but I was relieved that I'd made it through the night with enough money, though barely, and thankful that the drizzle had now ceased for the long drive back to Santa Monica . . . with no top.

I was thinking about the evening while driving home, and that first kiss, then that last kiss. They were electrifying, and what fun we'd had, too. This would be a humorous first date that we could talk about for a long time. *Yeah, what do you mean we could talk about it? I'll be lucky if I ever get to see her again. Shit . . . James Dean!* The thought then suddenly occurred to me, *You know, she could be marriage material. But I already have a girlfriend . . .*

CHAPTER 9
LIFE'S GETTING CONVOLUTED

Yes, life was getting a bit perplexing. I was now dating two girls. I'd gotten a second date, and then a third. I had two wonderful, magnificent, and beautiful girls, mind you; one a model, the other an aspiring actress. Could life have been any better? I was still nuts for my girl, the blonde, but falling very much in love with my new girl, the brunette. So, was it to be brunette or blonde? Or blonde or brunette? *I don't think it's going to be about hair color.*

It was getting to be a nightmare, juggling Friday nights and Saturday nights, and all the fibbing. I didn't like the fibbing. So, I started mixing in week nights when I could!

I called Joan early that week and we went out on Wednesday night for dinner to a place she introduced me to called Sargent's in Toluca Lake, just around the corner from Bob Hope's compound. A great casual restaurant with down-home southern cooking. They had fried chicken, chicken and dumplings, pot pie, chicken-fried steak smothered in country gravy, all the heart-clogging food I loved. What a fun place it was.

I took her home early since she had to be at the studio very early the next morning. She said she was currently dancing in a scene in *The Opposite Sex* with Joan Collins at MGM Studios in Culver City. She also mentioned she was taking acting classes twice a week in the evenings from Jeff Corey, a renowned acting teacher at his home in the Hollywood Hills, so there would be no date for a few nights, I guessed.

Upon bringing her home, we said goodnight at the front door and I got my first real kiss. This time we really connected. Though it was somewhat brief, it still sent a message to both of us. There was immediate chemistry between us. I was falling for her but didn't know how she really felt about me yet.

It was now Friday night and my real girlfriend's turn. We went to Hamburger Hamlet for a bite, then to the drive-in theater on Sepulveda. However, I don't think we ever watched the movie.

I suddenly realized that I had a huge problem. *How do I not let my girlfriend know I'm dating someone else? Or have Joan catch on that I have been in a long-time relationship?* I had been going with this girl for a couple of years now and we were seriously in love.

It's now amusing, but it wasn't funny at the time. I forget what day of the week it was, but I had just made love to my girlfriend, my real girlfriend, that is. I then went to see Joan. They lived somewhat close, both being in the Valley. I remember it being in the late afternoon.

Unknowingly, I had a spot near my fly on my pants—yes, that kind of spot, and I walked in and gave Joan a little hello kiss. As I did, her mom loudly exclaimed, "Where have you been?!" "Uh, where have I been? Why?" I replied. I was now afraid why she was asking that. She said, "What is that white spot on your zipper? And look, it's all wet!" *Oh, shit!* I didn't know what to say. I was frozen in dead fright that I was going to lose this wonderful girl because my goddamn testosterone had gotten the best of me again.

Looking down, trembling because of my pre-indiscretion, I calmly answered, "Oh, I just had a vanilla milkshake down the street at Du-par's. Guess it spilled!"

Thankfully, they both just chuckled. Whew, that was a close one! Not sure to this day just what they thought.

My God, what am I doing? I felt like a rapscallion, an unprincipled scoundrel. Well, I was.

One of the most tumultuous days that I can recall during this dating fiasco was the first Thanksgiving while I was dating them both. Of course, I declined staying home with my parents.

I had accepted an invitation from both girls to spend Thanksgiving dinner with them. Why, you ask? Well, they were my girlfriends—yes, plural.

The blonde's parents had me over early at four o'clock in the afternoon, because I said I had to be home—yeah, sure, home—by six thirty to spend some family time with them and for dessert. They kindly ate earlier just for me. I then had to be at Joan's house at a quarter past six, not too far away. At least I had them both situated close by.

I had a nice time at my girlfriend's—uh, the original one—and it was a wonderful dinner. Naturally, they served turkey, but with a European flair. Her mom was a great cook. For dessert, she'd made apple strudel, but I couldn't have any since I was supposedly going home for dessert. I would have loved to have had a piece of it. God, it looked good! Her dad had too much to drink, as usual, and started to drill me about my intentions with his daughter and if we were thinking of marriage. Yikes!

Excusing myself a little after six, I said I had to get home to Santa Monica for dinner. I was stuffed. *Why did I eat so much? Stupid!*

Arriving at Joan's house, I was greeted most warmly by her Grandma Ernestina, and her mom and dad were cordial. I could tell Grandma liked me, though I wasn't so sure about her mom or her father. This dinner now had an Italian theme, of course; so many appetizers, so many. Prosciutto and melon, salami, coppa, mortadella, prosciutto—mmm, I loved prosciutto—with French bread; all kinds of cheeses, olives, clams, and oysters on the half shell, calamari. Ugh, I hated fish. I know . . . they didn't understand, either.

Then, homemade gnocchi, which I love. "Just a few, please," I said. Obviously, they were putting on a wonderful spread just for me, the "Italian guy." But oh my God, where was I going to put all this food? I couldn't let it be known I'd just eaten a big dinner, especially since it had been at another girl's house! *Okay, Joan can act, so I'll give it a try . . . but I can only consume so much.* Well somehow, I jammed it all in; the appetizers, salad, gnocchi, the turkey again, with mashed potatoes again, and gravy again, and peas again. My future with this amazing girl was at stake.

I think I handled it all very well, even though I was about to burst. Then the typical Italian dessert came, cannolis. I couldn't, I just couldn't. I declined and said, "No more room." Little did they know! Hey, I'd gotten cheated out of two of my favorite desserts that evening. Yeah, I know, you're probably saying, "Oh, you poor thing."

This was getting way too convoluted. What was I doing? I wasn't being fair to either girl, and they were both wonderful. This couldn't continue. I felt like a creep, and I was.

I didn't want, and couldn't, hurt either one. I don't like hurting anyone, and especially the two women I was now involved with, who obviously had sincere feelings for me.

I had to decide.

The decision-breaker was on the third serious date with Joan after a night out. It was about midnight as we sat in the T-Bird on the dark, narrow, winding street just down from her house, when we experienced our first moments of passion. She captured my heart within a moment with the depth of the first *real* kiss. My life was instantly turned around, and I knew I'd met my life partner. That may sound hard to believe, how that profound revelation can come from a single kiss, but the connection we had was overwhelming, and I felt the same from her. It was genuine.

For the first time, *I wanted to touch a woman's heart—not her body.*

I never experienced anything like it before. It was as if a heavenly presence came over us and we were just adorned with our newfound love. As I looked into her eyes, I saw the innocence and the purity of her soul. We were then enraptured with emotion as we kissed.

I was now committed. I'd found the *love of my life*. We sat there for hours, never tiring of holding each other, our lips ever-so-eager to engage to express our feeling of affection. I remember not wanting to part that night. It was magical.

When you hold a woman in your arms and feel your entire body at peace while your head spins with the joy of contentment, and your heart aches to be with this person forever, not wanting to separate even for a moment . . . you know . . . you have found *her*. Of course, my extreme sex drive kicked in—but was quickly subdued!

Meanwhile, I still felt a responsibility for the girl I'd dated for over three years. I couldn't just walk away; we'd shared so many great times together and had had so much fun, but I was now in love with Joan, and she was the girl I wanted to marry. I had to break it off with the other girl, but how?

The thought of losing her wrenched my senses.

CHAPTER 10
MY FIRST LOVE DRIFTS AWAY

My girl had gotten busy modeling, and it took her out of town quite often. She was also dancing occasionally in some of the reviews in the local nightclubs.

I'm sure by now she knew I was out dating; however, possibly unaware that it was with just one girl and was now serious. My excuses for not being available on the weekends were waning. We eventually started drifting apart, and she started dating. That was okay, but not really. I hated it; the thought of her with another man tore me apart, if even just putting his arm on her shoulder, but I had to accept it. What else?

I heard she was now dancing in a review at the famous Moulin Rouge Night Club on Sunset in Hollywood. I don't know what the hell came over me, but I took Joan there one Saturday night and we sat in the front row—yes, the front row. I nervously downed a few drinks as fast as I could before the show started, now questioning my reason for being there. Maybe I missed her, maybe I just needed to see her. But why? To torment myself, and her, if she saw us. And why the front row? Of course she would see us!

The review started shortly after, and as the girls came out from backstage she immediately stood out with her indubitable beauty and blonde hair. My heart sank, seeing her. While the girls danced and swirled around for several minutes not thirty feet from us, she looked down at the audience and immediately saw us.

I can still see her shocked expression upon seeing me—me with another woman. Her piercing blue eyes locked onto mine with such a painful expression, a painful expression I will never forget—never.

Joan had noticed that she looked directly at me and stared for a few moments. She later asked if I knew her, and I said, "Well . . . somewhat. We dated a few times." Why did I bring Joan there? Why? How insensitive, how insanely irresponsible and foolish of me. I still loved that girl, and I was ashamed. I can still see the hurt on her face to this day.

A week later, I received a call while at work from the girl I'd once dated who had introduced me to her. She said she thought I would want to know that the girl I'd dropped her for, had just attempted suicide while living at the Studio Club in Hollywood. Her attempt was only thwarted because her roommate Ann, an upcoming actress at the time (now very prominent), had come home and found her sprawled on the bathroom floor with an empty bottle of sleeping pills beside her. She was rushed to the emergency room, and they pumped her stomach just in time to save her. As I write this, I experienced all over again those feelings of guilt, shame, and remorse.

The last time I saw her was both astonishing and discomforting. The very next year, in 1959, while watching the Oscars on television with Joan at her house in Studio City, my old girlfriend was walking in on the red carpet at the Pantages Theater in Hollywood, holding the arm of Hugh O'Brien, TV's Wyatt Earp. Joan was sitting next to me as I gasped! She asked what was the matter, and I said, "Oh, it's just some of the gowns these women wear." Joan then commented, "Oh, look who that is. It's Hugh O' Brien. I just did a stage play with him!" *Oh my God...*

La Cienega Boulevard was known as "Restaurant Row." My dad sold to most of the restaurants, and it was always fun to send my card back to the chefs and have them come out and sit with us, further inflating my ego. The Captain's Table and the Oyster House were two of his biggest accounts. We went to the Oyster House most often, and I would be greeted at the door with, "Hello, Mr. Paladini. How are you this evening." Though still a punk, it made feel good; no, it made me feel like a big shot, like a future heir to a giant food company fortune. *Ha!*

Joan's favorite was the blood-rare pepper steak at the Oyster House. No, we—or at least I—never ate the seafood. The waiter would prepare it at the table as the flambé from the Cognac warmed the surrounding tables as the diners curiously looked over, wondering who this beautiful ingenue actress was. We were being catered to as if we were celebrities. Well, at least she was.

Another favorite was Frascati's on Sunset and Fairfax, but on special occasions we would go to Romonoff's on South Rodeo Drive in Beverly Hills. Probably the swankiest, most expensive restaurant in all of Beverly Hills, with the exception of Perino's, which was a mile or so further south on Wilshire but it catered to a more snobbish, sedate type of clientele. I remember one evening talking with the chef in the kitchen as he showed me how they stored each entree item in individual refrigerated shelves. I had never seen that before. Romanoff's, much more modern and garish in décor, was most often frequented by many of the younger up-and-coming actors.

The very first time we went to the famed Romonoff's, Joan asked for an Amer Picon cocktail. The waiter and the bartender were clueless. "You would think they would know in a place like this!" exclaimed Joan in her stage voice. Amer Picon, is an aperitif imported from France and was more well known in San Francisco at the time.

She got up and promptly marched behind the bar without asking and made her own damn Amer Picon cocktail while the bartender looked on in amazement, hesitant to dare say a word. The waitstaff applauded as this vivacious brunette with long chestnut-brown hair flowing behind her, walked back to the table, proudly gleaming at me with those piercing brown eyes. Only a beautiful young woman could get away with something like that—and be applauded!

That night as we left Romonoff's, we pulled up alongside Robert Wagner and Natalie Wood a few blocks away on Wilshire as they were leaving Don the Beachcombers just up the street on Rodeo Drive. They were in their 1957 white T-Bird—the exact same car as mine. We all waved and gave a thumbs up, then raced one another down Wilshire Boulevard for a few blocks. What fun!

One night while out for dinner, Joan told me a funny story about what had transpired on the set of *The King and I*. She had danced in the movie, and during a lunch break between filming, she spilled a pistachio ice cream cone on Marlon Brando's lap while complaining it had almonds in it instead of pecans. As she reached forward to show him while saying "look!" the melting ice cream landed on his meticulously ironed white trousers. He didn't scream, "Stellla!"; it was, "Joannnie!" Sinatra loved it, while David Niven grabbed Joan to protect her from Brando's wrath! Brando, Sinatra, and Niven were filming on nearby stages and had stopped in on the set.

On occasion, I would pick up Joan from the studios. In 1958, while picking her at MGM in Culver City, they were filming *Cat on a Hot Tin Roof*. I remember large colored banners advertising the film waving in the gentle wind on all the nearby studio buildings as she seemingly danced her way to my car—yes, to lucky me. It was always fun hearing what had happened that day on the set and who she had met.

I recall in 1959 picking her up, again at MGM, and this time they were filming *Some Like It Hot*, with Marilyn Monroe and Jack Lemmon. I would see Jack occasionally on San Vicente Boulevard in Santa Monica around four thirty in the morning while driving to work. Coincidentally, he was driving a Thunderbird as well, but dark blue. We would look at each other and nod, approving of our choice of cars. Meanwhile, I'm sure his was paid for; plus, he was on his way to a movie studio and I was on the way to the grungy side of east LA to a wholesale fish market.

It was always fun picking her up at the studios, because most times she would still have on full makeup from the set, and she looked incredible! One night after picking her up at Universal in Burbank around eight o'clock, we went to dinner nearby at the Smokehouse Restaurant on Lakeside Drive, and during dinner people were staring at her! So was I.

One time during the week, Joan was shooting at Warner Bros. in West Hollywood, and she invited me to meet her for lunch. She said she would meet me directly across the street at the fabled Formosa Cafe. Celebrities were profoundly abundant, and as I walked in, I noticed some of the high-and-mighty patrons putting their delicate noses in the air, most likely thinking the fish of the day wasn't very fresh, smelling something rather offensive. Of course, I couldn't imagine what they were smelling. Joan was again in full makeup and made my heart flutter. I was ambivalent about anyone else in the café.

I recall one Saturday afternoon her asking me to take her over the hill into Hollywood to the Screen Actors Guild (SAG) office on Sunset Boulevard to pick up a replacement SAG card because she had lost hers. The building was rather oddly shaped, with two long ramps on either side leading up to the front entrance, quite modern architecture for 1960. I parked directly in front, and who came walking out but Ronald Reagan. He was the president of the Guild at the time. Joan said that he had been negotiating with the studios for residual and health benefits for the actors for films being shown on television after their initial release. Thankfully to Mr. Reagan, Joan still occasionally gets residuals to this very day.

Well, unknown to me at the time, Joan had a very bad automobile accident just before we met. As I understand, she was in her 1955 Chevy Bel Air Coupe one evening, stopped at a traffic light at the intersection of Rodeo Drive and Santa Monica Boulevard, waiting for a green light, when of all people, Audrey Hepburn, driving a rental car, was making a left turn off Santa Monica Boulevard onto Rodeo Drive. A car coming the opposite way alarmed her, and she rushed across the intersection, hitting Joan head on. Joan was taken to the hospital in an ambulance, with severe whiplash and a lower-back injury.

It was on the local radio and television news the next morning: "Two Hollywood Actresses Involved in Head-On Collision in Beverly Hills, One Taken by Ambulance to the Hospital with Undetermined Injuries." It also stated the names of those actresses, Audrey Hepburn and Joan Lora. It may have been good for publicity, but not for Joan's back. She suffers with it to this day. She was a professional dancer, as well as an actress, as I previously noted. Ever since the accident it was painful for her to dance in films, resulting in the need for her to decline several parts.

There was a settlement, but it was a pittance. Miss Hepburn, due to driving a rental car, had high-priced lawyers defending her, as well as her own personal lawyer.

Actress Joan Lora Awarded $6,250 As Result Of Accident

LOS ANGELES (AP) — Actress Joan Lora was awarded a $6,250 damage judgment against actress Audrey Hepburn Thursday in a suit resulting from a 1958 auto accident.

Miss Lora said she lost important acting roles because of back and neck injuries suffered in the collision. She said she specialized in dancing and in horseback riding roles in westerns.

Miss Hepburn said she was making a left turn in Beverly Hills when a car approached rapidly. She said she stepped on the gas to get out of the way of this car and hit Miss Lora's auto.

The trial took over a year to be heard. Joan and I were engaged by then, and I still recall Ms. Hepburn coming into the courtroom, surrounded by her attorneys. She was elegantly dressed, reserved, and soft-spoken.

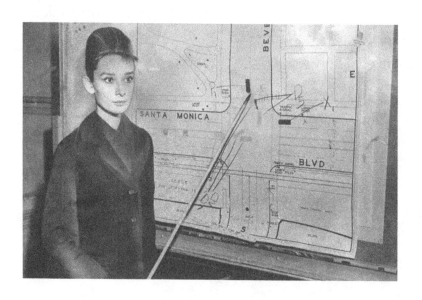

Joan wasn't asking for an astronomical amount, mainly repayment of the medical bills, plus some compensation. They showed a clip of Joan dancing in a segment of Sugarfoot, a western film made for television, and claimed based on that, that she hadn't been severely hurt; however, the scene had been shot a month prior to the accident, and just recently had been released.

Joan's attorney failed to bring up that fact. However, I think he was intimidated by Audrey Hepburn's imposing attorneys. Joan attempted to express the fact that the scene was shot prior to the accident, only to be silenced by the judge. So be it.

Joan could be a lot of fun, but was also mischievous. One Sunday, on the drive back after we'd gone to Palm Springs for the day, we stopped in at a Basque restaurant. They served family-style meals. The highlight of her day was when I commented on how good the thinly sliced roast beef was on the appetizer tray—and she quickly informed me that it was tongue! Oh my God, tongue! Who in the hell would eat tongue? Between you and me, it must have tasted pretty good, though.

Upon leaving, she asked if she could drive the T-Bird home, and I said sure. As she entered the freeway, she started speeding—I mean really taking off, like at eight-five miles per hour. Well, a California Highway Patrol officer soon pulled us over. As he approached the car, she promptly said, "Thank you for stopping me, officer. He was trying to get very fresh with me and wouldn't stop. I saw you and was hoping you'd pull me over!" I almost shit as I looked over at her, bewildered. The officer then proceeded to give me hell, and lectured me. He said I should behave myself, and told me to stop. He then went on and on, as she sat there with a smirk on her face. As he was about to leave and was now not going to give her a ticket, she looked over at me and loudly exclaimed, "Now are you going to behave yourself?!"

As we drove off, I said, "What in the hell did you just do? And why did you say that?" She replied, "It worked, didn't it? I didn't get a ticket—and after all, I *am* an actress, you know!

Oh my God, what am I in for?

CHAPTER 11
MY FIRST REAL GUY FRIEND

We became very close friends with Lisa and Pat, coincidentally both actors. Lisa Davis (she used her surname as her stage name as well) and Joan had met a few years earlier before Joan met me. They were first introduced while filming the television show *My Little Margie*, a hit series at the time. It was during a beauty contest scene when Joan Lora (my Joan) played "Miss Italy," and Lisa Davis "Miss England," and Joy Lancing, "Miss America."

The Gale Storm Show

They soon became the best of friends.

Lisa was a slim, magnificent, sexy blonde with pearl-white skin, and had a silky, soft, seductive voice—the epitome of femininity. She was born in England and had that wonderful, alluring English accent.

Pat Waltz (he also used his surname as his stage name) was six foot two, and a handsome, muscular guy with coal-black hair, and had been an Olympic diver when he was young. I was first introduced to him when we double-dated one evening.

Lisa and Pat fell in love on the set while making the movie *Queen of Outer Space* (1958), starring Zsa Zsa Gabor, with them ironically playing parts as lovers. Lisa played "Motiya," and Pat, the lieutenant of the space ship, was named "Larry Turner." Soon after filming, they married, and the following year had a baby girl, Carrie.

Between Joan, Lisa, and Pat, they represented well over fifty filming segments and were noticed whenever we went out. I was the only non-Hollywood outsider, but probably had the biggest ego, though unwarranted.

We double-dated most weekends, and loved going to Trader Vic's, a Polynesian restaurant in the Beverly Hilton Hotel. Their featured drink was called a "Scorpion," made with dark rum, light rum, and brandy. They were so potent, there was a limit of two! We all, of course, drank our limit, and it was always a difficult decision who would—or could—drive home. Looking back, none of us should have!

Lisa had been trying to get pregnant again with their second child but was having difficulty conceiving. During one of the outings while at Trader Vic's, it so happened that that night was during her six days of ovulation, so she needed to take her temperature occasionally. When it reached the predetermined desired temperature, she would then be apt to be more fertile. I recall her sitting at the table sipping her second mind-altering Scorpion, and occasionally would slip a thermometer into her mouth. The waiters found that very bewildering, but amusing.

Now, after a couple of hours of munching on Hawaiian barbecue ribs and hot-and-spicy Korean-style chicken wings, she popped the thermometer into her mouth and stood up, looked at Pat (and not at me, damn it), and screamed, "Let's go! I have to get laid—and *right* now!"

Her temperature must have been very high, or she was very drunk! I did wonder, however, if it was actually the heat from the hot-and-spicy Korean-style chicken wings that raised her temperature! But who was I to say? Pat was my buddy.

Several surrounding male patrons had a very envious look on their face because Lisa was knock-down beautiful. Who in the hell wouldn't want to satisfy her wishes?!

Unfortunately, Lisa couldn't get pregnant no matter what they tried, so they soon after adopted a baby girl. Life was now good, and they enjoyed parenting their two little girls.

Pat and I eventually bonded and became the best of friends, one of the few adult male friends I would ever end up having. We were sort of like a Mutt and Jeff; he was tall, and I was shorter—notice I said, short-*er*. I would often jokingly stand on paint cans to make myself taller. But he was still taller, and by several inches!

Joan and I were honored to be asked to be the godparents for their first daughter, Carrie, early the next year. Lisa's sister, Beryl Davis, was a well-known singer who sang in Glenn Miller's band. She also sang in a group with Jane Russel, Connie Haines, and Rhonda Fleming. Beryl married Peter Potter, of the Emmy winning *Peter Potter's Juke Box Jury*, a popular television show back in the late fifties and early sixties. Lisa was often on the show, as well. Beryl and Peter were also there the day of the baptism at St. Ambrose Catholic Church on Fairfax Avenue in West Hollywood.

Let's take a look at this scene. Pat was an actor. Lisa was an actress. Beryl was a singer. Peter was a television personality. Joan (my Joan) was an actress. Me, I was a fishmonger. Oh sure, I fit in!

I *must* flash forward for a moment: I so remember one day in particular, several years later after we moved up to San Francisco and I no longer worked for my dad (that's a hint of things to come). I was working for one of his competitors on Fisherman's Wharf as a salesman.

The wholesale fish facility was a disgusting, horrible environment, to say the least. Men would constantly scream profanities and holler in an ignorant manner to each other, while the smell of fish permeated your clothes and impregnated your nostrils to a nauseating affect—a sharp contrast to my posh, spoiled young life and the fairy-tale existence I'd just left in glitzy Tinseltown, and certainly a far cry from my aspirations of working downtown on Montgomery Street.

I was standing, not sitting, as there was no room for desks in the tiny sales office that had barely enough room for three men. I was dressed in a sport coat and thin slacks and freezing my butt off as the cold wind whipped in from the bay through the two open roll-up doors on the production floor. One of the owners sat on an old, creaky wooden stool at the front, facing the production floor, as his fat ass overlapped the strained stool he sat upon. He was a quick-tempered and violent, five-foot-four very rotund man from lower Italy. He was allegedly associated with some of the West Coast's underworld figures, so no one dared cross him. He could also hear every word you said.

It was about ten thirty that morning, and I was about to call a chef down the Peninsula for an order, when most unexpectedly I received a call, and it wasn't from a customer. It was Beryl! I don't know how she ever got the number for where I worked. She said, "Hi, Kiki, this is Beryl Davis, Lisa's sister. I'm up here appearing at the Fairmont Hotel with Jane and Connie and Rhonda. We're going to lunch and would love to have you join us."

I sank and got weak in the knees. Holy shit, my flamboyant bullshit past lifestyle was coming back to haunt me. I was now eating nineteen-cent McDonald's burgers every day, and probably didn't have fifty cents on me. I couldn't even pay for the parking at the Fairmont, for Christ sake. Anyway, they would probably direct me to the receiving dock, thinking I was making a delivery in the unsightly, old, faded-green Ranchero.

My clothes and every pore in my body were infused with the repulsive smell of fish. Oh, sure, I could sit up there on Nob Hill in the supercilious Laurel Court Restaurant and talk with these celebs as if I was still a big shot, and they wouldn't notice anything different. Hell, they would be holding their noses and gagging while reaching for perfume as I inauspiciously ducked out without paying the bill.

Yeah, remember back just a year or so ago? That illusory era where I thought I was the heir to a huge seafood corporation fortune? Ha! What a joke!

Having to think fast to get out of the situation, I graciously said, "Oh, Beryl, it would have been fun and so nice to see you, but I'm in an important business meeting, and it should last for several hours. I'm so sorry, but thank you. Please say hi to Lisa for me"—all the while, cupping the phone in my hands to attempt to drown out the screaming and cussing in the background. She even commented that she heard talking in the background and apologized for bothering me while I was in the meeting! Whew...

That incident depressed me to no end. It made me realize how low and what a nothing I really was. My six-year span in Southern California, having delusions of grandeur, was like a movie set—all up front and nothing in back. Like my back pocket. It was all just an illusion. I was just a stinkin' fish salesman now trying to support my wife and baby, with a second daughter on the way.

For a moment, I thought of my first girlfriend, and wondered where she could be now, maybe married, possibly to an actor or director or a producer, living a wonderful lifestyle. I guessed she'd gotten lucky that we'd drifted apart. And now poor Joan; she'd given up everything to move up here just for me. She left all her friends and her thriving acting career. She could have been a big star!

The revelation was devastating. I was depressed, beaten, bewildered, and more than anything, lost. More on that later, but for now we'll get back to what was at the time, the present day.

Unfortunately, Pat wasn't getting many interviews or auditions for roles anymore. He was ten years older than me; I was twenty-six, and he, thirty-six. I assume he was typecast as a good-looking young man, as that so often happens, and unless you're an incredibly good character actor, the parts seem to cease, not uncommon. The film industry can be cruel and merciless. Meanwhile, to make matters worse, he'd suffered his first heart attack, and was told he could no longer do any strenuous athletics. Being an Olympic swimmer, as I previously stated, this was devastating to him.

Depression set in and he started to drink heavily. But you know, we all drank; however, not to excess at the time. Well, one evening during an alcohol-induced stupor, he burnt down their adorable small home in Studio City. The home once belonged to Oliver Hardy, of Laurel and Hardy, the comedy team. Pat showed me a secret hiding place that Oliver had built for his treasured belongings in the hallway near the front door.

Of course, the home was all ashes now. This did not help his depressed state.

Lisa and Pat had fought that evening, so Lisa and the two little girls were sleeping in the master bedroom at the time of the fire, and fortunately were able to get out. Pat was sleeping in one of the girls' beds, which had a sheer veiled canopy on top. He was smoking and fell asleep, and the highly flammable, thin material caught fire. Pat suffered first-, second-, and third-degree burns on over 50 percent of his body and was in the hospital for over three months.

Now deeper in depression, he apparently started experimenting with anything that would let him escape his adversity. I'll never forget one evening when he handed me a pill and said, "Try this." I asked him, "So what is it Pat?" He passively replied, "It will just make you happy, that's all." Stupidly, and trustingly, I took it. A few minutes later, I thought my heart was going to come out of my chest. My heart was pounding so hard I thought I was having a heart attack. I have no clue what the hell he gave me, but never again. I didn't get happy either.

With Pat promising to stop trying to soothe his despondent state by numbing himself, Lisa apprehensively agreed to stay with him. He told her don't worry; "God just kicked me in the butt."

Within a couple of years, they surprisingly had another child; this time, a son. She'd always wanted at least two children, so Lisa was elated. It strangely seems that if a woman is relaxed, she can then conceive. The little boy was an added joy to their lives, and thus should have cemented their marriage.

However, within a couple of years, Pat's depression and addictions got the best of him, and he was totally out of control. He had also by now suffered his second heart attack and was abusing the medications prescribed by his doctors to help control his anxiety and mood disorders. His persuasive personality convinced the doctors to over-prescribe the medications, and he'd started mixing Valium (diazepam) with alcohol for a euphoric high and was soon addicted to it. Pat obviously used it to get high to try to escape his emotional issues.

Lisa had finally had enough, and they sadly divorced. He was forty years old.

The last time I saw Pat, he was a security guard at the La Brea Towers apartment complex near the farmers market on Fairfax Avenue. He was probably making minimum wage and was a broken man. From having been the tall, muscular look-alike stand-in for Elvis Presley in *It Happened at the World's Fair* (1962), and a handsome actor in his own right, he was now an unrecognizable, aging security guard at a paltry apartment complex.

This was so sad to see. I told him we needed to see more of each other, and tried to give him support, emphasizing that I was still his good friend. Then, trying to make him laugh, I jokingly said, "Friends are like bras: close to the heart and always there for support!" He chuckled, but the depression was still evident, and my banter had obviously made no impact.

He was now living in a small apartment on Coldwater Canyon, and had attempted suicide several times. The combination of Valium and alcohol was a potent and toxic cocktail. He was also no longer acting.

Pat not only lost his lavish career, but his beautiful wife and three young children to his enslaving addiction. Sure, addiction is not an uncommon scenario in Tinseltown; however, if you add a serious heart condition, the guy didn't have a chance.

He tragically died two years later after suffering his third heart attack at the age of forty-two at Saint Joseph's Hospital in Burbank.

We had long since moved to Northern California when we got the news. Oddly, he once told me he would never make it forty-five. I'd scoffed at his remark as we arm wrestled and fought for domination, always laughing with a high five at the end, no matter who won.

This was not all Hollywood or the entertainment industry's fault that lead to his pathetic and sorrowful demise. It was Pat, himself, behaving in an incredulous manner. He was unwilling to admit or accept being expendable, and move on from acting, as many actors have had to do. Pat was a well-educated guy. His escape into his addictions is what allowed him to disguise his perception of himself and his aging identity, and it eventually consumed him. His exodus from life was way too soon.

However, every man—no, every person—needs an *identity*. How well of this, I know.

To add to this sad segment, their first daughter, our godchild, now in her late twenties, was diagnosed with AIDS. It was discovered when her husband had pneumonia while doing a routine blood test, that he was HIV-positive. She had just given birth to a son a month prior, and it was then discovered that she and the newborn were also HIV-positive. It had been transmitted to her by her husband, and to the baby through pregnancy. That baby, now a grown man, is fortunately in remission.

At the time, the only drug available for Lisa's daughter was the primitive AZT, and it was totally ineffective, so there was little hope for her.

Lisa, however, had been estranged from her daughter for many years, which had been the case ever since her daughter had brought her fiancé to first meet Lisa. Lisa was unaware of all that was happening until her daughter called and told her she was sick.

Lisa told me that when her daughter had come to Lisa's house to introduce her fiancé, that he'd sat out on the street on the hood of his car with a six-pack of beer, and had raised the can he was drinking from, as an assumed gesture that meant "hello"—an apparent and obvious sign of disrespect and lack of decent upbringing.

Lisa was shocked by his actions, and advised her daughter not to marry him, but her daughter didn't abide by her mother's wish. They married shortly after and moved to Sacramento. Lisa, being disheartened by this, then had little contact with her daughter for years, until her daughter called and advised her mother about her irremediable diagnosis.

When Lisa's daughter called and told her mother about her HIV-positive diagnosis, she also told her, shockingly, that she had a third son; it was the middle child, and they had given him up for adoption at birth. She begged her mother to try and find the child and have him tested for HIV. What a double dose of tragedy; not only for the daughter, but for Lisa.

Well, now after hearing how very sick her daughter was, Lisa would drive for over six hours from Studio City to Sacramento every weekend to try to look after her. Upon arriving, she would go shopping and prepare meals for her and her family and try to console her as much as she could. Lisa would leave work at five o'clock every Friday and often arrive well after midnight. She would then leave on Sunday late afternoon and arrive back home around ten at night and get up at five the next morning to drive to work in the horrific LA traffic. This went on for three years.

Lisa told me that after seeing her daughter getting sicker and sicker every weekend, that she would cry after leaving her, often times from the Grapevine, a section of winding and mountainous Highway 5, all the way to her home just off Ventura Boulevard in Studio City. One can only imagine the pain of knowing you were going to soon lose a child, and one so young.

An obviously bad relationship existed between Lisa and her son-in-law, and how could it not? With Lisa now wanting to be with her daughter as her time on earth neared the end, Lisa had a hospice nurse tell her daughter's insolent husband she (the hospice nurse) was driving her daughter to a doctor's appointment, but instead drove her to the Sacramento Airport for a flight to Bob Hope Airport in Burbank, arranged by Lisa, where she picked her up.

Lisa then drove to her vacation home in Palm Springs, where she surrounded her daughter with pictures of her two handsome young sons and her brother and sister. Her daughter told her that she had hoped she could have one more Christmas, but she was failing and would obviously never make it, so Lisa decorated the house with Christmas decorations and a tree. This was in mid-September, and Palm Springs was sweltering in one-hundred-degree-plus weather, but she made the best of it.

Ten days later, on September 24, 1993, Lisa and Pat's beautiful daughter Carrie, still in the prime of her life, laid her head back and died in Lisa's arms just before midnight, with the pictures of her two young sons in front of her. She had just turned thirty-four.

After many months and much investigation, Lisa finally made contact with the son her daughter had given up for adoption. He was living in New York. Lisa has now formed a meaningful relationship with him, her newfound grandson.

She told me that when first seeing him, she saw the image of Carrie, and immediately knew it was him.

Upon their meeting in Southern California, Lisa asked if they could meet at a restaurant close to her home in Studio City due to the horrendous traffic in downtown LA where he was staying. She was surprised when he oddly asked, "You don't have a driver?"

It came to pass that he ended up being the heir to an affluent family's fortune on the East Coast. His adoptive parents had both tragically died relatively young; the adoptive father, from a brain tumor, and coincidentally, just ten days later, his adoptive mother, from breast cancer. He then was raised by the adoptive mother's first husband and new wife. She was a society matron of New York, and a larger-than-life figure in Washington, DC politics.

He has a home in the Hamptons, an apartment in Manhattan, and currently takes up residency in Beverly Hills. He is a very wealthy young man, and is fortunately free from HIV. Yes, he got tested—his mother's last wish was granted.

While he was talking with Lisa that first night during dinner, he went on to say that when he was about five years old, he'd found a tin box in the basement of his parents' home in the Hamptons that had documents inside stating that he was adopted. These documents also included his birth father's last name, but he didn't know where he lived.

Lisa asked him to please not try to find his birth father, explaining his life style was less than respectful, and it would only hurt. He didn't listen, and eventually found him. The meeting did not go well. All he said was that they didn't hug.

Looking back, I so remember Carrie, our godchild, as an angelic, beautiful little girl, with those big, piercing blue eyes looking up at us from her crib, filled with purity and innocence. What a shame her life ended so young, so sadly, and so tragically. How unforeseen and unfortunate one's journey can be.

I don't think I could ever recover from the loss of a child. My heart goes out to Lisa.

CHAPTER 12
THE PROPOSAL

One of Joan's and my special treats on Saturday night was the Windsor Restaurant, located just behind the Ambassador Hotel in Los Angeles. It was the ultimate epitome of class, with a five-star rating. No, of course I couldn't afford it! We would naturally start with the traditional Amer Picon cocktail with a brandy float—and yes, they knew how to make it—then start the meal with a caprese salad, with vine-ripened tomatoes and fresh buffalo mozzarella, skillfully stacked and drizzled with olive oil and balsamic vinegar, and garnished with basil leaves; then, the superbly baked, medium-rare Beef Wellington, a filet mignon coated with pate de foie gras and duxelles, cooked in a pastry dough. It was truly delicious. It was accompanied by oven-roasted baby potatoes and pan-sauteed vegetables of the day (that I ignored). Dessert was often a Grand Marnier souffle, with a warm white-chocolate sauce. Dinner was equivalent to just about two-thirds of my entire week's salary.

We would then swing around the corner to the Coconut Grove Night Club in the Ambassador Hotel to enjoy a cabaret-style floor show and blow the remaining one-third. The Grove would always be loaded with celebrities. Harry Belafonte was appearing on one of the nights we were there, singing his mood-altering sounds of calypso music, in his sexy cutaway shirt and tight pants, as the women in the audience relentlessly gazed at him. He eventually noticed Joan Lora, the young actress—my Joan—and toasted her.

She had just been in a film with him in which she'd danced. He also just happened to be married to her close friend, Julie, also a professional dancer with whom Joan took dancing lessons. However, just as most Hollywood marriages end up, they eventually divorced.

A bottle of Moët et Chandon Dom Perignon champagne appeared at the table a short time later, compliments of Mr. Belafonte. Well, that bit of luck allowed for gas money.

We then danced, and as I pulled her into my arms, everything felt right, so right. It just felt so damn good. The warmth of her body ever-so-close to mine felt as if we were one. I found the scent of her perfume intoxicating and her eyes mesmerizing. Her lips were now so close and enticing, I strained not to kiss her. As we now gleefully danced, her hair gently brushed against my face with a tantalizing sensation. My arm around her tiny waist drew her in even closer, and I could feel her femininity. She then sensually ran her hand through my hair with a hypnotizing affect, causing a feeling of total elation. This was the sensation, realization, and validation of love.

Of course, being a professional, she was a magnificent dancer, but respectively allowed me to lead.

Our favorite, more casual hangout was Dino's Lodge. Dean Martin had just opened the restaurant on the Sunset Strip. We would often go there for dinner, then go a few blocks further down to a small romantic lounge called the Interlude. It had a piano bar that we would sit around for hours listening to cool, rhythmic, soft jazz. It was owned by Bobbie Troupe and his wife, Julie

London. Bobbie was on the piano as Julie sang. She had a deep, soft, soothing tone that was enchanting. They had many record hits at the time, and we eventually got to know them both quite well.

It was there one night, while I was holding Joan in my arms as Julie sang, when I felt this overwhelming desire that I had to be with her for the rest of my life. I couldn't wait any longer. I didn't want to lose her. I was going to ask her to marry me. I wanted her to be the mother of my children, and a wonderful mother she would be. She was everything I ever wanted; not only beautiful, but was kind and had a heart of gold. My playboy days were over. I was going to buy her a ring! However, I didn't have any money, as usual . . . but that never stopped me.

That next week I shopped for engagement rings. Jeez! I hadn't realized how expensive diamonds were! I knew that several wealthy men had flashed big rocks at her, so I'd better get her a nice one. I had to be extravagant. So what if I had to pay for it until I collected social security?

I found a two-and-a-quarter carat marquis-cut diamond in a cool setting. That was the one! I then asked the man, "By the way, sir, how much is it?" When he told me, I remember saying, "Oh my, you're kidding, aren't you?!" I then asked if they had a payment plan. The ring was most likely half the size that she would have expected, but . . .

Joan and I went out the following Saturday night—to where else?—Dino's Lodge. Frank Sinatra and Dean Martin were there that night sitting at the bar, smoking and getting plastered.

We finished dinner and continued talking. She must have known something was up since I was so nervous and procrastinated with paying the bill. The waiter started bugging me, asking if I wanted the check. I repeatedly said, "No. Not yet. Not yet, damn it!"

Okay, the time is now, brave up and just say it! We sat there for the longest time holding hands, my heart pounding and my forehead sweaty, then I suddenly blurted out, "Honey, I want to ask you something." She then interrupted and said, "Yes!" "Uh, yes?" I replied. "Yes, what? I didn't say anything yet!" She then said, "Well, weren't you going to ask me to marry you? Isn't that why you haven't paid the bill for the past two hours?"

My God, she said yes! But aren't I supposed to formally ask her first? And, oh, the ring! I then opened the black velvet box and put the ring on her finger. I can still see her looking at her left hand, holding it up and saying, "Hmm . . . well, I guess it will do!" What the hell had she meant by that, "Well, I guess it will do"?

This was just her way of letting me know she'd had larger—much larger—diamonds thrown at her by the Hollywood bigwigs, even a five-plus carat. But she'd said yes to *me*!

She then asked if I had asked her dad. *Oh, shit. I didn't even think about that! Jeez, yes, I probably should have asked him first, but heck, she just said yes, so it doesn't matter. Or does it? He can't say no, can he? You know, maybe he could! Shoooot. He was never very fond of me!*

Now happy as can be and walking arm in arm out of Dino's, she walked up to Sinatra standing at the bar while holding her left hand in the air and said to him, "Look at what I just got, Frank!" He looked over at me and said, "What the hell is the matter with you, kid? You're not supposed to marry the broads, ya just fuck 'em! Joan then looked at him and gave him the Italian curse—with one arm in the air with all five fingers pointing up! He then grinned and said to me, "You have quite a spicy beauty there, young man." Hey, at least she didn't give him the middle finger! Maybe it was a good thing filming was finished!

Joan had met him earlier that week while filming the San Francisco segment in *Around the World in Eighty Days.* In the scene, he played the piano just inches from her, while she talked with Marlene Dietrich and George Raft. Michael Todd, Conteflas, and Red Skelton were also in that scene.

Dino, however, was very nice, and started singing while holding a cigarette in his left hand. "When the moon hits your eye, like a big pizza pie, that's amore. When the world seems to shine, like you've had too much wine, that's amore." He then ad-libbed, "Wedding bells will soon ring, ring a ding-a-ling-ting-a-ling-a-ling . . . " He then held up his now-empty martini glass and toasted us, and shook my hand.

We set the date May 14, 1960, as the wedding day. I needed a best man, so I called my best friend (or so I *thought*) up north while he was at work. Well, he didn't sound very pleased to hear from me, not even asking how I was, and then promptly said no, stating it was too far. He then dismissed my call without encouraging any further talk. I tried to reason, saying it was only an hour by plane, and even offered to pay for his flight down and the hotel for the night, but he still declined with an abrupt, surly attitude. Hurt again by a guy friend.

I then hesitantly asked my brother, and surprisingly, he said yes. Okay, what happened a few years ago had to be let go. I wanted it to be, anyway. I still loved him.

Joan's folks asked if we wanted a big wedding or a small one, with tickets to go to the Isle of Capri where her dad's family was from. We promptly said the Isle of Capri, of course!

The wedding day soon came, and I arrived early. We were married at the St. Charles Borromeo Roman Catholic Church on Lankershim and Moorpark in North Hollywood, a beautiful old church depicting Spanish colonial architecture.

As I was standing in front of the church on that warm Saturday morning waiting for everyone to arrive, including my soon-to-be gorgeous wife, a tall, rather scantily clad, sexy girl, dressed as if going to *Meet the Fleet*, walked up to me and asked if I was Kiki. She introduced herself as one of Joan's friends, a model. She obviously wasn't wearing a bra, since her nipples were piercing through her white silk blouse that exposed a hint of color beneath. She was a bit flat-chested, as most models are, but a knockout. For just a moment—but only a moment—I thought, *Maybe Sinatra was right?* Then I said to myself, "Hey, I love Joan with all my heart, and have the woman of my dreams. C'mon, get it together. You're getting married in a few minutes, for Christ sake!"

A half hour later, the white limo pulled up and Joan got out. Oh. My. God! She was beyond magnificently beautiful, and the epitome of femininity.

If ever the presence of an angel visited earth, this was the day, and she was mine. She looked like she should have been on the cover of *Bride Magazine*. I had never seen her so beautiful, so radiant, so happy.

What had I ever done to deserve her? How lucky could one guy be?

By the way, I did end up asking her father; however, while asking, his gray hair curled—a sign that he wasn't very pleased.

The marriage ceremony was a full one-hour mass; long, but all went well, except that I nearly passed out just before communion. I didn't know if that was due to not having had anything to eat, or if it was getting married—or I was afraid to accept Jesus in my soul, just as I'd been at my first Holy Communion when I was a little boy. Possibly all three.

We then went to Joan's folks' home for the reception. Everyone was having a great time, especially my dad. He was as happy and jovial as could be. Of course, I married the "nice Italian girl" he'd introduced me to! Thank you, Dad, for that, by the way.

One thing bothered me, however. The week before the wedding, my dad called me into his office and said, "Here's your wedding gift, Kiki." It was a check for approximately $600 that he had endorsed over to me from an insurance policy. I thought it was odd, since it wasn't for an exact amount; it was an amount down to a specific number of cents, something like $614.92. I never questioned why it was from an insurance company, or for an odd amount; probably never even thought much of it at the time. Looking back now, it must have been a return premium, or even possibly a policy he'd cashed in for me. Did he really not have much cash of his own? How totally stupid of me not to realize back then what was going on.

We had to leave everyone at the party that afternoon, since our flight out of LAX was departing early that evening.

We left the house in Joan's father's car, and my sister Kay had tied tin cans onto the rear bumper and put rocks in the hub caps. Joan's father didn't appreciate it, but that was something they did back then! We went down the street, clanging away, with everyone looking and waving, wishing us good luck.

CHAPTER 13
THE HONEYMOON

It was a long seven-hour flight from LAX to New York on the American Airlines Boeing 377 Stratocruiser prop plane. I remember halfway through the flight, cuddling up to Joan, taking her into my arms, and kissing her. I was so in love with her.

A moment later, she said, "No!" I replied by asking, "No? No what?" "You can't do it here, here on the plane!" she replied. "What? I was just kissing you, honey!" I exclaimed. To this day, she doesn't believe that I just wanted to kiss her. Actually, that really was all I wanted to do. Honestly!

Joan had a close friend in New York, Mia, who said she would have Bino, her fiancé, pick us up at the airport in one of the limousines from the mortuary his father owned. Yes, their names were Mia and Bino—so what do you think their nationality was?

That was cool, being picked up in a limo to be driven to the hotel, I thought. However, I was a bit dismayed but entertained with the thought of its use. It was now about ten o'clock at night and we were tired. It had been a very long day. At that point, any means of transportation would have been fine.

Now as we stood in the arrival area at the Idlewild Airport in New York, a long black limo pulled up with the passenger-side window rolled down. It was Bino, who said, "Hi, Joanie. Hi, Kiki. You'll both be sitting up here in the front seat with me." Hmm . . . the front seat. That was odd. Why? Well, maybe it was just that he wanted to talk with us up close, and not from the rear seat, I assumed.

I then glanced back at the rear of what I expected to be a limo and saw it was a hearse—not a limo! *Well, it's sort of a limo, I guess, just not for the living. Oh, shit. Well, okay, I'm sure it's empty back there. No big deal.*

Bino then said, "Kiki, bring your luggage to the rear." When he opened the rear hatch, to my utter astonishment, in there was an effing corpse wrapped in a white sheet! I stepped back and exclaimed, "Holy shit!" "What's the matter?" Bino calmly asked. "I had to make a pick up"—as they call it— "on the way to the airport."

On the way to the hotel, on one of the turns, both large suitcases fell over on our newfound reticent friend. That gave me the heebie jeebies! Yeah, our horizontal companion didn't say a word about it—that was the problem!

Arriving at the Waldorf Astoria Hotel, you should have seen the look on the bellman's face as we pulled up in the hearse. It was also obvious that Bino was a bit apprehensive about having to open the rear hatch to unload our luggage. The bellman jerked back upon seeing that the luggage had fallen over upon the dearly departed. Reluctantly and gently, he respectively removed our bags from its upper torso. Yes, I gave him a nice tip.

When I saw Mia the next morning, she unemotionally said, "Oh, yes. On our very first date, Bino had a pick up before arriving at my house. I've gotten used to it."

Checking into our rooms was quite an experience. It was now hovering close to midnight and I was tired—no, exhausted. We'd just gotten married, spent seven hours on a plane, and another hour in a hearse with a cadaver in the back. It had been a very long and intense day.

We were assigned a room on the twelfth floor with a king-size bed; an elaborate room, but it was rather odiferous smelling. It couldn't have been from the guy in the back of the hearse; we'd left him with Bino. It was possibly from mold. The hotel was rather old, but the room was spacious with a view—yeah, a view of the brick building next to us twelve feet away. I just wanted to crash. Who cared about a view? Joan went to the bathroom and I was now laying on the bed. It felt so good to lie down. She came out of the bathroom and proceeded to begin bouncing on the bed, bouncing up and down, up and down. I asked, "Darling, what the hell are you doing?" She said, "It squeaks!" "It does, what?!" I exclaimed. Then moaned, "No, it doesn't. Anyway, who cares? Please, let's just go to bed." She said, "No. I want to change rooms." *Oh, God. It's now after midnight. I'm shot, but okay, anything for my new bride.*

She had opened our suitcases earlier for something, and noticed my sisters, most likely Kay, had put what appeared to be at least a five-pound sack of white rice all over the inside of the bags. There was now rice all over the floor, and we were going to leave a once-perfectly clean room looking like a Chinese banquet had just been served!

I called the front desk, and they said for me to come downstairs and they would give me keys to another room. As we were changing rooms, now dragging the luggage (this was before luggage with wheels) from the room into the hallway, I noticed a trail of rice had followed us from Room 1218 to Room 1214. It now appeared like someone hadn't wanted to get lost in between rooms and had left a trail of rice to find their way back!

Opening the door of Room 1214, Joan said, "Don't get comfortable. I want to try out the bed!" *Ohhhh, no,* I thought.

So, there she was, sitting on the bed, bouncing up and down, up and down again! She then screamed in her stage voice—which probably awoke the six rooms adjacent to us—"This one's squeaky, too!"

All I wanted to do was to go to sleep. It was almost one in the morning, but I said, "Okay, honey, I'll ask for another room. But they're going to think we're nut cases."

The desk clerk was in hysterics when I asked for another room, explaining that my wife said the beds in both rooms squeaked. I can only imagine what he was thinking.

I forget now if the bed in our third room squeaked or not; I went to sleep. Forget about consummating the marriage. Maybe that had been her plan . . .

The next day after having breakfast with Mia, we saw some of the sights in the Big Apple. What a wonderful, exciting city. We were given a movie camera as a wedding gift—yes, a movie camera with film. There were no video or digital cameras or smart phones back then, so I was filming all of our experiences.

That first night, we met Joan's Aunt Lidia and her husband and their sons for dinner at Mama Rosa's, an old-fashioned New York Italian restaurant.

The next day we completed our short two-day stay with dinner at Gino's, where Joan's father had once worked as a waiter. We enjoyed another fabulous Italian meal, and we were treated like royalty.

The stay in New York was brief, and we looked forward to returning someday.

The following morning, we boarded our flight to Rome. Sometime later during the flight, I took out the movie camera and finally decided to read the instructions. Yep, it's a known fact that guys don't read instructions. I was reading the directions for how to use the movie camera and came upon a paragraph that said "Remove lens cap before using." *Oh, jeez. The lens cap! How do I tell Joan I didn't get any of New York? But I have to! She'll eventually find out when we get back. We're at thirty thousand feet—she can't storm out!*

I said, "Cara mia" [my dear]. . . " She then said, "What did you do wrong?" *Boy, does she know me.* I then braved up to admit what happened and said, "Honey, I left the lens cap on, on the camera. I didn't get any of New York." I then crumpled down in my seat so if she hit me, I would be a little farther away. However, she replied, "That's okay. Good thing you found out. At least you'll get all of Italy, won't you?" However, I sensed a bit of sarcasm in her voice.

Arriving at the Rome airport in the early morning, we were met by Joan's cousin Billie, who was living there at the time studying to be a doctor, and he drove us to our *albergo* (hotel). Exhausted by the long flight over the polar region, we checked into our room and rested for a few hours. Upon going up to the roof-top ristorante for lunch, I had my first experience feasting on the amazing breads of Italy and the sweet *burro* (butter), which I promptly poured salt on. It didn't take long to discover that I could forever live in Rome and be in paradise.

An hour or so later, Billie picked us up and we drove around magnificent Rome for a while. We saw churches and more churches, and then eventually ended up in Ancient Rome. I couldn't believe we were walking where the inhabitants of the ancient Romans had once lived. I was fascinated, and as a matter of fact, have always been intrigued with the history of Ancient Rome. This may sound odd, but I felt connected to old Rome, and more specifically, the Senate, and I needed to see the Senate building.

After walking for a half hour or so, we eventually came upon the Senate building, and with amazement, I saw that it was still in remarkably good condition. The door was open, and we were able to walk in about twenty feet or so. A velvet rope further corded off the area not allowed by tourists. I stood there, and a feeling of belonging came over me. I was mesmerized. I imagined what had transpired in that large rotunda so many centuries ago, almost like I knew, feeling that just maybe in a prior life I'd been connected to it. Could that be? Or was it just a fantasy? I had a difficult time leaving, but Joan had to go to the bathroom (something I'd gotten used to), so we had to leave.

It was now getting dark and Joan's cousin said, "I'm lost. I don't know how to get us out of here." This was back in 1960, and there were no lights, signage, or paths directing the way back to modern-day Rome.

I looked around for a moment, and without further hesitation said, "Follow me." What the hell? How would I know how to get out of there? But somehow, I knew, I knew exactly where I was, and promptly walked us out. Meanwhile, upon stepping back into modern Rome, I had no clue where I was. Go figure.

I wish I could have spent all the next day just wandering around the ancient city, but we still had to see the many other sights of Rome.

The next day, we went to Saint Peter's Basilica in Vatican City, the construction of which was completed in 1626.

The Basilica is the burial site of its namesake, Saint Peter, who was one of the twelve apostles of Jesus. The basilica is beyond anything you could imagine, as anyone who has visited knows. We climbed the several hundred steps to the very top of the spire and viewed the magnificence of Rome. What an experience that was.

The next day, Billie took us to the Capuchin Crypt, the catacombs that are located beneath the church of Santa Maria della Concezione dei Cappuccini that contain the skeletal remains of over four thousand friars buried by their order.

All the decorations are made from the bones of the monks from the past several hundred years. Many are piled high, as heads clamor together in various shapes, femur bones in the shape of tulips, leg bones, arms, wrists, feet, all in designs thought of by someone making a point, so I assume. It was eerie, cold, damp, and moldy—not a pleasant experience to say the least.

It made me realize how insignificant my life was, any life, and what a brief time we are upon this earth, as if our existence is "but a grain of sand on the beach" compared to eternity. Our individual life's term is so infinitesimal. If that was the point, it succeeded.

These were once living people, with feelings, desires, emotions, and at one time, with a purpose in life, and now they were just decorations on a wall. Just bones.

The revaluation came upon me that you must live and love, and even more, express your love while you can.

That experience may have possibly given me the inspiration to one day write about my life—that I lived—everyone should write something about their life, that they lived, that they existed. That they are not just bones, though someday we will all be just bones.

Coming back out and into the afternoon sun was more than a breath of fresh air. It made me want to breathe in deeply and embrace life, to embrace Joan. I grabbed her and put my arms around her and told her I loved her, and thanked her for wanting to spend her "grain of sand" with me.

The next day we visited the Coliseum. What a magnificent structure. How did the Ancient Romans build these structures with such massive blocks of stone? What civil engineering knowledge could they have had? I understand they had some sort of a huge wheel-like apparatus that slaves walked in. It looked like a water wheel attached to pulleys and winches, a holivela, that raised these massive stones so high with nothing but brute force.

Walking through the Coliseum, one can't help thinking of the horrific, tragic events that took place there many centuries ago, and just for entertainment. I can't imagine the barbarity of the Christians being attacked by starving animals, standing there with your family, your child, knowing the pain that would soon ensue, and that death was imminent. What atrocities, what inhumanity some people have had to endure, and then the inhumane brutality and slaughter of the animals, some to extinction. I now hoped I really had not been a part of this dreadful, abhorrent time in history.

A falsity about the "thumbs-up" gesture we all use suggesting approval or affirmation. Back in Ancient Roman times, especially in the Coliseum, a thumbs-up meant death to the gladiator. A "thumbs-down" meant swords down, thus he was spared. A thumbs-up was also an ancient phallic symbol for male virility! Maybe we should all reconsider this when using that gesture now.

Moving on into the countryside later that afternoon, we visited the Villa d' Este in Tivoli, a famous sixteenth-century villa with manicured terraced gardens and an amazing array of fountains and grottoes. It is a wonderment how the Ancient Romans were able to use gravity and the different-sized pipes to form the impressive fountains and water features.

It was constructed by Cardinal d' Este in 1550. I found that distressing. Why should—or how could—a member or ex-member of the church enjoy such a lavish lifestyle?

Ever wonder where the money came from? Well, from the poor; the poor peasants, of course, who crawled on their bloodied knees to give their coins, seeking atonement from hell and indemnification for their sins. The sinners were the hierarchy.

Our days in Rome had now concluded. We were leaving in the morning on the train down to Naples, and then over to the Isle of Capri where Joan's father had family.

A funny thing happened while at the train station. If you have ever been to Italy you will understand how confusing the train stations can be, with the constant changing of the tracks where the train you want to catch will be. Looking up at the display board up on the wall, it seemed as if they couldn't make up their minds as to what track the trains would be leaving from as the track numbers seemed to change every few minutes! I'm sure it was just us though that didn't understand the methodology.

Well, after a half hour of exhausting attempts, we finally found the right track for our train to Napoli, so we then ventured out to the open area where the trains were. Finding our train at track number seven, we then eventually found our car. It was again challenging due to the hectic rush of the rude Europeans pushing and shoving their way to get to their train. Thankfully, we were early as one should be when traveling in a foreign country, so we had plenty of time. While sitting in our first-class compartment, we looked around and noticed there really wasn't much difference from first class to second class, other than a little softer seat and the price. As we waited, Joan asked, "Honey, I'm thirsty. Would you please go and get me a beer?" I said, "You want me to venture out, out there, and get you a beer? I don't know how to speak Italian!"

She said, "Just say, 'Una birra, per piacere!'" Oh, okay, that's all I needed to say? Sure. So there I was, walking from the train on track seven, talking to myself, practicing, "Una bara perpe—una birra pepe?" I couldn't get the damn "please" right! Upon finding a man selling beer from a cart in the station, I walked up to him and said, "Una bara, perpe—una birra, perpa—" He then said, "What do you want? A beer?" In perfect English. Thank God, I got her a beer!

So now walking back to track seven—after all, seven comes after six and before eight, right? —well, wrong, this was Italy. I walked to track seven and the train was gone. The train was gone! All I had to myself was a beer! Joan had the passports, the money, and I couldn't speak Italian. Remember, this was before cell phones. So, there I was, standing at the end of track seven, with no train, just this beer, now spilling over. Yes, the train was really gone! But it had been scheduled to leave in twenty minutes from now. *However, this is Italy*, I thought. *Maybe they just leave when the train is full?*

Meanwhile, as I was standing there for several minutes, panic began to set in, and I was ready to drink the damn beer myself to help try and calm my nerves. Just then, I heard Joan screaming in her stage voice, "Keee! Keee!" What a welcomed sound that was. She was hanging out the window of our compartment, waving her arms, most likely just as frantic as I was.

It came to pass that they moved the train out of the station to connect the cars with a different locomotive. That was not a fun experience.

It was a pleasant train ride down to Naples, but we almost missed getting off the train at the Napoli station due to the strange way they announced the upcoming stops. They do so with very little notice, and we had to scurry to get our bags to get off the train before it left.

We now ventured to catch a taxi to take us down to the boat harbor. We were cautioned about keeping the windows rolled up, since the possibility of someone reaching into the cab and pulling off your watch or necklace could be a concern. That was a difficult task, since it was raging above ninety degrees that day and the humidity was horrible, with no air-conditioning in the taxi—remember, this was 1960. Unfortunately, and sadly, on the way to the harbor the taxi driver ran over a dog. Joan and I freaked out as we looked out the back window seeing this little black dog tumbling over and over. We asked the driver to stop but he just waved us off in a rude unconcerned manner. That was a downer. Fortunately, we made it to the harbor without another incident.

We then got onto the two o'clock ferry for the short nineteen-mile ride over to the beautiful and romantically seductive Isle of Capri. Sitting outside and up forward to take in the calming effect of the crystal-clear, deep-blue waters of the Tyrrhenian Sea, it tempted us to be splashed upon by the spray of the boat as it surged through the swells, cooling us from the intense summer sun as it persisted in scorching our skin. What an exciting sight it would soon be to see the Marina Grande, the history-filled ancient harbor of Capri, looming just ahead of us. Joan had been looking forward to meeting her two cousins for the first time and see her aging grandmother, whom she had not seen since she was seven years old.

Upon arriving, we were greeted with signs that said Congratulations on Your Wedding, in both English and Italian; "Congratulazioni per il tuo matrimonio," all along the dock as if we were exalted celebrities.

We then got into an awaiting old horse and carriage that was decorated with streamers to take us up to Ana Capri (higher Capri), where Joan's uncle owned the Hotel St. Michele, a charming, exemplary Capreze hotel facing Naples, overlooking the harbor below.

We will never forget the ride up that steep, winding, narrow road with hundred-foot drops on one side, with the horse losing its footing and occasionally missing a step. It was quite an experience. However, we both felt sorry for the poor old horse.

We were met at the entrance of the hotel by at least a dozen of Joan's relatives, who hugged and kissed us. My gosh, I felt so overwhelmingly loved by these people I had never met. I couldn't understand a word they were saying, but it had to be nice since everyone was happy and smiling!

We were given the king's suite, an enormous room facing Naples with a huge deck. Upon unpacking, we noticed that my sisters, most likely Kay, had put lipstick all over the fly of my pajama pants—yes, all over. It looked like we had had a wild old time before we'd gotten there! Joan asked her cousin if housekeeping could do some washing for us. We noticed when the wash was returned the next day, there was a funny smirk on the little old Italian lady's face.

It seemed as if we were never left alone, being surrounded by family every moment. The Isle of Capri is the epitome of romanticism, and this was our honeymoon, and romance was in the air (it always was with me, no matter where we were), and we looked forward to some alone time. We must have found it, because Joan alleges our first daughter Laura was conceived while we were there!

Wherever we went, Joan's family owned businesses. From jewelry and gift stores to restaurants, hotels and nightclubs, we couldn't spend a dime. That was great, because I didn't have many dimes left.

On one of the days we were able to escape the family, we hiked up to Tiberius's Castle, situated at the highest and furthest point of the island. It was quite a trek, but worthwhile once there. Though now mostly in ruins, you could see some of the mosaic floors and walls of the rooms.

At dinner that night, Joan's cousin Norma, the daughter of the uncle who owned the St. Michele Hotel, asked me what my favorite Italian food was, and I told her raviolis. Well, I ended up having raviolis for lunch and raviolis for dinner for the next three days, but thankfully not for breakfast. They were delicious—but for three days in a row?

They were all wonderful and treated us as if we had known them all their lives. Joan was delighted that she was able to visit with her grandmother, her father's mother, once again; she was now ninety-seven, and Joan knew she would never see her again.

After three glorious days in Capri, we left in the early morning and flew from Naples to Milan for one afternoon and night. That night we went to the La Scala, *Teatro alla Scala*, built in 1778. We were both in wonderment that we were actually sitting in the La Scala Opera House. That night, however, it was not an opera, but a variety show. One act was a dog named "Louie." His owner was trying to teach him commands, such as "Come, Louie." Louie would lie down when called and do the complete opposite of any command he was given—it was hysterical!

The next day we took the train to Torino and rented a car and drove up to the small mountainous town of Trivera Lora to visit with Joan's mother's side of the family. Part of our drive was on the historic Saint Bernard Pass high in the Italian-Swiss Alps. The "Great Saint Bernardo," as it is referred to in Italian, is the most ancient pass through the Western Alps.

If you noticed, the name of the small town we were visiting is called Trivera Lora; "Lora" is the last name of Joan's stage name.

The homes in this quaint village town were old and modest, and the people, simple and sweet. I remember Joan's aunt asking what I wanted for breakfast every morning, and I would say, "Oh, just a couple of eggs, please." I had no idea they were so expensive, and that she had to walk a half mile every morning to get them just for me. I learned about this later and felt badly.

After spending two days with Joan's relatives in the remote, chilly, oxygen-starved mountain town of Trivera Lora, we drove back to Torino and flew to Paris.

That night we went to the famed Moulin Rouge for the dinner show, and what an extravaganza that was. The next day we went where all tourists go in Paris: the Eiffel Tower, of course. It was quite a spectacle looming into the Parisian sky.

We then went to the Notre Dame Cathedral, Cathédrale Notre-Dame de Paris, "Our Lady of Paris." Fortunately, we didn't see the ghost of Quasimodo perilously hanging from the bell towers, as some people have claimed to!

We later visited the Musee du Louvre and saw Leonardo da Vinci's famed Mona Lisa. To be there live and witness the Mona Lisa's notable emblematic smile was awesome.

That night, the last night of our honeymoon, we went to the *Folies Bergere*. Les Folies Bergère is one of the city's most renowned classic cabarets. As we were seated, scantily clad women soon took to the stage and blew kisses at the men in the orchestra playing their saxophones during the pre-show fanfare. We then settled in and ordered a bottle of the cheapest champagne on the wine list, much to the disdain of the tuxedo-clad waiter. I was on a wing and prayer with money by now, and still had a taxi ride to pay for when we got home.

The Paris re-working of Cabaret was every bit as humorous and tragic as hoped, and with the orchestra being a seeming extension of the set, the audience was made a part of the action and drama as well, allowing one to partake. It was a nice way to end our amazing honeymoon.

We arrived at LAX the next morning with Joan unknowingly pregnant, and after experiencing a rock-star-like honeymoon, I had just enough money for the taxi ride home to the Valley. The driver wasn't very pleased with his tip, I'm sure.

CHAPTER 14
HOME NOW

Upon arriving home from our magnificent three-week honeymoon, we had to stay with Joan's parents until we found a place to live. We didn't want to waste our money renting, so we looked around for a little house to buy. Joan had saved some money from her acting career and I still had my playboy T-Bird that I had planned to sell.

We found a darling little home in Sherman Oaks on Murietta Avenue selling for $11,500. It was about nine hundred square feet, if that big—perfect for a starter home. So, I said goodbye to my past and sold the 57 Thunderbird for $2,500, combined that with Joan's money, and we had enough for the down payment on the house.

I forgot to mention, just before we got married, we ate at the Hamburger Hamlet on Van Nuys Boulevard one Sunday afternoon, and later, while walking around, came upon a pet shop that had a sign in the window that said Free Puppy. The lady told us the puppy was a six-week-old Staffordshire terrier. "Oh, a little Terrier," we said. "How nice! Sure, we would love to have him." Well, he grew and grew and grew, and was now eighty pounds of solid muscle with a neck on him like a weight lifter—and he was only six months old! We later found out that he was a pit bull! Yes, Staffordshire terrier is the formal name. We had to leave him with Joan's parents while on our honeymoon, and he proceeded to tear up the house! Our first bill as a married couple was a repair bill on their house.

When we moved into our little house, the first thing I had to do was secure the backyard fence to keep our "Sullivan"—named after John L. Sullivan, the fighter—in the yard.

I was now back to work for my dad as foreman, or production manager, as it is more formally called. It was a breeze of a job for me, but I wasn't making much money. Joan was still acting, and doing very well, plus she was getting some sizable residuals from her many TV and film roles. Combined with that, we were getting along fine, but still living frugally.

It was about the middle to late July of 1960, a month after we were back from our honeymoon, when Joan got a casting call to audition for the roles of either Anita or Maria in *West Side Story*, scheduled to be shot in 1961. They were looking for a young attractive brunette who could sing and dance. She was perfect for the part, and they were seriously considering her for it. This was her big break and would have certainly made her a star!

A couple of weeks went by and one night during dinner, Joan said, "Honey, guess what? I'm pregnant!" Well, so much for *West Side Story*. She had to notify her agent, and the Samuel Goldwyn Studios on Santa Monica Boulevard in West Hollywood and tell them she was not available for either role. Natalie Wood, as you know, eventually got the part as Maria, and Rita Moreno as Anita. Too bad. Joan Lora would have been wonderful as Maria, or even as Anita.

Yes, I screwed up her career! *Well done, as usual, Kiki,* I thought.

Time went on, and I was still working for my dad in LA. Sullivan was now getting out of our backyard and attacking anything on four legs, and Joan was getting bigger by the day.

Well, a few weeks later while I was at work, my dad called a meeting and unexpectedly said the San Francisco main office had informed him they'd decided to sell the Los Angeles branch to another seafood and poultry wholesaler.

Well, this was really great; my wife was about to give birth to our first child and I might be out of a job. Thankfully, Joan had a medical plan through SAG, the Screen Actor's Guild, that would pay the hospital bill for Laura's birth. Thank you, Mr. Reagan for negotiating this benefit into the contract for the actors, as well as residuals.

My illusions were now starting to become rash reality. I'd never thought until now that my dad didn't have control of his own destiny—or mine.

A few months ago, we'd been bride and groom. Now we were bride and gloom. But we would make it somehow, someway, I hoped.

My mom and dad were going back to San Francisco, and there we were, living in Southern California in a newly purchased home, with a mortgage and a child on the way . . . with no savings, and soon, no job.

I thought further. This was insane! The Los Angeles area has an ever-increasing influx of population, and the company was lacking sales! I knew when I first started working there that all the salesmen were dead on their ass. They were old and had no gumption to further themselves or the company. God, I wished I was older, knew more, and had some money. I would start the damn business up myself. I'd call on all those restaurants we used to frequent; hell, I knew the chefs by now.

I then attempted something unattainable and downright silly. I was angered and had drive and determination and decided to give it a try—yes, to open a small wholesale fish business.

I heard that the husband of Mitzie, my dad's secretary, had a truck for sale. I figured I would try to buy it, thinking maybe he would let me pay for it in installments. I met with him, he agreed, and I was now anxious to start. However, after thinking it through, the realization soon set in: *Come on, I have no money to buy inventory or to rent a place, and not just any old place, one with refrigeration. This is ridiculous.* So, my brief moment of entrepreneurship fell apart, and I had to give it up.

I was only twenty-five and had been living from paycheck to paycheck; there was no extra cash for this. *For Christ sake, how could Paladini not attain sales in a marketplace with such an insurgence of population?* This blew my mind, even way back then, being so young. The thought of an opportunity missed, haunted me.

I was now overtaken with fright of working for strangers. Yes, I had a job with the new owners, but I was a Paladini now working for someone else?! What the eff?

The new owners soon came in and took over. It was a wholesale poultry company that wanted to combine wholesaling fish with poultry. The concept was okay. However, they didn't have any knowledge of the fish business, so they depended on me to teach them. Ha! Me? I didn't really know that much. I'd never been taught; my dad had just thrown me into it, and I'd had to learn it on my own. I knew I was being used, but needed a job.

I remained on as foreman but was aware that would be short lived, because they already had a foreman, an older man who had worked for them for many years. They didn't need two of us. My future was dim; it was evident I would soon be unemployed.

A few weeks later, on February 8, 1961, Laura was born at St. John's Hospital in Burbank. What a beautiful little blonde daughter Joan had just gifted me with. I was overwhelmed with this newfound love; love never realized, or could have ever known existed, the love of your child, a whole new dimension of love experienced.

We were now a family and it was wonderful; however, it put me in a dire situation with new responsibility. As you recall, I fooled around in school, didn't take it seriously, and had no formal career training. What a dope I had been, and now I was a father, and my wife had put blind, loving faith in me. Why hadn't I followed my desire to become a lawyer? I was just a goddamn fishmonger now—and soon, I wouldn't even be that! What could be worse than an unemployed fishmonger?

Things got even more challenging when five months later, Joan said she was pregnant again. Her acting career was officially on hold, at least for now, so she applied for temporary leave from the Screen Actors Guild.

Oh boy, now what? I knew it was imminent that I was to be laid off. It had been over seven months, and they were paying two of us for doing the same job, which was awkward, to say the least. Their foreman and I were conflicting, and the company didn't need the extra expense. I liked him, and I think he liked me; we got along great. He was older and had been with the company for years, so it was my duty to accept departure.

That day soon came, and it was the following week. They were very nice about it and explained that it had nothing to with my job performance; that it was the obvious duplication of positions. I knew it, and understood it.

I was now unemployed, scared, lost, and confused. I went on unemployment for a month while trying to decide what direction to take, but that was scarcely enough for food, let alone a house payment. As I sat around the house, I couldn't help feeling what a waste of time it was, sitting there doing nothing. That's not like me.

One evening over dinner, Joan and I talked about our situation, and I asked if it would be okay if we moved up north, so I could work for my dad again in San Francisco. She was amazingly understanding and promptly said yes, of course. I was lacking in education, worldly wisdom, and informed judgment, and had nowhere else to turn. After all, I'd thought all my life I would be working for my dad. But, with this move, Joan's acting career would most likely be over.

We drove up to the San Francisco Bay Area the next week and looked around for an inexpensive home. We wanted to live in a warm climate as we were accustomed to in Southern California, so we decided to seek out Marin County. We luckily found a new tract development in Terra Linda, just north of San Rafael, that was affordable. We found a home that suited our needs for $17,000 and signed the papers that day. Back then, you could purchase a home on contingency of selling your other home, so that worked out fine.

Upon returning to Sherman Oaks, we immediately put our house up for sale and it sold within a few weeks for $13,750. So, we'd made a small profit, and the timing to move into our new home up north worked out great.

We then set a date to move during mid-week, so we could get settled in at the new home for a few days before I started working for my dad on the following Monday. I rented a moving truck and loaded it myself. We planned to leave early in the morning, because it would take most of the day driving on Highway 101 to get to Terra Linda, an extra half hour or so north of San Francisco. Joan, with Gina in her belly and Laura in the front seat next to her (before car seats in the rear) would drive our car, and Joan's grandma and eighty-pound Sullivan would drive in the truck with me.

We left Sherman Oaks about eight in the morning. It was a misty, cold morning, and slow driving on the coast. The dew was more like light sprinkles, and quite chilly, so the windows of the truck had to be kept rolled up to keep the heat in.

Well, after an hour or so on the road, Mr. Sullivan developed gas—very bad gas! It was a constant conflict to either open the window for relief from the noxious smell and freeze, or breath in Mr. Sullivan's aroma and keep warm! I'll never forget, at one point during the trip, Grandma was swearing at me in Italian because I had rolled down the window to escape from gagging, and she was now freezing. So, even though the smell was almost unbearable, I rolled the window back up. Then she started swearing at me again because of the unfavorable essence of Mr. Sullivan, so I then rolled the window back down.

I spent over an hour with this perpetual scenario of rolling down the window, then rolling up the window, then up, then down. At one point, I was crying laughing so hard, I turned on the windshield wipers, thinking it was raining! Grandma had a mouth on her like a drunken sailor. It was funny, all this time she'd been swearing in Italian and I had no clue what the hell she was saying, but knew it wasn't very nice! I finally stopped the truck and took Mr. Sully for a walk to relieve himself. Then he and Grandma were both happy for the rest of the drive.

Arriving at our new home in Terra Linda late that afternoon, I unloaded just what we needed for that night, had a bite to eat, and promptly crashed. We soon got settled in and started adjusting to our new life in Northern California. We had little or no money, but I would be starting work on Monday.

CHAPTER 15
A SHOCKING REVELATION

I called my dad that weekend and said I was all moved in and ready to go to work on Monday. He replied, "Let me see what I can do." *What the hell does that mean?* I wondered. "Let me see what I can do" . . . "Let me see what I can do." Those words repeated in my head over and over.

I immediately sensed a problem, but nah, why would there be one? I was too chicken to tell Joan of my suspicions. She had given up her career and had left her mom and dad and friends to come up there for me.

So, I thought, *Maybe, he wants to put me into a management position, and was figuring it out, so not to worry. I sure as hell hope so. I have a wife, a baby, and another one on the way, a dog that consumes a massive amount of food, and a mortgage—and nothing in the bank.*

A week had passed, and he didn't call, so I called him again on Sunday morning. I said, "Hi, Dad, can I come to work now? I'm really short of money." He said, "Not yet, kid, I'm bringing you over some groceries." *What? Bringing over some groceries? I don't want my dad to bring us groceries. I want a job!*

Now I knew there was a problem, but why in the hell would there be a problem? My dad was the boss, or at least one of the bosses. He owned the damn business, or part of it.

Or so I thought...

My dad came over that Sunday afternoon with my mom and had several large bags of groceries for us. I thanked him and said that was very nice, but mentioned that I could buy my own groceries if I could just get to work.

He obviously avoided what I said and didn't respond. I didn't pursue it any further. I now realized something was up. The next day, I called my mom and asked her what was going on. She said, "Kiki, the family is giving your dad a very hard time about you going to work there. They don't want you there!"

Thinking back now—yeah, after fifty years—it just dawned on me that my dad was the youngest in his family and must have been emasculated by his elder siblings. It wasn't his fault, and I feel bad now for having put him in that position at the time.

I'll give you some background information about the company: I mentioned in the prologue that my grandfather started A. Paladini, Inc., Wholesale Fish Dealers, in 1865, and was eventually given the title of "The Fish King."

SAN FRANCISCO CALL

NEWSPAPER

SAN FRANCISCO,. TUESDAY, NOVEMBER 15, 1921

TCHY BONDS ARE SOLD

HOW I BEGAN LIFE

A. PALADINI *tells* PAULINE JACOBSON·

The Story of His Early Struggles

orn in Ancona, Italy, the Son of a Stage Driver, Has Had Life of Adventure.

By PAULINE JACOBSON

PALADINI, the fish king, is reckoned the second wealthiest Italian on the coast.

He began life as a soldier in Garibaldi's army.

He was born in Ancona, Italy, the son of a stage driver. Being under age, fired by the war of independence, he ran away from home to join Garibaldi's army. He fought in several battles. At the end of the war he received his honorable discharge.

He returned home. He loved horses. But his father's calling and his home town failed to lure him after his experiences in the war. Grown restive in several months, he decided to follow the more adventuresome calling of the sea.

For five or six years he followed the sea as common sailor on ships plying in and about the Italian coast. Then one day he met with an engagement on a ship sailing for America around Cape Horn.

The ship in its journey anchored in the port of San Francisco.

Paladini came ashore with ten dollars in his pockets, all the wealth he possessed. His sole ambition in landing was none other than selling fishing after the long monotonous stretch of sea and sky

A. PALADINI, once a private in Garibaldi's army.

Second Wealthiest Italian California Was Once a S dier in Garibaldi's Army

length of the pocket, very wide almost to the knee.

He withdrew his hand and tied back once more into silen chewing the end of his unlit cig:

Paladini is 83 years old. He had a stroke. His sons sent him the country to recuperate. He mained three days. The fish m ket was his life. To remove from it was to kill him outrigh

He sits, clad in working clo: of rough serge, flannel shirt, an black felt hat, on a little side be at the wide open gateway of market, facing Clay street, a n row street, yet teeming with ac ity.

He leans, resting his hands the head of the cane between knees. He silently chews the of an unlit cigar. He speaks o when some one in the traffic t flows about him halts to speak him.

When the street is stilled of tra fic and the market of customers young Italian takes a packing b turns it upside down and seats hi self upon it at Paladini's feet. W the look of a devoted son and w all the animation he can muster given the scene for the old m reads to him news from t daily paper.

When yet another Italian, packing box at the long end, see

As the story goes, within a few short years, he had a flourishing business. His horse-drawn wagons (the only means of delivery then) were everywhere in the city, supplying fresh fish to all the major hotels and restaurants.

He also had eight fifty-to-seventy-five-foot fishing trawlers and named each of them after his seven children, plus one called the *Buena Ventura* [Good Fortune].

IL NUOVO MERCATO DEL PESCE DI A. PALADINI

Questa illustrazione rappresenta il grandioso mercato del pesce di A. Paladini, uno dei pionieri italiani che più hanno fatto per il commercio della città.. Egli è un veterano dell'industria e del commercio del pesce, con cui aveva accumulato, prima della catastrofe, una vera fortuna che si fece a salire a più di mezzo milione di dollari. . Nel disastro il Paladini ha subito delle perdite accertate per 250 mila dollari, a causa della distruzione per opera del fuoco delle sue numerose case le quali non erano affatto assicurate.

All'epoca del disastro il Paladini, su uno dei suoi vaporini adibiti alla pesca, fuggì a Sausalito dove rimase inerte per alcune settimane. Poi volle subito rimettersi al lavoro ed improvvisò un mercato provvisorio nello stesso molo di Greenwich Street, dove fanno scalo i suoi vapori. Vi rimase sette mesi finchè il giorno 11 Febbraio ritornò al vecchio posto dove costruì un magnifico mercato di cui diamo qui sopra l'illustrazione e che trovasi ai numeri 520-522 Merchant St. Quivi il Paladini fa nuovamente ottimi affari tanto nel commercio all'ingrosso quanto in quello al minuto. Punto scoraggiato dalle perdite subite, si è rimesso al lavoro colla stessa energia e buona volontà di trent'anni or sono ed è certo che ben presto potrà ricuperare quanto ha perduto.

He built his first wholesale fish plant on Front Street, operating from that location until the business increased to such a point that he then built a much larger plant at 542 Clay Street, between Montgomery and Sansome Streets, that consumed almost half of the entire block. He, of course, always paid cash for any real estate he bought. Remember the "deep pockets" phrase he coined!

The Clay Street location is the parcel that was eventually sold for the construction of the iconic Transamerica building. I have a picture of my grandfather sitting in a 1917 fish truck, directly in front of the old Clay Street plant, where the front entrance to the pyramid building exists today.

During my reign in the fish business, I was fortunate to find a similar 1920s GMC truck, and had it restored to replicate that exact same truck, including the old gold font on it displaying the name "A. Paladini Fish Dealer" exactly as it was back then.

After I sold my wholesale seafood business, I donated it to the San Francisco Maritime National Historical Park on Fisherman's Wharf, where it is now displayed on the old ferry boat, *Eureka*.

In the San Francisco Maritime Museum, directly across the street, there is a full one-story mock-up of his first wholesale fish plant on Sansome Street. Several old relics displayed, like a 1900s fish box, were items I was able to accumulate that were also donated.

To be included in both Maritime Museums, is indeed an honor, and a tribute to the history of the pioneers of California.

Achille then built a three-story cold storage facility on Sansome and Broadway streets, then a smokehouse on Gold Street, currently the Bix Restaurant. He then constructed a huge processing facility up north in Fort Bragg that employed over a hundred workers canning Dungeness crabmeat and California Shrimp meat and had a fillet line with forty girls filleting the local catch. Then, in time, he opened a similar-sized processing facility in Eureka, and eventually branched out with over a dozen receiving stations up and down the California coast, even venturing into Oregon. He also had an abalone processing plant in Monterey and a lobster receiving plant in Mexico. He then opened wholesale seafood distribution plants in Oakland and Los Angeles, encompassing all of California.

By the early 1900s, he was the largest wholesaler and producer of seafood in the entire country, thus from which came the title "The Fish King." He was, however, known to be an unscrupulous businessman. There are stories of him creating a monopoly, putting his competition out of business by selling at cost until his competitors went broke. He was charged with several so-called illegal business practices by the US Government, only to eventually prevail with the ruling in his favor. He is written up in many books about the history of California, one in particular, titled, *The Pioneers of California*.

He accumulated astounding wealth and amassed seventeen commercial real estate holdings in San Francisco. Such famous properties as Bimbo's 365 Club, Di Maggio's Restaurant on Fisherman's Wharf, the famous Tadich Grill (then) directly across from the plant on Clay street, the Le Bouf Restaurant plus the hotel above, the Black Cat Bar on Montgomery Street and, of course, as previously mentioned, the Transamerica property, plus many others. He then owned Paladini Real Estate Company that managed and held the properties.

On the morning of April 18, 1906, when the massive earthquake shook San Francisco, its immediate impact was disastrous. The earthquake ignited several fires around the city that burned for three days and destroyed nearly five hundred city blocks. Despite his vast real estate holdings, Achille was only worried about his horses, not the business, nor the properties. Upon recovering from the realization of what had just occurred, he immediately rushed to the stables to check on his horses, and fortunately found they were fine. He was obviously an animal lover. I'm sure that's where my father and I got it from, and now my daughters!

He had just built a huge mansion on Nob Hill, and was scheduled to move in within a few weeks, but he now found his new home in ruins. Unconcerned with lavishness, he never did rebuild.

My grandfather being a wise businessman, had a saying that he taught my father, who then taught me. It was: "The eye of the boss fattens the horse." When my dad told me, I said to him, "It doesn't even rhyme, Dad." He then said, "Don't worry that it doesn't rhyme, kid. Just never forget it!" Fortunately, I never did forget it, and followed the significance of it throughout my entire business career. A wise fact that all business owners should be cognizant of.

Turns out, that statement was a true aphorism. It meant: If you watch your business yourself, and don't let others, you will succeed. Literally, the "eye of the boss" meant "watch your business with your own eyes." "Fattens the horse" meant for him, he would then have the money to feed his horses. The horses were the only means of delivering the fish at the time.

Achille passed away in 1921. A. Paladini, Inc., and all the real estate holdings went equally to his seven children, which included four boys and three girls. Leaving the estate in equal shares was fine, but allowing the daughters to have equal say with the business turned out to be a mistake, in my opinion. The girls knew nothing about operating the fish business. Why would they? After all, it was a man's business at the time. More importantly, none of the second generation seemed ambitious enough to seek out new business, or to stay abreast of the changes in the industry, such as striving to increase the sales of the frozen fish and shellfish that was now coming on the market in the 1940s and '50s. Their concept was to only sell fresh fish, and only from their own boats.

During my grandfather's realm (1865 to 1921) the procurement of fresh fish was basically self-produced, which is why he had his own trawlers, and that concept was fine at the time. However, after his passing, new challenges were never addressed, and possibly never even noticed. The second generation was surviving off the past, and not looking into the future.

Well, they started losing money, and eventually began selling off the incredibly valuable real estate to keep the business solvent so they could continue to draw income from it.

My concept of business is: Take the excess profits from your business and buy income-producing real estate. You don't sell valuable real estate and put that money into a losing business to fund it without an optimistic future. You're better off shutting it down and stop the losses.

To make a very long story short, they obviously did not have the proficiency that their father Achille had. Though the company was once the largest on the West Coast, other companies were forming and were aggressively taking business from them. They were running the business with their heads in the sand, and did not, or could not, see the declining sales. They furthermore did not attempt to reduce expenses that they did not, or could not, see.

The fleet of trawlers were costing them a fortune to operate with the ceaseless, ever-recurring repairs, and those costs were most likely never factored in. The rents and managers for all the receiving stations along the entire California coast were another added expense associated with operating the trawlers, and most likely overlooked. One example was Pier Three in San Francisco; it cost thousands of dollars each month in rent and upkeep. Keep in mind, that during inclement weather and the off-seasons, the rents and the managers salaries continue.

The business existed for 109 years, fifty-six years under the supervision of Achille, and fifty-three years by his children. Sounds impressive, but the business should still be in existence, allowing it to be passed down to the third generation, and possibly even the fourth.

There were five sons in the third generation, my three cousins, one of whom became a priest, possibly the smartest one, avoiding all this bedlam, then my brother and me. We were the only two who carried the Paladini name since we were sons of a son; the other three were sons of daughters.

I was the youngest, "the runt," the last born, the mistake, by several years and was named Achille after my grandfather. That possibly may have caused the malignity that I felt from some members of the family. But it's only a name. I guess my brother wasn't a threat, with his passive personality. He had worked for the company all his adult life and appeared to be satisfied remaining in menial, routine positions.

Now that you know the background, let's return to the then-present time.

Working for them was not an option now. It was more than obvious I wasn't wanted. I was in turmoil and didn't know which way to turn. The thought of providing for my young family haunted me. I had now disposed of the intention of working for and with my dad. I still hadn't totally comprehended it though.

After thinking the situation through, it didn't take long to have the revelation that my dad was just one of seven owners. Why hadn't I picked up on that? I should have, but I was brought up in a life of lavishness and notoriety, and to be honest, my head was up my butt. I should have understood the corporate structure, but didn't, maybe I was too young, or more likely, didn't want to. It was my fault, no one else's.

This shocking revelation finally set in, and I was now bewildered. I had lived a youth of make-believe and self-delusions failing to recognize reality, and was now was experiencing an adulthood of very harsh reality.

I had no job, no future, and no plans. Oh, and no money. Ha! I'd said when I was born, I was omnipotent. And all I was now was useless and lacking any virtuous employment qualities. I was the court jester again, like I'd been in high school.

I now had to find a job—and fast—and obviously with another company. What, work for strangers? And for the rest of my life? Doing what?

My sister Waltina, "Tina," upon hearing that the family wouldn't hire me, was infuriated. I don't know how she knew, possibly my mom told her. She drove down the peninsula that same week and confronted our Aunt Henrietta. Henrietta was the oldest of my dad's family and the big cheese. Tina, as I was told, screamed at Henrietta, asking her what was wrong with her family not wanting her brother to work for the firm. She then asked her to talk with them. She said she would. However, nothing changed.

By the way, my sister Tina's husband Warren—"Red," as he was called—was the head of the Juvenile Probation Department for the City and County of San Francisco. He got me off from my many infractions that I was allegedly accused of as a minor. Little stuff, though, like breaking into the Palace of Fine Arts and driving my dad's car without a license. Yeah, little stuff. And notice I used the term "allegedly."

My sister Audrey and her husband Don coincidentally lived a few short blocks away from us in Terra Linda and also heard of my dilemma. Feeling sorry for us, they had us over for dinner. Audrey asked what I was going to do. I had no answer!

The next morning, she called and told me she might have gotten me a job working for friends of hers, the Zalezzi brothers, who owned O'Brien, Spotorno, and Mitchell. They were poultry wholesalers in San Francisco who had just started expanding into other lines, including frozen seafood. I was very touched that my sisters went to bat for me.

It was very nice of her, but I was concerned, not knowing what I would be doing. I had no job skills to speak of, and even worse, no self-confidence. I also feared stuttering; I stutter when things aren't right, or when distressed.

The next morning, with a mindset of apprehension and pessimism, plus a stomach with dyspepsia, I went to meet the Zalezzi brothers, Steve and Walter, at their office in San Francisco, a few blocks from the Embarcadero. Their building was new and clean, something I didn't expect. They were ever-so-nice, and surprisingly respectful—what a different response than the one from my own family. The plant was immaculate, and several food inspectors were constantly monitoring the hygiene of the poultry operation.

They sat me down and said they could use a salesman in the East Bay. I then quickly thought to myself, *Hmm, okay, a salesman. I know nothing about selling and often stutter. Plus, I don't know anything about the East Bay. Don't know anything about poultry. Don't even really know that much about seafood.* But hell, I took the job! I would be making a hundred bucks a week. This was in 1962. It was Thursday, and they said to come in on Saturday morning around ten; they would be having a casual sales meeting, and I could meet the other salesmen. Then I would start on Monday.

Saturday came, and for some reason I took Laura with me. They'd said it was casual, so I felt it was okay. She was about a year old, and just beginning to walk. I was waiting for the meeting to start and was nervously walking around on the loading dock while Laura hobbled around. She was about to get near the end of the dock, so I said, "Laura, come here, honey." She then ran and jumped up into my arms and put her arms around my neck and squeezed me with all her might.

She then said in her little baby voice, "I love you, Daddy!" To this day, I can feel her squeezing me, saying, "I love you, Daddy!"

I was overwhelmed with love for her, and from her. At that very moment, I closed my eyes and held her in my arms with all the love a father can exude, and said, "I love you, too, honey." Then, as my eyes teared up I mumbled to myself, "I *will* make it. I *will* make it. For you, for my wife, for all my children. Somehow, I *will* make it!" I must have *perseverance*.

I was angered that I had lived up to this moment thinking I was someone that I wasn't, that my dad was someone that he wasn't. I had wasted my youth with this illusion, and it was no one's fault other than my own. I now had a family depending on me. I now had to start life all over.

Monday came, and I was given a company car to drive; a real plus already. So I was a salesman for the East Bay. I asked one of the salesman how to get to the East Bay. He looked at me strangely and chuckled and gave me the directions to the Bay Bridge. I had never heard the Oakland area called the East Bay before.

Not having any clue where in the hell I was going, or who I was going to be calling on—or what I was even going to try to sell, or say—I ventured across the bridge not knowing what was in store for me. Suddenly I thought, *What if I stutter when I attempt to introduce myself to a buyer? Oh, shit!* I always had that fear, but now had to overcome it. A salesperson must talk! Talk? My heart raced.

There I was, driving on the bridge, and I saw in the far distance a large white building jutting out from the hillside. I then remembered that my dad had thrown a party there once a long time ago. Well, after stumbling around for an hour trying to find it (before GPS), I'd come upon the acclaimed Claremont Hotel.

My God, this place is huge, but hey, that's what you want. Start at the top, not with the little mom-and-pop places. Go for the big ones! Hmm, but c'mon, on the very first call?

I then bravely walked in the delivery entrance without further thought to meet my first chef; not only the chef, but the big executive chef. *Why in the hell did I come in here?* I now thought. *Maybe I should have started with that little diner I just saw down the street.*

As I walked in the kitchen, I was overwhelmed with how big it was. My God, it was massive! I stopped and thought for a moment, *I don't even know the prices of the poultry, or even the seafood, yet, and wait— how do you even start a conversation with a buyer, a chef?*

I knew the head chef wore the tallest hat, so I looked around and found this large, burly, imposing man, wearing a hat that looked like the Leaning Tower of Pisa; it was certainly the tallest one. His back was to me as he was talking to one of the sous chefs. As he turned around, I walked up to him and said, "Hi, chef, I'm Kiki Paladini." I hadn't yet gotten the chance to say what company I was with when he then replied, "Oh, hi, so you're a Paladini, huh? I just called in an order, so why are you here? I never see anyone from the company?" "Oh, shit. He's buying from Paladini," I murmured to myself. I then nervously said, "W-w-w-well, chef, I'm not with Paladini. I'm with O'Brien, Spotorno, and Mitchell." He looked at me and said, "Oh, well, then you're not *that* Paladini." I dismissed his comment and said, "I was selling poultry." He then asked, "Is that all the company sells?" I then honestly said, "Well, they now also carry a frozen seafood line."

Now becoming suspicious, he commented, "So what do you know about seafood?" Not wanting to lie, I then declared that I was indeed part of *that* Paladini he'd referred to. His eyes then opened wide and his face got flushed and he was obviously instantly angered. He then screamed at me, "So you want to sell me seafood? You're selling against your own family? What kind of fucking kid are you? You're a disgrace to the name! Get out! Get the hell out of here!" I tried to interrupt him and say that I'd just wanted to quote him some poultry prices, but he didn't give me the chance. He threw me out!

Oh, Christ, I thought, *is this what I'm going to be up against? I'm done for before I start. Maybe I just can't mention seafood to the chefs, but that's what I was mainly hired for! It's also what I know the best, and they want me to promote the new seafood line.*

I instantly turned around with my head down as tears streamed down my cheeks. I was also shaking in fear as I walked out. I got into the car and put my head back onto the seat and stared straight ahead with blinding thoughts of what was to come. I was petrified, and to say I was panic-stricken would be an understatement. *No one's going to buy from me. I didn't even get the chance to tell him I would be happy to sell him just poultry. I think they screwed up by hiring me, and my sister will have egg on her face. How long will I last if I don't get any orders? What the hell am I going to do?*

I sat there in the car for the longest time, my eyes now closed, pondering how I was going to handle the adversity with which I would most likely be confronted with upon meeting the buyers.

As my cheeks dried from the tears, I suddenly got the shakes. That was never a good sign. I was now angered beyond reason, and screamed out loud, "Fuck this! This is *bullshit!*"

I got out of the car and stormed back into the kitchen and found the chef, his back again to me, but this time I tapped him on the shoulder, and as he turned around, I screamed at him, "Okay, you want the fucking truth, chef?! I came up here from Los Angeles just to work for my father and my father's family. I have a one-year-old baby and my wife is pregnant, and the fucking

Paladini piece-of-shit family wouldn't hire me just because I *am indeed* Achille Paladini, and the ignorant bastards don't want me there because I carry my grandfather's name, supposedly because it would demean some of the family. Who in the hell knows? Now you know the truth, so just keep on giving them the fucking business. I don't give a shit! Anyway, I was going to try to just sell you some goddamn turkeys!"

I then turned around, and had started walking out, when I heard, "Kiki, Kiki, is that what they call you? Come back." I said, "For what?" The chef then said, "You want some coffee? Some breakfast?"

He sat me down in his office and ordered a pot of coffee. We talked about what had transpired and I told him the whole story—the truth—after all, it was the truth.

I walked out with the largest frozen seafood order O'Brien, Spotorno, and Mitchell had ever gotten. He also insisted we carry some fresh fish, and that very same day was when the company added fresh fish to their line, in which I was now also that buyer. I had the account for the duration I was with the company and—oh yes—the chef of the Claremont Hotel threw out Paladini! That was the start of my becoming their nemesis.

It came to pass that the Claremont Hotel was then the largest volume hotel account in the entire East Bay at the time.

I got thrown out of kitchens repeatedly, many times, but not in quite so dramatic fashion. I eventually learned how to deal with it in a more intellectually and psychologically beneficial manor.

I now had such vengeance for my family's company that it had grown into a vendetta. I couldn't help it. I had once been its greatest supporter.

I then followed the Paladini trucks around every day and waited for the driver to make the delivery, and on the way out, watch them drop the carbon copy of the invoice onto the floor or throw it into the trash. I would get the carbon copy and hold it up against the light, and could read everything the account had just bought, and the prices they'd paid. I would then innocently act as though I knew nothing, and walked into the account with a price list, knowing exactly what they'd bought, and undercut all their prices— I then promptly walked out with an order, and in most cases, totally took the account away from them.

I doubt if the Paladini Company even realized the business they were losing. They were too busy picking up paper clips from the floor, thinking they were saving money. (More about that later.)

Within just four months, I was the buyer and manager of the ever-expanding seafood department of O'Brien, Spotorno, and Mitchell. Things were looking up, and I got a twenty-dollar-a-week raise! I started feeling just a tiny bit good about myself, and was, for the first time, an individual not sucking off the damn name. I was now just Kiki.

However, still, deep down, my stomach churned, knowing I was selling against my dad—not the company—my dad.

I knew I was hurting them—and badly. My sales alone were well over $100,000 a month (this was in 1962). It was also now my function to direct the other sales people and teach them the seafood industry and how to sell it, which further deteriorated Paladini's client base. By the way, I never did stutter!

Gina was born about this time at St. Luke's Hospital in San Francisco, and I was gifted with a beautiful brown-eyed and brown-haired little image of Joan. She came out screaming and hasn't stopped since; another extension of love never realized or thought possible. I now had two beautiful little girls.

A few months later, I got a call one morning while at work from the owner of the second largest seafood wholesaler in California after Paladini, located on Fisherman's Wharf. He asked if I would meet him at Ott's Drive-In on Columbus and Broadway for lunch. I asked what it was about, and he said, "Let's just have lunch and we can talk."

Upon meeting with him, he asked if I would come to work for him as a salesman, possibly as sales manager. I asked him how many sales people he had, and he told me three. I then jokingly said, "Well, that's not much to manage." My comment most likely gave him the impression that it would be an easy task, though it had been unintended, but that was okay. In some ways, the job he was offering was a step down from what I'd currently been doing as a buyer and manager plus handling some sales accounts.

On the way back to my office, I suddenly thought this would mean I'd *really* be in the fish business, and not just working for a poultry company that was also selling seafood as a side line. This would be comparable to working at Paladini—and I could really hurt them. I would also be making double the money! That was quite an incentive with a new baby in the house.

After thinking it over for a few weeks, I gave notice. The Zolezzi brothers said it hadn't come as a surprise because they knew I was out of my element, and they respected that. They were both very nice, and I felt bad leaving them, but had to forge forward with my vendetta.

Two weeks later, I showed up for work on Fisherman's Wharf, my second job in Northern California. I found the environment to be very different, specifically the hygiene of the plant, and missed my nice office at the poultry company; however, this was the wholesale fish business. I had also forgotten about the reeking odor of the fresh—and the not-so-fresh—fish.

I immediately felt discomfort with the surroundings, especially the profanity and the ignorance of the employees, few shaved and their clothing ragged. It was also cold and damp all the time. *Jeez,* I thought for a moment. *What made me want to be here?* Maybe I'd had a clouded view of the industry, but I was here now and had to make the best of it. I needed now to focus, fixate, and intensify my vengeance strategy.

But then for another fleeing moment, I suddenly couldn't help imagining how different it would have been if I had truly become the lawyer I'd aspired to be. I'd most likely be dressed in a suit every day, and would be working in a nice, warm, plush office downtown in the Financial District and would eat at the ritzy Commercial Club or University Club every day with my fellow constituents. Well, that was gone now. *Just put on your fish smock and suck it up.*

The owner of the company assigned me the Peninsula, since they were weak in that area and wanted to build it up. Well, Paladini had a predominant presence on the Peninsula with the many restaurants and hotels, so this could end up being fun.

We lived in Marin County, and the Peninsula was the opposite end of the bay; it would be a long drive each day. But you must do what you must do.

As they say, "If your ship doesn't come in, you have to row out to it!"

CHAPTER 16
THINGS ARE LOOKING UP——A BIT

One of my uncles was the salesman on the Peninsula for Paladini. I soon discovered he preferred to call on just the small, insignificant mom-and-pop markets, leaving the larger restaurants and hotels without contact, which required them to call in their orders. Not wise! First of all, I didn't understand why an owner of a company would be a salesman, but more importantly, if a salesman, why he was calling on such small accounts and not handling the major hotel chains.

It was like taking candy from a baby, even easier—babies cry to make their point heard. I don't think Paladini was even the slightest bit aware that I was taking the large hotels from them in leaps and bounds on the Peninsula; the reason being, because Paladini allowed the large restaurants and hotels to call in their orders; no one had control or knew any better as to whether they were buying or not. (I will highlight that point later.) However, I do understand that occasionally—but only occasionally—you have no control if it is their policy. If so, then a trace system must be put in place to monitor what they are buying, and *are*, in fact, buying. Accounts should be called by an assigned salesperson on the day/days they need or want to place an order, regardless of the industry. This is a documented fact—by me.

I continued to run into chefs and buyers who questioned the fact that I was selling against my own family, having to hear the same old rhetoric over and over. I'd now mostly overcome it though, and had a well-rehearsed explanation, or better pricing, to shake them loose.

All the major hotel chains and major restaurants on the Peninsula were now buying from me. My sales soared to over $200,000 a month, and my paycheck doubled again, along with looking forward to receiving a nice bonus at the end of the year. I'm not bragging, just stating the facts.

Meanwhile, I was now officially the black sheep of the family; but hey, a black sheep within a flock of white stands out—*never be commonplace!*

It was funny that I knew all the delivery entrances to the nice restaurants, but never entered the front door. I was still eating nineteen-cent burgers at McDonald's trying to allow my family the best life possible. Often, while being in the kitchen talking with a chef, they would be cooking prime rib, and the mouth-watering aroma would drive me nuts. But that was okay, my little burgers were just fine.

Though things were looking up, money was still tight, but occasionally on Sundays we would be extravagant and take a ride to the city and treat the girls to a twenty-five-cent ice cream cone at the Thrifty Drug Store in the Marina, then go visit my parents.

On one of those Sundays, while crossing the Golden Gate Bridge I only had two dollars on me. I needed a buck for the three kids and Joan's ice cream cones—I opted out—and a buck to cross the bridge. I was driving the company El Camino that only had a front seat—enough room for four, and Gina, though cramped, was standing behind me. As I approached the toll booth, Gina asked if she could pay, so I gave her the dollar bill, and as she handed it to the toll taker, the wind blew it away! I then screamed at her, furious, because now we had no money for the ice cream cones. Was I really upset with *her?* No, of course not. I was upset with myself since I couldn't give my girls that little treat. I later apologized to her, feeling bad that I'd hollered at her so vehemently. She hasn't let me forget it to this day, and says I scarred her for life! Jokingly—I hope.

By the end of the first year, I was sales manager, and soon after, I added a few more people to the staff so that I was now directing six salesmen. I was feeling pretty good about it, but that damn ache in my heart was still there. I was brought up a Paladini, and constantly questioned myself as to what I was doing by attempting to destroy them. Every time I took a major account from them, though thrilled, I questioned myself and my stomach churned.

I must, however, mention that my dad was my biggest supporter. He cheered me on constantly. If my dad had expressed opposition to what I was doing, I would have immediately exited from the industry all together and done something else.

During this time of upheaval and drama, I stopped in every afternoon on the way home and checked in on my mom and dad. Knowing they were okay allowed me to stay brave and continue on my course; however, smelling the odor of fish on my dad's clothes was a constant reminder that we shared the same industry, but were in opposition. That was gut wrenching.

It was now August 13, 1964, and Joan had just given birth to our third daughter, Diana, at Marin General Hospital. She had the face of an angel, and like Gina, brown hair and those big brown eyes. What a joy to have three daughters; we were now a family of five. It was also Joan's birthday the very next day, the 14th. What a joyous birthday we celebrated.

With our newly expanded family, it was time to look for a larger home. Thankfully, I was now making enough money that we could afford to move from Terra Linda to San Rafael Park, about two miles further north, into a much larger and nicer home.

Things were going great, though I was constantly living with that subliminal heartache. It was bittersweet; sweet that I was doing well, yet bitter that I was almost singlehandedly destroying the family business. However, I wasn't really sure whether it was because I was *that* good, or they were just *that* bad.

Summer had now passed, and it was the beginning of autumn. And guess what? I got a call at home one evening from Lionel Shatz, the controller of A. Paladini, Inc. saying he wanted to meet with me. *Oh, really...* Lionel ran the complex intricacies of the business and did all the buying from the warm main office upstairs on the second floor, dressed in a suit, while my dad, an owner and vice president, now dolefully performed latent, laborious tasks out on the cold, wet production floor, wearing rubber boots, alongside the other menial workers. What the hell was he being punished for, I wondered? He once managed the Oakland plant, then the Los Angeles plant, before they shut them both down.

I could never comprehend why a stranger was upstairs in the main office and was trusted to do the crucial buying, and was never questioned, plus also conducted the entire overall running of the business. Mr. Shatz's title was "controller," and that position had to do with financial matters. That was all, at least as far as I was concerned. There were four brothers running the business, supposedly. Why didn't one of them do the buying, and why didn't they as a team run the business? Who am I to say. I was just a punk kid.

The position of controller is the designation held by the person most administratively in charge of daily accounting operations and all accounting transactions and financial reporting. It has nothing to do with buying or general management.

Anyway, so Lionel wanted to meet with me. Why would he have humbled himself to do so? Ha, well, I knew. I was putting them out of business. If not that severe, I was sure as hell hurting them, and badly. So, I'd had to almost decimate the company before I was recognized? *I'm still just Walter's youngest son; the youngest of the entire Paladini family. I'm just Kiki, or more formally, Achille Paladini. Oh hey, wait, wasn't that my grandfather's name?* They didn't give a shit about any of that. It was because my sales were now fringing on $300,000 a month—that's $3.6 million a year!

By maintaining a few of the original major accounts in the East Bay, and while almost certainly annihilating them on the Peninsula, that figure was easily achieved. I had almost every major account from South San Francisco to—and including—San Jose.

Paladini, at one time, sent five trucks a day down to the Peninsula, and was now down to one, with just two trucks on Fridays, and of course, loaded with only fresh fish.

Well, reluctantly—and possibly stupidly—I weakened and met with Lionel, and of course he wanted me to work for them. I'd had to damn near put them out of business before they humbled themselves to even recognize that I existed.

To this day, I don't know why I weakened and went to work for them—yes, I went to work for them. I guess I'd always wanted to, deep down. Maybe blood *is* thicker than water. But so far, I'd been treated better by water, than blood.

So, I gave notice. The owner commented that he'd known this day would eventually come, and that he enjoyed our relationship. He also mentioned that I'd made him a lot of money and said, "If you find it's not working out, call me." Then commented, "You know there's going to be a battle between us now, of course."

Well, that first day soon came. I was finally going to work at Paladini at the main office at 542 Clay Street, and I didn't know what to expect.

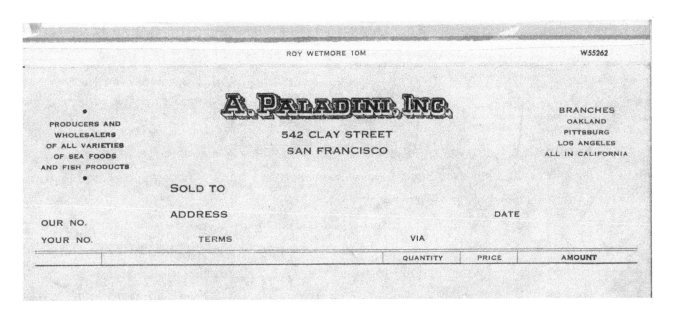

I was nervous, anxious, and pessimistic about what I was set to embark upon. I was used to the stench of fish by then, so it should have been an easy transition, but I didn't know the reception I was going to receive from my uncles and cousins.

I arrived at six thirty in the morning, and promptly proceeded upstairs to the small, shabby, ten-by-ten-foot cubbyhole they called a "sales office," which was barely large enough to fit the three dilapidated wooden desks paired with unmatched chairs. The floors creaked as you walked and were warped due to the moisture permeating in from the production floor below. Surprisingly, they had working phones—yeah, hey, working phones. They were the old black rotary phones, however. Everything was antiquated.

I will never forget how that morning started out for as long as I live.

I wasn't there any more than a few minutes, getting ready to "do battle," as my prior employer had said. I was about to call my multitudinous customers on the Peninsula extra early to beat whoever it was my former employer had assigned to call them. Just then, my two cousins suddenly barged in and abruptly said, "Hey, Kiki, let's go!" I said, "Go? Go where?" They both simultaneously said, "We have to go and unload the Catherine." (One of the company owned trawlers.) I said, "*What?!* You have to be kidding! I have all my customers to call!" In bold, demanding voices, they responded, "Forget it. Let's go!" This was like an order—no, not *like* an order—it *was* an order. I was stymied and confused, now wondering whether they were my bosses.

That action in itself showed their primordial, embryonic intelligence. My prior employer was going to have someone, if not several, salesmen on the phone early that morning giving my accounts some bullshit story as to why I wasn't there, and they would get all the orders.

More importantly, Mr. Shatz wouldn't see any orders coming in. *Hmm, wait. Maybe that's just what they want—so I won't look good. They're trying to set me up for failure!* They obviously didn't give a shit about the company surviving, either.

Well, they both dauntlessly continued to insist that I go. For a moment—but for just a moment—I thought maybe they were being nice by wanting to teach me something, but soon realized their intention was to sabotage me. It was evident by their demeanor.

For whatever reason, I went with them. I possibly didn't want to make waves on the first day, but knew I would sure as hell get back to the plant as soon as I could. Come to think of it, they never welcomed me, or even said good morning. This had obviously been planned.

I then thought, *I'm dressed in sport coat and slacks, wearing dress loafers, looking as a sales person should, and they want me to go and unload a fucking fishing boat on a wet dock and shovel ice?! I don't know how to unload a fucking boat, and I don't care to learn. Anyway, this is what the menial, servile hired help does, for Christ sake.*

We then all crammed into the front seat of an old faded-red flatbed fish truck, with torn seats that had springs piercing through that hit you in the ass as you sat down; the sun visors hung precariously and blocked most of the view of the road in front. There were open holes in the floor board, and you could see the pavement passing below as we drove to the pier. The gear shift made an annoying grinding sound when changing gears, as the floorboard stick shift loosely vibrated around and the motor deafened what little conversation was going on. The exhaust had you scrambling for fresh air and the attempt to open a window was futile since the handles were missing. It also wreaked of sour, decaying fish from the old carcasses that were embedded within the cracks of the deteriorating wooden truck bed just behind. As we proceeded the few blocks down to Pier Three next to the Ferry Building, we drove through parts of the Financial District, and with envy, couldn't help but notice the men in suits and ties walking to their most assured befitting offices.

Upon arriving at the pier, it was cold—no, it was damn freezing. It was only a quarter to seven in the morning. The wood floor of the dock was wet and slippery from the morning dew, and my thin-soled dress shoes soaked up the dampness, annoying me even more. As they nonchalantly talked to the skipper of the Catherine, taking their time getting ready to unload the boat, I noticed it was now just before seven, and I should have made over a dozen calls by now. The skipper, I guess surprised to see a guy nicely dressed, looked up from the cab and said to me, "Who are you?" I said, "Achille Paladini." I thought that would rub my cousins raw. The skipper then said, "Really? I didn't know about you. Whose son are you?" *Of course, he's never heard about me!*

After being there about a half hour, not having done a damn thing other than watch my cousins operate the winch unloading a mixture of thousands of pounds of rex soles and sanddabs, flounders, and petrale soles, and more Dover soles than they could sell in a week—meaning, at least half were destined for the freezer, something else they didn't control since a limit could been set—I finally said, "I'm walking back."

They both hollered, "No! No! You can't go! We still have to wash the fish bins out." I said, "Fuck the fish bins." I then heard them disparaging me as I left.

I walked from Pier Three on the Embarcadero to 542 Clay Street and was now well over an hour late calling my customers. I didn't know what to expect. Luckily, I'd told my customers I would be calling them on Monday morning from another company, and they had waited for me. Whew! I had also been deprived of my morning coffee, and that didn't help my mood.

The production floor was flooded with orders for the first time in years. The order packers were also astonished to see how much frozen shellfish went along with the orders—a point I ultimately tried to make to their other comatose salesmen. It increased sales by at least 25 percent and didn't cost anything more to deliver. The more product delivered at each stop, the greater the profit; simple business sense and logic.

The incident of them taking me to unload the trawler that morning during that pivotal time on my first day at Paladini showed the deceit they had for me. They inexplicably wanted to not only discourage me, but to extinguish any hope I had of bringing in the business that could ultimately save the company. How ludicrous and mindlessly absurd.

Another morning, within the first few weeks, one of my cousins came up to me (yes, while making calls) and this time said, "Kiki, run this paper up to Uncle Alex. He's up at Vanessi's on Broadway, having breakfast. They're not open yet, so just knock on the front door. He'll be sitting at the counter."

Again, to keep peace, off I went up to Broadway to Vanessi's. Looking in through the glass front door I knocked, and a tuxedo clad waiter answered saying, "We're not open yet!" Explaining I was there to see Alex, I then walked in and saw him at the counter with a few of his cronies, and said, "Hi, Alex, I was supposed to give this to you." He gave me a bewildered look and asked, "Who are you?" "I'm your nephew, Kiki, Achille, Walter's son." "Oh," he said. Nothing more. Nobody knew me!

I couldn't help but wonder why in the hell he was up there at Vanessi's at eight in the morning, and all dressed up in a suit and tie. Shouldn't he have been at the plant overseeing what was going on? He was the president of the corporation by the way. Even more of a reason to have been there. My dad was there. However, he was out on the fucking floor wearing fish boots and freezing his ass off, while Alex was nonchalantly eating breakfast at Vanessi's before they opened. As I understand, he spent most days at the Tanforan Race Track. You might now be starting to get a drift as to why the business was failing.

Well, thank God, I succeeded in bringing in all, or at least most of, the business on the Peninsula. Paladini was again up to five trucks a day, and six on Fridays—more than most of all their delivery areas combined.

My dad was beaming with pride, I know, though he never said as much.

I soon asked Lionel for a raise and he immediately said no—that quickly—no! I looked at him and poignantly said, looking directly into his eyes, "Do you want a moment to reconsider, Mr. Shatz?" He then sat back in his chair, rocking back and forth as it squeaked almost rhythmically to the tapping of his pen upon his desk, and thought for a moment. He then said, "How much?"

I had them, and we both knew it.

I'm sure if my cousins knew what I was making, they would have shit bricks. They can just continue having fun playing with the boats.

I must mention an amusing incident. One morning around eight, after one of my uncles—a rather rotund man—had just finished shoveling a huge breakfast into his enormous cavity across the street at the Tadich Grill (no, Tadich doesn't serve breakfast, but Paladini owned the property), came upstairs to the sales office while gasping for breath after climbing the thirteen steps to the second floor. He then sat on his old lopsided wooden chair with a roller missing on one leg, and as it precariously tilted, he leaned over and asked if I had a pen he could borrow. He had to write up an order for five pounds of fillet of sole—a $14.75 order. Note that in those days it cost twenty-five dollars to make a delivery. I naturally said yes and gave him my pen. I then sat there and waited and waited for the longest time for my pen to be returned. There was another salesman in the office, and by now we were chuckling finding it amusing. Finally, I said, "Hey, Unc, can I have my pen back?" He then looked over at me, and frowned while screaming, "What the hell kind of a salesman are you coming to work without a pen?!" I almost died. Now he was hollering at me for coming to work without a pen! I said, "But, Unc, *you* borrowed *my* pen." He impudently replied, "No, I didn't!"

That incident, though it may seem trivial and even humorous, was intended to cause hurt. It showed the lack of respect and harsh conditions that existed while working there. I found it difficult continuing to work in an environment with so much animosity and an obvious lack of appreciation. The invoice amount of just one of my orders amounted to more than his entire day of invoiced sales. Not bragging—it was just a fact.

Here's another genuinely funny story: One of my accounts on the Peninsula was the Hilton Inn just adjacent to the San Francisco Airport. The chef, Charlie, was a good friend of mine; a very nice, small-framed Chinese man. Every Friday he would order two dozen live Dungeness crabs, and always needed them to be delivered by ten thirty in the morning so he could cook them for the seafood lunch buffet that started at noon. Being Chinese, and as most Asians do, they want their crabs to be live so they can cook them themselves to assure the quality. Many times, if the truck couldn't make it there by ten thirty, I would run them down to him.

One Friday, the live crabs coming in from Bodega Bay were late due to traffic. The crabs arrived at eleven, and they were mostly all dead. Charlie had already called once, wondering when they were going to be delivered. He was going to kill me because he'd asked me the day before if we were going to have live crabs for him to cook for his Friday buffet. I'd said yes, so he'd put them on the menu. I couldn't call him now and say they were dead, so I grabbed twenty-four of the liveliest crabs I could find among them; however, they were mostly all limp—they had already passed on.

I rushed down Highway 101 to the airport Hilton, and as I pulled into the loading zone, Charlie, the chef, saw me and ran out, swearing. "Where in the hell have you been, Kiki?! I have to cook them! It's eleven forty-five already, for Christ sake!"

I was afraid to face up to it and admit to him that they weren't very lively. Very lively? They were dead! Well, I shoved the invoice in his face and said, "Thanks, Charlie," and proceeded to get the hell out of there. As I was getting into the El Camino, he hollered, "Hey, Kiki, these god-damn crabs are dead!" Oh, Christ, what the hell was I going to say now? Having to think fast, I jokingly said, "Charlie, they're not dead! They're just taking a nap!" "What the hell do you mean, 'they're taking a nap'?!" He screamed back. "Yeah, Charlie, they take a nap between eleven and two every day. Wait until two and they'll wake up!" He looked at me, bewildered, and said, "But I have to cook them now!" I replied, "Well then, I guess you'll never know!"

The next day, he called me up and said, "Kiki, you little son of a bitch, I asked another chef and crabs don't take a nap!" Thank God we were friends, and still are.

I worked for Paladini for almost two years and was in turmoil seeing most of the orders going out with only fresh fish. My average order would run, depending on the size of the account, anywhere from $500 to $2,500 because of the frozen shellfish that accompanied the fresh fish, which often supplied the customer with all of their seafood needs on their menu. By doing so, it also accomplished eliminating the threat of competition! If several companies call on an account, it ends up in a price war and having to deal with competitive pricing. By supplying an account with all its needs, it keeps the buyer unaware of competitive pricing. This is not illegal nor immoral, it's just plain clever and smart!

Their average orders ranged from $50 to $250, even to the huge hotels downtown. I would hear the aged, fermenting salesmen on the phone quickly say thank you and hang up after the buyer had bought only the fresh items, instead of working them over and asking about the other items on the menu. What a stupefaction of resources. It would have been such an elementary way to increase sales and profits. The hotels use a tremendous volume of frozen shellfish!

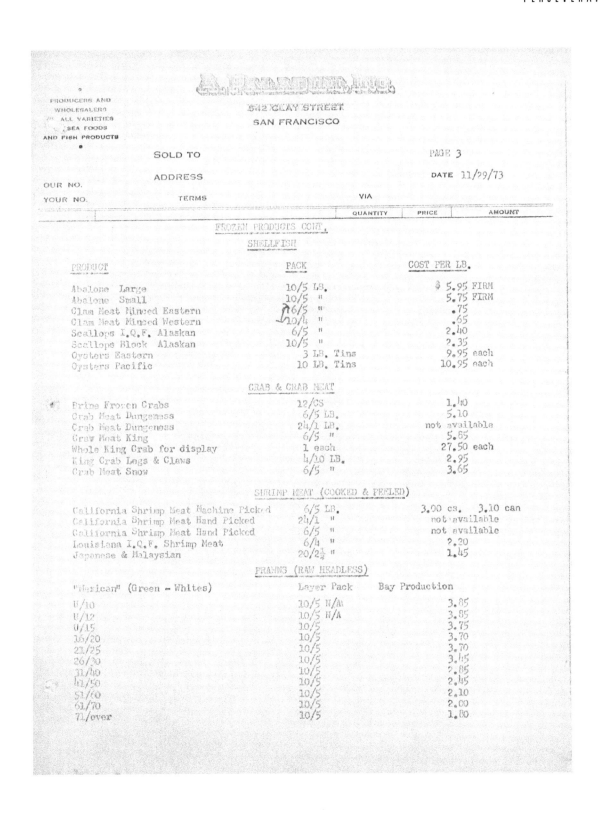

A. PARADISE, Inc.

542 CLAY STREET
SAN FRANCISCO

PRODUCERS AND
WHOLESALERS
OF ALL VARIETIES
SEA FOODS
AND FISH PRODUCTS

SOLD TO

ADDRESS

OUR NO.

YOUR NO.   TERMS

PAGE 3

DATE 11/29/73

VIA

	QUANTITY	PRICE	AMOUNT

FROZEN PRODUCTS CONT.

SHELLFISH

PRODUCT	PACK	COST PER LB.
Abalone Large	10/5 LB.	$ 5.95 FIRM
Abalone Small	10/5 "	5.75 FIRM
Clam Meat Minced Eastern	6/5 "	.75
Clam Meat Minced Western	10/4 "	.65
Scallops I.Q.F. Alaskan	6/5 "	2.40
Scallops Block Alaskan	10/5 "	2.35
Oysters Eastern	3 LB. Tins	9.95 each
Oysters Pacific	10 LB. Tins	10.95 each

CRAB & CRAB MEAT

Brine Frozen Crabs	12/CS	1.40
Crab Meat Dungeness	6/5 LB.	5.10
Crab Meat Dungeness	24/1 LB.	not available
Crab Meat King	6/5 "	5.65
Whole King Crab for display	1 each	27.50 each
King Crab Legs & Claws	4/10 LB.	2.95
Crab Meat Snow	6/5 "	3.65

SHRIMP MEAT (COOKED & PEELED)

California Shrimp Meat Machine Picked	6/5 LB.	3.00 cs. 3.10 can
California Shrimp Meat Hand Picked	24/1 "	not available
California Shrimp Meat Hand Picked	6/5 "	not available
Louisiana I.Q.F. Shrimp Meat	6/4 "	2.20
Japanese & Malaysian	20/2½ "	1.45

PRAWNS (RAW HEADLESS)

"Mexican" (Green - Whites)	Layer Pack	Bay Production
U/10	10/5 N/A	3.85
U/12	10/5 N/A	3.85
U/15	10/5	3.75
16/20	10/5	3.70
21/25	10/5	3.70
26/30	10/5	3.45
31/40	10/5	2.85
41/50	10/5	2.45
51/60	10/5	2.10
61/70	10/5	2.00
71/over	10/5	1.80

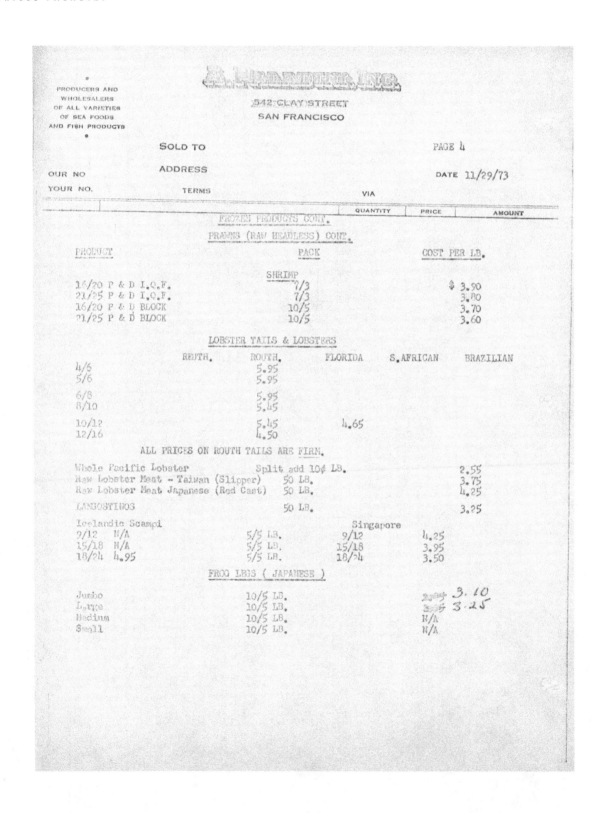

A. PALADINI, INC.

PRODUCERS AND
WHOLESALERS
OF ALL VARIETIES
OF SEA FOODS
AND FISH PRODUCTS

542 CLAY STREET
SAN FRANCISCO

SOLD TO

PAGE 4

OUR NO.

ADDRESS

DATE 11/29/73

YOUR NO.

TERMS

VIA

	QUANTITY	PRICE	AMOUNT

FROZEN PRODUCTS CONT.

PRAWNS (RAW HEADLESS) CONT.

PRODUCT	PACK	COST PER LB.
	SHRIMP	
16/20 P & D I.Q.F.	7/3	$ 3.90
21/25 P & D I.Q.F.	7/3	3.80
16/20 P & D BLOCK	10/5	3.70
21/25 P & D BLOCK	10/5	3.60

LOBSTER TAILS & LOBSTERS

	REUTH.	ROUTH.	FLORIDA	S.AFRICAN	BRAZILIAN
4/6		5.95			
5/6		5.95			
6/8		5.95			
8/10		5.45			
10/12		5.45	4.65		
12/16		4.50			

ALL PRICES ON ROUTH TAILS ARE FIRM.

Whole Pacific Lobster	Split add 10¢ LB.		2.55
Raw Lobster Meat - Taiwan (Slipper)	50 LB.		3.75
Raw Lobster Meat Japanese (Red Cast)	50 LB.		4.25
LANGOSTINOS	50 LB.		3.25

Icelandic Scampi			Singapore	
9/12	N/A	5/5 LB.	9/12	4.25
15/18	N/A	5/5 LB.	15/18	3.95
18/24	4.95	5/5 LB.	18/24	3.50

FROG LEGS (JAPANESE)

Jumbo	10/5 LB.	2.90 3.10
Large	10/5 LB.	3.05 3.25
Medium	10/5 LB.	N/A
Small	10/5 LB.	N/A

It was obvious to everyone at the time that the company had been losing money since they were selling off their precious real estate to stay solvent. Well, one afternoon—without permission—I called a sales meeting with the semi-vertical cadavers in the sales office. They were all in their mid-seventies, mostly ignorant, and talked with Toscani's in their mouth. I knew beforehand that it most likely was going to be futile, but I wanted to give it a try to help boost sales.

I used the Tadich Grill directly across the street as an example. I said, "You're selling all the fresh fish to them every day, totaling about three hundred dollars, but did you ever notice the other companies delivering the frozen shellfish? I know their orders are running well over $1,500 a day. Why can't we get that business, or at least part of it, as well? For Christ sake, Paladini owns the damn property! But not only Tadich, all the restaurants and hotels, as well. The Saint Francis Hotel would buy the fillet of petrale sole and whole rex soles, and our competitors are delivering all the high-volume shellfish to them. We could triple—quadruple—the sales if you guys just concentrated on it."

I continued to preach to them. "At the end of your conversation—remember this as if it's a song—quickly say, 'Hey, chef, how about the crabmeat, shrimp meat, prawns, scallops, abalone, and clam meat for chowder?'" I stated factually that they had eight to ten seconds—but only eight to ten seconds—to get something more out of a buyer. I made them repeat the saying out loud several times, as if singing. Well, they found that amusing and chuckled as they looked at their watches. It was now time to go home. It obviously made no impact.

What I sold after singing that song was often twice as much as what the buyer had originally intended to buy. I'd just have to remind the buyer that he or she might need a frozen item or two. Another company would have gotten that order when they called later. It was added profit with no added expense. I also told them to make the buyer their friend. I found it amazing the difference in attitude and the conversation when you befriended the buyer.

It annoyed me that they would not or could not comprehend what I was saying. Of course, there was also no incentive for them to sell any more, and I certainly didn't have the authority to offer it. After all, the sooner their calls were finished, the sooner they could play poker in the office. One day I observed that the phone rang eight times before one of them would leave their card game to answer.

As you may have by now comprehended, the company was rapidly shrinking instead of rapidly increasing. How foolish not to have capitalized on the capacious population influx into California. Of course, the constant siphoning of cash to reward the greedy stockholders for sitting on the sidelines watching the decline without engaging tactics to rectify and emend the diminishing returns, only facilitated the acceleration of its decline.

It apparently seemed as if the forces running A. Paladini, Inc. had no foresight, and yet possibly, simply had no desire to progress into the twenty-first century. They vitally needed the increased sales to offset the ever-increasing expenses. The exiguous approach they took to control expenses was similar to the story of the Dutch boy who held his finger in the hole in the damn to thwart off the impending leak.

Their preposterous thinking that they were infallible would eventually extirpate the company.

CHAPTER 17
DARK DAYS LOOM AHEAD—AGAIN

It was 1966. Laura was now five, Gina, four, and Diana, two. We had sold our home in Terra Linda and had now been in our new larger home in San Rafael Park for about six months. The kids loved the expanse in the backyard where they could play, and were especially happy since they each now had their own bedroom painted in their favorite color. Joan also now had a wonderful big kitchen to cook her heart out in, as she so enjoyed doing. Home life was happy. However, I was miserable at work.

The discontent working for the family plagued me. I hated the unremitting contentious animosity that I felt every day. I was continuously walking around with a nervous, unrelenting ache in my gut. The repugnance was obvious, and I knew I wasn't wanted. It was indeed a very uncomfortable atmosphere to contend with. Plus, witnessing my father, at his age, working as a common laborer was tearing me apart.

Be that as it may, the weekends were always enjoyable, a time to relax and get away from it all and be with my wonderful wife and three young daughters. Fixing up the new house was also a distraction, doing landscaping and the like. Joan was the boss when it came to the landscaping; I just did whatever she said.

I will never forget one Sunday afternoon. It was shortly after two, as a calming breeze soothed me from the warm afternoon sun, as I planted pyracantha bushes between the properties in the front of the house. My shirt was off, and my hands were immersed in manure and potting soil, mixing just the exact amount of each following Joan's instructions, when Joan frantically called out to me, "Kiki! It's your sister Audrey on the phone. Something happened to your dad!"

Stunned, I ran to the phone. Audrey told me that my dad had just had a heart attack at home while eating lunch, but she didn't know how serious it was. It was a horrible feeling that she couldn't expound about it in greater detail. My heart raced, and I felt flushed, feeling I was going to pass out. *Oh, Christ*, I thought. *No, no, not my dad.*

I immediately said to Joan, "I have to go. My dad had a heart attack!" I rushed off and as I was speeding to San Francisco to the home on Baker Street, I couldn't help but think of a conversation he and I had just had that past Friday. We'd had lunch together in a little coffee shop in Beldon Alley near the plant. As we were walking back to the plant crossing Clay Street, where the entrance of the Transamerica building is today, my dad had said something very odd. I'd mentioned to him that I felt he was working too hard and that maybe he should retire and enjoy life, and he said to me, "What the hell? How much more time do you think I have left?" That had concerned me, but I didn't question it further. I hadn't understood why he'd said that, because I'd thought he was in relatively good health. Now I wished I had. I had intended to pursue his comment further the following week.

As I approached the toll plaza, I was thinking, hoping. *But people survive heart attacks. Maybe it was just a mild one.* I came off the approach of the Golden Gate Bridge onto Richardson Avenue and turned at the first left onto Francisco Street, then drove the fifty feet to the corner of Baker Street.

The memory is as vivid as if it happened today. As I pulled in front of the house, I saw a black hearse parked in front. "Oh, God! Dad! Dad! ... NO!" I screamed.

My heart sunk, my breathing now shallow while I trembled and gasped for air as I ran up those twenty-one red brick steps I'd played on as a kid. The front door was open, and as I walked in and looked to the right down the long hallway into the kitchen, I saw what appeared to be a gurney. There was my dad in a zipped-up black body bag.

Oh. My. God! Oh my God. My dad is dead. My dad is dead. My dad is dead. I will never forget that image, and the sudden realization of how quick death can be.

I grabbed my mom, who was kneeling over him, frantically sobbing and trembling. She collapsed into my arms and said, "Kiki, Kiki, look at your father. He's gone."

They wheeled him out of the kitchen into the hallway. There was a wooden heater vent on the hallway floor. I remember as they wheeled him across the vent, his body shook from side to side in the black bag while crossing it. The wheels on the gurney made a deep cadenced sound while they rolled over each opening. I can hear that sound now as I write this.

I knelt, wanting to hug him as my mom held onto me, holding me so as not to fall. I'm not sure if I was holding onto her, or her onto me. I was just inches from him and wanted to throw myself over him and say I was sorry. I didn't know what for. Just sorry. Maybe for being the black sheep, maybe for the strife I may have caused him, maybe for *never telling him I loved him.* I so just wanted to hug him and say it. But it was too late now. It was too late.

When I stood up, my mom grasped onto me tightly, and as her head lay firmly against my chest, she tugged at my shirt, pleading for God to resurrect him. If only that could have been possible.

I followed the undertaker down the steps, then watched my father being placed into the hearse. As the hearse drove away, a feeling of complete emptiness came over me. My rock, my god, my father, was gone.

My mom and I and my sister Kay and her husband Jack then gathered in the kitchen—in the kitchen where he had just died. My mom told us that she had fixed lunch and called him to come upstairs from his stamp room to eat. He sat down at the kitchen table, put the fork in his mouth, and the fork suddenly dropped. She looked over and saw him gasping for breath and thought he was choking. She'd desperately tried to free his throat, but to no avail. He died instantly from an aneurysm. Oh, that poor woman, all alone when it happened.

Is life really that fragile? Alive one moment, dead the next?

Odd how things stand out in your memory: Jack turned on the fire under the small pot of coffee that my mom was going to warm up for my dad to drink... and made himself a cup of coffee with it.

That angered me. I found that to be so incredibly insensitive and ghastly that I ran out of the room. Possibly it was just my state of mind.

Sometime later, my mom asked me to go downstairs and make sure that the garage door was shut since my dad often left it open. I did, and then went to check the stamp room, as he called it. As I approached that small room, the door was ajar, and I noticed that the goose-neck lamp over his desk was still on, that same lamp that I'd hung over so many times as a kid, watching him work on his stamp collection, so wanting to tell him that I loved him, but never had. Turning off that lamp was a finality—He was really gone, and would never return. I literally felt the hair on the back of my neck stand up. Devastated, I threw myself across his desk as if hugging him and asked myself why men couldn't tell other men they loved them. Jesus Christ, he was my dad.

When the estate was settled many years later after my mom's passing, I only asked for two things: that very lamp and a little cast-iron bulldog door holder that had held the kitchen door open. When I was a kid, I would run my little toy tank through its legs and make the roaring sound of a tank.

I have that lamp on my work bench to this day, and every time I turn it on, I feel his presence.

Meanwhile, having to get my composure back, I went upstairs and joined everyone, including my sister Audrey and her husband Don, who had now arrived. My mom, being a mom, asked if she could fix us anything to eat. Even with her heart breaking, she was our wonderful, loving mother, still taking care of her kids.

A few minutes later, the doorbell rang. I went to the front door and saw that it was Lionel Shatz, the corporation's asshole pompous controller. *It's odd he's here*, I thought. He never came to visit my folks. I wondered if he knew, but how?

As I opened the door, I said, "Lionel, my dad just passed away." He said, "I know. Attilio just called me." Evidently my mom had called my dad's older brother, Attilio, for help, who lived just a block away, but was in ill health himself.

Well, without saying hello or that he was sorry to hear about my dad's sudden passing, he pushed the door open and abruptly stormed in. He then pugnaciously shouted at me in his deep, raspy, angry voice, "Did you know your father is deeply in debt to the company?"

Shocked and appalled by his callousness and insensitivity, I screamed back at him, "What the fucking hell are you saying?! My God, the man just died! Why are you saying this?! And now?! Is this the only reason you came here?" Now enraged, I screamed, "I want you to leave! We will sort this out later. How rude and malicious of you to barge in here, just minutes after he died, and want to give my mom this news. What the fucking hell is the matter with you, for Christ sake?!"

As he was walking down the steps, he looked back at me and said, "We must have a meeting." I shouted back, "What's the matter?! Are you running out of properties to sell?"

I had no idea of this alleged pecuniary fiasco and doubted if my mom did.

As I was walking back to the kitchen, my mom asked who was at the front door. I said it was Mr. Shatz; he'd come by to give his condolences, Attilio had told him. How could I tell her what he'd really come by for, and now? Anyway, even if what he'd said was true, they could have written the debt off—that is, if they'd been making money. Oh, what a concept—making money.

Alone later, with thoughts now to myself, I remembered my dad had lost a lot of money in the stock market crash of 1929 but assumed he had recovered from it. Thinking back, he'd always driven a Dodge or a Plymouth, and only ordered business Coupes. Of course, they were cheap. He couldn't afford anything more. Why hadn't I seen that when I was young? And stupidly, I'd ordered a more expensive car that time way back, just so I would look good. It also suddenly made sense that he had now been driving an old used Mercury. I'd asked him why he'd bought it and he replied, "It's just a car. A car is just for transportation." Of course, he'd had to say that, knowing what I now knew. This was the man who had once driven a big fancy Packard Sedan.

I knew my days at Paladini were now over, and forever. I was sick of the jealousy, deceit, aggravation, and ignorance, but now, more importantly, the lack of respect for my father and the insensitivity and inconsideration toward my mother. I was *done!*

Though totally devastated with my dad's sudden death, I had to comfort my mom. I knew I had to be strong for her. Hopefully, my dad had at least passed away content. My oldest sister Lorraine had just gotten married for the second time and had stopped in to see my mom and dad that very morning. She'd told them that she was finally happy. Mom said that Dad was very pleased to hear that.

He was laid out at Valente Marini Mortuary on Sutter Street in the city. The first time I saw him in his casket is another memory embedded within me. I went alone; I had to. Joan, naturally being a good wife, wanted to come, but I didn't know how I was going to react. If I cried—or should I say *when* I cried—I needed to cry alone.

I remember walking into the funeral parlor and seeing my dad's name on the sign in the entry foyer: Walter Louis Paladini—Room B.

Oh, shit. I got weak in the knees, and now wished Joan had come with me. I walked in and saw him lying in the casket as if he was asleep. I recall that he looked so young and quiescent.

Why did he look so young? How strange. His face was also relaxed. Possibly, he was finally indeed at peace. He was now released of any strain or pressure, any worries, any conflict. He was dressed in a dark-blue suit, with his hands folded, but I noticed that his gold jade ring was missing! He always wore it. He never took it off!

As a kid he would sit to my right, and it was on his left hand, on his marriage finger. He wore it instead of a wedding ring as many men do. I wondered why it wasn't with him.

I knelt next to him and put my hand on the rim of the coffin. My heart was beating ever-so-fast. I was looking at my father, knowing he would never hear the words "I love you" from me. Why wouldn't—why couldn't—I have said those words to him when he could have heard me? When he could have comprehended it? He would never hear again, never see again, never speak again, never feel emotion again, never know laughter again, or play those whimsical jokes on us as he so often had. He was gone. Like when I was a young boy and had asked my mom where our dog Corky had gone when he died; she'd said he was gone, and I then asked her, "Gone? Gone where, Mom?"

Death is so damn permanent, so eternal.

My dad was like a god to me. I must have spent well over an hour with my head leaning against his casket in a state of semi-somnolence.

Strangely, I suddenly felt close to him, almost as if he knew I was there. I wonder. It was as if he was conveying to me that he loved me, and knew I loved him, and that he was okay. That feeling was soothing. However, I must say that I'm a realist and not ignorant to the fact that we most likely conceptualize and visualize a mental fabrication of what we want. I do hope that's wrong.

The day came for the burial. He was to be entombed at Holy Cross Catholic Cemetery. He was not a religious man, but we were raised Catholic.

We gathered at the funeral parlor, the priest said a mass, and then it came time for the sealing of the casket. They asked if anyone wanted to approach the casket.

This was it. I would never see him again. My mom had given me a tiny twenty-four-carat gold bracelet when I was a baby, and it was engraved with *"Kiki."* I had gotten it earlier and put it in my pocket. This was going to be my personal way of expressing my love for him.

With everyone watching as I approached the casket, I was now ever-so-close to my dad, just inches from him, and I whispered, "I love you, Dad."

I then reached into my pocket and took my tiny engraved gold bracelet and surreptitiously placed it in the casket to be with him forever. *But . . .* I didn't reach in far enough and it slid down the inside of the metal casket, making a loud metal-on-metal sound! I'd tried to do it without anyone seeing me, and now I was sure everyone had heard it. I'd screwed up! My private expression of atonement to my dad was now irreversibly on the bottom of his casket. It lays there to this very day, and not next to him. I had nightmares about this for years. I will *never ever* forget that scraping sound as it slid down to the bottom, and not next to him. I can hear it as I write this.

As the days went on, I was having an extremely difficult time accepting the fact that he was really gone. The evocative, poignant, emotionally moving feeling of love and sadness was so difficult to escape.

PAGE 34 Tuesday, Februar
SAN FRANCISC

Walter Paladini Dies at 73

Walter L. Paladini, member of a pioneer San Francisco family and president of A. Paladini Inc., wholesale seafood firm, died of an apparent heart attack Sunday at his home at 3159 Baker street. He was 73.

A native San Franciscan, Mr. Paladini became president of the company in 1964 when his brother Alexander died after heading the firm for 40 years. Their father, Achille Paladini, founded the business in 1870. It supplies many Fisherman's Wharf restaurants with seafood, and maintains offices at 542 Clay street and a cold storage plant at 924 Sansome street.

Surviving Mr. Paladini are his wife, Jennie, and six children, all residents of the Bay Area Lorraine Richter, Catherine Bray, Walter Paladini Jr. Waltina Cain, Audrey Tomei and Achille Paladini.

There are 17 grandchildren.

A brother and three sisters also survive: Attilio Paladini, Henrietta Cavallero, Ercelia McGuire, and Yolanda Reed of Nevada City, Calif

Funeral arrangements were pending yesterday at Halsted & Co., 1123 Sutter street.

I went into a deep depression, into a cocoon, a cloister, shutting out everyone close to me. Joan told me later that I eclipsed her, totally closed her out for a long time. The one person I so needed. At the time, I didn't realize that I was doing that to her, or to the kids.

I needed to be alone and get through it on my own, as I have with most things in life.

I then meandered in a lonesome, nebulous dark fog for a very long time.

My dad was now entombed, and my expression of adoration now lay forever, not next to him, but somewhere beneath him, in the shallow cavity of his coffin.

CHAPTER 18

AFTER THE GAME, THE KING AND THE PAWN GO INTO THE SAME BOX

Within two days, a stockholders' meeting was scheduled by Mr. Shits—excuse me, Mr. Shatz. The entire Paladini family, representing all seven stockholders, was to be there; however, there had been no mention of the subject matter.

Alex and Hugo, my father's brothers, had passed away prior to him, and their daughters, now stockholders, chose not to attend. All three of my father's sisters were present, as well as Attilio, the last surviving son.

Attilio was now very old and hadn't worked in a long time, so was not up on business matters. He was also not very outspoken, or better yet, most likely intimidated by his sisters. The three sisters—Henrietta, who had no living children, Ercelia, and Yolanda—had one son each: my two cousins, who worked for the company. Remember them?

My mom represented my father's share of the business. Only she was to attend. I was candidly told not to attend. Well fuck them! I attended. Lionel promptly asked me to leave and I precipitously refused. I outright said, "Nope, I'm staying." I had no fear of him or the family now. I was the nexus between my mom and dad and had a notion of what the meeting was to be about. I knew they were going to rake her over the coals, and she was in no condition for that, nor would she understand. She had never attended a stockholders meeting. Actually, neither had I.

The meeting soon abruptly started with Lionel growling in his deep, raspy, annoying voice about the financial indebtedness of my father to the corporation. This was said without introduction of the articles of discussion, or outlining the purpose of the meeting, as would normally be the case. It was immediately obvious that it was the one and only purpose of the meeting, as I'd suspected! When he said that, I looked over at my mom, and the surprised painful expression on her face is still etched within me.

I must take a quick detour and give a briefing of what I'd learned of my father's debt: When my father was the manager of the Oakland plant, one of my sister's husbands wanted to open a retail seafood store in the East Bay city of Richmond. My dad agreed to sell him all the fish and allowed him to pay with extended terms. He did very well, and was making good money, but being the sort of man that he was, his character was such that he never finished anything. He got involved with another venture and let the store go. He was now indebted to Paladini in Oakland for approximately $25,000. This was just after World War II, and yes, that was a chunk of change, but a pittance for the corporation, especially considering the fact that a 25 percent profit margin was included, so about $18,750 in principal.

However, the family viewed it as my father's debt instead of a business write-off, so he ended up owing it to the company without any form of discount or consideration. All large corporations have a reserve for bad debts or should have. However, the family being the family they were, chose not to write it off. I assume, with trying to pay off that debt—with interest, by the way—and with what he'd lost in the stock market crash, my dad was compelled to draw money from the company above his salary to live on. After my asking what the current balance was, I was told it was $18,000.

The amount stated was not that capacious. Why did Lionel have to belittle my father in front of my mom? In front of everyone? Lionel spoke so indecorously, but what was even worse was that none of the family spoke up in defense of my dad. They were all multi-millionaires, yet wanted these few dollars from her. If aggregate and divided by seven, it would have been a measly amount to each of them.

I asked if the amount due the corporation could possibly be reduced, or even forgiven, but was abruptly and indignantly shouted down with contempt and disdain as they unanimously proclaimed that my mother had to pay it—and soon! It was as if the presence of evil demonic creatures suddenly arose within the room, emanating hatred as their eyes became inflamed with loathing and malice.

"Why is there so much animosity and contempt for my dad's family?" I asked. I then shouted, "Jesus Christ, you're all brothers and sisters!" I then got the shakes, and that wasn't good! I said, "Mom, let's go!" She started to ask me why, and where we were going. I said, "We. Are. Leaving!"

As I was walking out, I said to Lionel, "You're a man with polyorchidism [which means having three balls]. Shame on you, with your inequities toward my father. I quit! I assure you that the loss of my sales will make my father's debt look like a pittance, and you will soon regret this. Fuck all of you!"

As we were leaving, I heard a great deal of grumbling. They knew I was going to destroy them, and you bet I was! I didn't, for the life of me, understand this loathing. We were family—at least we were supposed to be.

As I drove my mom home, she was trembling and sobbing uncontrollably, and she asked what she should do. I said, "Don't worry, Mom. I'll take care of you . . . and I'll take care of them!

I then drove the car back to the plant and parked it dead center in front of the main loading door so they would know the next morning I surely wasn't coming back, and put the keys in the mail slot. I then went upstairs and cleaned out my desk. Just before leaving, I looked out that same window, as I had so many times, and again envisioned my dad laboring out on the production floor at seventy-two years old, like a common hired hand.

My poor dad. I hadn't known that he'd *had* to work.

As I walked back to my mom's house from the plant on Clay and Montgomery Streets through the litter-strewn grungy alleys of North Beach, I indulged in planning my vengeance. Tolerance was no longer an option, since any relationship with the family had now ceased. Walking further up the steep hill on Bay Street toward the Marina District, my legs tired, but my focus strengthened, knowing I must fulfill the silent promise I'd just made to myself, to my mom, to my dad. My malevolence would somehow turn this tragedy into a triumph, like a testament to the human spirit. I will *persevere*.

I was now exhausted, but at the same time, exhilarated that I was now free of the constant turmoil and disparagement, and was experiencing all the vast spectrums of human emotions. Meanwhile, I couldn't help feeling that I'd wasted many years bouncing back and forth between wanting to destroy the company to wanting to save it. My direction now, however, was unmistakably clear: I was going to finally destroy it, and I knew I could.

When I eventually got to the house, totally worn and weary after walking from the other side of the city, the back of my legs ached as I reached those ever-so-familiar twenty-one red brick steps, but climbing those seemingly steep steps was surprisingly easy. It was as if I'd had a sudden surge of stamina, as if the eternal flame at the Olympics had just been lit, and I was ready to compete.

I must mention that there was admittedly a hint of apprehension; apprehension because of the realization that if they indeed prevailed, there would be a rightful stigma against me for the rest of my life. After all, I was just one, little, young guy, fighting a century-old dynasty, hoping that that surge of adrenaline wasn't just another unrealistic fantasy.

Upon seeing my mom, we hugged, then cried together for a while. We both didn't know what was going to happen next, to either one of us. She had no idea what money my dad had, if much, if any. What was she to live on? she asked. She was also concerned about how I was going to take care of my family without a job.

I told her not to worry about me, and that I would try to figure out and decipher all this for her. I felt brave, and a feeling of solace came over me. My first concern was for my mom, as she was alone. I would have to be her strength. Yes, again, I was the youngest, but . . .

Here was this wonderful woman, who just wanted to be a wife and mother, who possessed only love, innocence, and purity. There wasn't an evil streak to be found within her. For her to be treated in such an abhorrent manner, with a total lack of compassion from the family, was abominable.

Well, to my complete and utter surprise, the very next morning my two cousins came over to our house in San Rafael unannounced. I hesitantly let them in, curious as to what they had to say. I didn't offer them coffee or anything—unusual for us. I abruptly asked what they were doing there? They simultaneously said, "Please come back to work, Kiki." I must admit that it felt really good to hear that... them pleading!

They admitted they needed me. I knew it, and they'd known it all along.

A flashback suddenly occurred. Were these the same two who hadn't even said hello or welcomed me when I'd first started working at Paladini, and wanted me to go and unload the fucking trawler? Did they want me for my sales? Or to assist them in running the business that they obviously knew nothing about? One cousin knew about repairing the boats. That wouldn't get them far. The other knew how-to pick-up paper clips to save expenses. I abruptly said, "No. Not now. Not ever. Please leave!" They departed with their heads down. They knew what was to come.

As good as it felt, I still had no idea what I was going to do, or how I was going to implement my plan of restitution. I had been in this situation a few times before, but never with such vengeance.

Meanwhile, I knew my mom needed money to live on since there wasn't a hell of a lot in the bank, and the only liquid disposable asset that I could think of was his stamp collection—yes, his cherished stamp collection. Unfortunately, I didn't have much money saved up, living from paycheck to paycheck, to help her, so I decided to have the stamp collection appraised by three professional collectors.

It was sold a week later at a sum that was surprisingly low. I'm not sure my dad would have been pleased, but it gave her some money to live on at the time. I hated having to sell his prized collection, but had no other options.

I'll never forget, my final paycheck from A. Paladini, Inc. had my dad's signature on it, and I had to cash it. I had no money. I went to the Bank of America on Chestnut Street to cash it. If I hadn't desperately needed the money, I would have framed it. Copy machines weren't readily available yet, unfortunately. My heart sunk as the girl took it from me.

It was now time to find a job, a job that would steer me on course to annihilate them.

Hoping my last employer would take me back, I called and said I was done with Paladini for good; could I have my old job back? He promptly said no. *Oh, shit!* I thought. He then said, "I want you to be the general manager of my new wholesale food distribution company in Oakland!"

The new operation sold fresh fish, frozen shellfish, and a complete line of frozen foods, including poultry, vegetables, and a new line of gourmet ready-to-cook entrees, a new concept. The operation had only been open a few months, and not having confidence with his current personnel in San Francisco, he'd been looking for a qualified person to run it. Me, qualified?

Taking over this new venture would give me the perfect opportunity of finishing off A. Paladini, Inc., especially since the company was jointly tied to a main producer of fresh fish. I wasn't going to have mercy on them this time. I immediately planned to go after their two largest accounts, Safeway Stores and Lucky Markets. The two combined equaled well over four hundred stores in the greater Bay Area.

I spent the first few weeks at my new position learning the frozen food industry, and it came easy.

The girls were now six, five, and three, with two of them in school. Joan was an excellent mother, and that allowed me to stay focused. I wasn't over my dad's passing by any means but needed to keep my head clear to support my family and guide my mom.

First, I concentrated on building a sales force, acquiring several employees from the competition since they had an established sales base, then trained others to cover every corner of the Bay Area. With an excellent sales force now in place, production was next. That was going to be more difficult because most of them had to be trained.

After several months, things were jumping, business was good, and the operation was turning a profit. I was standing proud knowing my job was once and for all secure, and my plan to decimate Paladini was right on course. The company was also naturally enjoying the increased sales and profits, not only from being aggressive, but as result of my intended vengeance.

Things continued going well, with sales escalating each month, and everything was good. My kids were healthy and growing, and my wife was happy.

Be that as it may, a very strange and odd thing happened concerning my boss after the second full year of operation. He'd received the profit and loss statement (P&L) for the year and said he wanted to talk to me. I looked forward to receiving praise because the net profit margin was exceptional being above the industry norm. Well, I expected it to be, since I'd watched every facet of the business. I had the overhead fine-tuned, from controlling expenses, doing competitive buying to monitoring selling prices to inventory control. It was running like a fine Swiss watch.

He came over to the Oakland plant and sat me down in the office. He said something was wrong with the P&L statement. Confused and concerned, I said, "What do you mean? What exactly is it?" He said, "You're cutting a better net percentage than we are in San Francisco, and that's not possible!" I remember looking at him and saying, "Wow, that's so great!" He said, "No, it isn't. It can't be." I then said, "So what are you saying?"

Evidently, he thought he and his partner were beyond invincible. How could a young punk who'd just turned thirty beat his percentage at the main office? The fact of the matter was that when I'd worked for him years ago in San Francisco, I'd thought his operation was very irresponsibly managed.

I was greatly disturbed. Instead of him complimenting me, he thought I'd done what? Falsified the figures? This blew my mind. I'd watched every invoice, making sure the prices were correct, monitored the orders going out to make sure there were no mistakes with the product, and carefully watched all expenses. I did all the buying, and many times actually refused to buy from his Northern California production plant because the prices were often too high. Maybe that was what he was upset about? But how could he be upset if I'd beaten his figures? This was a wonderment.

I was now pissed! What a slap in the face. I couldn't believe this was happening. *Is everyone in this fucking industry nuts?!* I thought. He came over the next day with a crew from San Francisco and took inventory. It had to have been the inventory that he may have thought I'd falsified. What was he thinking? That I'd overstated the inventory?

It couldn't be the accounts receivables. What the hell else? What hurt even more was that he walked in and didn't say a word to me, just walked by and went into my office and put his feet up on my desk, smoking his foul-smelling Cuban cigar—almost as to make the statement that this was *his* business and I was just his humble employee.

I damn near told him to go fuck himself, but wanted him to see that the results of the inventory were indeed correct, and that the net profit was indeed correct.

The inventory ended up being absolutely as stated, but then he had to deduct the sales to date, plus add on any new product. It was very laborious and convoluted, but it ended up being exactly as stated on the year-end inventory. It was beyond belief when he then said that he wanted to see the cold-storage withdrawal records. It took several days for the cold storage slips to show that everything again matched up. Well, my P&L statement was indeed correct, but he never acknowledged it!

As he was on the phone telling me everything was in line, I gave him the middle finger, an expression I despise and seldom use, but felt compelled to use it at that moment. How dare he question me. I was hurt and felt a loss of entitlement and allegiance, and gave him the finger again!

The mixed messages I received from my boss confused and enraged me. It also made me wonder if their intention in opening this branch was for a tax shelter, thinking it would take a long time to turn a profit. Or they'd possibly even hoped it never could and never would. Thinking back, the demand for me to buy from their production plant at inflated prices and my refusal may tell the tale.

Things were never the same, as far as I was concerned. I still watched their business but didn't have the same driving force. I got a nice bonus and another raise that year, but never heard a word about having done a good job. This is a perfect example of why someone loses interest; an occasional compliment can encourage one to do better. Having said that, in this case, maybe that was not their intention. Not their intention to do better.

At any rate, I hate gray zones or cloudy issues. It's either black or white. Even my food must be separated in specifically categorized food types on my plate. That's nuts, I know! I may, however, allow a pea or two, or possibly a little bit of the mashed potatoes to touch my turkey, maybe. Things must be defined, must be exact, and if not, must be explained. Their attitude thus became a cloudy issue that went without explanation.

Just about this time, I heard that the Paladini family had sold the entire Clay Street property to Transamerica to build the now iconic Pyramid Building. They had moved to a mammoth building leased by the state at 70 Rankin Street in San Francisco. I had also overheard they were paying an equally mammoth rent, something I knew they couldn't afford.

May I add that the family should not have sold the property out right, but should have exercised a 1031 tax-deferred exchange into a ninety-nine-year ground lease. This would have avoided the huge capital gain taxes they paid. Good job, Lionel. You screwed the heirs out of a massive fortune!

Sadly, my mom had a stroke around this time, and needed to sell her home since she couldn't live alone. She moved in with my sister Kay and her husband down in San Mateo, on the Peninsula.

I don't doubt that the turmoil she went through having to deal with my dad's estate and all the family bullshit caused the stroke, plus the lack of compassion and understanding shown by her husband's siblings must have hurt deeply.

CHAPTER 19
THE FAMED FAMILY BUSINESS GOES BUST

Whether it was indeed in part from my doing, or just a matter of time, the Paladini empire crumbled in mid-April of 1972, two years after I left the company. They had been faltering for many years, as you now know, however it was predestined to fail under the current management. The management had titles, just titles. Titles not earned. It doesn't take long to implode if you don't know what the hell you're doing. They even fired Mr. Shatz to gain control. Complete control . . . of nothing. How sad.

I was told by my brother Walter, who had been working for the company since his early twenties, that they were drowning in debt, with well over $3 million in arrears.

It came to pass that the Paladini family was approached by two investors who were good friends with the president of the factoring company that had been advancing funds against daily sales.

FYI, factoring is a corporate death sentence. It's like, as they say, throwing a champagne cork to a drowning person.

The two investors offered the seven A. Paladini, Inc. stockholders one dollar each for their individual share of the corporation. Yes, one dollar, or fifty cents from each investor. You heard me right—a grand total of seven dollars for the now-fading dynasty. Desperate to stay out of bankruptcy, they accepted and sold the famed iconic company and once industry leader for seven bucks, then the price of one steak dinner at the Blue Fox in the alley on Merchant Street just around the corner—in a building they fortuitously once owned. I often wondered if Mario Mondin, the owner, would have made that trade for a steak dinner. And remember my chef friend, Charlie, from the Hilton Inn, he was coincidentally the chef at the time. It's not relevant, just thought I'd throw it in to continue with the comedy of it all!

It was apparently agreed upon by all parties that they, the investors, would reorganize and pay the liabilities for receiving the assets.

If my grandfather had been alive, he would have dropped dead again to see his empire now in shambles. What a shame there would be no third generation taking over to carry on the business. Well, that's not true. Some of the third generation did take over . . . and put it under.

The real travesty is that over the years, all the extremely valuable commercial real estate holdings were now also gone—all seventeen, mostly prime San Francisco real estate—sold to fund the continuous depletion of the cash flow of the, to use a pun, floundering wholesale fish business.

The brilliance of my grandfather's investing was foolishly dissipated. The real estate was purposely and wisely set up by Achille to be held under Paladini Properties, Inc., a separately held corporation to protect the properties from liability for asset protection. What a farce. They lost the properties to themselves!

They could have, and should have, shut down the business long ago while still doing well enough to pay off the creditors, if they'd had the foresight to do so. That would have halted the depletion of the valuable income-producing real estate. They could have all lived extremely well from the income of the properties. I can only imagine and speculate what the properties would be worth today. Certainly, quantifiable and multitudinous in excess of hundreds of millions of dollars.

I couldn't help but wonder the purpose of the investors taking over the company for the assets. It didn't make sense to me. What assets? The trucks were falling apart, the equipment antiquated, the trawlers in disrepair, and the Fort Bragg and Eureka processing facilities were leased from the state, as were the receiving stations and now the main distribution facility, as well.

Now as an outsider, I questioned their intentions. But who was I to question, or care? I was working as a general manager, making good money for another company, though our relationship was now strained due to unresolved, bewildering, and amusing circumstances.

It was sometime in early May of 1972 while in my office one morning, when my secretary said, "Mr. P., you have a call from a Mr. Jesse Bertrano." "From who?" I asked. She responded, "He said it was very important." So, I picked up the phone and he introduced himself as one of the new owners of A. Paladini, Inc. Responding to his introduction, I then said, "So, Mr. Bertrano, why are you calling me?" He replied, "Well, my partner and I want you to run the corporation.

We want you to be the CEO and president." I sat there, dumbfounded, in silence for the longest time. I then replied with a simple, "Oh, really?" Then asked, "So why me, Jesse? Because of my name? Do you want me just as a figurehead?" He then said, "Hell, no. Not at all." He went on to say that he'd heard about my accomplishments and knew I could bring the company back. *That was quite a compliment*, I silently thought to myself. *Wonder how this guy knew*. I then said, "This comes as a real surprise. I really need to think about it, and I have to talk to my wife. I have a good position here now, you know." He then said, "We will make it well worth your while, and by the way, don't you want your name to stand proud again?" I knew at that point he was pushing my buttons. Before hanging up I remember him saying, "Kiki, money is no good without management, and management is no good without money. You have the management skills; we have the money skills!" Boy, this guy was very affable. He could have sold you a plow horse for a unicorn! I thought for a few moments. *I knew I could bring it back, but did I want to—again, and for strangers? As far as the name, fuck the name!* That was my feeling at the time. *Anyway, shit, I just destroyed it. What, now save it?*

Having thought it over, and after talking to Joan, we both decided that we had to at least meet with him and talk about things in greater detail, and more importantly, see what kind of a person he was, and if he and his partner were truly genuine.

Of course, then I would eventually have to meet his partner Jim Signet, an executive vice president with a major bank with its main office in San Francisco. I was impressed with his position but needed to verify it and be convinced they indeed had access to funds, whether theirs or borrowed. I couldn't give up such a good position that was now so easy and take on such a major and almost impossible undertaking. Anyway, why would I even want to do it, or should I say, try to do it?

We agreed to meet that Saturday evening for dinner, but of all places, at the Heritage House Resort in Mendocino. I assumed he had been at the Paladini plant in Fort Bragg a few miles away, and it was close for him. We would really have to struggle if we were to get two rooms and stay there for the night. It was a very expensive resort, one for lovers, since it was set back on a steep, majestic bluff overlooking the ocean and surf below. The movie *Same Time Next Year* was filmed there in 1978 with Alan Alda and Ellen Burstyn.

Well, off we went up the coast with the kids in the backseat of our little red Ford Pinto station wagon to Mendocino, a good three-hour drive. We arrived just in time, and of course, Joan and the kids had to go to the bathroom, so they rushed in ahead of me. We were to meet in the lobby of the restaurant, however I had no idea what Jesse looked like. I figured he would recognize me since I'd told him I was coming with Joan and the three girls, but they were now nowhere near by.

As I was standing in the lobby, an older, rather nice-looking, distinguished, gray-haired man, dressed in what appeared to be an expensive light tan suit, walked up and asked if I was Kiki. Yes, it was indeed Mr. Bertrano, a charismatic and impressively charming man, almost too much so, smiling most of the time. I hate when men smile all the time for no apparent reason. He was also quite the outgoing conversationalist, and pointedly shook my hand as he said hi and referred to me as "ole buddy." I hate to be called "buddy." Such a bourgeois reference. I soon dismissed my snobbish and imperious attitude, realizing that we'd driven up there in a used Ford Pinto station wagon, and had had to scrape up money to pay for the room. He'd driven up in a new Mercedes and was the man with the real money. We then all sat down and talked about everything but business for the first half hour. He occasionally put his hand on my shoulder as if we were old friends. I found that false and uncomfortable. Then it got time to get serious to find out just what he was offering me to take on this almost insurmountable challenge.

He repeated that I was to be the president of the corporation, like that fact would impress me, and that I would have a free hand to do whatever I wanted or needed to run the entire operation, including all the branches and receiving stations on the West Coast. They had over three hundred employees up and down the coast at the time, with almost a dozen locations, which included the main office in San Francisco, two large packing plants—one in Fort Bragg, the other in Eureka—plus eight receiving stations and six company-owned fishing trawlers. The Oakland and the Los Angeles distribution centers had been sold long ago. It was a huge operation; however, it was operating with a huge deficit. He was very convincing and persuasive in getting his point across. He said he interviewed members of the current management team and felt they were all incompetent, and obviously so, given the condition of the company. I guessed it was a compliment that he felt me capable, yet maybe not, compared to who he'd just interviewed. He then threw out an astronomical figure as my compensation, with the promise of a hefty bonus at the end of the year. This impressed me and allowed me to think they had money.

Nevertheless, I would never do anything without Joan's opinion. She is most of the time, if not always, correct with her observations and feelings. I then reluctantly on the way home asked her, "So, honey, what do you think?" She then strangely replied. "He's a tap dancer!" "A what?" I exclaimed. "A tap dancer!" she said again, only this time much bolder and louder. "What the hell does that mean?" I asked. "She then said, "You'll see."

Well, I knew what she meant. He was disingenuous. Better yet, he was, as they say, as fake as a politician's smile. Nonetheless, I was blinded by the opportunity.

CHAPTER 20
BACK AT PALADINI AGAIN, BUT THIS TIME . . .

Joan asked me what I was going to do, but she already knew. I said, "Honey, I have to. I think it was predetermined for me to save the name." She then asked, "But can you?" Hesitantly, I replied, "Yes, I think I can . . . *hopefully*."

However, my chance of actually saving the company was inconceivable, and it would be an insurmountable task. I was only thirty-four, rather young to take on such a challenge, especially with the woe of taking on the obligation of having to pay back the $3 million-plus in past due accounts payable. That alone could be an albatross, but Jesse said new funding would be coming into the company, ample enough to pay down some of the debt right away.

I would have to come up with a well-thought-out plan for both the immediate and the long-term future of the company. I knew my priority must be to meet with the creditors and perform a compromise and settlement, a legal term for an agreement to forestall an obligation that must have the same elements as a contract. Parties must have the capacity and authority to agree to an offer and acceptance. Thinking about this further, what choice would they have other than to agree? Without it, the company would have to be thrown into bankruptcy and they would receive nothing.

But this would be a monumental task. I'd be taking over Mr. Shatz's position as controller, Uncle Alex's as president, my father's as vice president—oh, and yes, of course, buyer and production and sales manager, as well. There was no one presently capable for any of these positions. I will have to build a totally new management team.

Hey, Uncle Alex, do you recognize me now? I'm the kid you didn't know who watched you fill your gut at the counter at Vanessi's one morning a few years ago. Maybe if you had been at the plant watching the operation instead of going to Tanforan at noon to watch the horse races, the business wouldn't be in this condition. Isn't it funny that the kid you didn't recognize, now has your position!

Well, before undertaking this tumultuous task, Joan called to my attention that I hadn't been taking much time to be with the kids, and they were growing up fast. I knew I hadn't, and that concerned me. I was missing their youth. I saw our children blossoming, and needed to luxuriate in it, and engage myself with them during this precious time.

That very next Sunday, I was sitting in our garden pondering whether to take the position and thinking about what Joan had said, when I noticed a magnificent peony in bloom she had planted. I remembered when she planted it she'd told me that its lush, full-rounded bloom was said to be regarded as an omen of good fortune and a happy marriage. What a beautiful, free, God-given gift it was, this creation of nature. Then I had a thought: *Just as our children, this amazing flower, with its incremental beauty, will only blossom for a very short time, then be gone. Our kids are now blossoming into young adults and their youth will soon be gone. I must make time to share their youth with them while they are still blossoming, I can't miss that precious time.*

My thoughts were now flashing back and forth like a thunder and lightning storm between spending treasured time with my kids, and taking on this absurd, preposterous challenge. Just a moment ago I'd been engrossed in thoughts of being with my family, and now I was back at the damn business. I hate that about myself. I so wanted and needed time with my wife and girls.

As a total distraction from my intentions to further the quality of my home life, the following week, Jesse called and insistently asked if I had decided. Well, I had surreptitiously been formulating plans in my head beforehand about it, but needed to meet the other partner, the so-called money man, before finally deciding. After all, the amount of the indebtedness of the company was only hearsay and inconclusive, never outlined with exact figures to me. I was only given an approximation at this point. I wanted a precise figure. Remember, with me, it's either black or white. No gray. I had asked prior if they did or were doing an audit. This would be paramount to assure me that the funds available would be copious enough to cover the outstanding debt, whatever it was, plus allow for some operating capital.

We then met within a few days at the main office of the bank in San Francisco. It was an ornate, early 1900s building with majestic Roman columns allowing you passageway to the steps of the entry. The interior was impressive, commanding a feeling of grandeur and excess with its white marble floors and large crystal chandelier hovering above the atrium from the two-story carved dome ceiling. The half-circle marble steps that led you to the second-floor executive offices persuaded you to believe that you were about to meet royalty. Well, banks equal money, and money equals wealth.

Upon entering Mr. Signet's cavernous office with rosewood-lined walls and Persian rugs overlapping the meticulously polished hardwood floors, there was a large desk set back many dozen feet, thereby presenting you with Mr. James Signet, the executive vice president of the bank. I was immediately intimidated and humbled.

He was a distinguished, gray-haired, very well-dressed man with $300 dark-brown tasseled loafers. He surprisingly greeted me with eloquence and respect.

I couldn't help but be anything other than overly impressed. Now believing that they were factually successful, astute businessmen, and had the avenue to money, I said, "Okay, gentlemen, I'll take the position."

My impression now was that they appeared as if they found companies that had greatly faltered or that were on the verge of bankruptcy, would then seek to find a good management team, and with their multitudinous money resources, the combination would allow the company to once again be successful and profitable.

It now all made sense. Jesse was the front man involved with the operations and Jim was the money man, and as Jesse had said, "Money is no good without management, and management is no good without money." I now understood his statement.

I called the owner of the company I was currently working for at his office in San Francisco and told him about the position I had accepted. To my complete and utter surprise, he abruptly said, "Oh yeah? Well then, just fucking leave right now!" Jesus Christ, I was so taken aback by his comment! I then replied, "But I wanted to give you a formal two-week notice." He then rudely blurted out, "Why, so you can plot and rape me?"

Oh, the joys of being in an industry with men who talk crass and bosses who act like mobsters. I tried to explain that my undertaking at Paladini was beyond the realm of taking his business, and only his business, that the complete internal structure needed to be revamped, and that would be my focus, which would possibly take a year, maybe longer. Then he blurted out, "So then after that you'll be going after my accounts." It was as if he either didn't want to accept my resignation, or he feared the consequences of the future . . . or both. I found that flattering, but you know, when it all came down to it, at one time most of his current accounts I'd taken from Paladini anyway, but of course I didn't say that.

He knew that he was now the number one company on the West Coast since Paladini had faltered. He was powerful and felt omnipotent, almighty, and infinite. Could he really have possibly feared little insecure me? Oh, but wait, I beat his profit margin, remember?

A. Paladini, Inc., the once powerhouse of the entire seafood industry on the West Coast, was now near bankruptcy. The family had been too busy these past years fighting for internal control and leadership of the company. The appointed third generation leader, the uncapable president, led the company to ruin. They felt they were invulnerable and couldn't be taken down. They should have allowed the third generation (the four sons) to work together, to commandeer the company as a team. Maybe one of them could have seen adversity looming.

Humans can possibly learn a simple lesson about leadership from the phenomenon of nature and migratory geese. Sound strange? Odd? Well, leadership is about helping others, not just yourself. Geese fly in a V-formation for a definite reason. Besides each flying at slightly higher altitudes behind the leader for wind resistance, they take turns as leader to conserve that bird's energy. In doing so, they can fly great distances. They work as a team!

The same approach applies to the role of corporate leadership. The function as a leader should be to do whatever is in his or her ability to help others succeed to reach the shared goal. We can also appreciate that leadership is not a position; it is a disposition that people can exhibit regardless of whatever formal title they may carry within their organization, i.e. each bird is given a turn in leading. Too bad the family couldn't take advise from a goose!

After accepting the position as president of A. Paladini, Inc., I was well aware that I had my job cut out for me, but I knew the industry and was fortuitous to be backed by two astute money-men.

The first day came, a Monday. It was a cold, drizzly San Francisco morning and I arrived at the Rankin Street plant at a quarter to five, fifteen minutes before the men were to show up to get ready for work. Upon driving up to this structure, I was taken back by its size; it appeared to be almost a block long. It was an old, ugly, three-story brick building, built well before any earthquake building codes. It was in China Basin with water access opening onto the bay, convenient for unloading the trawlers.

After parking my car and walking up to the building, I immediately realized that nothing made sense—nothing. The office was in a separate three-story tower, not attached to the building, so obviously it was impossible to watch the operation from there.

Walking way around the outside of this massive structure, I finally reached the separate entrance to the production area and loading docks. I immediately noticed that floor-to-ceiling walls separated the work area into a myriad of small sections, which, again, did not make sense, but of course the building hadn't been designed for a wholesale seafood distribution operation. It was a haven for product theft since so many work areas were split up and not visible from any one location. I couldn't help but wonder why they didn't take them down, opening up the space and allowing it to be one large area.

Well, no one had come to work yet, and it was just before five in the morning. The thought occurred to me that they should have shown up by then.

It was now five in the morning and the men started walking in, then more men, then more men. I immediately thought, *Holy Christ! They can't be doing this kind of business to support this payroll!* It looked like a New York subway station. The first thing I noticed that got my blood flowing was that the men were supposed to "start" work at five, but were *showing up* at five, punching the time clock, then going up to the locker room and changing, and getting down to the production floor at least ten minutes or so later, then walking around without direction. Okay—this was bullshit!

I then counted 120 time cards. This was beyond belief! It took only a moment to figure out that 120 men times ten minutes each equaled 1,200 total minutes. That, divided by sixty minutes (an hour), equaled twenty hours. Twenty hours times $12.50 per hour (including benefits) equaled $250 per day that was being wasted. The men hadn't done a damn thing other than change their clothes. That should have been done on their own time, even by Union rules.

Now let's calculate it for a week: $250 times five days in a work week equals $1,250. Now let's do it for a month: $1,250 times four equals $5,000. Now, for a year: $5,000 times twelve equals $60,000 total wasted in one year. It's simple math. This was the approximate Union wage back in 1972; wages have more than doubled and tripled since then. This would be more than $120,000 per year by today's standards.

Payroll also has other factors when calculating its overall cost. For example, the city's 1 percent gross payroll tax, the Union pension and health plans, plus unemployment and social security benefits, to name just a few. The need for each employee, and hours worked, had to be carefully scrutinized. I'd only been there fifteen minutes and had saved over $60,000 a year—and I hadn't even gotten up to the office yet. *Oh boy, no one is going to like me! But I'm not here to make friends, I'm here to make money.*

The next day a notice was issued that stated "All production workers are to clock in *after* changing from their street clothes and report to work promptly at 5 a.m."

By the way, take note: If possible, employees should be paid on the first and fifteenth of every month. There are thirteen weeks in a quarter. An employee, if paid by the week, gains four weeks' additional pay by the end of the year. Again, I said *if possible*. Union drivers and packers are normally paid by the week, but other departments within a company may not be unionized. Many industries follow this payroll pattern. It is not intended to cheat the employee; it is just wise business practice.

This was my first day, my first few minutes, and I was already trembling, experiencing the absurdities I was witnessing. Meanwhile, I did start to feel that turning the company around could be easier than I'd first thought.

I stayed on the production floor and watched the operation set up; no one was rushing, of course. Why would they? There weren't many orders to pack to speak of, and there wouldn't be any more for at least another hour and a half when the salesmen arrived. Why were there no orders in the day before? I wondered. I found that strange.

The three salesmen eventually walked in at six thirty to start making their calls for that same day's delivery, but of course not until after making coffee and bullshitting with each other for a while. I also noticed there was a dart board in the sales office. Most likely my face would soon be the bull's eye after I start reorganizing things. But no worry, the dart board would be in the dumpster that afternoon.

I then asked myself—I had to; my two cousins weren't there yet to ask—why had they scheduled the men, especially the drivers, to come in so early when they hadn't much to do for at least another hour and a half? The drivers, consequently, will be on overtime making the deliveries in the late afternoon. I couldn't wait to get into this now. It was so simplistic.

I then walked to the main office tower, having to go back outside and all around the entire almost block length of the building, to then take a very slow elevator up to the third floor. Upon entering, I walked into a dimly lit, drab office environment. Papers were strewn all over the half dozen or so desks, obviously without organization.

When the bookkeeper came in at seven that morning, I asked her for the payroll records, then for the sales figures. I was shocked at what I saw. The sales damn near matched the payroll. What the hell?! Unless the profit margin was 200 percent-plus, this didn't make any sense. The average gross markup, or profit margin, for a wholesale seafood operation was 25 percent. It didn't take long to see why they were obviously losing so much money. This was unbelievable.

An amusing thing happened, and this is the God's truth: It was about eight in the morning, and I went back downstairs to watch the operation. Men were scrambling here, scrambling there, and all around the many partitioned walls. It was total chaos. Who in the hell knew where they were going or what they were doing, since you couldn't see them once they disappeared behind the floor-to-ceiling walls. I was now standing there in total disbelief, watching the confusion and multitude of men scurrying about. The thought then occurred to me that maybe they were trying to look busy since I was standing there. They must have heard by now about the takeover and the new management coming in.

While I watched and planned my next move and thought about how to knock down the many cement partitions to open up the cavernous room, my older cousin, the president at the time, (who I was replacing) walked up next to me and started babbling. He had never been so friendly. Yeah, well a couple of years too late. He was also kissing ass now! Anyway, I wasn't interested in what he had to say and wasn't listening being so focused on my thoughts. Suddenly, I noticed that he bent down, and it appeared as if he picked something up. I then asked, "What did you just do?" He stood up and held out his hand, then proudly exclaimed, "Look! A paper clip, a paper clip. You have to watch expenses!" Oh, my God! I damn near fell over! They had 120 men working on the floor, more than double, maybe triple what was needed, and he was picking up a fricking paper clip—and was proud of it! Wow, he'd just saved a fraction of a cent! Thousands of dollars a day were being wasted with over-employment in front of his very eyes, and all he saw was a rusty old paper clip.

What does that tell you? Was he really trying to impress me with such a nugatory display of—of what? This was one of the idiots who'd wanted me to unload the trawler way back when I'd first worked for the company. Remember? Well, I was his boss now, and what he didn't know was that he was one of the first to go on the chopping block!

Later that morning, I had to tackle the most important element: the accounts payable. I asked my new secretary to give me a list of the outstanding product payable. Past-due product was paramount, because if I couldn't make a deal with the product creditors, there would be no reason to continue; it would be over before we started.

It was indeed confirmed that they were indebted to the brokers and producers for $2.7 million. There was also a balance of close to half a million dollars for general expenses, such as back rent, boat and truck repairs, utilities, and the like. A total of $3.2 fricking million dollars. But hey, my cousin had just found a paper clip—that would help!

There was going to have to be two creditors meetings separating each faction, but it was paramount to meet with the product suppliers first.

I had my secretary call each supplier to see if they were available the next morning at ten for a meeting with me at the plant to postulate a payment plan. They all, of course, jumped at the chance to meet with me.

I then spent a sleepless night going over in my head how I was going to implement and present a proposal to the creditors, while hoping the investors intentions were indeed honorable, as they'd presented. That morning I thought of sitting on my grandfather's old wooden chest for confidence as my aunt had said, but hesitated, still not totally convinced of their integrity. That old wooden chest was special; it was my "paladin" (which isn't related to my last name; it means "a determined advocate or defender of a noble cause").

I got up the next morning at four, and as I drove to the plant, my gut wrenched. I stopped in at the Happy Donut Shop on the way, figuring it couldn't hurt to have a couple of happy donuts in me before the meeting. Well, it ended up being four happy donuts. I still wasn't happy.

Nervous but oddly confident about the outcome, I stayed up in my office that morning, turning my back on the disaster going on down on the production floor. If I couldn't implement a compromise-and-settlement agreement with the product creditors, that would be a minuscule problem. No product, no business. The investors would have to immediately come up with at least $3 million if the creditors turned me down. I then wondered for a moment why *they* hadn't called a meeting with the creditors before hiring me. I now questioned myself for not having thought of that before accepting the position.

Well, ten in the morning soon came. I was expecting at least thirty representatives from corresponding companies, but only eighteen showed up, explaining that the other companies had agreed to go along with any agreement they made.

They were anxious to meet this kid called "Kiki" who had just taken over this behemoth, who they'd speculated was to be the savior of the money they were owed.

I introduced myself to those I didn't know, and thanked them for their patience with the company since it was so many months in arrears. I went on to explain that the corporation was sold, and that the new owners had hired me to bring the company back to a profitable state. At first, I heard gasps upon hearing that the Paladini family had sold the company. I urged them to go along with my endeavor, and outlined that if they chose to throw the company into bankruptcy, they would get little or nothing.

I proposed that all the outstanding debt be frozen until new funds would be available, and explained who the new owners were, and more importantly, their affiliation with a major bank.

I further proposed that if they would continue to supply us with product, anything I bought—and repeated, anything *I* bought—they would be paid within seven days of invoice. I gave them my word that I would do so. This would then allow us to operate and give time for the funds to come in to start paying off the old balances.

I further explained that I had a cost-cutting plan in place to greatly reduce the operating expenses, and was going to soon bring the company down to just the frame and rebuild from there. They seemed excited to hear that, and I hoped that they respected my resoluteness.

There was, however, some hesitation among them, but after outlining and explaining the background of the investors, they all anxiously agreed. It was basically very simple. They had no choice but to accept it, and they all left with an upbeat attitude.

Breathing a sigh of relief, the four happy donuts I'd eaten earlier now felt like lead cannon balls in my stomach. But hey, they'd agreed. Yeah . . . but now I had to perform.

I immediately called Jesse and told him, and he was elated. Things were off to a good start.

The next morning, I called Tony, the production supervisor, into my office up in the tower. I asked him how many deliveries were being made per day, and he respectfully answered. I then asked him for the Union seniority list for the production staff. It did indeed total just over 120 men. I drew a line in the middle of the schedule and said, "Effective Friday after the day's completion, all the men under this line are laid off." I wanted to see how successfully we could operate with 50 percent of the staff. More than likely, many more were to be soon laid off, as well. This was just the first step in the cost-cutting reduction.

Tony looked at me in disbelief, but respectfully said, "But Mr. Paladini, we won't be able to operate with that few men." I then said, "How can you say that? There isn't enough business to support all these men. As far as the drivers, just double the deliveries on each truck. They aren't going out with that many stops. The order packers will just now have to move faster and not walk in circles." He then said, "B-b-b but, boss—" "That's it!" I answered.

The entire corporation was soon to go under a complete restructuring. My goal was to eliminate at least two-thirds of the workforce. They could always be re-hired, if need be. Eventual permanent employment would be predicated against sales. As sales increased, so would employment, but cautiously.

Next, I had a sales meeting. There were only three salesmen, or should I say, "order takers."

I'd noticed previously that they often shot darts and played cards in the afternoon while waiting for the phone to ring, which greatly disturbed me, but I'd kept my cool until this meeting. My skull cap damn near came off upon witnessing that.

The meeting started with my announcing that effective immediately, all, or at least most, orders would have to be in the day before. They pounced on me, claiming that was impossible since all the accounts called in during the morning hours. I then said, "Well, no more! There will be *no* more call-ins! You will start this very afternoon telling your customers that you will be calling them after lunch every day for the next day's delivery. Only one of you will arrive at six thirty in the morning to answer the phones, since there should be very few calls coming in for the same day delivery now." I then told them, "The other two of you will arrive at eight, giving you both an extra hour and a half in the afternoon to make calls for the next day's delivery." They moaned and groaned with dislike, still claiming it was impossible. Well, I knew differently.

I then asked them for the playing cards and promptly discarded them in the wastebasket, then tore the dart board off the wall as their glazed eyes gleamed at me with deceit. I was now labeled a bastard—that was just fine.

I also stated, "Each of you will be assigned a territory; the city, the Peninsula, the East Bay, and Marin. In the morning hours, since you will now have no or very few orders to write up, you will open the phone book and start calling accounts in your assigned areas to which we aren't selling." As an incentive, I said, "The person opening the most accounts will get a bonus at the end of the month." Meanwhile, I knew I was attempting to make just order-takers into extraordinary sales people. I knew I needed to find and hire those extraordinary salesmen if I was to get the sales increased quickly. I needed to steal the best from the competition. *Talent is critical to success!* I knew they were going to be costly, but their core competence and performance would be an unparalleled asset. It was going to take time to accomplish this, and time could be my nemesis, but there's no shortcut to success.

Another incentive I employed was that the sales person who sold the most frozen shellfish would also get an additional bonus. I said, "Sing this song after they order the fresh fish [yep, my same old song]: 'Thanks, chef, but how about the crabmeat, shrimpmeat, prawns, scallops, abalone, and clam meat for chowder?'" They scoffed at the thought, but after a few weeks of singing that song just before ending each call, sales started increasing dramatically. I then exercised random positive reinforcement as encouragement.

New accounts started flooding in, and most accounts liked being called in the afternoon, especially because they now got a much earlier delivery. And guess what? We were operating just fine with the crew now half in number of what it had been, and overtime had been almost eliminated since the trucks were now getting out hours earlier.

Tony was astonished that we could operate with half as many men. Well, of course. The orders were now starting to be packed at five in the morning because they were mostly in the day before. There was now no down-time for the guys to meander about. They were kept busy, especially since we had so many more orders to pack and they now had to move faster since there were half as many of them. I explained to the men that the drastic cutbacks were for our—their—survival. I do believe they respected that. They were also thankful they still had their jobs, I'm sure.

That's how you increase profit margins: by drastically reducing expenses and dramatically increasing sales in a parallel manner.

I now needed to find those extraordinary salesmen I mentioned, because *nothing happens until a sale is made!*

I soon took the best sales manager in the industry away from one of the competitors; also, the four best salesmen from several other competitors, one for each surrounding geographical area. I then let two of the three order-takers go, but kept my brother. Next, I cleaned out the accounting staff and hired a new controller and bookkeeper. I trained a new accounts receivable bookkeeper to watch the accounts receivables in the manner I chose. It was paramount to keep the accounts current if I was to pay the brokers weekly, as promised. I kept Tony, the production supervisor, because he impressed me with his faithfulness and had expressed a desire to learn.

The next big undertaking was to get rid of all the current management team. I started from the top, with the decision-makers. Now I was hitting the big boys: first the president, my oldest cousin—yep, the paper clip guy—and the vice president, also my cousin, who wasn't that bad, but followed in suit and did what he was told, then the so-called general manager and buyer.

That afternoon, I called them all into my office up in the tower and unabashedly announced, "I'm letting all three of you go, effective immediately." They were, of course, astonished, to say the least. They gasped and sat there in disbelief over what they'd just heard, blindly gazing out the cracked dirty office window stained with seagull dung—a fitting sight for the occasion.

The general manager and buyer, a tall, thin, middle-aged man, abruptly stood up and slammed his fist on my desk, and said, "I've been running this business for the past eight years. It was me, me, running everything—everything!" I guess he was proud of the job that he hadn't been doing very well. I then said, "Well, that's exactly why I'm letting you go!" I then stated, "Did any of you ever come upstairs and look at the books? The sales? The payroll? The P&L statement? The balance sheet? What about the accounts payable to see how fucking far in the arrears the company was?" I then calmly asked, "So let me ask you guys one simple question: Why did you have so many order packers on the production floor and so many drivers? Were any of you even remotely aware that the payroll almost matched the sales?!"

All three then stormed out...

Next, I tackled the six drag boats that were dragging the company down, to use a pun, with their horrendous expenses keeping them in operation, not to mention the insurance. We had no need for them now, since so many producers on the Pacific Coast had recently gone into business to supply the distributors. This was in sharp contrast to my grandfather's days, when you also needed to be a producer of your local fresh products. We could now buy the product already filleted, packed and delivered to us cheaper than what we could have produced it for. We would also know our exact cost. The business had to return to basics and be simplistic, with defined product cost without anything eluding the true cost.

All the boats were soon sold at auction, not only eliminating a tremendous cost factor, but resulting in additional funds for cash flow. I heard that the family, upon hearing this, was appalled and aghast. Most likely, that was only due to vanity, since each boat was named after a family member. They loved eating at Scoma's on the wharf so they could look out the window and see the Paladini trawlers tied up nearby with their first names boldly displayed. Meanwhile, when a boat was tied up, that meant it wasn't working. It was then a costly non-producing expenditure.

Next, I closed the Eureka production plant, ridding us of forty-five employees, plus the on-site manager. The plant had been losing money for years, and there was especially no need for it without the company-owned trawlers. The State of California was in an outrage at my ceasing the lease years before it was up, so I simply told them there was no money to pay the rent. Meanwhile, being aware that I needed a receiving station in Eureka for Dungeness crabs and Chinook salmon for the smokehouse, I used the bargaining ploy of agreeing to keep just the receiving station. It worked! The Crescent City receiving station was also needed for crabs and salmon, so I kept that lease intact as well. I then needed to cease the leases that were still in force with the remaining four receiving stations along the coast. Of course, the state refused. So, I refused to pay. They agreed.

All the production plants and receiving stations had permanent managers on the payroll, whether in operation or not. Due to inclement weather, which was the case most of the time, the operations were shut down, and the managers were in the local bar playing pool.

I kept one production plant, located in Fort Bragg, California. It was also a receiving station, primarily for the producing and packing of the Paladini label of fresh local fish fillets, Dungeness crabs and crabmeat, local shrimpmeat, and for the freezing of Chinook/King salmon for the smokehouse.

All the raw products were now bought from individual privately owned boats. They took the brunt of the expenses.

Now that the overall operating costs were properly in place, we could be competitive with the industry norm of a 25 percent mark-up, and make a proper profit.

The company's entire overhead had now been reduced by the projected two-thirds, and the archaic business practices ceased. The rest should be easy: just bring in new business.

Each facet of the industry is a business within itself: boats, receiving stations, production plants, and wholesale distribution. These individual facets of the industry can, and do, work together, and in most cases allow for greater profits, since you have several tiered profit centers. That concept is certainly true, but there must be tremendous volume to support them. And they must be controlled—I repeat—they must be controlled. It is also understandable that once these operations are in place, it is easy to become complacent, especially over the years.

We would now concentrate on being just a wholesale distributor, and that's where the money is.

A few weeks had passed, and I noticed I was always walking around this huge contraption of some sort that was in the middle of the production floor. I asked Tony, "What the hell is this thing?" He replied, "An IQF [individually quick frozen] machine, boss." I then asked him, "How often do you use it?" He said, "Not often, not often at all. I can't remember the last time we did." "Then why did they get it?" I asked. He replied, "Because supposedly it freezes the fillets individually and quickly. It's also leased." I responded, "But we have a production plant in Fort Bragg. This is not only counterproductive, it's ridiculous." He then replied, "I know, boss."

I then went up to the office and looked up the lease payment. It was $1,500 a month. This was in 1972. I called the company that held the lease and introduced myself, then said, "Please pick it up today, this afternoon." They boldly responded, "Well, Mr. Paladini, your cousins signed a three-year lease and there's eighteen months left on the lease, and the lease can't be broken." I then calmly replied, "Well, I'm not paying for it any longer, so pick it up or I'll put it out in the parking lot in the morning." They picked it up the very next day, and that saved a previously wasted $1,500 a month, $18,000 a year.

I had been curious all this while what the lease payment was on the San Francisco distribution building—the behemoth, as I referred to it—but being preoccupied delving into production costs, I hadn't gotten around to it. Today was the day. I asked my controller what the monthly lease payment was on the building and he said, "It's $10,500 a month, Mr. P." That was complete insanity! (Again, in 1972.) The building was way too expensive and way too large, being three stories; the top two stories were a complete waste, especially since the lease was predicated on square footage. I then got on the phone and called the city port authority since the property sat on water frontage, and asked for whoever handled the property leases. After introducing myself, I said, "We must renegotiate the rent down—and down drastically." He abruptly and rudely said, "Absolutely not! The previous management signed a ten-year binding lease." I then said, "Well, let me advise you of something: The company can't afford it, and if I bankrupt the company, you'll have a huge empty building. It's your choice." And I hung up. Well, he called back a few hours later and we then went back and forth, with my wanting a 50 percent reduction while they were only willing to give a 10 percent reduction. We finally agreed on a 33 percent reduction, down to $7,000 a month, which would save another $3,500 a month and $42,000 a year. The rent was still too high, but I was in no position to move the business.

I then asked if I could take down a few of the cement partitions that were separating the bottom floor, and he said I could if the cement partitions weren't supporting beams.

I no sooner hung up and grabbed Tony, and we both got onto two fork lifts and started slamming the solid lead backs of the fork lifts, repeatedly and repeatedly, into each partition until it fell to the ground with a thunderous, deafening sound. One came down, then the second, then the third. The floor was now strewn with concrete slabs, and we had one hell of a mess on our hands, but we were overjoyed with the results, now having one large open area. There was now no place for anyone to hide and procrastinate. No, I had no clue if any were supporting beams!

The next challenge was a sensitive one. The smokehouse. It was run by a very likable gentleman by the name of Johnny Messina, but he was operating his department as if it were a separate company. They did their own billing, packed their own orders, and made their own deliveries, and most often to the same accounts. I had a meeting with Johnny and told him as of Monday the smokehouse invoicing and packing of orders would be done by the main production staff, and his deliveries would go on the same trucks as the ones making the fish deliveries. This eliminated the cost of making double deliveries to the same accounts. It also eliminated two packers and two drivers. However, I was greeted with great resistance. I knew he was angry; the famed Paladini Smoked Salmon was his baby; the product was the best in the nation, and he was the best in the business, and was very proud of the product, as was I, but it was ridiculous and too costly to duplicate expenses.

Most middle management don't realize, or possibly even care, about the expense of an employee, even one employee; it's much more than just their wages. My intention, of course, was not to eliminate the prudently trained men, or the age-old formula crucial to the product, but to just eliminate the unnecessary labor involved with it. The company had been operating like this for over fifty years. I asked him why. There was silence.

Well, after daily confrontations with him for the rest of the week, and my not backing off, the plan went into effect that Monday. It ended up working out perfectly, of course. Not one customer complained, and better yet, even noticed any difference. I sold two trucks and laid off two drivers and two packers.

I then insisted that the "hand-sliced" smoked salmon not be cut into perfect squares, as he was doing. This created one hell of an excessive amount of smoked-salmon trim, which would then be sold at one-fifth the price. He claimed the chefs wanted a perfect square to put on crackers and bread. I furthermore explained that besides producing so much trim, cutting it into perfect squares made it appear as if it had been sliced by a machine. Well, he fought me tooth and nail on it. I thought he was going to quit, but again held my ground, stating that the chefs would just have to absorb the cost of trimming it themselves. I also suggested he tell the chefs they could make smoked-salmon mousse with their trimmings, if indeed they were to cut it into squares, as he said they wanted.

As he was doing, the excessive trimmings were constantly backing up, resulting in the need for it to be sold to the Safeway Stores at a drastically reduced price; a fifth of the price of the hand-sliced that sold for $18.75 a pound at the time. The trim sold for $3.75 a pound. The monthly accumulation was approximately five hundred pounds. Do the math: a fifteen-dollar-a-pound difference times five hundred pounds equals $7,500 a month—times twelve months, that's $90,000 a year.

A month later, Johnny reluctantly came into my office and said his department's profit margin had surprisingly increased drastically due to that one little change, and more importantly, not one chef had complained. Why had he doubted the kid?

It can often be so simple, and often so obvious, how well-thought-out cost reductions can greatly increase your net earnings. Regardless of the industry, there are always factions to reduce costs if you conceptualize and thoroughly analyze your operation.

A simple one I have always used: When an employee went on vacation or took extensive sick leave, and if we were able to operate comfortably without him or her, that position would be eliminated and absorbed by others. Just because you have chairs in an office doesn't mean they have to be sat upon!

Now here's a management story, and somewhat humorous, but with a moral to it: A sales rep, an administration clerk, and the manager are walking to lunch when they find an antique oil lamp. They rub it and a genie comes out. The genie says, "I'll give each of you just one wish." "Me first! Me first!" says the admin clerk. "I want to be in the Bahamas driving a speedboat without a care in the world." Puff! She's gone. "Me next! Me next!" says the sales rep. "I want to be in Hawaii relaxing on the beach with my personal masseuse, have an endless supply of piña coladas, and be with the love of my life." Puff! He's gone. "All right, you're up," the genie says to the manager. The manager says, "I want those two back in the office right after lunch."

Moral of the story: Always let the boss have the first say!

Three months had now passed, and I received the first quarterly P&L statement. It showed a 25.5 percent gross profit and a 3.25 percent net profit—right on target for the industry. The corporation had made money for the first time in over ten years. Meanwhile, having to pay for the product in seven days as I had promised was a Herculean task while waiting for funding. I was, of course, very pleased with the P&L. It gave me the perseverance to continue, and now set the goal to be number one in the industry again—but was still far from it.

I suffer from "HAS"—High Achievement Syndrome. Unfortunately, I expect the same from my employees, which can make the work atmosphere tense.

Yes, things were going well with the job, but my promise to spend more time with my family wasn't happening since I was so consumed with the business. This concerned me, and time was moving on. What also was starting to be a concern was that *no* money had yet come in to make payments on the old debt, and it was now approaching six months. The only cash flow that was generated was from the increased sales and the reduction of the operating costs, plus by attentively watching the accounts receivables. This allowed me to stay current for what product I bought, as promised. But it was getting increasingly more difficult every month as new business came in, with most accounts wanting thirty-day terms. You can't pay for your product in seven days and extend thirty-day terms—simple logic. I never thought it would take this long for the funding process. There always seemed to be an excuse for why the funds hadn't come in yet. They were very convincing with their seemingly evasive rationalizations.

Something else also took place about this time that greatly disturbed and alarmed me. Jesse brought three hook-and-line black-cod boats that he evidently was building and tied them up to the pier at the plant. That was okay, at first; there was no cost in doing so, but I wondered why he was getting involved with this factor of the industry. He didn't know shit about the fish business—that's why he hired me. What was this all about? I wondered.

What put me over the edge was when I learned that one Friday he'd gone up to the tower office and had taken some of my weekly cash flow and paid the expenses for *his* black-cod boats. He didn't ask; he just did it. This was bullshit. But more importantly, *why?* Something was "fishy."

What the hell was going on? He knew I needed that cash flow to buy product. There must have been an explanation. Maybe it would be returned shortly into the company's account, I hoped.

I asked Jesse what the black-cod boats were doing there and he said, "This way you will have all the black cod you need." I replied—no, shouted—"I don't need any fucking black cod! I need money, Jesse! What the hell are you thinking?!" Hook-and-line black cod was a very small-volume item and used only for the smokehouse for kippered cod, and I bought just what we needed each week. The amount was minuscule. I then asked that he replace the funds he took from the cash flow. He then promptly did. The reason for the boats being there, however, remained a mystery.

Meanwhile, I was starting to become confused and disillusioned with him, now thinking maybe Joan had been right. I asked her that evening what she'd meant when she called Jesse a "tap dancer." She said, "He dances around. He's not serious. He's a phony!" *Oh, shit*, I thought. *She's mostly right with her feelings. Is he really a phony? But why? Why?*

Suddenly I had a flashback to when I'd been the manager of the last operation in Oakland and I was questioned about beating the percentages of their San Francisco plant. Were these men just wanting tax shelters? Did they not want to make money, but shelter other income? Was I being used again?

Just possibly, these allegedly smart, intellectual businessmen had thought it was totally inconceivable to turn the company around, and they were now in a quandary with it being profitable. Yes, we were making money, but it wasn't a huge amount yet; we still needed to increase sales even more. Having said that, I needed the funding to carry the new accounts. It made it extremely difficult to bring in new business and pay my bills in time without it. Sort of a vicious circle! Maybe that was why the black-cod boats entered into the equation: to increase expenses to destroy my progress. Was this takeover of the corporation just a ploy to reduce their income taxes on other profitable investments by showing a loss with this operation? After all, they'd bought the entire company for only seven dollars. What a perfect set up, I started thinking.

The thought haunted me. It was difficult to put aside. I now started having legitimate concerns regarding what moves he might possibly make next.

Regarding cash flow: When structuring or restructuring a business and dramatically increasing sales, you should have a cash reserve in place. When increasing sales at a normal, slower pace, it is not as dire; the cash flow usually works out if percentages are maintained. If a new account purchases $1,000 per month, it is estimated that the turnaround time to receive payment will be approximately forty-five days. Restaurants' average turnaround was fifty to fifty-five days at the time—not good, but an accepted industry practice. Consequently, you need $1,125 in reserve to pay for what you bought payable in thirty days, normal payment terms for an established wholesale operation.

The formula works as follows: Product cost is $750. Required gross operating markup is 25 percent from sales price, so $750 times 33.33 equals $250 (gross profit), equals the $1,000 sale. One-and-one-half times the $750 (product cost) equals $1,125 needed to carry the new account for a month and a half, allowing for the normal cash flow, plus the reserve to pay your creditor in time.

I obviously was very aware of this—I just explained it. Meanwhile, in my extraordinary situation, I was paying for all the product I bought as I had agreed to and promised within seven days, an extremely difficult task to continue for very long while increasing sales without any reserve funds.

This was a monumental and exhausting task, playing manipulation with the cash flow.

I recalled, as discussed during the interview with Jesse up in Mendocino several months ago, to quote him, "Insurmountable funds would be available soon after taking over." If you'll remember, he'd said at the time, "Management is no good without money, and money is no good without management." *Where in the hell is the money, Jesse? I'm the management, you're supposedly the money?!*

I had been operating the business with mirrors, and now had enigmatic thoughts about the intentions of the investors. I now had to act on my own, using whatever resources and knowledge that I possessed. I instructed my sales manager to concentrate in getting the Safeway Stores and the Lucky Markets and other chain stores that paid promptly within seven days to assist the ailing cash flow. My sales manager and I met with the Safeway buyer that very week, and fortunately he agreed to try us out in a few stores; a few stores to him meant seventy-five. We also met with the Lucky Markets and were given half of the stores immediately. That was another 127.

Thankfully, after only two weeks, Safeway was pleased, and we were now selling to all 237 stores, thus greatly facilitating the cash flow. But it only helped—it didn't cure the ever-increasing need for funds, since the restaurants and hotels paid so much slower.

Let me advise, in an ideal situation, *Never allow a single account to exceed one-fourth of your total gross sales.* So often companies rely on a single account to cover their expenses, and in some cases, expand due to the newly increased sales volume realized from that single account. That is a gross error in the fundamental of business. If you suddenly lose that single voluminous account, you will suffer urgent and crucial consequences. Because to expeditiously reduce expenses to offset the loss of those sales, can be exceedingly difficult, especially if you have long-term leases on trucks, equipment, and properties.

Attempt to have a well-rounded client base. In the meantime, yes, of course, enjoy that single large account, but don't rely on them, and don't depend on them, because most likely they won't stay with you at length. Buyers change, companies sell, procedures change. A myriad of conditions could prevail.

CHAPTER 21
FEELING VULNERABLE

I suddenly realized the need to get away from all this business crap and enjoy my wife and daughters that I'd so ignored during all the fiasco.

To be the father of growing daughters is to experience something of beauty. Nothing could make me so happy and exhilarated, yet so frightened. It is a solid lesson in the limitations of oneself to realize your heart abounds in their bodies. It also makes me quite astonishingly calm at the thought that I would die to protect them. That would not be a lugubrious act, but one of a father's devout love.

That Friday night, I insisted we spend the weekend just doing fun things together. Joan and the girls were overjoyed. After my breakfast of "eggs in a frame," made specially for me by Laura, the chef de cuisine, we hopped into our little red Ford Pinto station wagon and took a ride into the Marin countryside toward the coast. It was a beautiful, bright, warm summer day, with not a cloud in the sky.

We stopped in Bolinas for lunch, a little quaint town approaching the coastline. Many of the residents were left over from the days of the famed Haight-Ashbury in the city, and the distinct aroma of hallucinogenic drugs was ever apparent in the air. Everyone was notably happy and carefree—of course. We entered a small, ramshackle cafe that beckoned us in with a tie-dyed flag displaying the peace sign over the entrance. We sat in the back patio at an old wood table with open knot holes surrounded with burn marks, apparently to flick your ashes on the floor, then douse your joint. A brightly colored umbrella shielded us from the sun while the intermittent breeze coming in from the nearby fog-laden coast cooled us to the extent of occasionally wanting our jackets.

Joan and the girls were fascinated watching the array of strange—at least strange to us—long-haired bearded men and the scantily clad young women, who were sitting nearby, zoned out in trance-like states. An obviously bra-less girl with kinky hair from lack of washing, who was most likely high on Maui Wowie or Panama Red, sat on a stool in the corner, softly playing a guitar, its melody haunting and repetitive, while we snacked on our nachos and salsa and waited for lunch. I swear I saw Gina out of the side of my eye trying to wave in some of the pot smoke that abounded throughout the room into her nostrils, though she denied it! I also had to shush my girls several times, pulling down their hands, as they pointed at more than one anomalous couple portraying rather bizarre behavior.

As I sat there relaxing in this eccentric atmosphere, I was so enjoying every moment being with them. Their outgoing personalities and clever wit commanded all my attention, and I was having a lot of fun. I was also very proud of my family, even though a bit snobbish. Wonder where that came from? I then thought, *They are who and why I'm working so damn hard, and yet in doing so, wonderful times like this are too infrequent. Somehow, I must make the time. I'm too involved, trying to be successful, and in the process, the kids are rapidly growing up before my very eyes and will soon be off to college and have lives of their own. They must be my priority now, before it's too late.*

After lunch, we took a walk and found a field blanketed with a variety of wild flowers in an amazing array of vivid colors. The kids ran through the field, brushing the flowers with their hands as they happily played. I stopped for a moment and took a flower and caressed it in my hand. What a magnificent specimen of nature it was. While looking at this wondrous creation, I suddenly realized the paramount necessity of appreciating the free, God-given things in life, and sharing them with my family. Not just concentrate on worldly goods and accomplishments, as I had been.

However, the damn drive to better myself, still beheld me. Yes, I just experienced the realization of enjoying the free beauty of nature with my family, but also wanted to provide for them the very best I could. That didn't necessarily mean giving them possessions but wanted them in a good environment during their formative years.

Coincidently, around this same time, Mr. Bertrano—yes, Jesse the tap dancer—came up to me one morning all excited and said, "Hey, ole' buddy [grrr], I know you've been discouraged with no money coming in, but you're going to be very happy to know that I have a plan in place that will soon allow you all the cash flow you'll ever need!" I then replied, "So just what is this so-called plan?" He then said, "You'll soon see!"

Pleased to finally hear this, I suggested to Joan that I felt we could now move as I wanted to, possibly to a nice area down the Peninsula, explaining that the money was finally coming in and things were going to be great!

Now putting the stress and annoyances of the business aside, since the investors were finally stepping up and funding the company, the following Sunday we took a ride down the Peninsula and looked for a home. After spending most of the day looking for open homes in Burlingame and San Mateo, we were becoming increasingly discouraged. The homes were either too old, unattractive, or unaffordable. About to give up and return home, we drove around a little more and found a home under construction way up on a hill, in the appropriately called town of Hillsborough. The home was just being framed, so we were able to walk around in it. We loved the floor plan. There were four bedrooms on the second floor, with plenty of expanse for the kids as teenagers. We all loved it, though at the time it looked like it had been dropped by a helicopter, given the lack of landscaping and no fencing; just a big house plopped on an acre-and-a-half parcel of land.

We got the phone number for the realtor that represented the builder from the sign in front, met with the agent late that same afternoon, and signed a purchase agreement contingent on the sale of our home in Marin. I knew I had the business turned around and the money from the investors was finally coming in. I now assumed the delay was just possibly a conservative financial move, and the affordability of our new home was not an issue since my position should be secure and the future bright.

We were all really excited about moving down to the Peninsula into this plush country community. The construction of the home would be completed in about two months, so we promptly put our home in San Rafael up for sale.

The following week, I approached Jesse and asked him again, "When are the funds coming in? You said last week that you had a plan. The creditors are asking for a payment on the old balance." He jokingly replied in his usual irritating way, "Don't worry, ole' buddy, my partner and I just talked, and it's coming." I looked at him and said, "The creditors and I are running out of time and patience. It better be. I just bought a new home."

Another month passed, and still no funds. Now aggravated, disgusted, and starting not to believe anything he said, I called his partner at the bank and said I wanted to meet with him. He reluctantly agreed, but only after I was insistent and almost indignant.

We met the following day, and after the usual formal BS pleasantries, I emphatically expressed my concern regarding the fact that no funds had come into the company yet, and stated that my cash flow was alarmingly tight. More importantly, I was now being pressured by the creditors for payment on the old balance. I further asked why it was taking so long, especially with his position with the bank, and that I found the delay curiously aberrant.

He promptly and acrimoniously dismissed my questioning his position with the bank and the fact that it had taken so long. He then mentioned that Jesse already had a plan in place for funding. Nonetheless, he never went into detail exactly *what* the plan was. It was never made clear if the funds—which had to be in the millions of dollars—would be their personal funds or borrowed, and if so, presumably borrowed from the bank at which he held a prominent position. Possibly I should have asked, but he appeared to be sincere, and I wanted to believe him. I also felt it would be impolite to question him further. My mom raised me to be a gentleman.

I then asked what he knew about the hook-and-line black-cod boats that Jesse was building and had tied up at the dock near the plant. He replied while chuckling, "Oh, he's just having fun. He's something else, isn't he?" Then he stood, shook my hand, and flippantly said, "Oh, by the way, excellent job you're doing, Kiki. Nice seeing you again." I took that as a dismissal.

I walked out totally disgruntled, thinking of his comments regarding Jesse: "Oh, he's just having fun. He's something else, isn't he?" What the fuck did that mean? I now sensed that their intentions were incongruous to what they originally presented me with. They were demonstrating strange behavior. Something was amiss. Something wasn't feeling right, but I was in this mess now, and couldn't just take off and turn my back on the creditors and the employees who'd been working so hard for me. I was in one hell of a mess.

Within that week, Jesse came up to me and said, "Okay, ole buddy, this is the beginning of the influx of the funds for you, the plan that I told you was coming. I formed a holding company." "You formed a what?" I asked. He replied, "A holding company. It's called JAYCO." "What the hell does JAYCO stand for?" I asked. He replied, "JAY is for the J in Jesse, then CO for company." I didn't really care what the hell it was called. I didn't understand what he was doing, or why, and my first reaction was that I didn't like it—I didn't like it one bit. I then asked, "Okay, you formed a holding company, but that doesn't provide funding." He replied, "Funds will be now be advanced to JAYCO for anything you buy." I then asked, "Is this your and Mr. Signet's personal money or borrowed?" He avoided the question by changing the subject. I insisted in knowing and asked again. He finally replied, "Borrowed." "From Mr. Signet's bank?" I asked. I received no reply.

At the time, I didn't care where in the hell the funds were coming from, as long as they were coming—finally.

When I had some time to myself, I then thought and thought about this holding company setup. *Maybe there's something I don't understand about financing, but I doubt it. Hmm . . . why did they need financing? Where's their money? Well, maybe it's okay if they are borrowing it, especially if it's from Signet's bank, and at a good rate, even though that puts us further in debt. Borrowed money isn't free.* In the meantime, my head was spinning and filled with daily operational problems, so I didn't question it further, assuming this was what and how investors—or so-called money-men—did it. Maybe they just don't use their own money. That may be wise.

The question still stuck in the back of my mind, however, why he'd formed this holding company. Why couldn't the funds be advanced directly to Paladini? I wondered. This appeared to be an avoidance, a diversion. I didn't like this new JAYCO concept.

Jesse then told me to have the brokers and the producers charge JAYCO for anything I bought from now on. I asked, "Why? They know me—Kiki Paladini—not this goddamn JAYCO thing." He hesitated. I asked again, "Why?" He walked away. I felt a big hole was being dug at that point.

Days later, with my insisting that he answer, he shockingly told me that he had factored the accounts receivable, and JAYCO was the way of tracking it! Well, that was big time bullshit! I was only in my thirties, but I knew what factoring accounts receivable meant, and his forming a holding company released him and his partner from financial responsibility—it's a third-party involvement. Then, as the old expression goes, a light bulb came on. The factoring company he'd mentioned was the same one that factored the accounts receivable for the old Paladini company. They must have proposed that these two men take over Paladini. What the hell was going on here? They never had any intention of putting their own money into the company, and also had no intention of personally borrowing or taking any responsibility for it.

I immediately knew I was in trouble. Factoring is the last resort! Like hospice for the dying.

This was way too convoluted now, and against my basic, simplistic, straight-forward approach to running a business. Why had they taken over the business? Why? Was I now involved with another goddamn tax shelter scheme? The thought then came to mind that Jesse bringing the black-cod boats over and attempting to take substantial funds from my cash flow for their construction was an intentional move to erode my ability to continue to persevere in sustaining profitability. Well, thankfully, I was able to circumvent that cagy maneuver. It must have been a counteractive move to cause a stalemate, to stall me. Maybe they hadn't thought the company could ever be profitable, assuming it was too far gone, and the feat was unattainable. In one way, I guess that could have been a latent compliment—that the company had been turned around and was now profitable—and on the other hand, in doing so, I'd dug my own grave, and possibly those of the creditors that had had faith in me.

Allow me to *very* briefly explain the factoring concept: Factoring simply involves accounts receivable funding. Having said that, it is anything but simple. The application and calculations used to determine the weekly precise sum to fund is extremely convoluted and time consuming for accountants. Using accounts receivable factoring improperly, or choosing the wrong funding source, could literally cripple a company. It is in fact a transaction whereby a business sells its accounts receivable to a third party at a discount. Thus, further eroding your net profit, that you most likely weren't appreciating in the first place. That is why it is a death spiral.

Factoring differs from a bank loan, since the emphasis is on the value of the receivables, essentially a financial asset.

This absurd so-called funding plan, as Jesse captioned it, was a sham to falsely elasticize the cash flow to give me the impression of a cash influx. He didn't fool me. I just now needed time to figure out how to gracefully get out of this mess and try to pay the creditors for what I'd bought.

I was devastated; these guys were both con men. They either really had no money, or had too much and wanted a tax shelter. They were supposedly both smart men. I guess I had been the stupid one. My thought process had most likely been foolishly clouded with the desire to save the goddamn name. Pride and vainglorious superciliousness had gotten the best of me—again.

Now infuriated, I called Jim Signet at his office. His haughty secretary told me he was busy. I said, "I'll wait." I hate to wait, especially when agitated. I needed to talk with him—now.

When he came to the phone, I screamed at him and asked why they'd bought Paladini; why they'd taken me from a comfortable, secure position and put me in this mess. Was it because their only out-of-pocket expense had been seven fucking dollars? "What about the contract with the family obliging you to pay the past due bills? That's why they sold it to you—excuse me, *gave* it to you. They wanted to avoid bankruptcy. And now you're calling factoring the accounts receivables your way of funding the company." I wasn't giving him time to talk. I knew it was going to be bullshit anyway. I then hung up.

That evening, Jesse called me at home, wanting to take me out to lunch at the Commercial Club the next day with Jim. I'm sure their intention was to attempt to dilute my thinking that they were indeed honorable. I said, "I'll have lunch with you both when you put earnest money into the business as agreed, and I'll pay for my own lunch."

Our relationship was now strained, to say the least. I was only thirty-five, but felt like a fossilized diatom. The arduous task of holding the business together for almost two years with having to juggle what little funds I had was exhausting. Business was still increasing, and more backup funds were desperately needed to carry the accounts, not to mention paying the creditors on the old balance. I felt as if we were now a vaudeville act; Jesse was the tap dancer and I was the juggler. However, there would be no encore for this act.

It was a living hellish nightmare. But I never let it be known to my family. I didn't want to concern them and didn't want to admit to Joan that she'd been right all along . . . at least not yet.

Too bad, we'd almost been on the verge of being number one again, and the Paladini trucks were once again seen all over Northern California. Sure, I was proud, but at the same time, exceedingly worried about the near future of the company, as well as my future and my family's future. I couldn't hold it together much longer under the foreseen circumstances. I knew that if the factoring was the only source of funding to come, the company was doomed. I was probably the only one who knew, because it now appeared to be a successful operation.

I had appreciatively gained the respect from the employees, brokers, and the producers, but at the same time, the creditors were fervently insisting for payment, or at least a payment, on the old debt. After all, I had been stalling them for almost two years now. It was gnawing at me.

The newly implemented factoring of the receivables now made it impossible to attain any additional funds to even attempt to pay them, since every Friday I had to fill out a sheet of purchases made for that week that were to be paid on the following Monday, and only those invoices would be paid. As a matter of fact, if there was indeed any excess cash flow that was generated, it would have been needed to upgrade the now-aging trucks and equipment. Simple math outlined a blueprint for an impossible solving equation.

The factoring also took away my once successful control of the cash flow. Jesse now had the control since he'd hired the factoring company and could do whatever he liked.

During this chaotic and stressful time, we fortunately sold our home in San Rafael and soon had to move. Our Hillsborough home's completion date had been delayed due to weather for a few weeks, so my sister Kay and her husband kindly invited us to stay with them in San Mateo until it was completed. My mom had been living with them ever since my dad had died years ago. She had had several strokes by now and was bed ridden. It was such a heartache to see her in that condition. While living in Marin, I would drive down to San Mateo from the city after work as often as I could to see her.

I recall sitting at her bedside holding her hand. There were times she couldn't speak, but looked at me with such tender love while attempting to squeeze my hand to let me know she knew I was there. She was often confused, wondering why she couldn't express herself. With her now living in the cloistered world of her bedroom, life's adventures were limited to doctor visits and those few who stopped in to see her.,

Leaving was always difficult. Letting go of her hand tugged at my heart, not knowing if it would be the last time, I would hold it. While attempting to release my grasp, she would hold on tighter, as if not wanting me to leave her . . . ever. Here was this woman, who'd given six children their lives, and hers was about to cease. I couldn't imagine life without her. She gave the world her presence of purity and innocence and asked so little in return. If ever there was an angel, it was her, Jennie, my wonderful mom.

It was bittersweet when we eventually moved in with my sister; sweet, being with my mom and sister, and to some extent, a trace bitter, living with my brother-in-law, Kay's often cranky, contentious husband. We found it very cozy living there. There was my sister, her husband, their son, and my mother, plus Joan, Laura, Gina, Diana, and myself, and our two dogs, and their two dogs. Did I mention this was just a three-bedroom house? Fortunately, the downstairs den area where we lived was quite large, and our four beds fit, though tightly. We all lived in one room, and I snore when tired—and I was always tired. The poor kids.

While living with my sister and her husband, I heard that Jesse was up the coast in Eureka. The commercial Dungeness crab season had just started north of the Sonoma-Mendocino County line; it was December 1. I had no clue as to why he was up there, and really didn't care. He was out of my hair, and we weren't talking anyway.

During this time, the factoring that he'd set up had greatly inhibited my buying. No one liked it, neither me, nor the brokers. They had faith in selling me, as me—Kiki Paladini—not to this JAYCO entity. I was constantly being asked why it had to be that way and had to double talk so as not to divulge my disdain for it as well. I had to wear two faces: one of accepting it in front of the brokers, only because I had to, and the other, of contempt and disparagement for it.

I must advise so you will understand the sequence of events that follow: My brother-in-law had a small seafood brokerage, mainly selling fresh farm-raised Rainbow trout from Idaho to the seafood distributors in the Bay Area, but during the Dungeness crab season, he also represented a producer of Dungeness crabs. Their facility was near the Oregon border. I bought all our fresh trout from him, and occasionally if our production of crabs was insufficient, I would fill in and purchase crabs from him as well.

Keep in mind, when purchasing fresh seafood products of any sort under such monetary constraints, as well as the need to keep the product fresh, there was an extremely delicate balance of buying only what you could afford and what you could sell in the next few days, and no more.

Well, one evening when I arrived at my sister's house, my brother-in-law said he heard rumbles that Jesse had been talking with the crab fishermen's association in Eureka. I was taken back and of course, shocked!

So, the next morning I called Jesse in Eureka. I found that he was staying at the Eureka Inn, an expensive Elizabethan Tudor-style hotel built in 1922, the only rather swanky hotel in the small town. Of course, the first thought that came to mind was that he'd better not put in an expense chit for it. Well, upon his coming to the phone, and without my saying hello, I asked him, "So what the hell are you doing up there, Jesse?!" Now sounding like he was in defense mode, he annoyingly attempted to verbally fondle me, as he so often did, and tried to dance his way around directly answering the question. Meanwhile, during our brief conversation he mentioned that he was checking out black-cod boats. Still not understanding his fascination with them, nor caring, I then directly asked him if he'd been talking to the crab fishermen's association for any reason. He then laughed and said, "You know me, I like to learn about everything and was curious how they set the prices, since the season just opened." I then asked, "So that's all?"

Well, at least he had satisfied my curiosity. I dismissed it since he had a few of his absurd black-cod boats in San Francisco that he was supposedly playing with. Of course, none of this made any sense to me, since he'd never been in the seafood industry and had always been a chief financial officer, but I was too busy to be concerned with it.

Well, the very next evening when I walked into my sister's house, my brother-in-law was obviously very upset and exceedingly furious about something, but I didn't think much of it since it was somewhat his usual demeanor. Then within just a few minutes of my arriving, he blatantly confronted me with intense, vehement condemnation, and shouted at me, "You're living in my fucking house and raping my income by buying all the goddamn crabs on the West Coast, leaving me with no sales for commission!"

Shocked by his comment, I then said, "What the hell are you talking about?" He replied in his not-so-respectful manner, "Don't goddamn tell me that you don't know that your boss just signed a market order to buy *all* the fucking crabs on the entire West Coast at ten cents a pound over the originally agreed market order!"

Let me take a minute to explain. The recovery from a whole raw Dungeness crab to crab meat is approximately 25 percent, could be less, thus every penny must be multiplied by four as a cost basis for the meat. A ten-cent-per-pound increase in the raw product cost was extremely disproportionate. This was back in 1974 when whole Dungeness crabs were selling retail for ninety-nine cents per pound, so an additional ten cents in correlation was huge.

Jesse naturally had no clue of this, nor I'm sure cared. He was out of the realm and boundaries of his knowledge. In the meantime, it came to mind that there could be other factors as to why he was doing this.

Well, my brother-in-law wouldn't believe that I knew nothing about it and was obviously extremely furious with me, to say the least. I further tried to explain that he was surely aware of my cash flow problems and was struggling to pay everyone on time, so why in the hell would I agree to venture out and buy so many crabs each week when I could only sell so few? That thought process was insane! I further tried to explain to him that I needed a full rounded inventory, not just crabs. Having said that, I don't think he believed me. Indeed, he must have felt I was living in his home and was extorting him of his income. Yes, it was tense. No, I didn't eat dinner.

The very next morning, three tractor trailer loads with over thirty-thousand pounds in each truck pulled up to the San Francisco plant—almost a hundred thousand pounds.

This tonnage was enough to supply all the wholesalers in the Bay Area for several days. I then called Jesse and screamed at him, asking what in the fucking hell was he was doing? Then asked what he wanted to do with the excess of ninety thousand pounds. Obviously unconcerned, he then laughed, and seemingly proud, said—if you can believe this— "Ole' buddy, we have all the crabs on the West Coast!" He seemed to be as happy as a buzzard on a gut truck. I then said, "Well, ole' buddy, who in the hell are we going to fucking sell them to? Especially since you paid over market price. Plus, how am I—or should I say, *you*—paying for them? By the way, did you know that they have to be cooked, and quickly? They don't come out of the water ready to eat!" There was silence. As if someone shot the buzzard. At first, I thought I'd stunned him, but not true; he knew what he was doing. I was the gut truck, and he was the crafty buzzard, trying to consume me. Me, the president; me, the company; me as just me. But I knew that. I was on to his predetermined scheme by now. He didn't want a successful profitable operation. He had to put it back in shambles. And quite honestly, this one move just did!

The total due the fisherman was approximately $35,000, a fair amount of money back then. He laughingly replied to my query when I asked how he was going to pay for them, saying, "I'll talk to the factoring company. Maybe we can get an advance." I went totally out of my mind! I then said, "Do. Not. Buy. Anymore. You hear me?" And hung up! I was baffled by his reply regarding getting an advance on sales. You can't get an advance on sales that haven't taken place. And there was no way in hell we could sell a hundred thousand pounds! I knew it, and he knew it. Nice way to decimate a company. He was clever. However, I could be clever as well.

Meanwhile, to protect the fishermen up north, I immediately called and cancelled the market order he'd signed. I didn't know how they were going to get paid, and it was the Paladini name that they would remember.

I now knew without a doubt I had to shut down the company, the corporation. I was out of tools to repair it. It was hopeless.

I should have not hypothesized the assumption that the investor's intentions were honorable to provide a basis for my illogical reasoning in wanting to save the company and the fucking name.

My post-analysis was now unfortunately grim, and I would have to now carefully plan for the closing. I was the president and had the authority to cease all operations. My primary concern was for the creditors, especially those I promised to pay for whatever I bought.

In the meantime, there was no conceivable way we could pay for the crabs and pay the bills on time as promised. I needed time to think and get the goddamn crabs out of there, but I had to act quickly! They needed to be cooked, and soon. I also had to raise money. The only way was to call the competition and offer them the crabs at ten cents per pound less than what he paid for them, back to what the original market order had been, and hope they will buy them. It was the only way to dispose of them before they spoiled. I didn't care if we/he lost money now, and since he contracted with the crab fishermen, it was his responsibility to pay them. I hadn't made the deal, and now had bigger problems I was facing.

I had to move fast to unload them. I personally called all the wholesalers in the Bay Area and successfully sold off all the excess ninety thousand pounds and asked they bring a check when they were picked up since I'd discounted them to the original market order. I told my controller to take the checks totaling approximately $25,000 and immediately deposit the funds into the Paladini account. I was the only signatory on that account, so now I had control of these funds! The factoring company and the JAYCO account would never see it! Yes, it was totally against the contract with them, but who the fuck cared? I'd gotten him on this one! The crabs would have spoiled, resulting in a total loss anyway.

My intention was to now use these funds, along with the factored funds, as a way of securing payment for all the product that I bought, plus whatever I could on the company's old payable account.

Funds would be available from the factoring company every Friday late in the day after the verification and analysis of the week's sales and the necessary convoluted formula that equated the availability of the funds, less the deduction for their fees. Normally we would send out product payable checks on Monday morning for what I'd bought the prior week, keeping my seven-day commitment.

It was now Wednesday, and I had only three days to cease operations on that Friday at the close of day, as I had now effectively planned. My plan had better work! Since the funding transfer always came in late on Fridays, I anticipated to stay late along with a few of the office staff and mail the checks out on Friday evening, bringing all my payable balances I was responsible for to zero.

I also wanted to pay down as much of the old company's past-due payable balances that I could, so I had the men take inventory of our freezer at the San Francisco plant, then had it all delivered that same afternoon to the public cold storage, cleaning out our freezer. I then reviewed what we already had at the public cold storage. My strategy was to arrange to transfer frozen inventory from our account to the old company's creditors accounts at the same public cold storage, thus paying it down in the form of product, along with a check for as much as possible. I calculated the cost per pound of the frozen product that we'd originally paid times the weight and came up with a fair market value.

At midday Friday after all the trucks were out, I analyzed all the payable invoices for product that I had purchased during the week to make sure they would be accurately paid down to the penny, keeping my personal vow to them.

The prior old company's debt, though it now would have been significantly reduced since they received frozen product in cold storage, plus a check against partial of the balance, would be the debt of the tap dancer and his three-hundred-dollar-loafers partner.

I called up each broker and producer I'd bought from—they were now also my friends—and explained to them what I was doing. I had to be very short with them. I'm sure it didn't take long for them to figure out what I was doing.

I knew when Monday morning came, they would be grateful they'd gotten paid as promised. I had to also calculate to hold back enough funds to cover that week's payroll, including the Fort Bragg plant. The employees were now also my friends.

I could now postulate that my credibility was forthright. I could now walk out proud, though saddened with the outcome.

Friday morning, I had my secretary type out a formal letter and fax it to the Fort Bragg production plant, instructing them to fax back the payroll to us for payment, then to let everyone go and to cease operations at the end of the day, and to advise the receiving stations as well. The managers at the receiving stations were on the Fort Bragg payroll. So, every employee was paid.

I then had a meeting with my entire staff at the main office in San Francisco and advised them of my decision and why I was shutting the company down. It was simple: I could not be deceptive to them or the creditors and continue under these circumstances. I explained that eventually no one would have gotten paid if we continued under the present circumstances. Surprisingly, they applauded, and expressed they didn't know how I'd held it together for so long, that they had concluded long ago that Jesse and his partner were cunning, disingenuous phonies.

A. PALADINI, INC.

FRESH, FROZEN, MILD CURED AND
SMOKED FISH

CALIFORNIA BRANCHES:
CRESCENT CITY
EUREKA
BODEGA BAY
FORT BRAGG

MAIN OFFICE
P.O. BOX 24246, 2 RANKIN STREET
SAN FRANCISCO, CALIFORNIA 94124
TELEPHONE: (415) 285-8900

March 4, 1974

5:40 PM
3/4/74
*Telegram sent
to Mr. Wereson.*

Stockholders
A. Paladini, Inc.

Effective today, March 4, 1974, I Achille George Paladini do
hereby submit my resignation as President of A. Paladini, Inc.
I no longer will accept any responsibilities as a corporate
officer.

I refuse to sign any corporate papers, documents or checks
pertaining to A. Paladini, Inc.

I will remain on with A. Paladini, Inc., as overall General
Manager if so desired by the stock holders.

Respectively,

Achille George Paladini

Achille George Paladini

cc: James Wereson, Atty.   James Shields
     Robert LaVine, Atty.   J.A. Bertrand

Witnessed by:

Brent J. Wilson 3/4/74
Brent J. Wilson, Comptroller

Joseph J. Velo 3/4/74
Joseph Velo, Sales Manager

Beverly August 3/4/74
Beverly August, Sect.

I was despondent and felt demoralized that so many people, almost two hundred, including my brother Walter and cousin Tom, had lost their jobs. We would have made it. We already had! We were, though for a short while, number one again.

Oh, by the way, upon hearing of this from the Fort Bragg plant manager, Mr. Bertrano called from the Crescent City receiving station and screamed at me, "You fucking can't do this! You can't do this!" I calmly replied, "I am the president, and already have. Goodbye, Mister Fred Astaire!" As I hung up, I vaguely heard him saying, "Who? Who? Fred? Fred who?"

The disingenuous so-called investors then threw A. Paladini, Inc. into chapter 7 bankruptcy the following week. What a shame for the Paladini name. What a waste. This, however, possibly could have been averted if the family had verified that they were indeed accredited investors.

So, what was their actual motive or purpose behind acquiring the company? I understand it only cost them seven dollars, but why the effort, the time? Was it indeed for a tax shelter, to drain what resources was left and use the company's losses? Possibly, they'd originally indeed thought it really was beyond saving, and when it turned profitable, it ruined their original intention.

Maybe that's why Jesse had cleverly entered into the contract in Eureka to purchase inventory that was beyond the realm of our capacity to sell and pay for—to intentionally destroy the current profit structure. I had evidently been used, manipulated, and exploited. What a waste of years and energy.

Thinking back to that evening up in Mendocino when we'd first met Jesse, Joan had been right with her ominous prediction after all. She has always been very perceptive and empathetic.

I have often wondered what the two investors who acquired the company for seven dollars thought, or better yet, the expression on their faces upon opening the massive freezer at the San Francisco plant and seeing it empty?!

However, I did leave them fifteen pounds of frozen calamari, with a wholesale value of $7.50—more than enough to cover their cost. They even made a profit! Whoops, sorry, "profit" is a nasty word.

On April 19, 1974, after a 109-year reign, A. Paladini, Inc. Wholesale Fish Dealers, the once icon of the seafood industry, closed forever.

And I was once again unemployed.

CHAPTER 22
HERE I GO AGAIN

We'd just moved into a new home—and I had no job. This was now getting repetitive and rather upsetting! Not just a home, but a huge home, and of course the house payments were equally huge. Good timing, Mr. P.

Of course, since I'd closed the company before the end of the year, I hadn't gotten my bonus. Sure, I could have taken it, but there wouldn't have been enough to complete the payroll. It would have been a rather large sum since it was predicated on the net profits and could have carried us for several months. I had counted on it when buying the home, since we'd used most of our savings for the additional amount needed above the sale of our previous home. The first payment would be coming up soon. So now what?

Anyway, the kids were excited to be going to a new school, and Joan and I were pleased that they would be growing up in a nice area—that is, if I didn't lose the house—and they could meet other kids with respectable backgrounds during their evolving years. These friends most likely would be their life-long friends. Hillsborough is a beautiful, upscale area. Just down the street from us, was the Tobin Clark Estate, covering seventeen acres. We looked down upon the estate from our living room, giving us a feeling of grandeur. But that now may have possibly been an apocryphal presumption.

I couldn't help but wonder how the neighbors would feel if they were to ask what my source of income was and I replied, "Oh, I'm working with the State of California"—i.e., on unemployment. Sure, they'd invite us to socialize with them at the private country clubs.

The first house payment was soon coming due and I didn't have enough money to pay it, but I had a boat, not much of a boat, but nevertheless, still a boat—to sell!

Joan named it *Wrong Way*. She names everything, even has a couple of ones for me at times. She had always been very clever in naming our cars and such, and appropriately named the boat.

Here's a short story . . . sort of: I'd bought a seventeen-foot inboard-outboard, dilapidated, floating hunk of junk from a customer when I was manager at the frozen food company in Oakland. It was bargain priced; I had to get it. The first time I launched it—without knowing anything about boating or having taken a coast guard course. It was a total disaster.

While backing down the ramp near the exclusive Loch Lomond Yacht Club in San Rafael, the car started to slide down the ramp due to the combined weight of the car, boat, and trailer—no, the car didn't have four-wheel drive. It was Joan's car that I'd had a hitch put on without her knowledge. Fortunately, it stopped just inches before the entire rear end submerged into the murky bay. The boat curiously wouldn't budge off from the trailer upon attempting to launch it. It never dawned on me that this boat had most likely been sitting on the trailer for years and was now adhered to the trailer. Yeah, yeah . . . I know.

The trailer was now in the water, and the boat wouldn't come off, causing the trailer to float, and the back end of the car was now also mostly in the water and at a very odd angle. Joan was screaming, "Get my car out of the water! Get my car out of the water!" I was now trembling, realizing I'd really screwed up. My kids were watching with bewilderment at their father's boating skills—or lack thereof.

Meanwhile, there was a young, bedraggled drunk sitting on a boulder nearby, sipping from something covered with a brown paper bag and smoking a cigarette, watching this fiasco. He came up to me and asked if he could help. He wasn't very stable on his feet, but at that point Donald Duck would have looked good.

He asked me to drive the car back out and he would show me how to launch it. As I tried to pull the car out, the wheels were spinning from the slickness of the cement ramp. Joan was now again screaming, thinking her car may soon be immersed forever in a watery grave. Well, this Good Samaritan, though smelling like a distillery, finally got us up the ramp by helping push the car. We then quickly discovered we had to rock the boat to loosen it from its stronghold.

He told me to slowly back down the ramp and he would pull the boat from the trailer. Upon having done so, he yelled to me, "Where's the rope?!" Rope? I didn't know you needed a rope to hold the boat once it's free from the trailer so it wouldn't float away. Yeah, guess I should have taken a boating course or two.

It was now slowly drifting out into the muddy marsh with no one on board. The poor drunk swam out in the cold brackish water of the bay and grabbed the stern and pulled it into shore. I'm sure he was quite sober by now! During all this humorous calamity, the girls were sitting on the beach with their hands on their chins, holding up their heads with dismayed looks on their faces.

There was a party going on nearby on a luxurious sixty-foot yacht tied up at the yacht club's pier, and all the guests had been watching the entire scenario, laughing while they sipped on their mimosas. The garish women were adorned in lavish high-brimmed bonnets and the men in light-colored sport jackets, displaying their black-brimmed sea captain hats. They snobbishly looked down upon us as if we were the afternoon's entertainment.

After giving our now sober, well-soaked friend five bucks to say thank you, the motor eventually started after many attempts and we were off on our day on the bay. Yippee!

As I sat back, my heart now beginning to beat normally again, I proceeded out, turning sharply to the right near the shoreline, fearing not to go out too far. Well, I soon found that we were in the mud flats and the engine was kicking up mud and splashing on the kids sitting in the rear. Yes, they were wearing life jackets. I wasn't that dumb. Attempting to get us out of this dilemma, I steered to the left to turn around, but the boat went to the right—actually, it went wherever it wanted. No, I didn't check the steering controls after I bought it. The steering cable was busted! What the hell did I know about steering cables? The kids were now looking at me in disbelief and Joan wasn't very pleased. This was not turning out to be a very fun day, as planned.

Okay, so now the engine had conked out because we were mired in the mud. Now what? We all sat there looking at each other. I had more than mud on my face.

I'll never forget the look on everyone's faces. I was less than their hero that day, to say the least.

While sitting there trying to figure my next move, low and behold, along came the sheriff's boat. We were saved! Yay! The sheriff said, "Throw me a rope." I didn't have a rope. There went that goddamn rope thing again. He threw me one of his and tied us up to his much larger boat and tried to pull us free. It wasn't working. He then tried again, with no luck. By now, the sheriff's boat was also stuck in the mud! Well, of course, his was larger and had a much deeper hull. I then saw him swearing. Oh jeez, this wasn't really happening, was it?

Now this is the God's truth: The sheriff threw out an anchor and tried to pull his boat free by using the anchor like a winch, and it worked for a couple of times. Then on one of his pulls, he slipped and fell into the bay and into the inevitable mud. *Splash!* The sheriff was now in the bay, soaking wet and muddy. As he got back on board, wringing out his shirt, he glared at me and left us—without even waving goodbye!

Luckily, shortly afterward, while sitting there dismayed about how to get back to shore, a young boy in a small aluminum outboard skiff came by and pulled us free, then towed us back to the ramp.

Within a few short hours, I had succeeded in acquiring the assistance of a drunk, a sheriff, and a young blond boy in a skiff, and had entertained the aloof on our first day on the bay. No one was impressed.

There was silence in the car on the drive home. Thus, that's how *Wrong Way* got her name. I was also given a few new names, as well. I gladly sold *Wrong Way* for just enough to make the first house payment. Maybe she didn't perform well on the water, but she was the *right way* to make the house payment.

Several weeks after I'd closed the company, my two brothers, Walter and Tom came over to our house. It was just before noon. Tom was actually my cousin; my mom's sister passed away shortly after his birth and she raised him like her son, and we all considered him our brother.

We then sat around the kitchen table talking for some time, reminiscing about what had happened at Paladini, while Joan fixed us a Margherita pizza. It's a thin-crust pizza, created in the late 1800's to honor the Queen consort of Italy, Margherita of Savoy. It originated in Naples and resembles the colors of the Italian flag: tomato for red, mozzarella cheese for white, and basil for green. Joan likes to add a sprinkling of oregano on top for extra flavor. Yeah, guess that screws up the flag concept, but it sure tastes good!

While munching on this yummy treat prepared by Master Chef Giovanna, they both asked what I intended to do. I guess they were hoping I was going to start up something, however, I had no clue at the time what my future held. I explained that I needed time to let my head clear after what I'd just gone through.

I then asked if they had started looking for jobs, and they both said they hadn't been able to find anything anywhere. "Really?" I commented. Both Walter and Tom had only worked for Paladini all their lives. I guess they thought since I had been involved with management as of late that I had something up my sleeve. Well, the only thing up my sleeve was a cheap Timex watch.

I must go back in time for just a quick moment. Years ago when I was a salesman on the Peninsula, I stopped in occasionally at my Aunt Henrietta's, who lived in Menlo Park. She had been nice to me; the only one in the family, by the way. She was in her late eighties, and had difficulty getting around, so I would take her shopping on occasion. I would then often stay and have lunch with them, and that was a real treat, since the nineteen cent hamburgers were getting repugnant.

One day during lunch, she asked me what I wanted to do in the future and I commented that I would like to have my own business. She then surprisingly said, "I want you to have your grandfather's old wooden trunk. Sit on it each morning before going to work and it will bring you good luck."

She then went on to tell me the story about Grandpa Achille coming to America with nothing other than this old wooden trunk that contained just a change of tattered old clothes. She told me about him starting the fish business with nothing, and his eventual success. She said he sat on the trunk every morning while putting on his boots before going to work. It must have brought him good luck. Maybe it would do the same for you, Kiki.

I thanked her and took it home and told Joan the story. She said it would make a nice piece of furniture, though old and worn. I agreed. The thought of having my own business was far-fetched, to say the least. Consequently, at the time, I took what my aunt said with a grain of salt. I placed the trunk at the foot of our bed as a decoration piece and didn't really take her comment seriously.

Meanwhile, after my brothers approached me and asked what I was going to do, I remembered what she'd said about the trunk, and thought what the heck, maybe I should give it a try. I have to sit on something anyway while putting on my shoes.

Now far from the thought of opening a business, I was still collecting unemployment, and was ready to sell one of our two cars for the next house payment, when I unexpectedly got a call from Frank Alioto, a seafood broker, now a good friend. I had bought a lot of product from him while at Paladini.

He asked if I had any future plans or interviews. I said yes; my next interview was tomorrow . . . at the unemployment office.

He then said he had about two hundred thousand pounds of frozen fish in public cold storage that customers had refused upon delivery over the past year, and it was now frozen in a solid mass and needed to be properly re-packed. Thinking back now, I was one of those customers that had refused some of the fish due to poor quality. He said he would pay me to re-pack it if I could find a place with a small cooler and freezer, and pay twenty-five cents a pound on the finished weight, plus pay for the bags, master boxes, and any packing material. The product would have to be partially thawed, washed in cold water with a small amount of salt, then individually quick frozen (IQF), then glazed and placed in ten-pound bags, then packed in a master container and labeled.

Doing some quick math, I figured I could possibly make $50,000 gross, and about $30,000 to $35,000 net when finished, within the approximate three months I calculated it would take. That was a lot of money. But I needed to find a place with refrigeration and it had to be cheap—very cheap—and oh yes, rented on a month-to-month basis. What the hell were the chances of finding that? I didn't like the fact, however, that I would be handling someone else's crap, but you have to do, what you have to do.

If I'd only known my life would come to this, I thought. And I'm one of the Paladini grandsons—hell, not only that, I'm the namesake of the Fish King, and look at what I'm about to venture into! Don't frown upon me, Grandpa. I have a family, and I gave it my best to try to save your old company.

You know, I thought, what the heck, this would be something to do until I found another management job. It would also give me some desperately needed income for a few months, and if nothing else, I would be helping a friend. I could also give my two brothers a job and some income for a while, as well. Maybe it could also be the start of something. And, as they say, "It isn't how you fall; it's how you get up!"

I went to see my mom the next morning to see how she was doing. Not much change from a couple of days ago, except she seemed rather anxious that day, like something was on her mind. As I sat on her bedside, I asked her, "How are you doing today, Mom?" She grabbed my hand and put something in it that she had been holding in her palm for God only knows how long. It was warm. It was my dad's beloved Jade ring that he'd worn all the time, including the day he died. I was overcome with emotion. I broke down and sobbed. *My God, Daddy's ring.* She softly murmured, "Kiki, I want you to have your father's ring." I then said, "But Mom, Brother should have it. He's the oldest son." She whispered, "He loved you, Kiki, and I know you will make your father proud."

I tried not to let her see the emotion so evident on my face. My body trembled with fear at the possibility that she was now giving me his ring because she felt she might soon be gone. Regaining my composure, I graciously thanked her and told her, "I hope I really can make you and Daddy proud someday, in some way. Thank you, Mom. I love you."

Kay then said, "So put it on, Kiki." I couldn't! I don't know why, but I couldn't. Did I not feel worthy? I really don't know. I have *never* worn it, to this day. I. Cannot. Get. Myself. To. Put. It. On. Even with everything I've achieved, up to this very moment, is it possible I still don't feel worthy?

Well, later that afternoon, I had an appointment with Larry, the owner of a retail fish and poultry store on San Bruno Avenue in San Francisco. I'd heard that he'd had a small wholesale operation at one time behind his store, and it was now for rent. He was asking $700 a month. (This was in 1974.) I knew Larry well. He'd bought from me for years, and was a fine gentleman and family man, and a devout Catholic.

The small facility was just perfect. It had a small cooler with a bit larger freezer, plus an area to pack. To reach the tiny office upstairs you had to walk sideways up the steps because it was so narrow. Upon reaching the second floor, there was a space with barely enough room for one small desk and a teeny tiny separate office the size of a closet. I really got excited about it, but I had no money for the first month's rent. What little money we had, Joan needed for food. I had been out of work for some time now and had another large house payment coming up.

Knowing Larry so well, I asked him if there was any way I could pay him the first month's rent in two weeks, possibly even before. Thankfully, he agreed, and we then entered into a verbal month-to-month lease agreement. I may have nudged him a bit though by saying, "What the hell? It's going to sit here vacant, anyway!"

I planned that I would invoice Frank every Friday, then I could pick up a check on Monday morning and pay my brothers. That should work! Now needing a business name, I decided to call it a simplistic and generic "Seafood Services."

I called my two brothers and told them about it, and they were delighted. I told them to be at work on Monday morning at seven. Take note, I didn't sit on the trunk. This was not thought of as an ongoing venture. This was just temporary survival.

Monday morning came, and we were ready to pick up the first load at public cold storage; however, I needed freezing sheets and some racks, a glazing tank, and all types of packing materials. I still had the keys to Paladini on Rankin Street, about a mile away, so my plan was to borrow what I needed to get started. It would only be for a couple of months or so; the bankruptcy auction was not slated for some time yet.

I rented a large truck, planning to hopefully pay for it when it was returned, and off we went to go shopping for our needs. It took several trips to get everything over to San Bruno Avenue since the equipment was so large and bulky.

The first load was then picked up at the public cold storage: ten thousand pounds of random-sized rainbow trout. We had no fork lift, so it all had to be unloaded by hand. That was a back-breaking job since each case weighed well over sixty-five pounds. We then unpacked the trout and laid them out in the cooler to partially thaw overnight. The entire ten thousand pounds of trout had been refused by a chain store, and each case had been frozen in one solid mass.

The next morning, we separated each trout, gave them a dip in cold water to give a quick wash, then placed them on metal sheets and racked them to freeze separately overnight. The following morning, we dumped the sheets, several at a time, into the glazing tank filled with ice-cold water to glaze them. This process had to be repeated at least twice, since a ten percent glaze was required. We then packed and stencil-labeled the cases and returned the load back to storage. The load was now eleven thousand pounds with the glaze. That same afternoon, while dropping off the load, we simultaneously picked up the next load to repeat the process.

I had figured to make sufficient money we needed to complete ten thousand pounds within two and a half days, twenty thousand pounds for the week. With the extra ten percent for the glaze, this allowed me to charge twenty-two thousand pounds at twenty-five cents per pound equaling $5,500 at the end of the week. It was not an easy task to thaw, re-freeze, glaze, pack, weigh, and label, and have the load back at public cold storage within that time frame, but we did it. We stayed right on target.

I soon realized it would go even faster if we had a fork lift. We also wouldn't exhaust ourselves, so I needed to think. *Hey! There are four fork lifts over at Rankin Street!*

But how in the hell were we going to get one over here? It was over a mile away, and there was an incline on the way. I abruptly then said to Tom, "Hey, Thomaso, let's go!" In his normal, comical way, he asked, "Oh, Jesus. What the hell are you thinking?" I said, "You'll soon see!"

Upon arriving at the Rankin Street plant, we found that all the fork lift batteries were dead, of course, as it been a month since they'd last been used. We picked out the best lift and plugged it in, and fortunately the electrical power hadn't been turned off yet.

We then drove back to San Bruno Avenue. It was now just before ten in the morning, and it would take at least four to five hours to get a good charge on it. Tommie was funny. On the way back he said, "So you're going to want me to drive the goddamn fork lift all the way to the plant, aren't you?" I simply replied, "Tommie." He then said, lovingly (I think), "You little son of a bitch!"

We then went back around two thirty in the afternoon, and it was all charged and ready to go! Tommie now bravely took off on the fork lift, slowly, slowly, slowly edging his way on the city streets, attempting to avoid the occasional chuckhole that would have jarred the fillings out of his teeth. Forklifts were not made to drive on the street. There were no shock absorbers to cushion the bumps, so it certainly must have been a jarring ride. I recall seeing him at a stop light. What a funny sight it was, seeing him sitting on the fork lift among the many cars! Thankfully, no police were in the area at the time. How would an officer write that ticket up? "Vehicle: Forklift. Reason for citation: Driving too slow in the slow lane. No rear lights, no brake lights, no turn signals, actually no lights at all. No license plate, no registration, no proof of insurance." Wonder how a judge would have handled that?

About an hour later as he approached San Bruno Avenue, there was a long, gradual upgrade. I was aware of it, of course, but hoped the battery would have enough juice to get him to the top. Well, it didn't.

I had returned to the plant, and after over an hour or so, it dawned on me that he was probably stuck somewhere on that hill, waiting. Sure enough, there he was, having a cigarette, calmly watching the cars whiz by. I'll never forget the expression on his face when I arrived. He started swearing at me with his favorite, "You little son of a bitch! I've been bouncing around for a fucking hour on this thing and my ass is sore and I have to pee—and you forgot about me!"

I couldn't help laughing, and that didn't help the situation. I chained the back of the lift to the rear of the truck, and Tom then had to steer it backwards the balance of the way, which was about a good quarter of a mile on a busy city street during the commute hour!

That first Friday I was able to invoice Frank's company $5,500.

Monday morning, I went to his office and picked up a check. I then paid both my brothers an even $400 in cash for the week. They were making $350 a week at Paladini and paid by check with deductions, so felt that was fair. I also then paid Larry the entire $700 for the first month's rent, well before the promised date. The truck rental and gas cost approximately $450 for the week, plus some incidentals that cost $25, totaling $1,975. Expenses were obviously at a bare minimum, where they should have been.

My net profit that first week was $3,525. Keep in mind, the rent was for a full month, so pro-rated, that equaled $175 per week, which meant the net profit that first week was actually $4,050. Meanwhile, as in running any business, I had a utility bill, a small phone bill, the cost of invoices, etc. which may have added up to an additional $300 for the month, or $75 per week. Deducting the miscellaneous expenses from that first week's net profit, I could now anticipate a net weekly profit of approximate $3,375. That amount, times ten weeks to complete, equaled $33,750—exactly as previously calculated.

Keeping expenses at a bare minimum is paramount when starting a business!

There was a week we had more than we could handle because the item we were working with was small and labor-intensive. Joan and the kids came in one Saturday and helped. It was fun, having them there that day. The kids played their loud, annoying rock music and had a fish fight. Luckily, the fish were small and were thawed! We went out for lunch and had Mexican food. I hate Mexican food, but loved every minute of it, and have fond memories of that day, working as a family handling someone else's stinkin' fish.

One Friday afternoon Frank called me, after five weeks, having completed just over one hundred thousand pounds, and surprisingly, he said he had to stall me with completing the balance, that he needed to catch up on selling what we had packed. He hadn't thought we could do it so quickly.

Oh, shit—the income would now cease. This came as a total shock! I was anticipating earning at least $30,000 upon completion, of which only about $15,000 had come in so far, and I had spent most of it paying our personal bills. I had intended to save the balance that was still to come, to hold us until I found a permanent job; it would have lasted a long time. I'd had it all planned out.

Now I was sorry that I'd bought Joan a car; a used car, but I had to. The one she'd been driving was in bad shape, and she was driving the kids around. I also bought myself an old junker Ford Ranchero, a mini-truck, to get back and forth to work. We'd also had a fence built around the house since we had two dogs, bought some furniture and made two house payments. I hadn't expected this!

Joan asked me what I was going to do, as did my brothers. They were, of course, worried about an income again. We all had house payments and families to support. Well, I had no idea what I was going to do, guess I'll have to go look for a job again?"

Why does it seem that I'm always looking for a job?

It was now Monday morning and I went to the plant as if I had something to do. Hell, the rent was paid for a month. I sat downstairs all alone in my little tiny cubbyhole with my small desk gingerly forced into it. It sat upon a cold cement floor with cracks large enough for ants to build a colony. I had my feet on the desk, sitting back like a CEO of a large corporation. However, there was just me. Just me, and one old silenced, single-line black rotary phone, with a half cup of black coffee, listening to the subtle taunting hum of the compressor that was cooling the now-empty cooler and freezer.

A rat or two, the size of a raccoon, would occasionally run by to check up on me. In the passing of time, I'd named them. We'd oddly sort of become friends. I called one "Jesse," the other, "Jim"—how fitting. I'd also become much better friends with those two rats than the other two rats. At least I knew what they were up to.

I was again in a quandary, wondering what to do, what to do. Why was I always having to figure and think, think, think?

I had just paid the second month's rent and had three weeks left. I asked myself, *So what the hell do I do with this place?* I laid back with my eyes closed, my hands behind my head, and fell into a deep, trance-like state, most likely to escape the reality of failure that was setting in.

Well, I don't know what the hell came over me! I suddenly sat up and slammed my fist down on the desk and said, "Bullshit!" The rats now scattered for fear of their lives, and the ants ran for cover deep into the crack. I picked up the phone, called Joan, and said, "Hi, honey. Guess what? I'm going to start a wholesale fish business!" There was silence for a few seconds. She then hesitantly asked in a conciliatory, calm tone, "With what?" I then exclaimed, "Well, with um, n-n-n-nothing!" Now thinking I may have talked too fast without thinking this through, I then quickly replied, "We still have four hundred dollars, honey!" She answered, "Oh . . . okay, then. Well, good luck! Oh, by the way, we'll be needing groceries soon . . . bye." There was an obvious tone of trepidation and doubt in her voice, possibly even a hint of sarcasm—and with good cause. Her demeanor was equitable. We had nothing—nothing. Zero from zero is zero! How could I start a business? However, to achieve success, you must risk failure!

I then looked over at Jesse, who, by the way, had just recently been renamed "Julie" after I'd noticed she was lacking a couple of body parts, and Jim, who were scurrying by, and asked, "So what do you two think?" Well, they both ran like hell! I wondered at that point if I should, as well. Maybe that had been an omen. Ignoring the visionary wisdom of my two furry confidants, I sat back in my chair, and while sipping the now bitter cold coffee, soon came up with another generic name for the soon-to-be imaginary company. I decided to call it "Seafood Sales"—another nondescript name. Purposely named nondescript, so just in case of the *extremely* unlikely event that I would somehow, some way, become successful, I didn't want the remaining Paladini family to say my success was due to the frickin' name. It is said that we cannot predict the future, but we *can* create it!

CHAPTER 23
WHAT? START A WHOLESALE BUSINESS WITH FOUR HUNDRED BUCKS?!

That would be like trying to fly a kite on a day with no wind!

However, optimism is the faith that leads to achievement. Nothing can be achieved without hope and confidence. To build a company, start with the essence of a *big* idea! Successful businesses are created using your brain, not your brawn, by carefully forecasting and visualizing the future. It is the thought process of prudent and methodical planning with systemic fundamentals that is paramount.

You must also maintain the awareness of unintended scenarios that may occur, as defined by the Duck Underwater Theory: the unexpected incidents that were not or could not be predicted that will significantly affect your risk management and bottom line.

Implementing the basic business principles of governing sustainable percentages/profit margins, ultra-precise monitoring of expenses, maintaining and perpetuating sales growth, judiciously manipulating funds to create cash flow, and preserving earned capital, should allow one to be eventually significantly rewarded.

Exceptionable chief executive officers are rare, because they use their brains in their entirety—both sides. However, in doing so, they burden the left brain due to its ability to analyze, decipher, and calculate. As a normal person, we carry around either large left brains, which favor logic and analysis; or large right brains, which favor imagination and intuition.

One of the biggest differences between the right and left brain is the way they arrange information. If you are a left-brain thinker, you take in information early. When your brain receives a piece of information, it arranges the parts logically and then looks at the whole. If you have a project to complete, you will outline the tasks carefully before starting. This makes a good business leader.

Running a large corporation demands the use of both sides. Exceptional CEOs can be, as they say in baseball, "switch hitters." In management, the brain's two halves are the financial side and the human side. However, more commonly, managers are good with only one or the other. To be exceptional, you must have the ability to use both.

But remember, according to Thomas Edison, "Genius is one percent inspiration and ninety-nine percent perspiration."

Well, I was now thinking of starting up a wholesale seafood business with just that one percent inspiration, because I had no startup capital, as any entrepreneur should—that is, unless you call $400 capital. To mention brains again—you've heard all those jokes about the Italian brain. Yeah, well, good chance I had.

Things were looking a bit bleak at this point, but I knew that destiny was not a matter of chance; it's a matter of choice. I had to decry any defeatist attitude or thinking.

No matter what the odds, and despite the difficulty I may encounter, I must maintain tenacity, determination and most importantly, *perseverance* if I was to be successful.

I certainly realized the risk of attempting this, but more importantly, what was the risk of *not* attempting it? The risk would be staying stagnant and return being a salaried employee for the rest of my life.

So, with that dispiriting thought, I looked around at what I had. *Hmm, well, let's see. I have a single-line old black rotary phone, a tiny cooler full of holes, a small freezer that leaks freon, a dilapidated old Ford Ranchero, and three weeks left on my rent. What the hell? I'll give it a try! Oh, but I'll need a business license. Nah, not yet. I'll wait and see if I sell something first. What a minute, what the hell am I thinking? I don't have anything to sell!*

I was now feeling forlorn, as if lost at sea, aimlessly being tossed around from one nonsensical thought to the next. But then this idea occurred to me: On the open sea, there are no landmarks to guide you. You must make do with what you have, or helplessly drown. I couldn't let myself drown in defeat.

So again, I started plotting, thinking, thinking. There I went again, thinking. *Hmm, well, maybe I'll call up Vince. He was the owner of a large wholesale seafood company nearby in San Bruno. I know him well, and I bet I can make a deal with him in some way. It wouldn't hurt to try. So, I did. I* called up Vince and we chatted for a while, talking about the industry and what a shame that the Paladini investors had been such pretentious phonies. Vince was also a good friend of Frank Alioto, by the way, and we often had lunch together, so there was some camaraderie between us.

I then hesitantly blurted out, "So, Vince, I would like to start up a small wholesale fish business but have no inventory. Can I buy what I need from you every day at a bit of a discount and I'll pay you as I pick it up?" He immediately said, "Sure, Kiki. Anything you want." He paused and then jokingly said, "So you'll be my competition again, huh?" I laughed and said, "Vince, I don't have a pound of fish yet. That's not likely. I just need to make a few bucks for now. Frank ran out of things for me to do and I still have this small plant for a little while longer."

Okay, so have I thought of everything? I think so, but now I must plan and visualize just how much I want or need to accomplish . . . if anything.

I now stared at my one and only corporate asset, that single-line black rotary phone. That silenced lonely phone now stood between me and actually starting a business—or chickening out. I then thought over and over, *Pick it up. Pick it up and start making calls, for Christ sake! But, to who? And what do I sell?* How do you start a conversation with intent, without content? I then questioned myself as to whether I really knew what the hell I was doing. I'd never been taught the industry; I'd only learned as I went on. Could I really tackle this undertaking? For several minutes I questioned my ability, then I remembered in college, in psychology class they'd taught us that most everyone questions themselves with their ability to perform and the feeling of inadequacy. Then it came to me: *How about that 150-plus IQ they said you had at Saint Ignatius? Use it, for Christ sake!* But it takes more than just genius, it takes courage.

Now sitting there pondering what the hell to do, I rocked back and forth in my chair as it squeaked in an annoying repetitive manner as the sound echoed throughout the now-barren plant. I toyed with the pen in my right hand as I put my left hand behind my head and gazed up at the ceiling in befuddlement. *Hmm, looks like the storm last week dampened and discolored the ceiling, and it looks like the cracks have gotten even bigger.* Yep, I was stalling...

Then, suddenly and without further thought, I sat up and once again pounded my fist on the desk and said, "Goddamn it, do it! Just do it!

So, I did! I picked up my only asset and called the first customer who came into mind, more importantly, one I could pick up a check from for the order—that is, if I were indeed to get an order. It was George, the chef at the Elegant Farmer Restaurant in Jack London Square in Oakland. Now not really knowing what I was going to say—remember, I stuttered when unsure of myself—George was suddenly on the line. The conversation went something like this: "Hi, George, how ya doin'? This is Kiki." He surprisingly replied, "Hey, Kiki! Where in the hell have you been?" We then chatted for a few minutes before I courageously said, "George, I just started my own business, selling seafood, of course." As I talked, there was an ominous echo. I had hoped he hadn't heard it. It would have been difficult to explain that I was the only living creature in the building; well, human anyway.

He then replied, "No kidding! When did you start?" I said, "About a minute ago!" He laughed, then asked, "Okay, so what do you have? I said, "Well, what are you looking for, George?" I was avoiding the fact that I had *nothing*!

He said, "Well, I could use three cases of U-15 prawns, two cases of jumbo scallops, a case of shrimp meat, a case of Dungeness crab meat, a case of small abalone, and—let me go check what else." He came back and asked if I had fifty pounds of fresh fillet of Petrale sole for the luncheon special. I said, "Can I call you right back?" He said, "But why? I need prices." I then meekly replied, "I know, George. Please just give me two minutes and I'll call you right back. I promise!" I knew he was wondering what the hell I was up to, but we were friends—I hoped.

I then hurriedly called up Vince and asked what he would charge me for the same items, and he said he would give me a 10 percent discount on everything. Fantastic. I had no overhead to speak of, so I called George back and marked everything up a little over 15 percent, giving me some room to come down if needed—but he then said, "Okay, sounds good, Kiki! Get it here before noon, though. I need the Petrale for lunch." I promptly replied, "Of course, thank you very much for the order, George!" I then asked if I could pick up a check for the order. He chuckled and said, "Sure, no problem, Kiki!" *Thank God!*

I had my first order, but I had to move fast. Oh, Christ! It dawned on me that I had no invoices. That was okay. I would just use the Seafood Services generic ones that I'd bought at the stationary store and would just write in "sales" over "services." That was easy.

But wait—oh, jeez—if he writes the check to Seafood Sales, I need an account to deposit it into, and more importantly, I need a check to pay Vince. Oh, shit! I looked at my watch; it was already nine thirty. I then rushed to the Bank of America just down the street and quickly opened a business account under that name. I deposited ten dollars to open the account. I only had eleven bucks, plus some change in my pocket, and needed a buck to cross the Bay Bridge. No burger for lunch today. The bank then gave me a small book of checks with just the numbers on the bottom, with nothing printed on top. That was fine. They were checks.

I then sat back in the seat of the Ranchero for a moment and thought, *Anything else? Hmm, yes, get going! He wants the Petrale for the luncheon special!*

Then, without hesitation, I zoomed down the Peninsula to pick up the order. Upon arriving, I wrote Vince a check—yeah, a phony check (sort of)—for $1,280, paying the invoice. When they loaded the order onto the Ranchero, it was way over loaded. I found it rather funny that the first order I got was more than what my little truck could hold! Now speeding over the Bay Bridge, my tiny truck was squeaking and groaning with sounds I'd never heard from it before. Well, I got to the Elegant Farmer just a few minutes before noon. Now I hoped to hell I could get a check from them. It was almost lunch time and they were busy. *Oh, God! If not, I'm done before I start.* Thankfully, I did—for $1,490. Now I had to get back to the other side of the bay to the Bank of America and deposit the check to make my check good. I now hoped I had enough gas. I only had forty-seven cents in my pocket after the bridge toll. Fortunately, I did! As I walked out of the bank, I breathed a huge sigh of relief.

Arriving back at my little plant, it was time to figure out what I'd made on my very first order. It calculated out to be $210. Less a buck for the bridge, maybe a buck for gas, I'd made $208 net, almost a week's salary back then. *Hey, not bad. That was fun! A bit stressful, but fun.*

I then called Joan and told her how excited I was. She said, "Okay, that's nice. I have to pick the kids up from school now. Bye." What the hell? "Okay, that's nice"—what kind of a comment was that?

I called her back and tried to be calm. I asked, "So, honey, what did you mean with that comment, 'That's nice'? You said it sort of sarcastically." She said, "That's today. What about tomorrow?" I brusquely replied, "I'll just do it all over again with another account or two, or three, maybe even more!" After hanging up, my heart sank, because she was right—what about tomorrow?

She doubted me. I didn't blame her. It was highly unlikely I would be able to repeat that again, day after day. Not many restaurants would pay upon delivery. I also knew I couldn't run a company with just a 10 or 15 percent markup if employees were ever needed to be hired.

Sure, for now the low markup was fine, as long as I was the salesman, order packer, picker upper, plant cleaner-upper, deliveryman, and bookkeeper. I had no employees, so no benefits or government contributions. This buying from another wholesaler would only work if it was only me, but with my big head and aspirations, I knew it would either quickly grow or quickly cease. If

I was going to have a real business, I needed to buy directly from the brokers, and oh yeah—maybe get a business license.

I suddenly got bold and called my friend Frank Alioto. He was a broker, and I asked if he would sell me some fresh fish and frozen shellfish. He replied, "What? You're in business?" Not knowing if this was good or bad, I hesitated and finally slurred out, "Uh, yep." He responded, "How fantastic! I'm so happy for you, Kiki! That's wonderful!" Ooh, this was good! He then said I could have absolutely anything I needed, and with thirty-day terms.

Oh my God, that was sure nice to hear, but it was bittersweet—it also meant I just may really be going into business . . . my own business . . . yikes!

He then went on to say that he knew everyone would sell me and give me thirty-day terms since I'd kept my promise and paid everyone in full at the old Paladini company; that my credentials, qualifications, and capabilities were highly respected within the industry.

Wow, just moments ago I'd been down in the dumps, and this opportunity had just been waiting for me. I wanted to celebrate and buy my two rodent friends some Camembert, but they were nowhere to be found. Guess they'd left when the goin' was good!

That was beyond what I would have ever expected to hear, and it felt so damn good. It was now mid-September of 1974, just five months since the old company had closed, and I might really be going into business. Our three girls had just started in their new schools; Laura, a freshman at Aragon High in San Mateo, and Gina and Diana at Crocker Middle School in Hillsborough. Now, when their friends asked what their father did, they could honestly say he had his own business, as tiny as it may have been, but still a notch up from his government job—EDD unemployment. Meanwhile, I thought I had better start sitting on that old wooden trunk before I had to go back to my government job. I didn't know how this was really going to work out.

I had to start planning and visualizing what I wanted to accomplish in the near future. I found when lying in bed late at night, when relaxed and the house was silent, it was the best time to think, to plan. The ideas just seemed to come, and then it was up to me to ensure they played out.

However, I had to proceed slowly and with caution. I couldn't let my overzealous ways get the best of me. I needed to maintain playing the quick buy-and-sell procedure like I'd been doing. I also had to continue to be all employees in one, until such time it became impossible. Now, since I could buy directly from the brokers and the producers as Frank said, and get thirty-day terms, it would allow me to call all the accounts I wanted and carry them for thirty days. But I had to use discretion and sell only to those accounts that I knew paid promptly within thirty days, since I was required to pay all my suppliers in thirty days, and not falter in doing so. That was going to be tricky. I had to move wisely in expanding the business. I might eventually need a couple of employees, one for packing the orders in the morning while I called the customers, who would then take care of the fresh fish in the afternoon, then clean up the plant; the other, to assist him packing orders in the morning, then make the deliveries.

Deliveries! Plural—like I'd even have any. Well, deliveries meant sales. The next thing I had to search my head for was the accounts I personally called upon; hopefully, the chefs would remember and buy from me.

I would have to play the manipulation game again with the cash flow for a while and be very careful, since I didn't have the startup capital most experts claim you need. This would be crucial. I would be the salesman and the bookkeeper, carefully monitoring the accounts receivables and the accounts payable. Hopefully by sending out weekly statements, that would encourage the accounts to pay sooner.

I would have to do the brain work and leave the brawn work for my employees. Of course, I'd also get in there and work with them when needed, as any wise boss should do.

I searched my head, thinking what good paying accounts to call Monday morning. For sure, the three Hyatt House Hotels. Chef Heinz in Burlingame, the buyer Joe at Rickey's in Palo Alto, and Chef Julius in San Jose, then all the Hilton Hotels—San Francisco was the big one—and for sure my good friend Executive Chef Gunther would buy. I also had my friend Charlie at the Hilton Inn at the airport. Then there were the Safeway stores. *Hey, goddamn it! Slow down, Kiki! Not yet...*

Boy, these were all the big names. Why not start with the big ones?

Okay, I thought. *Let's see who else . . . Ken's Seafood is right next door, and of course, how about Larry up front in the retail store? He's my landlord, for Christ sake. That's a natural! Okay, that's enough for now. You know, what the hell makes me think they'll buy from me? Or even worse, that I can deliver what they order? I'm getting a sick feeling in my gut now. I must not screw up the first order or there won't be a second. These are temperamental chefs that everyone wants to supply. I must be careful. I must find that crucial, critical balance between having enough fresh inventory, but yet not too much. This is fresh fish I'm dealing with, and I can't afford to freeze any excess. I must give the impression that I have a large operation to maintain and keep these accounts—friends or not.*

The good thing about running a wholesale business is that you deliver to your clients; they don't come to your place of business, so you can be in a palace or a dump. Having said that, it's imperative that I perform and deliver everything they ordered, and on time, plus the quality of the product must be paramount.

I then sat back for a moment with my eyes closed, thinking that this was a huge undertaking. *Do I really know what the hell I'm doing? Why do I have this feeling of insecurity again? Well, dumb ass, it's because you only have four hundred dollars to your name, and you're going into business. Not just any business, but the fricken wholesale fish business. Who in the hell does that? On top of that, there's nothing more perishable than fresh fish for Christ sake. It's no wonder you feel like this! This time your insecurities are bona fide. Oh, by the way, the cost of the business license is thirty-five bucks, so now you only have three hundred and sixty-five bucks to start it with!* I then opened my eyes and sat up and screamed out loud, "Enough of this insignificant bullshit! Let's get going!"

Well, I then went and finally got the goddamn business license in the name of Seafood Sales and paid the wasted thirty five bucks, then went to the stationary store and bought one book containing 250 four-part blank invoices; one sheet for bookkeeping, one sheet for filing for sales referral, two sheets to go with the driver, with one for the customer to retain, and the other to come back with a signature for proof of delivery. Oh yeah, and I ordered a rubber black-ink stamp to stamp the top of the invoices with the company name. Shoot! That would take a few days to get. I would just write it in for now. Okay, what else? Oh, yeah, a truck. Of course, a truck! What do I do about a truck? I arranged for a weekly rental with Hertz, paying at the end of the week, hoping I'd have enough cash flow with a few COD accounts to pay for it.

I thought some more. I would have one truck and one driver, which equated to about twenty deliveries a day. I would have to try to get twenty orders each day, but no more, so the deliveries would be made in a timely fashion.

Knowing that my two brothers were still looking for jobs, I naturally hired them again. Tom would be the inside man, and Walt, the driver. Good combination. This should be an effective and proficient symbiotic relationship between us.

It was now Friday morning, the day for me to place my first order with the brokers for the fresh fish to arrive on Monday. I figured I would only purchase a minimal amount; if I needed to fill in, I would pay a higher price and get it from Vince for now. I needed just a small starting inventory, not knowing if I would sell anything at all. I also bought a small inventory of frozen shellfish to have in stock. I picked it up in the ailing Ranchero that afternoon, since Monday would be devoted to receiving the fresh product and hopefully making a few sales and delivering them. The planning was crucial to make this work. I sure as hell had better sell all the fresh fish coming in–I don't like to eat fish! Yes, I know, I'm odd.

I had a very restless weekend, to say the least. I now had a small frozen inventory in a freezer which had a difficult time holding a zero-degree temperature, and some fresh fish arriving on Monday morning to store in a cooler with gaping holes that allowed refrigerant to seep out, and Jesse—whoops, I meant Julie—and Jim to sneak in. I knew when they smelled all that fresh fish they would surely come back and invite the neighborhood.

Thankfully, no one would come to the plant to see the operation. I hoped. Don't get me wrong, the place was clean—well, sort of. It just needed some refurbishing. Actually, it should be torn down and rebuilt. Then, of course, I had my two brothers coming to work, and they would naturally expect to get paid on Friday. *Oh my God! What have I done?*

I tried to enjoy the weekend with my family but was too predisposed with worry. Joan puttered around in the garden and the kids had some friends over and did stuff as young teenagers do. Being attentive and interacting was difficult; all I could think about was Monday morning and the fiasco I'd started. If it flopped, we'd be living in a flop house.

Sunday night, I tossed and turned most of the night, rehearsing over and over what I was going to do the next morning. As I mentioned prior, if I imagined what needed to be accomplished the next day, it strangely happened, or possibly it was as simple as just having a plan to make it happen. I am convinced that there are three parts of every event: anticipation, participation, and culmination, i.e., the planning, implementing, and finalizing.

I now wondered if, in some strange fashion, whether I was shadowing my grandfather, paralleling what he'd done. Did he have these same feelings of consternation when he started? The anxiety, the apprehension, the fear . . . of failure?

I got to work at five in the morning, anxious to make my first sales call. I couldn't wait for six when the chefs started to arrive, so I went down the block and picked up a couple of glazed donuts—okay, three. Yeah, yeah, I know, they're unhealthy, the only healthy part is the center, but you have to eat it all to get to it! I also bought a cup of black coffee and brought it back to the plant to drink while I nervously watched the clock tick forward as I sat at my tiny desk.

Just then Rick came by, sniffing my shoes. Oh, Rick was another rat that I forgot to mention, Julie and Jim's cousin, who were the two that had skipped out on me, remember? Rick also had a girlfriend named Rita, and they had an illegitimate son, Guillermo; they had obviously had him when they were very young, since he was now almost the same size as they were. His manners were less than admirable. I had named most of them by now—yes, there were many. Heck, I would have been all alone if it wasn't for them.

Six in the morning finally came, and I anxiously dialed my first customer on that old forlorn, solitary black phone. As the rotary dial leisurely took its time returning to dial the next number, I became impatient, my nerves were raw. I was calling Heinz. I called him "Heinzi"; he was the executive chef at the Hyatt House Hotel in Burlingame, and a good friend. The phone rang several times before getting the switchboard. I then asked for the executive chef, and she connected me to his extension. Again, the phone rang and rang. No answer. I was too early. That was frustrating—my adrenaline was flowing, and I was anxious to get that first order. It might foretell how I was to be accepted.

It was the middle of the month, so I knew I couldn't count on getting any large frozen shell-fish orders since the chefs normally loaded up just after the first of the month, which allowed the product to eventually diminish, resulting in the lowest possible food cost at the end of the month. I now took a deep breath and settled back, realizing it was still a bit early, so I went down the street and got some coffee and donuts for the three of us. Yes, I had another donut. Heck, they were still warm. Tom and Walter would be arriving soon at six thirty.

Upon returning, I opened the one and only loading door on San Bruno Avenue. The sidewalk was just inches from the entrance, so we would have to be careful when driving in and out. The fresh fish could start arriving at any time and the truckers needed to see where to back in to unload. Then I had a horrifying thought: *Oh my gosh! Did I charge the fork lift?* I then ran to the back of the plant. Thankfully, I plugged it in before I left on Friday. I had so much to think about.

I then gulped down my last donut and tried Heinzie again. This time, he answered! My heart raced, and I did that imaginary magical click on my forehead to "turn on the charm." The conversation went something like this: "Hi, Heinzie, how are you? This is Kiki!" He replied, "You little son of a bitch!"—his way of showing affection, I think— "Where in the hell have you been? No one took care of me like you!" I then said, "Wow, that's a nice compliment, Heinzie! Thank you. So, what's been going on with you?" He then said, "Forget that shit. Why are you calling?" I replied, "I just opened my own wholesale fish business." He then blurted out, "Do you have a pen?" I excitedly told him yes. "Good, then send me . . . " It was one hell of an order. I think he must have ordered everything he needed for the entire next week. I profusely thanked him, and for his continued friendship. *Wow*. I felt good and was so exhilarated! I now thought that if only all, or at least most, of my chef friends would react that same way, I just may have a chance.

To make a long story short, that first day I was very fortunate to get twelve orders, short of the twenty to maximize the use of the driver and truck, but I only called twelve accounts! I wanted to get all the orders packed and delivered as early as I could. I concentrated on just the close Peninsula that first day. I would have to take it an area at a time, since I only had one truck and one driver. I couldn't have deliveries in different areas on the same day. I would handle that problem when or if it arose. That was also pretty far-fetched at the time anyway. Being a small operation, giving a big impression could have its flaws and improprieties. But no matter what, I wouldn't let a customer down.

Well, it happened the very next day. I was calling accounts in Marin County on Tuesday, and Charlie, the chef from the Hilton Inn near the San Francisco airport called and needed something for lunch that he'd forgotten to order on Monday. So, when I had ten orders in Marin, I stopped. Yes, again much short of my intended goal, but I had to deal with deliveries in two different directions now. After all, no one knew I only had two employees and one truck. So, I then got out on the floor and helped Tom and Walter pack the orders. At eleven, I had Tom take the order to the Hilton Inn in my Ranchero.

I then loaded Walter with all the orders for Marin County and got him on his way so that when Tom got back, he could start cleaning up and take care of re-icing and putting away the fresh fish, then give me an inventory to keep me abreast of what we needed for the rest of the week. This was now looking like it could be a serious business erupting and I'd be hiring more employees soon. It's time to get more proficient on my margins if I was going to start hiring employees.

To realize the overall 25 percent gross profit margin needed, I had to greatly reduce the amount of fresh product I was buying from the other wholesalers since it was at a much higher price than it would have been by buying direct. I now needed to get bold and only order directly from the producers.

The gross profit margin on fresh fish should average 30 percent, greater than frozen shellfish, averaging 20 percent. Fresh, 30 percent, frozen, 20 percent, equals 50 percent, divided by two, equals 25 percent. Gross profit margins would now be critical.

Business owners often confuse Gross Margin to Markup; however, the two terms greatly reflect profits differently. The markup must be enough to offset all expenses and generate a profit.

For example; a 25 percent markup would only equate to a 20 percent gross margin. Confusing I know. Markup is the percentage difference between the product cost and the selling price. Gross margin is the percentage difference between the product selling price and the profit. The markup percentage is higher, but the gross margin percentage is lower. For example; a 33.3 percent markup equals a 25 percent gross margin. Not being aware of this can greatly affect the net profit. I always used a 33.3 percent markup, thus giving me the 25 percent gross margin required to cover all the expenses for a wholesale seafood business.

Well, you may be wondering why I hadn't hit downtown San Francisco yet, since it was so close. It was because I had to be much more proficient with my operation before I took them on. The major hotels and clubs can be challenging, plus they needed a very early morning delivery, and I didn't have the staff yet. But believe me, they were on the list!

This was like playing Russian Roulette, trying to have enough but not too much fresh product. I couldn't afford to freeze anything, and couldn't and wouldn't mark anything out as unavailable, showing an inability to deliver. Fresh product came in on Mondays and Wednesdays, and occasionally also on a Thursday, so it was tight to figure. Let me add, this is not a business you choose to be in. It is a stressful and nightmarish way to make a living. I was born into it, and since I foolishly didn't take education seriously, I was stuck in it. It was also survival.

As I was making sales calls, many of the chefs of the finer hotels, restaurants, and clubs were asking what the different types of fresh fish were that I had that they could feature for the fresh fish of the day. The idea then soon occurred to me that I wanted to make it a goal to eventually be the first to bring in different, exotic fresh-fish species from other parts of the world. Air freight was becoming popular, and the cost should be coming down as time progressed. I would be like a transmigrate albatross, exploring the world's oceans for fish!

That move would not only allow me to be distinctive in having an array of fresh fish from around the world, it meant I would have the privilege of marking it up many times cost, even possibly over 100 percent, since it would most likely be an unknown new species in the United States with no competition or comparison pricing as an issue.

After completing my first five days in business, the sales for the week totaled $35,000. It was mind-boggling that the reception from the chefs had gone so well. Almost every account I called, had bought, and if not that day, they'd said to call again in a few days, meaning they just didn't need anything at the time. I was truly a lucky boy. I was honored and felt rewarded for all the years of grief. More than anything, I felt relieved. Somewhat.

The gross profit for those first five days was $7,000. I was only averaging 20 percent gross, but that was okay since my expenses were so low. The net profit that first week was $5,500. In 1974.

Was this what being in your own business rewarded you? I wondered. However, I knew it was because my expenses were currently extraordinarily low, and that would soon change. As business increased and became more professional, expenses would increase proportionately. The day would also come when I would have to give my employees a medical plan, sick leave, vacation pay, social security, and unemployment benefits. That was a scary thought. But why should that be scary? If I controlled the ratio between the increase in expenses with the increase in sales, my profit margin should proportionately work out to my past proven formula.

Percentages needed to be monitored carefully. I couldn't sell too cheaply just to attract customers. It was okay at first for a short while, but as time went on, they would have to be edged up.

I had to concentrate on eventually getting more customers, which meant spreading out. That also meant another truck, another driver. Come on Kiki, it's only been two weeks!

I still hadn't tackled the big ones in downtown San Francisco yet, the hotels like the San Francisco Hilton. I felt that account was a sure thing, since my good friend Gunther was the executive chef and could buy as much as $10,000 a week. Wow! That would be awesome. Then the Fairmont, Mark Hopkins, St. Francis, those may be more difficult, but if I was determined, I would crack them!

To succeed in sales, you must be persistent and consistent!

Then, of course, there were the Safeway stores and Lucky's to hit eventually. *Wait a minute, I thought to myself. Slow down for Christ sake, Kiki. You still only have one rented truck and two employees, and a broken-down Ranchero and a cooler full of holes. You're going too fast.* That's always been my problem—my mind drives me nuts. Try living in this body.

Monday came, and I was now in a bit of turmoil. Excited that I had gotten so many orders the past week from my chef friends but knowing I still had so many more to call, I started realizing that I couldn't handle all the calls, do the bookkeeping, all the buying, and stay on top of the overall running of this now somewhat-promising operation. I hesitated in hiring. Things were just still too unsure; it was too soon to add to the payroll, I felt.

So which area do I call this morning? The Peninsula, Marin, the city, the East Bay? Okay, that does it! I need some help making the calls, but the buyers want to talk to me! They know me. When I find someone to help, I'll have to call the buyers and explain my dilemma, and hope they understand. I also must make sure when someone else calls them, I'm close by to overhear the conversations, to quickly say hi so they know I'm in touch and in tune with them. I not only value their business, but their friendship. They have all been so loyal, it's unbelievable. I must also check out their orders since I know the little incremental details of what they want. This was going to be tough.

I decided to rent another truck for Thursday and Friday, knowing we would have to send trucks in opposite directions on those days, so I would have Tom, the floor man, make those deliveries, and I would handle the floor after he left. Okay, that wasn't going to work. I was splitting myself up into too many directions, and I was going to exhaust my brothers, as well as myself.

The word was out by now that I'd started up the fish business, and some of my ex-employees were stopping by, looking for jobs, so I hired a driver who lived close by. Then a young man called, asking if I was looking for a salesman. Of course, I was, but he was pricey for me at the time, but I needed the help and he knew the business. I wasn't a proven factor yet, so I couldn't steal a salesman from the competition. He then helped me with my morning calls and I assigned him the areas where I didn't know as many chefs, mainly the East Bay and Marin.

I was now starting to get a bit concerned; the business was looking very serious now, and I needed to make decisions for the future—if there was going to be one.

Never make decisions when you're tired! Get a good night's rest and tackle it in the morning when you're fresh. And that's exactly what I did. Over the next few days, I carefully strategized and planned the future momentum of the business.

Sales started increasing at an amazing rate, and we were really, really, busy! I remember so well the first time my truck picked up at cold storage and filled the entire truck. What a thrill that was! Could we really be selling that much? Soon after, one Thursday, we had to send a truck to each of the four areas. I had two rentals, an old Ranchero, and had to rent another truck for the day. The two drivers, the floor man, and the salesman all made deliveries on that day. I was left alone at the plant and had to re-ice and put away all the fresh fish, then take inventory and clean up. Now exhausted, I still had the bookkeeping to do and make calls for the next day. Okay, we need more help.

One morning, a short while later, I got a call from Beverly, a young woman who had worked for me in the office at the old Paladini company and asked if I had any office work for her to do. I immediately hired her part-time, doing the bookkeeping and sending out statements. I desperately needed to be relieved of that.

I was now up to five employees and things were humming. We were in inflationary times; it seemed as if whatever frozen inventory I bought was worth more the following week, and of course I priced it at replacement cost, allowing a greatly increased profit margin. Lucky boy! However, I don't believe that just luck is the spiral to fortune. I believe one makes their own luck by being opportunistic and wise enough to know when to take advantage of the opportunity.

Speaking of being lucky, the week prior I'd taken the family for a ride, and we ended up in Monterey. While walking around the old fishing pier after lunch, we came upon a shop that sold large models of fishing boats. Lo and behold, one was named *Lucky Boy*. I had to have it. I'll tell you later where *Lucky Boy* is today.

It was hard to comprehend this was all happening. I was now seriously in business and needed to prepare to properly handle it. I couldn't screw things up with late deliveries by not having the equipment or manpower. I had to seize the opportunity and solidify the future. These accounts were now relying on me to totally supply them.

Renting trucks was a waste of money, so it was time to buy a couple of trucks or three. I bought three used trucks in good shape and bought a used fork lift and paid for them upon purchase.

My theory was, and still is, if you can pay for new equipment or any expansion-related item, upon purchase and have it not affect the cash flow, then you're not over-expanding. This, of course, would and should only take place when and if excess cash was available. I wanted no long-term leases or payments that could suffocate me in the event of an unexpected slow down.

Meanwhile, business was still exploding. It was as if we were the only wholesaler. Accounts were aggressively calling in faster than we had a chance to call them. I'd never thought this was possible, and in such a short time. *Confidence doesn't come from what you knew you could do, but from overcoming what you thought you couldn't do!*

Within a few more months, we were up to five trucks that we owned outright, had five drivers, four order packers, two salesmen, and a bookkeeper; I was up to twelve employees now. Scary.

It was now getting ever-so-difficult to unload and load the trucks through the one door on such a busy street, with people constantly walking by. I was also getting tickets daily on the trucks because there was no place to park them, so we had to park them around the corner in a residential area. Things were happening so fast it was difficult to keep up.

Why this tremendous influx of business? I wondered. *Am I doing everything right? Or is my competition doing everything wrong? Maybe a little of both.*

Meanwhile, as my business was on incline, my mom's health was in decline. She had had another stroke. The perennial strokes were devastating her body and her mind. This was so hard to witness, to see this wonderful, kind person deteriorating before my eyes. It made me feel helpless and forlorn. Her life was now in God's hands.

I tried to visit with her each night before going home. I was very tired by the time I arrived, and felt I wasn't giving her the attention she needed. I would hold her hand and she would squeeze it tightly while looking at me, trying to smile. Her eyes had a look of desperation. She looked frightened and it sent chills down my spine. She knew she was failing, and I was helplessly paralyzed with that fear. It was difficult to find the right words to say to comfort her. Saying "I love you, Mom" now appeared to be fruitless.

I also needed to give Joan and the kids attention. The kids were quickly growing up into young adults, and my guidance was essential. I needed to be more involved in their lives.

Joan was doing an amazing job with the girls. The three girls were now in the Girl Scouts, and Joan was a leader. We were all going to Marin County that weekend for a Girl Scout camp out. Me, camping? Oh, boy. I had never been camping in my life. Well, I had once, long ago when I'd been in the Boy Scouts, but I'd gotten thrown out after the first night. I won't say why.

We arrived Saturday midday, and I started to set up camp. First, the tent. Okay, it was a disaster. The wind was blowing a gale, and of course, I didn't read the instructions how to set it up, and it was being blown all over. I would get one end staked up, then the other end would blow loose. This repeated itself time and time again. Joan and the kids were swimming and expected to come back to a tent all set up to change in. This was now ending up being more stressful than running the business.

So, you know how it went: They returned from swimming and came upon green canvas blowing in every direction, with me chasing the ends, trying to hold them down to stake them into the ground. Of course, they started laughing mercilessly at their now fatigued and weary father, as I laid back, exhausted from the ordeal. I have never been known to be much good with that sort of thing, the outdoors thing. Joan and the kids then took over and had it set up within minutes. "Woman power!" they proudly exclaimed. Yeah, but there were four of them!

It was now dinner time and I was told to start a fire. The goddamn wind was still blowing, and they expected me to start a fire . . . with a match! It seemed like the wind was a demonic force attempting to belittle me in front of my kids and defeat my every move. Joan, exasperated watching me, then stepped in and got the damn fire going, and all the girls took over the cooking while I sat back and watched. I said I would do the dishes—sure, paper plates.

We then had dinner and sat around the now blazing fire, warming ourselves from the chill coming from the ocean that never seemed to cease. All was good, and this was now fun. The kids made s'mores and we played games. It was so great to be able to share this time with my family and give them some fond memories of their father's (in)competence with outdoor skills.

Night time came, and it was time to hit the sack. We rolled out the sleeping bags in the now secured tent and attempted to sleep, but the ground was hard and full of rocks that jutted into our backs. I'd watched a program once that showed how to gather up leaves and brush to sleep on, making it soft to lay upon. It worked! I was now their ostensible hero, though briefly. I really didn't know a damn thing about camping, having spent most of my cloistered youth with my sisters. Heck, I knew more about bra sizes and nylon stocking lengths than this guy stuff! My brothers were uninvolved with me, and my dad, too busy.

As night fell, I was again to be challenged by several unexpected events. The food had foolishly been left in a cooler on the ground and could easily be opened by any prying paws and claws. Raccoons soon ravaged the cooler and knocked it over, spilling the contents. We were all awakened by the noise and scrambling about, so acting like a macho jock in front of my kids, I bravely attempted to scare them off, but they audaciously stood on their back feet, hissing at me in defiance. I recall being a bit daunted and intimidated by these small aggressive varmints, but I had to stand up to them. I was the big machismo paternal figure, the protector, and needed to show the kids I was fearless.

I then grabbed some pots and pans and started clanking them together, making lots of noise. However, the raccoons just continued munching on the carrot sticks and celery while looking at me like I was an idiot. The only thing I had accomplished was to wake up everyone in the campsite, who wondered who the idiot was, the same reference as the racoons accredited me with, that was making all the noise. Now I had a surrounding audience of at least twenty young girls in their jammies, as well as their parents, watching me foolishly clanging the pots together. Thank God, no one filmed this. I recall seeing a few of the girls with their hands over their mouths, chuckling, asking, "Whose father is that?" My girls quickly slipped back into their tent, so as not to be noticed.

I then thought I would outsmart those cagy critters. So, I took the cooler and tied it up in a tree, so it was hanging from a branch. *Ha! That'll fix them!* I thought. I then hollered to my attentive audience, "Okay, everyone can go back to bed now! Everything will be fine!"

We were all back into the tent now and freezing our butts off, trying to warm up again in our sleeping bags. Just as I started to doze off, I heard clambering outside once again. It can't be the damn raccoons! I'd tied all the food up in the tree. I went outside and there they were up in the tree, enjoying our breakfast. *What the hell?! I didn't know they could climb trees!*

Joan, disgusted, then abruptly came out of the tent and said, "Oh, Kiki." She then shined the flashlight on them, and they ran like hell!

Consequently, I was denounced as my girls' father for the weekend and was banished from attending any of the activities with the other scouts and their parents to save face. By the way, each Girl Scout leader had to have a unique individual name. Joan chose "Mrs. Beaver"—yep, *beaver.* Think about it! The other husbands thought that was quite a unique choice! That weekend somehow, actually ended up being a fun experience, even though the girls had briefly been fatherless as a result of the events that had taken place.

Monday morning came, and I went back to work to try to make some extra money to buy a self-erecting tent and a fire starter, plus some raccoon repellent, so I thought it may be time to call on the Safeway stores.

Safeway paid in seven days, therefore it would greatly augment the cash flow and give the volume I needed in placing the fresh fish orders directly from the producers up north. I made an appointment with the seafood buyer; I knew him, but not that well.

During the meeting in his office, he said he had heard of me, which was good. Well, good, if everything he'd heard had indeed been good. I admitted upfront that I had just started up. I had to admit that because I couldn't handle hundreds of stores; they had over 250 stores in the Bay Area. Of course, it was very unlikely he would give that many to me to start, but I had to move cautiously so as not to screw up this opportunity—if indeed there was going to be an opportunity. All I wanted to start with was a few of the San Francisco stores.

After talking for a while, he eventually asked about my operation and its ability to perform. Me, being me, I of course greatly embellished. Yep, a form of bullshit. My mouth often uncontrollably runs wild with garishly exaggerated things. Well, after hearing my upbeat, amplified ability to perform, he then said he would try us out in a few stores. Okay, a few stores, that was great! A "few stores" ended up being sixty-three. He then came up with a list of all the stores in Northern California and checked off the ones that had just installed new over-the-counter seafood departments. He then explained that I would be an additional supplier, along with two other wholesalers already supplying the stores, and this would only be a trial period; the stores would then report to him of my performance and quality. I knew that these new over-the-counter stores had huge volume, but at the same time were very demanding.

Suddenly, my gut tightened and my heart raced, now wondering if I had just taken on too much. I thought if I walked out with just a dozen or so stores to start, that would have been great. Me and my damn big mouth and pretentious ways!

I mentioned to him that I needed a week or so to get geared up for this opportunity. He took that well, and with respect. I now had to rush and get a couple more trucks, another order packer, and two more drivers, and—oh, yeah!—someone to call the sixty-three stores every other day. I was now up to seven trucks and sixteen employees. What had I just taken on?

This is a funny true story: A few weeks after supplying the stores—and yes, we had successfully performed thus far—the buyer called me and said he wanted to see firsthand some of my fresh products, and where I was operating from. I told him that I was temporarily renting a very small and somewhat shabby warehouse, and was looking for another location, and felt he should possibly wait. I assured him, however, that it was not affecting the quality or my performance, and obviously so, because the reports he was getting were very good. He said he understood but was considering giving me more stores and insisted upon seeing it.

I shuddered, thinking of him coming to where I was operating from, and hoped that the "rat pack" wouldn't come to visit that day.

A few days later, he unexpectedly called me one morning and said he was in the area and was stopping by shortly. *Oh, shit!* I screamed to Tom, my foreman, "Jesus Christ! Clean up the place—and quickly! The Safeway buyer will be here in a few minutes!" I felt I was screwed. He would never allow me to supply the stores after seeing the place; the holes in the walls, especially the ones in the cooler that we stuffed with cardboard, the one lonely door to load from, the scroungy little office, the cracked floors . . . the leaking ceiling. *Oh my God!*

Tom got right on it and had the men wash down the floor, ice up all the fresh fish, pick up the remaining orders and put them on pallets to elevate them from the oil-slicked floor, and close the cooler door, hoping he wouldn't go in, then calmed everyone down just in time for his arrival.

I then did that *little click* in my head when I must perform and got geared up for him. Thank God we were busy that morning, so there were plenty of orders that were packed and ready to load, possibly a sign of doing well, which might impress him.

Well, lo and behold, a few minutes later, in he walked. "Good morning! Good to see you again, sir," I said with respect. I then expressed my concern over his impending view of the place, and reiterated that I'd just started, and the location was temporary. Strangely, he appeared to be okay with it—at least for the moment.

I then showed him around. It only took a few seconds. There wasn't much to show him. I tried desperately not to bring him into the cooler where the fresh fish was kept, but he insisted upon seeing the fresh fish we had on hand and wanted to see where it had come from. Upon walking into the cooler, he asked to see the fresh local king salmon that I was sending the stores, so I told Tom to pull a box of medium king salmon over and take a few out to show him.

When Tom reached under the ice and grabbed a salmon, I was shocked—no, much worse than that—horrified and panic-stricken to see a salmon that was half eaten. Yes, *eaten*! That goddamn Guillermo had gotten into the cooler earlier that night and had eaten half the salmon. It was obvious from the teeth marks showing on the flesh. As Murphy's Law goes, the one goddamn salmon that Tom had pulled from the box had to be the one that Guillermo had dined on. I told you he had no manners!

Anyway, I now had to think fast—really, really fast! The head buyer now screamed, "Oh my God! What happened to that salmon, Kiki?!" Without hesitation, I immediately exclaimed, "Those goddamn fishermen snuck in another salmon that was eaten by a shark. Damn them! That's the second one this week!" He then said, "Oh, that's too bad. That will be a total loss for you, won't it, Kiki?"

Whew. If he only knew! Tom then looked at me and rolled his eyes.

You never get a second chance to make a good first impression! Had I just blown that? I don't think so. I was respectful and humble. Humility will guide you to the right path more often than not.

Tom always used to say to me, "You fall into a bucket of shit and come out smelling like a rose!" I explained to him, "That's because you have to be full of it to get out of it."

Well, happy that I'd just averted a tragedy, I jokingly said to Tom, "Hey, Tommy, talking about shit, why is it that a deer, a cow, and a horse all eat the same grass, yet a deer poops pellets, a cow poops a flop, and a horse poops a plop?" He replied, "How in the hell do I know?" I then answered, "Me neither!" Then he asked, "So what the hell does that have to do with anything?" I said, "Absolutely nothing."

The Safeway account eventually added more districts and more stores. My God, we were now swamped, and I was overwhelmed, and of course, we now checked every individual salmon we sent to the stores.

I'd only been in business less than a year and it was looking like I would have to buy another two trucks, which would now make eight. But where in the hell was I going to park them? There I went thinking again. *Okay, I know. I'll have the drivers take them home–perfect. That way I don't have to wait for them to come back to the plant. Better yet, I won't have to pay them overtime for driving back. It's also a plus for them, since they won't have to drive their cars to work and back home!*

I was feeling good about things, and this was all happening while running the business as Seafood Sales—no one gave a damn about the name "Paladini." I was just "Kiki." I would have loved to run my dad's family's noses in this. Their noses were certainly big enough! However, I can't talk.

Someday after I'd deemed the company successful—I mean, *really* successful—if ever, I might rename the company "Paladini Seafood Company," and have signs painted on all the trucks with a big red P. That would really get them. Oh, how I wished my Uncle Alex was still alive. Just a few years ago he hadn't known who I was, plus there were seven owners of the old company, and now just one. But I couldn't get a big head. I wasn't there yet. There was still so much more to accomplish before a phoenix rose from the ashes.

We all live under the same sky, but we don't all have the same horizon! I sure hoped I wasn't shooting for a distant star.

It was the end of September 1976, and we'd just passed the two-year mark, with sales exceeding $4 million—$350,000 a month. Who in the hell in their right mind would have ever imagined that?

Profits were levels never comprehended. All the trucks and equipment were paid for, and I had excess cash flow. This was also due to the fact that the operational cost factor was minimal, operating out of the small rented plant, but I knew we couldn't continue to operate like this. We had no room to move, not enough freezer storage, and certainly not enough cooler space, plus loading and unloading from one door was a nightmare. There was also no place to park all the trucks anywhere close by in the morning. The people in the neighborhood were constantly complaining to the police and we were getting tickets galore. I had to find another facility to rent, and as soon as possible.

I spent the next year searching San Francisco and the close Peninsula for an appropriate building to rent, but to no avail. None were suitable for a wholesale seafood distribution operation, plus they were mostly old, dilapidated buildings that would cost a fortune to renovate.

My Aunt Henrietta had passed away at the beginning of the year, and I was to inherit roughly $75,000. I wondered how far that would take me if I were to buy a piece of land, then design and build a facility to my specifications. I would certainly have to figure out some very creative financing. There wasn't much you could do with seventy-five grand.

I then looked around at vacant land all over San Francisco that would be suitable for a commercial wholesale seafood distribution operation. I luckily found a new business park in the city, which was called India Basin Industrial Park. Only one site had been built on at the time. It was a very nice-looking building, with setback landscaping, first class—just what I wanted to complete my dream of upscaling the seafood industry—a sharp contrast from the dumps on Fisherman's Wharf. I also felt a San Francisco identity was important. This could be perfect.

The thought then occurred to me that it looked like it could be a city-sponsored redevelopment project, which meant they just might offer some attractive financing. Intrigued, I made an appointment and met with the city planner and looked at sites. I found the perfect-size parcel of sixty thousand square feet, almost one and a half acres, at a price that I could pay cash for with my upcoming $75,000 inheritance. The city was offering heavily discounted prices for the land to encourage employing neighboring residents, and as I'd hoped, it was indeed confirmed that it was a redevelopment project with low-cost financing available. It was only for a small percentage of the overall project, however, since the redevelopment agency's funding was limited. This could then be a problem, arranging for the balance of the construction loan. I had hoped the process would be easier. I would be paying $1.25 per square foot for land that was worth $7.75 per square foot but had to conform to their restrictions and hiring demands—that was okay.

I now needed to figure out the construction financing of such a monstrous undertaking. I figured if I owned the land, I could get a loan from the Small Business Administration, combined with a bank loan to build the plant, and some funds would also be available through the redevelopment agency. It was worth a try. But before I committed to buying the land, I told the city planner I needed to get a commitment of construction financing before moving forward. I then gave him a refundable deposit of $15,000 (20 percent) to hold the parcel.

I contacted the Small Business Administration (SBA) regarding a construction loan for the new plant, then met with the Bank of America to try to team the two together for as close to a 100 percent loan as possible. Since the SBA only finances 20 percent on these types of projects, I would need possibly as much as 80 percent from the bank, given that it was difficult to determine just what the India Basin Redevelopment Agency's funding would be. It was captioned as a rather small amount, possibly 5 percent, and I didn't like the connotation of the word "possibly." You know I like things to be definitive. I was also finding the agency difficult to work with and unorganized, and felt apprehensive with their funding prospects, though supposedly arranged for through the city. The city required me to hire 17 percent of the employees from local residents, conforming to the redevelopment's requirements, so there must be remuneration for that, I figured.

This convoluted arrangement could only be possible if I owned the land mortgage-free—and I would soon.

I then found that this type of financing had never been done before—ever! Attempting to get three sources of financing to agree was looking like it was a preposterous, unattainable, overly ambitious goal. Another challenge!

I remember talking to the loan officers of all the three entities, and them staring back at me with blank expressions; and they were the experts. I was beginning to think that this may not work, but, never giving in, and having *perseverance*, I was going to pursue the idea and make it happen. No one so far had said no; however, no one so far had said yes.

After several months of planning and figuring, and refiguring, the SBA, the Bank of America, and the Redevelopment Agency granted me a $1.2 million construction loan. This was, of course, after hiring an architect to draw up plans to get competitive bids from contractors for the project, plus allowing a little extra for the inevitable unknown.

I was told that this would be the very first loan ever of its kind that the three lending institutions had teamed up and agreed to do jointly, anywhere in the entire United States.

I couldn't help but think that speaking up and nudging them, expressing the fact that "after all, it's all about creating jobs," may have been instrumental in the accomplishment of the loans from the three lending institutions.

I was later asked if the Bank of America could do a documentary and an interview with me and film the entire building process, given that it was a pilot program implemented after the many intense meetings between the bank officers and myself. I agreed. They wanted to use it in their branches across the nation as a training tool for these types of loans. I have a DVD copy.

I want to mention that my competition on Fisherman's Wharf had sweetheart leases with the city, paying somewhere in the vicinity of $600 to $700 per month, with little or no rent escalations each year. Lease contracts were allegedly arranged by the city a long time ago, exhibiting favoritism with some suspicious affiliations. All spaces were of course occupied, so I had to build my own plant. Not saying I would have even considered the wharf. I say "had to" build my own plant because we not only outgrew the tiny startup plant, but the constant city and state health inspections would have eventually closed me down.

Think of the difference in fixed expenses I was about to encounter: My mortgage would be more than $13,000 per month. I had to overcome a $12,300 fixed expense factor difference compared to my competition on the wharf. Having said that, I was building a $1.2 million facility with only $75,000 of my own money, by *being creative.*

I met with the architect and completed the final detailed drawings for the new facility, making sure I kept within the boundaries of the loan commitment. It would be, when completed, the largest, most modern wholesale seafood distribution plant on the West Coast. Construction was slated to start soon after competitive bidding was reviewed and a local contractor had been selected, who, by the way, also had to conform to the city redevelopment agency's hiring regulations of employing 17 percent from the neighboring areas. Don't ask me where the that odd employment figure came from?

I had met the then-mayor of San Francisco, George Moscone, several times at social functions, but befriended him after formally being introduced by my good friend Bill Armanino, owner of a large wholesale spice company in the city. He was also at the time co-owner of the Fior D'Italia, a famous old Italian Restaurant in North Beach. He enjoyed throwing lavish dinner parties for his closest of friends in the restaurant's small private banquet room, appropriately named "The Godfather Room" since most who dined with him were indeed Italian. Bill, however, was quite the opposite of what the connotation of the room's name insinuated. He was a fine, respectable gentleman.

The room only held ten people, so to be invited was an honor. One night during one of these affairs, we were treated to a private performance by Tony Bennett, an old friend of Bill's. It was a magical night, being in the small private room with Tony singing for only Joan and I and the three girls, George and his wife, and Bill and his wife. That same night during dinner, I asked George Moscone if he would do a ground-breaking ceremony for me at the site of the new plant in a couple of weeks. He said it would be his pleasure, and for me to call his office and advise his secretary of when and where. Moscone, Armanino, and Paladini are very prominent, old San Francisco names with abundant histories. And of course, everyone knows who Anthony Benedetto is.

A few weeks passed, and it was now nine in the morning on Monday, November 20, 1978. Mayor George Moscone arrived at the new property in a chauffeur driven black city sedan for the ground-breaking ceremony. Several local TV stations were there as well. About a dozen or so brokers also showed up to join in on the festivities. Joan had sprayed an old fishing pole gold, and we had the mayor throw it out onto the dirt of the property as he said, "San Francisco proudly welcomes back the Paladini Seafood Company to our great city!" Thinking back now, I'm not sure just why we used a fishing pole, and why gold? And why did we have him throw it out onto the dirt of my empty lot? It just may have been a pretty lame idea.

WILBUR W. HAMILTON, Execut.ve Director

GEORGE R. MOSCONE, Mayor

Howard M. Wexler, President
Joan-Marie Shelley, Vice President
Dian Blomquist
Rubin Glickman
Walter F. Kaplan
Melvin D. Lee
Hannibal A. Williams

SAN FRANCISCO REDEVELOPMENT AGENCY

939 ELLIS STREET • SAN FRANCISCO 94109
ADDRESS MAIL TO POST OFFICE BOX 646 • SAN FRANCISCO, CALIFORNIA 94101

(415) 771-8800

For immediate release

REFER TO:

A. PALADINI GROUNDBREAKING IN REDEVELOPMENT'S INDIA BASIN AT 11:00 A.M. TUESDAY

More than 100 years ago, a San Franciscan named A. Paladini started a commercial fishing business where the Bay then met Montgomery Street.

Over the years, the business grew so large that he became known as "The Seafood Tycoon," with eight plants and more than 1,000 employees --

And when a friend named A. Giannini wanted to start something called the Bank of Italy, he turned to A. Paladini for backing.

Later, the Bank of Italy became, of course, the Bank of America . . . but five years ago, A. Paladini, no longer a family enterprise, went out of business.

Then, a year later, in 1974, the grandson of the original A. Paladini -- Achille Paladini, an experienced food processor in his own right -- decided to start his own firm, using his grandfather's name, on San Bruno Avenue. It grew so rapidly that he soon needed larger quarters, and almost went to the suburbs to get them.

Fortunately, however, the Redevelopment Agency had India Basin Industrial Park available --

And so, on Tuesday, November 21, at 11:00 a.m., the A. Paladini Seafood Company will break ground (possibly with a golden fishing rod) for a 15,000 square foot fish processing plant, at the corner of Galvez and Mendell -- with the help of a $1.2 million loan from, appropriately, the Bank of America.

- more -

40% recycled material

Mayor George Moscone, Supervisor Robert Gonzales and other government officials will join with Achille Paladini and the Redevelopment Agency in the ceremony.

According to Wilbur W. Hamilton, agency executive director:

"The new plant will enable A. Paladini to double its work force, from 20 to 40 employees.

"And since the creation or preservation of blue collar jobs is a prime objective of India Basin, this is good news for San Francisco."

Hamilton also noted that A. Paladini is the sixth industrial plant to go under construction in India Basin.

Four have been completed and occupied -- McCormick-Morgan Inc., Western Electric, the Morgan Equipment Company and Pacific Western Engineering.

Another, De Narde Construction Company, is 10 percent underway.

And, finally, Hamilton said, construction will begin on four more over the next three months -- Western Boiler, Homestead Ravioli, Banker and Marks and Steam Specialties.

###

I invited George Moscone and his family to the opening party that would eventually take place the following year, and he said that he would be looking forward to it. It would have been fun having the mayor join us for the opening celebration.

However, sadly, as we all know, George Moscone, at age forty-nine, was assassinated the following Monday morning, November 27, 1978—exactly one week after the ground-breaking ceremony, and eerily almost to the hour.

Regarding the new plant, I now wondered how all this had happened. Yes, I was truly a lucky boy, but also a very scared lucky boy, as well. This was a huge undertaking. I don't totally believe in luck, as I said prior. Maybe in playing the lotto, but in real-life situations, you make your own luck by seeing an opportunity and acting upon it, not just by thinking about it. *If you think about it for too long, it may be gone.* Being an opportunist is assuredly a virtue.

Meanwhile, I knew this was a serious move and that my expense factor would greatly increase. I also knew that I needed to greatly improve sales to offset the expense by the time we moved in next year. *Any decision you make may have costs and consequences.* Having said that, I would now own my own facility, my own property to operate my business from.

I have always lived with the concept of controlling my own destiny. In this case, to strive to own my own property for my place of business. I have witnessed too many businesses being forced to cease their operation due to greedy landlords wanting to cash in, taking advantage when seeing a successful business, often increasing rents to absurd, unaffordable levels.

The girls were now all in high school and doing well, and Joan was happy because we were not only able to finally finish landscaping our new home, but completed furnishing it as well. Yay, we can invite the neighbors now!

We'd also just started construction of our vacation home in Lake Tahoe in the Homewood area. We had bought an ideal lot of three quarters of an acre in a cul-de-sac with a stream that flowed at the rear of the property. We had purchased the lot several years ago with a minimal down payment, and I'd had to work for my brother-in-law on Saturdays at the time to make the thirty-five-dollar-a-month payment.

Well, with what I was now confronting, it certainly was the time to sit on my grandfather's old wooden trunk every morning—and hope to hell it brought me the same luck it had given him!

CHAPTER 24
BITTER SWEET MONTHS

My mom's health was unfortunately deteriorating further. The mini strokes now persisted, with each one isolating her from the world around her even more. It was tragic to witness her leaving us slowly, yet surely. My own personal comfort was that she knew I loved her, contrary to never verbally expressing it to my dad.

Nevertheless, I was having feelings of guilt that I wasn't seeing her as much as I should. I also wasn't spending the time with Joan and the girls that I should, either. Is this what happens when you're consumed in perfecting the development of a business? Unfortunately, the way my mind works, everything must be perfect, and it was mentally consuming. However, this was survival, and the only way I could support my family. Plus, college was just around the corner for the three girls, and sure, I also wanted them to be proud of the name they carried.

Why was I so driven to succeed? I will never know. And why this obsession to preserve the damn name? They say, "There is only one success: to be able to spend your life in your own way." However, this wasn't how I'd originally intended to spend my life in my own way; working in a repulsive, cold, damp environment, with men screaming profanities and the redolence of fish.

I often wondered why this couldn't be a respectable industry while handling seafood products in an environment that exemplified cleanliness, as it should. Of course, there were state and county inspections, but for the most part, sanitation was over looked. If you'll recall, this was in the late 1970s. Hopefully I could make a difference with the new distribution plant and try to ameliorate the industry. It was going to cost a fortune, but I had to contemplate to achieve the goal of exemplifying cleanliness and respectability in handling seafood products. Everything in the plant would be new, with stainless steel tables and scales, attractive yet unpretentious offices, and clean white trucks exhibiting the ultimate of sanitary conditions.

It was Christmas of 1978, and time to thank my employees for working their butts off for me, several of them, for four years now. Of course, my two brothers were first and foremost. I enjoyed compensating those who gave all they could with a substantial bonus to show recognition of their efforts being appreciated. *Recognition of efforts encourages a positive, productive, and innovative work climate. It's also an incentive to do better.*

Faithful employees are the lifeblood of any business. We were doing well, and I wanted to spread the prosperity as much as I could.

Having said that, the business had been created as a private enterprise, an economic system based on operating for profit, capitalism—not socialism, the economic theory that a business is owned by the community and its production not used for profit or individual wealth.

Fortunately, business continued to thrive, and the company was now established in the industry as one to be reckoned with. I was eagerly looking forward to the completion of the new plant, but with apprehension. I couldn't stop wondering if I was taking on more than I should, and if I could handle it.

June 8, 1979

Ever since opening the business I've had the feeling of insecurity, since I started with basically nothing, as you by now know. At the same time, I knew others looked at me as being a strong, confident man, but they were looking at the outside, at my affable, gregarious, bullshit ways that may have emanated confidence. No one in the industry except for my controller and my CPA knew I'd started with absolutely nothing. That was my lonely, covert secret. I had to keep this allusion of wealth to keep the allure. I needed and wanted my competition to fear me. Money is power!

An unsettling incident happened one day that was very disconcerting and disheartening. My brother Walter called to my attention that an employee was stealing! I asked who, but he wouldn't say. He did mention that he felt he was working with just one customer, but again, refused to say who. On the other hand, why wouldn't he just tell me who, and with what customer, but appreciated him stepping up and doing so.

This was shocking, especially since I hadn't been in business that long and needed every dollar for cash flow. How devastating it was to hear this. Coincidentally, I had noticed weeks earlier that my gross percentage had slipped a bit, and this now made sense. We took inventory very carefully every month, and I knew it wasn't a mistake with the inventory. I'd been perplexed and puzzled by it for weeks and had been racking my brain and couldn't determine the cause. I'd also even started checking out the trucks myself as much as possible, looking for innocent mistakes, as well as reviewing all the pricing. Everything appeared to be right. It was illogical.

Most problems can normally be resolved with *logic* and *common sense*.

I sat back and thought about this unnerving, egregious scenario for hours. Then I remembered that we had a customer that came in every Tuesday to pick up his order. I thought that to be odd, since we delivered to his area three times a week. I recall asking him why he picked up his product, and he said it was because he liked to see the quality he was getting. That made sense to me at the time. *Hmm*, I thought. *I must give this some attention. Just maybe, somehow.*

I then looked up his past receipts. He had been buying about $2,000 worth of product every Tuesday, between both fresh and frozen seafood. However, for the past six weeks his invoices had consistently shrunk down to about $500. To occasionally be less was of course normal, due to business conditions, but not for it to be consistently lower. That is, unless the account was buying several items from another wholesaler at a cheaper price—but he never complained about my prices. This was now an immediate red flag.

I recalled noticing just a few weeks ago that he hadn't been buying the more expensive frozen items, and asked him about it, and he said he was backed up with it. Of course, there was also the possibility that he was buying it elsewhere and was embarrassed to say. But why? I'd given him good prices because he picked up, saving us the delivery up to Vallejo, a good hour east.

Thinking further, I noticed he would always come in at ten in the morning, just when I would go up the street for a cup of coffee and a donut. This was "fishy." However, he had to be working with the employee who packed his order and then checked out his truck to get the frozen product on his truck without it being invoiced. I immediately knew who that person was. This was distressing, disheartening, and devastating.

The next week, I decided when he came in I would leave for coffee as normal, but this time would wait a few minutes until the tarp was pulled all the way back on his truck, as he always did upon arriving. With the tarp now untied and pulled all the way back, an empty bed was exposed, which allowed me to confirm there was no other product on the truck from another wholesaler.

I went up to the coffee shop and bought a cup of coffee as usual, but this time, brought it right back to the plant and waited outside the loading door while his truck was being loaded. I listened to him now saying his goodbyes. I suddenly then appeared and could see the fright on his face. He quickly started the truck and attempted to leave, but I was blocking him so he couldn't get out of the only loading door.

I then approached him as he sat in the driver's seat of the truck and I asked him for his invoice. He asked me why. I said, "I have had some quality problems with the fresh fish, and I want to see what fresh items you bought so I can check it to make sure they gave you the best." Now obviously unnerved, he exclaimed, "Oh, Mr. P., everything is good! Everything is fine." I then insisted at looking at the load on his truck. He was already invoiced, had signed the invoice, and was tied down with the motor running, and he was ready to pull out and leave; he couldn't say there were charges still coming if I found anything that hadn't been invoiced. So up on the truck, I went. I immediately noticed a huge mound up near the front under the tarp. Obviously, the load was much larger than what was invoiced. Now tearing the order apart, lo and behold, there was the $1,500 worth of frozen shellfish that had been missing every week on his order—he indeed had it. He just hadn't been charged for it!

This was where my gross margin was going. Numbers don't lie. Now you see the importance of constantly monitoring your gross margin.

Now getting the shakes—and that's not good—I promptly pulled off the frozen shellfish and threw it to the ground, spitting mad. My hair must have curled as I used some very explicit, foul language toward him while he looked around for his cohort. I can still see the vision of him cowering as he leaned against his truck. It seems like when I get mad, I get a foot taller!

I demanded he write a check for $3,000 and told him he wasn't getting the product that I'd taken off; that was to only partially pay for what he'd stolen last week and the week before, and God only knows for how long. I then said, "It's that, or I'm calling the police." So, with compunction, he meekly wrote the check. Then I said, "Now get the fuck out and never come back!"

That week, I had at least gotten the product back, plus an extra $3,000. Who knows how long this had been going on. According to the back invoices that I later looked at, I figured at least eight weeks, so the loss could have been as high as $12,000—in 1978. However, I got back $3,000 of it. I had only been in business a few years and couldn't take this kind of a hit. I also soon confirmed who I suspected the malefactor to be—it wasn't difficult.

Loss aversion is the impulse to recall negative experiences, and to let those darker memories shape your expectations of the future. This can be averted by forecasting in advance for these challenges and setbacks. These bumps in the road are inevitable and should be expected and not feared.

The man involved with this was a close friend I had hired. I now started feeling that maybe guy friends just didn't like me and enjoyed the hurt.

The visible scars on our rescued racing greyhounds reveal the evidence of the pain inflicted upon them at the track. My hidden internal scarring inflicted by male friends was deeply embedded within me, and now formed an impediment and cautionary barrier for any new friendships.

Besides that bitter incident, life was sweet. Business even better. Sales were soaring.

Everything was going great, but my mom, my poor mom, wasn't doing well, and her time was near. *Damn*, I thought. *Why can't life always be perfect in every way? I must get over this fantasy of perfection. It is in fact just that—a fantasy.*

Meanwhile, almost every day after the trucks were out, I went to the new plant to observe the construction and make minor changes as it took place. It was going well. As the building took shape, I recall being astounded by how enormous and cavernous the building was. Oh my God! The freezer ran the entire length of the building, nearly the size of a football field. I would no longer need to store and pay cold storage charges for the frozen inventory. What a tremendous savings and convenience that would be. However, that was the intention when I'd designed the building. It was scheduled for completion at the end of 1979, and we could move in sometime in early January of 1980.

It was early on a Wednesday morning while at work when I received a devastating call from my sister Kay. She said that Mom was unresponsive and had been rushed to Mills Hospital for observation.

I hurried down the Peninsula to the hospital and met Kay. She said, "Kiki, it's not good." It was another stroke, and a bad one, one that could end up taking her. The doctor said there was nothing he could do but wait forty-eight hours to see if she regained consciousness.

They then moved her across the street to the extended care unit to await the results. We both knew there was little chance of her regaining consciousness. She was now eighty-four, and so frail.

Business didn't matter anymore—very little did. I just wanted to be with my wife and three daughters. I needed their love and comfort.

Losing a parent is devastating, especially your mom. The one who gave you life; the one who nurtured you since birth and guided you into adulthood with the skills and love that only a mother could do.

I know this is the cycle of life, but somehow you think your parents will live forever. You want them to, but that would be living in a utopia, just a phantasmagorical fantasy, an illusory, idealistic society where life never ceases, and everyone is free of pain and suffering. Not possible. You can wish all you want on those green bales of hay you see passing on the roadway, but one day that truck will be empty.

The next day, my mom was still unresponsive. It was heartbreaking to see her looking so delicate, and now so vulnerable to death. Her eyes were closed, her chest making sudden tiny movements as she attempted to breath, while a low, dire, soft moan seemed to pervade her body. I took her hand and softy said, "C'mon, Mom, take another breath. Now another, now another." While holding her hand, her frail, tiny hand. Then, alarmingly, there was suddenly no response. No normal, impulsive grasp; her hand just rested in mine. About to faint with the realization that she may be about to pass, I bent over and held her tightly, but tenderly, afraid of hurting her. I was now unsure if I was holding her, or as my mom, being my mom, was holding me, just like the morning my dad had passed away. My mom would only think about her children, their well-being; she would have done anything to protect them.

I then held her close once again for several minutes as if to say goodbye. She must have known I was there. Though helpless, I was there. Overwhelmed with emotion, I had to turn away to hide the tears flowing down my cheeks. My only peace was that I'd told her many times I loved her, because it appeared to be too late now to verbally express anything.

The following day, we met with the doctor and he said she was brain dead. That is something you never want to hear about a loved one, at any age.

The doctor said he wanted to have a meeting with the immediate family the next morning. I knew what he was going to say, and I didn't want to hear it.

Friday morning, we met with the doctor. He again confirmed she was brain dead, and wanted to take her off all life support, which also meant no liquids or nourishment. That meant starving her to death. How in the hell could I say yes to that? To starve my mother—starve her? The one who reverently put food in my mouth most of my life.

I said no; there had to be another way to let her go peacefully, without suffering. My God. Unfortunately, I was out-voted. My mom died the next afternoon. She was then entombed on top of my dad at Holy Cross.

Joan and the girls were wonderful and shared my grief. Laura was a senior at Aragon High, Gina, a junior, and Diana, a freshman at Crystal Springs Uplands School. They hadn't experienced or dealt with death before and didn't know how to process it. I'm not sure anyone does, at any age.

The finality of death is like trying to comprehend the infinity of space. How can it not have an end, not have boundaries? How can life end with such a sudden complete void?

The happy, wonderful, carefree days as a child with my mom and dad on Baker street were now only a memory. How fast time passes; how fast life changes. How bitter sweet it is.

Let's now move on from that deeply emotional topic to life and the living. We'll fast forward to near the end of the year, the upcoming opening of the new facility, and the challenges of the future.

The final inspections of the new plant were about to take place. It was December of 1979. I spent the next few weeks meeting with the city inspectors, making sure it was following in compliance with all the city building codes. I was shocked to find out that I needed to have a disabled persons toilet stall in the men's restroom. I said, "Do you understand this is a wholesale seafood plant? It would be impossible for a disabled person to work on the production floor!" It fell on deaf ears, one stall had to be totally redone at additional expense to accommodate a disabled employee, which held up the final inspection by a week.

I finally got approval by the city, but now the Occupational Safety and Health Administration had to come in, as well as the state and federal inspectors, to make sure it was up to code.

I asked the inspectors why they were being so tough on me when most of the wholesalers on Fisherman's Wharf were operating out of rodent-infested dumps. There were no disabled persons bathrooms, no stainless-steel packing tables, no steam-cleaning the plant at the end of the day, no women's lounge adjacent to their bathroom, no employee lunch room; none of these facilities.

I couldn't help but think that maybe some of the guys on the wharf had gotten to one or more of the inspectors. It's rumored that possibly one or two of the companies just might have been involved with some unscrupulous organizations. However, this was just an allegation. But I bet that was it; they were trying to prevent me from opening, or sure as hell slow me down. Well, tough chance! Hey, just maybe they were starting to fear me. Little me, with *no* financial backing—none, zip! I bet they thought I'd inherited millions from Aunt Henrietta. I then thought, *So let them think it!*

When all the inspections were finally completed, the new facility would be the largest, most modern wholesale seafood distribution plant in the United States.

The company now owned over a dozen white trucks with no name on them. So just in time for the opening, I sent the trucks to the sign man and had "Paladini Seafood Company" painted on them. I would use the big red P as my logo. Red was the color of the old Paladini company's trucks, so that would bring in some of the old. I'd have it designed with a salmon coming from the bottom, going up through the opening of the P and emerging with a crown on it, symbolizing my start at the bottom and my eventual rise to the top. Emerging as the king, as my grandfather had. Wow, was that just a lot of crap, or what! It sure sounded as if my ego was acting up again. However, I view it as aggressive positive thinking. It's also, most likely, an impossibility.

I made plans to buy five new white refrigerated trucks and have them backed into the five loading docks the day of the grand opening. That would set the stage and impress the customers attending, we would soon need them anyway. Hopefully. I also bought four new white cars, Chevrolets, three coupes and a sedan for my salesmen, the sedan would be for the sales manager, that didn't exist yet. Neither did all the salesman. I didn't need the five new trucks either—so, you see, this whole scenario was just a simulation. I wanted to create a vision of success. Success breeds success! But at the same time, I must remember; if you buy things you don't need, you may have to sell things you *do* need.

Ignoring that wise thought, doing so would give us eighteen trucks and four cars. There would be twenty-two vehicles parked in the parking lot the day of the party. That would give the image of having unlimited funds and would put the fear in my competition. More importantly, it would show the customers, especially the chain store buyers, that we could easily handle their business. Of course, I was putting the cart before the horse, and I knew it was a risk. But ya know what? I knew I could do it!

No other wholesale seafood facility built in the U.S. could compare, or even come close, to the new facility. The building was over twenty-eight thousand square feet, with another twenty thousand for parking. It had a twenty-five-thousand-gallon underground gas storage tank, so we could buy the fuel wholesale, saving a bundle. It sat on nearly one-and-a-quarter acres of prime industrial San Francisco land. The physical address would be 500 Mendell Street. It had setbacks for landscaping around the entire building. India Basin Industrial Park was a new, good-looking industrial park, also close to the freeway, allowing the trucks easy access to the on-ramps, and close to the San Francisco Airport for the daily pick-up of product we intended to have flown in from all parts of the world.

Fisherman's Wharf is now basically a thing of the past, and a farce with all the touristy gift shops, tattoo parlors, wax museum, and traffic. Very little fish is now received on the Wharf in comparison to the major production ports further north.

The freezer would be capable of holding almost a million pounds of product, or well over thirty tractor-trailer loads, and could hold a constant minus-ten degrees Fahrenheit. The blast freezer could freeze twenty thousand pounds of fish solid within twelve hours. The two coolers could hold sixty thousand pounds of fresh product, or two tractor-trailer loads.

The ice machine could produce twenty thousand pounds of crushed ice overnight, more than what we should need on any one day. The entire facility was naturally designed for future volume—certainly not the business I currently had.

The smokehouse would be capable of smoking a ton of salmon every seventy-two hours. The fillet room could process up to ten thousand pounds of whole fish a day, resulting in approximately 2,500 pounds of fillets.

The steaking room would be able to a take two-hundred-pound whole frozen Alaskan halibut, or a four-hundred-pound whole frozen swordfish and reduce them into four to twelve-ounce IQF steaks for custom orders.

We could load five trucks at a time instead of just one, as we had at the old plant. The receiving dock was at tractor-trailer level. Since the forklift could drive onto the bed of the truck, it could unload a forty-four-foot tractor-trailer containing up to thirty thousand pounds within twenty to thirty minutes.

All the new packing tables were stainless steel, as well as the scales and other equipment for ease of steam-cleaning. Two new battery-operated forklifts would be purchased as well. One would need to handle temperatures under minus-ten degrees and be able to stay in the massive freezer for many hours at a time, requiring a special type of battery. I hoped I'd thought of everything. Joan often asks me at two in the morning, "Why aren't you sleeping?"

The sales office had ten sound-proof cubicles to reduce the amount of noise emanating from the production floor, allowing the salesmen to clearly hear their customers. A center desk would be for the sales manager. Directly above him on the center back wall was an eighteen-by-eight-foot white board displaying the hundreds of daily fresh fish items from around the world to offer our customers. An adjoining small office was for my international fresh fish buyer that would keep the board current. I would also have a desk in the sales office to stimulate sales, as well as to over hear their conversations with the buyers and aid them if needed. My desk was strategically situated to face the production floor to watch the operation during the morning hours. It was also directly across from the extension desk, allowing me to read every invoice that came in from the production floor to catch any errors in weights and/or pricing before being extended, then going to the drivers' dispatching room just adjacent. These were just some of my thoughts at two in the morning.

The facility was thoroughly thought out in every detail for quality control and for properly expediting more than five hundred orders each day—in the event I was to ever accomplish that.

The upstairs offices were carpeted throughout and tastefully furnished by an interior designer. She bought all new matching desks, including a conference table with seating for fourteen. The accounts receivable had a private office, as well as the controller.

There were four desks in the center office plus a switchboard to receive the myriad of expected incoming calls. A hand-carved redwood plaque with the logo of the big P was placed at the top of the steps to apprise visitors of the firm's executive offices.

My office was rather imposing and most likely not one expected in a wholesale seafood plant. I guess when I'd designed it I still aspired to be an attorney, and this would be as close as I would ever get to it. It had redwood paneling on all four walls and a mini-bar. My desk was one solid piece of rosewood sitting on two triangular, chrome supports. A sofa with matching chair was strategically placed in front of my desk to interview brokers and entertain customers. Behind, were heavy drapes encasing the one-way glass bay windows that emerged out over the plant allowing me to observe the production floor operation without the workers knowing. As Oscar Wilde said, "Moderation is a fatal thing. Nothing succeeds like excess."

The facility was designed for efficiency, quality control, and sanitation in handling seafood products. My intention was an attempt to try to elevate the industry to one of respectability.

I wanted to have an opening party announcing Paladini's reemergence into the industry, and invite all my current customers, plus the chefs and buyers of every major hotel and supermarket chain on the West Coast—that I wasn't selling, to entice them to buy. Hopefully, they would, knowing their product would come from a new facility with their products delivered on clean trucks with uniformed drivers—everything symbolizing the epitome of sanitation and quality.

Meanwhile, I had to remember that no one cares how pretty the wrapping is, it's what's in the box that counts! We could have the largest and finest facility, but if we didn't deliver as promised, I would be done. You only get one chance.

I also wanted to invite the brokers to hold a pre-party display of their products. I felt it would be wise to include them to encourage their support.

The way it was looking, we would have at least 3,500 people attending between that afternoon and night. It was going to be costly, but it was all about the image, that mystical image of success that allows one to conclude that the company's performance *must* be excellent, creating the desire to buy its products. However, the challenge of bringing the company to this next level would not be easy.

The biggest challenges are never solved at one's current level of thinking. Its practical application in a business context would refer to the thinking and actions that got you to where you are may not be enough to allow you to get to the next level. The closer to the top one gets in any industry, strangely, the less uncensored feedback you get. Few employees tell the boss what they really think, or if they notice the potential for a problem. They may not even care. Without good feedback, you cannot properly adjust, plan, or grow. *You can't correct a problem, unless you're aware there is a problem.*

I knew I couldn't achieve the company's full potential by myself. I was working on a goal that I seriously knew I could achieve, but without the proper assistance, chances were, my aim could be limited. The better I was at attracting, developing, and retaining exceptional and capable people, the better the chances were of building the business to its full potential. Relinquishing and delegating responsibilities to the management team would also allow me to have an engaging life with my family.

These are truths in business management that I had to remember and employ to be successful in both business and family life. I must seek to find a good—no, an *exceptionally* good—management team to assist me in running the sales department, bookkeeping, and production, in that order of importance; sales first. Remember, nothing happens until a sale is made!

My God, had I really inherited my grandfather's driven desire to succeed? Desire? Hell, I *needed* to succeed.

It was summer of 1979 and Laura had just graduated from Aragon High School and was heading to Long Beach State College. Gina would be graduating the following year from Crystal Springs Uplands High School and would be going to the University of San Diego. Then Diana wanted to go to the University of Southern California. I would soon have all three daughters in college—at the same time. Then there were the sororities, food, books, and everything else that goes with college life!

I'm very proud of all our girls for doing so well in school. Joan did a wonderful job making sure they studied, which was unfortunately something I never did, or was forced to do.

Speaking of schools and education, let me tell you an amusing story about our darling, angelic youngest daughter Diana.

Diana emphatically did not want to go to Crystal Springs Uplands High School in Hillsborough, a private all-girls school at the time. Neither did Gina, but that's a whole other story. It was and still is quite the uppity, snobbish and rather garish of all high schools in the area. Also, quite expensive may I say. The main building of the campus was the Uplands mansion, originally built as a private residence for Templeton Crocker, scion of railroad baron, Charles F. Crocker.

Well, after much ado and Diana's indifference, Joan and I insisted she attend, since we knew it was the best high school in the area, scholastically, plus it would eventually involve the girls with a good social circle of friends. We unfortunately couldn't afford to send Laura to Crystal for high school since I had been in between jobs and had just started the business at the time.

We had to tell Diana that we wanted her to "try" the school for at least one year, and if she really didn't like it, then maybe we would let her go to Aragon. Well, we lied. That was never our intention. We hoped that once she was there and had made friends, she would like it. Well, she made plenty of friends . . . but still hated it!

The second year came, and we enrolled her again for the second semester. Well, she was furious with us. Her exact words were "You guys lied to me! You were both sneaky and tried to fool me." Then she said again, "You guys lied!" You might say that she was upset with us.

So, she decided she would just get expelled (sounds like me at Saint Ignatius). She must have thought for some time about what would be the most dramatic thing she could do to get thrown out of this "all-girls penitentiary," as she called it.

Well, she decided to sell the school. That's right, you heard me correctly—*sell* the school!

Since it was originally a Hillsborough mansion, and no renovation to speak of had been done to it yet, it still appeared to be just a mansion, not a school. So, she placed an ad in *The San Mateo Times* newspaper that read "For sale: stately, colonial Hillsborough estate; thirty-five thousand square feet of living space, with thirty-nine rooms, including twelve bedrooms and twelve baths. Contains a ballroom, library, and solarium. Large wine cellar with elevator and living quarters for service help. Has interior of matching marble walls and silk coverings. Italian ironwork and finely crafted German woodcarvings. The interior resembles an Italian Renaissance Palazzo. Price upon inquiry. By appointment only. Call (the school's main number)."

The school was soon inundated with calls, people asking the price and wanting more information, while the real estate brokers scrambled, trying to get the listing because they thought it was for sale by owner. She also stole—yes, our sweet, innocent daughter stole (she says "borrowed")—real estate signs saying House for Sale and placed them on the main street down from the school.

After the principal had received a multitude of calls asking the price and for more information, flabbergasted, he called a meeting of the entire student body. He stopped all the classes and stated that the school had erroneously been put up for sale; he was sure it had been a mischievous student behind it, and wanted that student to come forth. Of course, laughter erupted, infuriating him even more.

Well, no one came forward . . . that is, until he said he would keep the entire student body there all afternoon until he found who had done it. Several of the students then looked over and stared in Diana's direction as she sunk down in her seat, knowing she had now been found out. But that was okay. That's what she wanted!

I received a call at work that afternoon from the head office requesting—no, *insisting*—I go to the school to meet with the principal immediately.

I arrived at his office about an hour later, and as I sat across from him, I found it very odd that he was smiling as he told me of my daughter's insubordinate actions. He always had a smile on his face, even when supposedly upset. It appeared to be painted on him like the Joker in Batman.

As he proceeded to tell me that our daughter had put the school up for sale, and that it had caused significant disruption and affected the entire student body for most of the day, I couldn't help but discourteously dismiss his anger and said, "So did she ask a good price for it?" He then gleamed at me with that absurd smile, though most surely with disdain. Meanwhile, I now had to get serious. I apologized for my daughter's disruptive actions and asked how or what I could do to amend this outrageous act of rebellion (even though I thought it was quite ingenious and clever).

Consequently, I donated to the Crystal Springs Uplands School fund, and we also gave the school a large, original landscape oil painting. It hangs over the mantle of the fireplace in the grand entry hall to this day. Others that view it may admire the artist's work; we consider it a remembrance of our daughter's ingenious comedy that unfolded that day.

Though greatly disappointed that her attempted, furtive act to sell the school hadn't resulted in her expulsion, Diana now thanks us for insisting she go to Crystal Springs Uplands School, and realizes it was an asset in getting her into USC and Pepperdine University, where she majored in psychology. So maybe, just maybe, sometimes parents do know what they are doing and what's best for their children. Upon graduating, she thanked us. We grinned.

I must say that her performance that day was one to always be remembered. It was riveting and demonstrated both her technical prowess and her clear understanding of repellent behavior. Her demonstration was exquisitely sculpted, authenticating her effulgence for her profession, which resulted in a successful career as a marriage, family, and child therapist . . . despite her talent with selling real estate.

CHAPTER 25
THE NEW DISTRIBUTION PLANT OPENS

The opening of the new distribution plant was coming up just after the first of the year, in 1980, and would be the beginning of a new decade and the beginning of the re-emergence of the Paladini name in the industry; a very proud era for me. I had to incorporate for liability purposes, so the official name was now "Paladini Seafood Company," a division of Achille Paladini Enterprises, Inc.

Sounds impressive! But with it came a great deal of new responsibilities and challenges.

I hoped I hadn't shot for the sun—the moon certainly wouldn't do—and gone too far, like Icarus in Greek mythology. It is said that Icarus, being overly ambitious, didn't follow the advice not to fly too high, since his wings were made from pigeon's feathers tied by wax. As he eagerly flew and approached the sun, the wax melted, the feathers separated, and he fell back to earth.

I then started thinking, *Am I being overly ambitious? But heck, if my grandfather did it, why in the hell can't I? Aren't I just shadowing him? Yeah, but he started over a hundred years ago, for Christ sake. He didn't have much competition back then. Jeez, dodo bird, c'mon, this is the twentieth century. Look at all the damn competition you have now. Nah, they're the least of my problems. By the way, what the hell was the name of that Greek guy? Oh yeah, Icarus. Well, he had difficulty with the lack of wings. I'm worried about the difficulty with the lack of capital.* Then I said out loud, "So since when in the hell has that ever stopped you, Kiki?!"

It was now the end of 1979, and I received final approval from all the agencies and was looking forward to moving into the new plant, though I was dismayed at the tough time I'd had getting the permits to operate when most of the wholesalers were operating out of such deplorable buildings. I guess that proves a point that when you make changes, you call attention to yourself.

We soon started moving everything out of the old plant with great delight, looking forward to the first days of operation in the new building. It was a weekend when we moved, so we could start there on a Monday morning.

Back

I will never forget when we finished moving everything into the cavernous building. It looked so bare, so empty, and yet in the old place, we'd had no room to move. All my frozen inventory had fit into one tiny corner of the massive freezer.

Warehouse and Freezing Area

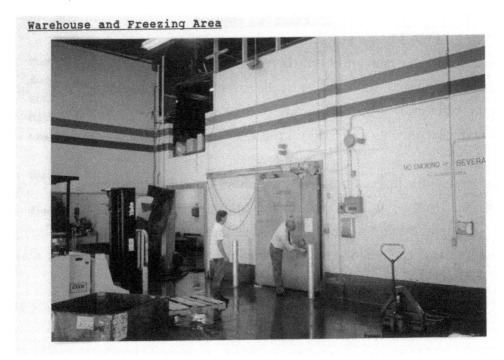

A feeling of fright came over me. How in the hell—or maybe, *why* in the hell—had I built such a huge building? "Well, to show off," I could hear my wife saying. But that wasn't true; I couldn't operate out of the old place anymore. We were simply doing too much business. But just how much more would we have to do to fill this damn place, I wondered?

I only had three sales people, and now had room for ten. I only had one bookkeeper and there was room for four. I had a switch board, but no one to answer it. The men's locker room could handle at least forty men and I only had eighteen. Oh boy...

The one welcoming sight was the five loading doors and the receiving dock. They would be put to good use right away. I was well aware that I had to do one hell of a business to fill this place, so I'd better get moving and load up the sales office. *Because nothing happens until a sale is made!*

I now had to steal the best salesmen in the industry, and if that wasn't possible, then I would have to train them. In the past I'd found that an order packer who knew the products, and if he had a good personality, would make the best salesman, since the chefs had little time to spend on the phone and needed someone with knowledge of the products to answer their questions quickly.

Monday morning came and the first day of operation in the new plant was now in full force. The incoming fresh fish arriving on the tractor-trailers from Alaska, Washington, and Oregon that had backed into the receiving bay were immediately unloaded with the ability to now drive the forklift onto the trailer. The product was then put off to one side to be properly checked in, then re-iced, and immediately placed into the cooler for quality control. This all went smoothly and as planned. The salesmen, yet still only three, now had a pleasant environment in which they could talk with the chefs and were now excited to represent the company. However, I strangely missed the "rat pack"—no, not Frankie, Dino, and Sammie, but my ex-cohorts Julie, Jim, Rick, and his lady friend Rita. They'd all had to be left behind to fend for themselves, even that mischievous, ill-mannered Guillermo. Sorry, guys.

It seemed like I had immediate respect from everyone in the industry, including the drivers who delivered to us; their attitudes had suddenly changed. I presumed that was from the amazement of the facility. I guess the illusion of success breeds respect, but now I had to live up to it.

My bank book was far from the illusion the new facility emanated, and my lack of accredited education still frightened me.

I kept vacillating from being assured to questioning my abilities. I couldn't help feeling intimidated by cultured, erudite men. I have always gotten by with using logic and common sense, and thankfully have an analytical mind, but this was big, big time business I was dealing with now.

I must fast forward a couple of years to 1982.

I remember the parties we gave at our Hillsborough home that had by then been greatly expanded. It included an enormous game room with a twenty-foot well-stocked bar, dance floor, and stereo system, plus all sorts of toys for the kids, such as pin ball machines, an air hockey game, and a juke box. In the center of the room was a wild, abstract-looking, custom-made stainless-steel pool table that we would cover with a sheet of plywood when we had a party. It would display an abundant variety of cold shellfish that included briny Bluepoint oysters on the half shell from the rich shallow bays of Wellfleet, Massachusetts, tender littleneck clams from the cold waters of Long Island Sound, local cracked Dungeness crabs on ice, as well as split king crab merus legs from the chilly waters of Alaska. Mounds of cooked and peeled jumbo prawns from Mazatlan flowed from a cornucopia, eventually converging into our cocktail sauce for dipping. The coup de grace was a copious amount of fresh Caspian Sea Beluga Malossol Caviar audaciously displayed in a chilled crystal bowl with a mother-of-pearl spoon to gingerly spoon the delicate eggs without harm. The mother of pearl's glimmering, incandescent whiteness was an aesthetically pleasing contrast to the shiny black of the caviar. Lemon was a no-no, since it would cook the delicate eggs, and was nowhere to be found. It was served with lightly toasted points spread with artisan butter, mixed with a couple drops of fine Russian vodka. Nothing else was served or available to our guests so as not to dilute the taste of the finest caviar on earth. Every single tiny egg should be like a juicy sphere, whose only aim is to explode onto your palate and give you a tiny burst of ecstasy. Sounds like oral sex! I was the fish guy, so we always had to put on an extravagant display of seafood, as our guests expected.

Back to the party: Our guests included doctors, lawyers, professionals, and successful businessmen, including several from Silicon Valley in the new tech field. When they talked about their days at college—and not just city or state colleges, I mean the prestigious universities like Stanford, Yale, Dartmouth, Brown, Georgetown, and the like—I would excuse myself and go to another part of the room, not only intimidated, but feeling I couldn't keep up with their conversations. I went to the déclassé Santa Monica City College for only two years, and now just sold fish—yes, fish. I seriously lacked self-confidence and self-esteem, plus they were all so damn tall!

Funny though, one evening during a party for the Hillsborough Chapter of the Lung Association, while sitting around the bar, a bunch of the men jokingly asked what I had in the garage, presumably impressed by the massive game room and all the toys. I seriously tried to change the subject, but the game room was just off the three-car garage, so without asking, they abruptly opened the door, which exposed an array of rather expensive modes of transportation. First in line was a Rolls Royce Silver Shadow, then a Lotus Esprit sports car, and then Joan's new Cadillac I'd just bought her since she wouldn't take the Rolls to the supermarket. What they didn't know, however, was that the girls' three cars were out on the driveway, and well hidden behind the tennis court was the Chevy Suburban, parked alongside the twenty-eight-foot Sea Ray boat to tow up to our place in Lake Tahoe, and my Jeep CJ-7, also for Tahoe, had my dirt motorcycle in the back.

Quickly hustling them out of the garage to downplay what they'd witnessed, I then showed them my favorite; this one certainly wouldn't be imposing. Parked off to one side out on the circular driveway was my old beat-up 1966 VW Bug that I'd paid $400 for and loved. I used it on weekends when I wanted to escape my businessman image and stress. The paint was faded and mostly primer, the seats were worn and torn exposing the sagging springs, and the headliner hung blocking the view to the rear window. The squealing brakes were certainly less than trustworthy, and I often slid through stop signs, and when raining, I had to manually move the wipers back and forth to wipe the cracked windshield.

I was stopped one Sunday afternoon by the Hillsborough police while driving my "getaway" car, and asked what I was doing in the area. I wasn't shaved and looked rather shabby. I also hadn't taken my driver's license with me, so the officer had to follow me home so I could prove where I lived. He apparently got a big kick out of it when, upon my opening the garage door and proving I lived there, he saw what was parked inside. He then drove away, laughing his head off.

However, even with all this *stuff*, I was still intimidated by these wealthy, successful, highly educated men. It wasn't the wealth, because I stood side by side with them in that aspect; it was the education. That damn sense of insecurity was still evident within me. When talking with these men, I often stuttered slightly due to my lack of confidence. Having said that, most likely with my imperious bullshit ways, I was able to cover it.

It certainly would have been less complicated if I'd gone to USF and had pursued the profession of my choice. I would then be referred to as a shark—hmm, wouldn't that have been a coincidence?

Let's get back to 1980 and the new plant. I immediately hired a couple of salesmen and one sales lady, which was a new concept. I thought having a girl with a nice voice on the phone with the chefs would charm them, it also added a touch of class and could even possibly liberate the food industry. Nonetheless, she had to be trained, and be knowledgeable of the product, or the chefs would decimate her in no time. My intention was to have a sales representative in each county of the entire Bay Area to attempt to capture every account possible.

The long-time vision of bringing in fresh seafood from other parts of the world now paid off. I was flying in an array of species of fresh fish never heard of in the US. The chefs were intrigued with the fact that they could get fresh imported Dover sole from Holland, grouper and orange roughy fillets, and green-lipped muscles from New Zealand, white seabass fillet from Chile, spiny lobsters from South America, and fresh scampi from Iceland, plus an assortment of amazing colorful fresh fish from Hawaii. Very little fresh fish had been brought in from the islands at the time. The air freight was expensive, but the uniqueness of these items allowed for higher prices to be asked from the many premier restaurants, such as Alexis, the Big Four, the Blue Fox, Doro's, the Old Ritz Poodle Dog, Domino's, and the Pacific Union Club, to name just a few.

The San Francisco identity, and being so close to the San Francisco International Airport, was working well, as planned. We were aggressively acquiring new accounts and business was escalating nicely. I needed to be careful to avoid an operational shortfall. Increased sales were now paramount to offset the huge expense of the new facility.

The opening party was soon coming up, and since we had only been in the plant a few weeks, the facility would look pristine. I had hired a chef friend, Armando, a month prior to plan the event. Everything was thought out to make this an opening party never to be forgotten within the industry.

It was planned that everything could be eaten holding just a plate and fork. Nothing had to be cut, avoiding the need for a knife, which was certainly not for security reasons, but for the ease of eating while standing. The main course was to be Veal Sinatra with mushrooms and madeira sauce, with the veal cut into bite-size pieces. We did have knives available, however, since a whole hind quarter of roasted leg of beef would be available for backup because we wouldn't know exactly how many people were coming. *Always have backup!*

There was to be a cold shellfish table containing three hundred pounds of 16/20 prawns, i.e., sixteen to twenty prawns to the pound, well over five thousand prawns; one hundred pounds of Alaskan king crab legs cut into bite-size pieces; one hundred pounds of Santa Monica fresh lobster tail meat sliced into medallions; three hundred pounds of cracked Dungeness crabs; and five thousand Bluepoint oysters on the half shell. It would be a display of shellfish that would bedazzle the finest of chefs.

There was also to be an abundance of Paladini's famous hand-sliced smoked salmon on baguettes to promote our fine smoked salmon. They would love it! It was the only smoked salmon to my knowledge that was still produced in the old-fashioned, cold-smoked, *old style* traditional manner.

A hot station would have a chef's helper preparing Clams Casino and steamed Maine lobster on skewers bathed in a warm lemon-butter sauce. There would also be a few non-seafood items handed out as well, such as warm cheese puffs, mini-meat balls, bruschetta, and more. There would be several ice sculptures by a few of my artistic chef friends, one of which would be the big red P logo, of course.

Joan had planned with Herbert's Furs to have a half-dozen mink coats (this was before the awareness of animal cruelty) available to keep the ladies warm during the tour of the enormous freezer. Of course, a uniformed security guard would be handing them out and would keep control of them. There were no free party favors!

There would be a five-piece orchestra with an elevated dance floor. Ficus trees would be brought in, along with shrubs, to give the party a feeling of warmth, depicting a garden setting.

There would be valet parking due to the surrounding neighborhood, which was less than desirable, for my guests' safety. Two uniformed San Francisco police officers, as well as two plainclothes officers, would be in attendance, again due to the area.

Every detail was thought out. It would hopefully be an amazing opening party and my competition would shutter with fear of what was soon to come to ravage their accounts!

I also invited all the local major brokers to have a showing of their products, and what was new, during the afternoon hours, which should cement my relations with them and also give the chefs and supermarkets buyers the opportunity to review what was available for them to buy through my company. That concept would be a win-win.

With just a week before the party, we still had to concentrate on business. I had a sales meeting on Monday morning and stated what I expected of them. I didn't want an account to get past us in any area, and that was all the areas now. I told them that they were to drive down the main streets in their specified areas and get—that's right, *get*, not *attempt* to get—every account. Start with just a few items if need be, then we would, over time, get the majority, if not all, the business by persevering.

I explained to the sales staff that a buyer always had one or two items that they seemed to focus on, and I do mean *always*—a proven fact going back to the days when I was in sales—so if they gave the buyer the first item they'd asked about just above cost, that would jerk them loose and they'd most likely walk out with an order. Even if that was the only item they ordered at first, that was fine. It would get them accustomed to Paladini calling them on a regular basis, and it would then be up to the sales rep to get *friendly* with them and eventually get all the business. *Always* attempt to make the buyer your friend!

I also instructed them to find out what specific day and time the buyer did the ordering. No sense calling the account on a Tuesday if they ordered on Mondays or Wednesdays, and no sense calling them in the afternoon if they bought in the morning. You had to discover the details of their buying habits using a psychological approach, thus making it easier to capture the account.

I also told them to check the garbage bin for the carbon paper copy from competitors. Back in the 1980s, many were still using carbon paper. I told them if they found it, hold it up to the light and you would see the items they'd bought, and at what price they'd paid. Then go in and quote cheaper prices only on the items they were buying, thus immediately getting their attention and eliminating the need to quote items they weren't using or interested in.

QTY. ORDERED	QTY. SHIPPED	✓	DESCRIPTION		UNIT PRICE	AMOUNT
10 cases	100	1/10	FR. FILLET BUTTERFISH	6904	2.09	209.00
45 cases	450	1/10	FR. FILLET DOVER SOLE	6908	2.39	1,075.50
2 cases	20	1/10	FR. FILLET OF HADDOCK	6916	2.65	53.00
33 cases	330	1/10	FR. FILLET OF PERCH	6918	2.49	821.70
1 case	30	1/30	WHOLE DRESSED RED SNAPPER	6920	1.05	31.50
7 cases	70	1/10	FR. FILLET TRUE COD	6922	2.29	160.30
7 cases	70	1/10	FR. FILLET LING COD	6924	2.29	160.30
32 cases	320	1/10	FR. SHARK FILLET	6932	2.29	732.80
19 cases	190	1/10	PAN READY CAT FISH	6934	2.19	416.10
22 cases	176	1/8	BAY SCALLOPS	6956	3.19	561.44
45 cases	450	1/10	FR. RANDOM TROUT	6987	1.69	760.50
7 cases	62	1/10	THRESHER	6997	2.89	179.18
25 cases	495	1/20	CARP	6971	.69	341.55

500 MENDELL STREET
SAN FRANCISCO CA 94124
PHONE (415) 821 1900

INVOICE

No. 168667

DATE 5-9-88

SOLD TO LUCKY STORES
1701 MARINA BLVD
SAN LEANDRO, CA. 94557

P.O. NUMBER 272484

A SERVICE CHARGE of 1½ per month (18% per Annum) on past due accounts and/or collection fees will be added.

TOTAL 5,502.87

POSTING COPY

ALL CLAIMS MUST BE MADE UPON RECEIPT OF MERCHANDISE. UPON ARRIVAL CALL COLLECT ON ANY DISCREPANCIES IN WEIGHT OR FREIGHT DAMAGE FROM AIR OR TRUCK HANDLING.

Well, it worked! We were getting literally dozens of new accounts every week in all areas. I also knew that we would embark on cementing relations with the Safeway and Lucky stores

after the party once they saw the facility. Things were looking good.

It was now Friday, the day before the big party. The brokers display started the next day at noon, then the opening gala was later that night. I kept the crew late that Friday afternoon and had them steam clean the plant twice and scrub the floors so there would be no odor of fish. Our guests would be highly sensitive to any smell of fish, and it certainly wouldn't be a very nice welcoming atmosphere if there was.

On Saturday morning February 2nd, 1980, I was at the plant to open at eight. The dance floor, Ficus trees, flowers, and all the tables and linens, as well as the four bars and liquor for the evening, were being delivered at that time. I had a crew come in to help set up and stage the plant and have it ready by eleven for the brokers show. The show started at noon and would end at three. Then afterwards, we would have to set up the numerous food tables, arrange the ice carvings that were being made during the exhibit, and get everything ready for the party, which would start at six thirty—and I was already exhausted.

The seafood brokers arrived as scheduled, and did their set-up, and the buyers soon started pouring in shortly after noon. I greeted as many as I could and took them around to the individual tables and introduced them to the brokers. The food show and demonstrations were a big success, and they all appeared pleased with the idea of sharing the day with them and appreciated the guest list to promote their products.

I was pleased, as well, that the brokers were in my corner now, and anxious to do more business with me. After all, that was the primary reason for having arranged all of this. Being shrewd is a virtue!

We then set up the plant for that evening's party. That was a job, but we got it done within an hour. An upsetting thing occurred, however, when I discovered one of the two immense candelabras that stood on the center long table was missing after the brokers had disassembled. The two candelabras were supposed to be the highlight of the planned decor on the self-serve appetizer table. It would be costly replacing it since they'd been rented for the evening. Why would someone do that?

I then went home and rested for about an hour and returned with Joan and the girls shortly after six. Joan looked beautiful and the girls looked amazing.

That evening was possibly the proudest moment of my life. I had my beautiful, loving family with me, and we were about to share not only the opening of the plant, but proudly the rebirth of the Paladini Seafood Empire. It had once again returned to the apex of honor and respect.

My *perseverance* had finally brought me success. I was bound and determined it would again soon be a dominant force in the industry.

God, how I wished my mom and dad could have seen this. Maybe my grandfather, too. I wondered what he would have said. By the way, I sit on his old wooden trunk every morning now.

Everyone of importance in the entire seafood industry was there, from as far away as Vancouver to Boston. All the head buyers of every major supermarket chain attended. Just what I'd wanted! Almost every executive chef in the Bay Area also came. It was Saturday night, so a few obviously couldn't. Several chefs brought their entire families, not just their wives; some even also brought their friends, who had not been invited—who had also brought bags. I guess it was time for payback.

They started arriving right at six thirty. I recognized immediately that this was going to be an overwhelming evening for me, but was overjoyed with the response.

It was estimated by the RSVPs we'd received that well over 3,500 people came that evening, as expected. We would never know the actual number since so many had brought uninvited guests. However, that was the reason for the planned backup for the roasted hind quarter of beef.

It was disappointing, noticing several women wrapping up dozens of jumbo prawns and other delicacies, like king crab legs, in napkins and putting them into their purses. Greedy bags were not figured into the equation of consumption.

It seemed as if I never stopped talking. I most likely conversed with hundreds upon hundreds of people that night. At one point my face hurt so much from smiling, it was an effort to even grin. But I needed to make the best of the evening, and entertain and capture the attention of my customers, since that was indeed the intended purpose of the evening.

Soft piano music set a relaxing background tone to the evening up until eight thirty. I then made a speech thanking everyone for coming, and shortly after, the live dance music started.

Most were feeling no pain by then. Might I add, I never drank that evening, or during any business function. I had to be Mr. P., and astute.

The evening went fantastically, and as planned, except for one little—no, not little, *major*—fiasco on the part of my executive chef, Armando. He'd forgotten the long-planned and very costly Veal Sinatra he'd made earlier that day at Ken's Seafood Restaurant, a few blocks away! Remember, I said it had been planned that everyone would stand and be able to eat with just a fork. Well, Armando was slicing and serving the goddamn roasted hind quarter of beef, that of course, needed to be sliced with a knife, and that was difficult to do while standing. It wasn't noticed until I had a moment to grab a bite to eat, and asked Armando if all the Veal Sinatra was gone already. He turned pale and said, "Oh shit, Mr. P . . . it's still at Ken's!" My face must have gotten flushed and my hair curled, because he immediately dropped his carving knife and left to go get it. I then stopped him and asked who in the hell was going to slice the beef while he was gone—we had to feed the people in the meantime.

I sent Ken, the son of the owner of Ken's Seafood Restaurant—yes, I'd hired him to get the account—to go get it, but by the time he'd gotten back, most everyone had eaten. Well, St. Anthony's Dining Hall in San Francisco had a wonderful treat the next day for the poor, unfortunate hungry souls.

You see, all the months of planning can be decimated by one thoughtless person. This applies to so many facets of life when you depend on others. And of course, my chef friends in attendance must have thought that Kiki wasn't very ingenious when it came to serving food. It always falls back to the guy on top!

All in all, I felt everything went well that evening, and I'm sure everyone had fun. I know the uniformed security officers gave everyone a sense of well-being ensuring they weren't bothered while waiting in front for their cars from the valet.

This is going to sound arrogant, so settle down, ladies, before you continue reading. Something strange happened that night; it seemed as if women were all over me. I guess the image of power, success, and wealth, is sexy. I know Joan certainly didn't appreciate it, but what could I do? I know what you're saying: "Oh, the poor guy, what could he do?"

Monday soon came, and the party was behind us. It was time now to get busy and capture more business. The trees and shrubs, stage, dance floor, and furs were gone. All the pomp and pageantry had vanished and it was once again just an austere wholesale seafood plant.

I soon discovered that I had oddly lost a couple of accounts due to the party, believe it or not. Two executive chefs felt I didn't need the business after seeing the new plant. That was certainly a reversal in my thought process! Then by Thursday morning, I also discovered I'd lost the prestigious millionaire's club, the Pacific Union Club on Nob Hill—my long-time good chef friend claimed he'd never received an invitation. I knew we'd sent him one; I'd gone over the list several times, but when you mail something without requiring a signature, how in the hell do you know it was received? Or if the front desk tossed it? I called him and tried to explain, but to no avail.

I eventually got the club back, however, by personally visiting with him several times, expressing how much I valued his friendship and insisting an invitation had indeed been sent. After all, why wouldn't I have sent him one? The other two were back within weeks because no one carried the hundreds upon hundreds of items we did, especially the exotic fresh fish from all over the world.

I was now up to seven salesman and one sales lady and had just hired a salesman who lived near Sacramento who'd been selling meat to all the casinos in Nevada. I convinced him to work part-time for me, selling the seafood to the clubs on the side on a commission basis.

This worked out very well. Within a few weeks, we had every casino in Tahoe, Reno, and Sparks, Nevada, and volume soared even further. I encouraged him to start calling some of the predominant supermarket chains in the Sacramento Valley, as well, and he soon captured most of them.

He then started calling all the restaurants, and surprisingly, they mostly bought on the first call after hearing of the wide variety of fresh fish we carried, which allowed them to have exciting new items for the fresh fish of the day. He now also needed an assistant to help him make all the calls. His sales of seafood were now surpassing his meat sales, and he was working for me almost full-time. I also hired his two sons to deliver the areas, locking in our relationship. He was doing well over $300,000 a month.

We were now sending three trucks a day into the Sacramento Valley, plus another two on Tuesdays and Thursdays up to Reno and Lake Tahoe—a total of five trucks delivering to well over one hundred and fifty accounts in this newly developed territory.

I soon concluded that there was an incremental amount of waste having the drivers drive back and forth to San Francisco every day, with the overtime and cost of fuel, so I arranged to rent a loading dock in Sacramento. I then bought a twenty-eight-foot heavy duty refrigerated truck to load the orders on at the plant. It would then meet the five trucks in Sacramento, since all five of the drivers had lived there. This immediately saved hundreds of dollars in overtime each week, plus drastically reduced the fuel cost. This strategy thus resulted in escalated net profits for the Sacramento and Nevada areas.

During the summer vacations while in high school, all three of our daughters would come in and work for their dad to make a little extra money. They also continued doing so while in college during their summer breaks. It was fun having them there. They found different miscellaneous jobs to do, mainly working upstairs in bookkeeping, and occasionally taking turns on the switchboard. I would never allow them to spend too much time downstairs in the sales office, since all the salesman would be drooling over them—unacceptable for an Italian father, plus they would procrastinate and not make their calls on time. I also tried to keep them isolated from the production floor, where profanity was prevalent. Of course, I never used that kind of language!

There were times when things would go wrong, very wrong, downstairs, either with the salesmen, or most often out on the production floor, and I would holler and cuss something terrible. The wholesale business can be very demanding and stressful, to say the least. Well, after I vociferously spewed a profuse number of expletives at whomever or whatever, and then went back upstairs to my office, as I hastily approached the top landing where the switchboard was, if my youngest daughter Diana was there, I would suddenly change my demeanor and softly say, "Hi, kiddo, how ya doin'?" She would always then say, "Dad, we all heard you!"

A frightening but amusing thing happened one afternoon. It was about two o'clock and I was in my office doing paperwork, as I did every afternoon. My secretary, Beverly, buzzed me to announce who it was, as she always did with any phone call, or if someone had stopped in to see me. She then said, "Three well-dressed African-American men want to see you." Not knowing what this was about, and since she said they were nicely dressed, I told her to show them in. I assumed they were from the local redevelopment agency.

The three men then came into my office and introduced themselves, then proceeded to sit down . . . without me having invited them to do so. I found that odd, plus they didn't have business cards. Two sat on the sofa directly in front of me, while the other was in the chair off to one side.

I then said, "So gentlemen, what can I do for you?" However, as I was saying that, I noticed that one of the men sitting on the sofa had a revolver in a holster that presumably he'd made visible on purpose, as he'd casually flung back his suit jacket to expose it. I then said to myself, *Oh boy, this isn't going to be good.* But I brazenly acted without concern.

The man in the chair was evidently the spokesperson, and said, "Mr. Paladini, we are here to offer you protection." I then said, "Oh, really? Protection? Protection from what?" He then said, "You are on the fringe of the projects, and there is a very bad and dangerous element less than a block away. We can assure you that you will not have any problems, like getting vandalized or robbed."

There was no way I was going to be extorted and pay anyone for any bullshit protection, so I needed time to think about how to get out of this situation. I then casually sat back in my large leather swivel chair, and while twiddling with my pen, I calmly said, "Hmm, no kidding? Well, isn't that interesting." I was now stalling for time, more time, while thinking, thinking . . . So, as a joke, because I wanted to make light of this and not show any sign of intimidation, I said, without smiling—since smiling is an indication of submissiveness— "Gentlemen, my name is Paladini, Achille Paladini. I'm Italian. See this phone?" (I had a private phone behind me with a roll-type cover to access the receiver, which was rather covert looking.) "This is my direct line to Chicago. Chicago! My Mafia friends can offer you guys protection anytime *you* need it!"

Remember, I was joking, with a bit of seriousness, just buying time to think about how in the hell I was going to get out of this! Then, to my total astonishment, all three men, now with pale complexions, suddenly jumped up and said, "Mr. Paladini, it was nice meeting you. Goodbye." They then rushed—yes, *rushed*—out of my office! I sat back in my chair and exclaimed, "Oh my God! Did that really just happen?!" I then called Beverly in and said, "Bev, you won't believe what just happened!"

We were now coming toward the end of the third quarter of 1980, and it was estimated that sales would easily exceed $10 million by year end. My eventual goal was to at least double that; however, it would take time.

It was about eight in the morning during the middle of the summer of 1980, and we had only been in the new plant six months. I had to go upstairs to my office for some reason, and upon returning to go down to the sales office and face the hustle and bustle of the morning's activities, I hesitated on the landing at the top of the stairs, then stopped and looked out the window.

I was dumbfounded. I saw a sea of white Paladini trucks wherever I looked—in the parking area and out on the street, and as far as I could see to the corner. There were also several forty-foot tractor-trailers from the production plant parked in front, proudly displaying the name as if they were billboards announcing a return to the industry.

Drivers were in line to gas up their trucks from the underground tank, as others were backing into the loading docks, and several more were leaving to make deliveries.

The scene I was viewing was one of an obviously very successful business that appeared to have been in business for decades—yet it had only been a little less than five years!

I sat on one of the chairs on the landing in the reception area that was close to the switchboard, and heard Doris answering call after call, saying, "Thank you for calling Paladini. May I help you?" She would then say, "Yes, sir, but all lines into the sales office are busy. May I ask you to wait just a minute, please?" My God, it was as if we were the only seafood wholesaler in the Bay Area.

I'd remained there for several minutes, maybe ten or so, staring out the window, mesmerized by the chaotic activity taking place, when my secretary Beverly came up behind me and said, "Are you looking at what you created, boss?" Bewildered, I looked at her and asked, "How in the hell did all this happen? And so quickly?"

My mind started to wander, remembering just a few years ago, sitting all alone in that tiny old dingy plant with just a single-line black phone, with *no* customers, *no* inventory, and *no* money. Then I thought back even further, at the intense struggle it had been getting to this point, and everything that had taken place, all the hurdles and all the disappointments. I never thought this could have ever been possible. My God!

I also thought back to my childhood days, without a care or need in the world, not knowing what the future held for me, just a little kid with no vision of my fate, playing on the steps on Baker Street, believing in Superman.

In the May issue of a *West Coast Seafood Industry Magazine*, there was a five-page article titled "Fishing Industry Phoenix: Paladini Seafood Company." The first paragraph stated, "A company that was once among the biggest factors in the West Coast seafood industry for more than a century, is now bigger than ever in 1981." It then went on to describe the resurgence of the company, and talked in detail about the new distribution plant, along with several pictures while in operation.

Fishing Industry Phoenix: Achille Paladini Seafood Co.

A company that has been among the biggest factors in the West Coast seafood industry for more than a century is bigger than ever in 1981. That, in itself, may not strike you as particularly exciting news, but the company in question caught a terminal case of bad management in the 1960's and wound up stone-cold dead in 1974. Now,

there is a new company, a new proprietor, a new success and a curious coincidence of names.

It was in 1865 that an immigrant from Ancona, Italy, with the formidable title Achille Paladini, started the original San Francisco seafood company that bore the same handle. Old Achille became known as a sea-

food tycoon and his firm "grew to be the largest bar none on the West Coast in the production and distribution of seafoods," according to a 43-year-old grandson who just happens to go by the name Achille Paladini.

The younger Achille says the old company had receiving stations and

The early morning rush to load the trucks and get them rolling.

Smoked salmon, specialty of the house. ➡

processing plants up and down the coast, produced the full complement of Pacific Coast seafood products and shipped them throughout the country

Old Achille died in the 1920's and his four sons—Walter, Hugo, Attilio and Alex—took over the business and ran it successfully Walter had a son whom they named Achille, after the old man, and who soon acquired the nickname "Kiki."

The current bearer of the historic name in seafoods shakes his head when you ask him about the origin of the nickname "Achille is bad enough," he says. "Where the hell they came up with Kiki I don't know Why couldn't it have been Bob or Tom or something else?"

Eventually, the young Achille joined the firm his grandfather had founded. Everything was prosperous until Walter's generation began to die off in the 1960's. Walter himself died in 1966 and young Achille left the firm at that time.

There began to be management problems, even while the company remained in family hands, and soon it was failing, suffering a declining reputation along the docks and in the marketplace. Finally, it was sold to a group of investors from outside the family, and the doors closed under their ownership.

The closure was a bitter event for young Achille to swallow The name Paladini had been "the most major name" in the West Coast seafood in-

Achille Paladini. ⬆

dustry, he says, and all of a sudden the name no longer existed as a brand or as a factor on the waterfront and in the marketplace.

Young Achille had worked for several other seafood and frozen food companies after he left the family business, and he had a strong background in the business of selling food, seafood in particular In 1975, he "had a bright idea."

He would recreate the old company, raise it out of the ashes. He rented a small, vacant warehouse in San Francisco and hired two employees. He had virtually no capital, no inventory, and it had been six months since anyone operating under the now suspect name Achille Paladini had made a sale.

Nevertheless, he began calling the restaurant chefs and other buyers that he knew and asked them what their needs were. Then, he called producers in an effort to find the desired seafoods at the right price Eventually he connected, made a sale, and the Achille Paladini Seafood Co was back in business.

"Now," he says, "a little more than five years later, I've surpassed the old company in sales and we're one of the two largest distributors in California."

The new Achille Paladini Seafood Co., 100 percent owned by its founder, will gross "well over $20 million" during the current fiscal year It has one of the highest ratings Dun & Bradstreet awards, he says, has a million-dollar line of unsecured credit with the Bank of America, carries its own receivables and inventory, and owns all of its own equipment.

"If I can't buy it [a piece of equipment], I do without," says the uncharacteristically candid seafood entrepreneur "If you lease and borrow you can easily find yourself in a trap."

The company buys frozen seafood from around the world and fresh products from this country's Pacific, Atlantic and Gulf coasts, from the Pacific islands and from Europe, stores the whole array in a new warehouse in San Francisco, and makes local deliveries in a fleet of company-owned trucks or re-ships the seafood around the country

The customers are more than 1,500 restaurants as well as supermarket chains like Safeway, according to Paladini, who says the company prides itself on selling to fine restaurants, to a "high class market," and doesn't go after big institutional sales where volume and cost outstrip quality as a concern.

The company "passes up a lot of

▲ *Dressed for a visit to the freezer, capacity 2 million pounds plus.*

The order desk at Paladini's San Francisco warehouse. ▲

sales" rather than fall into another trap that awaits unwary entrepreneurs today, according to Paladini, that of selling your products too cheaply

Even more exciting than the distribution effort, he says, the Achille Paladini company has once again "become a factor in production." Through a subsidiary called Seal Rock Fisheries, Paladini has within the past year opened up receiving stations at Bodega Bay, Fort Bragg and Crescent City and a processing plant in Santa Rosa.

The company is again producing fish fillets under its own label, is about to commence production of crab and shrimp meat, and is marketing what amounts to a small segment of the overall business but a big item in terms of pride, according to the proprietor Paladini's "world-famous, old-fashioned" smoked salmon.

Seal Rock Fisheries keeps a fleet of 6 trawlers busy and buys salmon and crab from numerous independent skippers, Paladini says, and the control of production enables the company to ensure the quality of the items that reach the marketplace; something that can't be done as effectively when you are simply distributing

someone else's product and don't know how long it has been on a boat and in a warehouse.

He claims that Paladini crab and shrimp were once regarded as the best on the market, and that he intends to recapture the title with the products processed in Santa Rosa.

His goal, however, is to remain a small producer, one who supplies about half of what he sells and buys the other half from other producers. That way, he says, Paladini seafoods won't fall into the same overproduction trap that has put so many seafood companies in jeopardy today

Producers are in worse shape than distributors today because of overproduction, according to Paladini, who says that as a distributor, he often gets numerous calls from producers trying to sell the same product. That makes it a buyer's market and means that interest rates soon eat up profits on inventories a producer can't move quickly

Only five years ago, Paladini says, the fisherman was "king" and a processing company would "do anything just to keep a boat." That situation spawned a tremendous growth in the number of new boats, he says, and now, in a complete reversal of what used to be the case, there are too many boats for the health of the producer and the market.

Among the new vessels operating to the north of San Francisco are the big midwater trawlers that harvest fish in much larger quantities than the old-fashioned draggers, according to Paladini, and their deliveries have

Circle No. 62 on Reader Response Card.

It was just about this time that Laura had started her second year of college in Long Beach, and was doing very well studying engineering design, but was also getting very serious with her high school boyfriend, who was coincidentally going to the same college. Gina had also started college in San Diego, majoring in business administration, and was being groomed to take over the business someday. Now two of our daughters were living away from home, which was a rather odd feeling.

It was now in late September, and I had an unannounced surprise visit from my former employer, the owner and president of a large wholesale seafood company on the wharf, which was currently the largest in Northern California, ever since the old Paladini's demise. I say "currently" because we were up and coming and I had designs to dethrone him. It was just after lunch, about one thirty or so, and I was upstairs in my office, when one of my salesmen called me from downstairs and said, "Hey, Mr. P., guess who's on the way up to see you!" After he told me, I was first shocked, then infuriated. It blew my mind that he'd had the gall and audacity to come to my place of business without asking me.

I naturally also wondered what the hell he was up to. He had just reached the landing on the top of the stairs as he saw me coming out of my office. It was as if we were meeting to do battle. It was apparent I was now his nemesis, who he couldn't conquer, and he must have come to spy on his adversary's armory. To cite history, Achilles met Hector in single combat and killed him. This was my archrival invading his adversary's boundaries.

With reserve, I said, "So, what brings you here?" He then took his long, partly chewed Cuban cigar out of his mouth, looked around at the elaborate office area, then looked at me and said, "I'm looking around at what I'll be taking over some day." He then turned around and walked downstairs and left. What the eff? Well, I had a few descriptive nouns I used as he walked away.

Years before, he'd been cut on his face from his left eye to his cheek by an outraged fisherman, very similar to old "Scar Face" Al Capone. Being a tall, large, portly man, he had an imposing profile, and talked very brazenly.

His sudden unexpected appearance and bold manner outraged me! I immediately went down to the sales office and called a meeting. I instructed my combat troops, the salesmen, to follow his trucks around in their respective areas every day and get the accounts. I told them to *get* the accounts . . . at any price. It wouldn't be costly, since we were going into all the areas now and would most likely be delivering close by.

I now wanted to slaughter him, as Achilles did to Hector. That was uncalled for, not so much his unannounced visit, but his comment. Just how did he plan on taking over?

In the weeks that followed, I enjoyed successfully taking away many major accounts from him, and his feared "don't-touch-me" organization. Several wholesalers were afraid of him and were afraid to even attempt to take any of his accounts. Well, bullshit!

This ultimately brought me even closer to the number-one position in the industry. I had a young and aggressive salesforce with whom I worked very closely. I took them out for lunch every Friday and treated them as a team. At the end of the year, I gave them hefty bonuses to keep the monetary incentive factor flowing.

He and his narcoleptic, short, plump partner had old run-down salesmen with little incentive, so their retaliation wasn't very effective. It was allegedly rumored that his rotund partner's cousin could have been involved with some of San Francisco's undesirables. A bar in San Francisco had the same last name as his and was supposedly the hang out. It was not a place for a respectable lady to stop in and have biscuits and tea, you might say.

I'll never forget one day, way back when I worked for them, directly in front of me in a rage of fury, for whatever reason, he went up to this guy with a fillet knife, held it to his neck, and yelled, "I'll cut your fucking neck like a chicken, you son of a bitch!" I don't know who the guy was or what he did, but that was intense. Nice work atmosphere, wouldn't you say?

Meanwhile, and back to my place, another year had passed, with 1981 sales continuing to climb, and I anticipated doing close to $12 million.

We were now kicking the excrement, defecation, fecal matter (you get the drift) out of all the competition, especially my vengeful ex-boss—and they were defenseless against our onslaught.

CHAPTER 26
A TRIP OF A LIFETIME

Joan and I had discussed taking the girls to Europe on a five-week vacation. The plant was running well and I felt my sub-management team could certainly handle the company in my absence.

We had to go; I needed time with my wife and three daughters. We had decided long ago to try to show the girls as much of the world as we could, especially outside the United States, figuring they could someday travel the US on their own, or with their eventual families.

I was so looking forward to being with just the five of us, enjoying quality time and having fun together. I wanted to bond with my girls and pay attention and pamper my deserving wife. A vacation like this I'd naturally never thought possible just a few years earlier.

I told her to plan through a travel agent, and that I wanted us to stay in the best five-star hotels wherever we went—and oh boy, did she!

The trip started with us flying to New York and spending three days seeing all the attractions and visiting with a few of Joan's relatives. On one of those days, we went to the Twin Towers and took the elevator up to the top floor observation deck atop the south tower. The view of Manhattan and the Hudson River looming below was awesome. You could see for miles. I remember looking down and seeing the people below looking like tiny ants and made me realize how damn high up we were. To think back to that day, and of the tragic events thought took place on September 11, 2001, is an eerie and deeply moving thought.

We then flew to Rome and spent four days showing the girls everything we'd seen when we were there on our honeymoon, including Ancient Rome, especially the Senate building, where I once held a position as a Senator in my first life. Amazingly, the building is still standing. Yep, we knew how to build them back then. Don't believe me, huh?

We then took the train up to Venice for two days and stayed in a magnificent hotel on the Grand Canal that was once a palace long ago.

We had been to all these places on our honeymoon and wanted to share with the kids what we'd experienced. The Isle of Capri would be coming up soon.

We then went down to Lago di Como and stayed at—where else but—the Villa d'Este, one of the grandest hotels on earth. The kids loved the swimming pool that floated in the lake, if you can imagine that. They had an odd experience while staying there, though. They claimed they'd seen a ghost hovering over them in their room while they'd been attempting to sleep. The next morning, when they asked the front desk clerk if they'd had any other reports of sightings, he scoffed and said something so fast in Italian that we couldn't understand it. He most likely said, "Pozzo Americanos"—However, when we asked, he got very flushed!

We then flew from Milan down to Naples and took the boat over to the Isle of Capri to visit Joan's cousins. When we'd been there on our honeymoon, Joan's uncle had owned the beautiful Hotel San Michelle, in Ana Capri. He had since passed away, so it now belonged to her cousin Norma. It sits on a bluff, facing Naples. When darkness surrounds the enigmatic ancient city of southern Italy, the lights of the busy hustle of Naples can be clearly seen as they glisten in the warm summer night.

We stayed in the Queen's Suite at the hotel, with the kids in one large adjoining room. The feeling of acceptance and warm affection was prominent from Joan's cousin Norma and her husband Franco. Their two sons, Massimo and Claudio, were twelve and ten at the time, and our girls in their mid to late teens.

The highlight of Capri for the girls was when we had a private boat tour around the island, and the girls were able to swim in the Blue Grotto, something that can't be done today due to the unbearable crowd of tourists. I remember the girls swimming in the crystal-clear, deep-cobalt-blue water, as the sun beamed in from the opening of the grotto and illuminated them in a prism of brilliant colors while they happily frolicked. What a wonderful memory.

We then left Capri and flew from Naples to the French Riviera, and stayed in Nice and visited Monaco, just fourteen miles further. The grandeur and elegance of Monte Carlo was breathtaking. The girls were enthralled to be able to walk freely through the exclusive atmosphere of the emblematic Casino de Monte-Carlo and experience its imposing magnificence and sophistication. Their snobbery was well lifted as a result. We spent two exciting, glorious days in Nice, eating mostly at the fine outdoor cafes while enjoying the warmth of the French Riviera during summer.

From Nice, we flew to Paris; "Gay Paree," as it's called in reference to the perilously risqué French attitude about sex and sexuality. We spent three days doing as tourists do, only we had a private guide and limousine touring us around the city. We had lunch atop the Eiffel Tower, which is nicknamed *La Dame de fer*—The Iron Lady. We also spent a commodious amount of time at the Musée du Louvre, located on the right bank of the Seine.

We then had a flight to Turkey and spent a day in Ephesus. Ephesus is a port town that housed different populations over time; Lydians, Greeks, and Romans. However, most of the ruins are Roman. It was an unforgettable experience witnessing the ingenuity of the Roman architectural skills and resourceful engineering; how they'd perspicaciously used gravity for the sewer system and aqueducts. You can also attempt to envision what the city would have been like when it was populated by the Ancient Romans by walking down the many roads and into the ruins of the buildings, and into the individual rooms that were once inhabited by families. We then wondered what had transpired in these rooms so long ago. Mothers cooking as their children played. Happy times, times of fear. It was such an uncertain time in history. The library was the most impressive building; the facade was two stories tall and very ornate. Its incremental beauty is still visible to this day. We also enjoyed visiting the terraced houses, where the more influential people once lived.

Then it was over to Jerusalem. Of all the experiences we encountered, Jerusalem and the Holy City was beyond anything one can imagine. It was awe-inspiring to be where Jesus once lived. Walking through the ancient streets and corridors where Jesus himself had walked, one could not help but feel humbled. The Via Dolorosa still echoes the agony he endured while carrying the cross to his crucifixion, being flogged by Roman soldiers.

Jerusalem is a city revered by Jews, Christians, and Muslims alike.

After visiting the Church of the Holy Sepulcher, the Garden of Gethsemane, the site of the Last Supper, and the Via Dolorosa, with the fourteen stations of the cross, you leave feeling exceedingly religious and overwhelmed with thoughts of what transpired there over two thousand years ago.

All of us were silent on the next flight over to Cairo, Egypt, absorbing and reflecting on the awe-inspiring experiences we just had.

Arriving at the airport—remember, this was in 1982—we saw that it was very small, and men were sitting on the floor smoking hashish pipes. We found this odd, but we were in Cairo. The men really pissed me off, the way they looked at my wife and daughters, like they were commodities.

The roads going to the hotel were mainly dirt, hardened from thousands of years of bare Masryeen feet and camel hooves. With the occasional swerving of the taxi to miss the camel dung on the road, and attempting to avoid the inebriated, befuddled men dressed in their galabias, we eventually got to our hotel. Beer was the drink of preference to water, likely due to the bacteria in the Nile. As I was about to pay the taxi driver, I said, "How much *faloos* [Egyptian money] do I owe you, Toot [jokingly abbreviating "Tutankhamen"]?" Well, I guess he didn't find that funny from the look he gave me, and mostly likely raised the price. I had no idea what in the hell I was paying anyway.

Our hotel was no more than a couple of thousand yards away from two massive pyramids that ominously loomed in the sky. It was awesome to look out the bedroom window at night and see the pyramids eerily illuminated, unimaginable thousands of years ago.

It was a bit unnerving, however, to discover that armed guards were not only posted outside the perimeter of the hotel, but there was one on each floor as well, plus one posted next to the inoperable elevator. Thankfully, we were only on the second floor.

We were told upon arriving that Cairo wasn't necessarily a safe city for tourists; the poverty level was high, making tourists a good target, plus there was much political upheaval and turmoil due to the assassination just a year earlier of President Anwar el-Sadat by fundamentalist army officers on October 6, 1981.

The next day, we naturally wanted to go see the pyramids, so we arranged for a tour on—of course—camels. I reserved three of them; one for Joan and Gina, and one for Laura and Diana. God forbid Laura and Gina would share the same camel, even if separated by a huge hump. I would then be alone on the third.

So off we went, bouncing, bouncing along together on these three dromedaries that were in dire need of breath mints and soap to eradicate their cloying smells, as our teeth jarred from the lack of a spring suspension. There were huge rippling formations of sand dunes that evoked images of the sea due to the desert surface constantly being sculpted by the winds, more commonly known in Egypt as Khamsin. Well, as I was just about getting used to the pacing gait of my camel (instead of trotting, they pace, moving both two feet on the same side of their body together), when all of a sudden I noticed that my driver, or puller, or whatever the hell you called them, was pulling me away from my family. I looked over my shoulder and saw my wife and kids now disappearing around the side of the pyramid.

Getting frantic—not for my safety, but for my four women—I attempted to jump off this huge beast, but the damn hump made it impossible to get my frickin' short legs over it. I now screamed at the driver, "Get me off! Where in the hell are they taking my family?" He paid no attention to me until I started using language like I had at the fish plant. I was really pissed off now, and started to get the shakes, and that wasn't good. I was about to lose control. I guess that finally got his attention, as I was ready to go into that fifth dimension of anger where I'm enraged and fear no one.

He then motioned to me that he wanted faloos. I wasn't about to argue; I needed to get to my family, who was now alarmingly out of site.

I screamed, "You motherfucker son of a bitch, get me to my family right now or I'll fucking kill you!" I'm not sure he understood English, but the spit coming from my mouth must have alarmed him. I threw him a twenty-dollar bill and he then turned around and took me to my family as my heart raced in fear for them.

I'd heard of vacations going terribly bad and wasn't about to let that happen to us. However, I knew I was in Egypt, and that guy could have slit my throat in an instant out in that barren, vast waste of sand dunes, and no one would have known. And God only knows what could have happened to Joan and the girls. I must admit, I was frightened for them.

The next day, we went on a tour of Cairo in a private car. We came upon a palace-like structure, so I got out of the car and snapped a picture. Well, holy shit! You would have thought I'd pulled out an Uzi! A guard came running over to me, screaming, "No pictures! No pictures!" "Okay, man, sorry!" I said, then asked, "What's the big deal?" Evidently you don't take pictures of government buildings in Egypt, as I found out.

I wasn't liking Egypt very much at that point, but we had a flight to Alexandria in the Valley of the Kings arranged for the next day, and we were all looking forward to that.

The next morning, we had to take a boat across the Nile to get to a small airport to catch the flight. Well, an amusing thing happened during this brief boating experience.

The young, rather good-looking, dark-skinned boy who commandeered the small skiff was enthralled with Diana. Diana is a brunette; her long, flowing dark-brown hair and brown eyes must have captivated him. While crossing the Nile he asked me (I naturally assumed he was joking) if he could "buy Diana for two goats and a cow." Don't get the wrong impression. By "buying," he'd meant "take her hand in marriage," even though she was just sixteen at the time. Guess that was okay there.

I thought I would play along with him and have some fun, much to Diana's disdain. So, while looking at her, I responded, "How about I double your offer? Four goats and two cows." He looked at me, then over at her, and thought for a minute, then replied, "How about three goats and one cow?" I then replied, "Will you throw in a chicken?" Of course, we were all laughing by now and only stopped when we saw Di tearing up.

Meanwhile, I couldn't even get a single old goat for Laura, the blonde; however, I possibly could have increased a bid for Gi, since she is also a beautiful, brown-eyed brunette! They sure did like dark-haired females.

Upon landing in Alexandria, we were all happy to depart the aging plane that seemed to creak and groan while in flight, which made us apprehensive about whether our final resting place would be with the pharaohs in the Valley of the Kings.

While in Alexandria, we soon experienced unbearable temperatures close to 120 degrees Fahrenheit. The mixture of the blistering sun and the sand and rocks we stood upon scorched us as we waited in the harsh desert heat for our guide to arrive.

We were very fortunate to have the extremely rare opportunity to be able to go into the four burial chambers with our private guide. Though empty, I must say, experiencing being in King Tut's burial chamber was unnerving, as well as a bit eerie. It was an awesome experience. People are no longer allowed to enter.

Waiting for our return flight back to Cairo, we sat in the plane on the tarmac in the scorching desert sun for well over two hours, with no water or use of the bathroom, while the doors of the plane remained open, allowing the heat to penetrate the interior of the plane. It was never explained why, and we dared not ask. It made you realize how vulnerable one can be, being subjected to the militant ways of a third world country. Unrest was not unknown during President Mubarak's reign at the time, so you never knew what to expect, thus it was wise to just remain silent.

For the next few days in Cairo, we intended to relax before our long flights home, and just lay around the pool every day. However, Laura suddenly became seriously ill, suffering from extreme abdominal pain. It came to pass that she had an ovarian cyst lodged in her Fallopian tube that proved to be excruciatingly painful in her lower back on one side of her pelvis.

She couldn't stop crying and was folding over in pain. Luckily, I'd brought my gout pain pills with me and they alleviated some of the pain, though temporarily. I called our doctor back home and he said not to let any doctor—and especially not the hotel's house doctor—touch her. He said to get her to Rome or Tel Aviv as soon as possible. He felt she may have needed tuboplasty to restore patency to the Fallopian tubes. He was concerned that it could rupture, exacerbating her condition. Well, that scared the hell out of us!

I called the front desk of the hotel and asked if they knew when the next flight to New York was, or if they could connect me with the airline. The employee started complaining in very broken English, and said, "It is Ramadan, and no one is working. Anyway, there is only one flight and that is on Thursday." He was rather insulting. It was Monday, and that wasn't very good news, and we were already booked on that one and only Thursday flight.

I later found out that the annual observance of Ramadan is regarded as one of the Five Pillars of Islam and is taken very seriously.

Please let it be known that I am not making fun of this very religious holiday, just adding some humor to the story by including the following paragraphs.

I called back and asked if I could charter a plane. He curtly replied, "No pilots, no pilots. It's Ramadan!" I screamed back, "My daughter is very ill, and I have to get her to Tel Aviv. How about a car rental?" He then disturbingly said, "They're closed. It's Ramadan. I told you, it's Ramadan!" I then said, "With all due respect, I must somehow get my daughter to Tel Aviv." He then replied a bit more calmly, "Sir, there is a war zone between Egypt and Israel, and it is impossible to drive there." Oh, shit.

We were now helplessly stuck in Cairo for two more days, awaiting our flight out on Thursday. This was back in 1980, and there were only one or two international flights to the US each week. Thankfully, my pills were helping to alleviate some of the excruciating pain Laura was suffering.

In the meanwhile, Gi and Di asked if they could go down to the pool to swim and hang out, and we of course said sure, since it was likely boring being up in the sweltering room. There was no TV, nothing. We told them not to venture out of the hotel grounds, and they assured us they wouldn't.

Several hours passed and I felt I'd better go down and check on them and see what they were doing, and if they wanted lunch. I went down to the pool area and found there were very few people there, and only tourists, no one handing out towels, no life guard, no one from the hotel. Well, of course . . . it was Ramadan! Gi and Di were not where they'd said they would be. Hmm.

Thinking they may have gotten hungry, I checked out the pool restaurant. Nope, not there. It was closed. Yep, it was, as you by now know, Ramadan!

There was one more place, the arcade where they had a few games. Well, it was also closed, of course. They were nowhere to be found. *Okay, so now what? Do I tell Joan and freak her out?* I sat there by the pool, contemplating what to do. They'd assured me they wouldn't venture off.

After sitting there for thirty minutes or more in the 110-degree heat of North Africa, without a hat and unable to buy a beer, I started getting hot—not hot from the sun's rays; I started getting mad. I was also worried. Where in the hell could those two be?

Thankfully, about twenty minutes later, I heard, "Dad!" It was them, walking in from the front entrance like nothing was wrong. Casually, calmly, and confidently, just walking in. I screamed, "Where in the hell have you two been?!" They assuredly responded, "We went downtown!" I screamed, "You did what?! You went where?! Are you both nuts? What the hell is the matter with you two? I told you not to leave the grounds!" I then asked, "By the way, how did you get there? It's several miles away." They then very meekly replied, "We hitch-hiked!" "WHAT?!?!" I now screamed, as the handful of tourists around the pool alarmingly looked at me. I exclaimed again, "You did what?!" They said this nice, older, dark-complected man with a cute little goat in the back of his truck had given them a ride. *Oh my God*, I thought.

Well, I was happy they were back safe, but I went on to say that most likely all serial killers and rapists in Egypt drive around with cute little goats in the back of their trucks to attract their young, virtuous prey! Then I thought, *How did they get back? No, don't tell me, not the same way.* So, I asked, and they said, "Calm down, Dad. We walked." Whew, well thank God for that. Then I had a frightful flashback; I remembered that young guy on the Nile who tried to buy Diana for a goat or two, then even started bargaining for Gina. Maybe he supplied the goats to these guys!

It seemed as if it took forever for the next couple of days to pass, as we awaited our flight back to the US.

After a very harrowing experience at the Cairo airport, combating the disparaging, immense crowds to obtain our tickets, we finally got on the flight to New York.

Laura, thank God, made it back fine, and saw our doctor the day after we arrived. Luckily, the ovarian cyst hadn't ruptured.

In 1983, Diana started USC, and was in a sorority and had a brand-new Volkswagen Goat—whoops, I mean Rabbit, convertible, and was a happy young girl.

All three of our daughters were now away in college, and it was just Joan and I; we were sort of back where we started. It was an odd feeling, being just us again, good, but strange with the large house now so empty and quiet.

CHAPTER 27
THE WEST COAST MAFIA ATTEMPTS A TAKEOVER

It was in late September of 1983, and sales were fortuitously mounting, when I had a very alarming and unexpected visit. It was about ten in the morning on a Thursday, the busiest day of the week. I was in the sales office, as always at that time, watching the operation, when my secretary called and said, "Mr. P., you better get upstairs. There is a well-dressed older man in an overcoat who wants to see you." I jokingly replied, "In an overcoat? It's hot as hell outside. Who is it?" She said, "He wouldn't say, but he appears anxious, and said he must see you—and now!" *Hmm, who could it be?* I wondered, especially given that it was someone acting in a rather strange demanding manner.

As I approached the top of the stairway, I saw a man dressed in a dark suit and overcoat, as if it was the middle of winter, wearing a hat. I'll never forget the *hat*, an obviously expensive Stetson. I immediately said to myself, *Holy shit! It's the don of the West Coast Mob family! The Cosa Nostra, the frickin' Mafia!* I remembered him well, seeing him when I'd worked on the wharf. Everyone would scatter with fright when he came in.

So, I politely, but not respectfully, said, "Hello, Mr. X, come into my office." I didn't smile and looked him directly in the eye. *Never smile when meeting an impassioned adversary and look them directly in the eye.* This shows no fear and gives you power over them.

He then took off his hat, revealing a thick thatch of unmistakably dyed pitch-black hair, his face now had a feral scowl that could have halted a charging bull. He followed as we went into my office and closed the door behind him. No one did that unless I wanted it closed. Overlooking it, I then said, "So what brings you here today?" He immediately replied in a soft but stern, deep, gravelly voice, noticeably never having said hello, and brazenly blurted out, "Look, I'm not gonna play games, Mr. Paladini. I'm here to take over your operation." He was obviously a man of few words.

Shocked and taken aback by his alarmingly bold statement, I didn't know what to say. I went silent. Meanwhile, I was rather exhilarated that I had indeed been recognized by their huge conglomerate, and felt complimented that he wanted my company, but at the same time unnerved and frightened by his audacious statement. But only a bit. I have never been frightened by any man. Then my arrogant and explosive temperament suddenly kicked in, and I immediately got the shakes . . . and that wasn't good! However, I had to control myself and stay calm, while thinking about what he'd said. "Take over my operation." That was bullshit! I didn't hear anything about buying it.

So, without any further ado, I calmly replied, "I don't know why you want my company, but I built this business from nothing, with nothing, and I am not about to be 'taken over,' as you put it, by anyone or anything. If whoever you're trying to protect got hurt by our aggressiveness, you—or they—were not targeted." (If you noticed, I never called him "sir.")

Without saying another word, he then just stood there and glared at me, obviously shocked and perturbed by my response. His left eye nervously started to cross and twitch, assumingly now realizing his reputation and power were unsuccessful in scaring me. I then said, "Uh, by the way, X [calling him by his first name, reducing the level of respect even further], when you said, 'take over' my operation, did you mean you wanted to make an offer to buy me out? I'm not sure just how you meant that." There was a moment of silence. I assume my response wasn't taken well. He showed no sign of consternation, most likely stunned and pissed him off. *I don't kiss rings!*

He then started to speak . . . but I abruptly interrupted him. "Anyway, I must profoundly refuse your offer. I take it that it was an offer, and not a demand?"

Obviously provoked and enraged, his jowls then expanded, almost in a demonic, distorted fashion. I guess I'd really, really pissed him off! For a moment, I thought I was going to hear a loud bang and see the vision of Jesus. However, he then just abruptly turned around toward the door in a huff and started walking down the steps. When he reached the landing, he turned around, looked up at me, and said, "This may result in dire consequences for you, Mr. Paladini!

By the way, did you notice he called *me* "Mr."? I then went back into my office and sat back in my chair, relieved he was gone. I thought about it for a few seconds, and never looked back at my reaction. I then wondered how they could just take over a business. Was there a buy out? Well, no matter now. In the meantime, I felt pretty damn good about it. I'd actually stood up to the Mob and the West Coast Mafia boss. But maybe that hadn't been smart. Maybe I could get, as they say, "whacked." But I wasn't going turn over my years of hard work building this business just because he felt he could intimidate me. My decision was one of justified rational confidence. I also knew it was a threat, and I was taking a risk.

I then suddenly rushed out of my office to the top of the steps and looked out the window at the parking lot as he drove away. He was sitting in the backseat of a large black sedan with three other men in the car. I now thought, *Oh, shit!* Then his departing words interminably repeated themselves in my head: "This may result in having dire consequences for you, Mr. Paladini."

So, who visited me that day in my office? Can't say, but there's a *hat*, whoops, I mean a *hint!*

I was very thankful that nothing ever happened regarding his statement, "There could be dire consequences." I feared for my family for some time, but never told them. If there was any indication of repercussions of any sort, or even a slight indication that harm could have come to them, I may have taken a different course and caved in to them.

A few months later, though, I started receiving calls at my home at two in the morning, supposedly from the security company, saying there had been a break-in at the plant. I would drive the forty minutes to the plant, of course, alone, intending to meet with the San Francisco police to investigate if there had indeed been a break-in. I carried a gun, a small .22 revolver that fit comfortably in my pocket.

I remember sitting at the entry gate of the plant in the Jaguar in the pitch-black of the night, with just the lights of the parking lot illuminating my car. The projects were just a half block away, so needless to say, it was a bit unnerving—no, it was damn frightening, sitting there all alone, awaiting the arrival of the police, that seemed to never come. After sitting there for about an hour, I would leave; after all, I had to be back in a couple of hours. After this had occurred for a third time, the next day I called the security company and asked if they had called regarding a break-in during the night. They said no! Thinking back, the last time this had happened I recalled seeing a black sedan circling the block a few times while I was there. This spooked me; that car sure looked familiar.

The following is a funny story, and unrelated to the assumed hypothesis just mentioned. A few weeks later on a Saturday morning, I was driving the Jag down the El Camino Real in San Mateo to my barber, and in the middle of the block, on the very busy street, I made a U-turn—yeah, I know, dumb thing to do, but no one was looking . . . or so I thought. As I pulled in front of the barber shop, a San Mateo motorcycle police officer pulled up behind me. He asked if I knew what I'd done wrong. What else could I say other than "Yes, officer!" He then asked for my driver's license and registration. The registration was in the glove box, and as I opened it, a towel covered my gun, but I guess not very well! He then ordered me out of the car and put me up against the wall and called for backup. Within moments, three additional police cars arrived with their sirens blaring and their red and blue lights flashing galore. My barber, hearing the commotion, came out of his shop and had a shocked expression on his face when he saw me being handcuffed. Many people thought that I was in the Mafia at the time.

The officer asked what a gun was doing in the glove compartment. I then explained who I was as he was looking at my driver's license and told him my place of business was near Hunters Point, a block from the projects; I said I often got calls at night advising me of a break-in, so I carried the gun in case of a confrontation while awaiting the SFPD. He then looked at me and said, "So you're Mr. Paladini of the Paladini Seafood Company, huh? I see your trucks all over." He then told the other policemen that everything was okay, and they could leave. He said, "I have to give you a ticket sir for the illegal U-turn, and I also want to give you some advice. Carry the gun unloaded in your trunk from now on . . . and get a bigger gun!"

Well, I found that amusing, but also good advice. A few weeks later, I did get a bigger gun, a much bigger gun, one that scared the hell out of me. I'm not a gun-savvy guy but thought it might be wise to have if something ever occurred at my home with my adversaries.

CHAPTER 28
THE FINAL STEP TO REPLICATE THE OLD PALADINI CORPORATION

By the end of spring of 1984, I was getting bored with the distribution end of the industry with things now going smoothly and sales continuing to do so well. Yes, I have a Triple-A personality, nuts, I know, and seem to get bored too easily, never satisfied with what I have. Needing a further challenge, I decided to open a processing facility. We now had the volume to necessitate such an expansion and doing so would allow us to double profits.

I always seem to want to do things fast, maybe too fast. And as they say, Rome wasn't built in a day. But I *did* try! I lived once before during Julius Caesar's reign. "Jules, he who rules," as I mockingly called him, would often come into the Senate chambers about noon every day and we'd do lunch, then play cards later over at the Forum. I was the one who suggested he be immortalized on playing cards as the king on the king of diamonds. Being so vain, he asked what his best side was, and I suggested he look to the right. Don't believe me, huh? Well, I also warned him to use a condom with Cleopatra and he didn't listen to me, and look what happened!

Okay, enough of my past for now. Before I continue with my explanation of the expansion of my company, I want to outline the parallel between my grandfather and my inceptive ideas and advent into the seafood industry. I told you in previous chapters how my grandfather started with absolutely nothing other than fishing off a pier for his dinner and his eventual phenomenal success. The only significant difference between us is that there was no defined seafood industry and little competition in San Francisco back in 1865. I am not in any way making less of what he accomplished; these are just facts. As also reading previously, I as well started with absolutely nothing, as he did. One can say that I may be shadowing my grandfather, paralleling his experience by creating my company in the same manner, and augmenting it into a premier status in the industry. I couldn't have started by fishing for my dinner, though. First of all, I don't know how to fish, and second, I hate to eat fish!

I also outlined in the prologue that my grandfather came from Italy to San Francisco with only his old wooden trunk containing just a change of clothes. The second generation may have, however, wrongly assumed or interpreted how he got started in the fish business. I will quote him, giving a slightly different version of the story, the one most likely to be true, since it came from his mouth, from an actual interview he gave less than two weeks before he died of a stroke in 1921. The journalist quoted Achille as having said, "I meet some friends. They tell to me money is to be made in the fish business. So, I stay. I buy fish on Fisherman's Wharf. I work to buy and catch fish on the Sacramento River."

Achille Paladini, my grandfather, was responsible for much of the development of the fishing industry on the West Coast in the late 1800s to early 1900s. He was one of the first to can tuna, to smoke fish, and to maintain a cold storage plant for the off season. By 1915, he had five fishing trawlers, eight trucks, and over sixty-five employees. It wasn't long before he became known as the "Fish King" on the West Coast, a title that has become his legacy.

Achille was known to pay for everything in cash and did not believe in borrowing or mortgages. He carried what assets he could in his pockets, which bulged from the heavy weight of gold coins. The often-used term "deep pockets" factually originated from him. When the great earthquake and fire of 1906 occurred, he was left with just the clothes on his back, and the gold coins in his pockets, though deep.

He now faced the dire prospect to rebuild on the parcels of property he owned in the city. Aware that it was the sea that had made it possible for him to prosper, he returned to the sea and what was hidden beneath to rebuild his fortune.

And rebuild he did. He purchased the land on Clay Street between Montgomery and Sansome Streets where he had once rented a space for his first fish stand and built his huge wholesale distribution plant. He then remarkably purchased the entire super prime so-called Montgomery Block. Many years later, and well after his death, the second generation sold the ultimate of prime real estate to the Transamerica Corporation in 1968. Thus, the Transamerica Pyramid was built upon it, and completed in 1972. It is 835 feet tall with forty-eight floors of office space. Upon its completion, it was the eighth tallest building in the world. The main entrance to the old fish plant was 542 Clay Street, and the Pyramid Building's main entrance is 600 Clay Street. The building is evocative of San Francisco and has become an iconic symbol of the city.

Shortly before his death, he was accredited to be the second wealthiest Italian in all of California, second to none other than his good friend, Amadeo Giannini, the founder of the Bank of America.

His life was not without controversy, however. At one point, he held a virtual monopoly in San Francisco's fishing industry. The newspapers referred to his empire as a "Fish Trust." He was said to have forced restaurants and retail fishmongers—who relied on him for deep-sea fresh fish, to go along with his price fixing schemes. Retail prices doubled, and consumers began to suspect that something fishy was going on.

The United States Senate investigated Achille, and the hearing revealed that the captains of the fishing trawlers were instructed to turn in only a given amount of fish each day and send the rest to the glue factory. One independent fish dealer was threatened by Achille's men when he sold fish for less than the price set by him. In another instance, when some of his associates attempted to go into business on their own, prices fell so low that they were forced to close. The following day, prices were back up to normal.

Some may say that Achille Paladini lent credence to the claim that "Behind every great fortune there is crime." However, there was nothing particularly scandalous about the way Paladini built his empire. His exploits were, of course, very much in the spirit of his age. It would be hard to say what made his trust any different—or more reprehensible—than the ones that, on a larger scale, were being operated by the likes of Andrew Carnegie, John Pierpoint Morgan, and John D. Rockefeller.

So, as you can see, there was a definite parallel between us. Our business principles were very much alike. Yes, some possibly a bit crafty and shrewd, but our personalities also seem to be consonant, with us both possessing outrageous tendencies. We also shared the firm conviction of not borrowing, but paying for, what you need for expansion, and owning your own properties from which to operate. My eventual investments into commercial real estate also replicated his strategy.

Possibly, I have in fact shadowed my grandfather. He may have even guided me. After all, I have his old wooden trunk. And yes, I am very proud to carry his name, even though it has caused much havoc. Having said that, it was my father I truly loved. As a matter of fact, I wish I had been named Walter after him, but my older brother, fortunately for him, was named Walter.

Now let's go back to my expansion plans. I was in no way being complacent and turning my back on the distribution business and moving on to another frivolous venture. I was adding another profit point and an important element of the industry—production—thus controlling the quality and ultimately furthering customer satisfaction and profitability.

There are five elements of the seafood industry: First; the boats sell the fish to the receiving stations; second, the receiving station sells the fish to the processor; third, the processor processes the fish and sells it to the distributor; fourth, the distributor sells the fish to the retailers; fifth, the retailers sells the fish to the end user. Five profit points. We would now have three of those five elements under our control. No need for boats or retail stores.

I concluded that if we had our own processing plant and receiving stations along the coast, we could have control of the quality by buying directly from contracted drag boats. We could then fillet and pack our own products, and also buy directly from the salmon boats and freeze the salmon needed for the smokehouse during the off-season. More importantly, it would allow us a much lower product cost factor, that is, if I was able to control the expenses of the additional plants and receiving stations. But why wouldn't I be able to do so?

I had been fattening up the other producers with our volume purchasing and could now enjoy the additional profits that I'd been allowing others.

We would then have three receiving stations. We would buy directly from the boats, then charge my processing plant a profit margin of 8 to 10 percent. We would have a processing plant, where we would process the fish, then charge my distribution plant a profit margin of 20 to 25 percent. We'd also have a distribution center, and would sell to the restaurants and markets with another 25 to 30 percent profit margin. I personally owned the San Francisco distribution plant and the Santa Rosa processing plant, and the corporation was paying me rent, similar to a triple-net lease. This equation was now a result of the additional profit centers.

I felt this would be an excellent move and started looking for a facility near the coast. I soon found a processing plant in Santa Rosa that had been out of operation for several years. The location was ideal since it was close to Bodega Bay, a major fish-receiving area, and fortunately there was a receiving dock available. Coincidentally, it was where Paladini once had a receiving dock long ago. It also wasn't very far from Fort Brag, the next desired location, where strangely enough, Paladini also had had a receiving station plus a large processing plant. I was ultimately able to locate a dock in Fort Brag as well, so things were going as planned.

But we still needed a receiving dock further up the coast. I soon found one available in Crescent City. I was hoping for Eureka to duplicate the old company, but there was nothing available. It didn't matter though; the concept was the same. These ports represented the highest-volume fish production areas on the entire California coast.

Now all I had to do was hurry and make a deal to buy the Santa Rosa production plant, which was pretty much ready to use without needing too much alteration. If successful, I would then immediately sign the leases on the three receiving stations, guaranteeing the product for the processing plant.

My controller contacted the owner and made a deal for less than the asking price of $150,000, if I paid partly in cash—green cash—for the three-acre site. But of course, I would need to conclude things in person. He then planned for us to soon meet.

My controller was twenty years older than I was, and very distinguished looking. When we arrived at the property owner's home, the owner stood, walked up to him, and said, "Hello, Mr. Paladini, nice meeting you." To which my controller replied, "*This* is Mr. Paladini. I'm the controller!" The owner and his wife were then taken back, I guess because I was so young at the time.

I had $50,000 in cash, and had placed it in a brief case, just as you would see in a movie. I opened the brief case and offered the cash to him. Shocked, he accepted. There was now a $75,000 balance due within a year. The total price for the plant was $125,000.

The property was titled to the Paladini Family Trust as a personal investment.

Buying this property was a win-win. Not only would the company pick up an additional source of profit, we would pick up another source of personal income because we personally owned the property, and it was leased to Paladini Fisheries.

An amusing thing happened on the drive back to the city that afternoon that I will never forget! My controller had driven his older Cadillac that day for some reason, and on the way back, needed to stop for gas in Novato. It was a very warm day, so all the windows were down. There was a car dealership directly adjacent to the gas station, and as I sat there while he filled his car with gas, I saw a wild-looking car in the showroom. I told him I would be over in the showroom, and if I wasn't back by the time he'd finished filling up, to come over.

Well, it turned out to be the new Lotus Esprit sports car. I fell in love with it and bought it on the spot. I told the salesman my controller would be coming over shortly, and he would make the arrangements for payment. I felt like a big shot. I'd just bought a piece of property, and now a new sports car—my first sports car. By the way, you should occasionally reward yourself for doing well.

Meanwhile, as I was waiting for my controller to arrive, I heard a sloshing sound. Slosh, slosh, slosh . . . Yes, it was my normally very distinguished controller who had driven to the nearby car wash while waiting for me and had gone through the entire car wash with the windows down! He'd evidently forgotten to roll up the windows before entering and had turned the ignition off, afraid to turn it on while in the wash for some reason. He was soaked from head to foot, including his fine sport jacket and expensive slacks, down to his loafers. As he approached, with his curly gray hair soaking wet, he asked me what the hell I had been doing. I then reluctantly introduced him to the salesman as my controller.

When we got back into his car, with the leather seats now saturated, I asked him why he hadn't just rolled up the windows when he'd discovered they were down. He said, "I got rattled and forgot that all I had to do was turn on the ignition!"

I picked up the Lotus the next day, and that was the start of my sports car fascination.

With the new venture for the production end of the business now initiated, I had to find a manager, but fortunately, I had already made prior contact with the best in the business, just in case I had indeed decided to proceed. He was running another processing plant in Santa Rosa, a huge operation connected with the prominent San Francisco wholesale company that I once worked for several years ago. Yes, it was the same company. Now I was hitting their processing operation, as well. That would really piss him off!

I named the processing company Paladini Fisheries, A Division of Achille Paladini Enterprises, Inc. The receiving stations didn't need a clever name since they would only be selling to the processing plant, so they were simply called Paladini Receiving, also a division of the main corporation.

Achille Paladini Enterprises, Inc. was the main corporation, with three subsidiaries, and Paladini Properties personally owned all the properties. The business would now be self-supporting from one entity to the next. *Control your own destiny!*

Sales immediately soared close to $20 million per year. And with the acquisition of the processing plant and the three receiving stations, this resulted in an additional $3.5 million in annual sales, with additional profits at each source. I could now expect a net profit of at least 5.5 percent, up an additional 2.5 percent from the once 3 percent net. At the end of this three-phase cycle, from raw product to processing to distributor sales, gross and net profits almost doubled.

To explain: One entity profited from selling to the next entity, and so on, starting with receiving to processing; processing to distribution; distribution to end user. Plus, there were two major commercial properties paying rent to me personally. Then there was the equity build-up with each mortgage payment and the ever-increasing land value. Thus the "magic" of volume!

However, they say the "safest and quickest way to double your money is to fold it in half and put it in your pocket."

None the less, volume was paramount and had to be maintained to produce this "magic." It was like going to a busy restaurant; because the restaurant is busy, you go to the bar while waiting for a table and have a drink, maybe an appetizer—furthering their profit margin. Success breeds success.

I was now paralleling my grandfather and had totally replicated the original A. Paladini, Inc. And it hadn't really taken that long. I wondered how long it had taken him to get to this point.

When running a successful business, any business, it is important that you—you, the boss, the owner—regress to what originally facilitated your success. You must ensure that your original concept has not changed, and that you don't lose focus on that concept that catapulted you to success. That ingredient that made you successful must forever stay within your formula.

Aristotle said, "Excellence is never an accident. It is always the result of high intention, sincere effort, and intelligent execution; it represents the wise choice of many alternatives. Choice, not chance, determines your destiny."

It is also wise to be involved with your flock and not totally depend on your Sheep Dog. Get out there and smell the sheep. Be involved with the daily activity, making certain the organizational parameters are kept in place.

Well, sure, things were going well at work, but I needed to pay more attention to my wife and kids and spend some quality time with them. For no success in public life can compensate for failure in the home. For better or worse, ambitious people always need to accomplish things. They are driven for results, wanting to do more, get promoted, and start new ventures. But they also have a personal life that can't be ignored. To achieve optimum balance and happiness there must be a correlation between the two. Ambition in this sense can mean taking care of family priorities, expanding social circles, and other interests. Guess I should listen to my own words.

The difference between successful people and very successful people is that very successful people say *no* to almost everything. I have said time and time again that no is the hardest word to say when conducting business. So, I now needed to say no to any further expansion.

In late June of 1984, Laura graduated from Long Beach State University with a Bachelor of Arts degree in Interior Architectural Design and was now working for a large engineering design firm in Los Angeles. Wow! Go, girl! I was also intrigued to hear rumblings there was an engagement brewing.

CHAPTER 29
MY IDENTITY

Everyone has an identity; what their profession is or was, i.e. a housewife, a shoe shine boy, librarian, or whatever. A fruit tree is identified by the type of fruit it bears; a person, by their profession, and most often, its subsequent success.

Oh, how I hoped my ego wouldn't get the best of me and let me forget the long hard road it had been to get to this point. I had to remain humble. *I must remain humble.* Maybe if I kept saying it over and over, it would get into my head. It was less than a decade ago that I'd been eating nineteen-cent burgers and was working Saturdays for my brother-in-law at his wood shop to make ends meet.

And how about the day when the dollar bill to pay the toll on the Golden Gate Bridge had flown out of Gina's hand? I hollered at poor Gina because after that happened, I didn't have enough money to buy the three girls their ice cream cone, as promised. I wasn't mad at her. I was mad at myself! Mad, ashamed, and frustrated for not having enough money for such a simple little treat for our kids.

As Will Rogers said, "If you're riding ahead of the herd, take a look back every now and then to make sure it's still there." I had to remember to look back and value this success, and not get overly confident or complacent. My competition was constantly going to be on my tail, trying to get their business back. *So, look back, Kiki! Look back!*

The Santa Rosa processing facility was now up and running after a sizable expansion by more than doubling the square footage with a new, much larger cooler and freezer, and a blast freezer for the individual quick freezing of local Chinook/King salmon for the smokehouse. A new smokehouse was also added to expand the production of the famous Paladini old-fashioned smoked salmon, and a slicing and packing room was built adjacent to it.

A forty-person automated fillet line was set up to pack fresh fish fillets in ten- and twenty-pound cartons, and a huge automatic bay shrimp peeling and cooking machine was installed for the Paladini brand shrimp meat to then be sealed in five-pound vacuum cans.

Two stainless-steel cooking tanks were installed to cook a ton of live crabs at a time, and a production line to pick Dungeness crabs for the Paladini brand Dungeness crab meat.

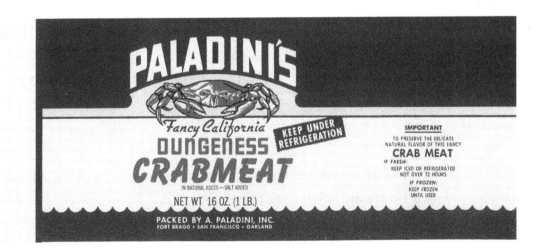

The processing plant now allowed for the total duplication of the original company by facilitating in having our own product label. All improvements and equipment were paid for, living by my concept that if you can pay for it and not have it affect the cash flow, you're not over expanding.

I'll now give a brief outline explaining the structure of the three profit sources and the order of the product produced and sold: The first was the three receiving stations, Paladini Receivers, which had their own built-in customer to sell the product to—me. The second, Paladini Fisheries, the processing facility, had its own built-in customer to sell the product to—me. The third, Paladini Seafood Company, the distribution facility, did not have its own built-in customer to sell the product to, thus we sold the product to someone other than one of my companies, the end user, i.e., the restaurants, hotels, and markets.

Fortunately, just about this time, the San Francisco main office and distribution center had just attained the Marriott Hotel chain contract, and this was huge. It included not only all the Marriott Hotels, but the facilities they subcontracted in Northern and Central California. The contract we signed would be worth well over a quarter million a month, three million a year. This kicked up the sales to a staggering $23 million a year, beyond my comprehension of what I ever would have achieved. This was in 1984.

Fast forward a year to 1985. I was now forty-nine years old, at the pinnacle of my career, and could rightfully say I was number one in the industry—an accomplishment of which my father and grandfather would have hopefully been proud. Paladini Seafood Company was now once again the largest wholesale seafood distributor on the West Coast. Against insurmountable odds, I fortunately was able to continue my grandfather's legacy. Somehow, someway, with unending *perseverance*, it miraculously happened! So, would that now make *me* the Fish King? Nah, I could never live up to that or take that from you, Grandpa.

Self-praise hath no honor. I am not in any way implying to give self- praise. This is just the true story of my life, and the factual way it went.

A company is also not one man, it is a team. I could throw the ball, but someone must catch it!

Sales eventually exceeded an unprecedented $25 million annually, equaling almost $60 million today. This is based on the inflation data calculator of the Consumer Price Index in 1985 to present, figured by extrapolating the data and applying the method of partial differentiation.

However, I now wondered, *was this it?* Was this really it? There was nothing more to prove. The challenge had been conquered. It now almost felt like a let-down, if that makes sense. It was like climbing to the top of Mount Everest, "The Goddess Mother of Snows," as the native

Tibetan call it. Few have ever achieved in conquering the lady's adversity of the overwhelming constant myriad of challenges, the freezing weather, the gale force winds, the misery and hardship, plus the slow, tedious, almost impossible ascent up to the twenty-nine-thousand-foot peak. Imagine being one of the very few to successfully reach the top (as I have), then upon looking down, saying, "Ho, hum. Is that it?"

Having said that, my goddamn audacious and tenacious personality still needed to augment the reckless rush of achieving, possibly even overachieving, killing the accomplishment. Always determined to make something greater. Why couldn't I ever be satisfied with what I had?

Success can indeed be attained with determination and *perseverance*, but also by being shrewd and taking advantage of opportunities as they arise. Remember, opportunities are never lost, someone will be there to take advantage of the ones you miss.

Case in point: We only had half of the Safeway stores, and I wanted all of them. The Santa Rosa production plant was starting to overproduce, and now needed the outlet for the product. The Safeway buyer told me he'd had to spread the business around, so the account was stalemated. A wholesale fish company in Marin County concentrated on selling only to chain stores, and mainly Safeway, and they weren't doing well. Selling only to chain stores often requires a less than normal gross markup, plus a commitment to recurring ad specials each week, and often having to take back product for any reason, valid or not. A seafood wholesaler, or as a matter of fact, any food wholesaler, needs a mix of restaurants and hotels for higher profit margins to offset the lack of margins selling to the supermarket chains. So, I bought the company to gain the accounts for pennies on the dollar! I kept the name and moved their operation into mine, and no one was the wiser. We now had all 450 Safeway stores! Thus, an example of being shrewd.

We were now, as you know, a receiver and a producer, as well as a distributor, enjoying a three-tiered profit margin. Nonetheless, the receiving and production plants depended on the sales volume of the distribution company.

I was lacking sales in the East Bay and tried to hire the salesman who worked for the now-aging company that had the majority stronghold of the restaurants in the area. He was a faithful employee, however, and would not leave. I found that they weren't doing well, so I bought that company as well. Again, for pennies on the dollar. Now we had it all—shades of my grandfather's tactics. Only perfectly legal.

Be that as it may, before making such bold moves, every detail, every tiny detail, must be thoroughly thought out. Even such transcendent spirits as Abraham Lincoln could not have produced history that did not rest on a foundation of *tedium* and *detail*, and even sheer drudgery. Like musicians using tuning forks to ensure that their instrument is perfectly in tune, a business relies on the brain of its master to ensure all functions are harmonious. Sounds melodramatic, I know, but just don't forget it!

However, be forewarned that there are some things that just can't be accomplished. No one has yet been able to produce wheat without chaff, simply because it just can't be done. So, think everything thoroughly through before making your moves, and ensure it is indeed possible before venturing further. So often, our imaginations and fantasies are far greater than reality, unless the reality can be achieved as a result of the fantasy.

I now started investing in commercial real estate from saved revenues to insure the future. Remember, do not save what is left after spending, but spend what is left after saving.

This was the beginning of a vision for long-term positioning, looking forward to retirement and eventually trading into only triple-net property investments. Thus, rewarding those years of working and planning. Also, a forethought of security for my family in the event of my sudden passing.

I thought it also wise to have a diversified income stream other than just commercial real estate, so I started investing in equities in a diversified array of tax efficient mutual funds. I didn't have time for individual stocks. A novice should use caution when maneuvering the corridors of Wall Street or trusting investments with strangers. I am of the opinion that self-management is one of the most important determinants of financial success. Investing is all about attempting to make the right moves at the right time, and of course, delimiting the wrong ones as much as possible. This is just *my* personal investment strategy and preference.

I would like to add just one more thing: Always remember, with any investment, the greater the return, the greater the risk. *Big mouthfuls often choke!*

Well, Gina had graduated from the University of San Diego, a Jesuit college, with a Bachelor of Arts degree in Business Administration. Wow, good goin', girl! And, as intended, she was coming to work with me. I was proud to now have my daughter as an incremental part of the company, and just possibly the first person ever in the industry with a college degree. I would finally have a manager with great intelligence. Someday she would be the future of the business and carry on its legacy.

Now when the banks asked me who my successor would be, or who would run the business if something happened to me, I could finally and proudly say . . . my daughter.

There was always concern with the bank regarding the fact that I was basically a one-man operation, though I had over three hundred employees amongst all the branches, and had a good sub-management team, but there was no one else with the capabilities to oversee the entire operation—that is, until now. I had a multi-million-dollar line of credit to purchase salmon for the smokehouse for the off-season that was reviewed and renewed each year by the bank, and Gina having joined me would ease their fears. I tried to use as little of the line of credit as possible; it was only my backup, if needed. The line of credit was, and always will be, the only borrowing I would ever do.

The first thing Gina did once she'd joined the company was to arrange to have the company computerized. Well, I knew nothing about computers; actually, not many people did at the time.

We had to put in air-conditioning in the head bookkeeper's office since the computer needed to be kept cool. Even though San Francisco rarely gets very hot, in went the air-conditioner and this mammoth-looking contraption called a computer.

It was a nightmare setting up a system to relate and correlate to the variables of the seafood industry. Weights aren't all even or consistent, and there are thousands of items that must be inputted. The variables were countless. I bowed out of this since I didn't know what the hell was going on. The system was soon finally up and working, but not without the occasional glitch, of course.

A few months later, it was Christmas, so I took the production supervisors, the salespeople, and the girls in the office to Dago Mary's for lunch, and naturally they mostly all had a few drinks—actually, far more than just a few. I did not, however. I never drank with the employees or during business hours. My accounts receivables girl got really blasted, so when I returned to the plant alone, I turned off the computer. I stared at this imposing, monolithic thingamajig for an hour before figuring out how to do it and was very proud when I finally found the "off" button.

Though suffering with a very bad hangover, my accounts receivable girl called me at home the next morning, which just happened to be a Saturday, and said, "Mr. P., I have to get into the plant and save the day's work and turn off the computer." I proudly said, "No worries, I did!" There was silence, then she gulped and said, "You did what?" Well, we lost the entire Friday's work, the biggest sales day of the week, and it all had to be re-inputted! Hell, I didn't know that little button was only the "on" button. So that was my first encounter with a computer, and it didn't go very well.

The company being computerized eventually proved to be a great asset, and I was proud of Gi to have had the gumption to do it. Nevertheless, I couldn't make Gina the general manager just yet. She had to *earn* that title. It would come only after experience and learning every aspect of the business. It would take a couple of years for her to gain that knowledge to achieve the respect of the employees. You can't lead your troops until you earn the stars on your shoulder. Respect must be earned.

In the interim, while she was learning the business, I made her my international procurement agent in charge of the acquisition of fresh fish from all parts of the world and researching possible new species to purchase.

Relating to procurement, we used one broker against the other, saving incremental amounts of money on an item. She and I both had phones with five lines, so when purchasing a volume item, we made sure we had several brokers selling the same item on the phone at the time and used one against the other. Thousands of dollars would then be saved on a single volume item with the purchase. However, we always used the average quoted price to predicate the selling price, picking up a few more percentage points. As sales volume increases, your purchasing power increases, to your advantage.

However, I really wanted Gina in sales. She has a fantastic—and I do mean, *fantastic*—outgoing personality, and has a wonderful way with people, plus, she's beautiful!

I explained that a family member must always handle the major prime accounts. Another salesperson would get friendly with the buyers, and if they were to leave the company, they could and would take a portion of the business with them. That would hurt, and also really piss me off!

The big hotel chains, including the Marriott account and the supermarket chains, plus the major clubs and country clubs, and cruise ships, and the inflight catering companies that supplied the airlines had to be handled by a family member. They were our bread and butter. Gina declined however, saying she didn't enjoy sales. I reluctantly respected that and didn't push her any further, though I got an ache in my gut knowing my sales manager would have to retain the accounts, not only putting them in possible jeopardy, but allowing him to feel omnipotent knowing I had to rely on him. I didn't like being in that position.

Gina, however, did a fantastic job as the fresh fish buyer for international species and was responsible for bringing in many new items from foreign countries, developing a demand for an otherwise unknown species. The profit margin was often as much as 200 percent. We priced the new items comparable to items such as Petrale sole and King salmon so the chefs would consider it a quality fish. The more expensive it is, the better it tastes!

As 1986 approached, my life had elevated to such a level I'd never thought possible. I remembered just a short while ago I'd been just a salesman for another fish company, calling on Draeger's Market in Menlo Park and meeting Frank Draeger, the elderly owner, and respectfully calling him "Mr. Draeger." I'd thought, *Wow, can you imagine owning a market like this? And I just met the owner!* I was so impressed.

Well, fast forward a decade, and Frank Draeger was now a neighbor of ours, living in Hillsborough, and he and his wife had been to our home several times—and strangely, he now called *me* "Mr. Paladini." It was a good feeling now associating with his element, and on the supposed same level as him. Well, my insecurity level was now compromised, and my head started to swell. Thankfully my nose remained the same size.

As you can see, I guess the being "humble" thing had been forgotten. I hadn't meant it to be that way, but I was now like a rock star in the industry. I know that sounds braggadocious, but I'm telling it the way it was. Upon reading this, my wife won't agree, however.

Please understand, considering how the company must have been perceived at the time, having sixty trucks on the road, including two forty-foot tractor-trailers, all displaying the big red P on them, the name was naturally well known, especially in Northern California. People would often say when introduced to them, "Gosh, I see your trucks all over!" Well, they were; they were ubiquitous. And yeah, it gave me a big head. When going to restaurants, not only would the owner and manager come to our table, but the executive chef and sous chef as well. Yeah, that was fun.

I can hear Joan saying, "You're bragging again." Not so, I'm just telling the story of my life, and that's just the way it was. And you enjoyed those times, too, didn't you? I'm listening . . . you're not answering . . .

Diana had now graduated from the University of Southern California with a Bachelor of Arts degree in Psychology and would be starting at Pepperdine University to get her master's degree. Then she would have to do an internship to be a professional family, child, and marriage therapist.

That was unbelievable! I'm so proud of her—of all our girls.

CHAPTER 30
MY FLIRTATIOUS WAYS BEGIN

To protect my wife and three daughters from any further hurt, and to not open old wounds, yet maintain some of the integrity of the events regarding my extramarital entanglements, I have chosen to not divulge all the experiences and/or totally go into detail about the graphic events during those years. This was a segment of my life that my narcissistic, bombastic, self-absorbed, and egotistical ways (was that negative descriptive enough?) got the best of me, and I am not proud of what I did, and am sorry for it. You may now also think less of me, and that is understandable, and I accept it.

Let me start out by saying that the women reading what I am now about to assert are not going to accept it as an excuse for my actions. But let me try to expound on my strange semi-transpicuous version of an explanation for it.

I honestly felt that if I gave my wife everything she wanted, and was good to her, and of course, still loved her, that I could do as I wanted in my free time, as the Italian men did in Italy. I saw it on our honeymoon, and every time we went there. Older men with younger girls, and the men were, of course, obviously married. Sure, it may have been presumptuous for me to assume that it was an endorsement for allowing it, but I felt it was like when smoking a joint—if you didn't inhale, it was fine. Yes, I know you're not buying that.

Something else: There has oddly always been some sort of extraordinary magical magnetism between me and women. I guess I needed to have used more vigilance and prudence, however, with this so-called bewitching polarity.

Reading what I just wrote, it sounds egotistical, yes, but it's true. Sorry. But don't judge in a negative manner, at least not yet. Wait until the end, then decide if I redeemed myself, at least somewhat. Having said that, I know men go to prison for murder, then claim they found God and ask forgiveness, which is indeed bullshit. Aristotle said, "To avoid criticism, say nothing, do nothing, be nothing."

I met a girl named Simone. She was working for a seafood brokerage company and called on me occasionally to look at new products. There was nothing going on—at first. However, I started casually seeing her occasionally for lunch. She gave me accolades about how I ran the business and made me feel good about myself. She was very nice, and a kind person, also intelligent and easy to talk with, she was twelve years younger than me, thirty-seven. She was also forthright, and a woman of values—an all-American girl.

Well, she invited me to her house one weekday afternoon for what I'd thought would be just a casual drink. She had bought an assortment of liquor that included my favorite bourbon. I had a few drinks, and before we knew it, one thing led to the next and my endorphins kicked in as if I was on an opiate.

The excitement was enthralling, and I soon got lost in her kisses. The depth of her passion for me was totally unexpected, but warmly received, and for whatever reason, I seemed to need this. She was a respite from the now serious responsibility of the business and I found solace being with her.

She told me that my sensitivity and gentle but obvious masculinity took her breath away (she said it—not me), and she couldn't help falling for me. She said that while calling on me at the plant, seeing me running that large operation and having men twice my size cowering in fear when I spoke, and to be soft and gentle with her, was alluring and seductive. Again, I'm quoting her, so stop twitching, ladies.

She took me away from the constant stress I was under running this now immense business I'd created and allowed me to be someone else. I could relax and just be me. It was fun being with her, not having to put on airs, not being that big, powerful businessman from upscale Hillsborough. Just a normal guy, wearing old, tattered Levi's, if I so wished.

The affair bothered me, however, but I couldn't stop it. I started drinking rather heavily about this time, possibly trying to mask what I was doing and escape my double life. It wasn't easy. I knew what I was doing was wrong, and didn't want to hurt my wife, but my highly fueled Italian testosterone, and that rush of euphoria, always got the best of me, and the alcohol allowed me to circumvent and eliminate any inhibitions.

I felt if I kept it quiet and no one knew, it may be okay. An aphorism from Mark Twain: "We ought never to do wrong when anyone is looking."

I still very much loved and adored my wife and wanted to be with her for the rest of my life. I was in constant fear she would find out. My God, I would never want to lose her.

I knew Simone never wanted to break up my marriage; she said so, many times. Nonetheless, it was obvious she still faithfully loved me. I was being selfish, enjoying the gratification of the adoration she gave me.

I had to fly to New York on business for a few days and asked her if she would like to go with me. It would only be for less than seventy-two hours, but I thought it would be exciting and fun to be there with her. We could meet later each day after the business had concluded. She said sure.

It was mid-week, and a storm was expected in the area of La Guardia Airport upon our arrival, and sure enough, it happened as predicted. What an experience, landing—or should I say, *attempting* to land. We circled for over an hour through dark, menacing clouds while lightning hit the plane, fiercely tossing us about. Passengers were screaming, and the flight attendants' expressions didn't help, as some of the overhead luggage compartments opened from the extreme turbulence.

Finally, upon landing, a flight attendant came on the PA system and said, "Now that you have completed the safest part of your journey, be careful on the freeways and byways of New York!" Uh, hello! I was tempted to ask her, "Miss, were you on this flight?"

Well, it was a whirlwind two days in New York. Simone went to see the New York Museum of Modern Art one morning, and the Gutenberg Museum the next, while I met for business. Later, during both afternoons, she had everything planned, and I followed like a caboose.

On one of the two nights, we had a fabulous dinner at the famed Rainbow Room on the sixty-fifth floor at 30 Rockefeller Plaza in downtown Manhattan. We then danced to the magnificent sound of the full orchestra with the conductor and musicians dressed in tux and tails, which led us to believe we were in a rendezvous scene from an old movie from the past. We then hopped a cab over to the Cafe Carlyle, many blocks away, and listened to the romantic piano playing and deep, throaty singing of the renowned Bobby Short.

The next day before the afternoon flight home, we had lunch at the famed Tavern on the Green in Central Park. I sent my card back to the chef since we shipped our smoked salmon to the restaurant, and he came out and said hello. It was certainly a fun few days in the Big Apple.

The affair went on for some time, and by the end of 1986, the drinking had increased. The toll of the pressures of the business and my double life were starting to get the best of me. Alcohol was now my elopement to impunity. However, I was still pretty much able to control it.

To briefly change subjects, some months later my brother Walter unexpectedly died. I remember one morning seeing him stumbling around the plant and asking him what was wrong, and he'd said he thought he had the flu. I told him to go home and take care of himself, and suggested he see a doctor. I remember him shrugging off that suggestion as he was leaving, holding onto the guard rail as he walked down the truck ramp. Thinking it was indeed just the flu, I didn't give it any further thought.

The next morning, I got a call from Tommy, my cousin, who said that Walt was in the hospital and had been diagnosed with leukemia.

"Oh shit, leukemia!" I screamed. How in the hell had this ever come about? Well, it seemed as if he didn't like to go to doctors, for whatever reason, and thus had no awareness of it. A simple blood test was all that had been needed. I would imagine that if it had been diagnosed earlier, they may have been able to help him, but evidently it was quite advanced.

I was asked if I could donate platelets for him but couldn't, since I'd had infectious hepatitis when I was eighteen. I felt terrible and helpless, but there was nothing I could do.

My brother died five days later—it was that fast. His widow, Adele, told Joan and I that as he was taking his last breath, he mumbled, "Hi, Mom . . . hi, Dad," as if they were greeting him into the afterlife.

That really got to me, and made me wonder just what happens when you die. Is there really an afterlife? His wife said he smiled as he said it, then drifted off. He was only fifty-seven.

I respectfully paid my brother's widow a full salary, with all Union benefits, for two full years.

As far as my brother talking with our mom and dad as he was about to depart, I did some research and found they claim that people who are dying may see things that the rest of us do not. People who are dying frequently speak to people who aren't really there, and it's not unusual for them to speak the names of people from their past who have already passed on. But how would anyone really know?

It was an odd feeling going to work without my brother being there. However, something he'd said to me a few months earlier had disturbed and haunted me. He came upstairs to my office one afternoon after a very busy Friday; everyone was working late that day. He was obviously mad and disgruntled, and growled at me and said, "I want you to know that I feel exploited." He then promptly turned around and left before I could even comment. I sat back in my chair, trying to understand what and why he'd said that. It wasn't that often he had to stay late, and even though he was on straight salary, I compensated him very well at the end of the year for days like this.

I'm not sure if that upset me or hurt me—actually, both. I would have never done anything to take advantage or hurt my brothers, at least not on purpose, or knowingly.

Well, if you can believe this, several months later, coincidentally, my other brother/cousin Tom was now in the hospital with cancer. He was diagnosed with non-Hodgkin lymphoma.

What the hell was going on? I wondered. First my brother Walter, now Tom! Tom was off for many months, first having extensive surgery, then chemotherapy and radiation. He eventually returned feeling pretty good, and felt that way for some time. However, one day several months later while on the job as head foreman, I noticed he was holding his back, and asked if he was in pain. I can still see him doing that. He shrugged it off and said it was just his back bothering him, and it was nothing. I had a hunch it was much more, and unfortunately, was right.

He was back in the hospital two weeks later and died shortly after. Tom was sixty-two.

I respectfully paid his widow a full salary, with full Union benefits, for two years, as I'd done for my brother's wife. I couldn't believe I'd lost my two brothers within a year and a half of each other.

I thought about that, and just how short life could be, and I realized you never knew what the hell was crawling around in your body, or what the next day might bring. It vastly stimulated my propensity to be even more drawn to women for fulfillment.

My sex drive was now in overdrive and caused my thought process to go astray without further analysis of consequences. I was forty-nine, so I must have been having my mid-life crisis, as they call it. I'm not making excuses, however. Just sayin'.

I now had a girlfriend on the side, and a wonderful, beautiful wife, and I still yearned for more—more? How could that be? Well, because I'm never goddamn satisfied.

My entire life has been like clinging onto the root of a tree while dangling off the side of a cliff, then looking up and realizing the damn root is rotten! That's living on the edge. It's insanity. I guess I'm a thrill seeker, drawn to activities that give me a rush, resulting in risky behaviors, like driving my 540-horsepower Aston Martin well over the speed limit. Or piloting a forty-five-year-old Cessna at seventy-five after a quadruple bypass with a seventy-seven-year-old instructor who had a pacemaker. So, I assume the key is that I had to channel that desire for excitement and engaging entertainment into activities that wouldn't jeopardize my work, and more importantly, my marriage.

Even though I'm admitting to being aware of the above, I still obviously couldn't control those impetuous desires. I really believe my brain contains an overabundance of dopamine. That's the pleasure-seeking neurotransmitter that is responsible for sensation, which can cause one to take risks. It can also be an addiction. See, so maybe I just couldn't help it!

Having said that, there was a cute young girl who worked in the office at British Motors in San Francisco. I met her the day I bought the Rolls Royce for Joan as a surprise for her birthday. I would then talk to her whenever I had it or the Jaguar convertible in for service. Upon paying for the service, she would openly flirt with me. One afternoon when I picked up the Jag, I playfully told her she was cute, and she unexpectedly responded by asking if I would drive her home. It coincidentally was coming up on five o'clock, and the office was soon closing. I amiably said sure—and no, I hadn't planned on this! Of course, I had no idea where she lived, but it ended up being down the Peninsula in Mountain View. I curiously asked why she was working in San Francisco when she lived in Mountain View, and she said she'd just moved since it was more affordable and would soon be working at the British Motors on Stevens Creek Boulevard in San Jose, not far from the apartment she'd just rented. She also mentioned that her car, a Toyota Camry, was in the shop that day. She possibly may have been enamored with the cars I drove, or the assumption of wealth. Her name was Leone, she was twenty-five—yeah, I know, twenty-four years younger than me. We ended up having a drink and dinner at Rickey's in Palo Alto. Afterward, we sat in the bar lounge and had another drink and talked while listening to live piano music for a while. When I brought her home, she asked me in. And...

Okay, okay, I know, you don't have to say it. But remember, all the Italian men did this back in Italy. It was in my genes for me to get into her jeans.

So, I was married to Joan, had a mistress named Simone, and now had a young girlfriend named Leone. Try keeping that straight, especially if you've been drinking . . . Joan, Simone, and Leone! You're probably laughing about now, but also think I'm a creep, and deservedly so. However, as the Greek philosopher Isosceles said, "There are three sides to every triangle."

I then ended up seeing Leone whenever I could. She was young—my gosh, so young—her skin felt like silk and her breasts were so magnificently teasing when she wore an open blouse. What a rush it was to be with her. I could easily make her laugh. Her laughter was contagious, and her innocence was refreshingly uncomplicated, and her sexual allure was seductive.

This was destined to be a sexually explicit affair ordained to extend my fateful term in purgatory; yes, in a deserved state of suffering inhabited by other souls of sinners who are expiating their sins as well.

She was another complete diversion and total escape from my serious and now complicated life, and made me feel young and carefree. She was twelve years younger than Simone, furthering my fascination for this evolutionary psychological phenomenon. I knew she was impressed with money, power, and my position in life, which fed my ego even more. Women seem to find money, power, and confidence to be the ultimate aphrodisiac.

I was embarrassed when we went out, since she was obviously so much younger than me, looking like my daughter, but not hardly, with her clinging onto me and groping my thighs while we were in public. Sounds like something out of one of those midday soap operas.

One night while at a swanky, conservative restaurant in Palo Alto, and after having several drinks, she was all over me as I was attempting to eat dinner. Her toes encased in shear silk black stockings were friskily hitting sensitive spots on the inside of my upper leg, my face must have been obviously flushed since she had also taken the maraschino cherry from among the ice in her Manhattan and was rolling it back and forth on her lips that were heavily laden with iridescent red lipstick. Looking around, it was apparent we were being noticed. However, being acutely saturated with alcohol changes one's behavioral demeanor, and diminishes the ability to distinguish between right from wrong, and morality from degradation.

I remember that a prominent politician was there that night, a state senator in Sacramento. I was impressed by his stature and notoriety and wondered who the big wigs were he was with, knowing I would never be in that company.

Fast forward fifteen years, and oddly enough he was just invited to a party at our home and is a very close friend of two of my best friends, who are also big in San Francisco and California politics. Who would have ever thought?

A month later, Joan received a call from her mother saying that Grandma, who had been in a rest home for several months, was not expected to survive but a few days. The very next day, Joan flew down south to be with her parents who lived in North Hollywood, so I knew I would then also have to go down. I said I would be there in a day or so, but could only stay for an afternoon.

Looking back now, I do not, for the life of me, know what the hell I was thinking. I told Leone I had to go down south and asked if she would like to come with me. She of course jumped at the chance, knowing I'd spent many years down there and could show her all the hot spots. I arranged for a flight into Burbank and rented a Rosso Corsa Ferrari Testarossa.

We stayed at the Bel Air Hotel in the heart of Bel Air. The hotel was nestled among twelve acres of beautifully landscaped gardens and was where some of the world's most celebrated personalities went to relax and rejuvenate in style. I was suddenly immersed back in time, when I'd been dating there, and it was exciting. However, I hadn't been married then.

We had lunch on Rodeo Drive, sitting outdoors in a trendy cafe with umbrellas shading us from the heat of the Southern California sun. I recall people looking at us, though the sight was rather common there . . . older guy, younger—excuse me, *much* younger—girl.

They may have thought I was a director or producer, or better yet a mobster, with my hair rather long. I was certainly dressed the part with the gold Rolex with my shirt open exposing the sparse brown hair on my chest with the big gold P hanging on a gold chain—a prominent statement of ostentatious gaudiness. Possibly the P stood for "pretentious," or for something else that starts with a P! Leone also looked the part of a young, imposing ingenue, her short skirt and cleavage gently exposed while dotingly staring at me like a young Hollywood starlet at her producer, soon awaiting the casting couch.

We spent the afternoon driving around as I showed her most of Hollywood, then I later made dinner reservations at the La Dolce Vita Restaurant in Beverly Hills. During dinner, I seriously got sick to my stomach with guilt, thinking of Joan and when we'd dated, and having taken her to the same restaurant when we were young. I suddenly so missed her and wanted to be with her. This was wrong—so wrong.

Now I wished I'd flown down and stayed at my in-laws with Joan instead of partaking in this charade, but it was too late now. I called Joan and asked how her grandma was doing and she said, "You better fly down here tomorrow. She won't be with us much longer." I said, "Okay, I'll see you tomorrow about noon at the rest home, which was on Ventura Boulevard in Studio City." Of course, I was already there, just on the other side of the Hollywood Hills that separates it from the valley.

If a person can ever feel like shit, I so did at that moment. I really, really did not want or enjoy what I had done.

The next day I drove over Laurel Canyon to the Valley and met Joan and her mom at the rest home. Walking in, I felt as if the devil was on my shoulder whispering, "Oh yes, this will assure you an eternity in hell with me."

I think I was in such a state of mind I may have looked over and told him to go to hell. Silly me, he was already in hell. I thought I saw a nurse looking at me rather queerly at that point. I now had to change my demeanor from an imperious, narcissistic, debauched asshole, to a married, austere San Francisco businessman.

As I approached Grandma's room, the door was ajar, and I saw Joan and her mom standing over this frail, crumpled little old lady. Jesus, I hadn't seen Grandma in some time, and was overwrought with shame and sorrow that I hadn't spent the entire afternoon with her as I should have with my wife and her mom. This was "Little Grandma," as the kids called her. I loved her, we all loved her, and she would soon be gone. I kissed her on her wrinkled forehead; it was cold and clammy. I then held her weak hand, and her skin was almost translucent, her eyes opaque. I whispered, "I love you, Grandma."

I then chatted with Joan and her mom for about an hour, then made the excuse I had to get back to a business meeting over the hill, then fly back home. I meekly left with that sneering devil still on my shoulder and could feel his pitchfork in my neck. At that point I had wished he had punctured my jugular vein.

As I write this now, I'm brought to tears. My gut just tightened, and I want to go hug Joan and say, "I'm sorry for what a shit I was." But I was someone else back then. I don't really know who. I have no excuse to plead forgiveness from her, or from you, for being a sociopath and such an egocentric prick.

"Little Grandma," as the girls fondly called her, passed away the following day.

One can only imagine how convoluted my abhorrent life was now, shuffling these women. I'm sure I can now hear you saying, "Oh you poor boy."

Be that as it may, satisfying them—all of them—and being afraid one would find out about the other was a horror. I was in constant fear that my wife would get suspicious that I was seeing someone. I was playing Russian Roulette with a Ruger Single-Six, but it was loaded with six bullets!

The drinking increased even more so after Grandma passed, maybe from guilt, maybe to hide, or maybe it was just a necessity to face life at that point. When I sneezed, and people would say "God bless you," I would reply, "He won't."

As Lucius Annaeus Seneca said, "The gem cannot be polished without friction, nor a man perfected without trials." Well, I certainly was no gem, but would soon be facing trials.

Joan doesn't deserve this. She's a wonderful person, and my love for her will live in perpetuity. Plus, I have three fabulous girls . . . and I'm putting all this in jeopardy! Why? How can I continue seeing Simone and Leone and go home to Joan each night and act like everything's perfectly normal?

I wasn't just cheating on Joan, but also Simone and Leone. Or was it just Joan? And not Simone or Leone? You know what... hell, it was all three!

It gets rather convoluted, doesn't it? *You can be financially rich, but emotionally broke!*

Before I experienced it for myself, I had always thought it would be impossible to be miserable while earning a high six-figure income. If you don't believe it's possible, I suggest you park outside the Betty Ford Clinic in Rancho Mirage, California and take careful note of who is getting in and out of those limousines that pull up in front. Also, why do you think it's called the Betty Ford Clinic? No one is immune. Misery, and the inevitable attempt to escape from it eventually results in addiction to drugs or alcohol.

The bottom line is this: If the emotional revenues you get from your work or business fail to exceed the emotional expenses your work is generating, you end up with an emotional net loss. Of course, I should have known this, being a businessman. I was running my emotions into the red, and not fully satisfying anyone, including myself.

It was unfortunate that my propensity to be so provocatively intrigued with women always overcame my better judgment and respect for morality. But the magnetism easily drew them to me, which made it too convenient and arduous to thwart off.

To make things even more complicated, I forgot that I'd left a photograph of Leone and me in the trunk of the Jag when I returned from Southern California. After I unpacked at home, I ditched it in the trunk of the car and intended to destroy it. The photo had been taken while we were at the Luau Restaurant in Beverly Hills. The Luau had a sophisticated Balinese vibe with Murano glass tiled walls with lamps made from puffer fish. The surreal atmosphere thrusted you into a far-off, romantic tropical setting. While there, we had consumed several mind-altering Mai Tais, sipped from ornamental coconuts. They were so strong that after drinking just two, you'd be thinking that little three-inch paper umbrella that came with the drink would shield you from an ensuing hurricane. The potency of the drinks obviously precipitated the absence of my good sense, having forgotten to destroy the photograph.

I picked up Simone a few nights after I had returned to take her out for a casual dinner, and it happened to be a cold damp evening. Since the Jag's tiny backseats were difficult to get to, she asked to put her coat in the trunk . . . and there it was. Bingo! I was nailed. The result: a very intense scene with lots of tears. She asked me to leave and never return. She was devastated. I was devastated.

Something was bound to happen sooner or later to reveal my overt deception and clandestine, risky behavior. I thought to myself, *You fool, Kiki, you had to be involved with three—yes, three—women at the same time. You always overdo it. What the hell were you thinking? How long could this go on? This self-indulgence? This womanizing? Forget that bullshit about the men in Italy!*

I returned a couple of hours later to try to talk with Simone, and she was crying her heart out. She wanted nothing further to do with me.

A few weeks later, Laura was getting married. It was an exciting, fun time around the house. The arrangements for the wedding reception had been made at the Crocker Mansion in Hillsborough, site of the Crystal Springs Uplands School where Gina and Diana had gone to high school. The interior of the mansion had remained intact as it originally was, and was a beautiful venue for a wedding, though no wedding reception had ever taken place there before. It had been allowed this time because the girls had attended the school, plus we'd made a donation and knew the headmaster well. Did we!

The evening of the wedding rehearsal, we were scheduled to all meet at the church at five o'clock. I came directly from the plant, but I'd had a few drinks before leaving. I'm sure my breath smelled of alcohol, and I was messed up. There was so much going on in my life at the time, I couldn't concentrate on the procedures that the priest was outlining. My mind was . . . I don't know where.

The day of the wedding came, and there were two hundred people at the church and later at the reception.

Our caterer friend, Charlotte Nassar, owner of a sizable catering company in Menlo Park that I sold to, catered the event. We had arranged for a magnificent pre-dinner seafood buffet that included a never-done-before fresh whole mahi-mahi from Hawaii, poached and served cold as was done with salmon. There were boundless amounts of chilled prawns, king crab legs, smoked salmon and Bluepoint oysters on the half shell, as well as other non-seafood appetizers that were passed around.

Everyone marveled at how incredibly beautiful Laura looked. She wore Joan's wedding dress, a meaningful decision, and it accentuated her tiny petite figure. Her long blonde hair gently cascaded down the back of the now twenty-five-year-old, magnificent handmade dress, adding to the allure. She looked as if she should have been on the front cover of Vogue magazine.

It was an elegant affair, to say the least. Live dance music played for hours, and by eight o'clock that evening, Laura and Mark had left for the airport and were on their way to their honeymoon in Hawaii.

Meanwhile, a shocking thing happened as we said our goodbyes to all the guests and were getting ready to go home. Joan got into the Rolls, which carried five people, with her parents and grandma, and she jumped into the driver seat. I thought it odd that she wanted to drive. As I approached to get in, though unsure of just where I would sit, she drove away and promptly gave me the finger!

What the eff?! *What's this about?* I wondered. Then suddenly I realized she must have known something and had waited until after the wedding to confront me. Holy shit!

I hitched a ride with someone, I forget who, but felt very odd asking for a ride home. I'm sure I made light of it so as not to cause a stir, saying something like, "Those damn cheap cars only carry four people." I recall whoever it was asking how I'd gotten there. I went silent.

I shuddered, arriving at the house, not knowing what I would be walking into. As I walked in, I received a very cold shoulder from Joan, and I reluctantly asked, "So what's up?" She replied,

"You don't know?" I then said, "Honey, don't be fooled with flawed assumptions and false narratives. What are you implying?" There was silence. I then trembled with consternation.

I presumed that she was definitely aware that something was going on but wasn't sure with who or what. I further surmised that she'd gotten the information from my secretary, who answered all my incoming calls and screened them. However, neither Simone nor Leone hardly called me at the office.

On that Monday, late afternoon, I went and saw Leone at her apartment and told her I wasn't going to see her anymore, that it had been a big mistake, and it was over. Well, she went totally nuts, slapping my face and beating on my chest. She was rather immature for her age and didn't realize how these things normally ended up. I'd told her long ago I would never leave my wife, but I guess her fantasies had taken over. Either that, or she felt she would miss the extravagant lifestyle she so enjoyed. Just before I left, she said, "Do you know how many guys want me? I just may go out with them now!" I simply replied, "I'm sorry," and left. The door loudly slammed behind me.

I had made up with Simone by that time, explaining that Leone was just a silly, casual fling, and she had reluctantly forgiven me, but I knew I had hurt her. I just couldn't say to her that I couldn't see her anymore—at least not now, not yet. She was a very nice and sincere person, and I still cared for her. I didn't want to inflict any further pain. There was way too much pain going on. I now needed to try to be a good husband and was hoping for forgiveness from Joan.

Thinking about what I did and why I did it, I wondered if all men were really like me and possessed the inability to circumvent the temptations. And yet, maybe most men just didn't have the opportunity, so their fidelity was never tested. Possibly, I was also just over-sexed, and lacked the propensity to thwart off the impulsive desire and say no to the invitation. I certainly have difficulty in controlling my sex drive, and of course, the women don't make it any easier being so receptive. Then add a few ounces of ethanol, and you have an extremely hazardous condition.

When I hold a woman in my arms and feel the arousing sensation of the warmth of her breasts against my chest and her nipples harden, hinting desire, and as the bouquet of her intoxicating perfume overwhelms my emotions and the scent of her lipstick draws me ever-so-close to her open lips and we engage, it enflames and incites my very inner being, and I have no self-control. I find the neurological chemical arousal and euphoria obsessive and addicting.

I should have probably sold my excess testosterone to the clinics, or better yet, should have had my seminal vessels severed long ago. The Roman gladiators used to sell their sweat as an aphrodisiac, rather crude, I know, but true. However, I refused and showered.

CHAPTER 31
NEVER KICK A COW FLOP ON A HOT DAY!

Several weeks went by and the atmosphere in the house was rather cool. Yeah, like my blast freezer at the plant. Joan and I were somehow talking, barely, but that was okay. I was frightened out of my skin that she would throw me out, but of much more—that I would forever lose her.

I tried to talk with her about it, but she would start crying before I could ever say anything. All I could say was, "Honey, honey, please," while trying to hold her hand, but she wouldn't take it.

One night she looked directly into my eyes, with tears in her own, and said—and I will never forget it, it was so profound and brought me to my knees— "I may hate you more . . . but I will never love you any less."

I was now bawling. Look at what I had done. How I had hurt her. She didn't deserve this. I prayed to God that she wouldn't leave me. My goddamn impetuous Italian heritage.

I had to remember to use logic and reason before acting out my fantasies, and to remember that the principle of cause and affect precipitates the outcome of the future.

Leone continued to call me at my office on my private line, even though I'd insisted she stop. Upon hearing her voice, I would immediately hang up. I had made it clear to her that it was over, and for her to get on with her life. I was now trying to get my marriage and my own life back in order and concentrate on business.

It was around that time when I heard rumblings that the Butcher Union was possibly targeting my operation when the contract was up. I suspected this could be the provenance, the *genesis* of something bigger; however, I couldn't be concerned with that right now.

A couple of months passed, and Leone unexpectedly called on my private phone. I hadn't heard from her in some time, so this came as a surprise. Before I could say anything, she screamed—and I do mean *screamed*— "Well, Kiki, *I'm pregnant!*" And promptly hung up.

I almost fainted. *Oh, no, no. Not again. At least last time I wasn't married, and it turned out to be a false alarm. Hopefully, this will be as well . . . but it has been a couple of months. Oh, shit.*

I immediately sank down in my chair and almost slid under the desk, reduced to tears, shivering, knowing my life had suddenly taken a drastic turn for the worse. I envisioned Joan divorcing me, and rightfully so, and my daughters never talking to me. I felt dirty and ashamed. I didn't want a child with Leone. I had my family.

So that afternoon I drove down to Mountain View to see her, and I suggested she get an abortion. I told her I would get her the best doctor and make sure she would have the best of care. She then emphatically shrieked at me from across the room, "*No!*" I said, "Please." She said no.

I offered to buy her a condominium. She said no. Then I said I would also buy her a new car. She hesitated and asked, "What kind?" Now I thought this might work. I said, "You like the new BMWs." She thought for a minute, then said, "You bastard, you want me to give up my child for a fucking car!"

I know abortions are frowned upon and against most theological principles, but the circumstances were overbearing. I was already going to spend three hundred thousand years in purgatory, so what the hell was another hundred thousand or so. The Catholic Church has always condemned abortion as a grave evil.

She was bound and determined to have this child. Attempting to reason with her further, I explained how a baby would impact her life. She blurted back, "So what! You'll be paying for it. So, I saw what was coming. Hmm, just maybe this had all been planned.

Nonetheless, I'm not a dumb man—stupid, but not dumb. After the child was born, I would arrange for DNA testing. This was a relatively new form of testing to determine a person's DNA, and I had a great attorney. We would just see. I needed to preserve the sanctity of my marriage, and my God, not have a child with another woman.

This would have a massive impact on my estate, and my will and trust that had been set up years ago. Oh, shit! Even more, my wonderful girls—how would they or could they accept this? I felt dirty, and a shower couldn't cleanse me. Everything was now in upheaval, and I envisioned my life in a cataclysmic adversity, and I could only blame myself. I'd had it all . . . for a short while.

I felt like running away and hiding. But as Joel Chandler Harris, the author of Uncle Remus said, "You can't run away from trouble; there ain't no place that far."

Now in a total quandary, on occasion I would stop in and see Simone after work. Nothing was going on; we were now just good friends and I needed her kind and gentle, comforting ways. She knew nothing about Leone's pregnancy, God forbid. No one did!

As if things weren't bad enough, Gina, unbeknownst to me, had followed me on one of those afternoons to Simone's house, high in the hills of San Carlos. She then told her mom where Simone lived! A few days later, Joan showed up at Simone's house and introduced herself as Joan Paladini, Kiki's wife. And as I understand, it was a sensible, non-abrasive meeting between two intelligent adults. However, Simone proceeded to tell Joan that she was, in Simone's own words, "old news"; I had a young, new "chick-a-dee" named Leone!

Now Joan knew about Simone, and Simone knew about Leone. And now Joan also knew about Leone, but Leone didn't know about Simone! Of course, when this had started, Simone had always known about Joan, but never about Leone, and Leone had always known about Joan, but never about Simone. Whew! See what I mean?

So next—yep, you know what's coming—Joan went and saw Leone at her apartment in Mountain View. Why, I'm not sure, however, I am sure she was shocked to see how young Leone was. As I understand, this confrontation didn't go as well as the one with Simone. Simone was much more mature and steadfast and down to earth. I don't know why Leone didn't tell Joan at the time that she was pregnant, possibly out of fear, or possibly women's intuition may have prevented her.

You may find this funny now, but at the time, it was anything but. Unbeknownst to me, sometime a short while later, Joan invited Simone and Leone, who was now pregnant but hardly showing, to our home. Yes, you heard me correctly, *to our home*. To discuss me, the son of a bitch, the bastard, the . . . well, you know. I'm not sure why, but she did. You would think it was three women just having afternoon high tea with crumpets, but of course, they weren't drinking tea. They were drinking champagne, and they weren't discussing the books they'd recently read.

It was just after five o'clock as I drove up Tournament Drive toward our home, and as I pulled into our circular driveway, I saw Simone's car . . . then Leone's car . . . yep, right there, parked directly in front of me. I pounded on the steering wheel, pushed my head back into the head restraint, and screamed, "Oh, shit! What the fuck?!"

I sat in the car for the longest time, getting up the guts to walk in. I didn't know what in the hell I was going to encounter. I imagined all sorts of scenarios, such as being stoned to death, or even being beheaded. Nah, they would have gone much lower! God only knew. No matter what, it wasn't going to be pleasant! I was in a real jam and had to face it. I got out of the car, took a deep breath, and imprudently walked in. *Forbidden fruits create many jams.*

They were sitting in the living room just off the entry, and as I approached the living room, I noticed they were already on a second bottle of champagne. There were also some assorted nuts and a cheese plate on the white marble table; they were having a good ole time. When they saw me, they lifted their glasses, looked directly at me, and simultaneously said, "Here's to the bastard!" Ya know, having presumed it was a party-like atmosphere, I would have thought they could have been more entertaining and said something like "Hail Caesar" (as the Plebeians did with my imperious, good friend Julius).

Well, I knew I had had it. While being toasted—or should I rephrase that, *while being roasted*— with her glass held up in one hand and giving me the finger with the other, Joan asked me in front of them—no, told me—to move out . . . *now.*

I guess you might have expected that, and you're probably saying, "Good for her. Go, girl!"

So, with my tail between my legs and all other hanging parts, I went to a dumpy motel alongside the freeway in east San Mateo and proceeded to get drunk . . . very drunk.

My life was now in complete shambles and turmoil, as one would expect. However, as Helen Keller said, "A bend in the road is not the end of the road unless you fail to make the turn." Yeah, but my road ahead doesn't just have a bend, I'm looking at a 45-degree turn!

I arrived at the office the next morning with an obvious hangover, and attempted to concentrate on business, which I couldn't do. I now had an I-don't-give-a-shit attitude.

The days came and the nights went, with me continuing to stay in that sleazy motel. I purposely wanted to be in the dumpiest of dumpy motels. I looked for the worst I could find, not for pity, no one knew where I was staying, but because I didn't feel I deserved any better. I was shit, and I felt like shit. I also wished I drove a shit car but had this fricking huge business and needed to maintain an image.

Joan's mother after having a few drinks, often screamed at me saying I was nothing but shit while dating her daughter because I wasn't a big Hollywood producer or director or even an actor. I was just a lowly little shit fish monger with no money. Yeah, that helped my self-confidence. So, she was indeed right, but now for even a better reason. Well, at least now I was a big shit!

CHAPTER 32
THE UNION TAKES ME ON

Meanwhile, to make matters worse—as if they could have gotten any worse—I received a formal notice from the Union regarding the contract that was coming due the following month. It had a list of demands, and they were extreme, impractical, non-functional, excessive, and unrealistic.

What really pissed me off was that for years, I had been telling the Union rep there was a wholesale fish company less than a half mile away that was rapidly expanding by undercutting prices to the chain stores and taking my business because they were bringing in foreign workers and paying minimum wage (which were, of course, non-Union). I'd further stated that all the wholesalers in the city should have the *same* labor cost and be on an equal plane with one another in terms of expenses. This fell on deaf ears, with the rep saying that no one spoke English. "Bullshit!" I told him. "Who in the hell speaks to the customers then?"

The Union wanted to organize not only the twelve members of my sales staff, but the six girls in bookkeeping. They already had the forty-five floor workers/order packers and the sixty drivers. If that wasn't bad enough, they also wanted the two hundred-plus employees in the Santa Rosa processing plant, which was totally and entirely out of the question.

You can't operate a seafood processing facility with organized Union labor rules and wages; it's impossible. The variances, mainly seasons and the weather, determine the unpredictable work load. Most of the employees were Hispanic women working part-time, making extra money, and they were happy working in that capacity. No other processing plant on the entire West Coast was unionized.

This was bullshit! How about the other large processing plant just a mile away? They were also connected to a Unionized similarly large wholesale distributor in the city—the same scenario as mine.

I suddenly had a flashback to the farcical encounter with the West Coast Mafia boss in my office, and now wondered if there could allegedly be some kind of possible affiliation with the wharf in some way. Could this be the complicit repercussion he mentioned as he was leaving? My relationship with the Union had been fine until my representative was oddly assigned a different area, and then I was strangely assigned the Union rep from the Wharf. Hell, I had more Union employees at the time than all the companies on the Wharf combined.

I thought back to my first meeting with the new rep. He'd arrived one day about noon and pulled all the floor workers out of the plant, shutting down the operation. I was out to lunch when I received a call from my plant supervisor, who said, "Mr. P., you better get back here. The new Union rep just pulled all the men off the job."

I was about three blocks away and was there within moments. When I arrived, the men were standing outside. I asked what the hell was going on, and while cowering, they meekly said, "Mr. P., the Union rep pulled us off the job and he's now inside looking for you!"

My monomaniac temperament suddenly took over and I got the shakes, and as you know by now, that wasn't good. This was destined not to be a pleasant first meeting! I sped up the truck ramp in the Jag and drove into the plant, sliding on the wet floor sideways while hitting fish boxes, and as they went flying, the new rep fled for his life. His eyes were now enormous and filled with fear.

I jumped out of the car and run up to him and screamed, "What the fuck do you think you're doing, asshole?!" He rebounded as if being attacked by a hungry, rabid cougar. After all, a lunatic was about to assault him—assault him? I wanted to fucking kill him. No one told my men what to do, except me!

As he attempted to get his composure back, he said while shaking, "We need to talk." I replied, "Talk? Bullshit. There's nothing to talk about. Why did you pull my men off the job?" He said again, now in a lower, meek voice, "We need to talk, sir." Good! He'd called me "sir."

I rushed him upstairs to my office, and the shakes had ceased a bit, but I was curious what he had to say. Now in my office, I stood behind my desk and asked, "Okay, so what is so important that you need to talk to me about? And why didn't you come up to my office and talk to me first before yanking the men? My secretary knew where I was."

He then boldly expanded his chest and approached me as I stood behind my desk. His legs were now pushing against the massive solid rosewood ledge of the desk as he reached over and pointed his finger in my face and brazenly said, "From now on, you're going to be doing what I tell you to do with your men!" I. Then. Went. Fucking. Berserk!

Talk about the shakes. I felt as if my skull cap was going to come off. FYI, I cannot be told what to do! I then picked up my desk, which was, by the way, extremely heavy, and dumped it over on him. He jumped back just in time as I screamed, "Get the fuck out of my office and my place of business, you motherfucker son of a bitch! You're not telling me how to run my fucking operation!" He then turned and ran out of my office, looking back to see if that crazed cougar was chasing him. By the way, I never got his name, and he never did give me his business card.

I then called the Union office and asked for the president. Upon talking with him, I could tell that his demeanor had changed from our previous conversation's months ago, a total about-face. I told him about the encounter with the new rep, and said it had been totally uncalled for, and it was unacceptable that he pulled the men off the job. I asked what the real reason and purpose for his provocation had been.

He then said, "You know, Mr. Paladini, you've been making your own rules for a long time, like having a dress code. What other fish company has a dress code? And the way you handle the coffee breaks. Anyway, we're now going to police your contract to the fullest extent." I replied, "Oh, really? You're going to tell me how to run my business? Well, fuck you, Mr. President." And I hung up.

By the way, I did somewhat have a dress code, as he said. I demanded that my drivers be clean-shaven and presentable every day; if they had a beard, they had to keep it groomed; and if they had tattoos, they had to be covered with long sleeves. (Tattoos were not as prevalent or as much of a fashion statement back then as they supposedly are now.) If a driver showed up unshaven, he was sent home on his own time to shave and could only punch his time card upon his return. I insisted upon the appearance of cleanliness; we were handling food products. My drivers represented me—me, as my company—and it was my fucking company and I would do as I liked. Those were *my* rules! It's funny, I'm getting pissed off all over again right now while writing this!

I want it to be known, I am well aware that the Labor Union(s) did a lot of good for thousands upon thousands of workers that were being taken advantage of and exploited years ago. The workers in many industries needed representation through collective bargaining to negotiate more favorable working conditions and workplace safety. I, of course, respect that. It allowed for equitable wages and working conditions that were at one time deplorable. And just so you know, I had no qualms with my operation being Unionized, as had been the case for many years, almost since inception, with little or no problem. It was only when they went too far and asked for too much that I became defensive, or should I say, aggressive. Their tactics and demands often did not recognize or take into consideration the fact that an employer's operating costs determined the longevity of a company's existence. It wasn't all about the employer's eagerness to make a fat profit, but often for survival to meet expenses, and to be able to have the funds to make payroll and pay all the Union benefits.

I have said countless times, "It takes just one employer to employ countless employees." One man's vision can create abundance. And one man's ignorance can create calamity.

Let me tell you a few things about the Union and how it worked back in the time I was in business. The poor young apprentices had to pay $250 up front just to join the Union when we hired them, whether they were kept in employment or not—no guarantees. Most didn't have the money, so we'd had to advance it. There were never *any* Union men available at the Union Hall to be hired for the seafood industry, so we had to find and train the apprentices ourselves. We voluntarily sent them to the Union office to sign up. I could visualize the Union reps rubbing their hands with joy every time one showed up.

The money I had to pay into the pension plan was mostly nonsense, as well. The men could not attain the pension unless they worked in the Union for ten years minimum; then it had to be "vested" or they would lose it. The percentage of men who eventually collected their pensions was very small, since so many left the industry or were terminated before their ten years were achieved. The hospitalization/medical plan had to be paid from day one for new employees, even though they didn't qualify to receive the benefits for ninety days.

As to why the rep pulled the men off the job that day, the men working on the production floor normally started at five in the morning and would get off at two in the afternoon. That equaled eight hours, including an hour for lunch. Yes, I had an agreement with the floor workers, but *they* came up with the following idea: Since they got two fifteen-minute breaks each morning and an hour lunch, they wanted to combine the two fifteen-minute morning breaks into one thirty-minute break, and have this longer break at eight o'clock in the morning, then work through their lunch to go home an hour earlier.

I thought this was a good idea and agreed. The men wanted it, and it would also help the company since we started loading most of the trucks around eight thirty, up until about eleven thirty, and could then do so without interruption. They could then clean up and go home by one o'clock in the afternoon.

Now back to my personal life. I was now separated from my wife, my mistress wasn't talking to me, and my once girlfriend, was supposedly pregnant, allegedly by *me*, and wouldn't have an abortion. My kids had turned their backs on me, and my business was now in dire jeopardy of a possible strike that could cripple the entire operation. I was now also an effing alcoholic. What a reversal of fortune.

I felt like I was helplessly entangled in a giant spider web, unable to move, waiting to be devoured. I was also unluckily amid the complexity of this labyrinth I created, trying to find a way out.

Looking back, however, I had been blessed with more than my fair share of good luck and fortune, and now just need to accept the consequences of my actions. My once sensitive, existential family values were now encapsulated in negativity, and my underlying ethos burrowed in isolation from my family.

Each day I went to work in the early morning, and would start drinking in the late afternoon, have an unhealthy dinner, then go to the little sleazy motel alone . . . and drink some more. I was Mr. Paladini, the big shit businessman by day, and a drunken, lonely, little shit, messed-up man at night. Problems seemed interminable.

They say that if you find yourself in a hole, stop digging. Well, I sure couldn't get much deeper.

I called Joan one morning and asked if we could go see a marriage therapist, and she said she would think about it. I said please. And she said she would think about it. I said please again. She hung up. Well, I hadn't totally failed . . . until I quit trying.

I spent another week from hell going to work, putting up a good front, acting as if everything was fine, but the girls in the office knew what was going on. Joan was good friends with one of my bookkeepers, and her aunt also worked for me in bookkeeping; coincidentally, her aunt's significant other just happened to be my controller. It seemed like everyone was working for me, so I guess everyone knew, but no one dared say a word. I guess I should have known since everyone would keep their heads down when I walked in, most likely frightened by my capricious personality.

Life wasn't very much fun now, to say the least, and now having the Union contract to deal with made things worse. A meeting with the Union president and his flock was coming up in a few days, and that wasn't going to be pretty. I called them his "flock" because that term is used to refer to sheep. Sheep have a strong instinct to follow the one in front. When the one in the very front decides to go somewhere, the rest of the flock follows. If it jumps off a cliff, the others follow. It's not something they think about.

One evening, I stopped in to see Leone in Mountain View, a good extra half hour or so from the motel in San Mateo and attempted to urge her to get the abortion before it was too late. But it again fell on deaf ears. I can't tell you the sickening feeling of sorrow I felt for my wife and kids. I could break into tears while writing this, those emotions return so easily. I had totally screwed up not only *my* life, but my wife's and my three daughters'. One man, *me*, had negatively impacted four women's lives.

After all this turmoil, I sincerely envisioned eventually moving away to a tiny cabin in the woods somewhere by a lake. I didn't know where this place would be, but I can still see it. I would be alone, a recluse, not shaving, not bathing, and most likely drinking myself to death. I really thought this through, like I do everything, even to the extent of not having a dog, because I would die alone, and no one would find me for God knows how long, and the poor dog would starve. I couldn't cause any more pain. It sounds dramatic, but it's true.

However, water turns into ice, and ice turns into water, so hopefully in time I could reverse this situation. I thought I'd give it another shot and ask Joan again if she would agree to therapy. And she shockingly agreed! *My God*, I thought. *There may be a ray of hope in salvaging our marriage, after all.* I was a happy guy for a few days, and looking forward to not only seeing her, but to hoping the therapy would help us. But I still had the damn baby thing to overcome.

It was a Thursday afternoon and we met separately, of course, at the therapist on Twenty-Fifth Avenue in San Mateo. As I approached, I saw the dark-brown Rolls parked in front and I pulled up in the Jag and parked alongside.

Joan was already talking to the therapist when I arrived, and hardly looked my way as I walked in. The therapist introduced himself . . . then we sat there in silence. I wondered who in the hell was supposed to be doing the talking now. Uh, wasn't this guy a therapist? I immediately found him incompetent, and I guess I exuded a lack of respect. To break the silence—or should I say, *ice*—I looked at Joan and said, "Honey, I love you with all my heart. I beg you for forgiveness." She looked at me with stone-cold, glaring eyes, obviously so hurt, and shockingly said, "I want a divorce!"

I sunk down in the chair, breathless, my heart about to jump out of my chest as she then got up and walked out. Oh my God!

Now slumped over with my head hanging between my legs, tears rolled down my face. I then looked away from the therapist, trying to regain my composure as I wiped the tears. After all, I wasn't about to let him see me crying, though I'm sure he knew.

I then remarked to him, "I thought we were here to seek help." (I really wanted to end that statement with "to seek help, asshole.") He then said, "Your wife wants a divorce. She came in here with that mindset." I then replied—no, screamed—at him, "You're the therapist! Why didn't you attempt to persuade her not to? Why did she need an audience to say that, for Christ sake?" I was devastated.

He then said a very odd thing. Remember way back several chapters when I said I'd felt inferior and intimidated by the well-educated and wealthy men at the parties we held at our home? Well, he said—to quote him verbatim— "Mr. Paladini, you're very intimidating!" Being shocked by his comment, I must have looked at him rather strangely, I'm sure thinking, *Me? Me, intimidating? What the hell is he talking about?*

I found this to be such a strange remark coming from him, the educated man. Since I hadn't understood his comment, I asked him, "What exactly do you mean by that?" He replied—and again, this is verbatim— "I saw your wife pull up in a new Rolls Royce and you in a Jaguar. You live in a big home in Hillsborough and have an immense business and have women all over you."

I'd never viewed myself in that manner; I'd never even considered it. And I still felt insecure and inferior to most successful men, regardless of what he said. I found it so strange for him to think of me like that. I got the impression he was actually envious, even jealous. But he was a trained therapist and wasn't supposed to judge. I felt more that he wanted me to give him tips on how to date women, than to try and help us.

It didn't matter what he thought, however. I had just apparently lost my wife and this asshole hadn't helped. I wondered later if she'd needed the support of another person, a professional, to tell me she wanted a divorce, and that was why she'd agreed to meet with me there. It now sadly appeared to be palpable.

Now completely and totally down in the dumps, I went to my sleazy motel room and laid on the unmade, lumpy old bed that was probably a mine field for bed bugs, and somberly stared at the water-stained ceiling as I looked back at my sordid life and reviewed what I'd attained and what I'd lost. I'd lost so much more than I had attained. My life was now like a Ferris wheel; I was on top with my business, and on the bottom with my personal life. Wanting to now drown myself in a mind-altering substance, I went out to the local 7-Eleven and bought a cheap fifth of vodka and a dried-up hot dog that must have been sitting under the heat lamps for six hours. I went out to the car and took a swig from the bottle and ate the unpalatable dog as the mustard stained my dress shirt. Why does mustard always get on everything? Now semi-sedated and fully depressed, I figured it wouldn't be long until I was down in the Tenderloin, drinking Thunderbird out of the bottle.

The next morning, I dragged myself to the plant, desperately in need of a cup of black coffee to try to quell the terrible hangover. It wasn't but a few hours until I had the first meeting with the Union. Funny, my ever-so-faithful secretary soon picked up on my daily needs when I arrived at the plant and would greet me with a hot cup of black coffee and two aspirins and put a pen in my trembling hands.

The meeting with the Union went as expected: They totally refused what I'd proposed and were playing hardball. And I'd flatly refused to allow the Union in the Santa Rosa processing plant, or for my salespeople or bookkeepers to be part of the collective bargaining agreement. Other items were just basically non-issues and would have been settled. It did not end well.

They were having a meeting at the Union Hall in a few nights to discuss the new contract with my Union members, and if they found my rebuttals to the proposed contract unacceptable, they may soon have a strike vote if I didn't back down.

The stresses from all of this had now caused a nerve disorder in both my arms, and on occasion they would go totally numb and I couldn't raise them. It strangely seemed to have resonated from the middle of my shoulder blades.

If there was anything that I had learned from all of this, it was that life comes with no warranty. There's no guarantee that your marriage, your business, or your health will last. You never know what's around the corner, or what's crawling around in your body.

Take my advice— I'm not using it...

CHAPTER 33
WHAT ELSE COULD POSSIBLY GO WRONG?

Would the Union vote to strike and decimate my operations? Would the baby be mine? Would my wife divorce me? Would my kids disown me? Would I ever recover from the alcohol addiction? What was the possibility of recovering from any of these devastating situations? I counted five. Well, using my lifelong hypothesis of common sense, logic, and deduction . . . not very good.

Who in their right mind would give any odds in conquering even one or two? Right now, everything appeared pretty bleak and dismal, and I was so damn depressed and ready to give up, though that wasn't like me. But this was so mentally and physically exhausting, and the alcohol only compounded things.

I felt detached from the world around me. All emotions were gone, at least the positive ones—love, affection, and joy—gone. Yet I can't say I had absolutely no emotions; of course, I did, but they were all the desperately negative ones. Most involved fear, anger, and sadness; the fear of never escaping this damnation; the anger at myself; the sadness at the realization I could lose my family. How could one not be depressed?

I tried to think how I could use all this as a valuable experience that would force me to take stock of my life and make changes in my lifestyle and desires, but I couldn't concentrate on anything. I couldn't even watch TV. I couldn't relax or unwind. To escape and hide, I would drink into oblivion. Sleep seemed impossible; so many thoughts were racing through my mind. I feared being alone with my thoughts, especially at night when everything seemed so hopeless. Everything to do with everyday life seemed like such hard work. I simply didn't have the energy to go to work. It all seemed pointless. What was the point in eating when I didn't want to live?

All alone, I would spend hours fantasizing about ways to kill myself. Yeah, I knew it was selfish, and what a hell of a mess I would leave. But alcohol is a depressant, and this was the mind of an aggrieved alcoholic. I was now desperately trying to be in survival mode. They say when a person is severely dehydrated that the thirst mechanism shuts down, so when you stop getting thirsty, that's when you must find water to survive, because the brain readies the body for death.

I couldn't allow my survival mechanism to shut down. I couldn't let my brain ready my body for death. I needed to counteract this psychological phenomenon and fight it.

I kept telling myself, *Don't give up! Never give up! Try to apply the same principle that got you here . . . no, not the unzipped-zipper principle; that guy must remain zipped up–that's the one that got you here in the first place. I mean the one about having the tenacity and perseverance to never quit, to never ever give up . . . if I want my family back!*

Mulling those thoughts over and over, I realized I needed to try. But damn, no matter how I pulled myself together, that couldn't or wouldn't change the outcome of the baby. Some things were now out of my control, but I needed to start, but where?

I had to face these demons head on. First, I had to stop drinking, or at least try; however, that was going to be tough, maybe impossible. If I could at least cut back, my head might feel clearer, then if nothing else, I would at least be able to deal with the Union in a more rational way without my explosive temper.

Yet how could I possibly concentrate on business when I had to deal with all these outside forces? I was trying to hold myself together and be tenacious but was being pulled in too many directions to concentrate on just one. To use an expression my father often used, "It's like shoveling shit against the tide!"

The Union would be meeting tonight, Friday night, to discuss the upcoming contract, and would be deciding if they want to settle, reject and continue with negotiations, or flatly reject and have a strike vote to determine to strike against the company.

How in the hell would I or could I handle a strike? I. Had. No. Energy. Left.

Well, it was Saturday morning, a few minutes before noon, and as I was driving on Highway 101, going under the overpass of Highway 92, my car phone rang (back then we had custom-installed car phones.) It was Tony, my production supervisor, and he said, "Hi, boss. Okay . . . well . . . your men voted to strike!" I damn near steered into the center divider; I couldn't believe it. Just as you remember where you were when President Kennedy was assassinated, I remember where I was that day, and what time it was. I was alone in my car and upon hearing that I impetuously started screaming and pounding on the steering wheel as passing motorists looked at me with strange expressions.

Okay, they wanted a fight, so a fight it would be. However, it's only when you see a mosquito landing on your testicles that you appreciate there must be a way to solve a problem without violence!

It was hard to believe that the men I'd thought I had such a great relationship with would vote to strike. To turn their backs on me. They'd come to me looking for jobs, many with no background in the seafood industry, and I'd taken them in and trained them for months, eventually allowing them to become journeymen and make top wages with full benefits. We never had a problem working together, that is, until now.

Tony was not allowed to attend the meeting since no one in management could be in the Union. We had an informant, however. Tony said all the Union reps from all the areas showed up "to rally against Paladini." The snitch said that they'd fed the men pizza and beer . . . a lot of beer . . . and then more beer.

By the end of the evening, they were mostly all drunk and pumped up, and just before the vote, they had the men chanting, "Fuck Paladini! Fuck Paladini!" Just like sheep, blindly following the head sheep right off the cliff.

The new rep from the wharf assigned to my company got up and asked the men how many of them had ever been up in my office. He said, "You guys are out on the cold, wet floor, packing fucking fish while he's upstairs in a warm, carpeted, rosewood-paneled office, and lives in Hillsborough and drives a Jaguar. Where do you guys live and what do you drive? He's the big king up there and you guys are just his little pawns!"

My reaction to that foolish statement was that they got paid—and very well—for being out on that cold wet floor, and for packing that fucking fish, and they drove a damn fish truck and got to take it home wherever, which saved them from having to buy a car to commute. If I hadn't created this goddamn business and given them jobs, they wouldn't have had the opportunity to falsely complain about me. Anyway, what did any of that shit have to do with the contract? Well, this was how they poisoned their minds with unrelated falsities and untruths and got them hyped up to vote for a strike!

And to set the record straight, at work I sat downstairs in the sales office among the salesmen the majority of the day and often went out on the "cold, wet floor," as he called it, and helped pack orders and checked out the trucks when busy. Oh, and by the way, without warm clothes or rubber boots.

Since they wanted to do battle, I would give them a fight. I immediately instructed Tony to put an ad in the *San Francisco Chronicle* for replacement drivers, the same paper where Herb Caen often mentioned me in his daily column. He was a journalist who wrote of local goings-on and insider gossip, social and political happenings, painful puns and offbeat anecdotes. He enjoyed writing about the fact that the "seafood tycoon," as he reverently referred to me, was not very fond of eating fish! He also loved our smoked salmon that I would send him during the Jewish holidays.

Having placed that ad now meant I would have an extra sixty drivers on the payroll; however, at much lower wages and with no benefits. I was well aware that would kill my cash flow and was also aware the Unions would be on my ass, claiming they had to go to the Union Hall and sign up to pay the ridiculous enrollment fee. Oh, sure, I'll send them right there. Wasn't that just a wee bit counter- productive? Anyway, what more could they do to me? Sure, maybe pull the men off the job. Well, they could go for it; that's what the replacement workers were for. They were going to pull them off one day soon anyway.

Well, I thought about my strategy over the weekend and started planning. My first plan was to have "strike drills," just as you would have "fire drills." A loud bell (a bell had been installed near the receiving door in case the doors were closed and a trucker needed to unload) would ring at my command, and since I figured we would never know when they were going to pull the men off, it would be a random judgment call as to when to ring it. Most likely, I expected it would be on a Thursday or Friday about eight or nine in the morning, prime time, and our two busiest days. The floor men/order packers and drivers would go outside as if they'd been pulled by the Union, and the salesman would go out on the production floor and pack orders. I, of course, had told them of the plan and had them bring a change of clothes to leave at the plant. The girls upstairs in the office would then come downstairs to call the customers and answer the incoming calls, leaving only my controller and one accounts receivables girl upstairs.

This was only the beginning. The brain, especially the prefrontal cortex, is responsible for logic, reasoning, and thinking, and allows us to conceive, envision, and plan. As Thomas Fuller said in 1661, "Logic is the armory of reason furnished with all defensive and offensive weapons."

Monday came, and all the Union men sheepishly arrived at work; not one would look me in the eye. By the way, there were all kinds of federal labor law rules that only I, the employer (not the employees or the Union), had to follow, so my management team had to be careful not to go against any of them. One of those rules was that I couldn't talk adversely to the men or say anything about the strike vote. I was supposed to act as if everything was just hunky dory and buy them their lunches as I did every Friday, and all the other goodies, like cigarettes, they snuck in that I'd previously chosen to ignore. The atmosphere on the production floor was cold, and I'm not talking about the cold, wet floor the asshole rep referred to. Sorry about some of the language lately, but adverse language was commonplace in the industry.

One employee in particular, the freezer manager, who received a premium wage, by my doing, not by the Union contract, only had ninety days to complete his employment before vesting his pension. As I said prior, a Union worker had to work in the same Union for ten years before vesting; if they left before, they would lose it. I heard that he'd foolishly been among the revelers against me, voting to strike. Well, how imbecilic and obtuse! Amazing what a plenteous amount of free beer and a couple slices of pizza can do.

It was very quiet out on the floor, with none of the usual jubilation going on. My men had all been very happy just the Friday before. I'd had a high-spirited and content crew until their heads were filled with non-truths. Ridden of their hangovers by now, they may have realized they'd made a mistake, a huge mistake, and may have opened Pandora's Box. Thinking about this further, the issues at hand could have been negotiated and resolved as we had done with all past contracts. There was a lot more behind what drastic action the Union took, almost like it had been staged and rehearsed. My Union workers were obviously followers and would do whatever the Union told them to, and not what they, the men, wanted or felt was in their best interest.

My prior position as their boss had now been cleverly displaced by the Union. Playing with their heads, they were led to believe the Union was their place of worship, their God to look up to and follow . . . yeah, to the beer hall. I knew my men wouldn't voluntarily turn their backs on me without being acutely coerced. There were no issues at hand that would had adversely affected them to this drastic level, to strike.

The normal 2 percent increase per year in wages over a three-year period equaled 6 percent; however, it was slightly more since compounding using the geometric average. The current Union wage was fifteen dollars per hour, which brought it up to $15.92 over the three-year period. And of course, the overtime wage would also be correlated upward as well. Keep in mind that the Butchers Union costly pension plan contribution that the company paid into was predicated on total wages paid as well. It wasn't just the wages that went up, but also all the benefit contributions, plus the governmental requirements, but most employees of course don't think of that, or care.

The employer's portion paid predicated on gross wages are as follows: Medicare and Social Security (FICA), state unemployment (SUTA), federal unemployment (FUTA), workers compensation insurance, health insurance benefits and pension plans, plus the 1 percent payroll tax paid to the city of San Francisco. In addition to those employer's costs, there are paid vacations, federal holidays, birthdays, sick days, maternity leave, and family death leave.

Of course, my labor cost and overall operating cost would increase as it did at the beginning of every three-year contract term—that was *not* the issue I was fighting, for this contract. At the end of every contract term a slight uptick in prices covered the increase and kept the expense factor at an even plane with sales. This was a normal industry-wide increase every three years and was acceptable.

Other issues could have also been worked through, like the arrangement regarding the coffee breaks and few other non-essential items. One in particular, the Union didn't like, was the arrangements we had for lay-offs. Wednesdays were very slow, especially in the summer months, so we laid off (just for the day) a few drivers. I had a meeting with all the men and asked if any of them with seniority (last to be laid off) would "voluntarily" consider taking the day off without pay. We usually laid off five to six men for the day.

The top driver with seniority had started back in 1974 and didn't like or know how to pack orders. He was single and didn't need the money and looked forward to time off to work on his car. We had several of these situations, and most would volunteer to take the day off, thus allowing the married men who needed the money to work. It made good common sense to me, but not to the Union. The men themselves had agreed, for Christ sake. They liked and approved of the arrangement. It allowed those most in need to earn another day's wages. I felt it was proper work ethics and helped the men with families. It was of no advantage to the company.

I understand I was not "entitled" to make my own rules per the written contract, and should have conformed to the wording in the contract; however, who was the Union protecting or defending if the men not only liked but had approved and agreed to the arrangements? After all, shouldn't the wording and stipulations written in a Union contract reflect the implicit desires between the employees and the employer? Not the Union and the employer.

However, to be fair, regarding wages, I do agree that the Union must debate on behalf of their members for a fair and equable rate during collective bargaining, plus other somewhat minor issues. That was the norm. But this contract was anything but normal. My main contention was that *all* wholesalers must have the same labor cost to stay equally competitive. Other overall operating costs would then be an individual choice.

The real thorn in my side was why they weren't attempting to unionize the foreign-owned wholesalers. Their labor cost was a fraction of mine. The owners brought over workers from their own country and put them up in old hotels in the tenderloin they bought, most likely, again, with a low-rate minority loan, plus who knew if they were here legally, another purposely overlooked issue. Think of that scenario: The poor men must have thought of the owners as gods. What else did they have or know other than being picked up every morning to go to work, then back again at night? They knew no one else other than those in their tight-knit little community and their bosses. I knew they worked six, possibly even seven days a week, as long as twelve-hour days, and were most likely paid minimum wage. Oh, sure, they were paid overtime—a sack of rice would have been more realistic!

To make this thorn even more painful, the companies, since minority-owned, allowed them to obtain low-cost startup loans from the government. Was that fair and equitable?

What pissed me off even further, was that some Union officials thought they were high and mighty, and walked into your place of business with their chests out, like they were the offspring of Hercules, both hero and god, one to be feared. Oh yeah? Well, bullshit. I'm Achilles. Let's go to war!

Regarding my contract, most of the non-essential points mentioned prior could have and would have been worked out without a problem. The only factual break point or stalemate was that I would not and could not allow the increase in Union membership with the Union gaining my salesmen and office workers, and certainly not the Santa Rosa processing plant. I had to go to war; I had no choice. As General Omar Bradley said, "In war, there is no prize for the runner-up."

This was obviously premeditated to demand the impossible, the impracticable. As I mentioned earlier, there had been possible "alleged" underworld ties to the wharf, and I'd been kicking the Jesus out of them. And ever since I'd refused to be "taken over" by that influence, the relationship with the Union had been noticeably strained. Let me be perfectly clear: I am not in any way insinuating there was a tie between them. I must clarify that. However, I couldn't help but wonder if they had been remotely somehow been directed and under pressure to purposely attempt to destroy me.

It was too bad. What a beyond amazing business we were doing. We had it *all!* The company had a tenacious hold on the market. Now it was all in jeopardy.

To make things ever-so-worse and mentally taxing, that same Monday I received a letter from Leone saying that upon the baby's birth, she expected all hospital expenses to be paid, plus child support, and she had already retained an attorney— it was the Santa Clara County district attorney. She also made reference to an outrageous sum of money at the time: $3,000 per month until the child was eighteen years old.

I did some quick math and concluded that over an eighteen-year period that would amount to $648,000, and with hospital expenses, it would exceed $660,000.

With my conscience bothering me, I called Joan to see how she was doing. She hung up. I was still drinking, and even more so. I was now totally fucked up.

I decided—no, my girls decided—that I needed professional help to overcome the alcohol addiction. They naturally knew about the strike; they knew about the extra-marital affair—sorry, affairs—and of course, knew their mom and dad were separated and their mom wanted a divorce. However, they did *not* know about the upcoming baby scenario. I had hoped they would never know. Not a pretty picture, is it?

The girls believed that an attempt to recover from the alcohol dependency would be a huge first step toward straightening out my life, and would possibly show their mom I was trying—trying to get my life back in order, if nothing else—and just possibly, she might stay with me. They naturally didn't want to see their parent's divorce. No child does.

I'll never forget that day. It was a Saturday morning and the kids asked me to come up to the house; Joan would be gone for the afternoon.

When I arrived, we all hugged and got a bit teary, then Diana, the leader of the pack, said, "Okay, Dad, let's take a ride." "A ride?" I asked. "Where?"

"Just get in, Dad," Diana said—no, not "said," *ordered*, as Laura and Gina also urged me. The girls knew I didn't take orders well.

They very cleverly had me get in first. We were going for this mysterious ride in Diana's VW Rabbit convertible, so they had me get into the backseat—yes, a coupe, no back doors, no escape route, and the top was up. I was screwed!

As we drove down the hill on Tournament Drive, I asked, "So are we going for an ice cream?" No one answered. There was silence. Then I said, "So hey, guys, what's up?" No one answered.

Then simultaneously, they said, "We're taking you to Peninsula Hospital to rehab. You're going to be there for a week."

"Jesus Christ!" I exclaimed. "I can't! I can't be away from the business for a week, especially not *now*! My God! There could be a strike anytime. Please, kids!" There was silence. Diana kept driving. Then Gina commented that she felt there was time before they would pull the men, and that my head would be much clearer to combat the nightmarish consequences. I knew I was doomed to enter the hospital, but a block away, I thought I'd give it one last attempt and blurted out, "Listen, kids, I'll try to stop on my own. I promise." Well, it didn't work. Silence . . . more silence . . . this wasn't good. I was goin' in!

We stopped in front of the hospital and they then all took turns admonishing me. Diana, the psychologist, took the reins and berated me, saying, "Dad, you know the years you took from us while we were teenagers, you would come home from the office and be blotto and pass out on the sofa. We wanted to talk to you and tell you how our day went at school, and wanted you to tell us how your day went, but couldn't because you were dead to the world. You made us miss wonderful years sharing our lives with you."

This tugged at me. It was so true. I was getting it . . . and it was well deserved. It hit home.

Then she said, "And remember the night when us kids were arguing about whose turn it was to set the dinner table, and you totally flipped out and pulled the dishes out of the cabinet and screamed at us? Do you recall what you did? You screamed, 'Are we having soup tonight?!' And slammed the soup dishes down on the table and broke them into a million pieces. Then you said, 'Here's the salad dishes,' and slammed them on the table and broke them as well. Then you said, 'Here's the main course!' and did the same. When you were finished, there were several dozen broken dishes all over the table and floor, and then the table collapsed, and Mom ran upstairs crying as we fled for our lives. You really scared us, Dad."

Jokingly, I said, "I see I missed the dessert course, didn't I?" They didn't find that amusing and just glared at me.

They were right. I was wrong. I deserved everything they were saying. And I was filled with shame.

Sheepishly, I got out of the car without saying another word. It was obvious I was badly addicted, and more importantly, I realized how much it had impacted my relationship with my daughters and my wife.

What a complete idiot I'd been all those years, and yet my girls still loved me. I could feel the love exuding from their beautiful hearts for me, desperately wanting to help their father.

In retrospect, I learned later in life that you can hurt someone or do something hurtful, not realizing you did anything wrong or with any ill intentions, until it is called to your attention and makes you realize it was pernicious and caused harm and hurt.

Well, I spent three days at Peninsula Hospital, with all good intentions, but I couldn't take it anymore, so I checked out. I knew my kids would be upset, but this propitious form of help wasn't for me. I found it very uncomfortable sitting in a big circle, in a room filled with alcoholics and drug addicts spilling their guts out about their lives, and why they drank and did drugs. Even more disturbing, they'd all started out by saying, "I am an alcoholic." Don't get me wrong, I was no better than they were, but I wasn't an alcoholic. No. Most alcoholics will not admit or accept the fact that they are indeed an alcoholic.

I also couldn't get myself to divulge all the shit that was going on in my life the way they were able to do so freely. I am a realist and knew why I drank. I didn't need to make excuses. I also didn't need to be told why I was an alcoholic by a so-called trained professional who, by the way, was once—excuse me, *is*—an alcoholic. The disease is with you for the rest of your life.

I drank because I wanted to get drunk, to escape, not to get gleeful or be in a happy state. Maybe they did, but not me.

I found the three days I spent in the hospital to be boring and yet comical, but more than anything, demeaning. By the way, the food was of course horrible. No salt, no butter, no fries, and no glazed donuts. They even served fillet of sole one night for dinner, that my company supplied them with! The first day they called us into a large room to meet the other thirty or so people who had entered the rehabilitation facility at the hospital. Sitting in a large circle, the therapist asked us to introduce ourselves, using only our first names. The introductions started across the room from me. Most names were naturally common, run-of-the-mill ones, such as Jim, Harry, Bill, Mary, and the like; however, there was one guy named Herb. I later jokingly called him Basil, but I'm not sure he got it. Then, it was my turn. I said my name was Kiki. Well, that got a good chuckle from them. Most, if not all, "Kiki's" are girls or dogs. Some babies say to their moms when they must go "pee-pee," they have to go "kee-kee." Seems like I had been referenced to more than just once as a "bodily function."

Then when it came to our individual turn to speak about our addiction, we were supposed to say why we were there. *Well, duh.* Anyway, the first person, a young girl in her late twenties, got up and starting out by saying, "Hi, my name is Jennifer and I'm an addict, a stoner." She then told everyone how her addiction had first started by smoking some weed, and then she'd tried coke, then did some smack, and experimented with other drugs. Blah, bah, blah. The next person spoke, a guy, and he started out by saying, "Hi, my name is Frank and I'm an alcoholic. I drink a fifth of vodka every day and now my wife is drinking with me, and we're about to be evicted." Then he oddly started sobbing. *Come on, what's this shit about a guy crying? Go get a fucking job,* I wanted to say.

Next, a gal stood up and said, "Hi, my name is Jasmine and I'm a base head. I was hooked on disco biscuits and did my snackies every morning, and occasionally snorted my liquid lady." She then said, "I was also a rock star." She then explained that meant she'd traded sex for drugs. She then revealed how much she loved the high it gave her, and blah, blah, blah—the same ole crap.

Then it was my turn to speak. I didn't want to speak, but sixty eyes were now looking at me. Trying to be funny and make light of things, I blurted out, "Well, I'm on caffeine . . . black!" Of course, the group immediately erupted in laughter. *That was a good beginning,* I thought. Nonetheless, the therapist was a bit perturbed and exclaimed, "Kiki, that was rather funny, but you need to get serious and tell us why you're here! And by the way, I noticed you didn't start out by saying you were an alcoholic." Well, first of all, as you know by now, I don't like being told what to do, even worse, scolded. This disturbed me, especially coming from this peon. Yeah, I know, that was bad for me to call him that.

Okay, so I had to get serious, but I intentionally avoided starting out saying what he'd said I should; So, I then said, "I drink to get drunk, not to get happy or high. It's my choice, and I really don't enjoy it." I then stated, "I'm drinking because I own a large business and it's about to undergo a massive strike that could decimate the entire company, and there's a lot more—a whole lot more." They were obviously taken back that a supposed businessman was in their presence and was admitting to be an alcoholic. *Hey, no, no, I didn't admit I was an alcoholic. I never said that.* As I mentioned prior, all or most alcoholics don't believe they are indeed alcoholics. Maybe something else, some other trait noun or metaphor that describes their emotional incompetency and why they were indulging in mind-altering substances, but certainly not "alcoholic." All I knew was that I could *not* say those words . . . at the time.

Then, continuing trying to make light of things whether the therapist liked it or not, and since everyone else was telling all their shit, I said, "Another reason is because my wife wants a divorce. I was having an affair with two women. Oh, and yeah . . . one of them is pregnant!" A loud, pronounced gasp came from the group. I now had their full attention. The therapist then asked, "Kiki, you said with two women?" I wasn't sure if he found this as just fantasy or intriguing, or even exciting. I then replied, "Yes, my wife's name is Joan, my mistress's name is Simone, and my girlfriend's name is Leone. That's right—Joan, Simone, and Leone. Try keeping that straight when you're drunk!"

Loud, thunderous laughter that must have disturbed the tectonic plates now filled the room, and most likely all the surrounding rooms! Several clapped, most likely thinking I'd made it up, joshing, like I had with the coffee joke. Several shouted, "More, more, tell us more!" Now having a captive audience, I then went on to describe having to buy three Valentine's Day cards that year. When I'd paid the girl at the check-out counter, she'd noticed they were all similar and asked, "Can't decide?" I replied, "You mean on the cards or the women?" Again, laughter filled the room, cheering me on! I guess it sounded like a fictitious soap opera to them and they found it amusing. Well, what the hell, it was better than all that boo-hoo crap!

Then I said, "But on the serious side, the love of my three daughters could be in jeopardy, and I could lose my wife, plus my business could be in jeopardy." Upon my saying that, the room went silent, and they all put their heads down. I guess they now felt it was, in fact, real, and wondered what else could possibly be going on with me. I didn't elaborate any further. For a moment, I thought the therapist was going to offer me a drink!

Meanwhile—a young girl in the group must have found this exciting, a turn-on, because after the class, she wanted to give me her phone number so I could call her when she got out! I told her I didn't think that was a good idea and declined. However, she was damn cute! Her name was Cilone. Just what I needed, another "*ohne*" in my life! Then there would have been Joan, Sim*one*, Le*one*, and Cil*one*! That I could not cond*one*. Okay, you're not believing me, huh? Well, it's the truth, except for her name. I just wanted to add a bit of humor to this forbidding tale.

But seriously, when it came down to it, everyone in rehab may have come from different upbringings and backgrounds, but we were all addictive souls, attempting to liberate ourselves from the fiend that was encumbering us from reaching our citadel. I was no better or worse than any of them.

Anyway, I didn't like the process, and knew I was now going to have to do it on my own to keep my promise to my girls, as difficult as it would be, someday, but not now. Not now.

After getting to the office the next morning, surprisingly, no one asked where I had been those few days. I assumed the girls had told my secretary and my controller, and they had known about it. I'm not sure what they'd told everyone else, but a couple of the salesmen asked, "What are you doing here, boss?" Obviously, they hadn't been expecting me until next week. I bet they'd thought they were going to have an easy week.

I shrugged it off. I had a lot of planning to do. The day went well; we were busy, and the thought of the upcoming strike had faded from mind, concentrating on the day's business.

As the day came to an end, I could feel myself being drawn to the thought of having a drink, and that meant not just having one. That goddamn five-o'clock alarm started going off in my head . . . time for a drink . . . time for a drink. My thoughts were suddenly lost and garbled, and I couldn't concentrate on anything, anything but having a drink. My bar was but a few feet away; it would be so easy. I weakened and opened the accordion doors that hid it. It was like a magnet, drawing me to it. I fought it and fought it as I trembled. I opened it just to see what was still in there, but to my surprise, all the liquor was gone, replaced with soda water and Diet Coke. Jeez, my girls were smart; they'd known I would peek in there. I was proud of them, and felt loved due to their concern for me, but only for a moment. The craving was paralyzing and screwed with my head, now only focusing on satisfying that unbearable craving. *You should have stayed in the hospital, you damn fool! Why didn't you listen to your kids?*

Dismissing that thought, I suddenly had to get out of there, now thinking irrationally. I needed to get a pint over on Third Street, as I usually did every night; yeah, where the local drunks bought their stuff. They staggered into the liquor store, some walking with canes, and I pulled up in a Jag. I hated the fact that the very polite African-American store clerk knew me by name and would say, "Good evening, Mr. Paladini. The same?"

I took a moment and thought, *Hell, no one will know. I'm living alone, and I have a really good excuse now, actually several . . . yeah, several. Think about it. The frickin' strike, Joan divorcing me, losing my kids, and especially if they find out I'm drinking again, and the baby. Oh, shit! The baby. Plus, I'm so goddamn bored at night being alone.* I then suddenly thought, *You jerk! Anyone can make up a reason or find an excuse to drink. But damn, this is hard . . . so hard. You know, maybe I really am an alc-alc-alc—no. No, I'm not. I just need to relax.*

I then locked up the plant and put on the alarm, then closed the front door and locked it behind me. I zoomed—no, *bolted*—down the few short blocks to the liquor store and looked for a parking place. Looked and looked. Damn, there was no place to park! Couldn't even illegally double park, as I normally did; there was too much traffic. Maybe this was a foreboding sign? Maybe this was good. It gave me an extra moment to reconsider. I was ashamed of the thought process that embraced me and endorsed the flight to the liquor store. I had just about gotten my head together and was about to pull away, when I suddenly found a parking place just up the street! With my will weakened by the disease and the acute, perennial, unmanageable craving, I backed in and parked.

As I started to get out, I stopped and said, "No. No. Goddamn it!" I got back in and drove off.

It felt good. Yet it didn't. What I really needed at the time was a psychological autopsy.

That five-o'clock craving I was fighting was unbearably agonizing. It tugged at my very inner being, causing my concentration to be warped in trying to thwart off the yearning that ensued. I couldn't understand or logically explain the phenomenon that was taking over me, but the memory of the alcohol's effects was evoked by such strong reminders of the state of mind it allowed me to be in. It allowed for a truce with my life—even though it was only a delusive, beguiling, temporary truce.

Alcoholics who drink daily avoid the craving, because they keep the blood alcohol level high enough to prevent the symptoms of withdrawal. Many of the symptoms of craving in the dependent individual are similar to the thought patterns and behaviors of persons with obsessive-compulsive disorder. That includes recurrent and persistent thoughts about alcohol and the inability of the individual to resist these thoughts and the compulsive drive to consume alcohol, and the ultimate loss of control over that drive.

Disgustingly, before I got onto the freeway, which was only about a mile, I would have downed a pint, usually vodka, thinking it didn't smell; however, it did. Several times I would stop at the second liquor store on Third Street just a few blocks before the on ramp to Highway 101 South and get a second pint. That guy didn't know me by name . . . yet.

I was fortunate to be able to drive after consuming two pints of any kind of alcohol, but nonetheless, had to concentrate on every move. I am certainly not proud of that. It was beyond stupid. Anyone who drinks and drives is a fool, and I was certainly a fool. But I was dealing with a mind-altering addiction.

If you ever ask someone who is drunk if they're okay to drive, they'll answer, "Ssssure, I haaaamm." The nescience factor of an alcoholic's brain overrides any realization or rationality to process the fact that they are drunk, even worse, that they are indeed "a drunk."

I must tell you a funny story that I was told by a drunk about another drunk, and it is totally true. This guy's friend would go on three-day binges, and on one of those binges, while he was in a bar, he was challenged by another inebriated cohort to a fifty-dollar bet that he couldn't commit suicide—yeah, suicide! Well, this guy's friend, being the sort who would take on a bet for just about anything for a few bucks . . . accepted! He was found later that night near the Crystal Springs Reservoir in San Mateo by a policeman, slumped over in his car with a hose coming from the exhaust, and was saved just in time. When the policeman asked him why he'd attempted to take his own life, the officer almost fell over upon hearing his explanation. Slurring his words, the guy replied, "A guy made me a bet that I couldn't do it, and I was going to show him!" The police officer, now holding onto the door handles with laughter, then asked him, "So how did you intended to collect?" Oh, the logic of a drunk.

Refusing to give in to my dependence that evening, I arrived at my apartment sober for the first time in a very long while. I also had moved from that dumpy motel and upgraded to a fairly nice apartment; not great, but okay. However, now looking at it sober, it showed many visible defects I hadn't noticed before! Amazing.

However, still stressed, to replace the alcohol I bought a gallon—yes, a gallon; I always overdo —of ice cream. After all, "stressed" spelled backwards is "desserts"! And I damn near finished it! Well, I made it through the night, though bored and lonely. I often got the desire for affection, but needed to fight that off, as well. I was feeling good . . . if only for one night.

Each afternoon, the similar scenario repeated itself, that damn tick, tick, ticking of the clock as it reached five o'clock drove me crazy. It was as if a fire alarm would go off in my head, ambitiously dictating to me that it was time, time to sooth that craving. That was going to be challenging to overcome.

I set my mind like a vise, never to loosen. I envisioned a vise in my brain and refused to allow it to open, not allowing the thought to drink. That may sound silly, but using my mind worked for me. But nevertheless I must clarify, it worked for only as long as I wanted it to. For only as long as I allowed my mind that option. Studies show that an area in the left frontal lobe of a sober alcoholic's brain lights up when thoughts of drinking occur, and most often causes intense cravings.

I'm now giving the impression that all was well, and that I never drank again. I wish I could say that was true. For now, I was okay, but again, only for as long as I wanted to be, and that thinking may change. Nonetheless, I truly believe that your mind controls every facet of your body.

CHAPTER 34
THE UNION STRIKES!

Several weeks transpired, and the impromptu-strike drills continued whenever I thought the time was right. I hated to do it but had to ring the bell at eight on a Thursday morning during prime time, because I envisioned that was the predetermined time they would most likely hit—the busiest time and day of the week.

It totally disrupted the operation, but needed to be done, and it had to be rehearsed over and over again. The bell rang, the Union men on the floor walked outside (of course, while making jokes about it), and the salesmen went onto the production floor and started packing orders. The girls in bookkeeping came down to the sales office and answered the phones and made customer calls.

If a chef asked during the drill where their salesman was, we said he was sick, not wanting to alarm them of the upcoming drama that was soon to unfold. It all went well, with each rehearsal getting better and more refined.

All replacement drivers were now hired after a laborious interviewing process and screening driving records. I now had over a hundred drivers. Oh my God! What was this going to do to the cash flow? The profits? Well, I knew. The replacement drivers were now sitting alongside the regular Union drivers while making deliveries. My Union drivers were instructed to show them the routes, and reluctantly they did. They had to. I often wondered about the conversations and the mood in the cab of the truck, given the Union driver was training his replacement. It must have been most uncomfortable, and animosity apparent, to say the least.

Curiously, it was brought to my attention that the Union drivers now felt they'd made a huge mistake after realizing they could easily be replaced, and they were now feeling vulnerable. Their only hope now was if the strike could possibly be averted, or only last a few days, and they would then be back on the job. What they didn't know was that they'd broken the bond between us, and I now felt no compassion or responsibility for them.

On Tuesdays and Thursdays, we delivered to over twenty-some odd different areas of California, often with several trucks in each area. To the west, we serviced all of San Francisco and down the Pacific Coast. To the east, Oakland and the entire East Bay, including Stockton, Modesto, and Lodi, and as far as Sacramento and the gold country, including Reno and Lake Tahoe. To the south, San Jose, Santa Cruz, Monterey, and Carmel, and as far as the Salinas Valley. To the north, all of Marin County up to Santa Rosa and up to Jenner, and naturally throughout the abundant restaurant and resort-rich Napa Valley.

Often trucks had to double-up in certain areas, so the need for the replacement drivers to know all the stops in all the areas was paramount in the event of a strike.

Meanwhile, I couldn't figure out why the Union was taking so long to pull the men but enjoyed the weeks it gave to prepare. Anyway, who was to say there was intelligence within the Union officials? If they had brains and gumption, they'd have their own businesses. I wonder if they would have been unionized? Couldn't resist that!

We were going to do battle, and they gave me the time to draft my plans, train my troops, and prepare for the counterattack. This would be a war without guns, without armament—this will be a battle of ingenuity and brains.

I needed to figure out how to get the delivery trucks across the picket line in front of the plant without the trucks being damaged, and even more so, without the replacement drivers being frightened or getting hurt. I also needed to figure out how to get my incoming product delivered without any impediments. Luckily, Paladini Fisheries, my processing plant would be bringing in most of the fresh fish with non-Union drivers, but not all the product. But hey, I could instruct the trucking companies to deliver what I bought from other producers to the processing plant, then they could send it down on my own tractor trailers. See there' always a way! Keep thinking...

Hmm, ya know what, I think I just figured out a way to get the trucks out as well, and in a stealth manner. This just may be fun, out-foxing them . . . that is, if I could pull it off.

The time may also soon come when I will have to hire the best labor law firm in San Francisco to defend the company. That wouldn't be fun and would be expensive and only further deteriorate the cash flow and the excess funds that had built up over the years.

In the meantime, I called Joan to see how she was, and if we could talk. With the brief time, the very brief time she gave me after saying "I'm fine" and not asking how I was, I rushed to tell her about the upcoming strike. She abruptly said, "So that's what you get when you think you're a big shot and invincible, Kiki." I hadn't expected that. So obviously she knew, and it was even more obvious she wasn't very fond of me. But she talked to me, even if she talked down to me. It was talking . . . maybe. Of course, she knew about the pending strike—her aunt worked for me and was living with my controller.

I still wasn't drinking but was fighting it every night. I hoped I could stay strong through all of this. It was getting a little easier every day, even at five o'clock. The cravings were waning . . . a bit. What I now had to resist was my own mind telling me to drink, dismissing my promise and well-being. I had to maintain the power over my brain and the demon that resided within. *You can use your mind to rewire your brain and shape your world into the one you desire.* I hoped. However, I tend to stretch and strain all things good, thus destroying all things good.

Back at work, my competition, now hearing about the pending strike, started trying to hire away my best production floor men and order packers by offering them a guaranteed Union job. It was difficult to find experienced men who understood the many items we carried, so they were very valuable to me, as well as the competition. We had to train most of them, and it had taken time and was costly. Most were once inexperienced in the seafood industry and had started as apprentices and ultimately become journeymen. It infuriated me to think that my competition would cash in at my expense.

A rather funny short story—at least it's funny *now*: There was a pay phone on the wall near the entry door in the production area for the employees to use (no cell phones yet). I had noticed that it rang several times over the course of that week. It never rang in all the time the plant had been open. Oddly, only one guy on the floor was answering it, the fresh-fish manager. This was the man who received and cared for all the fresh fish; he had to be extremely experienced and knowledgeable regarding the handling and care of the fresh product and was paid a premium. That premium was not a Union requirement. I found it odd that only he was answering the phone when it rang, so I asked Tony the supervisor if he knew who was calling.

He said it was a wholesaler in Oakland, and they were trying to get him to work for them. I blew my top at poor Tony and screamed, "Why in the fuck didn't you tell me? What the hell is the matter with you, for Christ sake? Why didn't you try to stop it?" He then cowardly looked down. Tony always meant well; he was just too damn nice.

Now I couldn't wait for that phone to ring again. A day passed, then another, then another, then sure enough, right around ten in the morning, it rang. I jumped up from my desk in the sales office and immediately sped over to the phone, almost knocking a couple of guys over to get to it, screaming, "I'll get it, I'll get it! I picked it up, then immediately slammed the phone down, then banged the receiver against the phone base repeatedly, trying to break it. I then proceeded to try to pull the receiver from the phone's base on the wall to snap the telephone cord. I pulled and pulled, tugging at it over and over again, and the damn thing wouldn't snap. Then I noticed the cord was encased in an aluminum accordion-type cover that stretched . . . so I walked a few more yards, tugging at it again, and it still wouldn't snap. Then I walked even further, pulling at it even more, and it still wouldn't snap. By now, I was about forty feet from the phone's base on the wall, almost to the center of the plant, stretching it, tugging at it, again and again. The goddamn receiver cord still wouldn't break! Now beside myself, and the men laughing their asses, I walked another few yards, and with all my might, gave it one more tug. Well, the cord that was intertwined in this accordion-like cover, finally snapped . . . and recoiled back at me like it had been propelled from a shotgun and struck me on my left shoulder. It sliced my shirt open and cut my arm in a pattern, like from a boat propeller! Damn, it hurt! It really hurt, and was bleeding, but I wasn't about to let the guys know just how badly it hurt—no, no, couldn't show pain. Anyway, I'm sure you've heard the story of Achilles, my only vulnerable spot is my left heel. I then unraveled the twisted cord from my shirt sleeve and then calmly tossed it into the garbage.

Of course, I heard snickering behind me as I walked away. Tony came up to me later and said, "That was quite a show, boss. Feel better now?" Then he said, "That really hurt, huh?"

This is another amusing story. This one *is* short, sort of: My major competitor in San Francisco had been trying to hire one of my Peninsula salesmen for some time, offering him more than I was paying him. He had worked for me for several years, but it had just only recently come to my attention that he was indeed the salesman who had been in contact with the rep from the Union that had precipitated attempting to Unionize my salesmen. I called him up to my office and said, "I understand you would like to be exempt from your job to go work for another company. Is that right?"

He meekly stammered, "W-w-well, boss—" I interrupted him and said, "Hey, that's okay, with everything that's going on here, I don't blame you for wanting out, and don't want to hold you back. It's a good opportunity for you." I wanted to get rid of this Union organizer! But of course, my competitor wasn't aware of that fact.

What I'd done was give my major competitor a gift, a "white elephant," and with pleasure!

Still waiting for the pending strike, we were now operating with a tremendous overhead. With every week that passed, my cash flow suffered even more. Paying the replacement drivers was taking its toll. Maybe that was their plan; maybe they weren't so dumb after all. Nah. However, I knew that without the replacement drivers, I couldn't continue to operate during the strike, and oddly enough, by now many of them had learned the routes very well and were making the deliveries on their own without a Union driver instructing them. There were no Union regulations that said I couldn't keep the regular drivers in the plant to pack orders, just as long as they weren't laid off. This was also my way of seeing if the deliveries would go well . . . and they were. Yes, the overhead was killing me, but it was a necessity for now.

So just maybe I could beat the Union, and this would all backfire on them, then I would be a non-Union shop. Hmm. That had never been my intention, but my consanguinity with my men had been broken, and not by me.

To add salt to an open wound, and to further screw up my numbed, taxed brain I received a notice from the Santa Clara County district attorney's office that a summons for suit would be forthcoming for child support upon the birth of said child. It was now about sixty days before the birth.

I immediately contacted my good friend and attorney Robert LaVine and told him of the upcoming crisis. He was very calm and cool about it. I'll never forget what he told me—and this is verbatim: "Anyone can sue you for anything at any time." Though he was calm, I was not. I realized what he was saying but hoped this suit didn't have merit.

I'd started getting heart palpitations a few months prior, but hadn't let it be known to my family. I basically had little contact with them now anyway. Most likely the emotional stress had started taking its toll on me. I also, for some time now, had occasionally been losing feeling in both arms, as I mentioned earlier. They would go completely numb and I couldn't move them.

Several months ago, when Diana was working for me during college break she'd borrowed my car earlier in the morning, then later when we went to go to lunch, as we walked out the front office door and approached the car, I said, "Toss me the keys, kid." Ironically, just as she threw the keys, my arms went numb and I couldn't raise them to catch the keys, which as a result, hit my chest. Alarmed and concerned, she asked, "Dad, what's wrong? What's going on with you?" I just shrugged it off. However, that didn't fool wise Diana; she knew something was up.

So, to recap: I now had five crucial situations facing me: Would Joan divorce me? Would my daughters indeed disown me? Would the baby be mine? Would the Union strike? Would I ever overcome my alcohol addiction?

The results to date: Yes, Joan was divorcing me, though I hadn't yet been served. Yes, my daughters would likely disown me, especially when they found out about the baby. Yes, the baby—oh, the baby would soon arrive. Yes, the Union was most likely striking and could put me out of business. Yes, no, well, I'd sort of stopped drinking, but the grip on the vise was loosening.

As you slide down that banister of life, you should hope that all the splinters are pointed the other way! Well, I have five big ones in me already.

So now fantasizing and thinking of life's joys and consequences; I envisioned sitting on a warm vanilla-white sandy beach, somewhere rather close within reach, on a beautiful sunny day with the sky so blue, with just the passing of a high cloud or two. I saw myself looking out at the magnificence of the calm cobalt-blue sea, and the serenity of softly splashing waves soothed my thoughts and defined who I was to be. But the water now so inviting and tranquil can be consuming, for if one ventures out too far one's fate may be looming. Never assume that all beauty be adorned, for one's judgment may determine one's destiny be forewarned.

Meaning; life may appear to be fanciful and beautiful, but if irresponsible decisions are made without considering the consequences of being intemperate, one can drown in the depths of the magnificence of the once calm sea.

CHAPTER 35
THE BATTLE BEGINS

It was a chilly, bright, fall day in 1987, and the local Dungeness crab season was about to start. The seagulls were eagerly circling around the crab boats docked at pier forty-five hoping to swoop in and grab a morsel of the smelly crab bait that was being loaded onto the boats that would soon be leaving to set their pots. A Thursday, about eighty thirty, right after the morning coffee break and the men were just getting back into the rhythm of packing the countless orders. We were swamped, as we were every Thursday, with over five hundred invoices to read, recap, pack, extend, and load to be delivered from San Francisco to as far as Salinas to the south; to the Napa Valley and Jenner to the north; to Lodi and as far as Lake Tahoe and Reno to the east. It was a real challenge every Tuesday and Thursday, since we only delivered to the far-out areas twice a week. It seemed like just about everyone bought on Thursdays.

I was downstairs in the sales office, as I was every morning at this time, busy with the daily buying and reviewing the completed invoices coming in from the packing desk for possible mistakes before they went to the extension desk just across from me. The sales office was humming with activity with the morning calls coming in, and the phones were ringing off the hook. We were so busy! Well, as I answered a call from a broker, I looked up and saw the men leaving the packing area, as if being sucked out like a tsunami had just occurred. Swoosh, they were gone! The packing floor now only had the replacement workers standing there, dismayed and looking around, and then looking directly at me.

Tony, my supervisor, came up to me and calmly said, "Boss, ring the bell. This time it's no drill. They pulled the men!"

The adrenaline quickly flowed, and we were ready for action, though under my breath, I said, "Oh, shit."

Before I even had a chance to ring the bell, the salesmen were already on their way out onto the packing floor, and within moments, the girls had come down and were in the sales office answering the phones. We were lucky that the early morning downtown hotel orders had already gotten out. It would have been mayhem if we'd had to deal with attempting to get them out and delivered in time.

Phil Gordon, my judicious Jewish controller, came downstairs, his gray hair curling from fright, and asked, "Did they really pull the men, Mr. P.?" I answered him, "Yep, Phil, they sure did. The exodus was as fast as Moses calling the Hebrews out of Egypt!" Don't know where this sense of wit came from at a time like that; maybe I was trying to downplay the conflict that was about to take place. Nervously, he giggled, but this was no time for joking.

I took a deep breath and prepared to lead my troops as planned. I was thankful that we had the time to train the replacement workers, as they were now eagerly out there packing orders, though still needing guidance.

I instructed Tony to close all seven metal roll up doors on the loading dock including the receiving door and the ramp, so they—the Union reps and the strikers—couldn't see what we were doing, or possibly not doing. We needed to get the orders packed and out. The salesmen were good, but we had a ton of orders that day.

I suddenly had an impromptu thought: If I got all the men in front of me at the packing desk and called out the orders to them, they just may go faster. I could fill in the weights not only for the hundreds of frozen items, but also for all the fresh items, avoiding costly errors that would never be caught checking out the trucks, especially working under these conditions.

Well, it worked fantastically, and I wondered why I hadn't thought of it before. I found I needed Tony to come up and assist me, however, because we were packing over twenty orders at a time and it took extreme concentration to keep it all straight.

Normally, the orders were packed in sequential order starting from the furthest areas to be delivered so as to facilitate getting those trucks on the road as early as possible. However, the downtown San Francisco orders always went out by seven in the morning, due to the times of the yellow zones, plus, the restaurants wanted the product early for their lunch business. Thankfully this was not a concern on that day, because those trucks were fortunately already out—but those drivers would be yanked upon returning to the plant.

Then it suddenly occurred to me, *How in the hell are we going to get the delivery trucks out and across the picket line without being blocked or damaged?* I ran upstairs and looked outside to see the configuration of the strike zone to figure how, or even if, I could get the trucks out of the parking lot. It was a sight to see my men, my friends—excuse me, my *one*-time friends—laughing and joking as they walked around holding signs that read "Local XXX On Strike - Unfair to Organized Labor."

Pictured on our A Paladini Seafood picket line are, left to right, John Moret, Gary Petrini, Robert Hutchinson, Don D'Angelo, and Gus Garcia. —UFCW Local 115 Photo

Day 'N Night They're On The Paladini Line

Pictured, left to right, kneeling are Jose Garcia and Gary Petrini, standing are Ed Bagby, Doug Thompson, Ed McGilvray, John Moret, James Mead, Gus Garcia, and Dave Camacho. —UFCW Local 115 Photo

U.F C W Local One Fifteen

a fraternal communication between the membership family and friends of United Food and Commercial Workers Local One Fifteen

Published By United Food & Commercial Workers International Union
Local 115
208 Miller Avenue
South San Francisco, CA 94080

THE BRIDGE
208 M ler Avenue
South San Francisco CA 94080

NON PROF T ORG
U S Postage
PAID
Perm t No 829
So San Franc sco CA

PALADINI SEAFOOD
500 MENDELL ST
SAN FRANCISCO, CA
94124

The Bridge — Page Four

A. Paladini Seafood Members On Strike!

Local 115 members are pictured in front of the A Paladini Seafood plant which has been the site of picketing since December 16th. Pictured, left to right, are James Mead, Ed McGilvray, David Camacho, Jose Garcia, Don D'Angelo and Local 115 President Dino Polizziani. —UFCW Local 115 Photo

On December 16th, members working at A. Paladini Seafood, Inc said no to the employer's final offer and went on strike for fair wages These members have stood together since then and have brought the employer's once booming business nearly to a complete halt!

In addition to the picket line in front of the plant, Local 115 has started to leaflet customers of stores doing business with A. Paladini. This action to notify the public of our dispute not only will affect Penninsula and Bay Area retail locations, but will be extended to Sacramento, Reno and Carson City.

We want everyone to know how A. Paladini treats its workers.

A. Paladini workers have not had a raise in 6 years and we are seeking a fair and equitable contract to bring these workers in line with our current area standards

"We are very proud of our A. Paladini members and their solidarity displayed on the picket line for the past seven weeks," stated President Dino Polizziani as we went to press. Don't buy A. Paladini fish products.

My emotions then ran rampant, from getting choked up because it hurt, to having a sick feeling in my gut, realizing the impending dilemma. What the hell had happened to turn the guys so defiantly against me? They were out there looking like they were actually having a good time. Or were they? I know men and know human nature. It's natural to team up in a pack; a pack gives a feeling of strength, of solidarity. But I bet deep down they didn't want this any more than I did. They followed who they considered their protector, their ruler. Most of these guys had families, families that were provided a favorable lifestyle, supported by this company for many years. They couldn't feel good knowing the position they were putting me in, as well as themselves. Meanwhile, *they* really had nothing to gain by this. Only the Union would gain, because what they were striking for, had nothing to do with them. The Union wanted more, more Union employees, thus more dues. I bet that never dawned on them.

Just a few minutes ago everyone had been working together as a team, as we had for years. They couldn't want to destroy the company. I bet most of them didn't even know why they were out there. Well, I did. They'd been told to. None of them had the gumption or the balls to say no. Originally, I hadn't wanted to hurt these guys. I really thought that if and when the time came, they wouldn't *all* walk out on me, maybe some, but not all. But when I saw them all out there laughing, it really pissed me off. Sure, it was all fun and games now, but winter would soon be here, and it was going to be miserable out there, and the Union was only paying them twelve bucks a day—that was per *day*, not per hour. That was a grungy hot dog, a Coke, and a pack of cigarettes from the gut truck.

Well, I couldn't let my emotions get in the way, we still had over four hundred orders to get out.

I thought and thought and thought. I needed to create a plan, visualizing every function and every detail, a plan that would work and completely think it through; no margin for error. I needed to get the trucks out and across that picket line!

In the background, there was the vociferous sound of the strikers annoying, repetitive shouting, "Paladini unfair to workers! Paladini unfair to workers!" Over and over again, it offensively impeded my now nerve-wrought thought process as I tried to concentrate and think. I then suddenly noticed that the Santa Rosa forty-foot tractor-trailer was still backed into the receiving dock, and the bed of the truck was floor level. I started to wonder.

There were at least a dozen or so of my trucks in the parking lot within the eight-foot cement wall at the time. I then told Tony to pull one of the Econoline vans up the ramp and into the plant.

I measured the outer width of the van, then measured the inside dimensions of the tractor-trailer. Okay, it would fit inside. I then measured the length of the Econoline van, then the inner length of the tractor-trailer; there was just enough room to pull three of them in. I told Bev, my secretary, to drive over to the wholesale produce mart a few blocks away to see if there was a rail-road ramp so the tractor-trailer could back into it and we could drive the trucks off. I thought I recalled seeing one there.

We then continued packing orders, and more orders, and more orders.

Bev eventually came back and exclaimed, "Boss, there is one! It's just as you come into the mart on the left."

We loaded up the first truck with the orders in reverse sequence so the last order to be delivered was the first to be loaded, and so on. Then the next truck, then the third truck. *Oh, jeez. How in the hell will the drivers open the door to get out of the van? Well, they will just have to stay in the van while in the trailer.* It was a little treacherous, and I bet even a bit spooky, being in there in the dark. Now I hoped the saying "There is no strong beer, only weak men" wasn't true.

The first van slowly, slowly edged into the trailer. Just as the cab of the van was about to emerge in, I suddenly screamed, "Stop, stop!" We'd forgotten to pull in the mirrors. Then slowly, it edged in. It was a tight fit, but it got in. Then the next, then the next. I told the drivers I was proud of them, and lunch would be on me. They gave me a thumbs-up as the door to the tractor-trailer closed like this was a kamikaze mission and they would never return.

Remember, all the roll-up doors on the loading dock were closed, so they, the strikers, couldn't see in, and we couldn't see out. Tony and I ran upstairs and looked out from the women's lounge so they couldn't see us. We didn't want them to get wise we were up to something. We needed to see if the tractor-trailer had gotten through the picket line okay. Of course, the bearded-tattooed Hell's Angels driver would have knocked any of them on their asses if they tried to stop him, plus, he must have pulled out at thirty miles per hour.

So yes, he, with all three delivery vans, made it out without a hitch, and best of all, they thought it was empty and returning to Santa Rosa!

I was now starting to feel more of a cohesive kinship with the replacement workers than most of the men who had worked for me for years. These men were very nice and not only needed, but valued their jobs, and thought the once faithful employees who'd walked out on me were foolish, not only for possibly relinquishing their jobs, but for abandoning the company that had supported them for years. The replacement workers would do just about anything to please me, and to illustrate their desire to learn.

You know what? I was now operating *without a Union contract*, and it felt damn good! And there was no one telling me what I *had* to do. If this worked out and I successfully beat the Union—sure, likely chance—but if so, I would make it right for these men. They would get a good privatized health plan, and instead of a Union pension, I would set up an IRA in each of their names and it would be theirs from day one, no ten-year waiting period or vesting. We would do similar vacations and sick days and holidays as per the old Union contract. *This just may work out. Settle down, Kiki. You have a loooooong way to go yet.*

There were no cell phones back then, so we had to wait until the Santa Rosa truck returned to find out if all had gone well—and it had! We still had to repeat this same process several times, and sure, they might get wise after a few more ins and outs, but so what? It was working, and it was actually fun!

But what about tomorrow . . . tomorrow? Damn, I need to think again. Can't do the same thing every day.

It was about two o'clock now and all the trucks were finally on the road, about two hours later then on a normal day, but that was okay; they were out. We were all exhausted and starved, so I told Bev to go get burgers, fries, and soft drinks for all the men. We needed to take a breather, then clean the plant before closing.

I told Tony to have each driver call him at his home at the end of their run, since they were going to be taking the trucks home. I still had to come up with an innovative plan for tomorrow, and may need to relay the plan to them.

It was three o'clock now and the plant was cleaned. It had been a mess and was disorganized, as you can only imagine. I told the salesmen and the few replacement floor workers just before they left that we would be calling them at home in a few hours about tomorrow, Friday's plan.

Friday was our second busiest day of the week and all the restaurants would be screaming, wanting their deliveries early, as they did every Friday. Meanwhile, the girls had been on the phone all afternoon getting the orders in for tomorrow to avoid a morning back log.

I was very proud of the girls and the salesmen. They'd all gotten in there and done as we'd planned, and without a gripe. I also think they enjoyed it; however, at the same time, they were dismayed about the production workers all walking out.

Exhausted, both physically and mentally, I went up to my office and fell sound asleep. I needed to clear my head and think about Friday. Christ, it was easier planning this stuff than actually implementing it. I'd forgotten about the exhaustion factor. We still needed to plan for tomorrow's downtown San Francisco early-morning deliveries. We had all the hotels and private clubs and dozens upon dozens of restaurants that needed their product before eight.

After twenty minutes or so, I suddenly woke up from a deep sleep, feeling as if someone had tapped me on the shoulder and whispered an idea in my ear: "Have the salesmen and order packers come in at three in the morning and pack all the downtown orders, then load up the six Econoliners that are here and drive them to Powell Auto Works, the mechanic's shop in North Beach. Then have the drivers be there at six, and leave their empty trucks there, then pick up the pre-loaded trucks and go on their way!" Was that you, Dad? Grandpa? Or was it both of you who tapped me on my shoulder? My God, that *would* work!

Getting that accomplished would take the pressure off us having to get all the early downtown deliveries out. The men on strike naturally knew of the Friday rush downtown, and if they could block us, that could possibly put us in jeopardy of losing many of the huge hotel accounts, that I couldn't afford to lose.

However, I still had to clear this with Leonard, my mechanic. He had the perfect place to safely park the trucks up on his rooftop parking area, where no one could see them. Leonard naturally said, "Of course!" He'd better.

The plan was in place. Tony told the downtown replacement drivers about the plan when they called and gave them the address and instructed them to report there at six in the morning; he would meet them there with the other replacement drivers to drive the empty trucks back to the plant.

I called the salesmen and the replacement packers and asked if they would please come back to the plant at two in the morning. They knew of the importance of this, and the salesmen sure as hell didn't want to lose their high-volume downtown accounts. All this activity, of course, was well in advance of the strikers scheduled to show up at seven in the morning to attempt to block the deliveries.

Again, it worked magnificently. The downtown hotels and clubs had never gotten their orders so early!

I heard that the strikers outside and the Union officials were under the impression that they had crippled us on Thursday by not allowing any orders to be delivered, and on Friday morning were out there gleaming, thinking the downtown orders were still sitting on the floor. Little did they know!

The entire day went well, but not without confrontation, since all the outlying area delivery trucks had to cross the picket line. There was nothing I could do about that. By now, the strikers knew the orders were being packed and deliveries were successfully being made somehow. The poor replacement drivers were verbally abused, and several trucks received dents from baseball bats that were swung as they passed through the gates. One striker even threw a lit flare into the open window of a truck as it drove out.

It was disturbing to see the guys once happily working for me out there doing these disruptive and damaging things, trying to cripple the operation that had supported them for years. I didn't think this was legal, however. As I understood, the federal labor laws regarding strike guidelines said they could not block entry in or out. But having said that, they were.

I had to call our labor law attorney that was now representing us with the negotiations to confirm it. He said to have one of the girls take pictures of them blocking the entrance so he could show proof to the Union officials and the National Labor Relations Board (NLRB). Well, it was the goddamn Union officials who were themselves encouraging this—yes, the same so-called abide-by-the-contract guys! I didn't need pictures to prove it to the Union, but I did for the NLRB and the Council on Labor Law Equality. They held superiority over the Unions. I could now show proof of the Union's actions and how they were not in compliance. They had to be put in their place and abide by the rules, as we had to.

FORM EXEMPT UNDER 44 U.S.C. 3512

FORM NLRB-501
(11-88)

UNITED STATES OF AMERICA
NATIONAL LABOR RELATIONS BOARD
CHARGE AGAINST EMPLOYER

DO NOT WRITE IN THIS SPACE	
Case 20-CA-23109	Date Filed 1/23/90

INSTRUCTIONS:
File an original and 4 copies of this charge with NLRB Regional Director for the region in which the alleged unfair labor practice occurred or is occurring.

1 EMPLOYER AGAINST WHOM CHARGE IS BROUGHT

a. Name of Employer A. Paladini Seafood Company	b. Number of workers employed about 10

c. Address (street, city, state, ZIP code) 500 Mendell Street San Francisco, Ca. 94124	d. Employer Representative Alan B. Levins, Esq.	e. Telephone No. (415) 433-1940

f. Type of Establishment (factory, mine, wholesaler etc.) Wholesaler of Fish	g. Identify principal product or service Fish

h. The above-named employer has engaged in and is engaging in unfair labor practices within the meaning of section 8(a), subsections (1) and (list subsections) _____ of the National Labor Relations Act, and these unfair labor practices are unfair practices affecting commerce within the meaning of the Act.

2. Basis of the Charge (set forth a clear and concise statement of the facts constituting the alleged unfair labor practices)

      Since on or about January 1, 1990, the above-named Employer, by its officers, agents and representatives, has granted pay increases and other benefits and/or has promised pay increases and other benefits in order to induce certain of its employees to testify falsely in an unfair labor practice proceeding and in spite of the majority status of United Food and Commercial Workers Union Local 115.

By the above and other acts, the above-named employer has interfered with, restrained, and coerced employees in the exercise of the rights guaranteed in Section 7 of the Act.

3. Full name of party filing charge (if labor organization, give full name, including local name and number)

United Food and Commercial Workers Union, Local 115

4a. Address (street and number city, state, and ZIP code) 208 Miller Avenue, P.O. Box 747, South San Francisco, California 94080	4b. Telephone No. 871-5730

5. Full name of national or international labor organization of which it is an affiliate or constituent unit (to be filled in when charge is filed by a labor organization)

United Food and Commercial Workers Union, AFL-CIO, CLC

6. DECLARATION

I declare that I have read the above charge and that the statements are true to the best of my knowledge and belief.

By _____ (signature of representative or person making charge)   Business Rep. (title if any)

Address 208 Miller Avenue, South San Francisco, 871-5730   Jan. 23, 1990
Ca. 94111   (Telephone No.)   (date)

WILLFUL FALSE STATEMENTS ON THIS CHARGE CAN BE PUNISHED BY FINE AND IMPRISONMENT (U.S. CODE, TITLE 18, SECTION 1001)

UNITED STATES GOVERNMENT
NATIONAL LABOR RELATIONS BOARD
REGION 20
…RKET ST SUITE 400
…RANCISCO, CA 94103-1735
…l Opportunity Employer

…AL BUSINESS
…for Private Use, $300

Is your RETURN ADDRESS completed on the reverse side?

CERTIFIED
P 468 801 169
MAIL

U.S.MAIL
POSTAGE AND FEES PAID
NATIONAL LABOR RELATIONS BOARD
NLRB 638

A. Paladini Seafood Company
Attn: Alan B. Lewins, Esq.
500 Mendell Street
San Francisco, CA 94124

RETURN RECEIPT REQUESTED

NATIONAL LABOR RELATIONS BOARD
REGION 20
901 Market Street, Suite 400
San Francisco, California 94103

Telephone Area Code 415 744-6810

January 24, 1990

A. Paladini Seafood Company
Attn: Alan B. Lewins, Esq.
500 Mendell Street
San Francisco, CA 94124

Re: A. PALADINI SEAFOOD COMPANY
Case 20-CA-23109

Gentlepersons:

A charge has been filed with this office alleging that you have engaged and are engaging in unfair labor practices within the meaning of the National Labor Relations Act, as amended. A copy of the charge is herewith served upon you. Also enclosed is a copy of Form NLRB-4541, describing our investigation and voluntary adjustment procedures.

Attention is called to your right to be represented by counsel or other representative in any proceeding before the National Labor Relations Board. If you have such a representative, please have completed, "Notice of Appearance" Form NLRB-4701 or "Notice of Designation of Representative as Agent for Service of Documents" Form NLRB-4813 and forward one promptly to this office. Failing to receive one of these notices, we will assume that you do not choose to be so represented.

Please submit promptly a complete written account of the facts and a statement of your position in respect to the allegations set forth in the charge. It is requested that your written account of the facts include the names of your witnesses and identification of any documents on which you are relying. Please also fill in and return one copy of the enclosed interstate commerce forms. All communications and submission should be made to Board Agent KAREN K. THOMPSON, whose telephone number is 744-7859.

If the preliminary investigation of this matter provides a reasonable basis for concluding that the charge has merit, the Board Agent assigned to this case will seek more specific information from you or ask that witnesses be made available. Your cooperation with this office is invited so that all facts of the case may be considered. In the event you decide not to provide evidence, a decision will be made on the basis of the evidence submitted by the Charging party and otherwise disclosed by our investigation.

Very truly yours,

Robert H. Miller

Robert H. Miller
Regional Director

Enclosures
CERTIFIED MAIL - RETURN RECEIPT REQUESTED.

LITTLER, MENDELSON FASTIFF & TICHY

A PROFESSIONAL CORPORATION

ATTORNEYS AT LAW

650 CALIFORNIA STREET 20TH FLOOR

SAN FRANCISCO, CALIFORNIA 94108-2693

(415) 433 1940

FAX (415) 399 8490

FRESNO
LOS ANGELES
MENLO PARK
SACRAMENTO
SAN DIEGO
SAN JOSE
WALNUT CREEK

LITTLER, MENDELSON, FASTIFF & TICHY
A PARTNERSHIP
BALTIMORE, MARYLAND

LITTLER, MENDELSON, FASTIFF & TICHY
A PARTNERSHIP
NEW ORLEANS, LOUISIANA

January 26, 1990

Ms. Karen K. Thompson
National Labor Relations Board
Region 20
901 Market Street, Suite 400
San Francisco, California   94103

> Re: A. Paladini Seafood Company and Local 115
> Case No. 20-CA-23109

Dear Ms. Thompson:

Enclosed you will find a fully executed Notice of Appearance in the above-referenced matter. Please be advised that I represent A. Paladini Seafood Company in all labor-related matters. This is also to inform you that the Union's charge is without merit.

In the unlikely event the Region determines that the Union has presented a **prima facie** case, please contact me. The Employer stands ready to assist the Region in dismissing the above-referenced meritless charge.

Very truly yours,

ALAN S. LEVINS

ASL/rty

Enclosure

Meanwhile, I knew I couldn't keep coming up with different innovative ways every day to try to avoid confrontation. It had been fun at first but was impossible to continue. I also had to remember the fatigue factor, not only for myself, but for the men and women who were collaborating with the company helping to facilitate with the daily strategy to fool them. The numbing in my arms wasn't getting any better, either.

The negotiations continued for months with no progress, as we were now operating almost normally since the replacement workers were now as good as the journeymen out there striking. The strikers were getting more and more disgruntled and bored, and it was getting colder and damper with each passing day, as it was now late fall. Their unemployment checks, plus the twelve dollars a day pay for striking, wasn't enough to pay their bills, and agitation was evident. Within time, we got used to them walking around out in front and paid no attention to them; it was like they were just strangers walking on the sidewalk.

Christmas was coming up soon, and it wasn't looking like it was going to be a very merry Christmas for them, or for anyone. Certainly not for me. I was also beginning to look more like Santa Claus every day, as my hair whitened, and waistline widened.

A very disturbing thing occurred a few weeks later, just a couple of days before Christmas. I would always buy all the employees their breakfast every Friday during the morning break when the coffee truck came, and of course, this had continued with the replacement workers, but not for the strikers, of course. The coffee truck would drive into the parking lot now when he arrived, where the strikers were no longer allowed. Well, this particular Friday, when the coffee truck pulled up and blasted its vexatious horn, being Christmas, I said to all the employees, "Get anything you want, anything, cigarettes included. You deserve it. I want you to know how much I appreciate you."

For whatever reason, I was in a pretty good mood for a change and felt sorry for the guys walking the picket line. They had been out there for several months and knew as followers, they had been led to the slaughter. I weakened and told the coffee truck driver that when everyone was finished in the yard, to drive out and stop outside and tell the men everything was on Mr. Paladini. I said, "And let them get whatever they want, as well," dismissing the no cigarettes rule. It was Christmas.

I was told most of the men exclaimed upon hearing this, "Wow! That's really nice of Mr. P." They got sandwiches and drinks or whatever they wanted and told the driver to say thank you to me. However, a few of them said, "Fuck him, I'll buy my own." I knew who they were, and that was okay. Most of the them were actually pretty good guys.

I then paid the driver and went up to my office to relax during the half-hour break. With my feet up on the desk and pushing back on my chair, I soon started to doze off for a few minutes, as I normally did. Suddenly, Bev came running in, screaming, "Mr. P.! Mr. P.! You've got to see what's going on outside!"

I rushed over to the window at the top of the steps and saw several men fighting. I looked closer and saw three of my salesmen fighting the three guys who'd told me to go eff myself!

I was flattered that my salesmen were out there defending me, then surprisingly saw Lou, a talented young man who worked on the production floor that I had intended to advance in the company, also out there defending *me* as well, yelling at the workers to stop. Lou was my brother Tom's son in law, now a part of the family. That felt good.

I then went flying down the stairs and ran out screaming for them to stop and pulled my sales manager off one of them. They were both bloody and both big guys. Several other salesmen and strikers were beating the shit out of each other as well by now, and blood was spurting all over. It was an ugly, disheartening scene.

After several minutes of scuffling, my daughter Gina and the girls upstairs screamed for them to stop and they finally separated. I was a bit annoyed that no one had listened to me—it had taken the girls!

What I'd thought should have been taken as a kind gesture, and viewed as a sign of possible understanding, especially during the holiday season, had turned into a free-for-all, with pain inflicted. I felt badly. That was most unfortunate, and not a pleasant experience.

As the old saying goes, "Don't misinterpret kindness as a sign of weakness."

Later that day, I took all the salesmen and the office girls out for lunch, as I did every holiday, to Dago Mary's Restaurant, which was in the naval shipyard about a mile away, the nicest restaurant in the area. Of course, we sold to them and the owner was a good friend. Well, everyone got plastered, all except me. I'm sure the strain of the strike was evident within all the employees, and it must have felt good to just let go. As I mentioned before, I never drank in front of the employees, needing to remain fully composed. You know, the respect factor.

After several hours had passed of consuming an abundance of potable libations and artery-clogging trans fats, we eventually got back to the plant. With the effects of the ethanol now waning, I gave the salesmen a generous Christmas bonus, not only to reward them for their performance over the year, but to also show my appreciation for their help on the floor, which was way beyond the call of duty. Of course, the office girls were well rewarded in like manner.

All the hoopla was now over, and after being surrounded by a magnitude of laudatory employees, I returned to the loneliness of my apartment. Tomorrow was to be a half day at work since it was Christmas Eve, and I was attempting to adapt to the thought of spending Christmas alone for the first time in my life. I had reached the pinnacle of success in the business world. In others' eyes, my life was the epitome of success, but aside from work, I had little joy.

I knew Laura was coming up from Long Beach and would be staying with Gina, who had just bought a townhouse in Foster City. Diana was already at the house, visiting with her mom, as well as Joan's parents, who had arrived earlier in the week from down south.

With Joan and I now separated, I could only imagine the conversations that took place about me with her parents, especially with her mom, who could now affirm and confirm that I was indeed a piece of that bodily function, as she'd so endearingly referred to me.

It was early the next morning and I had just taken a shower and was getting ready to leave my apartment and go to the office. I noticed there was a voice message from Diana, surprisingly saying that Joan wanted to know if I wanted to come over for lunch on Christmas Day. I was shockingly pleased, and naturally accepted. I also knew it was going to be extremely uncomfortable for everyone but needed to grasp at any chance to be with Joan and the kids. I was extremely happy, but also hesitant about how it would go. The thought then occurred to me why she hadn't invited me for Christmas dinner, but then I remembered that her mom started drinking in the afternoon, so maybe it was best I wasn't there. Recognized, acknowledged, and agreed!

This was the first time I was going to be with my family, all my family, in almost a year. I was actually looking forward to being with my in-laws, Mario and Livia, too—yes, even Livia, if you could believe that! Like old times. However, Joan's father could get very argumentative over just about any subject at any time. Oh, how I hoped he wouldn't start asking me questions about . . . about anything.

I told myself I wasn't going to drink, no matter what, even if Livia started in on me, as she had so many times before about so many things, even little things. I had decided to just ignore her, and maybe even agree with her, if anything came up, whatever it may be. Because most likely anything she had to say now . . . was unfortunately true.

It was Christmas Day, just before noon, and I was now standing at the front door of our home in Hillsborough, trembling, reluctant to ring the bell. It was an odd feeling that I had to ring the bell to my own home, like a stranger. Joan had changed the locks, so I was in essence a stranger, a stranger in my own home. Nevertheless, I then clicked that click in my head, that extraordinary ability to turn on the charm, and valiantly rang the bell. That familiar sound of the chimes sent chills through me. I had heard them only from the inside for so long, and now queerly from the outside. While waiting, I looked around at the circular drive and the landscaping, I had almost forgotten where I lived, well, once lived. Such a beautiful home, such a loss, such fond memories here. Just then, Diana came to the door with open arms and gave me a big hug and a kiss. She said, "Hi, Dad, Merry Christmas!" We hadn't hugged in so long. I got all teary eyed and emotional. Noticing, she wiped the tears running from my cheeks without saying a word. Such a perceptive, wonderful, sensitive girl. She also knew what I was about to be walking into. Jokingly, she said, "Brave up, Dad!" God, I love that girl!

Walking into the house, I was suddenly overcome with reminiscence of the wonderful, fun, love-filled years we'd had in that house. Then my stomach ached, realizing I may have thrown it all away, but I had to maintain my composure and try to be cheerful, even if my heart was breaking.

As I walked in further, I couldn't help glancing to the right at the living room, oh, that elegant living room. I had forgotten how magnificent it was. I then had a flashback to the last time I'd been in it, well, almost in it, when all the ladies had toasted me and said, "To the bastard!"

Okay, goddamn it! Get yourself together. I must dismiss those thoughts now, and boldly walk into the kitchen where Joan and Livia are and . . . and . . . and say what?

So, in I went, doing that click in my head even once again, making sure it was turned on, and gleefully, I said, "Hi, honey. Hi, Livia," and kissed them both on the cheek. They both coldly and flippantly pulled away and replied, "Helllloo," their voices deep, and then continued what they'd been doing, not looking my way. After all, what could I expect? I was lucky just to be there.

Now I had to go and face Joan's father, as my anxiety levels soared. I dauntlessly walked up to him with my hand out and said in an animated, effervescent way, like nothing was wrong, "Hey, Mario, how ya doin'?" Rather startled by my delusional entrance, he looked up from the couch and loosely shook my hand, first saying in Italian, "Sto bene." He then said, "Probably better than you!" Okay, so this was how the day was going to go.

We sat there for the longest time watching a college football game on TV, trying to make casual small talk. Actually . . . there was mostly silence. Laura and Gina did not come for lunch.

I wasn't sure if that was because of me or if it was true that they'd had something else going on. That hurt, but who was I to be critical?

It came time for lunch, and we all sat at the table in the large glass-enclosed sun room just off the kitchen. I started to sit in the middle of the table—not taking my normal spot at the head; after all, I was no longer the head of the family. I didn't really know at that point what the hell I was. Surprisingly, Diana said, "Dad, that's not where you sit." I was honored that she at least still considered me as, as . . . Have to say it again, God, I love that girl.

Joan and Livia cooked an amazing lunch that included an abundance of all the Italian appetizers I love. The conversations, however, were sparse. My food was lodged somewhere in my diaphragm; it certainly didn't reach the stomach. I was happy that Joan had allowed me to spend Christmas Day with her, though we hardly talked. It still meant so much, and it was evident what a wonderful person she was, though she now despised me.

The rest of the afternoon went surprisingly well, and the mood picked up as the day went on, almost like nothing had ever happened. This was so great. Gosh, maybe Joan was forgiving me—a little, sort of, and I could just maybe move back in . . . someday, maybe.

It was coming on four o'clock, so I felt it best that I leave, especially since a rather favorable mood was ever present. Livia would start drinking soon, and her aggression and negativity would most likely target me.

Gina, Laura, and Mark were coming for dinner, and I was looking forward to seeing them and being with all my family again. However, I wasn't invited for dinner and it would be awkward having to get up and leave my own home and not spend the evening with them once they arrived. Nevertheless, I procrastinated leaving, and milked every moment being there. It felt good being home.

I soon left, and was now back at my little abode alone, as my family celebrated Christmas dinner without me. Christmas evening was especially tough, being estranged. When most people were celebrating the birth of Christ, I pondered my possible crucifixion.

I'd never felt such loneliness. Today was the realization of what I could possibly lose.

The work week slowly came, and I was back to—back to what?

CHAPTER 36
WHEN ALL THAT YOU LOVE IN LIFE SEEMS LOST, YOU NEED COURAGE TO SURVIVE

Several months had now passed and there had been little contact with Joan or the kids. What a teaser it had been, spending Christmas Day with them. Oh, how I wished I could erase parts of my life's path, as easily as the tide washes away the path footprints leave in the sand. Like no one ever walked on it, like none of my wrongdoings ever took place. If even just one tiny footprint, a baby's.

Easter Sunday was in a few days, and I looked forward to another family day of celebration alone. I figured I'd now better get used to this. However, I unexpectedly once again received a call from Joan's communicator, Diana. She asked if I wanted to come over for Easter brunch. I then said, "Uh, Di, are you asking me, or is your mom?" She then said, "No, it's Mom, really! I was overly delighted, to say the least. It was April, and months since I'd seen any of them. Even Mario and Livia were coming up from LA.

Sunday soon came and once again I had the jitters walking into the home I'd once lived in, but the atmosphere seemed as if there could be forgiveness in the air, at least I so hoped.

But it was so hard being there hiding such a deep, dark grizzly secret within me. I felt like two people, one, a husband and father, the other, a maleficent philanderer. I was a twin, and I am a Gemini, but those are not improprieties.

All these aberrant thoughts were rushing through my head as I sat there attempting to enjoy the day, making small talk with my in-laws. If they only knew of the secret agony and fear that was looming within me at that very moment while having to smile. If they only knew what a nefarious, sick son of a bitch their daughter had married.

In the back of my mind, it haunted me, knowing the baby was about due. But having had no contact for such a long time, I had no clue of the date, but did the math, and it was soon, very soon.

Attempting to forget it and put it aside for now, I noticed that Joan was surprisingly in a pretty good mood, so that immediately thrusted me into a state of joy for the first time in over a year and a half. It was as if none of this had happened. Or maybe she had decided to divorce me, and this was the last supper.

I was in the cowboy room with Mario and Livia, a large den, decorated with original cowboy paintings and pencil drawings, a warm, comfortable sitting area with a large, natural-stone fireplace that was now roaring, setting the mood for a wonderful afternoon on this chilly day in early April. The blossoms were in bloom and the crystal-clear sky above made the day magical. I so just wanted to relax and sit back in my old comfy chair and snooze for a while. The girls would be arriving soon to enjoy a fantastic late brunch that Joan was preparing, starting with all my favorite Italian cold cuts, salami, mortadella, coppa, and prosciutto di parma, served with fresh ciabatta bread; then cheese raviolis like they make on the Isle of Capri; then turkey with mashed potatoes and gravy. These were the meals I so remembered she cooked. I couldn't wait, and oh, it smelled so good!

I was now relaxed—well, at least more relaxed—and talking with Mario about the SF Giants and LA Dodgers game on TV. The phone then rang, and Joan picked it up in the kitchen. She then told me to pick up the other line in the den, while unbeknownst to me, she stayed on the phone.

I naturally didn't know who it was, since Joan hadn't said. I then wondered, *Who would be calling me here?* Well, I soon knew why she hadn't announced it. She hadn't wanted to alert her parents that it was Leone's father!

Oh my God. No, no, no! Not now, not today, not here. Why did her father call me here? Here? Oh, shit.

I trembled as I picked up the receiver. As I was saying hello, I was defiantly interrupted by an abrasive, deep-throated man's voice in French: "I want you to know you are now the father of an eight-pound-two-ounce baby boy. C'est tout." He then hung up.

I instantly sank to the floor on my knees, feeling faint, holding my head in my hands. I then immediately tried to make it not look obvious that I'd just received devastating, life-altering news.

My God, my wife's parents were just inches from me; our knees were almost touching, and their son-of-a-bitch son-in-law had just had a baby with another woman. Jesus Christ! They were both now looking at me strangely with stares of wonderment. I naturally couldn't let them get any hint of this. Having to think quickly, I then said, "Oh, that was my sales manager, telling me that one of my best salesmen quit!" They didn't question why I'd fallen to my knees, thankfully. I'd possibly recovered quickly enough, I hoped. Talk about an Oscar-winning performance, though a bit over-acted.

I knew, of course, the baby was going to be born soon, but not today. Why today? On Easter Sunday, while I was with my family, finally with my family, and at this moment?

My body was now weak as I hyperventilated, and my face was ashen and wrinkled with agonizing distraught. I then went into the kitchen and found Joan on the floor, folded up in the fetal position crying, crying her eyes out. She then glared at me with so much intense hatred. Oh, the hurt, oh, the hurt I'd inflicted upon her.

I will never forget that one moment in time. I just cried...

She didn't give me the chance to say anything. She just looked up and said, "So an eight-pound, two-ounce baby boy, huh? Well, congratulations, Kiki, you really did it this time! Leave. Leave and never return."

I have no clue what she told her folks or the kids. I know she didn't mention the baby. She possibly could have said one of my girlfriends had called; everyone knew about them.

I may have just been to the point of beginning to have gained her forgiveness, but that was over now. The baby had done it. My woman, my wife, my life, was gone. As Christians around the world celebrated the Resurrection of Jesus, I contemplated my Dissolution with Joan.

I went to my apartment and spent the remainder of the day crying my eyes out, knowing divorce was now surely imminent, and I also knew that all those in life I loved may have just been lost. But at the same time, I had hoped that even if there were a hundred reasons for her to give up, she would find just one reason to hold on. But why should she?

I was now isolated with serious thoughts of suicide. What the hell was there to live for? The worst of it, though, wasn't the thought of taking my life, it was realizing I wouldn't be remembered by the person I'd never forget. Well, the ridiculous self-serving thought of suicide soon diminished; there was too much to be sorted, plus it was the chicken shit route of escaping this mess, only to leave my family with the problem—excuse me, *problems*. I needed to face it head on, as hard as it would be.

So now the Union *was* striking, and it could destroy my business, but I didn't care. Joan *was* divorcing me, and that would destroy my life, and I did care. The baby allegedly *was* mine, and that will destroy all our lives. And most likely, I *was* going to lose my daughters, and that may destroy our family. I then released the hold on that vise in my head, and drank myself into oblivion. I *was* now an alcoholic.

My life was now like a psychic fair: canceled due to unforeseen circumstances.

CHAPTER 37
THERE CAN BE NO FAILURE FOR A MAN WHO HAS NOT LOST HIS PERSEVERANCE TO SUCCEED

Well, Monday morning finally came after the horrendous Easter weekend, and by now I had greatly increased the common stock value of Old Crow Straight Kentucky Bourbon. Not that I particularly like Old Crow, it was just the closest to my reach while at the 7-Eleven.

After arriving at my office and attempting to recover from a brain-numbing hangover with a half-dozen cups of black coffee and an equal amount of aspirin, I tried to get my head together to deal with the current matters at hand with the business.

The loss of sales, thus the loss of revenue, I was now experiencing due to the strike could end up being devastating, most certainly indeed, if permanent. One never knew. My company was now employing well over three hundred people between the five branches, with a payroll of more than $2,000,000 a year; that's one hell of a revenue that must be generated just to cover payroll, not to mention benefits, taxes, and the like. Having originally started the company with just that meager four hundred bucks was now a haunting plague. Built up cash reserves were now depleting and cash flow was straining—without significant start up operating capital strains the ability to persevere and perpetrate the marketing of a company, any company.

The obvious thought now occurred to me that I needed to start getting a whole lot leaner if the cash flow kept depleting at this rate. The corporation fortunately had no operating loans other than the line of credit used only during the salmon season, and there was a zero balance, thankfully. Remember the business principle of not flagrantly over borrowing?

Having said that, I knew the Santa Rosa production plant manager would fight me cutting back, as he had when I'd once told him we had enough King salmon for the smokehouse for the off-season. I told him not to buy anymore, and he totally ignored my direct order and sent a truck to Eureka to pick up twenty thousand pounds that we did not need—and the fishermen didn't wait thirty days to get paid; they got paid on the spot. That was $40,000 instantly taken from the cash flow. Most employees don't understand cash flow or how it works. They seem to feel there are always magically unlimited funds available. When I questioned him about it, he said, "Oh, you young kids don't understand the game. If we don't take the fish, we'll lose the boats. They'll go elsewhere." I said, "Joe, it's best we lose the goddamn boats than the business." It fell on deaf ears.

When sales decrease, profits obviously decrease; when profits decrease, cash flow decreases; when expenses increase at the same time due to non-essential costs, as we were experiencing, a company is obviously headed toward a state of non-profitability. Expenses then become the villain for acute, uncompromising, and immediate containment!

Controlling expenses is rather like flying an airplane—yes, I took flying lessons! Weight and balance are paramount. The performance of an airplane is influenced by its weight and overloading will cause serious problems. The same as with overloaded expenses within a business. It can and will cause serious performance problems.

Normally controlling expenses can be a relatively easy equation of balance, but with unpredictable outside forces, such as the unforeseen strike requiring interminable and exorbitant legal counsel, it then can be almost impossible and uncontrollable. The strike was the duck that was underwater. Remember, I warned about those deceptive ducks!

The remote branches that were well established and once needed several years ago, due to the volume emanating from the influx of all the new business and to further advance quality and profits, had now become a liability, being non-essential and unproductive due to the decreased sales.

However, it's not so simple of an equation to balance expenses when sales plummet so quickly at such an alarming rate. It is always easier to increase employment and costs parallel to rising sales than it is to decrease employment and costs due to declining sales. Many fixed assets such as extra trucks, buildings, and leases cannot be easily dispelled of overnight.

Now I would have to call my plays using impromptu thinking when making decisions. I would have to be rational and logical, and exercise perseverance to get through this trying time.

Having said that, implementing and executing the moves was going to be assiduous.

CHAPTER 38
EAT DESSERT FIRST ~ LIFE IS UNCERTAIN

There was so much uncertainty, and yet . . . and yet . . . you know, I couldn't even think straight. My mind wandered. There was too much going on, too much serious stuff. I had to deal with the guys on strike, the Union negotiations, my marriage that had fallen apart, and the kids not returning my calls. Sure, Gina was just a few feet from me, but we didn't talk much lately. And now the goddamn baby situation. And on top of all that, trying to hold on to the business—what little business I had left. Sales were still plummeting since my accounts feared they would have consequences imposed on them by the Union if they patronized Paladini.

Everything was all falling apart.

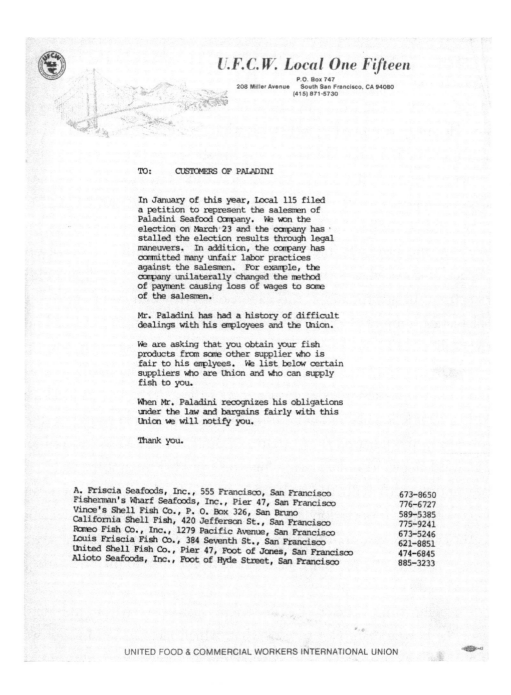

U.F.C.W. Local One Fifteen

P.O. Box 747
208 Miller Avenue   South San Francisco, CA 94080
(415) 871-5730

TO: CUSTOMERS OF PALADINI

In January of this year, Local 115 filed
a petition to represent the salesmen of
Paladini Seafood Company. We won the
election on March 23 and the company has
stalled the election results through legal
maneuvers. In addition, the company has
committed many unfair labor practices
against the salesmen. For example, the
company unilaterally changed the method
of payment causing loss of wages to some
of the salesmen.

Mr. Paladini has had a history of difficult
dealings with his employees and the Union.

We are asking that you obtain your fish
products from some other supplier who is
fair to his employees. We list below certain
suppliers who are Union and who can supply
fish to you.

When Mr. Paladini recognizes his obligations
under the law and bargains fairly with this
Union we will notify you.

Thank you.

A. Friscia Seafoods, Inc., 555 Francisco, San Francisco   673-8650
Fisherman's Wharf Seafoods, Inc., Pier 47, San Francisco   776-6727
Vince's Shell Fish Co., P. O. Box 326, San Bruno   589-5385
California Shell Fish, 420 Jefferson St., San Francisco   775-9241
Romeo Fish Co., Inc., 1279 Pacific Avenue, San Francisco   673-5246
Louis Friscia Fish Co., 384 Seventh St., San Francisco   621-8851
United Shell Fish Co., Pier 47, Foot of Jones, San Francisco   474-6845
Alioto Seafoods, Inc., Foot of Hyde Street, San Francisco   885-3233

UNITED FOOD & COMMERCIAL WORKERS INTERNATIONAL UNION

My controller called me into his office later that week and said the attorneys wanted a progress payment. I said, "What progress?" I then asked for the invoice to review it. Looking at it in detail, I noticed they were charging hours for the young paralegal they'd brought who was doing her internship. She just silently sat there taking notes during the negotiations while in the conference room the last few times. What the hell was this? I had to pay the law firm for them to teach their paralegals? "Bullshit, get them on the phone," I told Phil. By the way, why do attorneys state they are "practicing" law?

I then told the attorney assigned to my case that I had no intentions of paying for the paralegal taking notes. He abruptly replied that this was what they did. I said, "Well, maybe so, but it's not what I do. I'm taking it off the invoice, and if she shows up here again, be forewarned, I'm not paying for her. I then looked at my controller and said, "Great, so now we have to fight the goddamn attorneys supposedly defending us from fighting the goddamn Union!"

I always felt we—my controller and I—could handle the negotiations ourselves, but two factors intervened: first, my uncontrollable hair-trigger temper—yes, I admit to that; second, and more important, the lack of knowledge of the federal labor laws. So, I was stuck. I could see from the very first invoice from the attorneys that this expense factor would eventually propagate and be cash-flow problematic on top of all the other expenses I was incurring, but I had no choice.

The attorney called back a little while later, his voice harsh, most likely now upset with me. He said he had received numerous citations and claims against me personally, and as president of the corporation from the National Federation of Labor filed by the Union local, citing my non-compliance with several federal labor laws during the collective bargaining agreement sessions.

This was obviously in retaliation to my charges against them, I was sure. You see, it was all a game. We were awarded a court order stating that they couldn't disrupt the traffic flow in or out of the premises, and couldn't bully the replacement workers, thus losing any stranglehold they had with trying to disrupt the operation. That was against the federal labor laws, and they had to abide by it. So, the citations were an intimidation tactic. I later learned this is a tactical procedure they inflict on a company to attempt to persuade them to conform to their demands, a mere scare tactic. Well, I don't scare so easily.

Meanwhile, at night in my little studio apartment, just between you and me, I *was* scared. Certainly not of the boogie man. Not sure of what, which faction, but my gut would wrench. What facet of my life was causing that fear? Possibly the unknown, the unknown of what was in store for me the next day. Everything, and I repeat, *everything*, was in turmoil.

It also seemed as if I moved every three months from one apartment to another, possibly psychologically thinking if I didn't make it permanent, then it wouldn't be. It would then just be a temporary living arrangement. Oh yeah, sure.

Oddly enough, I owned an eighteen-unit apartment building in prime Burlingame on Trousdale Drive, but didn't want to be there, even though no one knew me other than the manager. I just wanted to be alone and a nobody.

The thought of reaching bottom and ending up down at the Tenderloin was looming within me, and it just could become a reality if I didn't pull myself and things together.

I remember driving to the Tenderloin in San Francisco one night to observe the unfortunate people walking around; actually, they were mostly just laying around. I don't really know why I was drawn to go there, maybe to envision my future if I didn't get it together, or possibly a subconscious scare tactic to jolt myself. I remember, though only momentarily, feeling a strange comfort in observing the simplistic life the bums had, if it was indeed a life those poor bedraggled forlorn men and women were living. It appeared they had no worries except where the next bottle of cheap wine would come from. No obvious responsibility, no one to worry about but themselves. And hey, free food at St. Anthony's dining hall. Ha. I wondered if they would remember I'd donated all that Veal Sinatra. They'd most likely not believe it had been me, anyway. I wasn't sure about sleeping on the streets, however; that was harrowing and nasty stuff. Who only knew what had transpired in their lives prior to having ended up there; maybe too much had been thrown at them, like it was at me now? I must say, it was a very sad sight, and a very sad night.

I know all this sounds melodramatic, and you most likely think I mentioned it for a reaction like "poor pitiful pearl" (Joan's phrase), but that's not true. I was in a terrible state of mind and feeling such intemperance. As I slowly drove looking at some of the unfortunates on the street, I noticed a few looking at me in the Jaguar. They may have thought I was looking down at them. If they'd only known. As far as me ending up in the Tenderloin, hell, the primary requirement was already in place: I was already a drunk.

Of course, most likely it wouldn't happen, I didn't think, but if nothing else, I now realized how life's path could result in one being there. I may have also had a death wish at the time. I may have also just been very inebriated . . . as they were. Nonetheless, it is said, "When you're down to nothing, God is up to something."

Back in the semi-sober real world I was facing every day, another month had passed, and still no progress with the negotiations. However, I was now deducing that the attorneys, upon approaching a possible settlement, would conceivably contrive to disrupt the negotiations without asking me, and would become argumentative, only furthering the distance between the Union and myself. Another tactic I unfortunately later learned was that some unscrupulous nefarious attorneys used to lengthen the negotiations for additional billing hours. Why, of course! If they settled, the cash register would close.

I was now wise to this and started taking over. I had to try to bring this to a culmination. If I couldn't convince the Union to back down on acquiring the salesmen, the bookkeepers, and the entire Santa Rosa plant, I would then legally, aggressively push towards going non-Union. They could continue to strike if they wished; it was currently ineffective anyway, and all the replacement workers were now as good as the once journeymen at twice the price that were walking around outside with their signs now at half-mast. Meanwhile, my sales were unfortunately also now at half-mast.

During all this, I sure missed talking with my three girls. I so needed to talk with them. It had been months, and my heart ached to know how they were and what was going on with them. I also wondered if they *knew*? Of course, I saw Gina every day, but we only talked business. It was obvious our relationship was strained with her mom and I separated; after all, she was the one who'd first gotten wise about my wandering ways. I couldn't push her into warming up to me. She was a very smart girl, and I sensed her pain. I had to call Laura and Diana, though. I waited until seven at night and called Laura at home, but she was working late at a design job. I then called Diana at the sorority house, but she was at the library studying. So, zip.

It was late one Sunday night about a year into the strike, and I was at my apartment with a dear friend, my old black bird, watching TV, and got a call from Joe, my Santa Rosa production plant manager. He said we had a fire at the plant!

This rocked me off my chair. How could that be? It had just been remodeled a couple of years ago, with all the updated fire code regulations installed. A nearby homeowner had supposedly called the fire department around ten at night. Joe said one of the firemen told him it appeared to be arson! Arson, but who in the hell—hmm, wait . . . The Union officials knew most of my fresh product was coming from there. Those goddamn dirty sons of bitches! It had come to this.

I then asked Joe how bad, and he replied, "Pretty bad." The entire west side of the building was badly damaged, and even worse, there was smoke damage throughout the building. I told him I'd be up there first thing in the morning. I then put the bird down since I needed a clear head the next morning. By the way, if you haven't picked up by now, the "old black bird" was my Old Crow from Kentucky.

Early the next morning when the arson inspector did his investigation, he found a broken window with the glass inside the plant with an accelerant where the fire had started. It was indeed arson!

I met Phil at the San Francisco distribution plant early on Monday morning, totally ignoring the strikers as I arrived. Surprisingly, a few noticeably nodded as if to say "Hi, boss." By now, most of them were tired of walking around in the cold, damp weather for twelve bucks a day, especially since it was obvious they weren't accomplishing anything. It was a sad sight. I also noticed there weren't as many of them. That was an odd feeling. Not sure if I was pleased, or if I missed them.

The name "Paladini," synonymous with seafood on the West Coast for well over 125 years, could now be in jeopardy of losing that acclaim if this strike wasn't settled soon. What the hell was the purpose of the strike anyway? Well, because I was being undermined by the Union with unwarranted demands, most likely since I wouldn't be intimidated by the mob, that just could "allegedly" be behind all of this.

It took well over the normal hour and a half to get up to Santa Rosa because we were in the height of the commute traffic. Arriving at the plant, I was shocked to see the devastation the fire had caused.

My obvious first thought was what impediment this would be to the operation. Salmon season would be starting soon, and we would be freezing hundreds of thousands of pounds, and now wondered if that could be possible. Meanwhile, to further confuse the equation, with the looming loss of sales, I also needed to figure how much of the plant's capacity would really be needed, and what volume of salmon we'd need—a difficult call to make.

Upon further examination of the premises, I felt we could still operate with only a few restrictions. We wouldn't need the entire plant any longer, anyway.

A funny scenario, if anything funny could possibly come of this: We had four thousand pounds of frozen salmon in the freezer slated for the smokehouse. Well, it naturally thawed since we'd lost power to the freezer and coolers. I called the insurance company and told the adjuster I needed to put in a product claim for two tons of salmon that was ruined due to the fire. Upon his arrival and approval of the claim and giving us the okay to dump it, I instructed the smokehouse manager to continue to finish thawing it . . . and smoke it. After all, it needed to be thawed anyway, and was already partially smoked! Well, at $3.25 a pound, that was a quick $13,000!

Oddly enough, one morning a couple of weeks later, two of my trucks were torched that were parked around the corner from the San Francisco distribution plant, and of course the strikers had no idea what happened.

So, we'd had several all-out fist fights with the strikers, a major fire at the Santa Rosa processing plant, and two trucks torched. They were playing dirty with serious, costly consequences. The Union's aspirations were now to attempt to blame and defame.

I recalled the words of Martin Luther King Jr: "The ultimate measure of a man is not where he stands in moments of comfort, but where he stands in times of challenge and controversary."

CHAPTER 39
"YOU WANT TO DO WHAT?"

Well, okay, so let's get back to another wonderful facet of my life at the time. One afternoon the following week, upon going up to my office after lunch, I found a certified letter on my desk that my secretary had signed for. It was from the Santa Clara district attorney's office. Of course, I knew what it was before I opened it.

It read that I had been petitioned by the courts to appear on such and such a day at the Santa Clara County Court House relevant to the case of paternity.

I then called my attorney and advised him of it, and he said to have someone drop it off at his office as soon as possible so he could prepare a response requesting DNA testing to determine the validity of the claim. He further said he was going to demand that the birth certificate not be filed until its credibility was established.

Foolishly, I'd never told my attorney that when I was told of the baby, I'd gone to my doctor to see if I was still virile, and I had been. Well, of course I was—I'm Italian.

You're not going to believe this: A few days later, Joan called me at the office and knocked my socks off when she said, "I want to see the baby!" "You want to do *what?*" I exclaimed.

Evidently, my secretary had told her about the certified letter from the DA's office. However, I don't think my secretary knew anything about the actual reason I'd received it. That is, I don't think so. She must have been talking with Joan all the while we'd been separated and kept her abreast of the goings-on at the office, such as any odd mail or phone calls. There had been none lately other than this, so Joan must have pieced the letter to the baby.

Well, upon my gasping for breath and asking her again what she'd said, she replied, "You heard me. Call Leone and make the arrangements!" And hung up. *Holy shit!*

So now I had to call Leone, who I hadn't talked to in well over seven months, and ask if we could come to her apartment and see the baby. I wasn't looking forward to talking with her, no less seeing her.

Of course, she didn't know about the DNA testing—yet. That notification would be coming from my attorney soon. Knowing her, she would freak out about me doubting the validity of who the father was.

Then I thought, *What the hell do I say to her? Especially with my wife there?* Can you imagine how frickin' uncomfortable this was going to be? Oh, God! Poor God, why do we always call upon him or her (must be politically correct) for such frivolous things? I'm sure God was busy with much more serious matters to attend to than my petty concerns. Funny, why do baseball players always look up after hitting a home run, like God assisted them? And why do women repeatedly scream, "Oh, God! Oh, God!" when having sex? Well, ignoring that claim about God being busy, I now screamed, *"Oh, GOD!"*

I was confused and scared out of my wits. I was soon to see the baby that could be mine by another woman, with that woman and my wife in the same room, the two of them right next to each other. And you wonder why I had a quadruple by-pass?

Why does my wife want to see the baby? Why? My God! There goes God again.

I braved up and called Leone. Oh boy, I didn't even get the opportunity to say hello or why I'd called before she went off, calling me every name you can think of, some I'd never even heard at the fish market. When she'd finally exhausted herself from malevolently calling me every negative descriptive noun in the dictionary, she then claimed I'd abandoned her and left her with all the bills, that she had been lonely during the pregnancy; and where had I been? I calmly interrupted and said, "So, how are you?" Well, that set her off again. "How in the hell do you think I am? I just had a baby and you were nowhere to be found. You never even called. I was all alone with *your* baby!" Then she started in again with, "You bastard." I interrupted her again and said, "Joan wants to see the baby." There was a hush . . . total silence . . . for the longest time. Then, obviously taken aback by this, she asked, "Why?" I truthfully replied, "I'm really not sure."

Then she started talking somewhat civilly, asking questions like what I had been doing, that she'd heard about the strike, and thought maybe Joan and I were separated.

When I acknowledged that we were separated, she started in again and asked, "Why didn't you call me then? I told her, "When I saw you the last time, I said it was over, and you refused to accept it. Then a couple of months later you called and said you were pregnant, and so here we are." I forget how the rest of the conversation went, but for sure not well.

I then repeated, "When can we come see the baby?" She reluctantly gave me a day and time. I then called Joan. She said she would meet me at the plant and we would then drive together to her apartment down in Mountain View.

Several days passed with several sleepless nights. I don't know if I was more nervous about seeing Joan, or seeing Leone, or seeing the baby. Most likely, all three, though I so didn't want to see the last two.

The day arrived, and it was about two in the afternoon. Joan showed up at the office and was talking nicely with the girls upstairs, then Gina came up, and everything seemed as if it was fine—that is, until I came out of my office and said, "Hi, honey." Joan just glared at me. Suddenly all the girls started shuffling papers on their desks, not knowing what the next reaction from her would be. I, of course, was cowering. I'm sure the girls enjoyed that. Joan then looked at me and said, "My car or yours?" I stammered, "W-w-well, mine."

I was now having a panic attack walking to the car. Then that sensation started at the base of my neck, stretching into the middle of my shoulder blades, then shooting to my arms; that odd vibrating feeling before both arms simultaneously went totally numb and I couldn't raise them to open the car door. Most likely it was a form of peripheral neuropathy, but I never saw a doctor regarding it. I know, not smart.

Joan noticed, and instead of the kind caring person that she is, she uncaringly barked out, "What's the matter? Are you nervous, little boy?" That's okay, I deserved it. I then replied, "I just have to wait a few minutes and it'll be okay." For just a moment while glancing her direction, I thought I may have picked up a glint of her possibly caring. Well, that hopeful glint was cut short by her saying, "Are we ready to go yet?"

We drove out of the parking lot and headed towards Leone's down the Peninsula. As we were driving, Joan broke the mute silence and asked, "So when did that start? The numbing in your arms?"

Ooh, hey, that's progress, I thought. *Yeah, sure.* We were headed to see a baby that could be mine, and not with her. *Sure, she cares about me.*

The absence of sound while driving to her house was unnerving. My nerves were raw and found the slight hissing of the wind passing against the driver side window annoying. It only accelerated the anxiety level of seeing Leone again, not to mention the baby for the first time.

At that moment we were like two sides of a coin; I couldn't face her, but we were still together.

Upon arriving, we parked directly in front of the platitudinous two-story apartment complex, then walked on the mostly uneven and cracked cement walkway that led to a center courtyard with apartment units facing each other. Joan sarcastically enjoyed being critical of the neglected and paltry landscaping on the way to her unit on the ground floor. It then took several attempts to ring the doorbell since my hand was shaking so violently. I couldn't believe I was standing in front of Leone's apartment . . . with my wife. Then it reoccurred to me, *Why, does she want to see the baby?* This was so aberrant, so strange.

The door very slowly opened, suggesting apprehension at allowing us in. It was now barely halfway open, but just enough to see Leone off to the side, almost hiding behind the door, as if in disbelief that we were both there. However, I'm sure more so because Joan was there. Then suddenly, I was facing Leone. She looked directly into my eyes, glaring at me with disdain while avoiding contact with Joan, and then hesitantly said, "Come in." She looked forlorn, without expression. I was so shaken that I hadn't opened the screen door and walked into it. Joan giggled. I'm sure she enjoyed seeing me so overwrought.

As we walked in, I immediately perceived the void of clemency or feelings from Leone.

The living room was just off to the left, and in the far corner, a white baby bassinet was visible. There wasn't much conversation going on; after all, it was in question why we were there, but it was certainly not a social visit. To say the mood was awkward and the circumstances uncomfortable, would have been an understatement. I was nervous, flushed and perspiring. A toxic environment was evident.

Can you please just try to imagine my state of mind at that moment? My heart rate must have been at three hundred beats per minute, experiencing arrhythmia. Sudden cardiac arrest would have been welcomed. My heart beat must have sounded like Native American war drums warning other tribes of an impending attack. Joan then suddenly broke the silent chill by saying, "Well, can I see the baby?" *Oh, shit.* Leone paused to answer, then with extreme hesitation said, "Okay." Just that one word: "okay." It was actually more like "ohh-kaaay," as her voice got noticeably higher.

The baby was naturally sleeping. He was a cute little boy, displaying an abundance of light-blond hair, and had big brown eyes. Oh, oh, brown eyes.

Upon my first seeing him, I couldn't and wouldn't let that feeling overcome me of the love you experience when first witnessing your own child. I didn't know whose child I was looking at other than Leone's at that point. I stayed stone-cold, without feelings.

Then Joan asked if she could pick him up. *Oh. My. God.* Yes, I needed to call upon God at that moment; this was not a frivolous request. I needed strength to just stand upright.

Leone then reluctantly and with a foul frown said, "Well, if you must . . . I guess."

If you can envision this scene. There was my wife, standing in an ex-girlfriend's apartment, about to hold a baby that could be her husband's—but not hers—by another woman. I stood there, now cowering.

You know, I must hand it to Joan. That took a lot of balls, and she had a hell of a lot more than I did at that moment.

She then held the baby in her arms. Witnessing that sight should have immediately induced chest pains, or so I wished. She then held the baby out from her and looked very closely at him. She was examining his every tiny feature. After holding him for a few minutes, she gave a curt smile while looking at Leone, and gave her back the baby. Joan then blurted out, "Okay, we can go now, Kiki."

We weren't there very long, but it was extremely intense for everyone those few minutes we had been there, except for the innocent baby who, of course, slept silently through it all.

We both simultaneously said goodbye, almost tripping over each other while rushing to leave. Thankfully, the screen door opened outward as I once again ran into it. Leone's reaction to the visit most certainly would have been to take offense, and to be confused as to just why we, especially Joan, were there.

As soon as we got into the car, Joan said something astonishing. *More about that later.*

Afterward, and while we were on the way back to the plant to pick up her car, she suddenly and without warning or indication said, "I want to sell the house." I knew what house, but diverted that thought by saying, "You mean Tahoe?" She said, "No, Hillsborough." All I could say was "Oh." There went my gut again.

Then she said, "That's *your* house, your party house, with the goddamn swimming pool shaped like a fish, with your white sandy beach and palm trees, your twenty-foot bar, and game room with all the toys, your three-car garage, and the parking area behind the tennis court for all your extra cars—oh, and what about the hot tub I caught you trying to fool around in with some of my lady friends?" I interrupted her and said, "So why can't we just sell the hot tub?" She then turned and gleamed at me with evil eyes. I cowered and said, "Okay, okay, enough. We'll sell it!"

The atmosphere in the car turned cold again . . . there was a hush.

By the time we got back to the plant, all the employees were gone. I asked her if we could go out for dinner. Yeah, you guessed right.

So, I went up to my office and got plastered. I had restocked the bar. About six o'clock, I left and carefully drove to my studio apartment to be alone. I was swamped with so many calls and surrounded by so many people during the day, yet at night it was just me and my aging friend, my black bird, my "Old Crow."

I was drinking, I was getting a divorce, I was not talking to my kids, I was dealing with the strike, and I was in a quandary about the baby.

My arms had just gone numb again, and I also had that severe pain in between my shoulder blades. I wondered if this was just from stress, or if it was little strokes, or possibly a sign of an impending heart attack. Heck, death would be welcome now...

CHAPTER 40
CRAZINESS, CONFUSION, CHAOS

I had to forget about the divorce and the baby for now and concentrate on bringing this god-damn strike to an end. The Union and my attorney's arguments had been relentlessly ongoing about irrational moot points, and we were at an impasse, while my attorney's bills were progressing. Somehow I had to end it before it was too late to recover.

The next morning, I called the attorney and said I wanted to bring the negotiations to a decisive pivotal conclusion, for better or for worse. He fought me, reciting several bullshit points that I no longer cared about. His answer was indicative of not wanting to close the cash register just yet. I clearly outlined to him why I wanted to end it, but also clearly let it be known that I absolutely would not allow additional departments or branches to join the collective bargaining agreement. I would, however, negotiate in a positive manner all other issues. I told him to just bring the negotiations to an end now, and let the Union convey both sides to the National Labor Relations Court for a resolution. I didn't give a damn about the small, exiguous extraneous items. I then firmly said, "That's it. I'm done. Just do it!"

Consequently, if the courts indeed decided I must conform to all the Union's collective bargaining agreement demands, we would experience critical increased labor costs with all the additional Union members that would inevitably devastate the ability to maintain profitability. Furthermore, and meanwhile, the non-Union minority-owned local wholesalers would continue paying their employees a pittance, allowing them to continue to undercut prices even more. As I said before, I didn't care what we paid our employees if *all* the wholesale distributors had the *same* labor costs, meaning *all* companies would then be Union shops. Equal costs would then demand and determine a fair and equitable overall wholesale price for the products for *all*. Having my salesmen and the bookkeepers in the Union, with the costly benefits package and the absurdity of a Unionized processing plant, would be my kiss of death. Thankfully I'd invested in some commercial real estate, because if I got overwhelmed and outraged, I would sell the business, or just shut the damn operation down and retire.

However, if the courts decided their demands were excessive, unreasonable, and unwarranted, I would have a non-Union shop. But what was the chance of that?

The court date was set to be sometime within the next sixty to ninety days. The strike and negotiations would have been ongoing for almost two years by then. It is said that I *shadowed* my grandfather, but he didn't have to deal with all this Union crap back in his day.

Now I had to wait a couple of months before they could do the DNA testing on the baby, then another few months for the results, and now also a couple of months or so before the court date deciding the future of my business. I also wondered how much longer it would be before I was served with divorce papers. My life now was filled with craziness, confusion and chaos.

The only thing that was currently for sure definitive was that my consumption of the elixir of life, the panacea or whatever the hell you want to call it, was ever-increasing. The anxiety of the unknown was taking its toll, and I now felt old.

Well, I did something stupid . . . really stupid. Oh, so you say that doesn't surprise you? The afternoon we saw the baby, I noticed he was in a dingy, run-down, and obviously used bassinet, and that bothered me. I was alone so much at night thinking so many negative thoughts that it became tiring and boring. My mind wandered, thinking of everything currently going on. I then thought, *I can't let the baby sleep in that old bassinet, no matter if he's mine or not.* I then called up Leone and said I wanted to buy a new bassinet for the baby. Well, naturally, she was at first floored to hear from me, but I made it very clear that my intention was to only see that the baby slept in a nice clean bed. I asked if I could go and buy a new one, but she said she would really like to go with me to pick it out. So, I said okay; after all, there was no sense in us being antagonistic. God only knew what the future may have had in store for me, or should I say *us*.

It was an odd feeling arriving at her apartment; after all, my wife had just been there a few weeks before. I was met by her that evening with an obvious outward climate of condemnation, and she manifested resentment, though she noticeably attempted to be somewhat civil under the circumstance.

While walking on the pathway to the street, she asked me to hold the baby. I stammered, "Y-y-y-y-you w-want m-me to, to hold him?" Oh, Christ. I really didn't want to. But I had to. What could I do? I didn't want her to slip and fall and hurt the infant.

As she passed the baby to me, I had an odd feeling; actually, I had many odd feelings. While I held him, my thoughts were running rampant. *Jesus, am I holding my child? I don't want another child. But what if he is my child? But what if he isn't? But why wouldn't he be?*

I couldn't think about that now. I would soon know whether he was or wasn't. I just wanted the baby to be in a nice bed. As soon as Leone got into the car, I passed the baby over to her, relieved I hadn't dropped him, and further relieved he wasn't in my arms anymore. I fretted having feelings for him. We drove to downtown Mountain View to a shop that sold items for infants and young children. I let her pick out the new bassinet and paid for it. Then I asked if there was anything else she needed for the baby. She then pleasantly said she could use some more diapers and Enfamil baby formula. *Jesus Christ, I'm fifty, and shopping for fucking baby formula.*

Arriving back at her apartment, we talked about the separation, and where I was living, the strike, and just stuff; it wasn't even ten minutes, and I left. It appeared as if she was copacetic with things now, but I didn't know how to play this. I was still awaiting word from my attorney when to advise her we wanted the blood test. I could only imagine the scene there would be when that occurred.

Just so you know, I didn't view what I'd done as nonsensical, but more as just having simple compassion. However, it is said that most wealthy men have more dollars than they do sense!

Well, I did something stupid again, and this time it had nothing to do with compassion. Since Joan was giving me signals that she was divorcing me, and wasn't warming up, I called Simone and asked her out for dinner. I was bored and lonely and scared of the many things coming up in my future. I had feelings for her; she was an extremely nice, down-to-earth girl, and had once adored me, and oh, did I need that adoration now. If that was still possible. At first she was adamant about not wanting to even have a conversation with me on the phone, but after a good half hour I convinced her to just have a casual dinner with me, and she reluctantly agreed.

I picked her up a few nights later. It was unnerving, seeing her after all this time, but she soon warmed up, somewhat. It even seemed as if she still may have even cared a bit, even though she'd called me a sociopath on that last night. We went to a restaurant in San Carlos. It didn't matter anymore if we were seen; all of Joan's friends knew she and I were separated and headed for divorce; no need to be stealth any longer. After dinner, we headed back to her house, and as

I walked her to the door, she didn't invite me in, much to my disappointment, but I convincingly insisted.

We sat and talked about everything that had transpired since we'd last seen each other. I then tried to kiss her, but she pushed me off and said, "You're still married." Let down, I attempted to reason and said most likely I would be in divorced soon, but she didn't weaken. I so missed her genuine caring and adoration.

No one liked me now.

She then said she was moving to Santa Fe, New Mexico, the following month to go back to college to get a degree in art and design. I commented, "Wow, that's impressive. I'm so happy for you." Though I wasn't happy she was moving away.

I was saddened, because if Joan indeed divorced me, I would have liked to have continued seeing Simone. We'd always had fun and gotten along so well. "When you're happy you enjoy the music; when you're sad, you understand the lyrics."

So back to my apartment, I went. I was now living in a triplex, a step up from the dingy places I had been living. Yep, I had moved again, and every time it got just a little bit nicer. I don't really know what I was looking for. I'd never lived alone, and I get bored and tired of things so easily.

Damn, I really missed my girls. Gina and I were conversing a little bit better, but there was still a wall between us, and I couldn't and wouldn't want to try to climb over it. We naturally talked business at work all day. She was doing a great job, and I was very proud of her. She's an extremely smart girl and a good business woman. I was going to make her general manager soon, since she'd learned the business so quickly and could now do just about everything. I also wanted to hug her and tell her I loved her so many times, but the business environment just wouldn't allow it, not that she would have let me.

I also wished she had just some glimpse of what I was going through at the time. Maybe she would have understood my foul moods and my bastard-like manner. Yet, she could never know.

So, I picked up the phone and called Laura. Luckily, she was home. Surprisingly, she was cordial to me. I said *cordial*, not nice, because that's the way it was. We talked about just stuff for a while. I then told her how much I missed her. There was silence, but I thought I heard her crying. Then I said, "I love you." She simply said, "Goodnight, Dad."

I called Diana and she was thankfully in her sorority house. She said, "Daaaad, how are you?" That response was happily accepted with open arms. I replied, "Well, kid, I've been better." She then commented, "Yes, I bet you have." Then I said, "I really miss you." She didn't respond. We then talked for a good fifteen minutes as she wisely tried to console me. She suggested I ask her mom for forgiveness, then asked if I'd learned from my mistakes. Oh boy, she was tough, but she was good. After all, she was soon to be a licensed family therapist. She then said, "Well, call again, Dad, and maybe we can talk further." I then said, "I love you." There was a dial tone.

None of the girls knew about the baby. None of the girls said, "I love you, Dad." Most certainly, none of them had any further respect for me, and that was understandable. I wonder if Hitler had had a daughter, would she have respected him?

I think what hurt the most, and what really drove the point across of just where I was in my girls' lives at the time, was Father's Day. Yes, I received a card from each of the girls, but they'd only signed their names inside the cards. The word "love" was obviously missing. And yes, of course, each card said "Happy Father's Day" in print, but the word "happy" should have been crossed out.

Respect is something a child usually wants from a parent, not a parent, from a child. Yes, of course there is the inbred love and respect for a parent, but that can have a propensity to be vulnerable.

Maybe the purpose for wanting to talk with my daughters, was that I needed to hear their voices—before they found out about the baby. I doubted if I would ever hear their voices again once they knew.

Let's get back to the business and the reality of facing the fact we'd lost many prime accounts due to the upheaval from the strike. We needed to start the challenging yet necessary cut backs. I had planned carefully so to allow for each cost reduction to be eventually reversed in the likely event we were successful in reacquiring the accounts.

When cutting back due to a slow down, *never cut back on quality*—never—and *never cut back on service*, and more importantly, *do not change what originally allowed your success*. Cut back on labor and non-essential items, but only where it won't affect the company's performance to the customer.

I had a meeting with my processing plant manager in Santa Rosa and told him within thirty days I would be closing the operation, though most likely it would only be temporary. The intention was to attempt to lease out the plant for a year, or until business resumed as it once was. It should be relatively easy to lease out since it was fully equipped, and I'd already previously had an inquiry about it. Coincidentally, I had been contacted a few months prior by a Japanese sea urchin roe company that wanted to lease out a portion of the plant, but I now intended to lease them the entire building for one year, then go on a month-to-month basis until ready to take it back to start up Paladini Fisheries again.

The plant was owned personally and was leased to the corporation, so now it would simply be leased to another credit-worthy company, and for a tidy sum, I must say.

This maneuver would take the pressure off the cash flow of the processing plant, because now I wouldn't have to pay the rent to me. Payroll and all other costs would also be suspended until the operation resumed next year. It was totally legit and within the labor laws to reduce overhead due to a slowdown. A slowdown they, the Union themselves caused!

If you can smile when things go wrong, you have someone in mind to blame.

Are you cognizant of what had just transpired? I bet you totally missed it! It was two-fold. Not only were the operating costs slashed, but I removed the employees that the Union wanted to be part of the collective bargaining agreement. Bingo! They were now gone! That equation, that segment of their demand, had now magically vanished. *Andato via...* Nothing further to unionize now existed at the Santa Rosa processing plant—a result of planning and being shrewd.

To explain: I totally removed the Union's largest stronghold contract demand with their attempting to gain so many members in Santa Rosa. This would now protect my distribution business, the real money maker, where I'd started. I removed the major target and we were now down to just the basics of a contract for San Francisco.

So, what did the Union accomplish? They caused the elimination of over two hundred jobs. Two hundred innocent men and women were happily working. Some full time, some part time. But working.

So, Mr. Union and *Mr. Hat*, how does that make you feel? Did that warm the cockles of your heart. To use a pun. I'll get back all the business once I defeat you, and my distribution business will be stronger and more profitable than ever! Thought you were playing around with just a punk kid, huh?

Remember when I gifted my competitor with the white elephant, the salesman who was behind attempting to organize my sales department? Well, now two major points of contention, the processing plant, and the mole in the hole in the sales department, are gone! *Ciao...*

Though not part of the bargaining agreement, but tied to the processing facility, were the three receiving stations. They also had to temporarily be dispensed with since they were no longer needed.

Oh, and yes, also several hundred salmon and crab boats and a dozen or so drag boats would have to find another company to deliver their products to—a ripple effect. Nonetheless, these were all reversible, when and if I so deemed to do so.

There wasn't much I could do in the San Francisco distribution plant to reduce expenses. I had to maintain the quality and service and keep most of the now experienced men. I might only temporarily lay off a dozen or so drivers, but no more than that, so as not to reduce service. It was a nice feeling having that freedom, and the Union couldn't do a damn thing about it since they weren't in the Union.

So far, well over 225 people were now out of work as a result of the two-fold decision to cut back and eliminate the Union's targets. It was, however, also necessary to stay solvent. Having a simpler, refined-and-defined operation, focusing only on distribution, and by carefully controling expenses paralleling sales, can result with similar net profits as having a larger operation.

That precise balance between expenses versus sales must and always be carefully and constantly monitored.

Now feeling some relief from the drain on the cash flow, I was ready and waiting to go to court to fight this sinister Union conspiracy, especially since their major targets had now been obliterated.

CHAPTER 41
YESTERDAY'S HISTORY IS TOMORROW'S MYSTERY

It was early on Monday morning a couple of months later when my personal attorney called and said he had received a response from the DA's office approving the DNA testing. He further said a copy of the letter had been sent to the baby's mother requesting testing, and she should therefore bring the baby to the laboratory in San Jose on such and such date. I also had a date set that same day to have my blood drawn. Oh boy! The s-h-i-t would hit the fan now!

Well, lo and behold, it was midday of the same day when my private line rang. There she was, screaming her head off, calling me every name under the sun, accusing me of doubting her faithfulness, and she went on and on and on. She finally hung up, but her last words were "You fucking bastard!" Then she called back a few minutes later and said, "I bet your Mafia friends will get involved and the real results never revealed!"

What the hell? Where had that come from? I'd fought the Mafia! Oh yeah, that's right. She'd always thought I was in the Mafia, and I just let her believe it for kicks.

So only time would now tell the truth. I had little doubt that the results would prove to be any different other than what I fearfully suspected. The only tiny tinge of a doubt that I had was my recalling what she'd had said when I told her we were through. She said, "Do you have any idea how many guys want me?" Just maybe she'd started dating right away in retaliation, possibly seeking some kind of reciprocal justice, validating the concept of proportional revenge. Like equality for suffering and hurt. *Hell hath no fury like a woman scorned!* Even the fires of hell couldn't compare to the wrath of an angry woman. But having said that, it was all just wishful thinking.

It's strange how things seem to always come together at the same time. My father used to say, "Problems come like bananas—in bunches." *Well, Dad, I have a truck full of Bananas right now!* That same afternoon I received a call from my labor relations attorney saying we had a court date set in two weeks. It wouldn't be long now until we found out if the Union had any factual basis of authenticity to call the strike.

Meanwhile, we put, as Joan called it, my "party house" up for sale. But when we'd added onto the house, it was our girls that we'd really thought of. The game room was designed for parties of course, but not just for my parties; it was to keep our daughters home and enjoy the dance floor with the surround sound and all the games, the air hockey and pinball machines and jukebox, and that magnificent stainless-steel, ultra-modern pool table, all the stuff teenagers loved. The pool was certainly for the kids. Okay, so it was shaped like a fish, but abstractly, somewhat, and the white sandy beach with the palm trees and the partially sunken row boat—the kids loved Hawaii, so I'd tried to emulate it for them.

Okay, okay, so the hot tub had been my idea, but they were "the thing" back then. And yeah, I knew, when I'd been drinking I'd gotten out of order a few times while in it. "So, then let's just sell the hot tub," I'd suggested. She then disturbingly replied, "You already said that, Kiki, and it's not funny." Whoops.

What greatly disturbed me, though, was when signing the papers to put it on the market, she made the comment, "We can split the proceeds from the sale. I want to get a tiny house that I can wrap around me, and you can get yourself a big fancy-shmancy playboy pad in Hillsborough." I wasn't exactly sure what she meant by a house that she could wrap around her. I envisioned she meant a small house just to herself. Of course, it was very clear what she meant by my "playboy pad."

I guessed that meant there was no chance of a reconciliation. Why would I think there would have been, anyway? It's odd how life works. I'd heard of these situations happening to men, but to other men, not me. Why do we always think things only happen to other people?

I was in a quandary. My thoughts were running wild, thinking that if my wife bought another home without me in mind, I'd never get her back. She would start a new life without me. *Will she date? Christ, she's beautiful. Oh, shit. I can't bear that thought. I'm more frightened now than I have ever been in my life. I'm about to really lose my wife.*

It was now the work week again and I had to try to put these thoughts aside. I had to; I was being hit by too many things and they were all pulling me in different directions. I still had to try to save the business, but I didn't give a shit about the business anymore. Now I wished I never had it. Anyway, I did what I had to. I brought it back, bigger and better, to prove—to prove what? That I could do it? Was that just for me, for my own ego?

No, goddamn it! I had a family to support and didn't know any other way; it was survival. I'd been blessed with my grandfather's business knack, and it came easy.

As these thoughts were spinning in my head, it made me want to drink; to get drunk, to hide.

A couple of weeks had passed, and it was now the day of the court hearing. As I approached the courtroom on the second floor of the San Francisco County Municipal Court, a sign outside the door read "San Francisco Union Local XXX versus Paladini Seafood Company. Judge XXX Presiding."

I gulped hard as I walked into the court room, my stomach churning. My attorneys were sitting near the front. As I joined them, they smiled and greeted me like we were attending a cocktail party. I guess this was all fun and games for them. Well of course it was; the clock was ticking at $550 an hour for each of them, and that's $1,100 bucks an hour. If I coughed or sneezed, delaying the procedure for just one minute, it cost me $18.33—that was a good dinner back then!

The president of Union Local XXX and the Union rep for my plant was present, plus their two attorneys, who acknowledged my presence with persnickety nods; however, a slight hint of respect and fear emanated from them. Possibly that was just an illusory assumption on my part.

The proceedings started with the judge calling the attorneys to a brief meeting in front of the bench. It wasn't revealed what that was about, but appeared to be just a formality.

A fault I have—yes, there are obviously many—is that my mind wanders off during matters like this. I remember being in school and the teacher calling on me to answer a question regarding what he or she was teaching, and I had no clue what the subject was, because I was off somewhere else. Anyway, all the time the attorneys were presenting their case, all I could think about was Joan and my girls, and that I no longer really cared how this was going to turn out. It seemed as if I'd lost my affection for the business and had lost my fight to continue. I was a beaten man, not business-wise, but in character and esteem.

Why would I even need the damn business anymore? I thought. My thoughts then brought me to thinking of selling or just closing. That inbred virtue to be so *driven* had vanished. My thoughts were all over the place, and I wasn't listening to the court proceedings.

The rep from the Union was now called to the stand by my attorney, and I felt I'd better get focused. It had been a long hard fight to get here, though that energy had waned. I suddenly perked up when my attorney questioned him about why he was so intent on causing the Paladini

Seafood Company so much unnecessary grief. He then abruptly stood up while timorously tucking in his shirt hanging out of his pants, evidently forgotten after taking a dump, and screamed, "Have you ever seen his palace of an office?!"

What the hell was that statement about? I wondered. How bizarre! The second floor is the accounting and executive offices. Sure, it's a contrast from the production floor area, but we also don't handle frickin' fresh fish up there. And of course, compared to the shacks on the wharf, I guess the second floor is nice, but my office, a palace? Come on. This guy is nuts, or just plain jealous. But why?

As I said many times prior, was he—were they—prompted by a sordid, unmentionable force?

Oddly, I suddenly felt energized again after absorbing the impact of his comment. That temper overcame me and the adrenaline flowed, and I got the shakes, and as you know by now, that isn't good! I then stood up and loudly exclaimed, "That's all horse crap! State the real reason! Put me on the stand!" The judge started banging on his gavel repeatedly, banging, banging. "Mr. Paladini," he said, "I will not tolerate any outbursts from you!" I then stood up again and this time, even louder, said, "But that statement about my office is not only baloney, but a diversion from the true reason for the strike, Judge—uh, excuse me, I mean, Your Honor." Bang, bang, bang, went the gavel again! Ignoring the judge's order, I then said, "Anyway, what in the hell does that have to do with the Union contract?" The judge then promptly stood up erect and said, "Mr. Paladini. Sit. Down. Or. I. Will. Have. You. Removed. From. This. Courtroom!" Christ, I felt as if I was back in high school again. That's okay; I'd made my point!

You ask why I stood up and made a scene? Well, first of all, I felt that if I had been the attorney I once wanted to be, I would have most likely been dramatic in a court room. You must be dramatic to make and get a statement across! I hate mundane, marshmallow-type, boring people, especially attorneys who just sit there like wimps. And after all, judges are people, too. They pee just like we all do. You must make your point, and at the right psychological time, or it just may go unsaid, missing the opportunity.

I also felt if we could play up the nonsensical issues, we could get them off track on the serious issues—a diversionary tactic to confuse the issue! Uh, hum... like my closing the production plant so they couldn't organize it.

The judge then turned on the rep, who was now cowering on the stand with his shoulders crumpled in, and his hands crossed, and questioned him. "Just what did you mean by calling Mr. Paladini's office a palace? And what does that have to do with the case being tried?" Ha! See, told you! Who was the lawyer here? The judge then further went on to outline that employer-employee relationships are always asymmetrical in terms of power and views, and most of the time, in lifestyles as well, and that we weren't there to discuss the amenities in Mr. Paladini's office or elsewhere.

I felt that knocked some of the proprieties out of the Union's case and was content to see that the judge wasn't taking sides. If anything, he, or was it in fact me, had set the tone for the rest of the trial.

Now, if I'd been the attorney, I would have followed that tone, the format, that the judge had set forth and pursued the case in that fashion. It was to our benefit; it exhibited weakness in their case as far as the cause to strike. Meanwhile, I had to sit down and shut up, but I nudged my attorney, hoping he would catch on, but he didn't.

I couldn't help thinking that in a court of law, you must pick up on the judge's thought process if it is indeed advantageous to your case, and play on it, especially if trial by judge and not by jury. I wondered if they taught that in law school. It made sense to me, and it was logical. See, there's logic again. Besides, shouldn't all law stem from logic and common sense?

The rest of the day, the attorneys argued their case, with the Union accusing me of interfering with the National Labor Laws by claiming that I allegedly tried to coerce my Union members, and blah, blah, blah. It was all a diabolical deception. It was difficult for me to run a business and not go against their rules since the constraints were so tight. If I offered the strikers a hot cup of coffee or an umbrella on a cold rainy day, it was of course, viewed as coercion and not kindness.

They also claimed I shut down the Santa Rosa processing facility to avoid Union rule, a direct violation of the NLR laws. Possibly, they were right about that one. *Shhh.* However, my claim was that they forced me to shut it down because they'd cut off my access to the major chain store sales, thus reducing my volume, making the facility non-essential. It was basically true, in part. While on the stand, I believe I proved that point. It was a basic simple equation of survival, also a diversion from the truth.

The trial continued for three days. We had one good day, one bad day, and a so-so day, so it was anyone's call how the judge would rule. It was said that it could take up to a month before we would have the ruling.

Well, we might survive the hurricane but drown in the storm surge. We might survive the Union's demands of the processing plant since the operation was now closed but might drown at the distribution plant due to an impervious and impractical binding contract. Now we wait.

Let's get back to the baby caper. The day came that I had to get the blood test for the DNA testing. I hoped I didn't run into Leone with the baby, because there would just be screaming—not from the baby, but from her, at me.

I arrived at the laboratory in San Jose and was given several pages of forms to fill out. I hadn't expected that. I'd thought it would be simple; walk in, roll up the sleeve, take some blood, and it would be done, but things are never that easy.

The technician said the mother and baby had just left. Whew, that was a relief. She then made an odd comment. She told me that the mother had asked if the test results could be rigged, meaning falsified. The technician had of course answered absolutely not, but as she was explaining how it was impossible, she was rudely interrupted by the mother, who'd said the father was in the Mafia and could get to anyone.

It's funny, I recall the technician being a bit nervous when taking my blood. She was probably afraid to hurt me after hearing that! I assured her I was not in the Mafia; however, as a joke, as I was leaving, I asked her if she had anyone she wanted eliminated. She giggled but gave me an odd look at the same time, probably wondering if I really was, or was not one of "them."

I then went to my apartment. This time I had moved (again) into the De Sabla Apartments, a twelve-story building cornering El Camino Real and De Sabla Road in San Mateo. It was uncommonly located near one of the Peninsula's most exclusive neighborhoods with private homes. It was built in 1950 on the corner of the once entrance to the former historic estate of Eugene J. De Sabla. The front door of the apartment led you out onto a charming, tree-lined, gently winding street that led into Hillsborough where I'd once fondly lived. The homes were most attractive, and several beautiful as you approached the extensive properties of Hillsborough, with their stylish, manicured landscaping and tall, mature trees that cascaded over the narrow roadway. I remember looking out from my apartment window thinking it would be a great street to live on. Anyway, I doubted there were any ostentatious playboy pads in the neighborhood, as Joan had acrimoniously mentioned.

Another day, another night passed. The clock was ticking, and I was punctiliously waiting to be served by Joan's attorney with divorce papers. My gut also wrenched, vigilantly anticipating the court's ruling about the Union. And appreciably even more dire, the DNA results. I was living in my hermit kingdom, shrouded with puzzling enigmas.

It was a wonderfully tormenting night as I aimlessly stared out of my fifth-floor window at the beautifully illuminated full harvest moon. What a great escape that would be. I now wondered if there were any apartments under construction on the lunar surface yet. Was I depressed? Was I drunk? Why would you even ask?

I then started talking to "Crissy." No, not another girl, for Christ sake. She was my dependable feathered friend, my old black Crow. You know, looking at her picture, I just noticed she wasn't looking any older than when I'd first met her. Yet it said right there on the label "aged in oak barrels." Maybe that was her secret? You know, when you're drunk and lonely, that's what happens: You start talking silly stuff to a similitude of a bird. But truthfully, I so wished I could conquer tensions without her, but her *spirit* (distilled alcohol) always lifted me and helped me through the forlorn desolate nights.

I had good taste, however—at least in bourbon—Old Crow is one of the oldest and the most historic bourbons and was served in the homes of many U.S. presidents. It's said that General Ulysses S. Grant received more than his fair share. See? However, I wonder if Ulysses had a name for his bird.

CHAPTER 42
WHEN LIFE GIVES YOU A HUNDRED REASONS TO CRY . . .

The days now boringly consisted of arriving at the office and immediately consuming several cups of black coffee and downing several aspirins to try to dispel the hangover that Crissy unwittingly seemed to demand I have, then procuring a pen and clicking the "on button" in my head to face the ensuing day.

The sales were now horrible and the cash flow even worse, and I had this monstrous building with a sizable mortgage. The only ray of encouragement was that the chefs were starting to call asking if the strike was over, and if not, when. They expressed they weren't satisfied with their supplier. I also received a call from the Safeway buyer asking about the strike.

In the meantime, talk about a Catch-22. Oddly enough, not too long ago, I'd thought of expanding the building even further by buying the property next to it. I now wished the plant would catch fire and burn to the ground. What a great excuse to shut down. Too bad, though, when I'd designed the building, we'd taken all the necessary precautions to prevent just that.

I was mentally exhausted and didn't care about the business anymore. I actually hated it. It was painful to just show up at the place I'd once loved and was so proud of, and now wished a giant rodent would come and swallow it. Hmm, wonder if big Rick was still over at the other place?

You're most likely getting tired of hearing the same old shit by now, aren't you? Well, so was I. This had all been going on for too long now, and I wanted to end it all just as much as you don't want to hear about it anymore.

Yep, every day at five o'clock, it was the same ole, same ole: that disgusting ritual of driving over to Third Street and picking up my bird, sometimes, two. Hell, I could have used a flock. Funny, Crows actually live in a group called a murder. Maybe that was Crissy's intention. That'd be okay. What a sad state. I couldn't help but laugh that the nice African-American man behind the liquor counter now called me by my first name, like I was a respectable social acquaintance. What a diametrically opposed indication of reverence when I had such disdain for myself.

When driving home, it was amazing that between being blotto and color blind, I could distinguish the color of the lights at a stop light. Thankfully, I remembered that the red was on the top and the green was on the bottom—or, uh, was the red on the bottom? I knew the amber was always in the middle, though. Right?

Meanwhile, one Friday afternoon after work, not wanting to be alone, I called up Simone in Santa Fe to see how she was doing. She had been on my mind for some time. We chatted for about an hour and she was quite congenial. I asked if I could fly there to see her and she surprisingly said sure, she would like to see me, but only after she quizzed me about my marital status, and I had explained I was separated and was just waiting to be served—and I didn't mean a meal.

She picked me up that Saturday just before noon at the Albuquerque International Sunport Airport, and though her welcome was rather cool, the temperature was hot. The contrast of leaving the damp, fog-ridden San Francisco Bay Area and arriving in this heat was unexpected. The bareness of the landscape was a sharp contrast to California. Everything was so dry and lacked foliage.

As she was driving, I couldn't help but notice that she obviously had no bra on. Her nipples were suggestively piercing through the thin, light-weight sundress precariously held up with a single strand over her neck, and her breasts were bewitchingly cradled loosely within. It caused me to speculate that her libido for me could still be lustfully aroused. Well, that got a few testosterone vessels pumping, but I held it in remission. This was just a platonic friendship now; none of that stuff.

We went to lunch in the square in quaint Santa Fe at a typical outdoor southwestern restaurant festooned with overstated, brightly colored umbrellas that shaded the tables from the blazing sun. As she walked in front of me while going to our table, I could see the outline of her long legs through the sheer sundress revealing her curvaceous body. Like the mythical primordial giant cyclops with his single massive eye focusing on his prey, my lustful thoughts started focusing on my covetous appetite, and I'm not talking about the chips and salsa.

While sitting under a phosphorescent-orange umbrella, a slight breeze attempted to cool us as we munched on tortilla chips. As we attempted to catch up from a long siege of not conversing, she brought me up to date on her going back to college to study art and design, her life-long passion. I was pleased to hear that she was going to make something of herself, and especially in such a highly regarded career. As she enlightened me of her current life, I couldn't help but notice that her dress was lifted on one side, exposing her upper leg, my favorite erogenous zone on a woman. She must have noticed me looking, because she tapped me on the knee and said, "Kiki, my eyes are up here!"

After lunch, she asked if I wanted to go for a swim; she had told me to bring swimming trunks since she had rented a house with two other girls that had a pool. Upon arriving at her home, I expected to meet the other girls, but they were working that weekend and wouldn't be home until late.

We put on our bathing suits then met out by the pool. It was very small, as was the house.

I couldn't keep my eyes off her. She was wearing a micro-string bikini and her firm yet soft breasts revealed more than a hint of their shapely form, and her accentuated nipples were scarcely covered from the lack of nylon fibers. The bottom was a thong, and the front, only the size of a pirate's eye patch. She looked sexier than a Victoria's Secret model; however, if she had any secrets, they weren't very well covered. Her firm, tanned body was so sensually exposed, my sexual proclivity for passion was now running recklessly rampant with the desire to make love to her. Forget that platonic shit!

We lay upon the chaise lounge—yes, singular—around the pool, the scorching sun beating down with such stimulating intensity, it seemed as if the incandescence of the abysmal heat manifested my need for intimacy. I so longed for the touch of a woman.

She then asked if I would put sunscreen on her back. I, of course, willingly obliged. She then untied the backside of her bikini, exposing her evenly tanned bare back that now extended all the way down to her buttocks. As I rubbed the oil on her back, I couldn't help but bring my hands around to her front, attempting to caress her breasts, only hesitating when she commented that her back didn't stretch that far in front. Her seemingly endless legs urged to be touched, and I satisfied that need.

Jokingly, I asked if she wanted me to do the front, and she surprisingly said, "Maybe later!"

Escaping the raging heat at the pool was challenging. The tall palm trees gently swayed from the soft breeze that attempted to cool, but only fanned its intensity even more. The sun felt as though you would blister within moments without shade or the refreshing effects of the water.

Sometime a bit later, the wind picked up and the fierceness of the heat eased as high swirling thunderclouds shielded the sun and darkened the sky. While we were in the pool watching this dramatic display of nature, I came from behind her and kissed the back of her neck, then slowly brushed my lips down one side as she turned her head, sharply exposing the full bareness of her neck now craving for more. My hands, once on her tiny waist, slipped upward under her bikini top and caressed her breasts. Her wet nipples were now lasciviously hard, penetrating the palm of my hands as if a semaphore for passion. I then gently turned her around and softly and tenderly kissed her, then suddenly enraged with fervor, entered her mouth with intense deep hard kisses, wanting to evoke her pent-up passion for me.

The already thermal temperature of the water felt as if it turned into steam as the sweat poured from our bodies. Her breath was now ever-so-warm, as if an inferno was burning deep within her. With her breathing heavy, our lips sealed in a suffocating, vise-like grip. We then emerged into that same deep void of salacious ecstasy that we once had. While gasping to take a breath, she started pulsating in spasm-like motions, swinging her nearly naked body backwards and forward in complete ecstasy, wanting me to violate her.

It was obvious we still had that zealous, sensual desire for each other. My lips now aggressively exploited her neck as I inched down and exposed her breasts, then gently cradled her nipples within my mouth. The eroticism was carnal and intense. This wasn't just lascivious foreplay we were experiencing; we had deep feelings for each other. I then pulled her out of the pool and headed for the bedroom. I could no longer wait to experience what I had so missed and desired for so long.

With her breasts now bare, I furtively slipped off her bikini bottom and threw her onto the bed. Without hesitation, I descended upon her and engulfed every inch of her still wet, naked body. Her legs were now open, eagerly wanting me to penetrate her. She was so moist, so ready, oh-so-ready—but then suddenly, without provocation, stopped and pushed me away. She then said, "Tell me again you're getting a divorce!"

"Not now," I said. She then sat up and shouted, "What do you mean 'not now'? You're not getting a divorce now?" I said no. She then screamed, "*No?!*" I then replied, "Oh, damn, I mean no, that wasn't what I meant! Jesus, honey, you were so ready."

There are only two-four letter words that are offensive to men: "don't" and "stop"—that is, unless they are used together!

Well, the mood suddenly changed. She got serious and refused to continue, assuming I was leading her on and was not really getting a divorce. What then totally blew my mind was her next comment. She said, "So, tell me about the baby!"

Holy shit! How in the hell did she know about the baby?

"God made man before woman so as to give him time to think of answers to their questions."

I gingerly asked, "Uh, so you know?" She said, "Joan called and told me all about it just before I moved. She said Leone's father called you the day she threw you out, supposedly for good." I lamely replied, "I'm sorry. It's not something I wanted, believe me."

She then said, "I think this was a mistake for you to come here. Anyway, I have a lot of studying to do." So that was it! As she dropped me off at the airport that same evening, she said, "Call me when you're divorced." That was the last time we spoke. The last time I saw her.

I'd been there for eight hours, maybe less, and now would be on my way back to SFO, but was looking forward to the foggy, damp weather to cool me off from the episode by the pool.

Arriving at the airport—keep in mind the Albuquerque airport was much smaller back then—while in the concourse waiting area, Murphy's Law kicked in. There were only seven people in the waiting area, and lo and behold, one of them was a close lady friend of Joan's. What were the chances of that? I shouldn't have gotten so frantic, but I did! Joan and I were separated, and I was supposedly soon to be served. Well, I spent the next forty-five minutes dodging her, hiding behind polls and reading the newspaper over and over again to hide my face. I had to go to the bathroom so badly but dared not because I would have had to walk in front of her to get to the men's room. It was like a funny scene out of a B-movie, a spy trying to hide, involved in a covert scheme! A little trick: I feared that she had her eye on me, so I yawned continuously, figuring if she then yawned, I was nailed, but she didn't. Strange how a guilty conscience works.

Arriving home, I mean at my apartment, I was now even more dispirited than before. I should have just stayed home with Crissy. She never gave me any crap. Just a few headaches.

"Desperation" is an anagram; when you rearrange the letters, it reads "a rope ends it." I seriously thought about it. However, you must remember, when you find things difficult, you often begin to think that life has no meaning. But life doesn't depend on outside circumstances; life is an internal process. What you must do is take a deep breath and hold it for as long as you can. You will then only think of your next breath. This way it will remind you of what life is truly worth. You will remember that it's worth the fight.

Meanwhile, we'd just gotten an offer on the Hillsborough home, almost full price. However, I didn't know what the hell to do about handling what Joan had said about us splitting the money and getting separate places. I was confused; if we were getting a divorce, everything would be split in two anyway. Maybe she wanted to do it that way because divorce took so many months to settle. What a mess.

Well, we accepted the offer on the house. Now we had to decide what to do about living arrangements—her living arrangements; mine wouldn't change. I'd gotten used to being a vagabond, constantly moving like a vagrant, a tramp, a wanderer, aimlessly drifting. Sounds like a song.

I decided that Joan could have my half of the proceeds from the house. What the hell. A vagrant didn't need cash, and then she could get herself a really nice home. After all, she deserved it. I loved her and wanted the best for her. Sounds gallant, but I mean it. I can hear Joan again now, saying, "Oh, *poor pitiful pearl*."

She didn't know of my intentions to let her have my half yet, and I didn't know when I would tell her, but soon. But she had to accept my calls so we could talk, so how was that going to work?

I would have to be innovative in how I approached this, knowing she may not accept it. We both had to meet with the realtor to sign the acceptance document, so I would bring it up then.

The following day, we met with the realtor at her office to sign the papers. Walking in, I was surprised to see that Joan was already there. I gulped hard and simply said hi, catching myself before I called her "honey." She barely glanced my way.

After signing the papers, we started talking to the realtor about finding another home. This was a good time for me to bring up my plan, so I said to her, "I don't know if you're aware of it or not, but Joan and I are separated." She acrimoniously said, "Oh, I know all about it. You'll be looking for two homes." *Oh, shit. So, this is really her plan*, I now mindfully thought.

I then told her that I wanted Joan to have all the proceeds from the sale of the house, so she could get herself a nice home and stay in Hillsborough with all her friends she'd made over the years. Joan then dispassionately blurted out, "Oh my! He's being a chivalrous ass now, isn't he!" Well that worked out like bringing a butter knife to a sword fight.

Looking away from Joan, I then said, "I think it's best. Please show her around and what's available in Hillsborough and the neighboring areas." She then said, "Well, it would make the property settlement a lot easier and save a lot of money in capital gains by trading up." I looked at Joan and said, "Come on, honey, it just makes sense." See, I had the balls to still call her honey. Joan didn't respond and just looked away, but I felt she had accepted. Accepted, not that I called her honey, but that I'd give her all the money. It even rhymes!

The realtor then told us to give her a day or so to compile a list of what was available. This was in the spring of 1988.

So that afternoon, the vagrant who'd just sold a million-dollar-plus large custom home in Hillsborough went to his tiny rented studio apartment with rented furniture and watched a rented eighteen-inch TV with rented rabbit ears on a rented small table. He then proceeded to consume libations and converse with his old obsidian, tranquilizing confidant. That's okay, Crissy and I had gotten used to living like this.

Surprisingly, the realtor called Joan the very next day and said she had a few exciting properties to show us. She requested she show us that very afternoon, and lo and behold, Joan called to tell me. She was short and curt, but nevertheless, she'd called me! *Don't get excited, Kiki. She had to.*

We met on West Santa Inez in Hillsborough in front of the Randolph Hearst mansion; yes, the same one that was the center of the Patty Hearst case years ago that showed Mr. Hearst on the front steps talking to the TV reporters. This was one of the homes now available. It was rather exciting seeing the now vacant home; however, after inspecting it, it was quite old and needed a lot of work, more than we, or should I say Joan, was willing to undertake at the time.

My gosh, we saw so many beautiful homes and estates. If it had been my decision, I would have bought one in particular, an elegant palatial estate high up in Hillsborough. It had a cobblestone circular drive with magnificent stately big gates. Ah, gates, I always had a thing for big gates. Okay, I know, you're saying exactly what Joan just said: "You always want big, everything big, big and grandiose and magnanimous!" Well, I guess to a point I do, but remember, I was raised in a large, lavish home. It was just what I was used to; it wasn't to show off. Really. Yes, really.

So, what's wrong with wanting nice? Anyway, I can't change my ways. There's a story about a turtle and a scorpion I must tell you. There was a torrential downpour and the stream where the turtle and the scorpion hung out was overflowing. The scorpion was sure to drown. He saw that the turtle was about to cross the stream to get to higher ground, so he asked the turtle for a lift on his back. The turtle said, "Sure, hop on." Well, as they reached the other side, the scorpion, now safe, stung the turtle on the back of his neck, assuring the turtle would die. The turtle then asked the scorpion why he'd done that, and the scorpion answered, "I can't change my ways. It's in my genes."

A metamorphosis or some type of mutation would have to take place to allow me to change my ways. Gina gave me a mounted scorpion in a glass frame for my fiftieth birthday as a reminder. I still have it. However, there could have been a bit of cynicism involved with her gift.

We looked at so many beautiful homes that day. I liked several, but it was Joan's decision. It was an odd feeling knowing I wouldn't be living in the home.

The realtor said there was a spectacular home with an amazing garden coming up for sale next Thursday and she would see if she could get us in to see it on Monday before it was listed. She cautioned us that it was a one of a kind and would be bid up. She didn't divulge where or what kind of property it was, however. This sounded intriguing.

Back to the business for now: It was late Friday afternoon when I heard from the labor law attorney. He said the court had had a ruling and we were waiting for a date to appear to learn of the decision. It was odd. I'd been so obsessed with it, and now I was strangely ambivalent about it. It certainly had been a challenge. If I am indeed victorious over the Union, it will be a first. *Ho hum.*

It seemed like once I achieved whatever it was, I lost the aspiration. I so wished I knew the answer for my inability to be content with what I had. I don't know why I push, push, and continually try to pursue in all probability, the impossible, like the "Paradox of Stretch Goals," in pursuit of the seemingly impossible.

Well, much more important than business, I had to now achieve the seemingly impossible to focus on being channeled with new standards of morality and ethics, creating new paths which might stimulate exploratory, radically new approaches to my life's path.

I heard a story some time ago about an old Cherokee man who was teaching his grandson about life. He told the young boy that a fight was going on within him. It was a terrible fight between two wolves. One was evil. He was angry and filled with regret, greed, arrogance, self-pity, guilt, resentment, lies, false pride, superiority, and ego. The other was good. He was joy, peace, hope, humanity, kindness, benevolence, empathy, compassion, truth, and faith.

The grandfather went on to say that the same fight is going on in most of us. The grandson thought about it for a few minutes, then asked his grandfather, "So what wolf will win, Grandpa?"

The old Cherokee simply replied, "The one you feed."

CHAPTER 43

YOU SHOULD SEARCH ALL CORNERS OF THE WORLD FOR ANSWERS

How could that be possible, the earth is round? I have often wondered about that statement. I gave this chapter its title, because at this point it was about searching for answers, mainly wanting to seek the answer as to why people repeatedly make the same mistakes. Like I had, such as my need to accomplish, then over-accomplish; the drinking that led to indulgent drinking; my arrogance that led to confrontation; the affair that led to affairs. There's a parable that states "A bedpost that has too many notches will one day fail."

Case in point, I was awaiting the court's decision regarding the Union fiasco that was most likely caused by my arrogance and having been so confrontational, not to mention unyielding, obstinate, and pragmatic. I most likely also shouldn't have been so retaliatory and hard-headed during the negotiations. But in my defense, there was much more going on than just a contract. They wanted to sabotage and annihilate the company, and I was consumed with justice and retribution, so my indignation and temperament got the best of me, extinguishing my better judgment. I should have known that emotional tangents don't allow you to think logically. But no, my idiosyncrasy took over again.

I would also sure like to know why I always need to do things *now*. I can't seem to wait. It can be as simple as a silly little thing like a picture being crooked on the wall, and even though I'm exhausted, I have to get up and straighten it—now. Another example: One Sunday while on a drive with Joan and the kids I saw a restaurant we weren't selling to, and I couldn't wait to get to the office the next day to ask the salesman why, so I had to call him, now. He responded, "Oh yeah, I've been meaning to call them. I will later this week." I screamed back at him, "No, I want you to call them now!" Maybe there are two parts to my question: Why do I always have to do things *now*? And why do people procrastinate and *not* do things now?

Forgetting all that, let's get back to the house hunting. Today we were to look at this supposedly magnificent home and garden that the realtor had mentioned. It was a glorious morning in mid-April of 1988. The sun shone through the hovering wispy clouds above, while a scattering of crepuscular rays reflected the brilliance of the morning sun. The blossoms were in bloom and accentuated the backdrop of the vivid blue sky. An early morning chorus of song birds were also refreshingly heralding in a mood of gaiety. I was hoping it was indeed to be a day of gaiety.

My thoughts were now happily focused only on Joan and her new home. We met the realtor near South School in Hillsborough to look at this "one-of-a-kind home," as she'd described it. We got into her Mercedes Sedan and drove down El Cerritto and made a right turn onto of all streets, De Sabla Road. *Hmm, where in the hell is she taking us?* If you recall, I was now living just further on down the street in a little studio apartment near the El Camino Real.

We then very slowly drove down this enchanting, gently winding, narrow street while commenting on the beautiful homes, and as we passed a huge redwood tree demanding its rightful place in the center of the road, I couldn't help thinking back just a while ago that this would be such a wonderful street to live on.

The realtor then made a sharp left turn immediately past the Town of Hillsborough sign, and pulled into the gravel parking area in front of this seemingly Japanese-style home. It had a prodigious, large, solid granite Japanese lantern in front, proclaiming the homes propinquity. The property was called Higurashi-En (in English, "Garden Worthy of a Day of Contemplation"), and it had originally been constructed in 1887 and was once owned by none other than Eugene J. De Sabla.

We then walked the gravel pathway and arrived in front of the double front entry gates that were obviously designed to credible standards of authenticity that introduced us to the genesis of this amazing garden. From the first hint of glancing at the home, it was evident that it was irrefutably constructed long ago by Japanese artisans. This was a great start, but little did we know that the best was yet to come. We both stood outside the gates marveling of the entrance, when the realtor said, "So let's go in!"

As we walked through the entry, it was as if we had been magically transported 5,200 miles into a fairy-tale setting in Japan. We both gasped as we first saw only a glimpse of the garden and the immense koi pond—pond, hell, it was a small lake! It was beyond anything we could have imagined, and we found it to be unbelievable that this gem had remained hidden for so long.

As we walked the almost one-acre property, we were both in complete awe of what we were experiencing. Joan started jumping up and down saying, "I want it, I want it. Oh, please, Kiki, please!" Little did she know, she could have whatever she wanted, and she didn't even have to say please! I would have been benevolent with anything she desired.

However, we hadn't looked at the house yet, and oh yeah, I hadn't asked the price yet, but we still had so much of the garden to see before getting to the house. We walked the garden and suddenly stopped, and I was taken aback as we gazed upon this impressive solid-granite, hand-carved bridge. The realtor told us it had been brought from Japan by De Sabla and was over four hundred years old. She pointed out that it had an inscription on each side, one in Japanese and the other in Chinese that stated "The Path to Eternal Tranquility." I then joshed, "Show me the path! Any kind of tranquility in my life would be greatly appreciated about now!" She chuckled.

We continued walking the paths winding up and down and around the garden. She showed us a granite lantern from the 1894 California Mid-Winter Exposition, San Francisco's first world's fair, then a small statue of a woman that had to have been well over two hundred years old. We then stepped on huge stones and crossed over what should have been the water from the cascading waterfall from above; however, none of the irrigation was working, so consequently it was dry and overwrought with growth. The garden went on and on and exuded the history that once played out on the grounds for over a century. The realtor didn't know too much of the history but was able to highlight a few things.

The pond, obviously in great disrepair, exhibited only mud since the piping had corroded, but it supposedly held close to a hundred thousand gallons of water. After closely observing the foliage of the garden, it appeared that it had also been neglected and needed a great deal of work to bring it back to its worthiness.

This was going to be a big project, and costly, I commented to the broker.

We went into the house, entering through the front door made of ornate wood, which then brought us into a portion of the home that had originally been outdoors but was now enclosed. It was an area where one would typically take off their shoes before entering the tea house, now a dining room. The tea house was magnificent. It was constructed entirely with aged redwood. No nails were used in the tongue-and-groove-style construction, and little copper doves cleverly hid the joints. It was told to us that Japanese artisans were brought over from Japan in 1888, a year after the garden was completed, just to build the very ornate and fastidiously authentic tea house.

The realtor further explained that the property sat basically vacant and unattended from the late 1920s until 1945, when a wealthy gentleman bought the property and built a detached guest house with garages below in a corner of the property. He lived there while he built a home around the fabled historic tea house. The entry area, living room, and second-floor master bedroom suite was exquisitely constructed, attempting to match the original fine Japanese artisan architecture of the tea house, and was finished with similar aged redwood in the tongue-and-groove fashion. Meanwhile, unexplainable and adverse to the rest of the home, a very small ground-floor kitchen and a tiny bathroom strangely veered off to one side with a short narrow hallway that led to the magnificence of the second-floor master suite.

Many years later under new ownership, the home was greatly expanded, adding a family room and two more ground floor bedrooms and full bathroom with a much larger, updated kitchen. However, it was apparent that the newer part of the house that was just expanded and updated had been poorly designed and constructed. The owner, now listing the property, did not follow the significant costlier fine craftsmanship of the older part of the home, now obviously illustrating its dire need to be entirely redone.

It was concluded before asking the price that hundreds of thousands of dollars would have to be spent enhancing the home's interior, as well as the garden, to aggrandize the property. Quite a task, and not one that I had the time for. But this would be Joan's house and her undertaking. Anyway, the way things were going, I would be at the undertakers before she got to the undertaking.

It was now time for the sticker shock, so we questioned the realtor, "What are they asking?" I surprisingly found the price to be less than expected and now viewed it as a good investment. We offered over asking, something uncommon in 1988. We then told her we wanted her to present the all-cash offer of just under $1 million that afternoon, and if accepted, wanted it signed tonight, if possible, but no later than tomorrow morning, Tuesday. We knew this was going to be a hot property and bid up if we didn't get the acceptance before it hit the market. She said she would try to do as we wished. Well, it was accepted that same afternoon, much to the disdain of a member of the Crocker (bank) family, who had heard of the property and was looking forward to purchasing it since her family Japanese garden in Hillsborough had been destroyed. So now, we, she, still had to remodel the newer part of the house and entirely redo the piping to the waterfalls and pond and build a filtration system, plus locate all the missing specimen trees and plants, and build a fence around the entire almost one-acre property.

Joan would now have her beautiful, prodigious home and garden, as I so wanted her to have.

The property in 1894 as part of the Eugene De Sabla estate.

The property today as a National Historical Site.

Meanwhile, still fearsome that the mob might take some steps to hurt or scare my family, I immediately had an eight-foot fence built around the entire property with an electrified wire on top, as well as secured front gates and an automatic heavy wood gate to the garage area installed. Closed-circuit security cameras constantly monitored any activity around the entire property, including the front entry gate. A security system was also installed within the home monitoring not only all the doors but glass breakage. It was now a secure compound.

The element on the wharf, the unions, and the underworld influence wasn't over by any means, so I wanted Joan to be protected since they didn't know I was safely tucked away in a little apartment.

Well, I decided to move again. It was too painful living just down the street from where I should be, especially since this was now looking permanent. However, this time I was moving into the apartment building I owned in Burlingame. Coincidentally, unit number one had just come available; it was a nice large front unit. I had a manager, so I could hopefully live there incognito.

By the way, this would be the sixth time I'd moved in a year and a half, only signing a three-month lease each time. They were all also furnished, so it was easy to pick up and move when I got tired of them.

I got tired of the Jag, as well, and bought a sexy black Ferrari Mondial convertible—but I wasn't tired of my little black crow yet, though. She was nothing to crow about but was good company.

CHAPTER 44

ROCK BOTTOM BECOMES THE FOUNDATION ON WHICH I REBUILT MY LIFE

My wife was now set up in a home she loved, and had happily departed the party palace. I was in an apartment, and yes, I owned it, but it was still quite different to my once supposed showplace. Don't get me wrong, my apartment building was lovely and in a nice area, but not high on a hill in exquisite Hillsborough, as I was used to. But whether I lived in a seven hundred-square-foot apartment or in a seven-thousand-square-foot mansion, the loneliness was the same. However, I'd gotten used to living in this manner, and it was okay. When I was in my apartment, I liked to imagine that I was just renting the unit, not owner of the building, working for someone, not owner of the company; just a regular guy, and it felt good, even if just for a few hours at night. But you know what, it also doesn't matter where you live or where you are, you take your thoughts with you; there is no escaping them. And within the lonely silence, you think, think, and the silence can be haunting if your thoughts are daunting.

I can never turn my mind off; that's why reading is an annoyance.

You already know that I'd received notice regarding the court's pending ruling on the strike and labor law issues, but I was also awaiting to hear about the *other* issue, and I don't mean the divorce.

It's too bad we can't cover up the shit we leave behind like my male dog does when he kicks up the dirt to cover up the shit he leaves behind.

Calm down, yes, I know, I'll pick it up!

Have you ever noticed that if you drop two sticks exactly the same size, shape, and weight from a bridge into a stream below that each stick doesn't go in the same direction? Life's fate can be similarly governed. However, there are many factors that can intervene to affect one's journey through life, the slightest shift in any of these can dramatically change the course of one's future. Any important decision one makes in life will bring you on a different journey, similar to choosing the right or left fork in the road will determine your journey's end.

A simple dramatization of how just an instant could change the course of one's life: Let's say you're in a coffee shop, and as you leave entering the sidewalk, while holding your cup of coffee lacking a cover, you suddenly bump into someone walking by, spilling the scalding coffee all over your shirt and sport coat. Then you stop for a moment to attempt to clean as much as you can with the one flimsy napkin you had, while apologizing to the person for the incident. You then suddenly realize your bus just left that was to take you to your job interview, a job interview that you have been waiting for, for months. Now catching the next bus brings you to the interview twenty minutes late with coffee stains on your shirt. So, you lose the once almost for sure job that you'd waited so long for because you were tardy and looked like a slob.

How could this scenario have changed? Well, a couple of ways: If you had asked for a cover for the coffee, it may not have soiled as bad, and you just may have caught the bus and not been late; however, you still may have appeared to be a slob, but not as bad a slob, thus you may or may not have gotten the job.

But here's a much better scenario: If the person you tentatively bumped into would have gotten a call on their cell phone and stopped, even if for only a moment, pausing to answer just before the entrance to that coffee shop, you would have walked out and not spilled your coffee, covered or not, made the bus, impressed the interviewer, and gotten the job you always wanted! You would have then made big bucks and later become president of the company. Of course, I embellished with the results to be humorous, but it illustrates how just a simple event can change the course of one's future.

It is truly astonishing how just an instant in time can alter the course of one's life, and how just a fraction of an inch can avoid a tragic accident. The decisions we make have similar consequences.

I made some wrong decisions and was trying to change the course of my life. I was also trying to be a "cock-eyed optimist," to use Oscar Hammerstein's phrase. But was it truly possible to remain optimistic in the face of such negative reality? The odds of resolving all the issues in a positive manner were on par with getting struck by lightning at the same time as seeing Bigfoot eating a meatball sandwich at a Subway!

They say when something bad happens, you can either let it define you, destroy you, or strengthen you. Well, defined I was, destruction was near, and strength—I had none. I had slipped into a camouflaged vortex of self-loathing and sought my escape through alcohol. Alcohol had turned into both my friend and my ominous demon, and demons are insidious. Self-loathing is a powerful emotion, and I was living in my personal hell right now. They say hell has many mansions, and the gates are always wide open to receive guests. My intellect and will power was now a casualty of my concupiscence, like I had reverted to my post-adolescent naivety.

Meanwhile, I finally resorted going to an AA meeting. I heard they had a twelve-step program that was helpful in guiding a person to sobriety. I thought I would try it and listen to the people asking God to help them resist the desire to drink. Several got up to speak, announcing their first names, then declaring, "I am an alcoholic." Then everyone clapped. I did not; I didn't understand that. Were they clapping because that was an accomplishment? I know, I'm being facetious; this was the protocol, but I just found it odd. Nevertheless, it took a lot of guts to get up there and admit it—something I could not do.

I know admitting that you're an alcoholic is the first step and is paramount to recovery, but I have always been a loner regarding learning and doing, and felt this was a private hell and not to be disclosed to the masses.

Though they were obviously stronger than me to be able to get up and admit the fact that they were indeed alcoholics, at the same time I found it a weakness for someone to not help themself, or at least try; try to click their brain and just say no more, no more. I know that's easier said than done, but I knew I could do it, but only if I wanted to. But did I? No, not yet; too many things to sort out. Maybe someday if I could change the perception of myself.

Meanwhile, I learned by going to AA, that I was not alone, not by any means, and was made aware that it was a sickness, a disease. I thought it was just a bad habit gone really bad and had just developed into uncontrollable urges and cravings. Hmm, am I describing an addictive personality? Or even possibly an alcoholic? Or both?

Let me make it perfectly clear: I respect those who attend AA. Alcoholics Anonymous is a wonderful organization that has helped and is helping millions of people. They are to be highly commended for the work they do helping those with addictive behavior. I give plaudits, kudos, and bravos to the volunteers and to the organization.

I had now hit rock bottom.

Rock bottom becomes the foundation for which I rebuilt my life.

CHAPTER 45
THREE THINGS IN LIFE ONCE GONE, THAT ARE LOST FOREVER: TIME, WORDS, AND OPPORTUNITY

Time: The time I lost when my kids were teenagers while I was passed out on the couch, is lost forever.

Words: The words that weren't said to my father and most recently my wife, are lost forever.

Opportunity: Opportunity is the one thing I took advantage of; however, I took advantage of several that I shouldn't have.

With some luck, I just might still have the *time* to have the *opportunity* to convince my wife I loved her and wanted her back, but finding the right *words* to attempt to heal the wounds could be difficult. I would have to challenge all obstacles.

Here I am saying, challenge all obstacles, but I felt like the circumstances were like playing chess. I felt like the single lonely pawn having to face the king, the queen, two rooks, two bishops, and two knights, and my other eight pawn buddies had just gotten knocked off!

I was thinking about my past while driving to work one morning, and as obscure as it may sound, I noticed that the windshield was very large, yet the rearview mirror very small. Well, the reason, of course, is obvious. You must look forward and clearly see where you're going, and not worry where you've been.

It was now mid-summer and an unexpected and shocking thing happened, something I *never* thought would occur. Gina came into my office and gave me notice that she was leaving the company.

I got weak in the knees. My first thought was to look back at my past, at having worked for the competition. It was a horrible experience, something my daughter should never have to go through. So, what was this about? My daughter, who'd wanted to be in the industry with me and take over the company someday, now wanted to leave?

She'd majored in business administration to be groomed for the takeover. All kinds of thoughts were now reeling in my head. Eventually regaining composure, I asked why.

She then explicitly expressed her discontent with my domineering ways and lack of ability to pass on the power of management and to accept change. I was shattered hearing this, now realizing my forceful psyche had caused her to lose her drive to be in the business with me. I would never have intentionally done anything to adversely go against her or hurt her. My God, she was my daughter. Nevertheless, it seemed as if I had that innate knack to do so, and to those I loved the most.

Sure, we butted heads as two hard-headed Italians do, but I'd thought that was just in the daily course of running such a hectic and stressful business together. Nonetheless, it obviously went deeper, much deeper, to the point she felt that she was causing me too much opposition and stress and was leaving to protect my health and for the betterment of the company. My gosh, she was thinking of what was best for *me*.

We were upstairs in my office at the time, and as I sat back in my chair, I said that I needed to think about this; it wasn't right. Attempting to quickly think of ways to salvage our business relationship, I suggested she take a few months off and go up to the Lake Tahoe house; maybe some time away from me would refresh her and would also allow me some time to reflect on my non-intentional magisterial and imperious ways, and how to correct them.

Meanwhile, I so wished I could have sat her down and explained the anguish I was encountering, and I mean above and beyond the divorce and the strike. That torment must have turned me into a lunatic at times at work. My patience was thin and temperament short. I was fighting too many forces and felt everything collapsing around me. She also didn't realize that the non-Union foreign wholesaler a few blocks away was simultaneously trying to get our Sacramento, Reno, Lake Tahoe salesman away from us. He and his staff now represented the majority of the sales since the area was out of the jurisdiction of the Union Local, so the accounts could not be threatened if they bought from us. It would have been a fatal blow to lose him, those accounts. To retain him, I had to humbly give in to his outrageous demands by meeting the commission he was offered by the competition, thus further raising our cost of operation. So yes, my patience was thin, and I was at times unreasonable to deal with.

Fortunately, Gina agreed with my suggestion and went up to Lake Tahoe to get away from her bombastic, adulterous asshole father. Being aware of the affairs, it was obvious she no longer respected me as a father, and now not even as a boss. It was apparent all my daughters no longer thought of me as the symbol of a dutiful husband to their mom, and sadly, I might have marred their relationship with men forever. My three daughters often said I was a good father, but a lousy husband. So, since there were three of them and just one wife, did that then make me three-quarters good? Okay, not funny.

Gi enjoyed the solitude and magnificence of Tahoe. The clean, crisp air and the smell of the pine trees with the gentle sound of the creek also allowed her the peace and contentment to concentrate on her dream of writing a book on recipes for seafood products from around the world. What better subject, and from what better source—the ingenious buyer of that very seafood from all over the world. Many species that Gi originally introduced to the United States are still on the menus in restaurants to this very day. Some of her recipes also now appear on the website for my sauce line.

In her absence, I resumed the buying of fresh fish, and now needed to arrive at work much earlier, since the brokers representing the foreign countries were mostly in earlier time zones. Needing a clear head to deal with this so early in the morning was difficult with the daily hangover and the spinning of the room, plus resisting the urge to run to the bathroom and barf. Yes, disgusting, I know.

CHAPTER 46
A FEW CONCLUSIONS TO ONE MAN'S TEMPESTUOUS LIFE'S PATH

Okay, it's time to divulge the status of the court's ruling about the Union, and even more captivating and intriguing, the results of the DNA test. I'll give the results to you one at a time.

I BEAT THE UNION! Yep, this little guy was decidedly victorious over the huge once feared Union, as well as the unscrupulous organization and the wholesale seafood dealers who'd planned to decimate my company. Their aggregate synergy had been intended to produce a combined affect much greater than the sum of their individual affects. It told a tale, it resonated a sinister plot. They wanted me out!

The collaborated efforts of all those compelling influential and formidable forces to attempt to put me out of business had failed, thus proving the Union's demands were not only excessive, but unwarranted, as I'd originally stated. The judge had gotten it right, after all!

LITTLER MENDELSON FASTIFF & TICHY

A PROFESSIONAL CORPORATION

ATTORNEYS AT LAW

650 CALIFORNIA STREET 20TH FLOOR

SAN FRANCISCO, CALIFORNIA 94108 2693

(415) 433 1940

FAX (415) 399 8490

FRESNO

LOS ANGELES

MENLO PARK

SACRAMENTO

SAN DIEGO

SAN JOSE

WALNUT CREEK

LITTLER, MENDELSON, FASTIFF & TICHY

A PARTNERSHIP

BALTIMORE, MARYLAND

LITTLER, MENDELSON, FASTIFF & TICHY

A PARTNERSHIP

NEW ORLEANS, LOUISIANA

April 26, 1990

PRIVILEGED AND CONFIDENTIAL

Mr. Achille Paladini
President
A. Paladini Seafood Co.
500 Mendell Street
San Francisco, California   94124

> Re: A. Paladini Seafood Company
>   and Local 115
>   Case No. 20-CA-22642

Dear Kiki:

Congratulations again! Pursuant to our telephone conversation of this date, enclosed please find a copy of the favorable Decision of the Administrative Law Judge, which I received in the mail today.

If you have any questions regarding the enclosed, do not hesitate to call.

Very truly yours,

ALAN S. LEVINS

ASL/rty

Enclosure

AGREEMENT FOR SETTLEMENT, RELEASE AND DISMISSAL OF ALL CLAIMS

1.   Plaintiff A. Paladini Seafood Company (hereinafter "Plaintiff") and Defendants Butchers' Union Local 115 (hereinafter "Union") through their respective counsels of record, and Gary Golden, Jose Garcia, Gus Garcia, Dave Camacho (hereinafter "Individual Defendant" or collectively, "Individual Defendants"), hereby enter into this agreement for settlement, release and dismissal of all claims alleged in the Complaint filed in San Francisco Superior Court, Case No. 901337, and all claims of each Defendant, if any, against Plaintiff. Agreement between Plaintiff and the Union and between Plaintiff and any Individual Defendant shall be evidenced by signing this Agreement and shall be binding as between them whether or not any other Defendant or Defendants has or have signed. No Defendant has the authority to settle for any Defendant other than himself or itself.

2.   Plaintiff and Union, in order to avoid the burdensome costs of litigation, hereby agree to completely resolve and settle any and all claims arising from this litigation.

3.   Plaintiff and Individual Defendants, each of them, in order to avoid the burdensome costs of litigation, also agree to completely resolve and settle any and all claims arising from this litigation.

4.   It is agreed and understood by Plaintiff, Union, Individual Defendants, and each of them, that this mutual release of claims cannot be construed as an admission of liability on the

Page 1 of Four

The truth, like oil, always comes to the surface. Here's a funny story about truthfulness to add a little humor to all of this: An elderly man introducing himself to a young woman, wanting to impress her, said, "Hi, I'm a politician and an honest man." The woman then replied, "Hi, well I'm a prostitute and a virgin."

Regarding my bout with the Union, it was a lesson learned: *Never give up on achieving your goal, nor give in to principles you believe in.* However, I must be explicit to mention that the consequences in doing so may have a premature effect on your health and the lifespan of your business. But to live in honor for a shorter time and die with respect is better than to retreat and back down and live longer as a coward.

I must say however, that my victory came at great expense, not only monetarily and emotionally, but health-wise. It resulted in almost bringing me to my knees as I suffered with acute alcoholism and now heart disease and kidney disease. I also received a final bill from the attorneys for over a half million dollars!

However, I was now non-union, though that was never my original intention. At first, I was shocked, surprised, and at a loss how to proceed, but that wouldn't last long. In the meanwhile, I knew I must make sure the current employees valued their jobs, so I had to take care of them. They were now *my* men.

With the distribution plant's labor cost now permanently plunging by over a third, I raised all the production workers and drivers wages substantially. However, nowhere close to the Union wages.

Meanwhile, the foreign companies were still wreaking havoc with their low-cost operating expenses allowing them to quote cheap prices cutting the gross mark-up to the bone. But we could now be highly competitive and start to get back the business we'd lost.

The still grossly unfair expedient to this synopsis, however, is that our government qualified these foreign companies, since minority-owned, for an almost interest-free loan for startup funding. Oh, yes. Startup funding. Wouldn't that have been nice?

Meanwhile, factors once never thought of or predicted were now changing the future of the entire seafood industry, and I'm not just talking about the gross over-fishing as a result of the greed of more foreign influences with no regard for future generations. I'm talking about the influx of people from other countries entering the United States, often illegally, qualifying for minimum interest loans to start a business, and the cleverness of their using their supposedly lack of understanding of the English language to avoid conforming to the rules we must, as US citizens, with many of us going back several generations born in this country. So, may I ask, how did they fill out the forms written in English? Oh, maybe they weren't in English after all.

As a consequence, many small wholesale seafood companies were now beginning to pop up on the West Coast not having to conform to any controlling factors.

Okay, enough of that. I immediately set up medical plans, as well as IRAs for all the production worker and drivers, same as I had for the salesmen and the bookkeepers. The simple virtue of the IRA exemplified the fact that the money was theirs from day one of the first funding, no need having to work for ten years before it became theirs, having to vest it. There was also a "work contract" designed since there had to be some standards set in place, very similar to the Union contract.

By expanding core benefits, I had hoped to secure employee retention. Wording in my work contract regarding vacation pay, sick leave, and holidays were comparable to the Union contract, but didn't have a nefarious force hovering over me.

The attitude of the workers was now better than ever, and I made a point of complimenting the men, often recognizing their efforts to reinforce their self-esteem and to let them know the "boss" knew they were doing well.

Now we had to get going and concentrate on getting back the business we'd lost due to the strike, and that alarmed me, because once an account gets accustomed to buying from another firm and is pleased with their quality and performance, and even more impacting, if the buyer gets friendly with their sales rep, it could be difficult—extremely difficult—to sway them to return. Most buyers dislike bouncing back and forth with purveyors. *It is much more difficult to get an account back that you lost than if you never had it.*

We also had to hope they weren't sympathetic for the workers who had lost their Union jobs, though no fault of ours. Keep in mind that most buyers are employees thus may take the side of the employee and not me, the employer. People can react strangely and unpredictably. Hopefully, those customers would be understanding and magnanimous and buy from us again.

Talk about people acting strangely: The majority of my ex-Union workers oddly went to work for non-Union companies. So what did they gain, other than causing me pain?

We *would* get the accounts back, but it would take time. Having said that, I was not sure I had the energy or the drive anymore. I was both mentally and physically exhausted, and simply put, burnt out.

I still also had so damn many dominos that had fallen and needed to be put back in place.

CHAPTER 47
EMOTIONALLY DRAINING MONTHS

My good friend and personal attorney, Bob LaVine, called early one morning while at work saying he had the results of the DNA test of the baby. I urged him to tell me on the phone, but he insisted he tell me in person, saying he had *good news* and *bad news*.

I had no clue what the hell that meant, but his statement regarding the bad news caused me to have a panic attack. My shoulders crumpled, and that sensation of shooting numbness ended in my arms again as I clenched my chest. Of course, my heart rate soared, and I felt severe pain in between my shoulder blades, as if an ax was trying to split them further in half.

For a moment, I wished my daughter Gina knew what I had been going through this past year that had caused my capriciousness and lack of patience. However, since I was the sole cause of the dilemma, most likely it wouldn't have changed the way she viewed the aspect of the predicament.

I asked my attorney if I could come to his office right then, and he told me I'd have to wait until eleven since he had prior appointments. Well, those two hours seemed like a week, like a week in hell. I found it difficult to concentrate on anything, especially the buying I still had to do. Every phone call I received was annoying. The morning business rush and the customers' priorities were no longer important, now only thinking how my life, our lives, could possibly change, and how the repercussions of what I was about to hear would affect my family and their future, and sure as hell, mine.

Ten thirty finally came, and I anxiously yet reluctantly drove downtown to Third and Market Streets to the Hearst Building. My attorney's office was on the third floor. During the elevator ride up I wondered what my state of mind would be on the ride down. Opening the door to his office felt like I was a prisoner on death row walking to my fate.

I was greeted by his secretary, who respectfully said, "Good morning, Mr. Paladini, how are you this morning?" I wanted to say, "I'll let you know on the way out!" She then asked if I wanted a cup of coffee and I jokingly said, "Any brandy?"

My attorney was running late with his prior appointment, of course, as all doctors and lawyers do. The suspense was killing me. I tried putting this out of my mind all these months, and now I would have to come to terms with it. I basically knew what I was going to hear anyway.

I waited . . . and waited. My hands were clammy, and I wanted to scream, "Why are you doing this to me, Bob?! Bob, you're my friend!" His door then suddenly opened. He was saying goodbye to a woman who was crying. Oh, shit, everyone was getting bad news today!

He then turned his attention to me and said, "Come on in, Kiki." As I got up, my head started spinning and I was seeing little black spots and thought for sure I was going to pass out as I had at my first Holy Communion. This time my house was filthy, and I had no clue what I was about to receive.

My good friend and attorney then warmly put his arm around my shoulder while walking me into his office. I viewed that as I was about to hear bad news, very bad news, and it was his way of comforting me, consoling me before the lethal injection was administered. I thought for sure he was going to ask if there were any last words I would like to say?

He then said, "Please sit down, Kiki." *Oh shit, he said sit down.* Okay, so now was he just being polite? Or getting me prepared? Either way, I wouldn't dare take this standing up.

He then sat down and pulled his chair up to his desk and leaned forward onto his desk with his hands clenched and stared at me. He didn't say a word, just stared at me, for the longest time. The black spots were now the size of bowling balls, and at that point I wasn't sure if I had already passed out or not. He hesitantly looked at me and said, "Well, Kiki, I have good news and I have bad news!" I then said, "I know, Bob, you already told me that on the phone. For Christ sake, please just tell me!"

He then sat all the way back in his large black leather chair with his hands now crossed behind his head and asked, "So which one do you want first?"

Suddenly, it was like I was hypnotized. I appeared to zone out and felt as if I was in a huge black hole; his voice resonated as if an echo. I didn't know what the hell had just overcome me. Christ, maybe I'd just died. And most likely that would have been okay!

Boundless heterogeneous thoughts were flashing in front of me, similar to what they say you experience upon your death. I envisioned the happy and fun times we had spent as a family when the kids were young. I suddenly ached to be with Joan, with my girls. I didn't want to be here. I didn't want to hear what was about to change our lives, now damning my flirtatious ways.

My thoughts flashed back to the summers we'd spent up in Lake Tahoe when the girls were teenagers. It was always so much fun, even with Laura and Gina having their daily bouts of attempted homicide. I think I actually giggled out loud, thinking of one of the times on the boat, and vaguely saw my attorney looking at me wondering what the hell had just overcome me. However, within that fraction of a moment, the remembrance came back of the time we were out on the lake in *Caesar's Chariot*, as Joan so aptly named our Sea Ray, and Gina was being towed off the back of the boat in an inner tube. Before she got into it she'd said, "Dad, when I do a thumbs-up, it means go faster, and thumbs-down, go slower." I said, "Okay, got it, kid!"

She was launched into the inner tube and the line stretched out tight. She then gave me a thumbs-up. I then slowly started going faster while looking in the mirror, checking if she wanted to go any faster. She gave a thumbs-up, so I sped up a bit. Now going about twenty-five miles per hour, Laura said, "Dad, just drive the boat and look forward and I'll tell you what she wants." Well, without thinking I said, "Okay, kiddo!"

A few seconds later, Laura said, "Faster, Dad," so I sped up. Then again, she said, "Faster, Dad!" I was now going about forty miles per hour and thinking that was damn fast for just an inner tube. I then turned around to check on Gi and found Laura laughing her butt off while Gina was uncontrollably bouncing up and down, holding on for dear life from the massive waves from the wake of the boat, about to be wildly tossed out of the inner tube! Laura's inept sense of humor and ceaseless dueling with her sister was now destined to meet with an unfortunate ending when Gina got back on the boat.

Upon picking her up from the freezing water, her faced was flushed and we all knew this was not going to be a pretty scene. She, of course, first screamed at me, "What the hell were you doing, Dad?! I was giving a thumbs down and you went faster! You almost killed me!" I mistakenly looked at Laura and that was the end of it. Laura had nowhere to run! What supposedly infuriated Gina more than anything was that we were all laughing our heads off!

This was all happening during that millisecond in my attorney's office.

Another flashback came, and this time it was Joan's grandma's birthday, "Little Grandma," as the girls affectionately called her, and she'd come up to Tahoe with us. I had prearranged with my chef friend, Gunther, once the executive chef of the San Francisco Hilton and now chef of a new casino hotel in Reno, to bake a special birthday cake for her since we were taking her there to gamble and celebrate her birthday. She must have been close to ninety.

The entire day went terrifically well. Grandma gambled with my funding, and it was now time for dinner. We went into the main dining room and enjoyed a great meal with Gunther coming to the table with his entire staff to sing "Happy Birthday" to little Grandma Romano.

The cake was similar to a Saint Honore cake, named after the French patron saint of bakers. Since grandma loved whipped cream, we asked Gunther to have his pastry chef add extra whipped cream on the sides of the cake and did he ever. Masses of whipped cream slid down the sides like an impending Sierra avalanche.

There was a live five-piece band playing in the next room, so as customary, I danced with Joan, then each of the girls. It was now Gina's turn and I said, "Okay, let's go, kid." She got up, and as she brushed by Laura, Laura grabbed a whopping handful of whipped cream from the cake and spread it on her butt. I also must add that Gina was wearing a rather alluring black dress, a bit much for her young age. I had no clue of Laura's perverse escapade until while dancing with Gina as she thought she was hot stuff, since several young guys were checking her out. I then noticed this huge white glob dangling off her butt, and may I add, very pronounced against the obsidian-black dress.

Well, I couldn't help it. I started laughing, then most everyone in the room started laughing, including the guys that were once checking her out! She was mystified why everyone was looking at her, and now not in a complimentary way, but giggling.

She eventually got wise and looked behind her since everyone was looking in that direction, and saw the whipped cream, now precariously dangling off her derriere!

Of course, knowing who the culprit was, she took off back to the table grabbing grandma's bag of silver dollars and slammed Laura repeatedly targeting her ill-fated forehead while Laura laughed uncontrollably.

Unfortunately, we were all laughing by now, not pleasing Gina. Laura said she didn't feel a thing since she enjoyed it so much! However, a large lump soon loomed on Laura's forehead as a reminder of her roguery of the evening.

Suddenly, I came out of this hypnotic trance, realizing I was in my attorney's office and those fun days were over and life was now serious, very serious and much more complicated. I now had to face it and hear the results.

My heart was now about to burst out of my chest, my breathing shallow, and I blurted out, "Okay, please give me the good news first!"

"THE BABY IS NOT YOURS!" He exclaimed.

Stunned, shocked, overwhelmed, joyous, exhilarated, relieved, then confused, I sat back for a moment and asked, "Then what the hell is the bad news?"

He said, verbatim, "She was fucking someone else!"

We both laughed for what seemed like an hour. Then I commented, "Thank you, Bob, and thank you, God in heaven above!"

Then the conversation got serious, not that it hadn't been. My attorney explained that the results also went to the Santa Clara County district attorney's office so he would request the immediate dismissal of the paternity suit. He would then petition the court to have my name that was listed as the father on the birth certificate be removed. He said he would make sure this was done properly by requesting a copy be mailed to him at his home, keeping it confidential. The real birth father of the child, if determined, would then be listed as whoever the mother stated.

Here's a funny story that I just recently learned while having dinner with Bob just a few months ago, after telling him I was writing my memoirs and the "baby thing" would be in it.

As I just prior mentioned, he said that the copy of the new birth certificate with my name removed would be mailed to his home to protect confidentiality. He then said when it arrived, his wife curiously opened it. After reading it she accused *him* of having an affair and of almost having an illegitimate child! His wife, who sat across from us at dinner the night he told me of this, looked over at me and said she was ready to beat the shit out of him, and only believed him when he said she could call me to verify it. Sorry, Bob, you're a good friend and a good lawyer!

Upon leaving his office, I of course couldn't wait to get back in my car and call Joan.

I got her on the phone and said, "Honey, honey . . . the baby isn't mine. The baby isn't mine!" She then casually said, "Told ya!"

The astonishing thing that Joan had said in the car after seeing the baby boy that day at Leone's house had been exactly that: "The baby is not yours!"

Well, being overly enthusiastic back at the time when she'd said that to me, I joyfully asked her, "But honey, how can you possibly know?" She straight forwardly answered, "He doesn't have your fat ear lobes! All our children do. Haven't you noticed?" Well, between you and me, uh, no, I hadn't, not even mine! Who in the hell looks at ear lobes?

However, back when we were leaving Leone's apartment that day, and hearing Joan's assessment of the baby, I couldn't help but feel that it just may have been my wife's voodoo perception and not a very scientific approach regarding biological pregnancy. Nevertheless, I have to admit, she's pretty damn amazing . . . *she called it!*

Back to me leaving the attorney's office and calling Joan and telling her of the good news: Joan then shocked me by saying to come on home and let's celebrate. Oh boy! My hands were shaking with excitement, never thinking I would get this news. I was elated, even more so that my wife had said, "Come on *home!*" My God, was she forgiving me? *Take it easy, Kiki. You can't get too elated yet.*

I then did something stupid, yes, again. You're not surprised? This seems to happen quite often, doesn't it? But I needed, I really needed, to know why someone would do this, not only to me, to anyone. I didn't understand it. Looking back now, I'm sure it was all about money, status, material stuff. I'm sure if I was a common guy, she would have found another wealthy man to blame. I'm sure the real birth father is indeed a common guy; however, I didn't have any idea who he was. But I wanted—I needed—to know why she'd named *me!*

I drove all the way down to Mountain View and stopped in at Leone's. She reluctantly answered the door. With the door open just slightly ajar, I said, "We have the DNA results." The door now opened a bit further and she delicately asked, "Well?" I then said, "The baby's not mine, Leone. Why did you do this? You almost ruined my marriage, my life. Why, why?"

The door now wildly swung open all the way, forcefully hitting the back wall as she verbally confronted and attacked me. She screamed accusations. "You liar! You fucking liar! You, with your big lawyer, you big Mafia guy, you had the Mafia falsify the results. You paid them off! I should have known. You fucking bastard . . . you fucking bastard!" I then calmly replied, "None of that is true. What is true, is that you were with someone else when we were together. How could you do that? You supposedly adored me, so you said."

Then she fell on her knees and broke down crying mumbling, mumbling, "You kept on breaking up with me. You were always breaking up with me. I wanted to get back at you, so I dated another guy." "So you admit you were with someone else?" I asked. She then said, "Yes, but only a few times. He was a nice guy, a mechanic at British Motors that liked me. It meant nothing to me."

The baby then started crying and I said, "I'm leaving. Contact the DA and drop the paternity suit." She screamed back, "Fuck you!"

I expected that I'd soon be on the Jerry Springer show, with all the proletarian women in the audience booing and hissing at me while Leone beat the shit out of me as another show-sponsored DNA result was soon to be announced!

When arriving at the house on De Sabla Road, I ran up and hugged Joan and said, "I love you, honey. Please, please forgive me." She said, "We'll see."

One thing that I never mentioned throughout all this, every time I saw her while we were separated, I looked to see if she still had on her wedding ring, not the engagement ring, but the wedding ring and she did!

Flash forward many years: In 2012, the baby boy who was once allegedly mine was tragically killed in a jet ski accident at Lake Berryessa, located just a few miles northwest of Napa, California.

He had just turned twenty-four.

CHAPTER 48
GIVING ME ADVICE IS LIKE GIVING A BALD GUY A COMB

Looking back, I wonder if things would or could have been different if my older brother had taken me under his wing at a young age and given me advice about life, about morality. Would that have changed many of the troublesome situations I'd just gotten through? *It's easier to build a boy than to mend a man.* However, thinking it through, that may have been too much to ask of him. Possibly he wasn't that experienced or wise enough yet, though he was thirteen years my senior. And if he had, would I have taken his advice?

Getting back to the remaining obstacles still challenging me, remember my previous words, to "always be consistent and persistent to attain your goals"? Well, that advice would now have to be precisely executed to persevere in attaining my goal to get my wife back, as well as defeat the damn alcohol dependency. Gaining back the respect and affection of my daughters would also certainly be predicated on the success of those achievements. However, I wasn't sure my three wise daughters would be so forgiving. These were still three huge hurdles.

Oh, and yes, the business. How about the goddamn fish business that I now detested? But how could it be that I now hated it? But I did. I guess I was just drained and it seemed to have somehow lost its luster. Nevertheless, I had to snap to it and get it back on track, then who knows what, maybe sell it? Especially now, since there was the possibility that Gina wouldn't be there to succeed me.

In the meantime, I found it a grueling task just to show up every morning.

There was a seafood convention coming up in Hawaii the following weekend and I asked Gi if she would attend in my place, and she agreed to go. She drove down from Tahoe, and the next Friday flew out of SFO early in the morning to arrive at the convention in time for the Friday evening festivities. The main convention days were Saturday and Sunday, and she would then return home on Monday.

Well, as soon as she arrived at the office that Tuesday morning, she said she needed to talk with me privately in my office. I immediately wondered what this was going to be about; it was odd that it seemed so urgent. As we entered my office she said, "Dad, sit down." *Oh Jesus, what the hell was coming now?* Well, she then shockingly told me that she was going to work for the foreign wholesale seafood company just a few blocks away!

There are no words to describe the feelings that jolted through my body. My initial concern was how she was going to fare working for another company within the same industry. Shades of the same thing I'd done long ago.

My God, this couldn't be happening! Was this deja vu? She then went on to explain that she needed to do this for not only my well-being, but for hers. She told me she wouldn't be in sales; she was to be their international fresh fish buyer.

Her final words to me were "Dad, we just don't work well together." How could I have done this? To my own daughter?

When she left my office, I immediately broke down, only getting my composure when there was a knock on the door. It was Gi again. "There's something else I have to tell you," she said. She asked if I knew that my sales manager and another one of my top salesman had attended the conference. No, I had not. I was totally flabbergasted! Why would they go? It was a weekend conference and the flights out and back were on Friday and Monday. Then I remembered they had both called in sick those days. I'd never thought of putting that together. Why would I?

Thinking about this further before calling them into my office, I now suddenly had the realization that I had vaguely noticed my sales manager hadn't been quite the same the past few weeks. Since he was the sales manager, he called on all the major hotels in downtown San Francisco, a major portion of my business that was now just starting to come back. My being involved with the overall running of the business and my head still reeling from all that had transpired recently must have caused me to overlook and dismiss the change in his disposition. I was also very tired.

I now had a hunch why they were there and dreaded finding out if I was indeed right.

Calling the two men into my office I asked, "What in the hell were you both doing at the seafood convention in Hawaii?" Their demeanor and attitude suggested they knew they were about to get fired and they obviously didn't care. That was bothersome.

They then both boldly blurted out, "Well, boss, we're going into our own business!"

I sat back in my chair and glared at them, then asked, "So why didn't you guys have the balls to quit and do it the right way, instead of planning and plotting on my time?" They didn't care; the ambivalence of their attitude showed it. I was no longer their boss and they were now out to take whatever business they could from me, especially the major hotels downtown.

They then looked at each other and just laughed. I then said, "Okay, guys, get the fuck out."

As they walked out, I knew I was going to get hit, and hit badly. The sales manager controlled all the major accounts for several years. That's why a trusted family member has to control all the major accounts, a point I brought up earlier. The revered large hotels downtown were going to be a battle to maintain, and we'd just gotten most of them back after losing them due to the strike. Even worse, I didn't have anyone to call on all the large hotels now except me. Shit!

Here we go again, I thought. *I have to fight all over again, and there's not much fight left in me. This is going to be a big hit that will hurt, and the timing couldn't be worse. The strike, now this.* I was screwed.

Things were falling apart, again, and my energy level was lower than the Salton Sea. If you notice, I didn't say Death Valley or the Dead Sea; both connote a sense of finality.

As expected, they opened the following week backed by an investor, and naturally took some of the hotel business with them, but only a very small portion, and that was unexpected.

Doesn't expecting the unexpected make the unexpected expected? *Okay, I think I'm losing my mind.*

Nevertheless, we were now doing a fantastic business again. Most of the accounts easily came back, presumably because we carried hundreds upon hundreds of seafood items from all over the world, and had the ability to service the accounts in entirety. Profits were once again good, even better than before due to the lower operating costs. I was also looking forward to opening the processing plant and the receiving stations again in the very near future, as planned.

But I was starting to get little subtle cues that hinted that it just may be time to dispel with those ideas and consider retiring while still at the top, in dignity and in good—well, at least fairly good—health, while I could.

Remember, there is always someone younger, stronger, with more energy, more desire, more need, wanting to take your place, regardless of the industry. Look at the famed boxer Mohammad Ali. He could have retired while on top with dignity as the heavyweight champion of the world, but no, he stayed in there and got the crap kicked out of him, lost his title and ended up with brain impairment.

Sell while on top when profits are soaring, when you're doing so well that the mere thought is preposterous! However, I was only fifty-four.

Now thinking further about this and more seriously, the thought occurred to me that all the employees I'd originally started with were now mostly gone. My long-time controller had retired last year, as well as Joan's aunt and bookkeeper, also another bookkeeper and friend, and my long-time secretary had moved to Oregon. My brother and cousin had passed away, and now Gina, my successor, was working for another company. So, what was the purpose or the need for the company now? I only had my two faithful sidekicks, my bird Crissy, and my supervisor Tony, who by the way, had been complaining about severe pain in his lower back and wouldn't see a doctor. We were all breaking down. Except Crissy that is. She's out of the barrel and into her bottle. She will no longer age.

All the other employees were relatively new, and I didn't owe any allegiance to them. I was basically there alone, not alone, per say; I was still surrounded by well over a hundred employees, but alone in the sense in the way I'd started. I needed to think about this. Time to go home, uh, I mean to my apartment.

I stopped in on the way and saw Joan. She was working in the garden, her passion. The place was starting to look really good. She had torn out tons of overgrowth and started to replace the specimen plants that had been lost over the years. I had to hand it to her. She went to the library and looked at old pictures of the property and descriptions of the over five hundred species once planted there and made sure they were exactly as they should be to preserve the authenticity of the garden.

She mentioned that she wanted to remodel the newer part of the home since it wasn't built with the fine craftsmanship as the older part was. I said, "Sure, get an architect to start on the drawings." She mentioned that Diana was currently dating an architect, and he supposedly was very good.

We then sat on the patio for a while making small talk and sipping on Manhattans, mine with two cherries. She sipped, I gulped, but I stopped with just one, wanting to impress her by showing I could cut back, and even stop if I wanted to, though I really couldn't.

I then said, "Well, I just wanted to stop by and see how you were." I then proceeded to leave. I was only at the house about a half hour, not wanting to push it. I had to try to ease myself back into her life, if that was even possible. I used all the essence of charm and charisma I could, almost like dating again, to make her laugh, though her laugh was reserved and cautious. It was like walking on egg shells, but I was pleased that she was being somewhat civil to me.

All the time when I was with her I couldn't help but wonder when or if I was going to be served with divorce papers. I certainly wasn't going to ask. But hey, the wedding ring was still on!

It was 1990, and we had now been separated for a couple of years. I was now seeking a philosophy box filled with miracles, as elusive as that may have been.

My days at the office were filled with discontent. Thoughts of selling the business were now constantly taunting me. I was drained, had lost my drive, and was sick of achieving, achieving, achieving. My daughter was now absent from the once drafted plan for takeover that had been paramount, so why keep it? I had inaugurated my own destiny. I had forced my daughter to leave by my impenetrable and obnoxious actions; it certainly was not her desire or fault. She left for *me*, for *my* salvation. There was nothing there that I cared for now.

How strange was it that I'd spent half my life building these walls, and now half of me wanted to see them fall.

Then goddamn it, just do it! Sell it. So I did! I put the business up for sale with a national business broker that very day.

I have always lived by the conviction, "Never look back on a decision once made."

In the meantime, I'd been spending a little more time over at the house lately and had actually slept downstairs one night. No, not upstairs yet.

Well, guess what, Diana was getting married! Her relationship with her fiancé had been on again and off again for some time, but it appeared she really loved this guy, so a wedding there would be.

The marriage ceremony was held at the Stanford University Chapel in Palo Alto. It was an elegant and moving ceremony with three trumpets playing "Ave Maria" as the ceremony concluded.

The reception was held in our garden at the new house, with the remodeling having just been completed in time. The garden was now in pristine condition after Joan's relentless work restoring it to its original magnificence. There were 120 people gathered on the patio and around the grounds with a catered sit-down early afternoon dinner. Diana was very happy, so we were of course overjoyed.

They then left the next day on their honeymoon to South Africa.

Gina surprisingly had invited a guy to the wedding. He worked for a seafood producer in New Zealand who she had been buying from for some time. I recalled her briefly mentioning his name to us and said he was in town. They'd apparently met in person at the convention in Hawaii. Yeah, the same one that my two salesmen had gone to while plotting to open their own business.

During the reception I couldn't help but look at him and try to figure out his intentions. It seemed like there was more going on than him just being an associate in the seafood business. I noticed a look of impertinence, and he was smoking incessantly, though a sign at the front gate clearly designated there was no smoking. I felt that to be disrespectful and a sign of impropriety, but knowing addiction, I chose to ignore it, but I couldn't help but be cynical of his misanthropic demeanor.

He stood in the background and only talked when spoken to. I found that odd since he was supposedly a salesman, but Gina's bubbly, outgoing personality more than kept the conversations going. Thinking further, I recalled Gi saying earlier that he came from a small farm town on the north island in New Zealand and that his parents were very cordial and nice. I then concluded he may have just been overwhelmed by the crowd and the intensity and large scale of everything here in the U.S. But I couldn't help but wonder if he'd really come from the other side of the world for business, or for the wedding, or just to see Gina. *Who in the hell is this guy?* I wondered.

Well, upon Di returning from her honeymoon, she and her husband bought a home on the Peninsula and appeared to be happy. She had her little dog, Meyers, and was doing very well with her own state licensed marriage, family, and child counseling practice in Cupertino.

CHAPTER 49
THE LEGENDARY BUSINESS IS SOLD!

Knowing when to walk away is *wisdom*. Being able to is *courage*. Walking away with your head held high is *dignity*.

It took many months to find a qualified buyer for the business, but I was finally successful. Working out the details of the sale took almost the remainder of the year. The business was sold to a large wholesale fish and poultry distributor in San Jose, California. The owners, along with my CPA and business broker, oversaw the transition and monitored the extremely convoluted formula. The due diligence process, however, felt like a colonoscopy gone bad.

The acquisition took place under the term Enterprise Value. EV is a way of figuring a company's net worth as an alternative to market capitalization. The formulation is very involved and convoluted, so I won't bore you with it.

The widely used measure EBITDA to value the company's worth was not used. EBITDA stands for Earnings Before Interest, Taxes, Depreciation, and Amortization.

This was an asset sale based only on the value of the accounts. Deciphering all of this was difficult, since they'd primarily only bought the immensely valuable and sought-after client/sales accounts. The acquisition of the accounts was predicated and calculated with a complex mathematical equation allowing for minimal variance using the squared deviation of a random variable from its mean by using the sales over the past three years verses the sales concurrently for the next two years paid over the course of two years, thus then consummating the sale.

I was to collect my own accounts receivable, pay the accounts payable, and sell the assets such as the inventory, trucks, and equipment myself. I clearly stipulated in the sales contract with the broker that the Paladini Seafood Company name was not for sale, thus would not be included in the purchase. I would not allow or take the chance that the name be extirpated if they were not able to satisfy the quality of the product, or service the accounts in the manner we did.

Since I personally owned the building, soon after the sale was consummated, the immense San Francisco distribution plant was leased to a large distributing company for several years and was eventually sold to a wholesale frozen fish, poultry, and meat distribution company. Then entered into a 1031 tax-deferred exchange into a large triple-net commercial income property out of state.

The following year, when the lease expired with my tenant at the Santa Rosa production facility, it was sold to a seafood processing company. I also personally owned that property, and again entered into a 1031 tax-deferred exchange into another triple-net investment property, also out of state.

I then formed Paladini Properties to oversee the management—by me.

I *shadowed* my grandfather!

Be that as it may, when all was said and done, I was a lost man without an identity. I said prior that every man needs an identity. You may not agree and think it's an ego thing. Possibly so, but I don't think so. I also must admit that I missed people saying, "Oh, I see your trucks all over," and even more so, going to a restaurant or country club and being swarmed by the owner, manager, and head chef.

The lack of that recognition was difficult to adjust to. I can only imagine how a has-been actor feels in Hollywood. I guess it's like what my actor friend Pat experienced. When on top they complain about the paparazzi, and I am sure they are in fact an annoyance and an invasion of privacy, but when that ceases, I bet they look over their shoulder and wish someone had recognized them.

From receiving virtually hundreds of calls a day and being a respected and noted leader in the industry and the business world in general, I went to my lonely apartment and received only an occasional, and now appreciated, call from telemarketers.

Okay, so I said I wanted peace and contentment, but jeez, the silence was deafening.

Nonetheless, I needed to ponder my shame in seclusion. I even found the faint sound of the buzzing in my head from the absorption of alcohol annoying.

However, I'd begun to realize that you can listen to silence and learn from it. It has a quality and dimension of its own. Silence can be comforting, yet silence can allow for deep concentration and clear thought processing, thus yielding commotion within. This is the great paradox.

How could life go from being so hectic and chaotic, filled with the daily profound trepidation, tension, and stress, dealing with the myriad of unforeseen trials and tribulations, to this? Nothing, nothing. To an unknown.

Was this what retirement was? Boring, boring, especially when I was alone.

It's okay, you can tell me to shut up . . . I *chose* to sell!

This page was intentionally left *blank*, because that's what life was like for many months.

CHAPTER 50
GINA MOVES TO THE OTHER SIDE OF THE WORLD

Joan called one morning and said, "Did you hear that your darling Gina is moving to New Zealand?" "*What*?!" I replied. "New Zealand?! Jesus Christ, could she move any farther away? Why New Zealand?" Joan replied, "You don't know? She was your international fresh fish buyer when she worked for you and was talking to this guy over there for over a year. Remember him? He came to Diana's wedding. Well, they apparently have a thing for each other, so there you go. She's moving—and soon. She also said she just may have found her husband." I replied, "How in the hell could she know or feel she loves him from just having seen him so briefly? And just for a few days, for Christ sake?" Joan then said, "Who knows what happened when she was in Hawaii, or while he was here." Hmm. I didn't want to go there.

If you took a BBQ skewer and stuck it in a globe of the earth from San Francisco, it would damn near come out in New Zealand—the other side of the frickin' world!

I was deeply saddened to hear of this. Was it her discontent that was causing her to seek a life on the other side of the world? I wondered. To get away from us? Or even more so, from *me*—and so damn far away? I mentioned this to Joan, and she snapped back at me, "Why does everything have to revolve around you? You?" Whew, okay, I hadn't meant it like that. Joan further barked at me, "Did you ever think that maybe she just wants to make a life for herself without the competition from her two sisters, or from you?" (Wasn't that sort of what I'd just said before she barked at me?) Joan then continued, "We have to support her wishes, and it just may be that she'll come back, anyway." I replied, "Okay, okay, honey. I'll support her wishes. I'm just going to miss her." Jesus Christ, New Zealand!

It was now fall of 1992, spring in the Southern Hemisphere, I guess a good time to make the move. Summer would be coming soon over there, a good time to get acclimated. I had to hand it to Gi, this was a monumental move. She was a brave girl.

She sold her lovely townhouse in Foster City, and her car, then ordered a container to be delivered to my apartment building in Burlingame to be loaded and shipped with all her belongings. I couldn't believe this was really happening.

Well, it did. She was soon on an hour flight from SFO to LAX, then almost fourteen hours over to Auckland and into the arms of a stranger, at least to us. That was a very uncomfortable feeling, but she was an adult and there wasn't much we could say or do about it, nor did we dare.

The container with all her belongings would take about three weeks to arrive in New Zealand if all went well.

She then settled in a quaint little Kiwi town on the north island called Whitianga (pronounced "Fitianga"), primarily a vacation spot for those fond of sport fishing and hunting during the summer months.

Joan and I flew over shortly after Gina had gotten settled in. We wanted to check this guy out and investigate everything, plus see where they were living. He appeared to be a nice man, but my father had a saying, "A new broom sweeps clean." However, they both seemed to be very happy and in love, and as parents, that's all you want—your children to be happy and healthy and respected by their significant other, especially if they're on the other side of the world.

After spending some time with them we soon found that he annoyingly smoked cigarettes almost incessantly and drank red wine as if it was tap water, but after a few days and meeting their friends, it appeared that most Kiwis smoked and drank as he did, and it was pretty much the norm over there. I also noticed that hardly any one wore shoes! Now that I found strange.

They were renting an adorable tiny old cottage, a "bach," as they called it, that was situated alongside a winding road just on the outskirts of the little quaint town. Well, one night as we slept, we heard strange noises coming from the hallway in the middle of the night and assumed it was just someone going to the bathroom or walking about. That morning, Gi asked us, "Did you guys hear the sounds in the hallway last night?" We both naturally replied, "Yes, we did. Why?" Gi then responded, "Well, the house has a couple of ghosts!"

The story goes, as she then explained, "It seems that two little girls liked to play in the hallway during the night, and they often rolled a ball up and down the long hallway. We've both actually seen them. They vanish once they notice us, though. We don't know if they died here in the house or not, but something strange happened here many years ago. The neighbors seem to change the subject when we ask."

It was a bit unnerving, sleeping there, but we soon got used to it; I chose however, not to get up in the middle of the night—for anything!

Fast forward one year: I received a call from Gina's fiancé one Sunday evening at ten o'clock. (Depending on the time of the year, the time in New Zealand is nineteen- to twenty-one hours ahead of California). It was five o' clock in the afternoon on Monday in New Zealand. They were evidently taking a walk on the beach and he wanted to ask Gi if she would marry him, and he was asking for my permission. He'd better! Well, a wedding took place a few months later, and again on the beach, and yep, of course, over there in New Zealand. I was happy for Gi, yet saddened because this was now looking very permanent. I wasn't liking that our lives were slowly slipping away, and we were missing precious time together, but perceived that she must be very happy and content and really loves the guy.

The family all flew over a few days before the wedding, and of course, slept in the house with the kids playing ball in the hallway during the night. I even thought of buying them a new ball. The next morning, Laura and Diana asked who was in the hallway making so much noise at two in the morning . . . we all just looked at each other!

It was a wonderful and meaningful wedding, though unfortunately it rained that day, as it often does, even in summer. Several of Gina's friends flew over and naturally, the groom's entire family was there, as well. The reception was held at the yacht club on the waterfront in the small harbor not far from downtown Whitianga. The entire quaint downtown area was only three blocks long.

I got up and made a short speech. I said, "This is the third happiest day of my life. The first was when Laura got married, the second when Diana got married, and now Gina." Well, a thunderous voice from somewhere in the crowd screamed, "How about when we got married?!" That was naturally Joan, in her stage voice! I then humbly restated my comment. "Excuse me, of course, the *fourth* happiest day of my life!" All the people chuckled—everyone except Joan. *Whoops!*

I remember getting choked up as I finished my speech as I looked at Gina. I forget exactly what I said, but I was suddenly overcome with emotion, loving her so much and finally seeing her happy. We'd gone through so much together. I still recall seeing Gi wiping her eyes, saying, "Wow, my dad doesn't normally get choked up like that!"

Gina had a nice chunk of money from the sale of her townhouse and they were talking about looking to buy a home. The currency conversion from U.S. dollars to New Zealand funds at that time was about two and a half times greater, so that was a big plus for them.

Things were looking good over there, and Joan and I were happy for Gi. We returned home content.

Shortly afterward, Gina started a business, a travel website that designed vacations for people with specific desires while traveling in New Zealand. She called her company "New Zealand Encounters." I was very proud of her. My gosh, she had only been there a short time, and was in a country she knew little about, in an industry she knew nothing about—and she had started a business. Our daughter was an entrepreneur! It wasn't long before she was doing amazingly well. The business was a cash cow, and she was employing seven people. I was amazed at what she'd created—from nothing with nothing. Déjà vu!

Oh, and remember that model fishing boat I bought in Monterey called *Lucky Boy*? Well, Gina now had it outside her office. Next time I was there I'd have to remember to strike out "boy" and replace it with "girl."

Gina would fly home to visit often, and we would go there as well, making it easier to accept her living so far away. It was always so joyous upon seeing her, yet so sad when having to leave.

On one of the occasions when Gi came home during the summer, Diana went back with her to stay for a couple of weeks. Diana had her own private practice and was doing very well. Summer was Di's slow time with family therapy, since the kids were out of school and on vacation. Gina had been staying with us, so Di and her husband came to the house on the day of the flight to New Zealand and we then all drove in their car to the airport. At the airport as they were about to enter the plane, we all hugged and said our sad goodbyes to Gi and wished Diana a fun trip.

Strangely, on the way driving back to our house, Diana's husband was driving rather fast and erratically. This bewildered me, though I don't think Joan noticed other than when she grabbed the arm rest a few times. As he pulled in front of our home, we invited him in for a beer. He loved beer, and after all, it was a warm summer Sunday afternoon, and he supposedly had nothing to do. Well, obviously anxious to leave, he imprudently declined, and his demeanor displayed his urgency to leave. That was odd; something was amiss; something strange was up! He then drove away in a hurried rush with his tires screeching. I watched him drive down the street, and as he disappeared around the turn, my suspicions grew. I stood outside for the longest time, blankly staring down the street as a sick feeling came over me at the thought that my daughter could soon be hurt, very hurt. But I never mentioned it, fearing it could just be my own guilt and sense of wrongdoing, and hoped I was wrong.

CHAPTER 51
THE DEMON GOES TO HELL!

It was time, so, I STOPPED DRINKING!—cold turkey. Yep, I'd finally gotten rid of that damn obsessive and domineering crow.

There was no need to escape from anything any longer, so I let Crissy fly away once and for all, and hopefully she would never return. However, I must admit, it wasn't easy letting go of that demon. It had embraced me when no one else would.

Let's review the challenges I'd vanquished so far: The Union; along with successfully selling the business. The baby; which freed me from possible life-changing consequences. Alcohol; no more whiskey to make me frisky!

But there were still two more huge and very important challenges to overcome: I still needed to win my wife back; and I still needed my girls' forgiveness. These are my paramount goals.

Now, with finally having prevailed over the disease of alcoholism, three of the five conjectured sequence of events had been circumvented. I must correct that statement; I did not prevail over alcoholism. The addiction is still ever so present, it is just psychologically and judiciously hiding.

The impulse to finally end this long siege of malevolent alcohol enslavement came to me late one evening on a fierce, stormy night, while driving—or should I say *attempting* to drive. The night was black, and visibility almost non-existent, while a heavy downpour belted intense rain against the windshield as the wipers flung back and forth. Harsh winds also blew the heavy coupe about as if being rocked by an enraged behemoth.

Unable to tell whether it was the wind and the rain that was causing the car to swerve about, or if it was my inability to properly control it under my impervious condition, I was now profoundly alarmed. I was, as a matter of fact, suffering from delirium tremens—sudden confusion that is paired with hallucinations and shaking resulting from the acute alcohol content in my blood stream. Yes, I was that bad. A near empty fifth of bourbon was also deceptively hidden under the front seat of the car in my attempt to camouflage my inability to drive. I was shamefully driving to the liquor store to replenish that seductive ethanol that deluded logic and mitigated the vexation of my spirit.

Something in the frontal lobe of my brain then suddenly snapped and caused a total realization of my idiotic insanity. I pounded on the steering wheel and screamed, "Goddamn it, stop it! Stop it! Just goddamn *stop it!*" I'll never forget that moment. I'll never forget where I was. I was at the intersection of Maple and West Fifth Avenue in San Mateo, and as I slowly drove by Bay Tree Park, a small quarter-acre park on the corner, I then grabbed the almost empty bottle of bourbon from under the seat, unscrewed the top, and desperately hoped that there was just one little drop left to taste for the very last time, because I now knew it was going to be *the* last time.

Thankfully, a minuscule drop moistened my tongue as I turned my head back and forth in disgust at the acidulous taste and said, "Never again—that's it!"

I then threw the devoid bottle of aqua vitae out the window and into the shrubs of the park. Yes, that was wrong. But I was drunk.

I then set my mind like a vise to *never* loosen, and now visualized alcohol as poison, and vowed to eschew alcohol until death do we part.

The mind is its own place, and in itself, can make a heaven of hell, or a hell of heaven.

It has fortunately been almost thirty years without that obsessive, controlling demon telling me what to do.

I must admit though, it wasn't easy to quit on my own. It took many months of constantly fighting the urges, especially when the alarm went off around five in the evening before it started to wane. It was as if there was a devil on my shoulder whispering in my ear, "It's time . . . it's time. C'mon, it's okay, it's okay. You can have just one little drink." However, once my body had been purged and purified of the alcohol in my system and that damn alarm had ceased, it was just a matter of mindset that has allowed me to prevail all these years.

Having said that, I must mention and caution, if you are indeed a heavy drinker, or possibly an alcoholic, whether you admit it to yourself or not, it is important to detox from alcohol under the supervision of a medical professional. The withdrawal from quitting cold turkey can lead to death. My quitting in that risky fashion was just me, with my foolish and reckless ways, having to do things my way and by myself, and without help. That was not and is not wise!

The one time I attended Alcoholics Anonymous it allowed me to understand that alcoholism is indeed a disease and can be controlled, but never cured. And most preeminently, it made me realize I wasn't alone. I commend Alcoholics Anonymous for the wonderful organization they are and say bravo to all the volunteers who give their support and help for those with addictions. I now admit that I was—no, that I *am*—an alcoholic. Like they say at AA, you must admit it—most importantly, to yourself—before you can conquer it. Correction, control it.

I am *so* very grateful to my three incredible, loving daughters who made me aware of how the effects of alcoholism had impaired and impacted our family life. That revelation, along with finally becoming cognizant of how alcohol desensitizes and anesthetizes all logic and common sense finally brought me to my senses. Without their love and support, I could have never defeated the demon.

My girls saved my life. They gave me a second chance. *Death begets life*. Like a tiny fir tree growing atop a dead log in the forest, emanating the powerful embodiment of determination, energy, and rebirth.

Oh, by the way. Joan is NOT DIVORCING ME! She had forgiven me.

M girls had also ACCEPTED ME BACK as their father!

I have very fortunately overcome *all five* insurmountable and impervious challenges, and against some most insurmountable odds.

You must never give up your determination to reach a goal.

My *persistence* finally prevailed...

CHAPTER 52
OUR FIRST GRANDCHILD ~ BEAUTIFUL SAMANTHA

Laura was now pregnant with our first grandchild. How exciting! A soon-to-be granddaughter named Samantha, and if she looked anything like her mom, she was going to be a knockout! She was due in early February of next year. This would be a whole new extension of love never experienced. We would be grandparents in a few months—ah, the cycle of life.

Well, I was living at home now; yep, the real home, on De Sabla Road. How nice to once again call it home. The ring was now on forever, thankfully. I never asked her, however, if she just hadn't been able to get it off?!

Meanwhile, we had been anxiously waiting for Samantha to be born. It was 1993, and the first week of February. Laura was due at any time. We anticipated her phone call to drive down to Long Beach at any moment to be with her when she entered the hospital.

The call finally came at 2 a.m. on February 4, a Thursday. It was Mark, Laura's husband, saying they were on their way to the hospital. Of course, we were sound asleep, so we jumped out of bed, got dressed, packed a few things, and got on the road. We hastily drove down to Long Beach and arrived at the Long Beach Memorial Hospital just before eight that morning.

Laura was already in the delivery room, but we were able to see her just before giving birth. She had been in labor for over eight hours, so was ready to give birth at any time, and sure enough, a few minutes later, in she went. After some time, we were called in to see little adorable Samantha. She had striking, platinum-blonde hair, with piercing, big brown eyes and a demanding cry.

Laura then made me hold her, and I was scared stiff I would drop her! While holding her and looking down at this miracle of life, this newborn infant, I was suddenly overwhelmed with an extension of love that I didn't know was possible, one never experienced, a love that captivated every cell in my body. I always thought the love of your child was the deepest, most revered love a father or mother could experience. Of course, it is, but this new revelation of life created from within our daughter allowed me to embrace this infant with all the love a grandfather could possibly possess. *A child born from within our child.*

A few hours later, Joan and I went to the cafeteria to have a cup of coffee. Joan then made a startling comment about Samantha, saying, "There's something wrong. I can't put my finger on it, but something's wrong." Taken aback by her comment, I repeatedly asked her what she'd seen, what she was thinking, but received no response. That was confusing and frightening, and it concerned and scared the hell out of me. I made her promise she wouldn't say anything to Laura or Mark.

As you know, Joan seems to have voodoo tendencies with sudden emotional rash responses, and most of the time, she is shockingly right. Well, this time, I chose to dismiss her observation about Samantha, hoping she was wrong.

We stayed with Laura and Mark for the first week and noticed that Sami was apparently having a difficult time sleeping. Laura was exhausted, staying up with her most of the nights, not allowing Joan to help her. It was only after Laura was weakened by the perpetual intense episodes of constant crying and tossing about that she finally conceded to let Joan help her.

We questioned the doctor, asking if the baby was in pain, but he said it was normal, and she possibly just had infantile colic, with paroxysms of irritability, fussing, and crying. He cautioned Laura not to overfeed her to lessen the crying, and to not give her juices with high sugar content. He also mentioned that the presence of excessive anger, anxiety, fear, or excitement in the household could worsen the colic symptoms. Well, it seemed as if Laura and Mark weren't getting along very well at the time. There appeared to be a lot of pent-up animosity between them, so possibly the baby was picking up the discontent in the house, or who knows. After all, she was just a newborn infant.

Thank God we stayed with Laura that week, but I feared how she was going to handle Sami without Joan's help. We wanted to stay longer, but we had a house sitter staying with the dogs who had to leave, and of course, Laura also insisted.

On the drive back home, I couldn't help but think about Joan's comment about her noticing something wrong with Samantha. As I said before, Joan has an innate second sense that I've learned not to question, *but* . . . there couldn't be anything wrong with our Sami. God forbid!

We would check in on Laura several times a week, not only to see about her, but to see how Sami was doing. Laura would always say everything was fine. However, I've learned that "fine" is a dismissal, meaning, "I don't want to talk about it." We knew she wasn't content in her marriage, and her life in Long Beach was strained, but we all go through some rough spots. Ha, do we! I felt it would eventually mend, and Sami would soon outgrow being so difficult.

We would drive down to Long Beach every so often to check on Laura and the baby since we were worried about them, especially with the apparent discontent in the marriage. Sami was now coming upon a year old and we couldn't help but notice a definite behavioral problem developing. Though Laura was a wonderful mother, we now hesitantly started questioning her mothering skills. We soon learned, though, that Laura was well aware of Sami's odd behavior and was totally exhausted and overwhelmed attempting to deal with it. She was consequently surrendering and giving in to Sami's every demand just to try to appease her to avoid another challenging, arduous, and trying tantrum.

Nonetheless, often nothing worked, and at times the tantrums seemed uncontrollable and extremely intense. This was very disturbing, and we were dumbfounded. We also thought possibly Laura just loved her too much, and the baby was influenced by all the attention. We naturally understood why Laura would put all her love into her child since the marriage was apparently lacking affection, so why wouldn't Laura give in to Sami and maybe spoil her a little? Especially when having these incredible outbursts that none of us understood. Laura was, at the time—and still is—an amazing mother and a loving, caring person. We all just assumed that Laura's mothering skills possibly needed some improvement, and we hoped the marriage would also improve so some of the love would be directed back to her husband; that in time, this would all pass.

Another year passed, and Sami now celebrated her second birthday. Shortly afterward, Laura and Mark decided to leave Long Beach and move up to Northern California.

Laura had been working for a large design firm in Long Beach and was doing very well before she'd gotten pregnant. She'd graduated with a bachelor of fine arts degree, with a specialization in interior architectural design and had designed several bank buildings in the area. Coincidentally, she'd done the schematics and design for the interior of the Long Beach Memorial Hospital where Samantha was born. She could and would have had a great future in Southern California, but wanted to be closer to us, her family. It's possible she also subconsciously feared or had preconceptions that Sami could have an impairment or pathological condition that had yet to be diagnosed and would need the closeness and love and support of her family.

Wanting a similar climate as Southern California, they bought a home in the East Bay, just on the other side of Mount Diablo in Danville, a chic community of young well-to-doers. They bought a charming, single-level, three-bedroom home in a lovely country setting, ideal to raise a family. Mark and Laura were trying to get their marriage back in order and were now talking about possibly having another child.

Sami was getting bigger, and even more beautiful, but appeared to be having some balance problems while walking. We weren't sure if it was our imagination or trepidation; however, at the same time, we also perceived that her learning abilities appeared to be very slow, but since the doctors didn't seem to be concerned or have any suspicions, we hoped it wasn't anything out of the ordinary.

The temper tantrums—we were now calling them "outbursts"—had not ceased. If anything, they were getting more intense and occurring more frequently. Laura was also having a more difficult time controlling Sami, since she was now so much bigger. Everyone was saying it was just baby stuff, little kid stuff, and she would outgrow it. We sure hoped so. One day while we were at Laura's, Joan, without forethought, blurted out in front of Laura that she felt Sami's eyes had an odd look. I immediately shushed her, only to be flagrantly given the Italian flag. Thankfully, Laura was busy doing something and didn't hear her. Well, Joan was right. I had noticed it, too. But jeez, Laura had enough going on.

Samantha was coming up on two and a half, and the sleep disturbance and the outbursts weren't getting any better. The outbursts— "episodes," as we now affably chose to call them—were much worse, now violent and very frightening! We categorically had to conclude that something wasn't right. I kept on thinking back to Joan's foreboding comment, "Something's not right." I started to believe it to be true. But what? None of the countless doctors Laura had taken Sami to could find anything wrong with her, even after all the endless tests.

Laura now started talking about seriously getting pregnant again. Of course, the fear that she may have another child with "something wasn't right"—the only layman's diagnosis we could come up with at the time—was foremost in our minds. Plus, the exhaustion factor that Laura was experiencing naturally led us to question her decision, but both Joan and I wouldn't dare say anything. Well, that's not entirely true. We did casually suggest that she and Mark be tested for . . . for what? However, we mentioned if she was in fact to get pregnant to have the fetus checked, but again, checked for what? No doctor had determined anything was out of the ordinary except for the possible behavioral problem.

The relationship between Joan and I now seemed to be going optimistically well, however, as expected, extremely cautiously on her part. I couldn't get enough of being with her. Why had it taken an almost cessation of my marriage to make me realize that? It took many years for me to finally understand that making a good living, is not necessarily making a good life.

A few months passed, and yep, Laura was now pregnant! Well, that hadn't taken long, and she was hoping for a boy.

Sami was still acting up and we were all now very seriously concerned. It was horrible to witness her being in this recurring state of what appeared to be a complete and uncontrollable *total sensory overload*. We all felt helpless and were baffled since all the tests continued to come back negative, showing nothing—absolutely nothing. The doctors now seemed frustrated and even annoyed when Laura called, since their only positive diagnosis was an assumption, she wasn't enforcing better behavior. This was now sounding repetitive, and a way to exculpate themselves from not being able to come up with an accurate diagnosis.

Laura was crying out for help, yet there was no help. A doctor or specialist couldn't help. When Sami was experiencing an uncontrollable outburst, she attacked her mother, biting, pinching, and hitting her, while incessantly slapping her own face, obviously causing a great deal of pain to both. Nonetheless, Laura's only concern was for her daughter's well-being as Sami tossed and thrashed about, out of control. Laura was only concerned Sami would seriously hurt herself. I so feared for Laura when Sami got bigger. It broke my heart to see *two people I loved so much, both being hurt at the same time.*

Let's now zoom forward seven months to April 17, 1996, to the birth of a very handsome baby boy named Maxwell. Yea! A boy in the family at last! What a thrill, but how in the hell did you play with a boy? All I'd ever known were my daughters and Sami! What a new and fun experience this would be. Now I could play rough with him, knock him around a bit, or him, me, maybe even arm wrestle. No gentle girly stuff!

Sami had turned three a couple of months ago, so there was three years and two months' difference between them. Laura was on double duty now, and I didn't know how she was going to do it.

CHAPTER 53
ANOTHER BUSINESS VENTURE ~ SAMI IS DIAGNOSED

I needed an interest. My damn mind was driving me nuts. Sure, I loved being a grandparent, but it would be some time until I could really do *stuff* with them. I also found that I was irritating Joan, being around the house so much. Oh no! No! I didn't want to do that!

I had two choices. The first and foremost involved Paladini's famous smoked salmon. We had the best, the very best. I'm not saying that because it's me talking; we, as a matter of fact, had the finest cold-smoked salmon possibly in the world. When you opened the wrapping, you smelled smoke. There's nothing on the market now that I'm aware of where you can actually smell the smoke emanating from the salmon. The methodology of the process goes back to the days of my grandfather, a time-consuming process of splitting the salmon, then mild-curing, washing, fan drying, then smoking the salmon for a minimum of eighteen hours at a temperature between seventy and seventy-five degrees, using only genuine redwood chips to slowly smoke the salmon.

Don't be confused with smoked salmon and the term "lox." Authentic lox is only from the belly of the salmon, and only salt-sugar cured, not smoked.

Also, paramount to our smoking process was smoking only the finest quality wild salmon, the King, or more formally named Chinook, dutifully and carefully hand selected without bruises, between fourteen and eighteen pounds. We chose the wild King/Chinook salmon that was caught only between Moss Landing and Crescent City, California. It is the finest of all salmon, since the fish consume the tiny bay shrimp that abundantly flourish within those waters which sweetens the salmon's reddish-pink flesh. The King salmon also has a fat content like no other salmon. It is also the most expensive.

The most widely used wild salmon for smoking today in the U.S. is the Alaska Silver, or Coho salmon, due to its abundant quantities and low price; however, it lacks the flavor and fat content of the more expensive and now scarce King/Chinook salmon. Most consumers today assume since the flesh of the Silver/Coho salmon is bright red, it's the best, but nothing is further from the truth. Quite possibly, they just don't know any better, since our product is now no longer being produced. If you never tasted better, how would you know?

Farmed salmon is also now abundantly being smoked. The current intensive "farming of salmon," is causing over production throughout the world, and has greatly reduced the price of the raw product. I personally feel harvested smoked salmon lacks the taste of the wild product, and certainly the fat content, which is crucial to bringing out the superior flavor.

If I was to choose to smoke salmon, my family and friends, especially my good Jewish friends, would be most happy, because they all loved it. However, I would need a cooler and freezer, refrigerated trucks, and a million-dollar line of credit to buy for the off-season. That would be a serious business. I didn't want serious. I wanted fun. Sorry, my good Jewish friends!

The second choice, and the right choice, involved a line of shelf-stable sauces to enhance seafood. No cooler, no freezer, no need for refrigerated trucks or a line of credit, just me and a brain—if it was still any good after almost being pulverized.

Joan had already developed a cocktail and a tartar sauce when I'd had the wholesale business, and it had gone rather well. It was called "Mama Paladini's," but we never pushed it; after all, we had tons of fresh fish that had to be moved daily, and the sauces were an afterthought. The Safeway stores and a few higher-end stores, however, did carry the line with success.

The process to produce the sauces would be relatively easy to initiate, since the bottling company in Gilroy would still have the two formulas, which would make it simple to get it started.

Joan is an accredited chef and a fabulous cook. She graduated with honors from chef's school at La Canada College, and I thought she would enjoy working with me to develop a line of maybe a half-dozen seafood sauces, which would make a compete line to offer the retail stores. I was thinking of an all-natural gluten-free Cocktail Sauce; an all-natural gluten-free Hot and Spicy Cocktail Sauce; a Tartar Sauce made with minced capers and dill; a Louis Dressing for crab or shrimp Louis salads; and an exceptional all-natural gluten-free Cioppino/Pasta Sauce. Directly out of the jar, it would be a fabulous pasta sauce with just a hint of heat as you swallowed. Instructions on the label to add lemon juice and a splash of white wine would turn it into an authentic old San Francisco Cioppino Sauce, or to be used with baked fish.

"Cioppino," for those of you who aren't familiar with it, is a type of seafood stew that contains Dungeness crabs, littleneck clams or manila clams, prawns/shrimps, chunks of firm-fleshed fish, as well as optional scallops or mussels. Basically, you can throw in just about anything, since that is how the dish got started. It was an accumulation of what was left over from the daily catch. The tomato-based sauce is enhanced with olive oil, onions, shallots, garlic, and red pepper flakes. My grandfather was influential in developing the dish back in the late 1800s in San Francisco, though this has been debated.

Maybe we would even come up with one more sauce, possibly a remoulade. My mind was driving me nuts, and I was heading toward making this big again. I had to remember, I didn't want big anymore. I didn't want big anymore!

Laura heard about the new venture and wanted to design the labels. She then hand drew the labels for the printer to make his proof and plates. What a talented girl! I originally said no to her because she had so much going on. Sami was now four and a half, and Maxwell, one and a half, and as you know, Sami was a hand full. But I really wanted Laura to design the labels, making this a fun family project.

I was thrilled with the concept of the sauce line, and it would be easy, but I had to get off my butt now and market it. I'd have to go and see the chain-store buyers to sell it. However, I'd gotten lazy and passive and really didn't feel like it. So then why was I doing this? Well, I had no idea!

The 1996 Fancy Food Show was coming up in January at the Moscone Convention Center in San Francisco, and I decided to introduce the line at the show. Meanwhile, it would be necessary to join the National Association for the Specialty Food Trade (NASFT) to be able to get a booth and have a display for the taste testing. Any respected retail food line is a member of the NASFT, so this would make a first-class introduction for the line.

Flash forward many months to the day of the Fancy Food Show—yeah, another funny, not so short, short story: On the opening day of the fancy food show, the salesman I had hired worked with me to set up the display. It was tedious since the tiny bay shrimp used with the sauces for the taste testing needed to be kept cold; our refrigeration was crushed ice that continued to melt all over the floor. We soon were able to deal with that, and eventually got the display set up, with no less than a combined hundred little cups filled with the tiny bay shrimp topped with the five sauces.

As the morning went on, our backs started acting up having had to stand there for hours being cordial to the hordes of people stopping by to taste the sauces, while giving them a pitch about the line.

Many people who are not commercial wholesale buyers attend the show to not only see what new products are available, but to consume the free food that is on display in abundance.

It was about two in the afternoon and a middle-aged lady stopped by and stood there for at least twenty minutes consuming no less than sixteen to eighteen samplings, while just saying, "Mmm, so good." She was rather rotund and not outstandingly dressed, and by now had spilled red cocktail sauce on her white blouse. I was getting perturbed because she not only was standing directly in front in the middle of the display, but we had to keep refilling the damn display since she was eating them faster than we could refill it. I was about to be rude to her and ask if she'd just enjoyed lunch, when she took out her card and said, "Call me for an appointment. I would like to carry your line." She was the head grocery buyer for a major supermarket chain with over three hundred stores! I don't want to mention the name, because I didn't talk very nicely about her!

Upon meeting with her the following week, she ordered two hundred cases of each item, which came to a total of one thousand cases. So, a lesson learned, you never know who you're talking to!

This was getting more involved than I'd thought it would be, but I had to do it right, and in my own way. I have always been autonomous, self-directing, and independent. Remember, you can't change the ways of a Scorpion. I was having that compelling feeling again that there were no gray zones; it was either black or white. That business philosophy drives me nuts. Everything must be damn perfect! However, my sister Kay has always said, "Perfection is boring!"

I named the line "Paladini Quality Seafood Sauces," and would use the phrase *"An Authentic Taste of San Francisco."* I would use the same logo, the big red P that was highly recognized on my trucks throughout Northern California.

The family name would now live on. No longer on large trucks, but on tens of thousands of little jars!

The product line could eventually just be the premiere line of seafood sauces on the market! It sounded like a lot to achieve, especially since I didn't know what the hell I was doing. But I hadn't known the seafood industry either, and I'd bluffed my way for over thirty years.

The sauces would be created using only the best quality ingredients, thus producing the finest of flavors. As a result, I knew we would be having numerous taste tests and adjustments to the formulas at the packer before putting it on the market. It would not be developed to be priced to compete with low-cost inferior seafood sauces for volume sales, but for the high-end, quality, knowledgeable, savvy clientele. Whatever the production cost ended up being, it would be marked up accordingly without competitive pricing. As I said prior, I wasn't aiming to compete for volume, but to appeal to the educated palate.

After all, an Aston Martin demands a high price because of its quality in workmanship and individuality of styling, it isn't competing with lower-priced, mediocre cars. They have a standard unto their own, and a market base accordingly. I fully understood that the level of affordability would be lessened, but that was the market base I'd chosen. I wasn't doing this as a money maker. It was only to have fun. Okay, and yes, maybe to get the name back out there again. See, I said it before you did!

Speaking of businesses, Gina's business was going great—she was now employing twelve people. Her husband, however, had unknowingly started to deplete her cash flow to pay his expenses after his most recent failed attempt to compete with her entrepreneurial ingenuity. It seemed as if each flippant idea he had had so far had failed, causing Gina to make up for his lost revenue, having to pay his payroll and general expenses out of her exceedingly profitable company.

Gina and I discussed this many times, and both knew it couldn't continue. It appeared as if whatever he attempted ended poorly.

He had two, very nice, clean-cut handsome sons from a prior marriage. Gina had taken them in and taught them about family bonding and proper manners. They were both very fond of Gina, and obviously respected her. That was amazing, because let me tell you, when Gina reprimands you, you know you'd better straighten out—and quickly! However, they adored her and appreciated the love they received from her; she loved them as if they were her own.

Diana—I wasn't sure about Diana, or what was going on with her and her husband. On the surface, everything seemed fine, but I wasn't so sure. Diana was a strong-willed and very smart girl, and also very private; she would never let it be known if anything was wrong unless she was ready to divulge it. I so hoped her marriage was okay, but I strongly doubted it.

Laura was still struggling with her marriage. She wasn't happy, and it was obvious.

I so hoped my three daughters' marriages weren't heading for collapse. My God, could that be? There was an instinctive sense of uncertainty that I perceived from them. *All* of them. That was unnerving; I couldn't bare seeing them hurt. How could all three marriages be strained?

Well, "Massimo," as I call him, was going to be three years old in a few months, and was running all over the place, as boys do. It was a lot of fun being with him and thank God there was nothing wrong with him. He was as normal, handsome, and as healthy as can be.

Samantha was now coming up on six, and was running Laura ragged. She was sadly not getting any better, and if anything, worse.

One day we were at a supermarket, and when Laura went to pay the cashier, Sami freaked out and threw herself to the ground, screaming and tossing about while banging her head on the hard floor. She then went after her mother, hitting and pinching her relentlessly. A woman in line, also a parent, came up to Laura and said, "If that was my child, I would give her the spanking of her life!"

It was always horrible and an embarrassing scene when this happened in public, especially since most observers assumed it was just a child behaving badly. What set her off, we all wondered? In that incident, all Laura had done was pay the cashier. Was it that they'd briefly interacted? It was an enigma. Most people just don't understand. It's too bad there isn't more awareness of specials needs children and adults. Most people live in a cloister, not projecting themselves into the lives of others; others' needs, their pain, or mental conditions at the time, or what event that could have just transpired to cause unexplained upheaval. When you see a child, or even an adult in obvious distress, if you can't help, at least attempt to use your thought process to try to analyze the situation and understand before passing judgment.

Well, after several years of exhausting all avenues to obtain a diagnosis for Samantha, Laura finally contacted Children's Hospital in Oakland and talked with a child behavioral counselor. They discussed Sami's explosive outbursts and self-injurious behavior, the nightly sleep-deprivation problems, and the delay in developmental progress. He thereupon recommended she be tested by a specialist in childhood disorders. Making a diagnosis for a genetic or rare disease can be difficult.

We had to determine what was going on with this poor child. This couldn't continue. The doctors were baffled, and we were at our wits' end.

Then, after six and a half years of living in disquietude, a molecular genetic testing was done, and beautiful little Samantha was finally diagnosed. She had Smith-Magenis Syndrome.

SMS is a rare neurobehavioral disorder. It affects one in approximately every twenty-five thousand births. The syndrome, however, likely remains under diagnosed. It is the partial deletion of chromosome 17p11.2, which contains the gene RAI1. The deletion is not inherited, but random, forming in early fetal development. It fortunately does not shorten life span. Our first concern.

It was told to us that she will most likely remain at a developmental age of about eight. We were devastated, of course. This only happens to other people.

Our beautiful Samantha will be *a child forever...*

Samantha, a child forever, so innocent, so pure, so trusting, and so unnervingly vulnerable. The beauty of the purity of her innocence and trust in people, causes great apprehension and trepidation. She just turned twenty-five and still believes in Santa Claus, and we hunt for Easter Eggs.

She will be excused from the burdens of adulthood, but, sadly, will also never realize the emotions of falling in love, dating or marriage. Her world is an illusion, one where the "yellow brick road" leads to no-where, and Mickey Mouse, Pluto and Snow White are her best friends. Money has no value nor need. She has no cognizance or desire for independence. It would never be attainable anyway.

She must feel torment living in her isolation, not being able to verbally express the turmoil within. When she implodes it is the result of *a complete involuntary sensory overload.*

Sami started having Grand mal seizures a few years ago, adding to the frailty of her debility. Last year she had precarious brain surgery to remove Cerebral Cavernous Malformations, a rare type of vascular malformation. A tangling of capillaries. If they were to hemorrhage it could cause stroke or even possible sudden death. This was discovered accidently while doing an MRI after an ophthalmologist suspected Sami had pressure behind one eye.

It was a very tense five-hour operation. It was only after the surgeon came from the operating room smiling when we all started breathing normally again. Thank you, God.

It takes a *special* parent to care for a *special* needs person. It is a life changing event for the parent or parents.

When I can make Sami laugh, it is like what sunshine is to flowers. She warms my heart, and her slight imperfection goes unnoticed. I am of course her "Papa."

Have you ever seen a small child acting up, tugging at the mother, tossing about or kicking and screaming uncontrollably? Sure, it may indeed be a temper tantrum or just a spoiled child, or it just possibly may be a symptom of SMS. This rare and little-known syndrome.

I immediately changed the labels on my sauce line to include a brief story about SMS and the symptoms, hoping to get the word out. If we only could help one child, one person, one parent, from the torment we went through, of not knowing.

I then donated all the net profits from the sales of the sauces that were now nationwide, to PRISMS. Parents and Researchers Interested in Smith Magenis Syndrome.

CHAPTER 54
A TRIO OF DIVORCES—SI, TRES

Laura's was the first, and it wasn't a surprise. About a year after they'd moved into the Danville home—yep, the one with the spirited grandma—her husband moved out and the aged poltergeist now comfortably settled in, becoming a frequent visitor watching over Samantha.

Oh, I had forgotten to mention that Laura had a spirit, a ghost, residing with her, didn't I? Silly me. Evidently the prior homeowner was an elderly women who passed away in the home. Laura was told by a neighbor that she always wanted a grandchild, and after her son married and they had a child, for whatever reason, the wife refused to allow his mother to see the baby. She evidently died distraught not being able to see her only grandchild.

Laura said that when walking down the hallway from the kitchen to Sami's bedroom in the rear of the house, she would often see a vision of bright lights emanating in a large circle similar to party sparklers. Having to get to Samantha, she had no choice other than having to walk through it. She said as she walked through, it was ice cold. I'm getting the shivers just thinking about it!

She further said that she didn't feel threatened by it and wasn't scared. Quite the opposite, she found it comforting and felt the old woman was watching over Sami and was finally happy that a young child was now in her home. I guess you can believe whatever you wish?

Well, shortly after her husband left, the home was sold and Laura moved into a townhouse in nearby San Ramon with the two children and her two very large dogs.

It seemed that Laura was constantly plagued with problematic scenarios. The dogs, Astro, a mature German shepherd, and Buckwheat, a stout, muscular rottweiler, now lived most of the time in her one-car garage. During the day she would leave the garage door half open or half closed, whatever way you wish to call it, with a removable, four-foot-high, heavy screened barrier to keep them inside. Both dogs were quite passive and non-threatening, contrary to the reputations of their breeds.

A woman neighbor living several doors away was a nut case, and disliked dogs—all dogs, big, small, any color, any breed. Well, she expeditiously claimed that Laura's dogs barked most of the day and were a nuisance. It was, however, quite the opposite; they slept most of the day because they were both mature animals.

Well, after numerous voicemail complaints, notes, and verbal confrontations from the woman, Laura got a restraining order against her, but to no avail. As I was told by my attorney many years prior, restraining orders, for the most part, don't work. Often it just provokes a situation and makes it worse. But Laura was beside herself and worried about her dogs' well-being while she wasn't home, and rightfully so.

Several months later, Joan and I were out for dinner with Laura and the kids. Upon returning to her home, we were horrified to find Buckwheat, the rottweiler, dead, apparently poisoned! It was a morose and heinous scene. Laura dropped to her knees and hysterically sobbed while holding Buckwheat's now limp body, his eyes open, blindly staring, while his tongue, moistened with blood, hung out of his mouth, staining Laura's dress.

Sami was now in a full-blown crazed meltdown, screaming to the point that several neighbors came out to investigate and wanted to call 911 because they thought she was being harmed. Maxwell, just a little boy at the time, was trembling as Joan comforted him in her arms, his head deeply embedded in her chest, not wanting to see or hear anything.

I was now in a rage, and got the shakes, and that wasn't good. I was out of control. I stormed over to the woman's house and rang the doorbell, then loudly banged on the door when they didn't immediately answer. Her husband then eventually opened the door to prevent it from being knocked off its hinges, as he cowered. I then, inches from his face, confronted him about his wife having poisoned Buckwheat. He stepped back, his face grimaced with consternation, and hollered to his wife to call the police! Ignoring his order, I demanded to know why she did it. I then heard her holler from the back room, denying it, screaming that the police were on their way, presumably to scare me. I tried to look for her to confront her, but her husband's protruding belly and robust frame blocked the way. We dodged back and forth for a few moments since I couldn't see over him. I wanted to push him aside but had to use restraint; I was in their home and could be arrested for assault and battery—not that I cared.

I'm not sure what would have taken place if I'd indeed had the opportunity to confront her. Maybe it was best that I didn't. I guess I was in such a state that I sounded physically threatening to the perplexed coward. But there was no doubt she'd done it!

I finally left, but she had indeed called the police. I was soon being questioned in the back of a police car. Seeing her papa in the police car, only fueled Sami's frenzy even more. I think the police only let me go because I explained that my granddaughter was a special needs child, and the episode was obviously causing her to have a paroxysm and she could convulse. I was then instructed to not go anywhere near the woman's townhouse and was released.

We now had a very large dead dog on our hands and the local animal control center didn't have an after-hours drop off for deceased animals. We had to drive over to the Peninsula Humane Society in San Mateo on the other side of the Bay, an hour away. It was heartbreaking hearing Laura and Sami sobbing in the backseat of the SUV as we drove over the bridge while Laura held Buckwheat, his reticent body slowly stiffening as blood seeped from his nose. It was now obvious that he had indeed been poisoned and had ruptured an internal organ.

Having to leave Buckwheat in the outdoor wooden enclosure in the cold dampness of the night as fog permeated the air from the nearby bay, was anguish for us all. Yes, he was gone, but still.

We then drove back to San Ramon in a silent, solemn mood as my temper raged within. It was extremely difficult for me to not be able to express anger to the perpetrator, but I'd had to abide, or I would have only made matters worse. Upon arriving back at Laura's townhouse, we then had to clean the garage floor where Buckwheat had vomited and bled to death just hours before. Joan tucked Sami in bed, trying to explain death. Naturally, being so young, neither she nor Maxwell understood the concept. Does anyone? We told them that Buckwheat was now playing with his pals up in doggie heaven. That was difficult, since Astro was now whining, looking for her partner.

It was a traumatic and exhausting experience for everyone.

Now let's get to what was happening with dear Diana. I will never ever forget it. It was just past eleven thirty on a Saturday night, and the phone rang. Naturally, it was startling to get a call that late.

It was Diana. She said, "Dad, please come pick me up." I started to ask what was wrong and she interrupted me. "Please don't ask me anything, please." Her voice was trembling, and she was obviously holding back from crying.

I immediately knew what it was. Joan then asked, "Kiki, what's wrong?" "I have to go pick up Diana at her house," I said. She then loudly exclaimed, "Why?!" I responded, "Something's up and I think I know what. I have to go!" Joan wanted to come, but felt it was best I go alone.

I arrived at their house, about a half hour away, and she was waiting for me on the corner. I could see she was trembling, and it wasn't cold. As she got into the car, she again said, "Please don't ask me anything, Dad . . . not now." I of course said, "Okay, kid." It was a long and silent half-hour ride back to our house. It was obvious her heart was broken. It took all the restraint in my body not to drive back and have a confrontation.

Meanwhile, Joan had made up the bed for her and greeted us at the front door. I looked at Joan and shook my head no, meaning don't ask or say anything. As difficult as it was, we left her alone that night, knowing she was crying her eyes out and needed to be alone, not questioned.

It was the middle of summer, and very warm the next morning when Joan and I got up, yet we found Diana sitting in the center of the living room all wrapped up in a blanket, rocking back and forth, shivering as she stared out the window, blindly gazing toward the garden, tears flowing down her face. She muttered something we perceived to be the bemoaned sound of heartache. That remembrance is etched within me to this day.

We sat in the living room with her for the longest time in complete silence. Joan then sat alongside her, taking her hand and rubbing it, then pulled her into her arms and hugged her. Diana most willingly collapsed into Joan's arms and cried and cried. I sat next to her and pulled her into my arms, and she cried even more . . . then I cried . . . then Joan cried . . . then we all cried together.

We didn't ask. We knew.

We sat there with heaviness of heart in reticence. The only sound was that of the waterfalls in the garden that could be remotely heard, attempting to dulcify the emotions we were experiencing. After some time had passed, Diana had started to regain her composure and said, "Well, Mom and Dad, you should know." Joan and I simultaneously said, "Only if you want to talk about it. Maybe let's just sit here a while longer." Diana then responded, "No, no, I want to tell you. We were sitting in the hot tub late last night and I mentioned to him that we had been married almost three years now and asked if he was ready to have children. Well, my supposedly loving husband hesitated, then replied, "No, I don't want to have children . . . with *you*."

Naturally, being shocked and taken aback by that stunning comment, Diana had asked him, "So just what does that mean?" Well, it meant he didn't love her anymore, if he ever had. He wanted a divorce.

Upon hearing that, my gut wrenched, and my fists clenched. I slammed them down on the marble table and wanted to immediately drive to his house and confront him! Diana naturally noticed my raging anger, seeing me get the shakes, knowing what that meant, and halted me. It would have been an ugly scene, and nothing would have been accomplished. His decision had been made, his desire expressed, and it had been acutely noted.

To this very day, I have pent-up anger toward him for the hurt he unduly inflicted upon Diana. She didn't deserve it. If ever there was a warm, loving, and compassionate girl, it was Diana.

I always had the feeling of uncertainty regarding his affection for her. His vagueness about their relationship was perplexing. Diana was dedicated to him and had given him her total commitment and faithful devotion, only to be burdened by his ambiguity, ambivalence, and incertitude.

I knew a good year earlier he was up to no good when he rushed off from dropping Joan and I off at the house after Di went to New Zealand. Who better than me to know?

Okay, so now let's talk about Gina. Yep, Gina also got divorced! But it didn't happen for a couple of years later. I'll eventually get to it, and boy was it a *doozy*!

CHAPTER 55

WE HAD ANOTHER WEDDING ~ THEN ANOTHER WEDDING ~ THEN ANOTHER WEDDING ~ THEN ANOTHER WEDDING

Nope, I didn't stutter up there. You heard correctly—another four weddings! Even though daughters, we have three.

To date, there have been seven weddings. Possibly even an eighth sometime in the future. So far there have also been five divorces. Oh, no more divorces, please. They cost more than the weddings!

You know, I just had to count all this on my fingers and concentrate with my eyes closed; it's rather difficult to keep track of. You're probably laughing about now.

I have to wonder how Joan and I stayed married, especially after all you've heard. Maybe it's old school, possibly tenacity, persistence, or just true love. It seems like getting married nowadays is like "going steady," as they called it when I was young. Breaking up was easy, sort of.

Diana was the first to get married again. A year or so after her divorce, she fortunately met a wonderful man, Brian, and oddly enough, they met through a close friend of her first husband. It was but a year after their courtship, and we were planning another wedding. This one was a keeper!

I'll never forget the day when Joan and I, Diana and Brian, and Brian's mom and dad were at my grandfather's old haunt, the iconic Palace Hotel in San Francisco. We were enjoying a lavish Easter Sunday brunch in the hotel's exquisite late-nineteenth-century Garden Court, just off the hotel's main lobby. The grandeur of the Garden Court is unparalleled, with its three-story, intricately detailed, stained-glass domed ceiling, and elegant accents wherever you look—an amazing setting for any occasion.

Everyone was affably sipping on their perpetually filled glasses of imported French Champagne, and I, on imported Italian Pellegrino—yeah, sparkling water—as we discussed where the venue should be for the upcoming wedding and reception. This was certain to be a joyous event, since Diana was adored by Brian, and she adored him as well.

Rather jokingly, I mentioned to Diana, "So kiddo, why don't you have the reception here at the Palace Hotel? It would be a magical setting, and you deserve it!"

I'd no sooner gotten those words out of my mouth before she darted off and was gone! For a second, I thought she had suddenly gotten ill from having eaten the abundance of chocolate decadence she'd consumed from the extravagant dessert table.

Well, where she went was not to the lady's room, but to see if the catering manager was in! When I mentioned having the reception there, I'd sort of been joking at the time, and never thought she would take me up on it! However, I was glad that she had.

Diana and Brian were married the following year on March 7 in the French Parlor, one of the hotel's most delightful venues.

Diana's two sisters were her bridesmaids, and her maid of honor was a close friend. Brian's daughter from his former marriage, Kira, now our "bonus" grandchild, seven at the time, was the flower girl. Our hearts were filled with joy. Brian was a fine gentleman and a good husband, and it was obvious they both respected and deeply loved each other. Thank God!

Brian graduated from the University of California Berkeley with a degree in engineering and is now extremely successful operating his own lucrative construction business.

Two years after they were married, Dianna gave birth to an adorable baby girl, Gianna. She was born on October 17, 2000, just three days before I had quadruple-bypass heart surgery. Well, we all knew way back that this had been coming.

Let me tell you how it came about. When Diana was pregnant with Gianna, Joan and I went out for dinner with Brian and Diana in Berkeley, close by where they lived at the time, to a noisy, spirited Sicilian restaurant about a half mile away. We walked to the restaurant, since Diana was late giving birth, in order to induce labor, as walking supposedly does. It was a warm, balmy Sunday evening in early October in the East Bay, so it was an easy and pleasant walk to the restaurant, especially since it was downhill, at least going there.

We all enjoyed a wonderful spicy meal, chowing down on all the cholesterol-laden, unhealthy food, starting with the multi-assorted antipasto plate, with the salt-saturated black olives, prosciutto, salami, mortadella, and celery—celery? How in the hell had that snuck in there? I've since learned however, that celery has long been touted as a nerve-soother and aphrodisiac, and it contains male pheromones believed to attract women. "Pass the celery please!"

Then there was the fresh, crispy San Francisco sourdough French bread with sweet butter that I topped off with a sprinkle of sea salt. Then the Caprese salad, the meat balls and spaghetti, and lastly, the dolce, the rich, creamy desserts that tempt you to overindulge, followed, of course, by a cup or two of the caffeine-riddled double espresso that would get my heart racing for the uphill trek home.

On the way back to Di and Bri's as we approached the uphill section, I started getting severe pains in the middle of my shoulder blades. I'd had similar pain in that region before, when my arms would go numb, but I'd never experienced anything quite like this. I wondered if this was a warning that I was about to or could soon have a heart attack. Then thought maybe it was just the devil hitting me with a pitch fork reminding me of my past, and was pissed off that I denounced him.

I then seriously started falling behind on the walk. Diana was talking and hadn't noticed that I was now several yards behind her. She soon looked back, noticed, and said, "Hey, Dad, what's wrong?" Not to alarm her, I said as only a man would, "Oh, it's nothing. Just my back acting up, kiddo. I'll soon catch up."

There was Diana, now power-walking uphill, her stomach staunchly protruding, feeling nothing—apparently no labor pains were in the forecast for that night.

Fortunately, a few minutes later I found a street sign and rested against it for a while, then started up the incline again. Upon reaching the house, I immediately sat down and caught my breath as the pain now slowly started to cease, but not entirely.

Diana and Joan both insisted that I see a chiropractor for my back the following week. But I knew better; it wasn't my back—it was my heart. I had to see a cardiologist!

Intending not to alarm Joan or Diana, I casually mentioned that it may be a good idea for me to have a stress test. I was at that age now, sixty-four, so possibly it wasn't my back. Well, that *did* alarm them, and now thought maybe I shouldn't have said anything.

I called a cardiologist my friend had recommended and advised him of the symptoms I was having. He took me in that same day, Monday. He immediately took my blood pressure, which was of course, normal—always was—and an EKG. The doctor never mentioned the results.

He then arranged for a treadmill stress test. Let me tell you, you could die taking that test. Oh my God, it was grueling! I never was much of a jogger. I had to sign a disclaimer that stated I was aware that on rare occasions while taking a stress test heart attacks may occur and could ultimately be fatal. There was a doctor and a technician constantly monitoring every activity during the test—I guess to catch you as you keel over.

Well, the cardiologist didn't like the results of the test, so he immediately arranged for an angiogram. I then asked what the procedure was, and I surely didn't like what I heard! He said they go in from the groin and follow an artery to and through the heart and inject dye. I then said, "Oh, so sort of like getting an internal tattoo, huh?" He then laughed and remarked, "You might say that, but this one's not permanent." I then replied, "Uh, the tattoo or the heart?" Yeah, I was nervously joking. He just grinned. He was obviously looking to see if I had coronary artery disease.

There are two kinds of tests for the diagnosis of coronary artery disease. One group includes different kinds of stress tests, and the other includes tests that look at the anatomy of heart arteries. The latter group includes coronary angiogram, also known as heart cath, short for catheterization, and CT angiogram. I had both tests, and the conclusion was that I needed immediate quadruple-bypass surgery since three arteries were over 90 percent blocked, and one was 95 percent blocked.

I guess it was a good thing I'd taken that walk with Di after dinner. It must have been the celery that had brought it on though—certainly not the salami or the fresh mozzarella or the bread with salt sprinkled on the sweet butter.

The cardiologist then recommended one of the finest cardiovascular surgeons in the area. I met with him the following day, and he wanted to operate the very next day, commenting that my condition was very serious. However, I insisted that I wait until Gianna was born, since I wouldn't know if I was going to indeed survive the open-heart surgery. I wanted to see my granddaughter.

I was told to take it *very* easy, and not do anything strenuous. Okay, sure. I was running the sauce business basically alone, apart from my nephew, who packed and drove, and the three people calling customers. The business was going amazingly well by now. The line was in most of the major supermarkets and was in all the upscale markets locally and in Southern California, including Whole Foods, and we were now starting to ship nationwide.

My purchase orders to the packer went from what'd I'd original feared, selling just seventy-five cases each of the original two sauces, to now ordering thousands of cases of each of the five sauces every few months. I had a warehouse and a new truck for local deliveries, and was under contract with three major distributors, as well as several smaller distributors locally and across the nation. I'd also contracted a sales representative in New Jersey who was now doing tremendous volume in the Northeast that included New York, New Jersey, and Connecticut.

Things were going very well, and I now feared that this "toy" of a supposedly fun business was getting out of control.

So, Mr. Cardiologist, how do I take it easy until Gianna is born? I wondered.

On the seventeenth, adorable "Gigi" was born. I lived to see my granddaughter, and I loved her from the very moment I saw her. What joy she has brought into our lives. I so remember when I first held her. Let me tell you, when your newly born grandchild holds your little finger tightly in her tiny palm, you're connected for life.

Surgery was then scheduled for the twentieth of that month. I guess it's obvious everything went well, since I'm writing this book.

In between all of this, Laura got married for a second time. However, they divorced twelve months later. I won't go into detail or mention anything about the marriage since it was so brief, especially since I choose to act as if it never happened.

Two years later, she married yet again! Now it's sounding like Hollywood marriages, isn't it? However, that marriage lasted a bit longer—yeah, two years. It abruptly came to a sudden end the day his lack of tolerance for Sami's condition became apparent. He erupted in a rage and caused a confrontation with her. Samantha's innocence and paucity were unfairly challenged. His declaration of love for Laura, and faux affection for her special needs child, was dutifully exposed. It is noteworthy, that a person with a disability, is what someone *has*, not what someone *is*.

My heart goes out to Laura. Her misfortunes with her husbands and having to care for a child with cognitive disabilities while trying to make a living—is a wonderment to me how she does it. We all know—actually, no, we don't know—what a difficult, all-consuming responsibility it is to take care of a child with SMS, handling the daily repetitive outbursts, the medical issues, the demands, exhaustion, pain—no, we don't know. It takes an extremely loving and dedicated *special parent* to care for their *special child* with the compassion that Laura does; especially with the realization that the umbilical cord of her daughter will forever be joined.

I sincerely hope if Laura marries again that she will know the *depth* of the man's love for her, and the true *extent* of the compassion, tolerance and tenacity he has to live with her child, as well.

If I was ever again to be asked for her hand in marriage, let me tell you, it will be one hell of a long lunch. As I said prior, the most difficult word to say is *no*, and I should have said no to a few of my three daughters' previous beaus.

How could we have ever known that *our little girl* would have *a little girl*—who would forever be *a little girl?*

CHAPTER 56
THE FAMILY JOURNEYS TO ITALY—GINA'S TURMOIL

It was early spring of 2006, and we all got together and planned a two-week family vacation to Italy for later that year. The first week we would be staying in a small villa overlooking the splendor of beautiful Lago di Como. However, only Joan and I, Diana and Gianna, and Gina, coming in from New Zealand, would spend that first week in Como.

Brian and Kira, Laura, Maxwell, and her then *current* husband were to meet us in Umbria the second week, where all of us would be staying in a two-hundred-year-old seven-bedroom farmhouse-style villa with a swimming pool, surrounded by a hundred or more acres of olive trees. The villa was called "Antica Quercia," and was close to the small town of Ponte Ferro between Orvieto and Spoleto. The magnificent countryside of Umbria was centrally located, allowing us to take daily trips to Pisa, Florence, and Rome, and the many surrounding historic places of interest.

It was now mid-August and the vacation started with Joan and I, Diana, and Gianna landing at the Milan airport a few hours before Gina. I picked up the rental car and we then waited for Gi to arrive. Upon her arrival, it was discovered that her suitcase was lost. She'd had to go through a maze of flights to get from Auckland to Milan by first going to Los Angeles, then to London, then to Milan. The total travel time was nearly twenty-four hours. She was tattered, tired, and now very upset that her only bag was lost, but we convinced her that the airline would be in touch and would eventually forward it to the villa in Lake Como. We were all tired from the long flights, but certainly nothing like Gina.

When we arrived at the villa, we soon discovered it was a 102-step walk up to the front entrance—not good when you're suffering from sleep deprivation and jet lag. Oh, and yes, we all had two huge suitcases to drag up, except Gina, of course. I guess that was a break for her; however, she had no change of clothes.

It was now evening and dinner time, so we walked down the steps, which was easy, and had a great meal. Where don't you have a great meal in Italy? We then walked around the nearby tiny piazza and just had to have a gelato before taking on the task of those steps.

Gina called Air New Zealand regarding her lost suitcase the next morning on my international cell phone I'd acquired before leaving. I mainly bought it for Laura when she arrived so she could talk with Sami when she called. We expected it would be frequent, since she thought her mom and Maxwell were at a soccer camp somewhere in California in the same time zone, not nine hours ahead. We also knew that she would be calling during the middle of the night, crying for Laura to come home.

Well, it turned out that Gina couldn't get confirmation of where her bag was, or when she would receive it, so we ended up buying her all new clothes. Her made-in-Italy new wardrobe made her look noticeably fashionable in the sexy, upscale resort area. The local lecherous Italian men also found her quite alluring, much to my aversion.

On one of the days while in Como, we took a ride to Villa d'Este, the magnificent resort hotel we'd gone to with the girls when they were teenagers. Gi and Di remembered the pool that floated in the lake and also the ghost that alarmingly had visited their room one night. I wanted to take a picture of everyone in front of the entrance to the hotel, so we found a great place, with the magnificent manicured landscaping as a back drop. Well, Gianna started posing like it was a photo shoot for an international fashion magazine, and she did it so well! The poses seemed to come so naturally to her. We all started wondering if this was to be her career someday. The truth is that she is just an exceptionally smart and talented young girl and adopts to whatever the situation may be. Little did we know that someday Gianna would seek a career in design of one sort or another with her incredible and amazing artistic talents.

Overall, Villa d'Este hadn't changed much since we'd first visited it, except for the fact that the price of the rooms and the food and drinks had tripled.

The week at Lake Como went quickly, and we soon got used to the steps climbing to the villa as our calf muscles now protruded like we were professional runners.

It was now the second week, and Brian and Kira, and Laura, her *then* husband, and Maxwell were arriving. We'd made prior arrangements that Brian would also buy an international cell phone, so we could communicate easily while there. It was also arranged that we would meet at a given time in the little town of Ponte Ferro close to the villa, since the villa was difficult to find with the confusing signage and narrow, winding roads that often dead-ended on a dirt road in someone's vineyard or olive field.

Driving to Ponte Ferro from Como was an adventure, especially with Diana driving. We never got out of the fast lane! But what allowed it to be an even more memorable experience was what happened when we had to stop for gas. No, of course, that in itself was not the memorable part. This is how it went: When stopping to get petrol, naturally, Joan and the girls had to go to the bathroom. Well, the simultaneous sudden exodus out of the car would have made one think a Black Friday clothing sale was taking place! That then left me alone, unable to converse with the unshaven burly attendant that I soon discovered spoke no English. "No englese, no englese," he rudely shouted at me while waving his hands in the air. There was no distinguishable marking on the gas cap of the Fiat stating what type of gas it took, or if it took diesel, so I attempted to ask the disparaging young man, "Petrol or Diesel?" He looked at me, disgusted, and mumbled, "Stupido Americano," and grabbed a hose to a pump. I naturally assumed he was putting in the proper fuel, of course. Why wouldn't I? I certainly knew you had to be careful in Europe, since many of the cars used diesel as well as gasoline/petrol.

May I mention that no one believes that part of the story to this day!

Well, the girls eventually came prancing out after several minutes, but not until after having gone into the little shop that was attached to the gas station that sold Italian trinkets that were made in China. They then sarcastically asked, "So did you figure out what kind of fuel it took, Dad?" I told them that I'd asked the young boy and he'd taken care of it. Then in a wise-ass way, they asked me, "So what kind does it take, Pop?" I responded, "Something flammable!"

We then started off with me driving, and still had about another sixty miles to go to get to the little town of Ponte Ferro. Well, after driving about twenty miles, I noticed that the car was acting up, jerking and making strange, belching-like sounds. I sensed that the young arrogant Italian boy had put in the wrong fuel—diesel when it should have been petrol. I also knew who would be blamed for it!

I now feared that the car would conk out at any time but didn't say anything, hoping we would get to the villa, or at least to the little town to meet the others. Brian was driving one car with Kira, and Laura and her husband were driving in another with Maxwell.

About five miles out from Ponte Ferro, it was obvious we had a serious problem. The car was now constantly sputtering, almost stalling and backfiring! Every time it backfired, Joan, with her stage voice, would scream, "What was that?!" Well, the girls had now sensed a pretty significant problem was ensuing and the sarcastic remarks began!

This wasn't good. I was afraid we weren't going to make it. We then came upon a sign that read "Ponte Ferro, three kilometers." I was now silently trying to figure what one kilometer equaled to one mile. What was even more worrisome, was that the others were coming from the opposite direction, and wouldn't pass us, and there was no guarantee the damn cell phones would work out there in the country, and it was going to be dark in a couple of hours.

Finally, just as we came around a bend in the road, a sign read, "Ponte Ferro, one kilometer, popolazione 102." Okay, that was scary—population 102. Well, at least we'd made it! I soon noticed that the town was less than a block long, and didn't see a petrol station, just a supermercato, a pizzeria, and an il bar—that was it!

I chugged up in front of this tiny grocery store and the car conked out with a last dying gasp. But we were there, and early. Maybe I could get someone to drain the tank, but who? There was no one in sight, and sure as hell no petrol station.

The girls were thirsty, plus we needed some food for dinner that night and something for breakfast the next morning, so they went into the supermercato. I was again left alone, sitting behind the wheel of a car that had just suffered cardiac arrest. The thought then suddenly occurred to me that my insurance didn't cover rental cars out of the U.S. and I hadn't taken the rental car company's insurance and signed a waiver. Oh, shit! I then wondered what the hell it would cost to replace a Fiat engine.

As the girls came out of the supermercato, I saw Joan go into the il bar next door. The bar was bigger than the supermercato; actually, it was the biggest structure in town. I then screamed, "Where in the hell is your mother going now?! For a goddamn bira?" The girls sweetly but rather sarcastically gleamed at me and said, "No, Dad, she's just seeing if she can get help. She's the only one who can speak Italian, remember?" I then meekly replied, "Oh."

Moments later, she emerged from the il bar, followed like the Pied Piper by six rather intoxicated, overweight, middle-aged Italian men. Several had no shirts on, apparently proud to expose their hairy sweaty chests. Accumulations of cigarette ash prominently clung to their obtrusive bellies that bulged over their belts. Most were still holding glasses of vino roso, while half-lit cigarettes loosely dangled from their parched lips.

Upon seeing Gina and Diana, with their long, flowing dark-brown hair and brown eyes, wearing shorts and tank tops, they now hurried toward the car, even more anxious to help!

One of the *inebriato grosso* ("inebriated plump") men disrespectfully hollered at me while flaying his hands about in the air saying, "Aprire il vano motore, aspire il vano motore!" "What in the hell is he saying?!" I harshly exclaimed. Joan calmly yet arrogantly said, "Open the goddamn hood!" "Oh!" I placatingly replied. It seemed as if my favored expression of the day was now, "Oh!"

I will never forget what took place next. I have a picture on Facebook to prove it.

The crowds had now surged to nine men, most with guts distending so far they couldn't even get close to the car's fender, not to mention the engine compartment. Nonetheless, they were all struggling to get a better look at the impending perplexity. This assemblage now represented almost one-tenth of the entire town's population, hovering over the now silenced engine that smelled as if it had just regurgitated cheap alcohol after partying too hard the night before.

All nine men, plus now two little old Italian ladies with gross hairy legs and strands of unsightly black hair protruding from their chins, had joined in, to ambitiously encroach upon the engine. They all just stood there intently staring, staring, deeply engrossed with this baffling yet obviously entertaining enigma. One of them would say something to the other, who would then shake his head in disagreement as he spilled his vino roso upon the steaming engine while talking with his hands.

Ten Italians looking at a non working motor!

I had to get out of the car and take a picture of this. No one would ever believe this scene! I took it from several feet behind so as to show all the fat butts up in the air with their cracks showing as they bent over, looking at the engine with obvious bewilderment. It would have made a great Norman Rockwell painting!

However, as I was taking the picture, one of the Italian men looked at me from the side with chagrin and I heard him whisper, "Stupido pazzo ignorante" [stupid, crazy, ignorant man]. It was apparent I was deemed guilty of the cause by the jury of eleven.

But you know what, if those guys had been back home and worked for me, I'd have reduced them to tears in a heartbeat; they didn't know who in the hell they were dealing with! I'm joking, of course.

At the moment, though, I was at their mercy, and had to just sit back and remain acquiescent like a nice little boy. I also felt badly that my wife and daughters were out there and not me, but you can see how far I would have gotten with those insolent, semi-sedated, brash Italian men.

Finally, one of the men called his friend, a *meccanico*, to come and figure out the problem. I tried to explain that I knew, but between the language barrier, and their lack of interest, and even more so, the lack of respect for me, it was to no avail. Meanwhile, they were all being very nice and respectful of the situation, at least to Joan and the girls.

The mechanic finally showed up several minutes later. A small man in his forties or so, his grease-laden jeans and dirty T-shirt smelled of a mixture of gas, oil, and body odor, and caused me to back away when shaking hands. I then hoped I hadn't offended him; he was our only salvation. Well, he soon came to the same conclusion that I had known all along. The diesel had to be pumped out of the engine and replaced with petrol. He then said we had to get the car to his garage two blocks away.

Unbeknownst to me since it happened so damn fast, Diana must have been told to get behind the wheel of the car and steer. I had looked away for just a few moments, only to turn around to see her being pushed up the street by six of the men. It was only six manpower, but it was amazing what a few pretty young girls, some vino, and Italian testosterone can do to propel a car uphill so damn fast! I screamed, "Where in the hell are you going with my daughter?!" Diana motioned with her arm out the window for me to calm down; it was okay.

After an hour or so, the engine was drained and filled with petrol, and it cost two hundred euros. I gave the mechanic an extra fifty euros and bought each of the remaining six men a large bottle of vino roso for their kindness. They loved me now! Not sure if you noticed, but three of the men had taken a hike when they'd realized they had to push the car up the hill! *Uomini Italiani figa*. You can look it up.

We eventually met my sons-in-law like nothing had happened, but before the evening was over, the girls naturally ratted me out. But I didn't do it! I know all the criminals, the thieves, and the like, all say they didn't do it! And of course no one believes me to this day.

We all spent a wonderful week together. We had three cars, and journeyed daily in caravan to Rome, Florence, Pisa, and Sienna. Well, as expected, we first went to Ancient Rome, *Roma antica*, and I was anxious to show my three grandchildren where I used to work. I was a senator, yes, a senator in the Roman Republic, so I spent my days in the Curia Julia in the Roman forum, the seat of the imperial Senate. It wasn't that big of a deal, I explained to the kids. Since I'd started as a Roman magistrate and served my term in office, I then had an automatic appointment to the Senate. It wasn't like nowadays, when senators are elected. I really tried to downplay it! I then got strange looks from them as I explained that you only live once or twice, and this was my *second* time.

You don't believe me either, do you? Well, smarty pants, let me tell you what happened next. While standing in front of the ancient senate building, Gina wanted to take a picture of me, so I proudly folded my arms and gave a noble pose. Gina then screamed, "Dad, you have to look at this!" I then looked at the screen and saw that everything was in full color, except me. My image was all in white! So, later that night at the villa, my son in law Brian said it was just an over-exposure. He tried to automatically and even manually correct it, and it wouldn't change. *So there!* I still have that picture.

Speaking of things ancient or old, it turned out that the two-hundred-year-old villa we'd rented was haunted! During the night, we heard strange, loud banging sounds, so in the morning we all accused each other of slamming doors going to the bathroom. Kira had us in hysterics, wanting to sleep in Diana and Brian's room in bed with them. Gianna cared less; all she needed was her "BB," her baby blanket she'd had since she was an infant. I pulled the covers over my head like a coward and grabbed onto Joan.

Laura and her husband and Maxwell slept in the guest house, and though it wasn't haunted, we could hear occasional screams during the night—scorpions had taken up refuge in the guest house and we assumed they found the guests intrusive! The next day, as Maxwell and Gianna and I played in the pool, we had to evade more scorpions while trying to bask in the rays of the intense sun of central Italy. However, we later discovered they weren't scorpions at all, but just insects with three pairs of legs and two pairs of wings . . . still not comforting.

Continuing with our daily journeys, the following day we went to Florence. While viewing Michelangelo's lifelike statue of David, I wanted to run up and hide his private parts from Gianna, fearing she was yet too young to see a man's anatomy! We then all walked across the Ponte Vecchio and ogled at all the gold in the store fronts and ended up having lunch at a little corner ristorante just at the end of the ancient bridge.

On the day that everyone else went to Sienna, Gina, Joan and I ventured out over to the coast to Ancona on the Adriatic Sea to the seaport town where my grandfather Achille was born. It was an arduous three-hour drive on a narrow winding badly maintained country road as blinding low fog burdened the ability contemplate the confusing signage. Gina and I were anxious to see where our heritage had begun and to authenticate our ancestry. We were surprised to see that it was no longer a little town, but now a bustling seaport city. Unfortunately, there was nothing that we could associate with my grandfather's description of it, but enjoyed seeing where he was born.

Okay, so now let's get to Gina's divorce!

We had all noticed that Gi was tense during the trip to Italy, and was on my cell phone almost constantly, obviously unable to enjoy much of her time with us. Something was up.

Nevertheless, none of us ever thought it could be a serious personal problem between her and her husband. Meanwhile, I knew there could possibly be some financial problems, since Gi would call and ask me for advice about cash flow, etc. However, her business was doing fantastic, so this was an enigma. She was and is a very astute business woman.

Three years prior, her husband decided he wanted to start a business of his own. When she explained the concept, it sounded like a good idea. However, at the same time, I explained that even though all things start with a good idea, a marketing plan, a well-thought-out marketing plan must be put in place. You can have the best idea and or concept, but without exposure, without aggressive marketing, it won't go anywhere.

He saw how successful tourism businesses could be and didn't want to work for someone else anymore and wanted to start one of his own. It was an innovative and good idea, but as I explained, it takes more than just a good idea. He didn't know about running a technology company or had the exposure to the systems and processes for developing software or the costs that were required to not just build, but to market and support a software system.

While we were in Italy, we all assumed—*never assume*—that the myriad of conversations Gina was having with him were about the cash flow problems that existed as a result of his now failing business that had put them in dire financial straits. Well, the calls were about that, but they weren't *all* about that.

It then also became apparent that some of the phone calls included his "phantom" illnesses. In the past three years, first he thought he had a brain tumor. Then he thought he had Multiple Sclerosis. His next imaginary illness was bone cancer in his shin. I think, he was trying to make Gina feel badly that he was ill *again...* and she was away.

I paid for Gina and the rest of the family to be on the trip for my 70th birthday. Gina had said that her husband couldn't come because of work, but we soon learned that Gina told him he wasn't invited. She knew the marriage was coming to an end.

Joan and I had no clue about a marriage problem, or what she had been going through. To the best of our knowledge, none of the family had, unless she'd told Diana, who would never have said anything if she'd been told not to.

It wasn't until the very last night of our two-week excursion in Italy that I learned about what was, and had been, going on for a long time, a very long time.

Everyone else had returned home a day earlier, while we—Joan and I, Diana, and Gianna— were leaving the following morning for SFO. Gina was departing that very evening on her almost-around-the-world journey back to Auckland.

It's odd how certain moments in life are embedded within your memory. Sadly, it seems like those moments mostly involve tragic events. It was about eight o'clock in the evening, and just starting to get dark in Rome, as I walked Gina from our room at the Michelangelo Hotel down to the lobby to catch a cab to the Fiumicino International Airport for her departure. She was obviously dismayed, shaken, and distressed, but had refused all the time we were together to disclose the agonizing circumstances she'd been going through for many months, if not years.

There are obvious drawbacks to having a child on the other side of the world. By not physically being with them or involved with their lives on a daily, even weekly basis, it is difficult to pick up or sense ill health, unhappiness, or wrongdoing.

As she handed me back my cell phone, she said, "Thanks, Dad, for letting me use it. You're going to have one hell of a bill!" I then firmly replied, "Okay, kid. What's up? There's obviously something very distressing going on in your life, and I don't think all those lengthy conversations were just about business. Please, please tell me. I'm your father, for Christ sake."

Like dropping a bomb, she then said, "Dad, I'll be filing for divorce when I get back."

I just got choked up as I wrote that, feeling her anguish all over again. What made it worse was that she was alone, so alone, and so damn far away.

She then briefly explained how bad the past few years had been, and his demands to keep all of it private. He said it was no one's business about their marriage, that they lived in a small town and it could further ruin them financially if it was known.

She then said they needed to sell their home as soon as she got back and the boat I had sent them three years ago as a gift. Upon hearing that, I got the shakes, and that wasn't good. I'm not sure if it was because of fright for her, or if I wanted to catch the next flight to Auckland and pummel him. My God! That beautiful home they'd spent years designing, building, and loving . . . damn.

I'd had absolutely no clue of any of this, and now felt I should have been more assertive and involved with her life.

She then shocked me even further by saying, as she attempted to hold back tears, that she will also need to sell her business, the business she started with nothing from nothing that was such as success. Due to the financial situation and her Sarcoidosis diagnosis, she didn't have the health or the desire to go though a marriage split up, financial chaos and trying to attend to the needs of the staff and business.

I didn't tell her that he had borrowed a quarter of a million dollars from me, and it was stilled entirely owed.

She then said, "Dad, I can't talk about it anymore now. I'll break down right here in the lobby. I'll call you and Mom and tell you all about it when we all get home."

The memory that is so fixed in my head to this very day is the vision I have of my daughter getting into that cab after telling me what had transpired for so many months, her heart breaking, knowing she was returning to face a multitude of problems on the other side of the world alone, then driving away without me next to her to help.

As she got into the backseat of the cab, I reached in and hugged her and said, "I'll come over and be with you." She said, "Please don't, Dad. I need to do this by myself."

I hardly had the chance to close the door as the damn rude Italian cab driver aggressively sped away, cutting off several approaching Vespas as their resounding trumpet-like horns annoyingly blared, echoing in the narrow cobblestone alley. Everything annoyed me now.

I then watched the taxi quickly disappear into the crowded street while I tried to get a last glimpse of my daughter, as my stomach ached and my heart wrenched.

The once seemingly South Pacific tropical seaside paradise had now turned into a diabolical hell hole for her. There are other acrimonious details, but I chose not to discuss them and open old wounds for the sake of both sides of the family.

If you'll recall, Gina had mentioned that they'd had to sell the Chris-Craft I'd shipped them. Well, a few years back, she had been worried about his incessant smoking and getting lung cancer. Since we hadn't been using the boat in Lake Tahoe much anymore—which, by the way, only had sixty-eight hours on it—I told him that if he stopped smoking for one year, and promised to never smoke again, I would ship it to him. Yes, to New Zealand. Well, he took me up on it.... and stopped smoking!

For the next year or so, when everything was assumed to be happy and hunky-dory with them, they'd enjoyed the boat, fishing most weekends during the summer months. I was happy that they were happy. I really liked her husband—*then*.

I actually caught my first fish while on that boat in Mercury Bay. Yes, I don't like eating fish, and had never caught a fish before in my life. Yes, I was in the wholesale seafood business most of my life, responsible for the mass butchery of possibly billions of fish but had never caught one myself. I must be honest and tell you that I really wanted to throw the fish I caught back, if you can believe that. I felt sorry for it. I looked into its eyes and didn't want to take its life. I can't kill or hurt animals, even a cold-blooded, gill-bearing aquatic craniate—at least face to face. But the excitement on board with my catch—and by the way, it was the *only* catch of the day—was that everyone was looking forward to a barbecue; the fish was doomed. It was a New Zealand snapper. Poor thing.

Now back to (then) present time: Gina called a few days after we'd gotten home from Italy and told us of the abhorrent details of her life for the past couple of years. She also finally told us how badly her lungs were riddle with sarcoidosis as she didn't want to worry us when she was first diagnosed. This can be, and was, serious. *Holy shit!* I thought. *Another worry, and we're on the other side of the world.*

We now hoped she would come home.

CHAPTER 57
SO MANY WEDDINGS ~ SO MANY DIVORCES

It was about ten in the morning on Sunday, the fog had just burned off and the sun was now beginning to shine through the ever-persistent low-hanging cumulus clouds. The ducks had now begun to arrive for their morning feeding, and the squirrels attempted to nibble on the half loaf of bread Joan had put out for them earlier, as the industrious crows assertively swarmed in to try to swipe any unclaimed stray chunks.

The pigeons were also combating the aggressive crows for the birdseed intended for the unfortunate swallows, now late on arrival. Of course, the koi were fed much earlier, as was the dog. I, meanwhile, was still waiting for my breakfast. So, you can see how the food chain goes.

As Joan now watered her beloved potted plants—yep, even the potted plants came before me—I patiently waited for my waffles. As I sat there sipping on a cup of coffee watching the Sunday morning news, the phone rang. It was Gina. At first, I was a bit concerned, since it was rather early back in New Zealand. Upon answering, she excitedly said that she'd met a wonderful man, his name was John. "Oh, wonderful!" I exclaimed. However, my first thought was, *Here we go again.* Then I asked, "Is he from the Bay Area?" Of course, I had hoped she'd somehow met a local man and would be coming home. Anywhere in the States would have been well received!

She then said, "No, Dad, he's another Kiwi!" "Oh no!" was my response. Gi then half-jokingly sighed and said, "Daaaad." I guess she'd picked up the disappointment in my tone.

Now don't get me wrong, we love the Kiwi's. New Zealander's are warm, friendly, wonderful people, but we had hoped she would be coming home, maybe for good.

She said she had met her "man" while attempting to sell the business, named Availability, what little there was to sell. Besides the measly client base, the only intrinsic, concentrated value of the business was in the potential of its concept. Wanting to settle the debts, the accumulated liabilities would have to be assumed by the buyer and eventually be paid as part of the sale agreement. Most likely, larger creditors would have to enter into an agreement with the new owner on payment terms mutually agreed on by both parties. This left little room, if any, for Gina to walk away with any funds as a result of the sale but would allow the creditors to be paid.

John had come to Gina's office to look at the books, but had inadvertently looked at Gina's looks, and forgotten about the books! The potential of the company was now secondary. He obviously ended up being more interested in Gina's availability than the availability of Availability!

Well, John eventually had taken his eyes off Gina and taken notice of the potential of the on-line booking service. He then successfully arranged for a buy-out, agreeing to the terms of the sale as she wished. Flash forward ten years and today, the business is known as "ResBook," which is a subsidiary of John and Gina's now ten-year-old co-owned massive parent company, Tomahawk Brands, based in Auckland, New Zealand. ResBook is a reservation management system for accommodation providers and property managers worldwide. While not directly tourism-related, JobSafe, another of Tomahawk's subsidiaries, is a responsive cloud-based system that allows businesses to manage their health and safety. Tomahawk is also a digital web design, search engine optimization, branding, logo design, and tourism consulting business.

Their talented salesmanship, organizational skills, and combined acute business principles, along with their alliance in working together, has brought their tourism-related venture to a premier status, not only in New Zealand and Australia, but the entire South Pacific region, and they just recently tapped into the U.S. market and opened offices in New Orleans and San Francisco. They currently have well over fifty employees—a real success story. *Bravo to you both!*

Well, we hadn't seen Gina since we'd parted on that harrowing night in Rome well over a year ago, and we were anxious to go to New Zealand and see how she'd been doing since the break-up. It was so hard to properly determine the truth over the phone, and she could naturally hide so many things so as not to worry us, as she so did. However, she insisted that we not come at the time, saying she still had too much to sort. This was disappointing; we needed to know what was going on in her life—where and how she was living, her health, especially with the new worry, sarcoidosis, the condition she had just been diagnosed with—but we had to respect her wishes. That was a difficult time for us. I can only imagine what it was like for her.

Much to our surprise, several months later, she said she wanted to come home for a few weeks, and John was coming with her. We were overjoyed to finally meet him, and of course to see Gi.

We wanted to do something to embarrass Gi when they arrived at the airport. As I recall, Laura enthusiastically encouraged the idea! It has been a custom that the first meeting with a new possible suitor, we do something to test his "fragility."

My "many" sons-in-law—prior, current, de facto, extant, and future, I think that covers them all—always assumed I was involved with the Mafia. I was not—well, not entirely. Anyway, I liked to play it up and say that I was, thinking maybe it would put some fear in them. So, Joan and I decided that we would dress as mobsters when picking Gina up from the airport, me as a mob boss—the "Don," the "Alpha Mafioso," the "Coppo di tutti Capi," the feared "Boss of Bosses"—and Joan as my "mob princess," as a mob wife is so called. Oh, and of course, we would have a dead guy in the trunk of our black Cadillac sedan. No, not a real stiff. I wouldn't have a guy knocked off just for a practical joke. It was a blow-up doll that we dressed in shirt and slacks with his arms tied with a rope, bloodied, of course. This guy hadn't died of natural causes!

We figured we would wait for Gina and her new beau in the arrivals section at the international terminal, and as they walked out from immigration and customs, we would casually be standing there to greet them in our mobster roles. Naturally, I would be smoking a cigar—I was the Don.

We arrived a little early, however, and I started feeling a bit faint from smoking the disgusting, smelly cigar, having ignored the clearly visible no smoking signs, as only a mobster would, while Joan gasped for breath. This was not a good scene, I was thinking, as John's first impression of me would now be of a sissy mobster, passed out from smoking a cigar, instead of the impenetrable tough guy! So, I tossed the cigar. Joan was exceedingly pleased. I then hoped he would at least pick up the scent of it, adding to my guise. I must say, we certainly looked the part. I was dressed in a dark pinstripe suit with a black dress shirt and white tie, and Joan was decked out in a short skirt, with bobbed hair. She looked like an ex-brash hooker flaunting her disdain, with her obviously excessive makeup. We had attracted a large crowd by now, who wondered if we were for real or were just from San Francisco, where odd scenes are a norm.

As they walked from around the high wall separating the inspection area from the expanse of the reception area, Gina looked for her distinguished, reserved parents from Hillsborough to proudly show us off to her new beau. Well, upon seeing us, she let out a scream! At that point, the surrounding crowd scattered, with some ducking behind chairs while looking for the security officers, most likely thinking I had a machine gun! She then started laughing as the crowd now realized it was a joke, or at least hoped.

Well, that was John's first meeting with Gina's refined parents. I must say, we did get several rather apprehensive looks from him as we walked to the car, but the best was yet to come. As we approached the car, John lifted one of the suitcases to put it in the trunk. I then remotely popped the trunk release, exposing the bloodied dead guy lying in a fetal position! Gina then let out a blood-curdling scream and used several profanities not heard since the fish business days. With a quick, unsuspecting glance, it really did look a real body. Gina then asked, "Did Laura put you guys up to this?!"

By the way, speaking of looks, you should have seen the look we got from the young girl at the party store when I'd bought the blow-up doll!

Once things had settled down, we then went to lunch in Burlingame—yes, we changed our clothes, somewhat. After talking with John for a while, I was very impressed with him. He appeared to be a gentleman, clean cut, and more importantly, sincere, and very much in love with Gina. However, I remembered my father's expression, "A new broom sweeps clean!"

No offense, John. I'm just spooked, as I think you can understand. We've experienced six marriages so far, and we only have three daughters.

We had met the children, mothers and fathers, the brothers and sisters, their husbands and wives, cousins, uncles and aunts, the entire family, and even some of the friends, also a few dogs, of a half-dozen men so far. We'd hugged them, gave them Hollywood faux kisses, entertained them, and taken them into our family and trusted them with our daughters, to no avail. What a waste of time and emotion. So, did I have any trepidation or apprehension? What do you think? All the brooms—or should I say, *grooms*—swept clean at first, but didn't last very long.

Having said that, during lunch Gina showed us pictures of where she was living. It was a very small home, a "bach," as they call them, like a vacation rental home. It was apparently clean and okay, however a far cry from the beautiful hillside home she'd once had. We all know though; a home doesn't make a marriage—it's the marriage that makes a home.

Gina was now very happy in this little bach, and that was fine with us, as long as she was away from the stress of that unhappy and unhealthy marriage. John appeared to adore her, and we so hoped he was indeed sincere, and his veracity, righteous and genuine. I liked him because he seemed to be unpretentious and forthright.

He had two young children by a former marriage, a boy, Jarred, and a girl, Taylor, and had filed for a divorce a year prior. Both Gina and John's divorces were not final, and coincidentally, would not be for another year. In New Zealand it takes two years for a divorce to become final.

The concept behind the ruling is the hope the couple will reconcile. It apparently has worked, since the law has long been in effect.

After lunch, we went home and they both crashed, reeling from jet lag.

They got up rather late the next morning, and Joan served the typical all-American scrambled eggs and bacon for breakfast. I was astonished when John asked if she had a can of baked beans. "Baked beans?!" I exclaimed. "What in the hell are you going to do with them? And for breakfast?" He then replied in his Kiwi accent, "Mr. Peee, you don't know what you're missing, mate!" He then asked for a tomato. He proceeded to pour the warmed baked beans on top of the tomato, which was now on top of the scrambled eggs, which was on top of the bacon—and then mix them all together. I had to look away.

Then Gina, obviously now a Kiwi to the core, did the same, saying, "Dad, you should try it!" Are you kidding? You know me. If I had, I would have had to separate the eggs from the bacon, and the bacon from the tomato, and tomato from the beans, and eat them all separately. Anyway, I hate beans!

That afternoon, we took John around San Francisco and showed him our beautiful, picturesque city, and ended up at the Cliff House for lunch. We waited for some time for a window booth, but it was well worth it. It was a beautiful, crisp spring day and we were able to clearly observe countless seals catching some zzz's on nearby Seal Rock and see past the Farallon Islands out to the horizon. While looking out at the far reaches of the Pacific Ocean toward New Zealand, many thousands of miles away, we marveled at how you could now get on an airplane in San Francisco and within thirteen hours, be on the other side of this vast ocean in the South Pacific.

John and Gina both ordered the broiled swordfish and Joan, sautéed petrale sole. I, however, looked forward to a scrumptious, medium-rare New York steak sandwich on sourdough, with crispy French fries. I was the only one that ate healthy.

The famed Cliff House used to be a good account of mine, and the chef, also a friend, was once the chef at Tadich's Grill, one of the oldest restaurants in San Francisco and another fantastic account.

As they were enthusiastically enjoying their appetizers of lightly battered, fried calamari and an order of Dungeness crab cakes with remoulade sauce, John looked over at me and said, "Mr. Peee, there's something I want to ask you." *Oh, shit.* I'd heard that tone of voice six times before. Here goes another wedding speech I'll have to give. He then said, "I'm very much in love with your daughter and would like to marry her and would like your blessing and permission."

My acute old-school formality was respectfully embedded within my daughters that a future spouse must ask their father for permission for their hand in marriage. Better yet, they should have had to ask their mother, with Joan's sixth sense.

I then looked over at Gi and asked if she was in on this. She answered, "Of course, Dad. That's one of the main reasons we came here!"

Now having mixed feelings, knowing she most likely would never return to live near us, and realizing she'd made a life of her own in New Zealand and obviously loved John very much, what else could I say but yes? Actually, saying yes was a delight. She'd gone through enough heartache. They were both mature adults and didn't really need my formal permission. But God rest their souls if they hadn't asked me!

I possibly should have suggested they wait, but their love for each other was apparent and genuine. However, I would be giving a false impression if I didn't say that I was ambiguous with my answer. Joan and I hadn't really had the time to know this man. However, we'd known the others, and look what had happened.

Gina and John had our blessings.

We enjoyed the week with them and felt that we'd gotten to know John very well and liked him even more by the time they left to return home. Joan and I were pleased knowing Gina had finally found a trusting relationship and could now leave her mother and her father feeling contented.

A wedding—yes, another wedding—was now to be planned for the following year, since they both had to wait for their divorces to be final.

In the meanwhile, I was getting bored with the sauce business. I love the challenge of creating, organizing, and building a business, and once it's successful, like I said, then it's, *ho-hum!*

I was now seventy-five years old—Jesus Christ, three-quarters of a century, and it just may be time to retire for good, or at least until the next idea popped into my head. Hmm, I'd always wanted a seafood restaurant. Better yet, and so much less stressful, maybe I'd write a memoir! Oh, sure. How in the hell would I write a book? I'd never read a book. Plus, I didn't know how to type. It would take forever, and what the hell would I write about? Me? That's so self-serving. *Don't you dare say a word!* Anyway, who wants to read about someone else's life?

In the meantime, I'd had several opportunities to sell the sauce line, and decided to take advantage of an offer, but I was hesitant whether I really wanted to. However, I'd learned long ago that you must sell your business when you don't want or need to. You must sell when everything is going well, when sales are at their pinnacle, when cash flow is abundant, and profits are soaring. As I just said—when you really don't want or need to! Reason being is that you never know what the near future holds. There could always be someone younger, with more energy, with ambitions, with a more aggressive marketing strategy who just may come along and take you down. I said all this prior.

There's always someone to take your place. I used that theory while running the seafood business, having key personnel feeling they were indispensable and/or couldn't be replaced. I made sure I always had "obvious" ready backup, someone who could easily move into their position. It not only lessened the idea that they were indispensable but solidified the fact they were indeed *dispensable*. It also made them strive to do better to ensure their job.

Paladini Quality Seafood Sauces – "An Authentic Taste of San Francisco" – was successfully sold on June 28, 2010, to Golden West Specialty Foods, a specialty food wholesale distribution company near San Francisco, California that focuses on selling high-end product lines.

I retained the rights of involvement, as well as the restriction that formulas not be changed. Labels cannot be changed and or any new products developed without my sanction since they would bear my name, as well as other issues of significant importance.

The product line continues to expand to upscale markets and specialty food stores throughout the entire United States.

Coincidently, the line was just recently exported to a distributor in New Zealand.

CHAPTER 58
YEAH, I KNOW—TAKING FLYING LESSONS AT 75 IS NUTS!

Yes, I was now bored again. Looking for excitement, I wanted to take flying lessons, so Joan gave them to me for my seventy-fifth birthday. Thinking about this further, I now wonder if there was an ulterior motive behind her urging me to do so!

The instructor, Orville, was a friend of ours, a retired general practitioner who took people flying with him for a fee. He wasn't a professional instructor, by any means, but had been flying for well over thirty years, so what could possibly go wrong—especially since his name was Orville? You know, like the Wright brothers, Wilbur and Orville Wright, "Founders of Flight." Sure, they crashed onto a sand dune on their first attempt, but heck, look what happened after that! And they were smart enough to make sure it was a soft landing, or crash, if we must be precise.

So, I was seventy-five with a quadruple bypass in my history; Orville was seventy-eight and had just recently suffered a heart attack and wore a pacemaker. His plane, a Cessna 175 Skylark single-engine, four-seat, high-wing aircraft, was built in 1962, so forty-nine years old; its big fiftieth was soon coming up. The thought suddenly occurred to me that between myself, him, and the plane, it represented 202 years, and we would soon be up there dancing among the clouds. I hoped none of us would soon be gasping for oxygen and end up eternally above the clouds.

Before taking off, there were pre-flight inspection procedures that had to take place to assure the aircraft's air worthiness. There are myriad basic individual inspection points, both in the cockpit and outside, encompassing the fuselage and empennage, right and left wing, nose, including fuel samples, etc., then in the cockpit again that must be inspected before starting the engine. The most amusing is the one when you must undo the canvas cover for the air intake and check if a bird nested or if a little rodent took refuge in there. It would take an entire page to list and explain all of the inspection points, so I won't bore you with them.

My first impression, sitting in this tight-fitting little four-seater, was one of amazement at how tiny the interior was. Our elbows were touching as we put on the noise-canceling headsets and looked out at the two-blade propeller less than thirty inches away. It made one feel it was more of a toy than a real flying machine.

However, that perception was soon dismissed, observing the complicated instrument panel and noticing the multitudinous gauges, such as the altimeter, altitude indicator, airspeed indicator, magnetic compass, heading indicator, vertical speed indicator, course deviation indicator, and radio magnetic indicator.

Whew, and a bird keeps all that in its tiny head.

After "Orv" finished explaining all the instruments to me, the functions of which I had by now already totally forgotten, said it was time to taxi out to the tarmac. His plane was based at the Palo Alto airport, a tower-controlled airport.

He then opened the small window and hollered out, "All clear!" At first, I wondered who in the hell he was screaming at, since no one was to be seen, but later learned it was the procedure in case someone was indeed nearby before starting the engine. Yes, *the* engine, singular. There was but one lonely engine just inches away, but it was now violently shaking the entire plane as if a Tyrannosaurus was pouring salt on its meal and we were the salt shaker. The intense sound of the roar of the engine, even with the headsets on, alerted you that it was indeed a true flying machine and not my flight simulator I'd been playing with!

Orv turned on the Aircraft Communications Addressing and Reporting System (ACARS), and just then I heard something like, "Charlie delta strength five taxi via Charlie and hold at bravo four for zero four?" Well, there just happened to be another plane communicating with the tower in an alien language. Of course, that was the phraseology they use to properly identify themselves and the runway by accurately distinguishing the first letter.

It was then our time to call the tower and ask permission to taxi out and hold. Orv called the tower and said, "Palo Alto tower, this is Cessna 310 Foxtrot taxi to the active for takeoff."

After getting clearance to proceed to the active runway, we then taxied out and sat in "position and hold." On this, my first flight, I was of course to just watch (so I thought) and get the feel for being in this motorized bird that, with some luck, would soon take us aloft.

As we sat there waiting for instructions from the tower, I couldn't help but look out my side window and observe how frail and flimsy this thing was, and how easily it bounced around from the wind. What the hell was it going to be like when we were airborne? *But never be afraid to try something new.* Remember, amateurs built the ark; professionals built the Titanic.

At this point I couldn't help thinking that this Cessna may have been experiencing its mid-life crisis; it was rather mature for a flying machine. I also hoped it had observed a healthy diet without any arterial plaque buildup, as both the instructor and I had experienced, and that all its fuel lines were clear. Well, Orville assured me that the plane had been properly serviced all the years it had been in operation, mitigating at least some of the stress level before taking off.

As we sat at the end of the tarmac waiting for clearance, Orville unexpectedly told me to take the controls and do what he said. I almost shit. "WHAT?!" I exclaimed. I then said, "Y-y-you w-w-want m-m-me t-to take the controls and t-t-take off?" He calmly replied, "Sure! You can do it, Kiki!"

The palms of my hands were now sweaty, and my legs were trembling—and not from the engine. My heart felt like it was going to jump out of my chest. I was now officially scared to death.

Orville then said, "Flaps at ten degrees, ailerons into the wind, and elevator about half back from the gust lock hole. Apply smooth full power, then check for at least 2,300 RPM's and oil temperature and pressure in the green. Maintain runway alignment with rudder. Put carburetor heat to cold. Slowly decrease aileron deflection as the airplane accelerates and at 55KIAS pull elevator back to pull nose wheel off the ground and place the top edge of the cowling on the horizon. Establish wind correction angle to stay over the runway. Keep the top of the cowling on the horizon and the wings level. Climb speed will be at eighty miles per hour," to which I replied, *"Huh?"*

I had been playing on my flight simulator for a couple of years, so I knew most of this; however, this was the real deal! Surprisingly, it went well, except I found it difficult to keep the Cessna on the center line at slow speeds dealing with the rudder pedals, but once reaching thirty-five to forty miles per hour, the aircraft control eased, and before I knew it, we were up!

Upon climbing up to a thousand feet, and now at 110 miles per hour, we ventured northwest toward the Half Moon Bay airport. Orv said the airport had a long and wide runway and would be good to practice landings and take-offs. Okay, so now my mouth went dry and my hands got wet, thinking I had to land this thing!

As we flew at 3,500 feet, now over the mountain range separating the Peninsula from the coastline, turbulence was bouncing us upward, then downward, then to the left, then to the right. We were instantly dropping several hundred feet, then elevating several hundred feet. Instinctively, I climbed to a higher altitude, not wanting to get the top of a tree up our butts. That was not fun. We finally got over the mountain range and were now skimming the coastline, heading for the Half Moon Bay airfield. The ride was now smooth and pleasant, and the beauty of the coastline below was calming. I found flying exciting, and a complete diversion from the now boring days of retirement.

As we approached the Half Moon Bay airfield, that calming feeling soon came to an abrupt end when Orv said, "Throttle back to eighty, flaps at ten degrees, slowly descend and maintain a thousand feet, mixture rich, hold at 2,000 RPMs, landing lights on. Use pitch to maintain air speed. Use power to control altitude. Use the ailerons to correct for any crosswind and the rudder pedals to keep the plane aligned with the runway center line." Now panic stricken and terrified, I said, "Holy Christ, Orv, quickly tell me again what comes after 'throttle back at eighty'!"

Ignoring my request, he then told me he would announce our intention to land to other planes that may be in the area since there was no tower. I guess he felt I had enough to think about. Then he said, "Approach and land downwind, Kiki." *Oh, shit. He really does expect me to land this thing! Flying level and making a few turns was fun, hell anyone could do it, but landing—yikes!*

Well, somehow, someway, I landed, but not without difficulty. It was hard to keep the plane lined up to the center line with the crosswind sweeping in from the nearby Pacific Ocean causing me to have to side slip or crab the plane to stay on alignment for final. That was a harrowing experience.

I now looked forward to lunch at the little cafe at the airport. I hadn't had a drink in years, but I must say, a good stiff one would have certainly felt good right then!

As time went on, I had taken over a dozen or so flying lessons with Orv. By the way, if you recall, I mentioned prior that Orville was not a professional flying instructor. He was just an *old* friend, who was *old*, who owned an *old* plane, who said he would teach an *old* man, to fly. Find that unnerving?

Well, let me tell you, I had several unnerving experiences flying in that small old Cessna with Orv. A couple frightening and almost life threatening. I made the mistake of telling Joan, and she made me stop taking lessons.

The book is already too long, so I won't expound on those experiences. Too bad, you would have laughed and would have gasped!

CHAPTER 59
MARRIAGE NUMBER SEVEN!

So, marriage number seven took place. This was now starting to sound like the musical *Seven Brides for Seven Brothers*. Well, fortunately these men weren't brothers!

The marriage would take place in Lake Como, Italy. Yes, Italy. No, not in Auckland where they lived, or the Bay Area where we lived, of course not . . . in Italy! The other side of the world for them, and not exactly around the corner for us and the rest of the family.

Evidently, Gina had fallen in love with Lake Como when we'd all been there back in 2006. That was unfortunately during the time when we'd been unaware of what she was going through. She said she fantasied if she was to ever marry again that she would want it to be there, as obscure as the thought may have been at the time. I was happy her fantasy had eventually come true.

Well, after many months of planning and their divorces being final, the wedding occurred on June 20, 2012, at the Villa Balbianello in Lago di Como, a private villa on a private island in Italy. No, not at a local funky YMCA or Elks Club, as many do, or better yet, at the drive-thru chapel in Las Vegas, where you can get hitched without leaving your car for $34.99. There was also a package deal I found on the internet for $67.99, where Elvis would even sing three songs to you. Okay, well, she obviously nixed those choices. I was joshing of course! Do you really think one of our daughters would have had a marriage ceremony like that? Or that I would have allowed it? Hmm, but you know, that package deal for $67.99 sounded interesting.

A number of feature films had used the Villa Balbianello for locations, including *A Month by the Lake*, *Star Wars Episode II*, and *Casino Royale* in 2006. I recalled near the closing scenes of *Casino Royale*, when Daniel Craig as James Bond, and that incredibly sexy, beautiful brunette Eva

Green as Vesper Lind, lounged on the pristine lawn behind the villa overlooking the lake. It was supposedly a sanatorium where Bond was recuperating. What a way to recuperate!

Well, leave it to Gina to have found such an amazing venue for a wedding.

The wedding ceremony took place at one in the afternoon, with the reception immediately following. It had to be limited to only twenty guests, due to the confined area where the wedding ceremony was held, a magnificent yet tiny outdoor chapel overlooking the terraced gardens and the lake below.

We were all brought to the island by prearranged private chartered boats from Aregeno, with the men dressed in tuxedos and the women in formal gowns. Upon arriving at the private dock of the villa a professional photographer met us and snapped away as the paparazzi do. Gina was naturally the star. She looked like a movie star; she was beyond amazingly gorgeous, her hair and makeup done by a professional hair stylist and makeup artist as if for a movie scene at the famous villa. Her one-of-a-kind, hand-sewn wedding gown was beyond magnificent. I hardly ever notice wedding gowns, but Gina's was most elegant and resplendent.

I had never seen her look so beautiful, and more importantly, so genuinely happy. She glowed with joy. Gina was a star that day, and I'm sure the gawkers certainly thought she was. She was even more beautiful than Eva, James Bond's woman who'd lounged with him at the villa just months before.

John also looked very handsome and debonair in his black tux and tails, and even attempted a few Italian expressions with his Kiwi accent . . . which didn't work. Though sweating profusely and constantly wiping his brow from the ninety-plus degree mid-summer heat and the torturous humidity, it was apparent he was filled with anxiety and delight. His love for his soon-to-be wife was obvious.

I also wore a black tux and felt the steam dispensing from around my shirt collar, as I coyly attempted to loosen it without being noticed. It was almost unbearable, and I wanted to tear the stiff, starch-laden shirt off, but knew my chest and muscular arms would alarm and excite the women, so I had to bear with it—just adding some humor; no egomania intended, ladies! This time.

My heart was filled with joy to see our daughter not only looking so beautiful, but filled with such happiness—*at last.* That's all a parent wants for their child.

The mayor of Lenno looked very esteemed and dignified in his long black tux, who by the way, also served as the minister. *Sorry, Elvis!* He conducted the ceremony in Italian with an interpreter translating into English. Two guitars softly played Gina and John's favorite sentimental music, setting the magical mood for the fairy-tale-like wedding at this enchanting villa overlooking the calming waters of magnificent Lake Como.

As the ceremony took place, it was hard to hold back tears of joy for Gina and John. Their love exuded from within and was evident to all who were present.

Gina's three closest girlfriends had flown in from the Bay Area, as well as most of our family, except for Samantha and Maxwell. Sami would have loved being there, but unfortunately could have never made the long flight. John's mother and step-father had flown in from New Zealand, and his sister and brother-in-law had come from England. His brother and sister-in-law, and his two children, Jarrod and Taylor, were unfortunately unable to attend.

At the end of the ceremony, their good friend Monique Rhodes, a famous singer and guitarist from New Zealand and France who'd attended the almost week-long celebration, sang a song she'd composed just for them as the ceremony concluded. It was very moving and meaningful. There wasn't a dry eye by the time Monique finished.

After the ceremony, pictures were taken for at least an hour in different locations around the magnificent terraced gardens. No matter where you looked, it was surreal.

The buffet reception then took place on a meticulously groomed lawn, while the azure-colored lake below peeked in between the fir trees as a back drop. Typical Italian appetizers of the region were passed around, along with fine champagne. The young girl tending the buffet insisted I try the lightly seared beef fat . . . *ugh.* I precipitously commented I'd rather not, but she insisted. Not trying to look like a pansy, I picked up a toothpick and jabbed it into this disgusting glob of near-raw fat and downed it. I then gasped. It was disgusting! Apparently not noticing my expression of utter repugnance, she asked, "So Mr. Paladini, what did you think? Would you like another?" I mumbled, "Hmm, well . . . is the Pelligrino cold?"

Upon leaving Villa Balbiennelo later that evening, we were ushered by chartered boat to the private dock of the shoreline Locanda La Terlindana Ristorante in the Piazza of Giacomo Matteotti in Lenno for *cena*—dinner—and what a cena it was!

Just so you know, the traditional structure of an Italian meal consists of: Numero uno; aperitivo. Due; antipasto. Tre; primo. Quattro; secondo. Cinque; contorno. Sei; insalata. Sette; formaggi e frutta. Otto; dolce. Nove; caffe. Dieci; digestivo. *And you wonder why most Italians are chubby.*

Thankfully, Gina and John—oh hell, we were in Italy, let's call him "Giovanni"—did not follow the typical Italian meal structure for dinner. However, it wasn't far from it, or lacking in calories. It started with more lavish appetizers—more, because we'd already had an abundance at the villa, if you recall—then insalata lightly tossed in a vinaigrette dressing with scattered pine nuts and glazed walnuts encompassing a round of baked teleme en croute; then ravioli limone in a sage butter sauce sprinkled with finely grated lemon zest and grated Parmigiano-Reggiano. I'd never thought of lemon ravioli, I must say, but they had just a hint of lemon and were delicious.

All during the meal, and well after, the abundance of the proficiently selected wines effectively allowed one to disavow the myth of moderation.

We were then served a fresh peach sorbet to cleanse our palates—yes, we had to cleanse our palates, not our souls, from the overindulgence.

We now sat up and prepared ourselves to consume the main course, consisting of perfectly roasted medium-rare New York strip loin encrusted with Italian cremini mushrooms shrouded in a red wine reduction, with roasted fingerling potatoes garnished with a sprig of fresh rosemary. We were then served dessert. Oh my! The dessert was divine, scrumptious, beyond delicious, the absolute best Gateau Saint Honore cake we'd ever had, and by we, I mean *everyone*! Then, to top it off, there was limoncello, but for me, just caffe nero.

I, as well as several others, then got up and said a few words wishing Gina and John all the happiness, health, and love that life would allow.

We were then escorted into taxis and driven several miles to a private beach club to dance and further indulge. The club was over the top, I must say; it mixed an obvious sophisticated elegance with a youngish, esoteric ambiance. Great care had been given to every detail, creating a unique and magical atmosphere. The striking white canvas gazebos set up on the grainy, white sandy beach were lit with soft up-lights to appear as candlelight, setting the mood for romance as a live quartet softly played in the background.

Everyone danced barefoot on the beach under the warm night sky, lit only by the crescent moon and the stars. I can only imagine how good that felt for the ladies who'd worn high heels all day.

John's brother-in-law had a wee bit too many libations, and while playfully frolicking in the sand, continued to take off his trousers. Not knowing what was yet to come, the girls shockingly hid their eyes, only to be soon tempered by the fact he had on long, colorful plaid boxer shorts.

Several weeks later, Gina and John received the shorts framed as a remembrance of the good time had by all! Dry cleaned, they had hoped.

Gina and John purchased a dozen mini hot air balloons to send aloft while making a wish. They were at least thirty inches high and contained a small basket with an ignition source. We were to light the flame with a small butane lighter near the bottom of the basket, let it heat up the envelope above, and just before it began to rise, make a wish, then let it go. We were all now gathered around the shoreline, flicking our butane lighters, and several of the more than slightly intoxicated revelers were burning their fingers instead of the wicks. Eventually all the balloons got aloft.

It was such a meaningful and beautiful sight to see them lit as they rose high into the pitch-black night sky. As they ascended into the darkness, only the shimmer of the burning flame allowed you to follow your wish. What a wonderful way to have brought the curtain down on such an amazing fantasy wedding, so beautifully planned by Gina and Giovanni. That day and that night would never be forgotten.

During the time while at Lake Como, we had rented three apartment-like villas in nearby Argegno to accommodate the family. Ours was just on the outskirts of the little ancient town, high on a mountainside, with a mesmerizing view of the lake clearly visible below. A roof-top pool conveniently allowed us to refresh ourselves from the daily humidity that drained the moisture from within.

After a non-stop five-day celebration surrounded by family and friends, the newlyweds departed on Saturday morning and drove up to Venice, then over to Croatia to honeymoon for a week. The rest of the family returned home, and Joan and I went south to the Isle of Capri to visit with her cousins for a few days.

After their week exploring Croatia, John and Gina then flew to San Francisco to spend another week with us. It was planned to have a second wedding celebration on July 7 in our garden. The intended purpose was so Samantha could be Gina's maid of honor since she hadn't been able to fly to Italy. It was originally planned for just the immediate family and a few friends, no more than maybe a dozen or so. Well, we ended up with over fifty people.

They were married *again* on the center island by a real minister who performed a mock wedding. Samantha looked beautiful, as did Gina, in the same wedding gown she'd worn in Como, and everyone again marveled at how amazing she looked.

As John and Gina were standing on the island, with the minister about to conclude the faux ceremony, it had been planned one evening two weeks prior back in the little piazza in Arregno,

Italy, that we would surprise them and fly Monique, their friend and singer, over from France to sing the same song she'd sung after the wedding at the Villa Balbianello.

The plan was that I would go onto the island and read an email that Monique had supposedly sent and asked me to read to them at the end of the ceremony, saying she wished she could be there. Well, she then suddenly emerged from behind them, singing that same song she'd written and sang to them in Lake Como! John and Gina were genuinely surprised and overcome with emotion as they both openly cried with joy.

The next day, Monique gave a concert in our garden for again, well over fifty people, singing from the island on a stage that was set up with a professional sound system. We invited all the neighbors to the concert as well, since we knew it was going to be very loud. It was our way of appeasing them.

Fortunately, now two of our girls were happily married and had men to watch over them.

Now my only hope was that Laura could meet a fine, compassionate man who would truly love her, and finally find peace and solace with him.

CHAPTER 60
IT'S ALMOST TIME TO SAY GOODBYE

Yep, we're nearing the end. No, not of the book—well that, too—but I'm talking about the finality of life. Heck, it happens to all of us; there's no escaping it. I must admit, however, that it's an odd feeling wondering how many more Thanksgivings and Christmases I'll have with my family. I now revere every one of them.

So many things can now be the last. It's bewildering, having the notion that even my next car may be the last, the next trip, the next—the next what? Birthday? When Frank Sinatra was asked what he wanted for his birthday, he said, "Another birthday!" Happily, though, for the first time, our dog will outlive me.

Oh, the aging process. The aches and pains—but hey, maybe they allow us to realize that we're still alive. I've always said, "When you die, you're the last one to know!" And of course, tomorrow is not promised; like my sauce line, life has an expiration date. However, I'm not ready to change my address to an earth's view quite yet. Okay, that was a presumption that I was going to make it to heaven, wasn't it?

And for my more mature friends, don't worry about old age; it doesn't last that long. I think old age was the most unexpected of all things that happened to me. It came so damn fast! It seems as if youth was just yesterday. Now, over eight decades later, I wonder where life went. When I was a kid, it seemed like time took an infinitude to pass. When you're eight, you want to be eight and half, and those six months seemed like they took forever! Now it seems like a year was just a month ago.

When you buy something online and have to give the year you were born, as you scroll farther and farther back, you witness all the years you have lived. It seemed as if it took me forever the other day to get to 1936. However, it led me to wonder what memorable event occurred in each year. A lot of years, and a lot of memories, yet I was fortunate to have lived to experience those many years and many memories.

I must now try to maintain my sensory and mental acuity and try to optimize my brain's fitness, keep it stimulated and creative, as well as stay physically active. I feel someone is not old until regrets take the place of dreams. Well, I'm still dreaming, now envisioning ways to give back and help the less fortunate. The children and adults with special needs, discarded animals needing forever homes, those who can't help themselves. Form a non-profit organization to accomplish just that, possibly a place where people with special needs can help care for animals in need. What a great combination and concept. But I must get going on that soon.

As far as my regrets, well, they're in the past. I can't punish myself any more than I have, and hopefully in my mature years, there won't be anymore. I must now make good of the wisdom that I've learned through my mistakes, but I have learned that it's easier to get older than it is to get wiser!

As far as death, I don't fear death. I do fear losing my wife before me, or God forbid, a child or a grandchild. I can't even let my thought process go there. With my passing, the only fear is the overwhelming heartache of never being with my family again. That is beyond comprehension, to never hug my wife, my daughters, my grandchildren again. When I hug them now, I often don't want to let go.

Before I depart, I have an enigma that haunts me. I must soon try to find the solution for Samantha's future, her security and well-being. My other grandchildren will be fine; they're all individually smart and independent, will support themselves, marry and have families of their own. Sami cannot and will not be able to enjoy any of these normal aspects of the cycle of life.

This has been perplexing. Laura certainly can't take care of her forever, and Sami will never be able to take care of herself. Every time I try to figure it out, it's like a box full of pieces to a complicated puzzle that dropped on the floor, and I can't find all the pieces, though I know they're there.

Money alone is not the answer for her long-term care; money can't guarantee proper aid. A family member, a devoted loving someone must monitor the quality of the care, her individual needs, and ensure there would be no abuse, emotional or physical, or God forbid, molestation. That is of paramount concern. I'm stymied with this, always reaching a stalemate. I hope I can live long enough to come up with the solution, if there is one. However, lately I seem to have this overwhelming feeling of urgency, the need to complete things, anything, even this book, because you just never know. I'm a realist.

Why should emotional and physical abuse be such a factor and such a worry? Because I'm now concerned with the general morality of mankind and the abusive behavior not only toward one another, but how it's affecting the future of our God-given planet earth. And concerning family values, morality, and sexual perversion; look back at the Roman Empire. It consumed itself. Could this happen in America? The entire world?

Have you noticed you don't hear about the old-fashioned fist fights anymore that resulted in only a black eye or a broken nose, at the worst? No, now they shoot, and shoot to kill, and for no reason. The depraved shooting of innocent masses. Of course, man killing man has been ongoing since the beginning of time. Wars for religious beliefs, ego, militant power, and genocide, the almost complete extermination of ethnic groups. And for trivial land boundaries. We can't be happy staying within or on our own property; it's never enough. Countries taking over other countries' land, like neighbors fighting over inches on a property line. *Oh, the sinister shadows of war.*

Then there's the slaughter of young children in our schools by someone mentally challenged or deranged, someone unhappy. A school is supposed to be a safe place, possibly the safest, not a battleground where killing is mandated. A fearful fourth grader in Littleton, Colorado, recently shouted, "God, why aren't you protecting us in school anymore?" God replied, "I am no longer allowed in your schools."

Let's talk for a moment about what we—we, the people who occupy this tiny space in the universe—are doing to it. Made in just *seven days* by our higher power, who gave us this once beautiful Garden of Eden, we have now turned it into a dystopia. We have oceans of waste material, with those very same oceans being over-fished, causing many species to be decimated in order to feed the masses. Then global warming, and its obvious effect on our planet, plus the near complete deforestation of our wilderness areas, causing innocent animals to scrounge for survival. Scientists now say we've entered a sixth mass extinction, and humans are the primary cause. Previous mass extinctions were due to natural climate changes, huge volcanic eruptions, or catastrophic meteor strikes, but this one is due to human activities. The massive loss of animal populations and species reflects our lack of empathy to all the wild species that have been our companions since our origins. It is a prelude to the disappearance of many more species and the decline of natural systems that make civilization possible.

Look at how many natural disasters have been happening worldwide lately. It seems as if the planet is rebelling against the parasites that are destroying the natural environment—and the parasites . . . they are us, us humans.

Another major concern is the straining of our natural resources by the apathetic proliferation of the earth's population, currently well in excess of seven billion. Every day, a quarter million people join us on planet Earth. Earth's population has more than doubled in just the last forty years—doubled! And that figure is quickly compounding. We must question the sustainability of further world population growth, citing the growing pressures on the environment, global food supplies, and energy resources.

Our natural resources cannot maintain the growth. How many more poor chickens must be slaughtered each day to satisfy the appetite of this ever-increasing obese population? How much more water will be required to quench the thirst? Water will eventually be the paramount concern; people need water to survive, not oil. Severe water shortage will eventually cause mayhem.

To prevent widespread misery and catastrophic biodiversity loss, humanity must practice a more environmentally sustainable alternative than we now do. This prescription has been well articulated and forewarned by the world's leading scientists many years ago, but in most respects, we have not heeded their warning. We must avert irreversible damage to our earth before it is too late. A shift away from our failing trajectory is paramount; time is running out. We also must recognize in our day-to-day lives and in our governing institutions that earth, with all its life, is our only home.

Another obvious and scary reality to me is true to fact. Soon, with technological advances, human logic won't be able to deal with the controlled artificial intelligence, and it will affect human mentality. No one will need to think anymore. Human brains will be digitized, and society will be vulnerable to robotics. Our brains will shrink as the CPU, the central processing unit of computers, will increase. We could possibly become mutations of our own DNA, it could simply and naturally change through the course of evolution and the heritable characteristics of biological populations over successive generations. Penguins used to fly, but the lack of use of their flippers for flight now only allows them to swim. You have obviously heard the expression, "Use it or lose it!" Well . . .

Human perceptual thinking is on the threshold of artificial intelligence, voiding reality. I heard a prediction that robots will someday be smarter than humans. Well, of course, they are computers. Can they take over the world? I also saw where a company is now making robots to replace a woman and a man for sex. Don't have to feed them, entertain them, compliment them, or communicate with them. We will become anomic, a state or condition of individuals or society characterized by a breakdown or absence of social norms and values.

Have you also noticed many young people don't communicate "live" anymore? They can be sitting next to one another but choose to text instead of talk. "Devices" have taken the place of personalities, and cursive handwriting is being eliminated in schools because it's being replaced with keyboards.

It just may soon be time for the earth to be refreshed and purified . . . again.

But no, surely not yet. Those were just the negatives I mentioned. There are so many good and kind people in this world, doing wonderful benevolent deeds for others. So many more fine, caring, and loving people than those with malevolent imperfections. If God purifies the world, the altruistic must remain, like angels and demons struggling over good and evil—the good must prevail.

If you look into the depths of the soul of a young child, you will see purity and credible innocence. Take the hand of a special needs person and feel the love exuding from within as they squeeze your hand ever-so-tightly, with total and unmitigated trust. Look into the eyes of a puppy just rescued from a shelter that was saved from euthanasia, and you will experience unparalleled love as it looks back in blind adoration without judgment of your race, color, sex, religion, wealth, faults, or your beauty—or lack thereof. The special needs child, the shelter dog, so often they are the unfortunate, overlooked *throwaways*. But they behold the inner beauty, goodness, and love we're looking for.

Yes, of course, I know I may have gotten overly philosophical and could be overreacting at this time, but Noah may have also overreacted to drizzles just before the great flood occurred.

Upon my eventual secession from this earth and involuntary abandonment of burden, my vexation regarding the future of mankind, and the turmoil humanity may have to endure, is indeed a concern. Our children and grandchildren, as well as yours, will be living in it. We must remember that the earth does not belong to man, but man belongs to the earth. Man did not weave the web of life, he is just merely a strand in it. Whatever he does to the web, he does to himself. The air is precious to us, the air shares its spirit with all the life it supports. The wind that gave us our first breath will also receive our last sigh.

And as I take my last sigh before entering the black void of eternity, I hope that just one last time, I see the faces of all those I love; my wife, my daughters, my grandchildren, even you.

I want to sincerely thank my wife for having the *perseverance* to stick with me through all this perplexing nonsense and drama.

I also want to thank all of you for giving me the time in *your* life to read about *my* life. For those I love, to those I have loved... *It's almost time to say goodbye.*

But wait, hold on! Don't say goodbye just yet. There's one more page—okay, two! Of course, an epilogue...

EPILOGUE

Don't worry, this *is* the ending to the ending. Why does it take just a moment to say hello, and forever to say goodbye? I've heard that the last page of the book is the hardest to write, and I'm struggling with that now.

So, what prompted me to write my memoirs? Well, everyone should. Everybody should at least leave a few words behind about what they've experienced on their journey here on earth. Of course, my "few words" were well over five hundred pages, but I had a lot to say, and I even left a *lot* out!

You should disseminate your remembrances of happy times, sad moments, your opinions, dislikes, and fears, or just thoughts about life in general. Even your predictions of the future of mankind, as I did, worthless as it may be! Your wording doesn't have to be articulate, just simply in your own words. Aristotle said, "To write well, express yourself like the common people, but think like a wise man."

The single most important purpose of writing my memoirs was that I wanted—no, I needed—to express the veneration of love to those whom I love, and from whom I receive love in return.

I am a very lucky man, indeed, to be married to such a beautiful woman, both outwardly and inwardly, and to have been blessed with her interminable love for almost sixty years. That is a lifetime. I can never thank her enough for gifting me with three such amazing, wonderful and loving daughters. They have given me more joy and happiness than I ever thought possible. A father could not love his children any more than I do. They in turn gave me six remarkable and awesome grandchildren.

I know I used the word "love and loving" repeatedly in reference to my emotions for my family, but I truly believe the seven natural *human* wonders of the world are the ability to see, to hear, to taste, to touch, to laugh, to feel emotion, and foremost, the ability to love. Without love, life is meaningless.

Remember, time will fade memories. Time will also fade the memory that you lived. We must write to leave our thoughts and inner feelings and expressions of love, of anything, so they can be read after we can no longer speak. The memory of you, your footprint, *will* eventually wash away. But better hurry! The tide is coming in.

In closing, I hope you were inspired, possibly even motivated, by my life story that proved regardless the challenge, even if insurmountable, anything is possible with *perseverance*.

You must never give up. Bravely meet your challenges face to face, and with tenacity, you will conquer. This is true with business, marriage, and relationships, even with enigmatic personal issues.

Just never give up! Defy obstacles and never stop dreaming, and never stop believing. Also realize that life will find a way to test you, so the urge to quit during these times is the highest, but don't give in—don't give in. Adversity is what you need to face to become successful.

Keep in mind, there is no express elevator to reach success; you must exhaustively climb the steps one at a time.

Go beyond what you thought you were capable of, even if you think it is *beyond the bounds of possibility.*

PERSEVERANCE

ACHILLE PALADINI was born in San Francisco in the mid-1930s, into a family whose name was renowned throughout the Bay Area for being synonymous with the seafood industry. A very successful businessman, he spent his life following in the footsteps of his famous grandfather, who was once known as the "The Fish King."

CPSIA information can be obtained
at www.ICGtesting.com
Printed in the USA
BVHW050211310321
603712BV00008B/852